Optimality Theory

Optimality Theory

Phonology, Syntax, and Acquisition

Edited by

Joost Dekkers
Frank van der Leeuw
Jeroen van de Weijer

OXFORD

UNIVERSITY PRESS

OXFORD
UNIVERSITY PRESS

Great Clarendon Street, Oxford OX2 6DP

Oxford University Press is a department of the University of Oxford.
It furthers the University's objective of excellence in research, scholarship,
and education by publishing worldwide in

Oxford New York

Athens Auckland Bangkok Bogotá Buenos Aires Calcutta Cape Town
Chennai Dar es Salaam Delhi Florence Hong Kong Istanbul Karachi
Kuala Lumpur Madrid Melbourne Mexico City Mumbai Nairobi
Paris São Paulo Shanghai Singapore Taipei Tokyo Toronto Warsaw
with associated companies in Berlin Ibadan

Oxford is a registered trade mark of Oxford University Press
in the UK and in certain other countries

Published in the United States
by Oxford University Press Inc., New York

British Library Cataloguing in Publication Data

Data available

Library of Congress Cataloging in Publication Data

Optimality theory : phonology, syntax, and acquisition / edited by Joost Dekkers,
Frank van der Leeuw, Jeroen van de Weijer
    p. cm.
    Includes bibliographical references.
    1. Optimality theory (Linguistics)   2. Grammar, Comparative and general—Phonology.
    3. Grammar, Comparative and general—Syntax.   4. Language acquisition.   I. Dekkers, Joost.
    II. Leeuw, Frank Reinoud Hugo van der.   III. Weijer, Jeroen Maarten van de, 1965–

P158.42.O684 2000
415'.01—dc21   00–044075

ISBN 0–19–823843–6 (hbk.)   ISBN 0–19–823844–4 (pbk.)

10 9 8 7 6 5 4 3 2 1

Typeset in Minion
by Peter Kahrel, Lancaster
Printed in Great Britain
on acid-free paper by
Biddles Ltd., Guildford and King's Lynn

Preface

This book took a long time to complete. First of all we would therefore like to thank the authors for their tremendous performance—and for their patience in waiting for the final result.

We are also grateful to staff and students of the Holland Institute of Generative Linguistics (HIL: Leiden University, the University of Amsterdam, and the Vrije Universiteit Amsterdam) for providing the academic framework in which this study was conceived and brought to fruition. Among other things, HIL provided a home page at which the abstracts of the articles collected here were presented, with the aim of publicising this book and fostering discussion between editors, authors, and others. Second, HIL provided a stimulating open academic environment which allowed for 'fringe' activities such as editing a voluminous publication like this. Most of all we would like to thank our colleagues in both Leiden and Amsterdam for ample discussion on all topics related to Optimality Theory and their continued moral support as this project progressed.

We are very grateful to John McCarthy and Alan Prince for wise advice in the initial stages of this project regarding the general set-up of this volume.

We would like to thank all those linguists—many of them no less eminent than the authors in the present volume—whom we bothered for reviews, more often than not at short notice. We would especially like to thank Paul Boersma, of the Department of Phonetics of the University of Amsterdam, for his invaluable help with the language acquisition studies and for writing the introduction together with us.

Finally, we are much indebted to OUP's Linguistics editor, John Davey, for his enthusiasm, advice, patience and continued support for this project.

Leiden and Amsterdam
May 1998

Joost Dekkers
Frank van der Leeuw
Jeroen van de Weijer

Contents

Part Two
Phonology: Segmental Phonology

Part Three
Syntax

Part Four
Acquisition

Introduction

Optimality Theory: Phonology, Syntax, and Acquisition[1]

Paul Boersma, Joost Dekkers and
Jeroen van de Weijer

A. General Introduction

The introduction of Optimality Theory (OT) by Prince and Smolensky (1993) can be considered the single most important development in generative grammar in the 1990s. It has profoundly changed (morpho-)phonological inquiry, and it has given an important impulse to the study of language learning. Although its impact on (morpho-)syntax is not as overwhelming as on phonology, the success of OT is remarkable. Perhaps the key to its success is its applicability in all areas of grammar, offering a new perspective on a wide range of problems in linguistics.

The major shift OT brought about in phonology is that from a rule-based to an output-based model—a move that was also foreshadowed in several other publications (see Prince and Smolensky 1993: 1). In Chomsky and Halle's (1968) influential *Sound Pattern of English* it was assumed that phonology consisted of sequentially ordered rules. In the decades that followed there was increasing attention for so-called phonological *conspiracies*—i.e. the phenomenon that several phonological rules together aim at the same representational goal. In an output-based approach, such as OT phonology, constraints on surface forms can express these conspiracies.

Not only does OT allow us to acknowledge the existence of conspiracies, it also enables us to formalize the idea that these conspiracies are the result of the interaction of grammatical tendencies which exist within as well as across languages. Many potentially universal statements about language are not always true: they are context- and language-dependent. For instance, languages tend to avoid codas. In some of them, this leads to a strict CV-syllabification. Other languages are more liberal, although the aforementioned pattern remains the

---

[1] By way of acknowledgement, we would like to thank Peter Ackema, Hans Broekhuis, Frank van der Leeuw, Géraldine Legendre, Ad Neeleman, and Marc van Oostendorp for their valuable comments on versions of this article as it approached finality. The usual disclaimers apply.

unmarked option: codas are avoided if other tendencies do not interfere and prevail. The assumption in OT that constraints are violable can be considered the formal correlate of linguistic tendencies, whereas constraint ranking expresses the degree to which individual languages exhibit these tendencies—the higher the rank of a constraint in the individual language, the more contexts there are in which we can observe its effect. In other words, OT is a theory of markedness.

In the most general of terms, OT states that decisions are made on the basis of a parallel evaluation of available options with respect to a hierarchy of conflicting requirements. As such it is applicable to domains other than grammar but also too general to provide us with a substantive theory of grammar. Only after thorough linguistic inquiry can we determine the specific properties an OT grammar should have. In the present volume a range of scholars study the theoretical questions that arise in this line of inquiry.

This introductory article consists of a phonology, a syntax, and an acquisition section. In each section we briefly introduce the field in general as well as the issues addressed in the corresponding sections of the volume. First, however, we introduce some of the basic notions to be found in an OT grammar.

A.1 *Some Basic Notions*

An OT grammar can be schematically represented as in (1). For every possible input, the generator (GEN) produces a candidate set. Inputs are in principle unconstrained linguistic objects such as lexical items in word phonology. However, if a grammar has to perform increasingly complex combinatorial tasks, the exact properties of the input become less and less evident. In syntax, for instance, it is not clear that inputs that consist of sets of words suffice to evaluate entire sentences. Hence it might be desirable to structure the input to a greater or lesser extent (see Section C).

(1) Input → GEN → Candidate set → EVAL → Optimal candidate

A candidate set contains output structures. These structures are possible analyses of the input (e.g. words in word phonology, or sentences in syntax). According to the principle of inclusiveness, GEN produces all those analyses of the input that 'are admitted by very general considerations of structural well-formedness' (McCarthy and Prince 1993), which could include universal properties of, for instance, syllable and phrase structure.

The evaluator (EVAL) evaluates candidate sets with respect to particular rankings of the constraint inventory Con. It is often assumed that Con is universal (see, however, Boersma, this volume, and Ellison, this volume). Its members are simple and conflicting statements about the form of the output (well-formedness constraints) or the relation between the output and the input (faithfulness or correspondence constraints). Because of the conflict between constraints, all conceivable linguistic structures will violate at least some of the constraints.

However, constraint violation *per se* does not lead to ungrammaticality, since constraints are violable and strictly ranked; those structures that minimally violate rankings are optimal, and by definition grammatical. An output structure minimally violates a ranking if all alternative structures that have an equal or better score on the lowest-ranked constraint score worse on the ranking dominating this constraint. Parametrization is brought about by differences in constraint ranking, and rankings can be taken to define grammars of individual languages.

Let us illustrate this with an abstract example (concrete examples are given in subsequent sections). Let us suppose that Con consist of CON_1, CON_2, and CON_3, that the language L is defined by the ranking $CON_1 \gg CON_2 \gg CON_3$, and that we have to evaluate a candidate set which contains the output structures A–D with respect to the input I. The violations each of these structures incurs are given in tableau (2). In OT tableaus the top row gives the constraint ranking from left to right. In subsequent rows constraint violations are given for each output structure. Each asterisk (or 'star') represents one violation.

(2)	CON_1	CON_2	CON_3
☞ A		*	*
B	*!		
C		**!	*
D		*	**!

It is easiest to determine optimal candidates by reading tableaus from left to right. For each column we have to determine which candidate(s) incur(s) the lowest number of violations. In (2), B is the only candidate that violates the highest-ranked constraint CON_1, even though candidate B has a smaller number of violations than the other candidates. This violation is fatal, which is indicated by an exclamation mark (cells to the right of fatal violations are irrelevant for evaluation, and are therefore shaded). This leaves us with three remaining candidates, which will be evaluated with respect to the next constraint, CON_2. Candidates A and D violate this constraint only once, whereas C does so twice. This means that the second violation of CON_2 by C is fatal, and only A and D continue. When we move on to CON_3, this constraint turns out to decide between these two candidates. D incurs two violations of CON_3, whereas A violates it only once. Hence A is the optimal candidate and therefore grammatical. Note in passing that the total number of violations is irrelevant. The fact that A incurs two violations and B only one has no influence on the evaluation.

On the assumption that rankings define grammars of individual languages, all six possible rankings of our three constraints represent distinct grammars. For instance, the ranking $CON_2 \gg CON_1 \gg CON_3$ defines the language L', distinct from L. In L', the evaluation of the candidate set {A, B, C, D} with respect to I proceeds as in (3). In this tableau, B is evaluated as optimal because it is the only candidate that does not violate CON_2, the highest-ranked constraint.

(3)	CON_2	CON_1	CON_3
A	*!		*
☞ B		*	
C	*!*		*
D	*!		**

B. Optimality-Theoretic Phonology

Optimality Theory was first developed with respect to phonology. There are good reasons why the phonological domain should have been very susceptible to an Optimality-theoretic treatment. Phonology is a rich hunting-ground for potential conflict. There is, for instance, the conflict between ease of articulation and the necessity of perceptual distinctness, which plays a role in most assimilation processes. Second, there is a potential conflict between phonological regularity (e.g. in terms of syllable structure) and morphological needs. Finally, the different demands of segmental and suprasegmental phonology may conflict.

In this section we examine some cases of constraint conflicts in phonology to illustrate these different sources, and to establish why constraint-based approaches are preferable to rule-based approaches.

B.1 *Constraint Interaction*

A prime motivation for a constraint-based approach is the long-standing problem of so-called conspiracies (see also above). This refers to the phenomenon that different rules of a language may interact to result in the same kinds of output patterns (Kisseberth 1970). For instance, a language may have a ban on consonants clusters in the output. In a rule-based approach, several different rules breaking up clusters—for instance imported in loanwords or resulting from morphological concatenation—may be postulated to break up such clusters by various means (such as vowel epenthesis or consonant deletion). Other conspiracies may involve the fact that outputs respect some well-established principle, such as the OCP (Myers 1997), or that outputs are properly metrified (Kager 1997).

Rule-based phonology can describe different such conspiracies, but does not account for the fact that these different rules are all geared towards an optimal output situation—e.g. one in which there are no consonant clusters in the phonetic signal. Optimality Theory, on the other hand, captures such regularities by postulating a single output constraint—e.g. that in (4):

(4) *COMPLEXONSET: *[$_\sigma$CC

This constraint forbids two (and, by implication, three or more) onset consonants. Candidate forms which violate this constraint will be weeded out in favour of candidates which have, for instance, an epenthetic vowel between the consonants, or in which one of the consonants has been deleted; other constraints (e.g. a constraint forbidding deletion from underlying forms, which would prevent the latter type of scenario) will take care of further selection.

Let us examine a case in point to illustrate the interaction of this constraint with other ones. In Sinhalese, loanwords from Dutch with obstruent + liquid are broken up by epenthesis (Sannasgala 1976; van de Weijer 1996; cf also Jacobs and Gussenhoven [this volume] and LaCharité and Paradis [this volume] for the treatment of loanword phonology in Optimality Theory and other frameworks):

(5) Dutch   Sinhalese
    plan   *päläna*   'plan'
    procuratie *perakala:si-ya* 'procuration'
    kraan   *kara:ma-ya*   'tap' (i.e. cock or fauset)
    vrouw   *porova*   'queen' (in cards)

Sinhalese obviously experiences the effects of *ComplexOnset. In addition, this language requires open syllables, and forbids resolution of the consonant cluster by deletion of a consonant. The conflict that is at stake here is one between the syllable structure of the target language, on the one hand, and the integrity of the incoming form on the other, i.e. the pressure to preserve the loanword as unaltered as possible. The latter constraint could be regarded as a general Faithfulness or Correspondence Constraint (McCarthy and Prince 1995), forbidding deletion and epenthesis in general.

(6) Max-IO   : Preserve lexical segments[2]
    Dep-IO (V) : Do not insert a vowel

In Sinhalese, the *ComplexOnset constraint dominates the Dep-IO constraint:

(7) /plan/	*ComplexOnset	Max-IO	Dep-IO
[plän]	*!		
[pan]		*!	
☞ [päläna]			*

Although the third candidate deviates from the input form, and therefore violates Dep-IO, this violation is not fatal because the candidate respects the two higher-ranked constraints, *ComplexOnset and Max-IO.

Interestingly, the data from Sinhalese are complicated by the behaviour of

---

[2] Or, technically, 'every segment in the input appears in the output', for Max-IO, and 'every vowel in the output has a correspondent in the input', for Dep-IO (V). The formulations in (6) only serve expository purposes.

loanwords with initial *s* plus consonant clusters. These are presented in (8):

(8) Dutch   Sinhalese
   spatie   *ispa:su-va*   'space'
   stoep   *sto:ppu ~ isto:ppu-va*   'footpath'
   strijkijzer *stirikka-ya ~ istrikka-ya* 'iron' (of the household variety)
   schop   *sko:ppa ~ isko:ppa-ya*   'spade'

These data show that initial [s] plus stop clusters are either not broken up or receive a prothetic, instead of an epenthetic, vowel. This indicates that the syllabic cohesion between [s] and stop is stronger than the cohesion between obstruents and liquids, a tendency which is observed in language after language (Broselow 1991, van de Weijer 1996). This may be formulated as, for instance, a constraint forbidding epenthesis between a syllable-initial [s] and a consonant, DEP-IO(V / s_C):

(9) DEP-IO(V / s_C) : Do not insert a vowel between [s] and a consonant

Note that this constraint is itself dominated by a constraint of the type MAX-IO(V), which forbids deletion of lexical vowels. Thus, like DEP-IO(V) (see above), this constraint must compare input and output: it says that every segment in the output must have a correspondent in the input. The constraint is unviolated in Sinhalese, although it may be violated in other languages (see below).

(10) /skop/	DEP-IO(V / s_C)	*COMPLEXONSET	DEP-IO(V)
soko:ppa-ya	*!		*
sko:ppa-ya		*!	
☞ isko:ppa-ya			*

This constraint ordering yields the attested form with prothetic /i/ (and with, presumably, resyllabification of *s* and *k* into different syllables) as optimal. Note, however, in (8) that the candidate /sko:ppa-ya/ also occurs, apparently in free variation with the prothetic form, although it violates the *COMPLEXONSET constraint. The problem of variability is a precarious one in Optimality Theory (see Hayes [this volume], Boersma [this volume], and a number of contributions to Hinskens *et al.* 1997, for instance). One way of formalizing it is by leaving certain constraints unranked, or by assuming different constraint rankings for different speech registers. Variability therefore touches on the heart of Optimality Theory, since it bears on the nature of constraint ranking within a language or on different constraint rankings within the same language. We will not address this here.[3]

---

[3] Note that another solution would be to assume that *s* plus stop clusters are single segments, so that they do not violate the *COMPLEXONSET constraint. This would account for the fact that forms like /sko:ppa-ya/ also occur, but it does not account for the fact that /isko:ppa-ya/ is also possible. It is important, however, to point out that the representation of segmental properties is crucial to a correct interpretation of constraints: see also Smith (this volume).

Given the hypothesis that constraints are universal, the tendencies they express are also expected to play a role in other languages and other processes. Given the hypothesis that constraint rankings are language-specific, it is expected that in other languages other tendencies are predominant. This is shown by similar loanword phonology data from Saramaccan, a creole language spoken in Surinam (Smith, p.c.):

(11) Dutch   Saramaccan
     schroef   *sukulufu*   'screw'
     schout   *sikɛutu*   'bailiff'
     schopp(en)   *sikopu*   'spade(s)'
     portret   *pɛtilɔti*   'portrait'
     melk   *meliki*   'milk'
     verstaan   *fusutan*   'understand'

In this language all clusters, regardless of their content, are broken up. In Optimality Theory terms, the constraints DEP-IO(V / s_C) and *COMPLEX ONSET must be reversed in this language. In addition, the language obeys strictly a constraint demanding open syllables and a constraint barring /r/ (which is realised as [l]). The constraints demanding these latter properties of the output are not shown in the tableau below.

(12) /skruf/	*COMPLEXONSET	DEP-IO(V / s_C)
skulufu	*!	
☞ sukulufu		*

Hence, Sinhalese and Saramaccan have the same constraints, *COMPLEX ONSET and DEP-IO(V / s_C), but these constraints occur in different orders in both languages.

B.2 *Phonology-Morphology Conflicts*

Another source of potential conflict is in the realm of phonology-morphology interaction. A standard example here is infixation in Tagalog, according to the analyses by Prince and Smolensky (1993), McCarthy and Prince (1993a, b), *et seq.*:

(13) *um + aral*   →   *um-aral*   'teach'
     um + sulat   →   s-*um*-alat   'write'
     um + gradwet →   gr-*um*-adwet 'graduate' (French 1988)

In McCarthy and Prince (1990), such data are analysed using 'prosodic circumscription' (see also McCarthy [this volume] for discussion). A prosodically circumscribed unit is divided from the base, after which the infix is prefixed to the remainder of the stem. The prosodically circumscribed unit is then attached again to prefix+base, giving rise to surface infixation. McCarthy and Prince (1993b) note that in this case the prosodically circumscribed unit must be an onset. First, the status of this constituent is rather unclear: in a mora framework such as that advocated by Hayes (1989) there is no unit that formally corresponds to this unit. Second and more importantly, it is not possible (according to McCarthy and Prince) to prosodically circumscribe just a single consonant in infixation processes like these (giving rise to *g-um-radwet*). Instead, Prince and Smolensky (1993) and McCarthy and Prince (1993b) analyse Tagalog infixation as the interaction of two constraints: one phonological, requiring that all syllables are open, and one morphological, requiring that prefixes are located at the left edge of the word. These are reproduced (from McCarthy and Prince 1993b: 120) in (14) below:

(14) a.   No-Coda
           Syllables are open

     b.   Leftmostness
           Prefix is located at left edge of the word

These constraints interact to select the candidate *grumadwet* over other possible candidates such as tableau (15) illustrates (from McCarthy and Prince 1993b: 121)—only No-Coda violations induced by the infix are given in the tableau:

(15) Candidates	No-Coda	Leftmostness
um.grad.wet	*!	
gum.rad.wet	*!	g
☞ gru.mad.wet		gr
grad.wu.met		gradw!

The first two candidates have closed syllables due to pre-/infixation of -*um*-. The last two candidates have no violations for this constraint (induced by the prefix), and the candidate in which the prefix is as leftmost as possible wins out. The difference between a rule-based approach and a constraint-based approach is that constraints such as those in (14) are well motivated and have a broad scope of application, while the mechanism of prosodic circumscription has to be specified for every separate affix, often cannot be independently motivated, and makes predictions—as we saw above—that are not borne out.

B.3 *Further Outlook*

Let us, finally, recapitulate briefly the papers in the phonology section of the present volume.

The notions of cyclicity and 'derived environment' have had a long and controversial history in phonological theory (see Mascaró 1976, Kiparsky 1982, Kaisse and Shaw 1985 for discussion). In his article in this volume, Burzio argues that Output-to-Output correspondence constraints are not only useful in accounting for 'cyclic' effects as has been shown in recent literature, but can also provide a principled account of 'Non-Derived Environment Blocking' effects, descriptively the mirror image of the cyclic ones. Both accounts hinge on the calculation of morphologically derived forms via surface-to-surface comparison rather than from underlying representations (see also Burzio 1994, 1996, 1998). Kager (this volume) deals partly with the same kinds of phenomena, and provides evidence in favour of a correspondence-based account over a derivational/cyclic theory on the basis of stress and affixation in Dutch. Certain stress-governed blocking effects in affixation, Kager argues, cannot even be captured in Lexical Phonology while they follow naturally from the interaction between phonological and morphological constraints.

As observed above, both the contribution by Jacobs and Gussenhoven and that by LaCharité and Paradis deal with loanword phonology. Jacobs and Gussenhoven (this volume) show the superiority of a constraint-based account over a rule-based one because the former avoids having to state the constraints to which adapted loanwords have to conform twice: once as a morpheme structure constraint of the language, and secondly as a rule which is applied to loanwords (see also Section D.13). LaCharité and Paradis (this volume) focus on another aspect: they argue that the concept of 'rules' has not disappeared in OT, as is sometimes claimed, but rather that rules have received another status: in particular, rules have been relegated to the Generator GEN (see above). Thus, they argue, the way in which candidates are generated should receive greater attention, and the fact that rules are tucked away in GEN should not be used as a criterion to distinguish between OT and other constraint- or rule-based approaches (cf also Broekhuis and Dekkers [this volume] for a similar stance in Optimality syntax: see also Section C.2.1 below).

McCarthy (this volume) focuses on prosodic faithfulness constraints, and shows how they account for a number of phenomena that were formerly analysed under the heading of Prosodic Circumscription (see above; see McCarthy and Prince 1990). While conserving the insights of the circumscriptional analysis, McCarthy shows that a correspondence account relies on more general, and therefore more attractive, constraints and principles. Finally, Smith (this volume) ties together Optimality Theory and Dependency Phonology, and aims to show that in this connection the issue of segmental structure is far from trivial.

C. Optimality-Theoretic Syntax

The recent birth of OT syntax can be attributed to two developments in the study of grammar. On the one hand, Optimality Theory has proved to be successful in the domain of phonology. Given this success, and given that there is no reason whatsoever to assume that Optimality Theory is applicable only to phonology, investigating the possibilities of applying this theory to syntax can be considered a logical next step.

At the same time, the emergence of OT syntax seems to fit into the general tendency in syntax to blame the ungrammaticality of a sentence on the existence of a better alternative. This view on grammaticality is also found in Chomsky's Minimalist Program (Chomsky 1995), although Chomsky takes optimization to play a much more modest role than OT syntacticians do. Whereas Chomsky's only criterion for evaluation is derivational cost[4], the inventory of violable constraints assumed in OT syntax is richer. As a result, the OT constraints interact and conflict with each other. This interaction is exploited by the assumption that constraints are ranked, and that parametrization can be reduced to differences in ranking between languages. Chomsky's economy conditions, on the other hand, have no such direct parametrizing effect. In the Minimalist Program, the locus of parametrization is the lexicon.

This section consists of two parts. In the first part, we give a brief introduction to OT syntax for those readers who are not familiar with it, by illustrating that the application of OT to syntax enables us to successfully account for a diverse set of syntactic phenomena. The second part should be seen as an introduction to the syntax section of this volume. We discuss several issues that are addressed there (and elsewhere) which pertain to the way in which OT could or should be applied to syntax.

C.1 *The Scope of OT Syntax*

Chomsky and Lasnik (1977, henceforth C&L), constructing their theory of filters, remark that 'filters seem to have the property that at least some outcome is possible for any "reasonable" base-generated structure' (p. 465). In OT syntax, we can attribute this to the very essence of the theory, in which at least one member of every candidate set survives evaluation. In this light, it is not so remarkable that—as we will see below—OT syntax is well-equipped for analysing the phenomena that C&L attributed to their filters: pronunciation patterns in the complementizer domain. And more generally, it turns out that OT does well in all domains that they accommodate in the 'phonological' wing (3a, 4a, 5a, 6a) of their grammar, given in (16):

(16) 1.   Base
      2.   Transformations (movement, adjunction, substitution)

      3a. Deletion   3b. Construal
      4a. Filters   4b. Quantifier interpretation, etc.
      5a. Phonology
      6a. Stylistic rules

We will therefore start by examining phenomena that C&L (would) analyse in terms of deletion and filters on the one hand (Section C.1.1), and stylistic rules

---

[4] Such as (i) Minimize the number of movement steps (Fewest Steps); (ii) Minimize the length of movement paths (Minimal Link Condition); (iii) Minimize overt movement (Procrastinate).

on the other (Section C.1.2). In Section C.1.3, it will be illustrated that OT can in principle be successfully applied to all areas of syntax, including those that C&L would accommodate in the transformational component.

C.1.1 The Complementizer domain

Pesetsky (1997, 1998) proposes to reduce several of C&L's filters to the interaction of a small number of faithfulness and alignment constraints. He thus revives the investigation of constraints on deletion—a topic that has not received much attention in recent years. In fact, the view on syntax Pesetsky lays down is largely consistent with C&L's. His OT system (just like C&L's filters) operates on already-formed structures, that is, on structures delivered by the transformational component. Pesetsky proposes that terminal elements in these structures may be deleted in an arbitrary fashion (cf C&L's rule of free deletion in COMP) and that subsequently, the OT system (again just like C&L's filters) narrows down the number of potential surface forms. Both the OT system and C&L's filters thus prevent the transformational component from having to become too rich. C&L explicitly state that filters 'will have to bear the burden of accounting for [. . .] all contextual dependencies that cannot be formulated in the narrower framework of core grammar' (p. 432).

An important point Pesetsky makes is that the question of whether the complementizer is pronounced or not depends on whether it appears in clause-initial position. This is illustrated by the French examples given in (17): the complementizer *que* is only pronounced in the absence of an element in SpecCP.

(17) a. l'homme que je connais
          the man that I know
      b. l'homme avec qui j'ai dansé
          the man with whom I have danced

Pesetsky explains this phenomenon by using the three violable constraints given in (18). Rᴇᴄ makes a distinction between deletion of relative pronouns embedded in a PP and deletion of those that are not. Only in the former case is a meaningful element, the preposition, deleted, which leads to a violation of Rᴇᴄ. The second constraint, LE(CP), is an alignment constraint (see McCarthy and Prince 1993a) which is violated whenever the first pronounced element in a CP is not a head from the extended projection of the verb. And finally, Tᴇʟ prohibits the pronunciation of function words, such as the complementizer *que*.

(18) a. Recoverability (Rᴇᴄ): A syntactic unit with semantic content must be pronounced.[5]

---

[5] We have simplified Pesetsky's definition of REC. The original definition, given in (i), seems to be too complex to qualify as a possible OT constraint, since it expresses matters that can be captured in terms of interaction of simpler constraints (cf Broekhuis and Dekkers [this volume]).

(i) Recoverability (Rᴇᴄ): A syntactic unit with semantic content must be pronounced unless it has a sufficiently local antecedent.

b. Left Edge CP (LE(CP)): The first pronounced word in CP is a function word related to the main verb of the CP.

c. Telegraph (TEL): Do not pronounce function words.

Pesetsky argues that in French these constraints are ranked as in (19):

(19) French: REC >> LE(CP) >> TEL

This ranking gives the evaluations in the tableaus (20) and (21). In tableau (20), deletion of the relative pronoun does not violate Recoverability because it is not embedded in a PP. Furthermore, LE(CP) prefers elements in SpecCP to be deleted because this ensures that the complementizer occurs in CP-initial position. As a result, candidate (c) comes out as optimal, and TEL is not relevant.

(20)		REC	LE (CP)	TEL
	a. l'homme qui que je connais		*!	*
	b. l'homme qui que̶ je connais		*!	
☞	c. l'homme qu̶i̶ que je connais			*
	d. l'homme qu̶i̶ qu̶e̶ je connais		*!	

In tableau (21), a different pictures emerges. When *avec qui* is deleted, the preposition is not recoverable, which excludes candidates (c) and (d). The second constraint, LE(CP), does not decide between the two remaining candidates (a) and (b), because it is violated by both. In this case, TEL plays a crucial role because it prefers candidate (b) over candidate (a), since only the former involves the deletion of the function word *que*. Note that this is an example of the emergence of the unmarked (see McCarthy and Prince 1994).

(21)		REC	LE (CP)	TEL
	a. l'homme avec qui que j'ai dansé		*	*!
☞	b. l'homme avec qui qu̶e̶ j'ai dansé		*	
	c. l'homme a̶v̶e̶c̶ ̶q̶u̶i̶ que j'ai dansé	*!		*
	d. l'homme a̶v̶e̶c̶ ̶q̶u̶i̶ ̶q̶u̶e̶ j'ai dansé	*!	*	

One of the advantages of an OT analysis along these lines is that it is compatible with a fully endocentric approach to phrase structure. In the 1970s it was assumed that the left periphery of the (relative) clause had the structure in (22a), whereas currently the endocentric structure in (22b) is standardly associated with the complementizer domain. Now, if the complementizer is taken to project, as in (b), there is no syntactic node that dominates both the relative pronoun and the complementizer but not the rest of the clause. Consequently, C&L's Doubly

Filled COMP Filter, given in (23a), cannot be invoked to exclude candidate (a) in the tableaus above.[6] As Pesetsky shows, an alternative analysis in terms of alignment is successful.

(22) a. $[_{S'} [_{COMP}$ *Wh*-phrase complementizer] . . .]
     b. $[_{CP} [$*Wh*-phrase] $[_{C'} [_{C}$ complementizer] . . .]]

(23) a. $^*[_{COMP}$ *Wh*-phrase φ], φ ≠ e
     b. *[for-to]

Another advantage of Pesetsky's analysis is that it refers to a small number of general and in principle universal constraints which turn out to be relevant for many more left-periphery phenomena than the one presented here. For example, Pesetsky shows that C&L's *For-to* Filter, formulated as in (23b), can be reduced to the interaction of the three constraints given in (18), which falsifies C&L's remark that the two filters in (23) 'are [. . .] minimal, in the sense that there seems to be no simpler way to state the facts' (p. 450).[7]

And finally, we predict that alternative rankings (co-)define other languages. Let us illustrate this for LE(CP) and TEL with clausal complements of epistemic verbs. In the French (24a), the complementizer is obligatorily pronounced, which is consistent with our assumption that LE(CP) outranks TEL in this language. A language that has the opposite ranking lacks complementizers. Chinese fits this description (Rint Sybesma, p.c.), as is shown in (24c). In English, both options are available, which indicates that LE(CP) and TEL are in a tie. If two constraints are in a tie, both rankings are valid.

(24) a. French: LE(CP) >> TEL
         Je pense *(que) le Président de la Republique a déguisé la vérité.
         'I think that the French president covered up the truth.'

---

[6] One could reformulate (23a) as in (i). However, (i) is far from surface-true. Cross-linguistically as well as within individual languages, it seems to hold only for a subset of heads and their specifiers. In other words, (i) would have to be interpreted as a violable constraint.

(i) Do not pronounce both a head and its specifier.

Further, if we substitute the hierarchical (i) for the linear LE(CP), we would lose part of Pesetsky's empirical coverage, such as his account for the facts formerly explained by the *For-to* filter in (23b). Note, finally, that neither (23a) nor (i) explains the ungrammaticality of candidates (b) and (d) in tableau (20).

[7] Furthermore, it is well known that neither of the two filters in (23) is universal, which had to be stipulated by C&L. In an OT approach, this can be attributed to a difference in ranking of the relevant constraints. Note that this is a principled advantage of OT which Pesetsky does not exploit in his analysis; any ranking of the three constraints in (18) bans doubly filled COMP configurations. In tableaus (20) and (21), the (a) candidates are harmonically bound by the (b) candidates (see below for a definition of harmonic boundedness). The fact that there are languages in which the (a) candidates do surface leads Broekhuis and Dekkers (this volume) to the conclusion that Pesetsky's constraint inventory needs to be revised.

b. English: LE(CP) <> TEL
   'I think (that) the President covered up the truth.'
c. Chinese: TEL >> LE(CP)
   Paul juede zongtong sahuang-le.
   *Paul thinks president lie-*PRF.

C.1.2 Information structure

Another domain in which OT does well is the syntactic encoding of information structure. It has often been pointed out that in cases like (25) (Heavy NP Shift) and (26) (Italian 'Free' Inversion), word order optionality is only apparent. Although C&L do not discuss these cases, they would probably analyse them in terms of stylistic rules (cf Rochemont 1978). The application of these rules is not optional if their interpretational effects are taken into account.

(25) Zubizarreta (1994):
   a. Max put all the boxes of home furnishings in his car.
   b. Max put in his car all the boxes of home furnishings.

(26) Grimshaw and Samek-Lodovici (1995):
   a. Gianni ha gridato.
      Gianni has screamed.
   b. Ha gridato Gianni.

Zubizarreta (1994) argues that movement applies not only for morphological but also for interpretational reasons.[8] The main difference between these two types of movement is that only the former is self-serving, in the sense that it applies to satisfy the needs of the moved constituent. The latter, on the other hand, is part of a syntactic conspiracy that targets a specific representation.

Let us start with the examples in (25), where (25a) displays the unmarked order. In (25b), *all the boxes of home furnishings* is interpreted as narrowly focused. Such pragmatic information is marked syntactically by the inverted order of the NP and the PP. This inversion can be analysed in two ways. Either the NP is moved rightward, or the PP is moved leftward. In either case, a syntax based on the hypothesis that movement applies in order to check features (Chomsky 1995) will not be able to map this pragmatic information onto syntactic structure in a straightforward manner.

Let us suppose that focused elements are endowed with a [+foc] feature, which must move to the checking domain of a Focus Phrase. Now, if the NP is moved, it should end up in a right-branching specifier of this FocP to check its feature.

---

[8] Zubizarreta actually argues that movement only indirectly applies for interpretational reasons; she associates focus with primary stress, and stress assignment with depth of embedding. By suggesting that information structure is directly responsible for the marked word order in (25b), and that linear order, rather than depth of embedding, is relevant here, we are simplifying matters considerably. This is done for expository reasons only.

However, right-branching specifiers are not uncontroversial from a conceptual point of view. And even if we allow them in our theory, they are not very likely to occur in an SVO language like English. If the PP moves, on the other hand, it is even less likely that the NP will be able to check its [+foc] feature.

It seems more plausible that the focus interpretation of the NP in (25b) is due to its right-peripheral position. In OT syntax, relatively much attention has been paid to the tendency across languages to align focused constituents with the right edge of the clause, which is generally attributed to an alignment constraint such as ALIGN-focus, given in (27a). This constraint is in conflict with the well-established economy constraint STAY. STAY can be held responsible for the fact that (25b) is syntactically marked. Irrespective of the question whether it is the NP or the PP that moves, (25b) involves one more movement step than (25a). Given that this order nevertheless surfaces indicates that ALIGN-focus outranks STAY.

(27) a. ALIGN-focus: Align focused constituents with the right edge of CP.
b. STAY: Traces are disallowed.

Just as in (25), the difference in word order in (26) gives rise to interpretational differences. In (26b), the subject is focused, whereas in (26a) it is not. Again, focus interpretation is associated with the right edge of the sentence. Grimshaw and Samek-Lodovici (1995) argue that there are two forces at work. On the one hand, focused constituents tend to appear in clause-final position, to satisfy ALIGN-focus. On the other hand, subjects have a preference for the preverbal (SpecIP) position, which they attribute to the constraint SUBJECT, given in (28), which can be considered a violable counterpart of the Extended Projection Principle.

(28) SUBJECT (Grimshaw and Samek-Lodovici 1995: 590):
The highest A-specifier in an extended projection must be filled.

In Italian, ALIGN-focus outranks SUBJECT; focused subjects appear at the right edge of the sentence. In English, on the other hand, SUBJECT outranks ALIGN-focus, since subjects appear in SpecIP, irrespective of whether they are focused or not.

(29) a. *Has screamed John.
b. John has screamed.

The difference between English and Italian is captured by assuming opposite rankings of these two constraints, as is illustrated in tableaus (30) and (31).[9]

(30)		ALIGN-focus	SUBJECT
☞	a. Ha gridato Gianni$_{[+foc]}$		*
	b. Gianni$_{[+foc]}$ ha gridato	*!	

[9] For a more detailed discussion of the possibilities of accounting for the interaction of information structure and syntax in OT, the reader is referred to Costa (1996, 1997), Dekkers (1997), Grimshaw and Samek-Lodovici (1996), and Samek-Lodovici (1996).

(31)	Subject	Align-focus
a. Has screamed John$_{[+foc]}$	*!	
☞ b. John$_{[+foc]}$ has screamed		*

Another interface issue where edges seem to play an important role is clitic placement. In this volume, both Anderson (this volume) and Legendre (this volume) argue that clitics have an affinity with edges of prosodic and syntactic domains, and should therefore be analysed in terms of alignment. This causes a conflict with the co-existing tendency not to parse clitics as the first element in a given domain (Anderson) or the Intonational Phrase (Legendre). Anderson extends this approach to Verb-Second phenomena. According to Legendre, alignment and non-initial constraints interact with syntactic and phonological constraints, although constraints belonging to different modules of grammar do not intermix (all syntactic constraints must outrank all phonological constraints, or vice versa, etc.).

C.1.3 Head and operator movement

Although OT syntax enables us to explain interface phenomena such as the ones presented above in a natural way, it should by no means be considered to be only a theory of 'surface syntax'. Since the first syntactic OT studies (Legendre *et al.* 1993; early versions of Grimshaw 1997), it has become clear that OT can provide us with a general theory of syntax—in fact, the broad empirical scope of OT syntax contrasts with the more specialised nature of the also recently developed minimalist syntax. This section will be concluded with an OT analysis of some aspects of head and operator movement, traditionally localised in the transformational component of syntax.

A remarkable property of Germanic subject-auxiliary inversion is the fact that it is contingent on constituent preposing. This is illustrated in (32) and (33) for English. In the interrogative in (32), the *Wh*-element is parsed in its left-peripheral scope position and the auxiliary precedes the subject. In declaratives, on the other hand, no such preposing takes place, and subject-auxiliary inversion is illicit, as is shown in (3).

(32) What will John read?
(33) a.   John will read books.
      b.   *Will John read books.

Grimshaw (1997) gives the following analysis of these facts. In her view, *wh*-movement takes place to satisfy the constraint Op-Spec, given in (34a). It should be noted that the definition of this constraint is of a general nature: it simply demands that operators, such as *Wh*-elements, be in a specifier position. Since there is no specifier position available inside the IP (SpecIP is occupied by the subject, and SpecVP by its trace), an additional projection is needed to host the *Wh*-element. However, this projection—let us call it CP—lacks a(n overt) head, and therefore violates the constraint OB-HD.

(34) a. Operator in Specifier (OP-SPEC): Syntactic operators must be in specifier position.

 b. Obligatory Heads (OB-HD): A projection has a head.

Grimshaw argues that the auxiliary is moved to C to satisfy OB-HD. Since movement is considered costly, this movement will entail a violation of STAY, as defined in (27). The fact that it nevertheless takes place should be attributed to the fact that OB-HD outranks STAY in English. Also OP-SPEC outranks STAY in English, since *Wh*-preposing is obligatory. In other words, the English ranking is as given in (35).[10]

(35) English ranking: OP-SPEC >> OB-HD >> STAY

The evaluation of English interrogatives is given in tableau (36), in which candidate (d) is evaluated as optimal, since it is the only one that violates neither OP-SPEC, nor OB-HD. In tableau (37) it is illustrated that the presence of CP in English declaratives does not serve any purpose; all candidates vacuously satisfy OP-SPEC. The projection of CP will therefore always entail a(dditional) violation(s) of either OB-HD or STAY (see also Section C.2.2 below).

(36) Matrix interrogatives	OP-SPEC	OB-HD	STAY
a. [John will [t read what]]	*!		*
b. [e [John will [t read what]]]	*!	*	*
c. [what e [John will [t read t]]]		*!	**
☞ d. [what will [John t [t read t]]]			***
e. [will [John t [t read what]]]	*!		**

(37) Matrix declaratives	OP-SPEC	OB-HD	STAY
☞ a. [John will [t read books]]			*
b. [e [John will [t read books]]]		*!	*
c. [will [John t [t read books]]]			**!

Again, alternative rankings (co-)define alternative grammars. In principle, this gives each OT analysis a typological flavour. On the basis of Grimshaw's analysis of matrix interrogatives, we can make predictions that go beyond the syntax of English. For instance, in a language in which STAY outranks OP-SPEC, *wh*-phrases remain in situ, as in the Chinese example in (38a), taken from

---

[10] For an argument in favour of the ranking OP-SPEC >> OB-HD, the reader is referred to Grimshaw (1997: 396).

Huang (1982). Alternatively, if STAY outranks OB-HD, I to C movement does not take place. If so, the language may resort to other means to prevent a violation of OB-HD, such as the insertion of a complementizer. A Canadian French example, taken from Lefebvre (1979), is given in (38b). The question of whether this insertion is actually permitted will depend on the rank of a constraint like TEL, given in (18c).

(38) a. Ni kanjian-le shei?
          *you see-*PRF   *who?*
          'Who do you see?'
      b. Quand que Marie viendra?
          when   that Marie will-come
          'When will Mary come?'

Grimshaw's analysis of *Wh*-raising can be extended to multiple interrogatives. In a *Wh*-in-situ language like Chinese, both *Wh*-phrases remain in situ, as predicted. The example in (39a) is due to Rint Sybesma (p.c.). Among *Wh*-raising languages, three strategies can be distinguished. In some languages, all *Wh*-phrases move to clause-initial position, which is illustrated for Bulgarian in (39b), taken from Rudin (1985). In others, exactly one *Wh*-phrase is raised, as is illustrated by Rudin (1988) by means of the English (39c). And finally, there are languages that do not allow multiple interrogatives. Rizzi (1982: 51) reports that Italian is one of those languages.

(39) a. Ni ji-le   shenmo gei shei?
          *you send-*PRF *what   to whom*
      b. Kogo na kogo e   pokazal Ivan?
          whom to whom pointed out   Ivan
      c. What did you give to whom?
      d. No multiple interrogatives

This suggests that there is a constraint that disprefers multiple fronting of *wh*-phrases which conflicts with OP-SPEC. Legendre *et al.* (1998) argue for the constraint *ADJOIN, prohibiting adjunction in SpecCP. If this constraint outranks OP-SPEC (and STAY), raising of a single *Wh*-phrase will be preferred over multiple fronting.[11] On the opposite ranking, the reverse will be true. At first sight, the absence of multiple interrogatives in a language like Italian is unexpected, since a priori one would expect that each language evaluates one of the possible multiple *Wh*-structures as optimal. We will return to this point below.

C.2 *Consensus and Controversy*

So far, we have seen that the acceptance of OT *can* lead to a general theory of

---

[11] For expository purposes, we have adapted Legendre *et al.*'s analysis to Grimshaw's (cf. Legendre *et al.* 1995, 1998). See also Ackema and Neeleman (1998).

syntax with important typological power.[12] However, OT does not provide us with a substantive theory of grammar right away, nor does it automatically lead to a unified view on the set-up of syntax. This makes it possible for Pesetsky to argue for a much more modest role of OT in syntax than for instance Grimshaw does. Pesetsky's main argument against a fully-fledged OT syntax is based on the existence of so-called *absolute ungrammaticality* or *ineffability*.

Syntactic objects are not always ungrammatical because of the existence of a better alternative. Sometimes ungrammaticality seems absolute, sometimes, a sentence is ungrammatical without there being a grammatical alternative available in the language. The absence of multiple interrogatives in Italian noted above is a clear example. This leads Pesetsky to argue that OT syntax deals only with matters of deletion and pronunciation, whereas some other module of grammar determines which structure-building and movement operations should apply. By assumption, this module consists of inviolable conditions, which would account for ineffability. However, it is not clear that Pesetsky's line of thought holds water. Several scholars have shown that ineffability can be captured in a fully-fledged OT syntax in terms of underparsing. It is not obvious that an explanation for ineffability in terms of OT is inferior to an approach that refers to inviolable conditions. It seems that this issue just attracts more attention in OT, and not if that is necessarily a more fundamental problem for this theory than for others. In the section, we review the possibilities of underparsing as well as the closely related issue of the role that semantic interpretation should play in candidate evaluation.[13]

Because the syntactic studies written within OT are so far small in number, it is not surprising that disagreement has arisen concerning the exact properties OT syntax should have; in part this is due to the influence of independently existing (non-OT) syntactic theories. We illustrate this in Section C.2.1 below by presenting different views on the role that derivation could play in OT syntax. It is not unlikely that these differences will disappear once the body of work grows, the influence of other theories is channelled, and OT-specific answers to general questions become widely accepted.

C.2.1 Derivation

Although OT is generally associated with a representationalist view on (modules of) grammar, most OT syntacticians do leave room for derivation. Müller (1998), for instance, assumes a multi-level syntactic model which consists of D-Structure, S-Structure, and LF, and argues that derivations, rather than representations, are evaluated. Grimshaw (1997) adopts a model of syntax where the

---

[12] Typological studies in OT syntax include Ackema and Neeleman (this volume, 1998), Costa (1997), and Legendre *et al.* (1993, 1998), among others.

[13] See Legendre *et al.* (1998) for an extensive discussion of the questions that are raised in this section.

levels of S-Structure and Logical Form co-exist (a heritage of the Principles and Parameters framework). Contrary to Müller, she does not explain her choice for this multi-level model of syntax. Although Grimshaw alludes to LF, she does not make crucial use of this level of representation. LF seems relevant only in the determination of the candidate set, because she assumes 'that competing candidates have non-distinct logical forms' (p. 376). However, Grimshaw also proposes that argument-predicate information is given in the input, and leaves the possibility open that the input 'should include a specification of LF-related properties, such as scope' (*ibid.*), which might be considered a redundancy in her system.

Another, related, heritage of the Principles and Parameters framework is the hypothesis that syntactic representations are transformationally derived, and that constraints—e.g., STAY given in (27)—may refer to traces of the transformations. However, Bresnan (this volume) argues that OT can more naturally be applied to syntax if a parallel correspondence theory is assumed, rather than a transformational syntax. More particularly, Bresnan (this volume) develops an OT syntax based on LFG, in which the optimal correspondence mapping is determined between two parallel structures: a feature structure (f-structure) which constitutes the input, and a categorial structure (c-structure) which serves as the output. F-structure is comparable to the structured input assumed by Legendre *et al.* (1995, 1998)—although the former is more precise than the latter: see also Section C.3 below—while c-structure is expressed in terms of extended X-bar theory, more or less along the lines of Grimshaw (1991). As Bresnan (this volume) shows, it is possible to translate Grimshaw's transformational theory into a non-transformational one based on imperfect correspondence mapping without losing the essence of Grimshaw's analyses. Those constraints that seem to presuppose a transformational syntax can relatively easily be recast in terms of extended X-bar theory and correspondence.

As we have already noted above, Pesetsky (1997, 1998) takes a direction that is entirely different from Bresnan's. He argues that OT syntax should not be concerned with building syntactic structure but rather with the way this structure is spelled out. Broekhuis and Dekkers (this volume) follow Pesetsky to a large extent. They argue that if one accepts (the essence of) the Minimalist Program, it is desirable from an empirical point of view to consider Chomsky's computational system to be the Generator of OT syntax. This enables them to (re)consider the division of labour between the Generator and the Evaluator. For instance, whereas Pesetsky assumes that the Evaluator determines the optimal pronunciation of one single LF representation, Broekhuis and Dekkers (this volume) present arguments in favour of the idea that pronunciation patterns of several LF representations may be compared with each other, so long as they receive the same semantic interpretation. They reach this conclusion by arguing that, among other things, it has empirical advantages to assume that economy of movement is not part of the computational system but rather an OT constraint. Similar considerations could ultimately lead to an important simplification of both OT syntax and the computational system in which the constraint inventory is seriously reduced and feature strength abolished. In short, whereas Bresnan (this volume) eliminates derivational residue by arguing for a non-transformational OT syntax, Broekhuis and Dekkers (this volume) consider derivation a crucial property of the Generator, responsible for building syntactic structure.

C.3 *Evaluation, Semantic Interpretation, and Ineffability*

To apply Optimality Theory in the domain of syntax after having done so in phonology is to encounter at least one intrinsic difference between these two modules of grammar. Whereas the essence of syntax is to combine simplex elements into complex ones, the basic task of phonology is not of such a combinatorial nature, since it is dependent on morphology (lexical phonology) and syntax (phrasal phonology) on this point. Through syntax, words are combined into sentences. On the null hypothesis that its input is a set of words, we could take OT syntax to associate optimal syntactic structures with sets of words. We are then faced with a large discrepancy between the input (unstructured on our null hypothesis) and the output (highly structured).

Broekhuis and Dekkers (this volume) illustrate the problematic nature of this discrepancy with the following example. Let us take the set of words in (40), selected in an in principle arbitrary way from the lexicon. From this set of words, at least two grammatical English sentences can be formed, which are given in (41). Let us suppose that these two sentences have the partial structural descriptions in (42). The question now is: why does one of these output structures not block the other? At least economy must prefer (42b) to (42a), because it involves fewer movement steps of the *Wh*-pronoun *who* (or, alternatively, *who* moves along a shorter path).

(40)   {game, Bob, the, wonders, thinks, who, Hank, lost}

(41)   a. Bob wonders who Hank thinks lost the game.
       b. Bob thinks Hank wonders who lost the game.

(42)   a. Bob wonders [who Hank thinks [t lost t the game]
       b. Bob thinks Hank wonders [who lost t the game]

The fact that both structures in (41) surface suggests that they have survived distinct evaluations. This follows directly from Pesetsky's assumption that distinct syntactic structures do not compete. However, let us focus here on the repercussions the grammaticality of the two structures in (42) has for the evaluation procedure in a fully-fledged OT syntax. Notice that although the two sentences are composed of the same words, they receive distinct semantic interpretations. In this light, it seems plausible that the semantics of output structures play a crucial role in the evaluation procedure in one way or another.

And indeed, there exists a broad consensus that semantic interpretation has an influence on the evaluation procedure, although the formal implementation of this idea is subject to debate. Roughly, two viewpoints can be distinguished.

Some authors (e.g. Ackema and Neeleman [this volume], Broekhuis and Dekkers [this volume]) argue for a semantic identity requirement on Candidate Sets (henceforth the Semantic Identity Approach). According to this requirement, only structures that have an identical (or non-distinct) semantic interpretation may enter in competition with each other. The two structures in (42) are thus in distinct candidate sets and will not be in competition, simply because they have different meanings. Others propose that the input is structured (henceforth the Structured Input Approach). According to Legendre *et al.* (1995: 610), 'Inputs consist of [. . .] skeletal structures containing predicate-argument structure and scope information'. Along the same lines, Bresnan (this volume) identifies the input with an LFG-based feature structure (see Section C.2.1).

Let us illustrate this with our example of multiple interrogatives. Legendre *et al.* assume that the input for multiple interrogatives takes the form in (43). Some outputs that are faithful to the input are given in (44). These structures correspond to the Chinese, Bulgarian, and English examples in (39) which we have repeated in (45).

(43) Input:
$[Q_i \; Q_j \; [\ldots V \ldots x_i \ldots x_j \ldots]]$

(44) Faithful outputs:
a. $[Q_i + Q_j \; [\ldots V \ldots wh_i \ldots wh_j \ldots]]$
b. $[wh_i \; wh_j \; [\ldots V \ldots x_i \ldots x_j \ldots]]$
c. $[wh_{i[j]} \; [\ldots V \ldots x_i \ldots x_j \ldots]]$

(45) a. Ni ji-le   shenmo gei shei?
          you send-PRF *what   to whom*
      b. Kogo na kogo e   pokazal Ivan?
          whom to whom pointed out   Ivan
      c. What did you give to whom?

Along these lines, we are able to distinguish between the input of (42a) and (42b). The structure in (a) is faithful to the predication and scope information given in (46a), and in (42b) faithful to that in (46b).

(46) a. $[\ldots V \ldots [Q_i \; [\ldots V \ldots [\; x_i \; V \ldots]]]]$
      b. $[\ldots V \ldots [\ldots V \ldots [Q_i \; [\; x_i \; V \ldots]]]]$

At first sight, the two approaches seem to be notational variants—Legendre *et al.*'s input structures could be reformulated as a restriction on candidate sets. However, although in many concrete cases both approaches have the same net effect, they are not quite interchangeable. First, contrary to the Semantic Identity Approach, the Structured Input Approach presupposes a syntax for inputs:

if the input is structured, this structure must be generated in one way or another. Under the Semantic Identity Approach, the task of establishing scope and predicate-argument relations is attributed to the syntax system itself. This means we do not need an additional generative device to structure the input, but rather an algorithm that prevents the comparison of semantically distinct structures.

Second, within the Structured Input Approach, unfaithful analyses of the input structure may compete with faithful ones. Legendre *et al.* argue that *wh*-elements may be realised as non-interrogative quantifiers, in which case *to whom* would surface as *to someone*. Hence, the unfaithful analysis (47) of the input structure (43) competes with its faithful counterparts in (44), and may even win.

(47) Unfaithful output:
    a. [wh$_i$ $\langle Q_j \rangle$ [x$_i$ V NP/$\langle wh_j \rangle$]]
    b. What did you give to someone?

On the assumption that underparsing has an effect on the interpretation of output structures, candidates conveying different meanings may block each other. Because faithful parses are clearly unmarked, Legendre *et al.* propose that in structures in which *who* surfaces as a non-interrogative quantifier, the constraint PARSE-*Wh* is violated. Now, in *Wh*-raising languages (OP-SPEC >> STAY) in which *ADJOIN has a high and PARSE-*Wh* a low rank (more precisely: if *ADJOIN and OP-SPEC outrank PARSE-*Wh* and STAY), a simple interrogative will surface whenever a multiple interrogative is targeted. These languages therefore lack multiple interrogatives. We established in section C.1.3 that Italian is such a language. The Structured Input Approach thus provides us with an explanation for language-specific ineffability which exploits the possibilities of partial underparsing ('sometimes it is best to say something else').

Within the Semantic Identity Approach, this type of ineffability cannot be explained in terms of partial underparsing, since competition between for instance simple and multiple interrogatives is not allowed because they are semantically distinct. However, Ackema and Neeleman (this volume) present an alternative explanation in terms of total underparsing, which they illustrate with a typological study of passives. In their view, all candidate sets contain a fully underparsed structure because this so-called null parse is consistent with any semantic interpretation. This enables them to claim that if well-formedness outweighs faithfulness, the null parse, instead of a party underparsed structure, may come out as the optimal candidate ('sometimes it is best to say nothing'). In this way they explain why languages lack (certain) passives.

Ackema and Neeleman (this volume) mention two drawbacks of the partial underparsing approach that do not arise in their analysis. First, they argue that the partial underparsing approach does not acknowledge the autonomy of syntax because it presupposes interaction of semantic and syntactic constraints. Second, they remark that it is not obvious what underparsed structures should look like. For instance, in a language that lacks multiple interrogatives (they take Irish as an example), the second *Wh*-phrase in (48a) cannot be fully deleted, as in (48b), because it is not the case in Irish that otherwise obligatory arguments may remain silent in interrogatives. Nor is it true for Irish that (48a) is allowed to surface if *what* is interpreted as a non-interrogative. Finally, there is the option Legendre *et al.* actually plumped for, according to which the second *Wh*-phrase is realized as an existentially quantified expression, as in (48c). Ackema and Neeleman argue that this option is not unproblematic because there seems to be no phonological relation between for instance *what* and *something* in Irish.

(48) a. Who destroyed what?
      b. Who destroyed?
      c. Who destroyed something?

Be this as it may, the total underparsing approach seems to have a more fundamental flaw, as noted by Legendre *et al.* (1998). Let us return to our analysis of multiple interrogatives. If *ADJOIN and OP-SPEC outrank PARSE-*Wh* and STAY, this does not necessarily lead to the election of the null parse as the optimal candidate. All things being equal, whenever some other parse constraint (for instance Ackema and Neeleman's PARSE-Passive, which requires that passive morphology be parsed) outranks *ADJOIN and OP-SPEC, the null parse will not come out as optimal so long as it violates this parse constraint. As Ackema and Neeleman (this volume) point out themselves, this leads to the presumably false prediction that there could exist languages which lack multiple interrogatives in active, but not in passive, sentences. To repair this, they propose a cyclic evaluation procedure which ensures that parse constraints do not interact with each other.

The terms *absolute ungrammaticality* and *ineffability* are thus used to refer not only to the language-particular absence of specific constructions, but also to the universal ungrammaticality of specific syntactic structures. There are at least two potential sources for universal ineffability. First, it can be due to harmonic boundedness (see Prince and Smolensky 1993). A candidate C_1 is harmonically bound by some candidate C_2 iff C_1 incurs all constraint violations C_2 does and C_1 incurs more constraint violations than C_2 does. In that case, C_1 will lose on any ranking. If the constraint inventory is universal (see Boersma [this volume] and Ellison [this volume] for claims to the contrary), C_1 will be ungrammatical in all languages. In most of the tableaus given above concrete examples of harmonic boundedness can be found. For instance, in tableau (37), repeated here as (49) for convenience, the candidates (b) and (c) are harmonically bound by candidate (a), because they both incur the violation of STAY that candidate (a) does (which is given in parentheses) as well as some additional violation. Hence, they are predicted never to surface (cf footnote 7).

(49) Matrix declaratives	Op-Spec	Ob-Hd	Stay
☞ a. [John will [t read books]]			(*)
b. [e [John will [t read books]]]		*!	(*)
c. [will [John t [t read books]]]			(*)*!

Second, syntactic structures may be universally ungrammatical because the Generator simply cannot produce them (see Broekhuis and Dekkers [this volume]). For instance, if X-bar theory is taken to be a defining property of the Generator (see Grimshaw 1997), any phrase marker that is not in accordance with the X'-schema will be an illicit output. Given the standard assumption that the Generator is universal, this structure is predicted not to appear in any language.

D. Learning in Optimality Theory

In generative grammar, one task of the learner is to determine which of the possible grammars allowed by an innate Universal Grammar is compatible with the language she is learning. In a Principles and Parameters (P&P) framework, this task amounts to determining the correct settings of a number of usually binary innate *parameters*, while in an Optimality-theoretic (OT) framework, the task amounts to determining the correct relative rankings of a number of innate *constraints*. We will now have a look at the problems that arise with several P&P learning algorithms, and see that some of these problems vanish with OT-specific learning algorithms. The increased learnability of OT grammars with respect to P&P grammars supports the correctness of Optimality Theory as a model of grammar.

   As an example, we will look at the learning of the parameters or constraints in a phonological problem: that of tongue-root-harmony systems. The results apply equally, however, to the learning of syntactic parameters and constraints.

D.1   *Seven Possible Tongue-Root-Harmony Systems*

For the phonological contrasts in their vowel inventories and for natural classes in phonological phenomena, tongue-root languages use the binary opposition *advanced tongue root* (ATR) versus *retracted tongue root* (RTR), next to the usual height and front/back oppositions. We will have a look at the non-back vowels only, in which case the maximal relevant inventory of a tongue-root language is

(50)

	ATR	RTR
high	i	ɪ
mid	e	ɛ
low	ə	a

A tongue-root-*harmony* language is a language that avoids disharmonic words like [etɛ]—i.e. words with ATR as well as RTR vowels. In constraint terminology, there must be a strong constraint like HARMONY. Such a language can be *ATR-dominant* or *RTR-dominant* depending on whether an underlying /ete/ would surface as [ete] or as [ɛtɛ], respectively. In constraint language, ATR dominance means that a constraint like MAXATR 'an ATR value in the input should appear in the output' dominates the analogous MAXRTR; we also see that HARMONY must dominate MAXRTR in such a case.

Many tongue-root-harmony languages lack the advanced low vowel /ə/, or the retracted high vowel /ɪ/, or both. Archangeli and Pulleyblank (1994) ascribe these asymmetries to the phonetically motivated *grounding conditions* LO/RTR 'if a vowel is low, then it is retracted' and HI/ATR 'if a vowel is high, then it is advanced'. Pulleyblank (1993, 1996) translates these grounding conditions directly into OT-able constraints: if a language honours LO/RTR, it has the ranking LO/RTR >> MAXATR, so that any underlying /ə/ will normally surface as [a]; if a language honours HI/ATR, it has the ranking HI/ATR >> MAXRTR, so that an underlying /ɪ/ will surface as [i].

We can now generate eight grammars from the following three binary *parameters*:

(51) a. whether the language is ATR- or RTR-dominant;
      b. whether the language honours HI/ATR;
      c. whether the language honours LO/RTR.

There is one ambiguity to fix, however. In an RTR-dominant language that honours HI/ATR, an underlying /ɛti/ has the surface candidates [ɛtɪ], which violates HARMONY; [ɛtɪ], which violates HI/ATR; and [eti], which violates MAXRTR. Since we already know that HI/ATR dominates MAXRTR in such a language, there remain two candidates: [eti], which would mildly *suggest* ATR dominance, and [ɛti], which is a surface violation of harmony and increases the vocabulary. Now, Pulleyblank and Turkel (1995, 1996) interpret the dominance parameter in such a way that it influences the surface vocabulary—i.e. /ɛti/ surfaces as [ɛti]. In other words, RTR dominance is expressed as the ranking MAXRTR >> HARMONY >> MAXATR (this is a slight simplification of Pulleyblank and Turkel's constraints).

Table (52) shows the eight possible grammars, with their seven possible surface vocabularies of VtV words; the labels A through G follow Pulleyblank and Turkel's (1995, 1996) typology. For instance, language B is a Wolof-like language: it honours the HI/ATR grounding condition and is RTR-dominant. The grammars A1 and A2 generate the *same* vocabulary: if there are no alternations, they describe the same language, which we will call A. Language C is the intersection of A and B; D is the intersection of A and E; G is a proper subset of E; and F is a proper subset of B. Pulleyblank and Turkel cite instances of real languages that more or less match each of the seven languages in the typology (52).

The first three rows of the surface vocabulary in (52) enumerate the harmonic words. The surface forms in the first row are always possible; forms with [ɪ] are

(52)

Grammar	A1	A2	B	C	D	E	F	G
HI/ATR parameter	−	−	+	+	−	−	+	+
LO/RTR parameter	−	−	−	−	+	+	+	+
dominance parameter	ATR	RTR	RTR	ATR	RTR	ATR	RTR	ATR
iti, ite, eti, ete, etɛ, ɛta, atɛ, ata	+	+	+	+	+	+	+	+
ɪtɪ, ɪtɛ, ɛtɪ, ɪta, atɪ	+	+			+	+		
itə, əti, etə, əte, ətə	+	+	+	+				
itɪ, ɪti, ɪte, etɪ, ɪtə, ətɪ, etə, ɛte, ɛtə, ətɛ, əta, ata								
itɛ, ɛti			+				+	
eta, ate						+		+
ita, ati			+			+	+	+

ruled out in languages with high Hɪ/Aᴛʀ, and forms with [ə] in languages with high Lo/Rᴛʀ.

The last four rows of (52) enumerate the thinkable disharmonic words. Most of them do not occur in any of the languages. However, the disharmonic forms [itɛ] and [ita] are licensed in RTR-dominant languages with high Hɪ/Aᴛʀ (B and F), and the disharmonic forms [ate] and [ati] are licensed in ATR-dominant languages with high Lo/Rᴛʀ (E and G); in the RTR-dominant language D, by contrast, underlying /ate/ would give [atɛ].

Note that P&P learning algorithms can be used for learning constraint grammars provided that the constraint rankings are translated into parameter settings first. This strategy is discussed in D.2 to D.7. OT-specific algorithms follow thereafter from D.8.

D.2   *The Triggering Learning Algorithm*

Gibson and Wexler (1994) proposed their Triggering Learning Algorithm (TLA) in order to account for the acquisition of three syntactic parameters (subject location, object-verb order, verb-second). Pulleyblank and Turkel (1995) applied the TLA to their three-parameter grammar space of tongue-root-harmony constraint grammars.

According to the TLA, the learner can, at any moment during acquisition, have as her current hypothesis any of the eight grammars A1 to G, and she may replace it with a different grammar only if incoming data conflicts with it—i.e. the algorithm is *error-driven*. Suppose, for instance, that the learner is currently in grammar F, and that the language environment is A. A possible datum, now, is [ɪtɛ], with a probability of 1/18, if all possible words are equally likely. This input conflicts with her current assumption of high-vowel grounding, which forbids [ɪ]. The conflicting input is a *trigger*: the learner will try a different grammar which she chooses randomly from the set of grammars *adjacent* to F (i.e. the algorithm is *conservative*), and will only accept that new candidate grammar if it does allow [ɪtɛ] (i.e. the algorithm is *greedy*).

According to the binary parameters in (51), grammar F must be considered adjacent to B, D, and G because a transition to any of these would involve changing a single parameter setting. We can represent the adjacency of all eight grammars in a graph:

(53) Adjacency

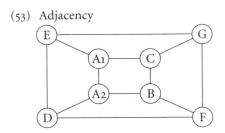

For instance, any shortest path from E to B involves three parameter flips.

Now suppose that the learner's environment is language A. Confronted with the A-datum [ɪtɛ] while her hypothesis is F, she will try the adjacent B, D, or G, all with probability 1/3. She will only change her grammar if the new grammar does license [ɪtɛ] i.e. if the grammar that she tries happens to be A1, A2, D, or E. Combining these, we conclude that she will only make the plunge if the new grammar is D. Since the data [ɛtɪ], [ɪta], [atɪ], and [ɪtɪ] trigger the same grammar change, the probability that the learner's grammar after the next datum (randomly taken from the vocabulary of A) is changed to D, is $5\times1/18\times1/3$ = 5/54. The complete transition graph in an A environment is:

(54) Language A

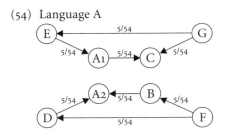

For simplicity, the self-loops are left out of (54): the probability, for instance, that the learner, if her current hypothesis is F, will cling to F after the next random datum, is 44/54—i.e. 1 minus the sum of the probabilities of going to B or D. If we compare figure (54) with (53), we see that the connection between the hypotheses D and E is broken, because the difference between the vocabularies of D and E consists solely of data that do not occur in A; the same goes for the pairs B-C, and F-G. The pair A1-A2 is a special case of this: in an error-driven learning scheme, the learner can never replace a grammar with a grammar that would generate the same language.

Pulleyblank and Turkel propose that 'any of the set of possible languages is equally likely as the starting hypothesis of the TLA'. The transition graph (54) shows that in the environment of language A, all grammars have a finite probability of being replaced with the grammar A after one or two steps, and that grammar A will never be abandoned once the learner has reached it. All learners will therefore eventually settle down in language A if the environment is A. Thus, language A will always be learned correctly.

D.3 *Unlearnable Languages*

According to Gold (1967), a language is *learnable in the limit* if the learner is guaranteed to find the target language if exposed to an infinite amount of data. Language A is thus learnable in the limit, and we will now show that the others are not.

Suppose that a learner in a homogeneous C environment starts out in grammar B. Because language C is the intersection of A and B, no data from the environment C can ever falsify the initial hypothesis: our learner will never get out of the unrestrictive hypothesis B because language C is a *proper subset* of language B. The complete transition graph for a homogeneous C environment is:

(55) Language C

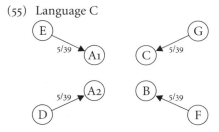

Starting from a randomly chosen grammar, 1/2 of the learners will end up in an A grammar, 1/4 in B, and only 1/4 in C.

The learning graph for language G shows three *sinks* or *local maxima* (B, E, and G):

(56) Language G

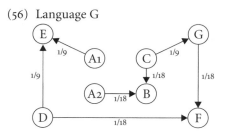

If the distribution of initial states is uniform, the probabilities that the learner ends up in each of the eight grammars is: 7/24 for B, 8/24 for E, and 9/24 for G.

The learning of the correct grammar for language B ('Wolof') is not guaranteed either; the learner may end up in the *absorbing cycle* E-A1:

(57) Language B

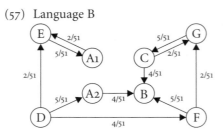

This graph shows that a learner can go back and forth between two adjacent grammars: if she is in grammar C (so that an underlying /ita/ would have to surface as [itə]), the B-datum [ita] may cause her either to reject her hypothesis of ATR dominance (and go to B), or to hypothesize that harmony is dominated by Lo/RTR (and go to G); conversely, if she is in G (which disallows [ə]) and is confronted with a B-datum that contains [ə], she will have to cancel the Lo/RTR grounding condition by going to C.

The learning graphs for the three remaining languages D, F, and E, can be obtained from (55), (56), and (57), respectively, by replacing all instances of 'B' with 'E' and vice versa, and doing the same for the pairs C-D and F-G.

D.4 *Supersets and Other Local Maxima*

The TLA proved non-convergent for most language environments. This does not have to be a problem for learning theories (Clark and Roberts 1993). It is possible that languages which allow learners to end up in local maxima do actually exist; they would simply be unstable, since a part of the next generation would speak a different language. If this new language is learnable without local maxima, the original language would die out in a few generations. Because no such instabilities have been reported for the instances of the languages B, C, D, E, F, and G identified by Pulleyblank and Turkel (1995), we will assume that the non-convergence *is* a problem in the case at hand.

The fact that language A is learnable in the limit is largely because it is the least restrictive of the seven languages: there is always positive data around to wipe out any grounding constraints. In graph (56), however, we see that if the learner's hypothesis is E, she will never have any reason to go to the target grammar G, since no data of G are incompatible with the hypothesis E—the vocabulary of G is a proper subset of that of E. In an error-driven learning scheme, the non-occurrence of certain forms ('negative evidence') cannot be signalled by the learner. Starting from a uniform grammar distribution, this will lead to a high probability that the learner will end up in a too unrestrictive grammar.

Apart from the superset problem, there is a more generic source of concern. The current hypothesis of the learner may be a grammar from which she cannot get out because all adjacent grammars are worse. This is a problem of conservatism and greediness together: if you are at a hilltop and want to reach the top of the higher mountain instead, you can choose between jumping the valley or climbing down—being conservative will disallow the former, and being greedy will disallow the latter. We can see this in graph (57). Suppose the learner's current hypothesis is B. According to table (52), she will only be urged to change the grammar if the incoming G-datum is [eta] or [ate]. Conservatism tells us that she cannot go to G directly because that would require flipping two parameters. Greediness, however, tells us not to go to the adjacent languages A2, C, or F because these do not allow [ate].

D.5 *Improving Convergence: The Most Restrictive Initial State*

To reduce the superset problem, we can try to start in the most restrictive grammar. In syntactic theory, this *subset principle* (Berwick 1985, Wexler and Manzini 1987) was confronted by the problem that pro-drop languages are supersets of non-pro-drop languages. This means that a child would have to start with a non-pro-drop hypothesis, although most children do not produce any pronouns when they start to speak. (A possible line of defence is that the empty subject in 'it rains' provides positive evidence for the negative setting of the pro-drop parameter.)

Gibson and Wexler (1994) applied the idea of a maximally restrictive initial state by requiring their learner of constituent order to start with a negative setting of the V2 parameter. In the tongue-root-harmony case, we could start with undominated grounding conditions. Such a restrictive grammar will be changed only if positive evidence is found of the occurrence of ungrounded feature combinations. We would thus start in language F or G (both with a probability of 1/2), with positive settings of both grounding parameters HI/ATR and LO/RTR.

We can easily see from graphs (56) and (57) that if the learner starts in F or G, she will always end up in the target language. From graph (55), however, we see that with a probability of 1/2 of starting in G, the chance that she will end up in the correct grammar C is also 1/2. This is an improvement over the random initial state, but is not our ideal, because if the learner starts with hypothesis F, she will end up in grammar B, which again represents a superset of the C language.

We can now compare the probabilities of convergence for all seven languages in the cases of the uniform and restricted initial distributions:

(58)

		initial grammar						
		A	B	C	D	E	F	G
target language								
randomly chosen from	A1 A2 B C D E F G	1	8/11	1/4	1/4	8/11	3/8	3/8
randomly chosen from	F G	1	1	1/2	1/2	1	1	1

Learnability is not perfect yet. There is no initial parameter setting that makes all languages A to G learnable.[14] The source of this problem lies in Pulleyblank and Turkel's 'packaging' of the tongue-root constraints: ATR dominance stands for MAXATR >> *HARMONY >> MAXRTR. In Smolensky's (1996b) proposal, structural constraints (like HARMONY) should initially dominate all faithfulness constraints (like MAXATR and MAXRTR), so that the languages F and G are not perfect candidates for the initial state.

The initial state should therefore have the harmony constraint on top. However, if the structural constraints are innate and binary, they are inherently conflicting. For example, consider the underlying forms /ita/, /ɪta/, /itə/, and /ɪtə/, which, according to the principle of the 'richness of the base' (Prince and Smolensky 1993), should all be possible inputs to a universal set of innate constraints. If the grounding constraints are honoured, the output in the initial state should be [ita], perhaps violating some MAX constraints. But [ita] violates the harmony constraint. A system of binary feature values cannot meet Smolensky's requirement of initially undominated structural constraints.

D.6 *Improving Convergence: Relaxing Conservatism or Greediness*

To tackle local maxima, the validity of both the conservatism constraint and the greediness constraint was challenged by Berwick and Niyogi (1996): 'If the learner drops either or both of the Greediness and Single Value Constraints, the resulting algorithm [. . .] converges faster (in the sense of requiring fewer examples) than the TLA' (p. 607). They go on to show that this statement is true for Gibson and Wexler's (1994) example of a three-parameter constituent-ordering problem.

However, Berwick and Niyogi's criticism does not seem to hold for larger parameter spaces. We can see this if we compute the expected number of examples (data) the learner needs to arrive at the target grammar, in the two competing algorithms.

In a space of N_p binary parameters, the number of possible grammars N would be equal to 2^{N_p}. In Berwick and Niyogi's algorithm, which does not use the conservatism and greediness conditions, the average number of triggers (conflicting data) required for reaching the target grammar (from any non-target grammar) would be 2^{N_p-1}. For a three-parameter space this is 7, but for a more realistic 30-parameter space this is 1,073,741,823.

For Gibson and Wexler's algorithm, we can compute the convergence under the simplifying assumption that the parameters have independent influences on

---

[14] Note that the problem cannot be solved by an initial unsetting of the dominance parameter, along the lines of Gibson and Wexler, who start with the specifier-head and complement-head parameters unset. If the learner starts with a combined FG hypothesis and encounters the C-datum [itə], she will flip the LO/RTR parameter and go to a combined BC hypothesis, from which she will never get to the target grammar C.

the language. In such a case, the worst initial state is one in which all N_p binary parameters have the wrong value. With every trigger, there is a probability of $1/N_p$ that the correct parameter change will be chosen. Thus, the target grammar will be reached after at most N_p^2 triggers. For a three-parameter space this is 9, which may be worse than in Berwick and Niyogi's algorithm, but for a 30-parameter space this is only 900, to which Berwick and Niyogi's alternative constitutes a drastic deterioration.

With respect to the quantity of *data* needed to reach the target grammar, the difference between the two algorithms is somewhat less dramatic because in the TLA the probability that a datum is a trigger decreases as the hypothesis approaches the target grammar. Even if the quantity of data thus becomes proportional to N_p^3, a polynomial dependence of the learning time will always outperform an exponential dependence as soon as realistic degrees of freedom are involved.

We must conclude that without the conservatism and greediness constraints the acquisition time of realistic grammar spaces would be prohibitively large. Besides, Berwick and Niyogi's alternative does not solve the superset problem (they were fortunate in the lack of superset languages in their three-parameter constituent-ordering problem), so in the case of our tongue-root-harmony problem it does not even converge (and it crashes on the absorbing cycle of (57)).

D.7 *Improving Convergence: Genetic Algorithms*

The local-maxima problem is smaller if the learner is allowed to maintain multiple hypotheses at the same time (Clark and Roberts 1993). For example, suppose the learner arrives at two different local maxima X and Y in a 20-parameter space. Apart from the usual parameter swappings within the hypotheses X and Y ('mutations'), which will not help her out of the trap, she will have the option of creating a new hypothesis Z that copies, say, 11 parameter settings from X and the remaining nine from Y (a 'recombination'). If this hypothesis is better than X and Y, the learner will have succeeded in getting out of a local maximum without sacrificing either conservativeness or greediness. After each generation, the least *fit* candidates are removed from the pool of hypotheses.

Pulleyblank and Turkel (this volume) propose an algorithm with OT-specific mutations (swapping the rankings of adjacent constraints), without any recombinations (not really genetic, therefore), and with an involved OT-specific measure of fitness. The learner of the tongue-root-harmony system of Yoruba has to maintain 32 hypotheses at a time, and will usually converge upon the correct ranking of the ten relevant constraints (in six strata) within a few thousand data. Interestingly, Pulleyblank and Turkel show that in their example the learner correctly achieves any subset grammar in the majority of trials.

As everyone acknowledges, the genetic approach does not guarantee convergence onto the global maximum. Moreover, it places a large burden on the learner, who has to maintain several, possibly very distinct, hypotheses. By contrast, some OT-specific algorithms (Sections D.8 and D.11) are guaranteed to converge, even with a single hypothesis.

D.8   *OT-Specific Learning Algorithms*

If parameter grammars have learning algorithms that fail in local maxima, and we cannot do without conservatism and greediness—there is but one conclusion: grammars are not built around parameters.

The alternative is, of course, that grammars are built around ranked constraints. Tesar and Smolensky (1993, 1996) and Tesar (1995, this volume) developed an algorithm that can sort constraints. We will describe here only the error-driven variant of this algorithm, which is called Error-Driven Constraint Demotion (EDCD). Like the TLA this algorithm is error-driven, conservative, greedy, and oblivious, but unlike the TLA, it always converges upon the target grammar: OT grammars are learnable with a number of triggers that relates to the square of the number of constraints (which is as fast as the grammars with independent parameters described in Section D.6), without ever getting stuck in a local maximum.

As an example, we will show how an OT learner can go from hypothesis B to the target grammar G—something impossible according to graph (57). In grammar B, the five constraints are completely ranked: HI/ATR >> MaxRTR because [I] is not allowed, MaxRTR >> Harmony >> MaxATR because of the 'packaged' RTR dominance, and MaxATR >> LoRTR because [ə] is allowed. Now suppose that the language environment is G and the learner encounters the datum [ate], which is not in her current hypothesis. Assuming that the underlying form is also /ate/, we get an evaluation of some relevant candidates in the following tableau:

(59) /ate/	HI/ATR	MaxRTR	Harmony	MaxATR	Lo/RTR
✔ [ate]			*		
☞ [atɛ]				*	
[əte]		*!			*

In the learner's current hypothesis, the winner is [atɛ], which is shown by the pointing finger (☞). The correct adult form, however, is [ate], which is shown by the check mark or tick (✔). So our error-driven learner will have to change her grammar. The EDCD tells her to *demote* all the violated constraints in the learner's winner that are higher than the highest violated constraint in the correct form (which is MaxATR) to the *stratum* immediately below that constraint. In (59), the constraint Harmony is demoted below MaxATR, ending up in the same stratum as Lo/RTR. This is the (nearly) minimal change that ensures that in the new grammar, the form [ate] will become better than the previous winner [atɛ] (though not necessarily better than a third candidate):

(60)	/ate/	Hɪ/Aᴛʀ	MᴀxRᴛʀ	MᴀxAᴛʀ	Hᴀʀᴍᴏɴʏ	Lᴏ/Rᴛʀ
☞ ✔	[ate]				*	
	[atɛ]			*		
	[əte]		*!			*

Now that harmony is ranked low, the new hypothesis is not a tongue-root-harmony grammar! The learner will now need evidence of harmony—for example, the underlying form /etɛ/, which surfaces as [ete] in language G:

(61)	/etɛ/	Hɪ/Aᴛʀ	MᴀxRᴛʀ	MᴀxAᴛʀ	Hᴀʀᴍᴏɴʏ	Lᴏ/Rᴛʀ
☞	[ete]				*	
✔	[ete]		*!			
	[ɛtɛ]			*!		*

The learner now demotes MᴀxRᴛʀ (the only high violated constraint in the adult form) below Hᴀʀᴍᴏɴʏ (the highest violated constraint in her own winner, so that this constraint becomes crucially violated in her new evaluation), giving the ranking in (62).

When comparing this learning algorithm with TLA, we can see that something very different is going on: we need an underlying form. Moreover, an underlying /etɛ/ suddenly becomes [ete], while it would have become [ɛtɛ] in the original hypothesis B.

The new grammar is already ATR-dominant (in fact, it is language C). The datum [ate] is relevant again, though the learner now chooses a different incorrect winner from before:

(62)	/ate/	Hɪ/Aᴛʀ	MᴀxAᴛʀ	Hᴀʀᴍᴏɴʏ	Lᴏ/Rᴛʀ	MᴀxRᴛʀ
☞ ✔	[ate]			*		
	[atɛ]		*!			
☞	[əte]				*	*

Since Hᴀʀᴍᴏɴʏ and Lᴏ/Rᴛʀ are in the same stratum, two candidates are both optimal in the learner's hypothesis. One possible interpretation of this (Anttila 1995) is that the learner can choose freely from [ate] and [əte]. If she chooses [əte], this will be different from the correct adult form [ate], so that Hᴀʀᴍᴏɴʏ will be demoted below Lᴏ/Rᴛʀ, into the stratum of MᴀxRᴛʀ, as we see in (63). After that, the underlying form /etɛ/ is relevant again:

(63)	/etɛ/	Hɪ/Atr	MaxAtr	Lo/Rtr	Harmony	MaxRtr
☞	[etɛ]				*	
☞ ✔	[ete]					*
	[ɛtɛ]		*!			

Since only [ete] is the correct adult form, MaxRtr is demoted to a lower, new stratum, giving the ranking of (64).

We may still want to learn low-vowel grounding. For this we need the underlying form /ətə/, which the speaker can produce faithfully, but which surfaces as [ata] in G:

(64)	/ətə/	Hɪ/Atr	MaxAtr	Lo/Rtr	Harmony	MaxRtr
☞	[ətə]			**		
✔	[ata]		*!*			

Now, MaxAtr will be demoted below Lo/Rtr, into the stratum of Harmony, giving the ranking of (65). The two grounding constraints are now on top of the learner's grammar, as they are in the target grammar G. But we need the datum [ate] again, because for the underlying form /ate/, the candidates [ate] and [atɛ] tie for optimality:

(65)	/ate/	Hɪ/Atr	Lo/Rtr	MaxAtr	Harmony	MaxRtr
☞ ✔	[ate]				*	
☞	[atɛ]			*		
	[əte]		*!			*

We see that Harmony must be demoted below MaxAtr, giving the grammar of (66). Finally, we need the underlying form /etɛ/ again:

(66)	/etɛ/	Hɪ/Atr	Lo/Rtr	MaxAtr	Harmony	MaxRtr
☞	[etɛ]				*	
✔	[ete]					*
	[ɛtɛ]			*!		

This demotes MaxRtr below Harmony, and the learner has arrived in the target grammar G. If she had started with five equally-ranked constraints instead (i.e. all in a single stratum), the grounding constraints Hɪ/Atr and Lo/Rtr would have stayed on the same height, and the learner would have ended up in the ranking {Hɪ/Atr, Lo/Rtr} >> MaxAtr >> Harmony >> MaxRtr, which is the way to represent the language G with the minimal number of strata.

D.9 *Comparison of Parameter-Setting and Constraint-Sorting Algorithms*

The good thing about Tesar and Smolensky's algorithm is that it resolves every conflict: there are no stressy local maxima like B in graph (57). The algorithm is guaranteed to converge. However, superset hypotheses may still be stable: if there is no morphology that produces underlying forms like /etɛ/, the harmony constraint may stay in a low stratum. Also, if there is no evidence for the ghost segment /ə/, the learner will feel perfectly well in the hypothesis of tableau (64). The superset problem will partly be gone if we follow Smolensky's (1996b) proposal of an initial state with structural constraints in the higher stratum and faithfulness constraints in the lower: starting from {HI/ATR, LO/RTR, HARMONY} >> {MAXATR, MAXRTR}, the learner will never arrive in a grammar that allows [ə], though in the absence of alternations, she will still arrive in the insufficiently restricted grammar {HI/ATR, LO/RTR} >> {MAXATR, MAXRTR} >> HARMONY after a single [ate] datum, and stay there.

The reliance of the constraint-sorting algorithm on underlying forms has been criticised by Turkel (1994: 7): 'From the point of view of a model of language acquisition, the assumption of having the optimal parse available as part of the input is problematic.' This is also the rationale behind Pulleyblank and Turkel's (this volume) use of the genetic algorithm, which does not involve the postulation of prior knowledge of correct input forms. The proposal by Tesar (this volume) of an iterative strategy of combining EDCD with the reconstruction of underlying forms (see Section D.14) may silence some of the criticism. We must note, however, that making reference to underlying forms is not a property of the learning algorithm itself but follows from the use of faithfulness constraints, which evaluate, after all, the relation between input and output forms; for (partial) grammars that contain structural constraints only, EDCD determines the ranking without ever referring to underlying forms.

D.10 *Optionality and Variation: Stochastic Evaluation*

Optimality Theory can easily be extended to incorporate *stochastic grammars*— i.e. grammars that allow optionality in their outputs. Hayes (this volume) and Boersma (1997, this volume) observed that this can be achieved if each constraint has a *ranking value* along a continuous scale, and at each evaluation, a random number is temporarily added to this ranking value, so that two constraints whose ranking values are close to each other can have reverse rankings at evaluation time. Hayes (this volume) applies this idea to acceptability judgements for dark [ɫ] and light [l] as reflexes of an underlying /l/ in English: the well-formedness judgement of native listeners is not an all-or-none matter: depending on the position of /l/ in the word and in the morpheme, each of the candidates may be judged 'acceptable', 'unusual', 'unlikely' or 'impossible'.

D.11 *Gradual Learning Algorithms: Acquiring a Stochastic Grammar*

While EDCD is the fastest available algorithm, it cannot inform stochastic grammars very well: the rankings would be reshuffled at each learning step. The EDCD is not very *robust* against errors either: a single error may destroy the grammar in such a way that it can cost on the order of N^2 learning steps (though usually much fewer; N is the number of constraints) to climb out of the wrong grammar. For instance, if the learner has reached the target grammar B (Hɪ/Aᴛʀ >> MᴀxRᴛʀ >> Hᴀʀᴍᴏɴʏ >> MᴀxAᴛʀ >> Lᴏ/Rᴛʀ), an erratic [itɪ] datum, if taken as correct by the learner, will demote HɪɪAᴛʀ past MᴀxRᴛʀ, into the stratum of Hᴀʀᴍᴏɴʏ, and it will require an additional se-quence of e.g. /itɪ/ → [iti], /ita/ → [ita], /etɛ/ → [ɛtɛ], and /ətə/ → [ətə], to arrive at the correct grammar again.

The gradual learning algorithm by Boersma (1997, this volume) makes use of a continuous ranking scale. When the learner's winner conflicts with the adult form, all constraints violated in the adult form are demoted by a small step along this scale, and all constraints violated in the learner's winner are promoted by the same small step. In tableau (59), this would mean that Hᴀʀᴍᴏɴʏ is slightly demoted and MᴀxAᴛʀ is slightly promoted; if the form [ate] was ad-ministered repeatedly, the two constraints would ultimately swap places.

For a continuous scale to make sense, evaluation must be *stochastic*, so that constraints can maintain a safety margin in their ranking difference. If the target grammar is a stochastically evaluating grammar, the gradual learner will always converge upon that grammar—i.e. she will learn to exhibit the same amount of variation as she hears in her language environment.

Although the gradual algorithm is much slower than EDCD, it is quite resis-tant to errors in the data: the number of learning steps needed after an error is typically *one*, and this single step may come at a later date. For instance, if the learner has reached the target grammar B and takes an erratic [itɪ] datum at face value, the constraints HɪɪAᴛʀ and MᴀxRᴛʀ will approach one another by a small step. This causes an increase in the probability that MᴀxRᴛʀ will outrank HɪɪAᴛʀ at some future evaluation. When that happens once, HɪɪAᴛʀ will be promoted and MᴀxRᴛʀ will be demoted so that the original rankings are re-stored.

D.12 *First-Language Acquisition*

A strong theory of Universal Grammar maintains that all the constraints the learner will ever need are available from the beginning (Tesar and Smolensky 1993: 1). Under such a theory it is found that structural constraints must be initially high-ranked (Gnanadesikan 1995, Smolensky 1996b). However, a non-nativist viewpoint could identify this situation with the initial state in the acquisition of speech production, when articulatory gestures have still to be learned.

Boersma (this volume) argues that the learner starts out with an empty grammar without any constraints: as soon as the learner manages to categorize a perceptual phonological feature, the relevant faithfulness constraints will enter her grammar from the bottom; and as soon as the learner starts to master an articulatory gesture, the relevant articulatory constraints will enter her grammar from above, where they have been waiting in a virtual pool irrelevant for the learner but possibly playing a role in what Ellison (this volume) would call 'ease of communication between linguists'. Thus, Boersma argues that sets of constraints are constructed from the data. These sets will contain unusual constraints like 'a low vowel should be ATR'; it is the task of the learning process to put these at the bottom of the hierarchy, where they can do no harm.

D.13 Second-Language Acquisition

When confronted with a different language, a speaker could take over the lexicon of this second language, and run the underlying forms through the constraint system of her first language. In the phonology, an underlying form would probably equal an adult form of the target language, *as perceived by the learner*. Differences between the learner's output and the native output of the target language could then arise either by differences in the perception or by differences in the production. Jacobs and Gussenhoven (this volume) tackle this indeterminacy by showing that if a learner perceives the target forms exactly as they were uttered, the constraint system can still produce the correct surface form. They hold a universal perceptual parser responsible for categorizing the foreign input into a set of feature values supplied by Universal Grammar.

D.14 Acquisition of the Lexicon

In a language that disallows coda consonants, the surface form [ka] could come from the input /ka/ or from the input /kat/. When confronted with the output [ka] for the first time, the learner has to put this in his or her lexicon as /ka/ or as /kat/. According to the principle of *lexicon optimization* (Prince and Smolensky 1993: 192), the learner will choose /ka/ (in the absence of dominating morphological considerations) because the input-output pair /kat/ → [ka] violates a FAITH constraint, whereas /ka/ → [ka] violates no faithfulness constraints at all, and both pairs violate the same structural constraints (which evaluate only the output, which is the same in both cases). The learner's strategy is to find all the inputs of which the optimal output form is [ka], and to determine which of these creates the most harmonic input-output pair with [ka].

To implement this strategy, the abstract learner has to generate a possibly infinite number of inputs (*richness of the base*), and for each of these inputs, she has to determine the winning output after generating a possibly infinite number of candidates, effectively squaring GEN. This procedure can be represented in a *tableau of tableaus*:

(67)	[ka]			
		/ka/	No-Coda	Faith
»→		[ka]		
		[kat]	*!	*
		/kat/	No-Coda	Faith
»→		[ka]		¡*
		[kat]	*!	

Following Smolensky (1996a), the turned exclamation symbol (¡) is put *before* the crucial violation mark for the input candidate /kat/, and the pointing feather (»→) identifies the winning input /ka/.

In the procedure exemplified in (67), there must be at least one input that leads to the output [ka]; otherwise, the parse will fail. In first-language acquisition, this will be a real problem. The remedy is to allow the output forms to be sub-optimal, so that we can simplify (67) to

(68)	[ka]	No-Coda	Faith
»→	/ka/		
	/kat/		¡*

Apart from needing only a single input generation, this move allows the learner to parse adult data that she cannot personally produce. For instance, the adult form [kat] will be perceived as /kat/, although the child would never produce this form:

(69)	[kat]	NoCoda	Faith
	/ka/	*	¡*
»→	/kat/	*	
	/skati/	*	¡**

If /kat/ is already in her lexicon, the learner will recognize [kat] as /kat/; otherwise, she may create a new lexical entry /kat/. In either case, she will pronounce it as [ka]. Because of the possible richness of the perceived underlying forms in relation to the produced forms, this technique for using OT grammars for comprehension is called *robust interpretive parsing* (Tesar and Smolensky 1996, Smolensky 1996a). It invalidates the argument by Hale and Reiss (1996), who believe that a faithful recognition of an adult [kat] as /kat/ would need high-ranked faithfulness constraints, and who conclude from this that the production system must be separated from the grammar. Robust interpretive parsing thus seems to save Gnanadesikan's (1995) analysis of unfaithful child utterances with high-ranked structural constraints, and Smolensky's (1996b) idea of an initial state in which all structural constraints outrank all faithfulness constraints, although Hale and Reiss (1998) continue the discussion by noting that tableaus like (69) would always force a German listener to recognize the utterance [raːt] as /raːt/ 'advice' and never as /raːd/ 'bicycle', which adults pronounce as [raːt] as a result of final devoicing.

In Section D.8, we saw that the constraint-sorting algorithm needed to know an input form. In general, however, it is the *correct parse* that has to be known; for Tesar (this volume) this is the correct metric interpretation (division into feet) of an overt surface stress pattern. Tesar uses robust interpretive parsing to find this correct parse: interpretive parsing may result in a metric interpretation that is different from the adult's because of the incorrect constraint ranking, but this is better than no interpretation at all, since the constraint demotions that arise if the learner's surface stress pattern (as computed with her constraint system) does not match the adult stress pattern may lead to an improved metrical interpretation on the next cycle of interpretive parsing. Tesar claims that such an iteration of interpretive and production-oriented parsing often leads to the correct acquisition of the grammar, especially when the learner starts from a suitable initial ranking.

In their genetic learning algorithm, Pulleyblank and Turkel (this volume) use the strategy exemplified in tableau (69) for determining the underlying forms that are compatible with the attested adult output forms. They limit the number of possible input forms by adhering to the assumption that a young learner will only posit inputs that contain a subset of the phonological content of the encountered output.

E. References

Ackema, P. and A. Neeleman (1998). 'Optimal questions'. *Natural Language and Linguistic Theory* 16, 443–90.

Anttila, A. (1995). 'Deriving variation from grammar: A study of Finnish genitives'. Ms, Stanford University. ROA-63. Revised version in Hinskens *et al.* (eds).

Archangeli, D. and D. Pulleyblank (1994). *Grounded Phonology*. Cambridge, MA, MIT Press.

Beckman, J., L. Walsh Dickey and S. Urbanczyk (eds) (1995). *Papers in Optimality Theory*. University of Massachusetts Occasional Papers 18.

Berwick, R. C. (1985). *The Acquisition of Syntactic Knowledge*. Cambridge, MA, MIT Press.

—— and P. Niyogi (1996). 'Learning from triggers'. *Linguistic Inquiry* 27, 605–22.

Boersma, P. (1997). 'How we learn variation, optionality, and probability'. *Proceedings of the Institute of Phonetic Sciences of the University of Amsterdam* 21, 43–58. [Earlier version in ROA-221.

Broselow, E. (1991). 'The structure of fricative-stop onsets'. Paper presented at the Conference on Phonological Feature Organization, LSA Summer School.

Burzio, L. (1994). *Principles of English Stress*. Cambridge, Cambridge University Press.

—— (1996). 'Surface constraints versus Underlying Representation'. In Durand and Laks (eds).

—— (1998). 'Multiple correspondence'. *Lingua* 104, 79–109.

Chomsky, N. (1995). *The Minimalist Program.* Cambridge, MA, MIT Press.

—— and M. Halle (1968). *The Sound Pattern of English.* New York, Harper & Row.

—— and H. Lasnik (1977). 'Filters and control'. *Linguistic Inquiry* 8, 425–504.

Clark, R. and I. Roberts (1993). 'A computational model of language learnability and language change'. *Linguistic Inquiry* 24, 299–345.

Costa, J. (1996). 'Word order and constraint interaction'. Ms, Leiden University/HIL.

—— (1997). 'Word order typology in Optimality Theory'. Ms, Leiden University/HIL and University of Lisbon.

Dekkers, J. R. M. (1997). 'French word order: A conspiracy theory'. In J. Coerts and H. de Hoop (eds) *Linguistics in The Netherlands 1997.* Amsterdam and Philadelphia, John Benjamins, 49–60.

Durand, J. and B. Laks (eds) (1996). *Current Trends in Phonology: Models and Methods.* Salford, Manchester, University of Salford Press.

French, K. M. (1988). *Insights into Tagalog reduplication, infixation and stress from nonlinear phonology.* Summer Institute of Linguistics and University of Texas, Arlington.

Gibson, E. and K. Wexler (1994). 'Triggers'. *Linguistic Inquiry* 25, 407–54.

Gold, E. M. (1967). 'Language identification in the limit'. *Information and Control* 10, 447–74.

Gnanadesikan, A. (1995). 'Markedness and faithfulness constraints in child phonology'. Ms, U.Mass. [Rutgers Optimality Archive 67, http://ruccs.rutgers.edu/roa.html.]

Grimshaw, J. (1991). 'Extended projection'. Ms, Brandeis University.

—— (1997). 'Projection, heads, and Optimality'. *Linguistic Inquiry* 28, 373–422.

—— and V. Samek-Lodovici (1995). 'Optimal subjects'. In Beckman *et al.* (eds), 589–605.

Hale, M. and C. Reiss (1996). 'The initial ranking of faithfulness constraints in UG'. Ms, Concordia University. ROA-104.

—— —— (1998). 'Formal and empirical arguments concerning phonological acquisition'. *Linguistic Inquiry* 29: 656–83.

Hayes, B. P. (1989). 'Compensatory lengthening in moraic phonology'. *Linguistic Inquiry* 20, 253–306.

Hinskens, F., R. van Hout and W. L. Wetzels (eds) (1997). *Variation, Change and Phonological Theory.* Amsterdam and Philadelphia, John Benjamins.

Huang, C.-T. J. (1982). *Logical Relations in Chinese and the Theory of Grammar.* PhD thesis, MIT.

Inkelas, S., O. Orgun and C. Zoll (1997). 'The implication of lexical exceptions for the nature of grammar'. In Roca (ed.), 393–418.

Kager, R. (1997). 'Rhythmic vowel deletion in Optimality Theory'. In Roca (ed.), 463–99.

Kaisse, E. M. and P. A. Shaw (1985). 'On the Theory of Lexical Phonology'. *Phonology Yearbook* 2, 1–30.

Kiparsky, P. (1982). 'Lexical Phonology and Morphology'. In I.-S. Yang (ed.) *Linguistics in the Morning Calm I,* 3–91. Seoul, Hanshin.

Kisseberth, C. (1970). 'On the functional unity of phonological rules'. *Linguistic Inquiry* 1, 291–306.

Koutsoudas, A. (1976). 'Unordered rule hypothesis'. In A. Koutsoudas (ed.) *The Application and Ordering of Grammatical Rules,* 1–21. The Hague, Mouton.

Lefebvre, C. (1979). 'Réanalyse de *que/qui,* inversion stylistique et mouvement de *Wh* en français'. *Montreal Working Papers in Linguistics,* 73–90.

Legendre, G., C. Wilson and P. Smolensky (1993). 'An optimality-theoretic typology of case and grammatical voice systems'. *Proceedings of the Nineteenth Annual Meeting of the Berkeley Linguistics Society*, Berkeley, CA.

—— —— —— (1998). 'When is less more? Faithfulness and Minimal Links in *WH*-Chains'. In P. Barbosa *et al.* (eds).

—— —— —— K. Homer and W. Raymond (1995). 'Optimality and *Wh*-extraction'. In Beckman *et al.* (eds), 607–36.

McCarthy, J. J. (1986). 'OCP effects: Gemination and antigemination'. *Linguistic Inquiry* 17, 207–63.

—— and A. S. Prince (1990). 'Foot and word in prosodic morphology: The Arabic broken plural'. *Natural Language and Linguistic Theory* 8, 209–82.

—— —— (1993a). 'Generalized alignment'. *Yearbook of Morphology*, 79–153.

—— —— (1993b). 'Prosodic morphology I: Constraint interaction and satisfaction'. Ms, University of Massachusetts and Rutgers University.

—— —— (1994). 'The emergence of the unmarked: Optimality in prosodic morphology'. Ms, University of Massachusetts and Rutgers University.

—— —— (1995). 'Faithfulness and reduplicative identity'. In Beckman *et al.* (eds), 249–384.

Mascaró, J. (1976). *Catalan Phonology and the Phonological Cycle*. Doctoral dissertation, MIT, Cambridge, Massachusetts (distributed by the Indiana University Linguistics Club, Bloomington, Indiana).

Müller, G. (1998). 'Order preservation, parallel movement, and the emergence of the unmarked'. Ms, University of Stuttgart.

Myers, S. (1997). 'Expressing phonetic naturalness in phonology'. In Roca (ed.), 125–52.

Pesetsky, D. (1997). 'Optimality Theory and syntax: Movement and pronunciation'. In D. Archangeli and D. T. Langendoen (eds) *Optimality Theory: An Overview*, Oxford, Blackwell, 134–70

—— (1998). 'Some Optimality principles of sentence pronunciation'. In Barbosa *et al.* (eds).

Prince, A. S. and P. Smolensky (1993). 'Optimality Theory: Constraint interaction in generative grammar'. Ms, Rutgers University and University of Colorado at Boulder.

Pulleyblank, D. (1993). 'Vowel harmony and Optimality Theory'. *Actas do Workshop Sobre Fonologia*, University of Coimbra, 1–18.

—— (1996). 'Neutral vowels in Optimality Theory: A comparison of Yoruba and Wolof'. *Canadian Journal of Linguistics* 41, 295–347.

—— and W. J. Turkel (1995). 'Asymmetries in feature interaction. Learnability and constraint ranking'. Ms, University of British Columbia.

—— (1996). 'Optimality Theory and learning algorithms: The representation of recurrent featural asymmetries'. In Durand and Laks (eds).

Rizzi, L. (1982). *Issues in Italian Syntax*. Dordrecht, Foris.

Roca, I. M. (ed.) (1997). *Derivations and Constraints in Phonology*. Oxford, Clarendon.

Rochemont, M. (1978). *A Theory of Stylistic Rules in English*. Doctoral dissertation, University of Massachusetts.

Rudin, C. (1985). *Aspects of Bulgarian Syntax: Complementizers and Wh-constructions*. Columbus, OH, Slavica Publishers.

—— (1988). 'On multiple questions and multiple *Wh*-fronting'. *Natural Language and Linguistic Theory* 6, 445–501.

Samek-Lodovici, V. (1996). *Constraints on Subjects: An Optimality Theoretic Analysis.* Doctoral dissertation, Rutgers University.

Sannasgala, P. B. (1976). *Sinhalese Vocables of Dutch Origin.* Colombo, Kularatne.

Smolensky, P. (1996a). 'On the comprehension/production dilemma in child language'. *Linguistic Inquiry* 27, 720–31.

—— (1996b). 'The initial state and "richness of the base" in Optimality Theory'. Technical Report 96–4, Department of Cognitive Science, Johns Hopkins University, Baltimore. ROA-154.

Tesar, B. (1995). *Computational Optimality Theory.* Doctoral dissertation, University of Colorado.

—— and P. Smolensky (1993). 'The learnability of Optimality Theory: an algorithm and some basic complexity results'. Ms, Department of Computer Science and Institute of Cognitive Science, University of Colorado at Boulder. ROA-2.

—— (1996). 'Learnability in Optimality Theory (long version)'. Technical Report 96–3, Department of Cognitive Science, Johns Hopkins University, Baltimore. ROA-156.

Turkel, W. J. (1994). 'The acquisition of Optimality Theoretic systems'. Ms, University of British Columbia. ROA-11.

Weijer, J. M. van de (1996). *Segmental Structure and Complex Segments.* Tübingen, Niemeyer.

Wexler, K. and R. M. Manzini (1987). 'Parameters and learnability in binding theory.' In T. Roeper and E. Williams (eds) *Parameter Setting.* Dordrecht, Reidel, 41–76.

Zubizarreta, M. L. (1994). 'Some prosodically motivated syntactic operations'. In G. Cinque *et al.* (eds) *Paths Towards Universal Grammar.* Washington DC, Georgetown University Press, 473–85.

PART ONE

Phonology: Prosodic Representation

1

Cycles, Non-Derived-Environment Blocking, and Correspondence[1]

Luigi Burzio

1.1 Introduction

The notion of morphologically 'derived' environment plays a role in phonology in two different ways. In some cases the phonology 'misapplies' precisely in those environments, as in the celebrated example *cònd[e]ns-átion* (Chomsky and Halle 1968), where the bracketed vowel is unreduced despite its lack of stress, in contrast to morphologically underived *hápp[ə]n*, where reduction occurs as expected. In other cases one finds the opposite situation, in which the phonology misapplies to *un*derived environments, as in *v[áy]tamin* or *sén[ay]le*, where a certain vowel shortening does not occur, in contrast to derived *sen[í]l-ity*, where it does.

As Kiparsky (1993: 278) notes, rule-based phonology grants no theoretical status to the notion of 'derived environment' and thus needs to be supplemented with additional machinery. The traditional supplements have been the 'cycle', to account for the type of misapplication of *cònd[e]ns-átion*, and the 'strict cycle condition' to account for the other type, as in *v[áy]tamin*. Matters are different in a certain specific version of Optimality Theory, in which 'derived' environments are simply those to which the notion of output-to-output 'Correspondence' is applicable. In that version of OT, formally developed in McCarthy and Prince (1994, 1995), McCarthy (1995), Benua (1995, 1997), anticipated in some ways in Burzio (1991, 1992, 1993, 1994a,b), Burzio and DiFabio (1994), and to be further defended in this chapter, the basic architecture of the theory consists of three types of constraints: purely phonological constraints: PHON; constraints imposing Input-Output faithfulness: IO-F; and constraints

[1] Work related to this article was presented in the Spring of 1997 at the University of Massachusetts, Amherst, and at MIT. I am grateful to both audiences for kind and valuable comments. Parts of this material were also presented in seminars at Johns Hopkins, whose participants have helped my understanding in measurable ways. For especially stimulating discussions of many of the issues addressed in the paper, my gratitude goes to Laura Benua, Greg Childress, Linda Lombardi, Robert Frank, Paul Smolensky, and Colin Wilson. The responsibility for any errors remains mine.

imposing Output-Output faithfulness: OO-F. These constraints interact in ways established by their relative rank as usual in OT. The range of interaction among the three types is then defined by the six logical possibilities in (1) and (2).

(1) a. PHON >> OO-F >> IO-F
     b. OO-F >> PHON >> IO-F
     c. OO-F >> IO-F >> PHON

(2) a. PHON >> IO-F >> OO-F
     b. IO-F >> PHON >> OO-F
     c. IO-F >> OO-F >> PHON

In a theory such as this in which there are no derivations, generalizations which were formerly expressed derivationally should follow from constraint ranking, with the rankings in (1)–(2) as the source of major generalizations. More specifically, one might expect that generalizations such as those proposed within Lexical Phonology in terms of rules differing by systematic clusters of properties such as cyclicity, non-application to derived environments, structure-preservation, having lexical exceptions (the 'lexical'/'non-lexical' distinction), should reduce to the variation in rankings of (1)–(2).

This chapter takes on a portion of that task, by claiming that all observed 'misapplication' of phonology consists of PHON constraints holding an intermediate rank, as in either of (1b), (2b), in fact generalizing the results achieved within the domain of reduplication in McCarthy and Prince (1994, 1995, 1999). Each of (1b), (2b) characterizes a situation in which some PHON constraint prevails over the domain of constraints it dominates, respectively some IO-F and some OO-F constraint, relating to underived and derived environments respectively. Furthermore, in each case, that PHON constraint will be blocked over the class of complementary environments, controlled by constraints that dominate it in turn. The other cases in (1)–(2) will not be quite as intriguing. Those in (1a) and (2a) will be cases where a given member of PHON always applies, and those in (1c) and (2c) the cases where it never does. As for the difference between (1) and (2), the ranking 'OO-F >> IO-F' versus the opposite ranking, it turns out to be important in its own right, as discussed in Burzio (1997), and in the Conclusion below.

Beside asserting the necessity of output-to-output Correspondence in OT, this chapter further asserts its sufficiency in dealing with allomorphy, leading to the rejection of the traditional notion of 'Underlying Representation' (Burzio 1994a, 1996, 1997, 1998).

The chapter is organized as follows. In Section 1.2, I consider the 'Correspondence' account of cyclic effect, essentially reviewing recent literature. In Section 1.3, I compare the notion of 'input' in OT with the traditional notion of underlying representation, giving reasons why, unlike the former, the latter is dispensable. In Section 1.4, I turn to blocking in non-derived environments, distinguishing two different subtypes. One of the two subtypes, addressed in 1.4.1 and instantiated by English vowel shortening, will be shown to follow from the proposed approach, reducing to one of the expected ranking possibilities, but crucially only if there is no underlying representation. The second subtype, reviewed in 1.4.2 and represented by Finnish assibilation, will be shown to be consistent with that conclusion, but to require a somewhat different account, along the lines of Kiparsky (1993). Subsection 1.4.3 briefly reviews the theoretical history of blocking in non-derived environments, while 1.4.4 addresses the special status of affixes, which do not appear to behave like other derived environments. Section 1.5 concludes.

1.2 Cyclic Effects

In Burzio (1994a) (henceforth 'PES') I provide detailed arguments that the stress of the boldfaced vowels in both (3b) and (4b) reflects a direct, surface-to-surface 'metrical consistency' with the corresponding items in (3a), (4a) rather than the principle of the 'cycle' or some other special provision.

(3)   a. medícinal   b. medìcináliy
         divísible   divìsibíliy
         napóleon   napòleónic
         accéleràte   accèlerátion
         antícipàte   antícipatòry
         phenòmenólogy   phenòmenológic
         persónify   persònificátion
         assímilable   assìmilabílity

(4)   a. accépt   b. accéptable
         propagánda   propagándist
         américan   américanìst

Specifically, the organization held responsible for the patterns of stress preservation in (3), (4) is the constraint hierarchy in (5) (PES: 165f, 312f).

(5)   a. METRICAL WELL-FORMEDNESS   (MWF) >>
       b. METRICAL CONSISTENCY   (MC)   >>
       c. METRICAL ALIGNMENT   (MA)

The MC of (5b) is an instance of OO-F, imposing metrical identity of related surface forms. The metrical constraints in (5a, c) each standing for a small cluster of constraints, are both instances of PHON. Roughly speaking, the first defines the range of well-formed feet, and the second imposes alignment of metrical structure with phonetic edges. Given the ranking in (5), MC is correctly predicted to succeed in misaligning the metrical structure at either edge as in (6), but not in enforcing exceptional feet as in (7).

(6)   a. me(dìci)(nálity)   b. a(mérica)(nìstɸ)
(7)   a. *(cómpensa)tòry, *(làryngo)lógic   b. *ca(tàs)tróphic, *e(xìs)téntial

In (6a) the metrical structure is misaligned at the left edge as an overt syllable remains unparsed, while in (6b) there is misalignment at the right edge as a non-overt syllable is parsed. (On non-overt syllables, see also Giegerich 1985; Kiparsky 1991; Kager 1993). In (6b), there is also a misalignment at the left edge, but that is independent of MC. In (7), on the other hand, each of the marked feet, which would satisfy MC relative to the base (i.e. *cómpensàte*, etc.) is disallowed by higher-ranked Metrical Well-formedness (there are neither unary feet nor ternary feet ($\sigma H\sigma$) in the PES analysis). Hence MC must be violated, as in *compénsatòry*, etc.

The hierarchy in (5) of PES is an instance of the ranking schema in (1b) above in the way illustrated in (8).

(8)   a. MFW >> MC   >> MA
        b. OO-F >> Phon >> IO-F

The OO-F of (8b) is instantiated by MC just above it, while Phon is instantiated by MA. As for the IO-F of (8b) it is implicitly instantiated by the assumption of PES that English stress is prevalently regular rather than lexicalized. In OT, this entails that the phonology must dominate IO-F.[2]

This reanalysis of 'cyclic' effects carries over to the noted failure of vowel reduction in *cònd[e]ns-átion*, assuming the partial grammar in (9).

(9)   OO-F >> *V >> IO-F

In (9), *V is taken to refer to full vowels and to be a member of a markedness hierarchy under which [ə] is the least marked vowel. Vowels will correctly fail to reduce in stressed positions assuming a higher-ranked ('positional') IO-F constraint at work in those positions, along the lines of Beckman (1996; see also Alderete 1995). In *cond[e]nsation*, failure of reduction will be compelled by the higher-ranked OO-F in (9), given in *cond[é]nse*.[3]

The above account of cyclic effects mirrors the account of misapplication of

---

[2] It is worth noting, however, that there is a certain degree of irregularity, especially where lower-ranked MA is involved. Many nouns and adjectives exhibit the misalignment of *ro(bústɸ)*, *ce(méntɸ)* (while that of verbs and of adjectives in -*ic* follows from MC: PES, Burzio 1994b, and below). Since this occurs in a minority of cases, the facts are consistent with the ranking in (8), abstracting away here from the problem of exceptions/lexical variability, to which I return.

[3] Matters are more complex along several different dimensions, though, as noted in PES, 4.4. Reduction does not fail in all such cases, e.g. *inf[ə]rmátion*, and does not otherwise succeed in all unstressed positions: *pród[ʌ]ct*. This would seem to require further elaborations on the notion of positional IO-F. Note also that minimal pairs like *mór[ʌ]n*, vs. *ápr[ə]n* raise a variability issue similar to that of the preceding footnote.

phonology in reduplicative systems of McCarthy and Prince (1995; henceforth 'M&P'), who develop the formal Theory of Correspondence. They identify two instances of correspondence, each imposing identity or 'faithfulness' constraints: Input-to-Output correspondence, and correspondence between Base and Reduplicant. The first results in IO-faithfulness constraints, which take over the role of the PARSE and FILL constraints of Prince and Smolensky (1993). The second results in BR-faithfulness, now an instance of the more general OO-faithfulness of the present and other recent discussions.

M&P note misapplications (*over*applications) of phonology such the one in (10) in Madurese.

(10) ỹāt-nēỹāt 'intentions'

In Madurese, vowels are generally nasalized if and only if they follow a nasal, as in the base form *nēỹāt* in (10). In reduplication, however, they can be induced by reduplicative identity, as in the reduplicant *ỹāt*, where no nasal precedes. Cases like (10) will receive a Correspondence account in terms of the ranking in (1b)/(8b) above. By dominating IO-F, certain members of PHON will give rise to the regularity observed in the base *nēỹāt*, while by being dominated by OO-F they will allow the apparent violation of that regularity in the reduplicant *ỹāt*. Just as the phonological cycle once seemed applicable to some of the cases in (3) above, so it may at first seem applicable to cases like (10) as well. Nasalization would apply on the root cycle, only then followed by reduplication. M&P point out cases like (11), however, in Klamath.

(11)   a. hoscənwa 'makes vomit'   b. Wic-Wicl'i 'stiff'

In Klamath, vowels are reduced in non-initial closed syllables, as in (11a). Under reduplication, this part of the phonology misapplies (*under*applies), however, as in (11b). This case is different from the Madurese one in (10) because here misapplication occurs in the base. That difference makes it completely intractable in derivational terms, because morphological and phonological operations cannot be ordered relative to one-another (a standard impasse of serialism). In (11b), correct reduplication presupposes the correct form of the base, and vice versa. In contrast, the misapplication of phonology in (11b) continues to follow from domination by OO-F as in (1b)/(8b).

The difference between (10) and (11) is not captured by the present discussion, which somewhat simplifies M&P's. Our PHON of (1b)/(8b) actually lumps together two of M&P's constraints: a general markedness constraint and a context-specific constraint. The full ranking is actually: PHON$_{\text{CONTEXT}}$ >> OO-F >> PHON$_{\text{MARK}}$, where the PHON$_{\text{MARK}}$ constraint rules out nasalized vowels in Madurese and unreduced vowels (in closed syllables) in Klamath, while the PHON$_{\text{CONTEXT}}$ constraint imposes nasalized vowels in post-nasal contexts in Madurese and non-reduced vowels in initial syllables in Klamath. The ranking OO-F >> PHON of the present simplified discussion in fact only holds relative to the more general markedness constraint, the more specific one remaining undominated. On this more fully articulated account, the specific, undominated $\text{P}_{\text{HON}_{\text{CONTEXT}}}$ constraint will now correctly apply in whichever component—base or reduplicant—it is applicable to. Misapplication will occur in the other component, only targeted by the dominated $\text{P}_{\text{HON}_{\text{MARK}}}$ constraint, whence the difference between (10) and (11) (see M&P).

The Klamath case in (11) refutes rule ordering and the cycle in ways similar to the pairs in (12) on the PES analysis.

(12)   a. pre(véntɸ)/pre(vénting)   b. aca(démicɸ)/aca(démical)

Verbs and adjectives in *-ic* have exceptional stress patterns, a 'misapplication' consisting of a violation of Metrical Alignment (5c) above. Their affixed forms in *-ing* and *-al* respectively, however, have regular stress patterns. This behaviour can be shown to follow from OO-F under the same ranking needed for the cases in (3) and (4) above if each pair in (12) is evaluated as a whole, like the base-reduplicant pair in (11). Other initially similar pairs behave differently, however. Foe example, *paréntal* does not result in **pa(réntɸ)*, despite similarly misaligned *ce(méntɸ)*. The nature of the distinction seems clear at least intuitively, although it will not be pursued formally here. In general, calculation by correspondence seems to activate only items that are immediate substrings or (co-strings) of the candidate, as in the cases in (3) and (4). Activation of superstrings, as in (12), seems to occur only with closely related items, strictly sharing syntactic category and semantic content. A different view is taken by Benua (1997), who maintains a general principle of 'base-priority'. Although the latter is certainly consistent with the bulk of the evidence as just noted (no *parént from *parént-al*) it is challenged by (12).[4] Both the cases in (11) and those in (12) would then point to the generalization's being not quite in terms of 'derived' environments but more broadly in terms of environments to which OO-F is relevant. It is this broader generalization that proves the 'cycle' ineffective.

M&P's theory of OO-Correspondence has been extended beyond the domain of reduplication in McCarthy's (1995) study of Rotuman, in Benua's (1995, 1997) comprehensive study of 'Transderivational Identity Effects' and in McCarthy (this volume), bringing M&P's line of work, direct descendant of Prince and Smolensky (1993), closer to the already similar, if less formally developed, positions of PES. Other researchers have also effectively asserted the role of OO-Correspondence within OT over that of derivations, notably Buckley (1995), Duanmu (1997), Kenstowicz (1996), Itô and Mester (1997), Kager (this volume). See also Padgett (1997, and references cited).

In sum, a clear consensus is emerging within OT research that phonological

---

[4] As a reviewer notes, the stress of the items in (12b) is predictable in the sense that it is the one typical of each class (*-ic* and *-ical*). The same holds for the items in (12a). However, it is the classes that are exceptional compared with the rest of English. The text aims to account for that exceptionality.

calculations relate surface forms to one another. This conclusion is fully consistent with the 'parallel' character of OT, and removes one of the last vestiges of the derivational theory—the cycle. Empirical arguments against the cycle have relied on the observation that the actual generalizations are broader than the cycle could express, as shown by (11)–(12), while other arguments have made the opposite type of observation, that the actual generalizations are narrower than the cycle can express. As noted in PES: 187f, from the point of view of the cycle there is little reason why stem stress should be preserved in *medìcinálity* and the other cases of (3), but not in **catàstróphic* and the other cases of (7).[5] [6]

The empirical inadequacies of the cycle have an expected echo at the conceptual level. A long tradition of use (insightfully reviewed in Cole 1995) has tended to obscure the fact that it is a stipulatory provision.[7] It does not follow from a general theory which has underlying representations and rules that the rules should apply in cyclic order. The conclusion that in a structure '[B . . . A . . .]' the surface form of A must first be calculated to correctly calculate B, is an admission that surface rather than underlying representation is relevant, contradicting the main premise. In contrast, OO-Correspondence is part of the main architecture of the theory, at least in the version of it defended here. It is not an ancillary notion alternative to the cycle but rather a central one alternative to underlying representation, as we see in the next section.

1.3 The Input Versus Underlying Representation

Reliance on OO-Correspondence by phonological analysis raises the natural question of whether morphological analysis should not just follow suit. That is, if the sound structure of *condensation* is calculated from the surface form *condense*, couldn't its morphological structure also just consist of the word *condense* plus -*ation*, dispensing with underlying representation (UR) altogether? M&P's analysis of reduplication certainly suggests that morphology and phonology go hand in hand, the identity between base and reduplicant being equally relevant to both. The present approach will explicitly assume an affirmative answer to

---

[5] Note that suggesting that **catàstróphic* is ruled out by 'clash avoidance' would be stating the problem rather than giving a solution. 'Clash avoidance' is an output constraint—in the present context, a surrogate of the claim of PES that there are no unary feet. The fact that the derivational apparatus is ineffective unless supplemented (and ultimately supplanted) by output constraints is the point of the text.

[6] The present approach is able to correctly broaden predictions that were too narrow (*prevént* ← *prevénting*) by generalizing over representations rather than derivations; and to correctly restrict predictions that were too broad (**catástrophic* ← *catástrophe*) by employing violable constraints of which the effects are automatically suspended under domination.

[7] Cole (1995: 80) notes that '[In Lexical Phonology] cyclicity does not have to be stipulated; it results automatically from the interleaving of morphological and phonological processes.' This is true but simply makes the 'interleaving' the relevant stipulation. From the present perspective, the reason 'interleaving' proved useful is that it provided some approximation to the full parallelism advocated here.

that question. On such UR-less, but OO-Correspondence-based theory, words sharing a stem can be seen as in correspondence over that portion, and similarly for words sharing an affix. This conception, independently proposed in the context of an analysis of English stress in PES, turns out to be in essence the conception long advanced by J. Bybee (see Bybee 1988, 1995). In turn, the latter seems implementable along OT lines under Correspondence Theory. The proposed conception also has points in common with Aronoff's (1976, 1994) 'word-based' morphology.

The type of misapplication of phonology reviewed above, then, suggests, by invoking OO-F constraints, that UR may be superfluous. The other type of mis-application, to be discussed in the next section, will indicate more explicitly that UR must not exist. Before turning to that case, however, it will be useful to compare the notion of UR, which need not exist in OT, with the notion of input, which obviously must.

1.3.1 *Active and Inactive Input*

The first relevant notion to consider is that of the 'base'. In OT, the latter refers to the class of possible inputs to the grammar. Since all systematic properties of lexical items are attributed to the grammar in OT, none is attributed to the base, which is thus taken to be 'rich' (Prince and Smolensky's 'richness of the base'). As the class of all possible inputs, the base thus includes every possible structure. Each grammar is then such as to partition that class into possible and impossible lexical items, schematically as in (13).

(13)   base $\longrightarrow$ GRAMMAR $\Big\langle$ possible lexical items

        impossible lexical items
        (class of ungrammatical outputs)

The grammar has this effect by virtue of being an input-output device. Some structures fed to the grammar as inputs will survive as outputs, while others will not. The class of *actual* 'outputs'—i.e. lexical items—will then be some (presumably random) subset of the class of possible ones. The question that arises at this point is what is the class of *actual* inputs, given the class of actual outputs, graphically, as in (14).

(14)   ? (actual) input $\longrightarrow$ GRAMMAR $\longrightarrow$ (actual) output

That class is indeterminate as things so far stand because although the grammar gives a unique output given the input, it does not do the reverse. For example, the output [əmérəkə] could result from the exact same input, or from *æmerikʌ*, given an appropriate grammar able to assign stress and reduce unstressed vowels. Some additional hypothesis is therefore necessary to identify the class of actual inputs given the class of actual outputs.

Let us address this problem in two steps, and put aside for the moment morphologically-derived or dependent items, such as those considered in the previous section, whose calculation requires comparison with other items (via OO-F, on the present approach). Concerning the other class—i.e. underived items— Prince and Smolensky (1993) (henceforth 'P&S') advance the hypothesis known as 'lexicon optimization'. On that hypothesis, the actual input, among all the ones that would yield the correct output, is the one that does so 'optimally', that is with the least amount of constraint violation. It is easy to see that (remember: aside from allomorphy) this means that the actual input *equals* the actual output. The reason is that any input different from the output, like *æmerikʌ* for [*əmérəkə*] would only add violations of IO-F without ever avoiding any other violation in return.[8] Under P&S's lexicon optimization, then, the input-output relation is schematically as in (15).

(15)   input ⟶ GRAMMAR ⟶ output

This expresses the fact that there are two conditions conjunctively relating input and output: identity and grammar-relatedness. Hence the grammar, in conjunction with P&S's 'lexicon optimization' hypothesis, defines a class of possible 'input-outputs', in which an input-output is a representation such that, when fed to the grammar as an input, it is returned by the grammar unchanged as an output. So, for example, [*æmerəkə*] is not a possible input-output because it fails to satisfy grammar-relatedness. The reason is that if it was given to the grammar of English as an input, something different would be returned as an output, like [*əmérəkə*], or perhaps [*æmerik*]. In contrast [*əmérəkə*] is a possible input-output given the grammar of English.

Now the claim illustrated for P&S in (15) appears to be non-distinct (again, allomorphy aside) from the PES claim that there is only surface representation and no UR. The reason is that if input and output are identical, then surely there is only one representation rather than two, and the grammar is to be understood as a structure-checking device (e.g. like the 'binding theory' of syntax) rather than a structure changing (or filling) one as in derivational theories.

Before putting allomorphy back into the picture, one further important distinction related to the notion of input must be introduced. The grammar as given so far has one major internal partition: that between Phon and IO-F

---

[8] This discussion is based on the first of two formulations of lexicon optimization P&S consider. The second formulation embodies the hypothesis that, everything else being equal, the input is minimally specified. So far as I can see at this time, this alternative would not lead to the conclusions drawn in the text. On the other hand, P&S do not provide concrete arguments to support such a minimal specification hypothesis.

constraints. That partition is reflected on the input-output in the following way. While the latter can be thought of as a single representation, it is a *complex* representation, involving features and their temporal distribution, prosodic structures, and so forth. Each aspect of that representation will have its own standing relative to the internal components of the grammar, thus far IO-F and PHON. In particular, given lexicon optimization, IO-F will always be satisfied by every aspect of the representation. However, PHON will not be. For instance, in *əmérəkə* there is one violation of ONSET, and there are further violations involving the greater than minimal number of syllables, the marked character of various segments and so forth. Hence, not all input-output is alike. All of the input-output satisfies IO-F, but some of it additionally 'activates' IO-F constraints into compelling violations of PHON, while the rest of it satisfies PHON. Hence, the complex representation that is the input-output has an internal partition that mirrors the grammar-internal partition—schematically as in (16).

(16)

INPUT-OUTPUT Internal partition:	GRAMMAR internal partition:
a. [ACTIVE: compels violations of PHON]	[IO-F]
b. [INACTIVE: satisfies PHON]	[PHON]

Clearly, the 'active' input-output in the above sense is the unpredictable part of the representation, which must thus be associated with memorization, while the inactive input-output is the predictable part and hence only possibly, though not necessarily, memorized. As P. Smolensky (p.c.) notes, the active/inactive distinction in (16) may be indeterminate, due to the massive parallelism of the system. So for example in [ærəzównə] there is a violation of a PHON constraint '*V: ' barring long vowels, but there are two possible aspects of the input-output that could force that violation. One is the long vowel itself, the other is the stress. A non-derivational grammar of English that allows stressed penultimates only if they are heavy would be able to calculate either aspect from the other, thus leaving it indeterminate, which is actually an active input, alias memorized. No general problem arises from this indeterminacy, however, so far as I can tell.

There is an important respect in which the distinction between active and inactive input is quite unambiguous. It concerns the difference between contrastive and non-contrastive variation, illustrated in (17a,b).

(17)   a. **Non-contrastive variation**: English p/p^h: [$p^h it/spit$]
        b. **Contrastive variation**:   English p/b: [rip/rib]

Under lexicon optimization, both types of variation are present in the input-output and all four sample words are represented only in their phonetic form. The difference between the two cases is that only in (17b) is the variation due to active input. Specifically, the [*b*] violates a markedness constraint barring voiced obstruents, so that that feature combination must thus be active in the input. In contrast, the [*p*] satisfies that constraint and hence involves no active input, at least relative to that constraint. The variation in (17a), on the other hand, is not due to active input. Rather, the marked member of the pair—that is, p^h is present in the output because of a specific phonological constraint imposing aspiration of obstruents in onset position. Hence non-contrastive variation instantiates the ranking PHON >> IO-F, where the input is inactive, namely unable to induce a violation of PHON. Contrastive variation instantiates the opposite ranking IO-F >> PHON, where the input is active, inducing a violation of PHON. This is what makes the former variation predictable or 'allophonic' while the latter is unpredictable.

Variation that is contrastive and unpredictable in general could still be predictable in specific contexts. For instance, the distinction between nasals *n*, *m* in English is contrastive in general: *dine/dime*, but is neutralized in nasal-obstruent clusters: *cou*[*n*]*t*, *ba*[*ŋ*]*k*, *ca*[*m*]*p*. This results from the fact that, while IO-F dominates the a-contextual markedness constraint that—let us say—rules out more marked *m*, it is in turn dominated by a specific constraint ruling out non-homorganic nasal-obstruent clusters. In contrast, IO-F is dominated by both contextual and markedness constraints in the aspiration-type variation. The three different situations are summarized in (18), where the intended effects of individual constraints are given in parentheses. (For related discussion, see also Kirchner 1995; McCarthy and Prince 1995.)

(18)   a. **Non-contrastive variation: English *p/ph***

PHON$_{\text{CONTEXT}}$ >>   PHON$_{\text{MARK}}$ >>   IO-F
(aspirate onsets)   (*aspirated obstruents)   (aspirated obstruents)

b. **Contrastive variation never neutralized: English *p/b***

IO-F >>   PHON$_{\text{CONTEXT}}$ >>   PHON$_{\text{MARK}}$
(voiced obstruents)   (e.g. final devoicing)   (* voiced obstruent)

c. **Contrastive variation neutralized contextually: English *m/n***

PHON$_{\text{CONTEXT}}$ >>   IO-F >>   PHON$_{\text{MARK}}$
(nasal assimilation)   (labial and nasal)   (*labial and nasal)

Note that (18b) presupposes the existence not only of a markedness constraint, but also of some contextual constraint(s) such as the one(s) responsible for final devoicing in languages like German or Russian, although neither PHON constraint will have any effect under that ranking (e.g. in English). This enables us to take the same constraint types to be involved in all cases, each type of variation resulting simply from a different ranking schema.

In this way, the expressive power once held in terms of whether or not some variation was 'underlying' is retained in terms of whether or not that variation is present in the *active* input (all variation being present in the input at large under lexicon optimization). Note here that, similarities notwithstanding, the 'active' input is not just the old UR under a different name. The reason is that, unlike UR, the active input cannot be characterized as a level in any meaningful sense. While a 'level' is generally defined by its inherent properties, the active input has no inherent properties. The latter consists of any array of features (using this term broadly to include prosodic and autosegmental structures) chosen from the range of possibilities permitted by the grammar. So all the properties—in the sense of anything that is systematic—that the active input may have are grammar-given rather than inherent. For instance, the *p/b* distinction in English is part of the active input by virtue of the ranking in (18b), a property of the grammar. In contrast, the *p/ph* distinction is *not* part of the active input, and that is by virtue of the ranking in (18a), again a property of the grammar. Matters are quite different for the traditional UR. In terms of the latter, the difference between the two types of variation—*p/ph* and *p/b*—is only partly attributable to the grammar, alias the 'rules'. One may presume the existence of a rule turning *p* to *pʰ* in contrast to no rule turning *p* to *b*, but, to correctly characterize the facts, one needs to postulate in addition that *pʰ* cannot be present in UR, while *b* can. That is to say, one needs the notion of 'underlying' inventory, a notion which is not defined by the rules of the grammar and is hence an inherent property of UR. To the extent that inventories appear to be principled rather than random sets, some principles will be needed, but traditional rules prove ineffective in subsuming such principles (Kisseberth 1972)—whence a need for a UR, which thus not only collects the idiosyncratic and unpredictable but also has specific inherent properties.

In sum, under 'richness of the base', all systematic properties are grammar-given. To the extent that a 'level' is defined as a coherent representation of specific properties, there is no level of UR in OT, aside from allomorphy. The reason is that although one can refer to the unpredictable aspects of an output representation as the 'active' input, there are no inherent properties to that notion, since active input is simply that input for which the ranking IO-F >> PHON holds—a property of the grammar.

1.3.2 *Allomorphy: Predictable versus Suppletive*

Let us now turn to the general problem of allomorphy. The latter can be phonologically predictable, as in *cat*[s]/*dog*[z], or unpredictable ('suppletive') as in *go/ went*. There are many cases where the unpredictability is only partial, as in *compel/compuls-ive*. On the radical version of Correspondence Theory that has no UR altogether, the overall architecture of the system will remain as described above. The only addition needed to express morphological relations among words will be a second set of correspondence relations, parallel to the Input-Output correspondence relations. These will be word-to-word or 'Output-to-Output' correspondence relations, resulting in a set of OO-F constraints, parallel to the IO-F constraints. Just as IO-F constraints interdigitate with PHON constraints, so OO-F constraints will interdigitate with the other two types to yield the overall hierarchy. Then, just as it partitioned the 'input' representation in the way illustrated in (16) above, the set of PHON constraints will also partition the representation of the 'correspondent', where the 'correspondent of α' is a representation β referred to by OO-F constraints in the calculation of α. Within the complex representation of the correspondent, some aspects will be active relative to PHON, others will be inactive.

On the present approach, that does not have UR, morphologically-related items like *electric/electric-ity* will in be principle allowed to have independent inputs. This enables us to account for the 'irregular' aspects of allomorphy. In *go/went*, the input to each member of the pair is 'active' over OO-F, evidently due to the ranking IO-F >> OO-F. On the other hand, in regular *walk/walk-ed* the opposite ranking OO-F >> IO-F must hold, a general characteristic of all the Germanic or 'level 2' affixes as I will further note below. Under the latter ranking, any encoding of idiosyncrasy in the input is overruled, forcing faithfulness to the base.

For this reason, in the present theory, all functions of the traditional UR reduce to interaction among the three constraint blocks: IO-F, PHON, and OO-F. The role of UR in defining segmental inventories reduces to relative ranking of IO-F and PHON, specifically the markedness constraints of PHON, holding over features, feature combinations and combinations of prosodic elements. The role of UR in carrying exceptional features of lexical items as in the case of the past tense of *go—went*—is reduced to IO-F dominating OO-F, and similarly for phonological, rather than morphological, irregularity as we see below. Finally, the role of UR in expressing the fact that non-suppletive allomorphs have substantially similar sound structures is played by OO-F, which in effect would ban allomorphy. Idiosyncratic or unpredictable allomorphy results when IO-F dominates OO-F as just noted, while phonologically regular or predictable allomorphy results when PHON dominates OO-F.

Note that there is no escaping the conclusion that the lexicon is heterogeneous, privileging memorization in some cases (*go/went*), calculation in others: (*walk/walked*). The present approach expresses this factual heterogeneity by means of heterogeneity of constraint ranking. One major innovation being proposed here is the treatment of morphological irregularity and phonological markedness with the same formal means: dominant IO-F—domination being over OO-F in one case, and over PHON in the other. The crucial empirical issue is how to characterize the exact balance of morphological regularity and irregularity that exists. From the point of view of any of the extant formal devices designed to express regularity, there seems no reason why irregularity should exist at all. From the present point of view, on the other hand, where the ranking IO-F >> OO-F can be freely utilized to express irregularity, there may seem little reason why regularity, in the form of the opposite ranking, should be as prevalent as it is. The problem then is to understand why the input active over OO-F is relatively restrained, as stated in (19).

(19)   **Restrained Input:**
Within the domain of application of OO-F, the active input is relatively restrained.

I will assume here the solution to this problem I advance in Burzio (1997). In essence, that solution is based on two ideas. One is that violations of OO-F compound class-wise, in the following sense. A morphologically irregular word, like *compUlS-ive*, in which the portions in capitals fail to correspond to the base *compel*, will result in a violation of OO-F indexed to the class of stems that are suffixed with *-ive*. Violations within such a class are allowed to compound, so that, given a sufficient number of them, say *n*, OO-F will effectively prevail over IO-F at *n*.[9] On the other hand, there can be no comparable compounding of IO-F violations, given lexicon optimization. Consider hypothetical *combust/ *combELL-ive*, with the capitalized portion in the input. At *n*, the grammar will simply suppress that hypothetical input, regularizing to *combust/combust-ive*, and leaving no trace of the violation of IO-F that may have compounded with some other. On this view, irregularity is thus capped at some *n* within each lexical class, accounting for (19). For cases like *go/went*, there is no affixational class, but there is still a class semantically defined: that of 'past tense'. We may presume this is also relevant for capping irregularity. The second idea in Burzio (1997) is that the rank of OO-F (or perhaps constraints in general) is tied to the number of satisfactions. With a relatively large affixational class (i.e. a large number of items appearing with the same affix) there is bound to be a large number of satisfactions of OO-F due to the cap on violations just discussed. With rank tied to such number, that of OO-F will automatically climb above that of IO-F, hence in effect suppressing all irregularity. This seems to correctly predict that large classes, such as those involving the English 'level 2' affixes or the first verb conjugation in the Romance languages, should be entirely regular —another manifestation of (19).

1.3.3 *Multiple Correspondence*

There is evidence that OO-Correspondence can apply multiply. For instance, in Italian, several formation based on *-ere* conjugation verbs are transparently in correspondence with both the participle and the infinitive simultaneously, as with *ascens-ore* 'elevator' based on the participle *asces-o* 'ascended', but featuring the *n* of the infinitive *ascend-ere* 'ascend', as discussed in Burzio (1998). This raises no formal problem within OT, since multiple sets of OO-F constraints,

---

[9] These ideas are attempts to derive constraint domination from independent considerations, and thus represent an alternative to Prince and Smolensky's (1993) hypothesis that domination is simply 'strict'. See also footnote 15.

with independent rankings, can all apply simultaneously. It does raise the empirical problem of determining, independent of what is needed for the phonological analysis, which items are allowed to be correspondents to which others, and by what ranking of OO-F constraints.[10] The general assumption underlying the present conception is that OO-Correspondence relations are established by shared content in sound and meaning, and that independent proximity of sound and meaning determines the strength of the correspondence, implemented in the rank of the OO-F constraints. A formal characterization of proximity in both sound and meaning is of course a complex matter, beyond the goals of the present work. It is easy to see, however, that this notion would in effect enable correspondence relations to yield a morphological parse. So for example *prevent-ing* will correspond simultaneously with both *prevent* and *develop-ing*, but only over each of the portions where the overlap obtains, namely *prevent* and *-ing* respectively.

By making no distinction between stems and affixes in the application of OO-F, the present view accounts for the fact that affixes tend to be metrically stable just as stems do, as argued in PES and illustrated in (20).

(20)   títan   ti(tánicφ)/   *(títani)c
        tríumph   tri(úmphan)t/*(tríum)(phàntφ)

The failure of the stems in (20) to preserve their stress under affixation (in contrast to the cases in (3), (4) above) requires postulating that the affixes themselves are being metrically consistent (OO-faithful), parsing as they do in other items (see PES 226f, 263f, 302f). In a system without UR, affixes are simply parts of items that, collectively, stand in mutual correspondence over that part—another instance of multiple correspondence. The question that arises perhaps generally, but perspicuously with affixes, is the following. When items stand in OO-Correspondence such that the active input of one results in some output in others because of OO-F, to which of the items must the active input be assigned, and which of the others are to be taken to have merely OO-faithful representations? In the specific case of affixes—e.g. English *-ic*—the question will be which of *academic, Napoleonic, tonic,* etc. has the active input, specifying segmental content and metrical properties of *-ic*, and which others merely inherit them via OO-F?[11] The answer is that, in the general case, the issue is indeterminate, and it will in fact not matter which of the above items has the active input, so long as OO-F is satisfied. This is similar to the indeterminacy of the active input in *ærəzównə* noted above (either the long vowel or the stress). As in that case, no adverse consequence seems to ensue from this indeterminacy—a chicken-and-

---

[10] The problem is independent of theoretical choice. It also arises if UR is used, in the form of establishing how much weight to give to each surface allomorph in the determination of UR, independent of the specific facts at hand.

[11] Thanks to Paul Smolensky for bringing this to my attention.

egg situation due to the parallel architecture with its mutual interdependencies. The only cases where it will matter which item has the active input for an affix are those in which OO-F is violated (segmentally or prosodically). For example, for the item *cátholic* there must be some active input specifying the exceptional metrical parse *-i)cφ*, which would otherwise give **ca(thólicφ*). As another example, the *in-/il-* allomorphy of *in-active, il-legal* will require that the nasal be specified in the input of at least one member of the class of prevocalic *in-*s. The class of *il-* allomorphs will arise as a violation of OO-F compelled by a high-ranked member of Phon imposing assimilation. Hence theirregular allomorphy of *académic/cátholic*, metrically: *-icφ*) versus *-i)cφ*, results from the ranking IO-F >> OO-F, while the regular one of *in-active, il-legal* is due to the ranking Phon >> OO-F.

1.3.4 *Base Neutralization*

There is one particular class of cases that may seem to reassert the existence of UR against the present proposal, illustrated by the pair *dam(n)/damN-ation*, in which the *n* is phonetically present only in the derived noun. More generally, this is the class of cases involving 'base neutralization'. Here, the contrast *mn/m* observable in *da[mn]ation/su[m]ation* disappears in the bases *da[m]/su[m]*. An analysis based on the UR */damN/* will account for the neutralization in terms of a constraint or rule simplifying word-final clusters. In contrast, the present approach needs to postulate that the *n* is part of the input (active, relative to OO-F) of the noun, raising the question of why, alongside of this contrast, one does not find, for instance **confir/confirM-ation*, where the *m* would also be in the input just for the noun. The latter pair is correctly excluded by the UR-based approach since word-final *[rm]* as in *confirm* is not banned. The advantage provided by UR in this connection proves illusory, however, once we evaluate candidate pairs in the manner of (21).

(21)	with UR		without UR	
	Phon	IO-F	Phon	OO-F
a. dam[n] damn-ation	*		*	
b. ☞ dam[ ] damn-ation		*		*
A. ☞ confir[m] confirm-ation				
B. confir[ ] confirm-ation		*		*

The two systems (with and without UR) are equivalent because they give equivalent evaluations of each set of candidate pairs. It is clear from this comparison that the pair in (B) is more marked than the one in (b). The reason is that (B) loses to (A) in a way in which (b) does not lose to (a). What makes the difference is the phonology, which blocks (a) by means of the prohibition against final clusters *mn*, not matched by a comparable prohibition against the final *rm* of (A). Hence the asymmetry between (b) and (B) in (21) is traceable to the phonology in the UR-less system, just as it is in the UR-based one. It is true that the present system can also characterize hypothetical but unattested (21B) by specifying diverging inputs (with and without *m*) for base and derived forms. This, however, will violate Restrained Input (19), and hence correctly assign such pairs the status of exception. Although the specific pair in (21b) does not exist, many other comparable ones do, like the noted *compel/compuls-ive*, requiring various measures of independent input in violation of Restrained Input. In contrast, there is no such violation in (21a, b) since the *m* is specified only once, and that happens to be in the derived noun.[12]

In sum, in the class of cases like *dam(n)/damNation*, in which some element of UR would have surfaced only in an affixed form and not in its base for phonological reasons, the present approach will postulate an active input in the derived form which, in effect, will fail to generalize to the base also for phonological reasons, under the ranking PHON >> OO-F. So there seems no loss of generalization in the reinterpretation of this class of cases that has many other members in English, like *bom(b)/bomBard, lon(g)/elonGate* (see Borowsky 1993), and other languages. English vowel reduction also gives rise to this sort of case rather massively. E.g. in *par[é]ntal*, the *e* must be present in the active input of this item, given its absence in the base form *[pærənt]*. A further similar case (noted by one reviewer) is that of Dutch final devoicing, as in [ret] 'I save', versus [red-en] 'to save-INF', [red-ing] 'salvation', [red-er] 'saviour'. Here the voicing will be specified in the input to—let us say—the infinitive. Suppose, as seems (semantically) plausible, that the two nominalizations are in primary correspondence with the infinitive: they will then retain the voicing under OO-F, while 1-SG [ret] will devoice—a violation of OO-F compelled by PHON (demanding unvoiced final codas).

To recap this section, P&S's conclusion that, under 'lexicon optimization', and aside from morphological relatedness, the input equals the output, and the PES conclusion that there is no UR, appear to be non-distinct conclusions. If input equals output, then there is a single representation which the grammar 'checks' for well-formedness. Some of the input-output is 'active' relative to phonological constraints, in the sense of inducing their violation, while some is inactive. 'Non-predictable' or contrastive variation is registered in the active input, while 'predictable' or non-contrastive variation is that which is present only in the non-active input. The 'active' input is similar to the old UR in some respects, but is not a 'level' in any meaningful sense because it lacks inherent properties.

In dealing with allomorphy, on the other hand, P&S's use of the traditional UR does constitute a substantive difference from the position taken in PES. However, the further developments of OT in McCarthy and Prince (1994, 1995, 1999), Benua (1995, 1997), McCarthy (this volume), and others, point to further

---

[12] Thanks to Laura Benua for stimulating discussion of this class of cases.

convergence, by acknowledging at least the superfluousness of UR in various classes of cases. In this section I have argued that UR is *entirely* superfluous, all of its functions reducing to interaction among the three constraint types IO-F, PHON, and OO-F. In the following section we see an argument that UR is not just superfluous but false.

1.4 Derived Environments

Many cases have been brought to light in which some phonological regularity occurs only in morphologically derived environments, an effect labeled (Kiparsky 1993) 'Non-Derived-Environment Blocking' (NDEB). Although all such cases have generally been regarded as constituting a single generalization, it now appears that two different subcases need to be distinguished. The first subcase is illustrated in (22).

(22)   a. electri[s]-ity, lyri[s]-ist, opa[s]-ify
        b. [k]ick, a[k]in, bas[k]et, tro[k]ee, leu[k]emia, ar[k]eology

In the derived environments of (22a) velar softening occurs (compare *electri*[k], etc.), while in the underived environments of (22b) it does not. The environments of (22a) are derived not only morphologically by involving affixation, but also *phonologically*, in the sense that affixation crucially creates the structural conditions relevant to the velar softening generalization: '*k /__ i'. Matters are different for the cases in (23), which exemplify the other subcase.

(23)   a.   (i)   div[i]n-ity, n[æ]tur-al, t[æ]bul-ar,
              (ii)   blasph[ə]m-ous, asp[ə]r-ant, molec[yə]l-ar
              (iii) im-m[ə]grant, bi-c[ə]cle, anti-th[ə]sis
              (iv)   expl[ə]n-ation, prov[ə]d-ential, volc[ə]n-ology

        b.   v[ay]tamin, d[ay]nosaur, d[ay]namo

As argued in PES (esp. 10.3), the vowel shortening of each of the cases in (23a), contrasting with the lack of shortening in (23b), reduces to the single constraint in (24) (I will henceforth use the colon to mark long vowels, ignoring their diphthongized status).

(24)   **Generalized Shortening**: *V: in affixed environments

If this account is correct, the cases in (23a) are 'derived' in an exclusively morphological sense, the affixation contributing nothing specific to the phonological environment.

   In this section, I will first consider this second case of NDEB—in 1.4.1 below, arguing that, within OT, it reduces to the 'emergence of the unmarked' in the sense of McCarthy and Prince (1994), though only if UR does not exist. In 1.4.2,

I will then turn to the other case of NDEB, exemplified in (22) and similarly by Finnish assibilation, adopting in part the analysis of Kiparsky (1993). In subsection 1.4.3, I will then briefly review past accounts of NDEB. In 1.4.4 I turn to the special status for NDEB of the affixes themselves.

1.4.1 *Morphologically Derived Environments*

A very long tradition had distinguished the 'trisyllabic' shortening of (23a.i) from the other cases of shortening (which had also not received a unitary account—see Burzio 1993). If one accepted that distinction and focused attention on the trisyllabic cases, it would then appear as if the phonologically relevant environment arose via affixation (which always adds some syllables). As argued in PES, however, that distinction is spurious since there is no phonological environment in which shortening is not attested—foot antepenultimate, penultimate, and final—each illustrated in (25), exhausting the range of possibilities (see also Kager 1989: 120).

(25)			GS	MC
a.	diví:ne	di(vínity)		
b.	blasphé:me	(blásphemou)s		*
b'.	desí:re	des(í:rou)s	*	
c.	expláin	(èxpla)nátion		*

There is one important *descriptive* difference among the various environments, though. Shortening in foot penultimate syllable as in (25b, b') is sporadic as shown by the (b/b') contrast (and *excí:tant, homicí:dal, bipó:lar, únicy̆:cle* compared with (23a, ii, iii), while the other two cases are considerably more regular. But this follows from the fact that, in (25b, b'), Generalized Shortening (GS) (24) is in conflict with Metrical Consistency (MC) (5b) above, an instance of OO-F (see PES, 10.3; Burzio 1993, where MC is also referred to as Stress Preservation), simultaneous satisfaction of both being excluded by undominated Metrical Well-Formedness (5a), constraining the range of possible metrical feet. Assuming then that GS and MC tie in rank, the choice of short or long vowel will fall upon the input, hence accounting for the lexical variability of (25b, b'). In contrast, no conflict between GS and MC arises in 'trisyllabic' (25a) or in (25c), in the former case because both can be satisfied simultaneously under Metrical Well-Formedness, in the latter because violation of MC is compelled independently of GS by Metrical Well-Formedness (PES, 10.3).

The PES analysis thus reduces the considerable descriptive complexity of English vowel shortening to GS (24). The question it leaves open is the nature of GS. The answer to that is now clear in the wake of both Prince and Smolensky (1993) and McCarthy and Prince (1994). The first part of GS, given in (26), is a markedness constraint of the kind proposed in Prince and Smolensky (1993, ch. 9; see also Rosenthall 1994).

(26)   **Markedness:** *V:

The second part of GS, singling out morphologically derived environments, can be viewed as the same effect as found in the 'emergence of the unmarked' cases that McCarthy and Prince (1994) attribute to the ranking in (2b) above, repeated in (27).

(27)   **Emergence-of-the-unmarked schema:** IO-F >> PHON >> OO-F

McCarthy and Prince (1994) arrive at (27) by considering discrepancies between base and reduplicant such as those in (28) (See also Alderete *et al.* 1996).

(28)   a. Diyari: tʲilpa-tʲilparku   (less marked prosodic structure)
        b. Nookta: či-čims-ʻiːħ   (less marked syllable)
        c. Tülatulabal: ʔɨ-pɨtita   (less marked segment)

They argue that such discrepancies follow from the schema in (27), where the specific instances of OO-F involved are among the constraints that regulate the identity of Base and Reduplicant (Max, and Base-Dependence). The base is able to display more marked structure than the reduplicant because such markedness is defined in terms of (some members of) PHON which is dominated by relevant IO-F constraints—the usual account of marked structures. The reduplicant, on the other hand, exists solely by virtue of its relation with the base, a relation separate from (though similar to) that between input and output and thus subject to separate constraints, apparently lower-ranked for each of (27), whence the stronger effects of PHON over the reduplicant.

Now, on the present approach, shortening as in *diviːne/ divinity* will receive the comparable account of (29).

(29) input: *diviːn*	IO-F	PHON: *V:	OO-F
a. dívin	*		
☞ b. divíːn		*	
correspondents: *divíːnity*	IO-F	PHON: *V:	OO-F
c. divíːnity		*	
☞ d. divínity			*

Tableau (29) assumes that calculation of unaffixed *diviːn* does not rely on OO-F. Recall that this is generally true, though the issue remains to be explored further, as bare verbs like *prevént* exhibit correspondence effects with their affixed forms like *prevénting*. (The calculation of *diviːn* in (29) would in any event remain unaffected under participation of OO-F. See, however, the discussion of (35) below.) On the other hand, the calculation of the affixed form *divinity* crucially requires non-participation of IO-F, and this in effect entails the conclusion in (30).

(30)   There is no 'Underlying Representation'.

The reason is that UR is precisely the hypothesis that there is a common input to predictable allomorphs of the same morpheme. But on that hypothesis, *divinity* would violate IO-F, just like *dívin, and the restrictive character of GS (24) would remain a mystery.

In the particular case of 'trisyllabic' shortening, an alternative may seem available that would not exclude UR. One could take the stress to be the active input, common to both basic and derived items. A long vowel, violating GS, would then be compelled in *diví:n* by undominated metrical constraints, but not in *divínity*, given the antepenultimate syllable. As argued in PES (ch. 5 and 10.3), an analysis that derives vowel length from stress is viable in many cases but ultimately fails, however, as can be seen from (31).

(31)   a. rábbi: rabbínic
       b. syllábify: syllàbificátion
       c. blasphé:me   blásphemous

Neither of the long vowels in (31a, b) are stressed, as argued in PES: 48–52, hence vowel length rather than just stress must be part of the active input. Those long vowels will now be predicted not to surface in the affixed items only if they do not share that input (UR) with the basic forms—the conclusion drawn for (29). While input stress is thus insufficient for (31a,b), it is false for (31c), where it would yield a ranking paradox, since IO-F for stress would have to dominate *V: for *blasphé:me*, but be dominated by it for *blásphemous*. In contrast, the account of (29) extends directly to each case in (31), the variability of penultimate shortening shown by (31c) versus *desí:re*/*desí:rous* following as in (25) above.

This account of English vowel length allomorphy has thus eliminated all language-specific properties, leaving only constraint ranking. GS (24) reduces to a universal markedness constraint targeting long vowels. In English, this constraint will be violated in underived environments through being dominated by IO-F. It will be satisfied in derived environments in general because it dominates OO-F, and will be violated again in a specific set of derived environments where it competes with METRICAL CONSISTENCY, a specific instance of OO-F. Cross-linguistic variation due to re-ranking of *V: will be expected to yield the following three basic types.

(32)   a. IO-F >> OO-F >> *V: (Latin)
       b. IO-F >> *V: >> OO-F   (English)
       c. *V: >> IO-F >> OO-F   (Italian)

The case in (32a) is that of a language with distinctive vowel length in all environments, such as Latin. The case in (32b) is that of English, with distinctive vowel length neutralized in derived environments. That of (32c) is the case of a language without distinctive vowel length, like Italian. A comparison of English and Italian is in fact of further relevance.

Italian does have long vowels in stressed open penultimates—e.g. *anc*[*ó:*]*ra* 'still'—like English, but, unlike English, only in such environments. This follows from the two different ranking schemas for contrastive and non-contrastive variation given in (18) above and repeated here.

(33) a. **Non-contrastive variation:**$\text{PHON}_{\text{CONTEXT}} >> \text{PHON}_{\text{MARK}} >> \text{IO-F}$
      b. **Contrastive variation:** $\text{IO-F} >> \text{PHON}_{\text{MARK}}$

While in English variation in vowel length is due to the ranking (33b), in Italian it is due to (33a), namely to the fact that although the markedness member of PHON, *V: dominates IO-F as in (33a), it is itself dominated by a contextual member of PHON that excludes stress on light penultimates—in the PES analysis, the ill-formed trochaic foot *(Lσ). Such constraint will compel a violation of *V: exactly in stressed open penultimates, whence the fact that long vowels exist only in this context. Some other constraints must impose stress on those syllables, however, and that must be $\text{IO-F}_{\text{STRESS}}$, also dominating *V:. Hence Italian has 'contrastive' stress, as shown by minimal pairs like *ancóra/áncora* 'still'/'anchor' (with *o* phonetically long in the first item), while it does not have contrastive vowel length. One could not have claimed that Italian had 'underlying' stress, however (again revealing the inadequacy of UR), because the contrastiveness of stress is neutralized elsewhere. So there is no antepenultimate stress over heavy penultimates (**ágosto*), and no pre-antepenultimate stress (**américa*). This follows from taking $\text{IO-F}_{\text{STRESS}}$, which dominates *V: , to be in turn dominated by constraints on well-formed feet—the PES's METRICAL WELL-FORMEDNESS (MWF) set of (5a) above, including the *(Lσ) just mentioned. The overall ranking in Italian is then as in (34).

(34) $\text{PHON}_{\text{CONTEXT}} >> \text{IO-F}_{\text{STRESS}} >> \text{PHON}_{\text{MARK}} >> \text{IO-F}_{\text{V-length}}$
      (MWF)   (*V:)

In (34), the constraints relative to vowel length (first, third and fourth) instantiate the non-contrastive variation schema (33a), while the stress constraints (first and second) instantiate the schema for contextually neutralized contrastive variation (18c) above, except for the absence of the markedness constraint (for stress), inconsequential given its bottom rank.[13]

---

[13] To instantiate it, one could simply postulate a '*metrical structure' constraint.

A reviewer wonders about the possibility of a language in which vowel length is non-distinctive, but which is transderivationally preserved, as predicted by the ranking in (i).

(i) $\text{PHON}_{\text{CONTEXT}}$ (stressed V:), $\text{OO-F}_{\text{LENGTH}} >> \text{PHON}_{\text{MARK}}$ (*V:) $>> \text{IO-F}_{\text{LENGTH}}$

The present approach predicts this to be possible only with 'level 2'-type items, which instantiate the ranking OO-F >> IO-F (see Conclusion below). With level 1-type items, the opposite ranking holds, contradicting (i).

Note that if we take English to simply reverse the ranking of the last two constraints in (34), we will expect that English could also compel long vowels by IO-F$_{\text{STRESS}}$ like Italian, in addition to doing so by IO-F$_{\text{V-LENGTH}}$. This is in fact the indeterminacy of *arizó:na* noted above: either the long vowel or the penultimate stress could serve as the active input. In its Italian counterpart *arizó:na* there is no such indeterminacy: stress is the active input.

In sum, while it may have seemed completely impossible to reduce the radically different distributions of vowel length in English and Italian to the same 'rules' (say with different orderings), they do reduce to the same constraints, with different rankings. Italian vowel length is non-contrastive because IO-F is subordinate to PHON. In English, it is contrastive in non-derived environments because IO-F is superordinate to PHON. The contrastiveness disappears in derived environments because those generally invoke lower-ranked OO-F, subordinate to PHON.[14]

Derived forms can still exhibit some idiosyncrasy of vowel length in English, as in *desi:rous* versus *blasphemous*, or *obe:sity* versus *divinity*, though not in Italian. This follows from the same ranking IO-F >> PHON of (29)–(32b) for English versus the opposite ranking for Italian, the idiosyncrasy coming from active input associated directly with the derived form. Note here that the ability to associate active input directly to morphologically complex forms may seem to void the asymmetry that GS (24) correctly expressed (if only by stipulation) by making explicit reference to 'affixed environments'. That is, the question is now 'Why aren't pairs like *blásphem/blasphé:mous* attested, violating OO-F, but satisfying *V: in one member, just like the actual pair?' This asymmetry can be reduced to the one needed for *parént/paréntal—that is, to the fact that in general unaffixed forms seem to be calculated solo rather than by OO-Correspondence. Consider the two pairs in (35).

(35)	IO-F	*V:	OO-F
a. blasphé:me		*	
blásphemous			*
b. blásphem			
blasphé:mous		*	*

In (35) both *blasphé:me* and *blásphem* are optimal for their inputs. However, there is a crucial difference between actual *blásphemous* and *blasphé:mous*. The

---

[14] Of course, within a rule-based system, the vehicle of cross-linguistic variation would be not only rule reordering but choice of rules as well as what is represented in UR (as one reviewer reminds me). Such closer scrutiny simply confirms the text conclusion, though. For one thing, a rule-based system would need shortening for English and lengthening for Italian—surely two different rules. Secondly, while it would need to postulate underlying stress for Italian open penultimate syllables, Italian stress is substantially regular, requiring assignment by rule elsewhere as noted in the text (see also PES: 2.4).

former is optimal so long as *V: and OO-F tie as we are assuming. The latter, however, is optimal on an input long vowel only if IO-F dominates not only each of *V: and OO-F but also their conjunction. I will assume that this is not the case, and that the latter conjunction (a 'local conjunction' in the sense of Smolensky 1995, 1997) dominates IO-F. So for a hypothetical base *blásphem*, the optimal affixed form will be only *blásphemous* (as in actual *cáncer/cáncerous*).[15] On this account, input long vowels in affixed items will only be expected to surface when they correspond to long vowels of the base item, exactly as in *obé:sity* and *desí:rous*. Our discussion thus correctly predicts that there should be idiosyncratic lack of shortening, but no idiosyncratic 'lengthening'. Note here that the lengthening of *elìzabé:than* (PES: 327) is different, in that it is motivated by MC (5b), as the alternative *elìzábethan* would fail to preserve the stress of the base *Elízabeth*. What is needed for this type of case in the present context is the assumption that while the conjunction (*V: &OO-F$_{\text{LENGTH}}$) outranks the single IO-F as claimed for (35), it is in turn outranked by the conjunction (MC&IO-F). This is perfectly consistent with the pairwise ranking of the conjuncts, which is *V: = MC (discussion of (25)), and IO-F >> OO-F (discussion of (29) generalized to level 1 affixation, see Conclusion below). Lack of relevant input will predict no lengthening and hence violation of MC, indeed as in *Hércules/hercúlean*, attested alongside of *hèrculé:an*, parallel to *elìzabé:than*.[16] The lengthening of *Cana:dian* is also not idiosyncratic but due to the special status of vowel hiatuses relative to high-ranking metrical constraints, as is the one of *mani:acal* (PES, 5.5).

One important restriction exhibited by NDEB is that it is only found with 'contrastive'-type variation—that is, variation that neutralizes contrastive distinctions, such as English vowel shortening, which neutralizes the distinction between short and long vowels. NDEB is not found with the other, 'predictable' type of variation, like English aspiration, which applies to all environments, derived or not (*p^{h}it/rap^{h}idity*). This restriction is directly accounted for by the above discussion, specifically by the inconsistency of the ranking schemas in (18a) and (27), repeated in (36).[17]

(36)   a. **NDEB:**   IO-F >> PHON >> OO-F
       b. **Non-contrastive variation:** PHON >> IO-F

In order to be confined to derived environments, a variation must fit the schema in (36a), but in order to be non-contrastive it must fit the one in (36b)—a contradiction. We have seen that there is a sense in which Italian also has vowel

---

[15] Note that PES does not presuppose strict domination of constraints but rather numerical ranking. See the analysis of items in *-ary/-ory*, p. 237–9. Smolensky's 'local conjunction' is a way to allow numerical-type ranking under specific circumstances.

[16] As expected, *Prométheus* only gives *prométhean* and not *pròmethé:an*, since lengthening is not needed to satisfy MC (PES: 328).

[17] In (36b), PHON conflates a contextual and a markedness constraint: see (33a), (18a).

shortening, like English. However, Italian shortening is non-contrastive, and as we now expect, it makes no distinction between derived and underived environments.

The above account, which sees NDEB essentially as phonological regularization in derived environments, will carry over to cases like (37) (PES: 323, footnote 7).

(37)   a. órchestra
       b. orchéstral

The underived item in (37a) is a relatively rare case of antepenultimate stress in the presence of a heavy penultimate—a foot $(\sigma H\sigma)$ in the PES analysis. As in the shortening cases, the morphological derivation of (37b) contributes no phonologically relevant material, the overall number of syllables remaining just the same. The account of (37) will consist of taking the prohibition '*$(\sigma H\sigma)$', part of PHON, to be dominated by IO-F, but to dominate OO-F, whence the 'regularization' of (37b).[18]

Note that there is no ranking contradiction in the fact that (37b) requires PHON >> OO-F while the cases in (3) and (4) above (*medìcinálity*, etc.) require the opposite ranking, since the PHON constraints involved are different: high-ranking METRICAL WELL-FORMEDNESS (5a) in the case of (37b), versus low-ranking METRICAL ALIGNMENT (5c) in the case of (3) and (4) above.[19]

Other cases amenable to the same 'Emergence of the Unmarked' account are listed in (38).

(38)   **Other 'Emergence-of-the-unmarked' cases:**
       a. Italian syncopated participles (Burzio 1998)
          as-cen-dere 'ascend'   *as-ce-so* 'ascended' (less marked syllable)

       b. Catalan stressed vowel lowering (Kiparsky 1993: 293 and refs; Mascaró 1976)
          séntrə 'center'   *séntric* 'centric'
          direktó 'director'   *direktóri* 'directory' (segmental regularity)

---

[18] Not all feet $(\sigma H\sigma)$ are allowed in this manner, however. Syllables closed by sonorants and *s* seem to be special in this respect, yielding less than fully-fledged heavy syllables (PES: 206ff).

[19] The case in (i) is slightly more complex, but ultimately reduces to a similar ranking schema.

(i)   a. cátholic   b. cathólicìsm

The item in (ia) is exceptional (compared with the penultimate stress of most adjectives in *-ic.ascétic, erótic*, etc.), and this will be by satisfaction of IO-F. The PHON constraint responsible for the regularization of (ib) is PES's: 166 'Strong Retraction' that imposes a binary foot before a foot which is 'weak' (i.e. which has only secondary stress). The latter is normally outranked by OO-F, as in *a(mérica)nìst*, but here it appears to prevail. The reason for this would seem to be that the sequence *icism* is strongly associated with stress on the immediately preceding syllable (*ascéticìsm, erótìcìsm, exótìcìsm*, etc.), thus yielding that same pattern in (ib) by OO-F across *icism* items, perhaps in 'local conjunction' with the noted Strong Retraction. In turn, the general pattern of *icism* items comes from both Strong Retraction and to OO-F with the *-ic* adjective (*ascétic, erótic*, etc.).

c. Catalan unstressed mid-vowel reduction (Kiparsky 1993: 294 and refs;
   Mascaró 1976):
   bostón 'Boston'   *bustun-yá* 'Bostonian'
   kátedrə 'academic chair' *katədrátic* 'holder of an academic chair'
                                              (less marked segment)

d. French *h*-aspiré (Kiparsky 1993: 294 and refs)
   Hitler 'Hitler'   (*h*)*itlérien* 'Hitlerian'
                                              (loss of marked segment)

e. Turkish disyllabicity condition (Inkelas and Orgun 1995: 770).
   ham 'unripe'   *fa-n[20] '(note) fa-2sg.poss'
                              fa-dan '(note) fa-abl'
                              (avoidance of marked prosodic structure)

f. Japanese two-mora requirement (Itô 1990; Kiparsky 1993)
   su 'vinegar'   *choko* 'chocolate (truncation)'
                              *cho
                              (two mora requirement satisfied)

These cases seem to be like English vowel shortening, and unlike the cases to be discussed in the next section, in that affixation does not seem to alter the environment in any phonologically relevant way. The case in (a) involves emergence of a less marked syllable. The one in (b) the emergence of a language-specific regularity, and the one in (c) a typical simplification of vowel inventory. (See, however, Kiparsky 1993 for an alternative view of the relevant environment for cases (b, c)). Cases (d, e) involve elimination rather than the repair of a marked structure.[21]

To conclude, I have argued that the GENERALIZEDSHORTENING of PES, which captured most of English vowel length allomorphy under a single constraint, now itself reduces to a universal markedness constraint barring long vowels, whose workings under various ranking circumstances are visible in other languages. Its effects in English are restricted to morphologically derived environments (NDEB) by virtue of the 'Emergence-of-the-unmarked' ranking schema of McCarthy and Prince (1994, 1995, 1999) given in (27) above. Intuitively, in the pervasive interplay of lexical storage and lexical calculation, the long vowel of *divi:ne* is independently stored as such (active input) and this entitles it to exist under language specific arrangements (IO-F >> PHON). The corresponding vowel in *divinity*, however, is not so independently stored but rather calculated in relation to the one of *divi:ne*. That relation is subject to a different type of arrangement (PHON >> OO-F), by which a comparably marked

---

[20] For some speakers cases like this become grammatical with a lengthened vowel: *faadan* (Inkelas and Orgun 1995: 771).

[21] The violation of OO-F compelled by the phonology would consist of a null or empty output.

structure (*divi:nity*) would lose. This account crucially presupposes the PES surface-to-surface conception of morphology. On the traditional, UR-based conception, the two items in question would share the input morpheme /*divi:n*/, essentially by definition of UR, excluding a principled account of shortening. The well-known limitation of such NDEB to variation which is contrastive directly follows from the fact that the latter is by definition the variation in which lexical storage can play a role (IO-F >> PHON), entailing a ranking consistent with the Emergence-of-the-unmarked schema, while non-contrastive variation entails just the opposite ranking, inconsistent with that schema.

1.4.2 *Phonologically Derived Environments*

A second type of NDEB, exemplified by English velar softening (22) above, involves environments which are 'derived' not only morphologically, in the sense of containing an affix, but also phonologically, in the sense that the affix provides some of the phonologically relevant material. The proposal presented above will be insufficient for at least some of those cases, for which it is clear that the phonological aspects of the derived environment are crucial. Kiparsky (1973a, 1993) notes the following type of paradigm with Finnish assibilation.

(39) a. *halut-a* 'want-INF'   *halus-i* 'want-PAST'
      b. *tilat-a* 'order-INF'   *tilas-i* 'order-PAST'
      c. *tila*   'room'
      d. *äiti*   'mother'

Assibilation turns *t* to *s* before *i*, but in general only when the latter belongs to a different morpheme. In particular, the form *tilas-i* in (39b) shows that the above 'Emergence-of-the-unmarked' account is insufficient, since the word-initial sequence *ti* is in a morphologically derived environment, hence subject to OO-F rather than IO-F, and yet does not undergo the assibilation. The relevant factor here thus seems to be whether or not the assibilation environment is created morphologically.

Kiparsky (1993) proposes for (39) the account in (40) [my paraphrase, LB], which I will partially adopt below.

(40) a. The first *t* of *tilat-a* is fully specified underlyingly as *t* (otherwise it would turn to *s* in this context). The second *t* is underspecified as an archi-segment *t/s*.
      b. The assibilation rule works only in a feature-filling fashion, hence only with *t/s* and not with *t*, whence *TilaS-i*
      c. A general default rule applying after the specific assibilation rule turns *t/s* into *t*, whence *tilaT-a*.

This account would have the following direct (though crude) translation into the version of OT that has UR, under the same specification/underspecification assumptions (assuming that underspecification is possible with forms that exhibit allomorphic variation, while lexicon optimization excludes it otherwise):

(41)   IO-F >> PHON$_1$: *ti >> Phon$_2$: *s

The t's which are fully specified in UR surface as such thanks to the undominated IO-F. Those which are underspecified as t/s surface as s before i due to PHON$_1$, and as t elsewhere due to PHON$_2$.

This account, in either version (rules or constraints), cannot be quite correct, however. The reason is that in order to correctly exclude *[$tilat$-i], which would result from full specification of the second t, one must make the crucial assumption in (42).

(42)   UR contains the minimal specifications *consistent with the surface form of the 'base'.*

This assumption is necessary because underspecification cannot be determined on the basis of UR alone. The reason that the initial t must be fully specified is that it would otherwise turn to s. That, however, is a fact about the phonology, not about UR. Hence determination of UR must be permitted to 'look ahead' at the surface, where the t has not assibilated. Among the surface forms, however, there could in principle be a *$tilat$-i forcing full specification of the second t as well. Such a form must be excluded from consideration, whence the need for (42). Under (42) the base form would be the infinitive $tilat$-a, where the t is not followed by i and thus can—and therefore must—be underspecified. This then makes it a prey to the assibilation rule/constraint, whence $tilas$-i.

The assumption in (42) cannot be maintained, however. Any definition of 'base' that is met by infinitive [$tilat$-a] but not by (hypothetical) past tense *[$tilat$-i] will be equally met by English $dam(n)$ rather than $damNation$, yielding no specification for the N, and hence excluding any account of the contrast with, say, sum/$summation$. Rather, in general UR needs to take account of all surface allomorphs, including potential *$tilat$-i, which will, however, invalidate the account in (40).[22]

To overcome this problem, Kiparsky's analysis needs to be re-thought along the following lines. The relevant specification for the morpheme /$tilat$/must be not each of the t's in particular, but rather the transition in continuancy between the first t and the i. Let us for the moment take the traditional view that there is a lexicon of morphemes, rather than one of full words (as in PES). There will then be no comparable specification for the second t since no i follows it within that morpheme. We may then naturally attribute a different status to IO-F constraints that deal with sequences than to those that deal with individual segments, and postulate the ranking in (43). (On constraints referring to segmental sequences, see also Lamontagne 1996).

---

[22] Thanks to Paul Smolensky for help on this point.

(43)   IO-F$_{TI}$ >> PHON: *TI >> IO-F$_T$

The first *t* of *tilat* will now be immune to PHON (assibilation) in (43), by invoking the higher-ranked IO-F in (43), while the second one will not be immune, by invoking only the lower-ranked IO-F, thus undergoing assibilation before *i*.

If we now turn to the (PES-inspired) version of OT that does not have UR, we will simply need to convert (43) into (44).

(44)   OO-F$_{TI}$ >> PHON: *TI >> OO-F$_T$

On the ranking in (44), surface form *tilasi* will be unfaithful to the surface form *tilata* in exactly the same way and for the same reasons that it was unfaithful to the UR /*tilat*/ on the more traditional version of the theory. The sequence *ti* must be part of the active input of either item *TIlasi*/*TIlata*, the other item acquiring it via OO-F, while the single *t* must be part of the active input of *tilaTa*, thus making this alternation similar to that of *dam(n)*/*damNation*. The ranking in (43) is also needed alongside of (44), to avoid *Silasi*, etc. In addition, OO-F$_T$ will have not to dominate IO-F$_T$ to avoid the leveling of *tilaSa*/*tilaSi*. Exclusion of the form *tilaT-I*, in which the second *ti* sequence is specified in the active input just like the first, follows in the manner illustrated in (45).

(45)			OO-F$_{TI}$	PHON: *TI	OO-F$_T$
	a.	tilaT-i		*	
		tilaT-a	*		
☞	b.	tilaS-i			*
		tilaT-a			

In (45a), the input specification for a *ti* transition cannot be maintained in the related form that has no *i*, thus yielding a greater number of violations than in the competing pair in (45b).[23]

Note that the restriction to contrastive or 'neutralizing' variation, which seems general to NDEB, follows for this second case as well on the present analysis (as it would on Kiparsky's). The reason is again that non-contrastive variation results from the ranking PHON >> IO-F (36b) above, now inconsistent with the ranking in (43) (needed to maintain the sequence *ti* in *tilasi*).

We have so far seen two of the three logically possible cases of 'derived' environments: morphologically only, as with the shortening environment of *div*[*i*]*nity* and the assibilation environment of [*t*]*ilasi* (where assibilation fails);

---

[23] Of course the alternation in (45a) would be possible under independent input specifications in the two items. That, however, would violate Restrained Input (19), placing this alternation on a par with exceptional cases like *go*/*went*. A reviewer is correct in seeing some 'loss of generalization' in allowing such independent inputs. This, however, is an asset rather than a liability. Cases like *went*, *compuls-ive*, *obe:sity* show that familiar regularities are not fully general. There seems no point in formulating a theory that claims that they are.

and both phonologically and morphologically derived, as with the assibilation environment of *tila*[*s*]-*i*. It remains to consider environments which are 'derived' only in a phonological sense. Kiparsky (1993) discusses the alternation in (46a, b), contrasting with the one in (a′, b′), and providing such a case.

(46)   a. *vesi*   'water-NOM-SG'   a′. *kuusi*   'fir-NOM-SG'
       b. *vete-nä* 'water-ESS-SG'   b′. *kuuse-nä* 'fir-ESS-SG'

The cases in (46a, a′) are both monomorphemic and yet are phonologically 'derived' because of a phonological rule raising final *e* to *i*, in Kiparsky's analysis. The latter *i* does assibilate a preceding *t*, while the underlying final *i* of *äiti* in (39d) above does not. The cases in (46a′, b′) differ from those in (46a, b) by having an underlying /*s*/ rather than /*t*/.

While in the present system there are no phonological derivations, these cases follow as well. The contrast in (46a, b) is again similar to the *dam*(*n*)/*damNation* case, as shown in (47).

(47)			PHON			
	IO-F$_{TI}$	OO-F$_{TI}$	*e#	*ti	IO-F$_{T}$	OO-F$_{T/E}$
a. (i) ☞ vesi						**
(ii) veti				*		*
(iii) vete			*			
b. (i) ☞ vete-nä						
(ii) vese-nä					*	

There is active input, in the form of *t* and *e*, in the derived form (47b). The effects of the latter input are then suppressed in (47a) by the two PHON constraints (outranking OO-F$_{T/E}$), which turn both word-final *e* to *i* and a preceding *t* to *s*. The sequence *ti* is not enforced in (47a) despite dominant IO-F$_{TI}$ and OO-F$_{TI}$, because it is absent both in (47b) and in (47a)'s active input. Hence Finnish assibilation occurs in (47a) despite the fact that it is not a 'derived' environment in the morphological sense because, as in morphologically-derived environments, there is no relevant active input *ti*.

The pair in (46a′, b′) above is the same as the one in (a, b) for the *e* part of the active input of the derived form. However, here *s* rather than *t* is in the active input. It could be in the active input for either form, passed on to the other via OO-F.[24] Note that the paradigm in (46) again contradicts Kiparsky's implicit assumption (42) above that UR contains the minimal specifications required by the base form. Here it is rather the affixed forms *vete-nä*, *kuuse-nä* that provide the crucial evidence for UR (underspecified *s*/*t* in the first case, fully specified *s* in the second).

---

[24] It is therefore easy to see that this excludes hypothetical *mati*/*matena*, like Kiparsky's analysis. With *ti* in the active input for *mati*, *matena* would violate OO-F satisfying nothing else.

In sum, certain cases of NDEB require an account partly along the lines of Kiparsky (1993). What makes this account necessary is the fact that in such cases, like Finnish [*t*] *ilas-i*, environments which are only morphologically but not phonologically derived are immune to the alternation, requiring a phonological solution. On the other hand, the account proposed in the previous subsection is not supplanted by the present one, to the extent that the earlier cases were derived in an exclusively morphological sense, making a purely phonological solution impossible. This second account of NDEB does not provide an argument against UR, but the first one does. On the other hand, the second account does not provide an argument *for* UR, since it can be straightforwardly cast in UR-less terms. Note, however, that the UR-less account differs from the UR-based one in *not* excluding that phenomena like assibilation could occur on a purely morphological basis, as in hypothetical *TIla/SIla-na*. If it turns out that there are no such cases, a principled distinction will remain to be found between them and the cases of the previous subsection.[25]

The literature provides a considerable number of cases of NDEB beside the ones discussed so far, a non-exhaustive list of which is given in (48) below. While the Polish case in (48b) in which only the second *s* palatalizes is just like the Finnish assibilation case, for most of the other cases it is not clear at the moment which of the two above solutions should apply (underived items are given on the right for comparison).

(48)   **Further NDEB cases**
  a.   Korean palatalization (Kiparsky 1973a; Iverson and Wheeler 1988)
       /*kot-i*/→   [*koc-i*] '(sun)rise'   *mati*'knot'
  b.   Polish palatalization (Kenstowicz 1994; Rubach 1984)
       /*serwis-e*/→   *serwiś-e* 'service-LOC.SG'
  c.   Swedish *k* → *ç* (Kiparsky 1973a)
       /*kämp-a*/→   [*ç*]*ämp-a* 'fight' (verb)   *kitt* 'putty'
  d.   Pre-coronal laminalization in Chumash (Poser 1993)
       /*s-tepuʔ*/ →   [*š-tepuʔ*] 'he gambles'   *stumukun* 'mistletoe'
  e.   Finnish C gradation, affecting onsets of closed syllables (Kiparsky 1973a, 1993)
       /*hattu-n*/ →   [*hatu-n*] 'hat-GEN'   *sitten* 'then'
  f.   Sanskrit *ruki* rule (Kiparsky 1973a, 1993)
       /*agni-su*/ →   [*agni-ṣu*] 'fire-DAT-PL'   *kisalaya* 'sprout'
  g.   Icelandic umlaut (Anderson 1969; Kiparsky 1993)
       /*hard-um*/ →   *hörd-um* 'hard-DAT-PL'   *akur* 'field'

---

[25] The same issue or question arises for the reduplication cases just as well on McCarthy and Prince's analysis. If reduplication cases like *si-tila* (with assibilation only in the reduplicant) do not exist, principled reasons will have to be found. I know of no such cases at the moment.

h. Chamorro vowel lowering in stressed closed syllable (Chung 1983;
   Kiparsky 1993)
   /*lapis-su*/ →   *lapés-su* '(my) pencil'   *lístu* 'quick'

i. Indonesian nasal substitution (Pater 1999)
   /*məN-pilih*/ →   *məm-ilih* 'to choose'   *əmp*at 'four'

j. Consonant gradation and V lowering in Estonian (Kiparsky 1973a)
   /*lugu*/ →   loo 'story-GEN'   *luu* 'bone-GEN'

k. Finnish cluster assimilation (Kiparsky 1973a)
   /*pur-nut*/ →   *purrut* 'bitten'   *horna* 'hell'

l. Mohawk *kw* → *kew* (Kiparsky 1973a)
   /*k-wi'stos*/ →   *kewi'stos* 'I am cold'   *rúːkweh* 'man'

n. Basque vowel assimilation (Hualde 1989)
   /*lagun-a*/ →   *laɣun-e* 'the friend'   *muɣa* 'limit'

1.4.3 *Past Accounts of NDEB*

As Kiparsky (1993) argues, earlier accounts of NDEB had proved inadequate. He
finds some degree of empirical adequacy in the Revised Alternation Condition
of Kiparsky (1973a), given in (49).

(49) **Revised Alternation Condition** (Kiparsky 1973a)
    Non-automatic neutralization processes apply only to derived forms.

However, the condition in (49), Kiparsky notes, 'is really no more than a
descriptive generalization dressed up as a principle and unstatable as a formal
condition on phonological rules'. In contrast to this impasse, we have seen
that NDEB reduces to constraint ranking. We have also seen that the restriction
to 'neutralization' processes follows from the fact that other processes instantiate the ranking PHON >> IO-F, antithetical to both of the accounts of NDEB
given above. The restriction to 'non-automatic' processes also follows in the
same way. A process which is not automatic is by definition one for which
there are lexical exceptions. As mentioned above, 'exceptions' are analysed
here as allomorphs that have separately specified inputs, as with *obeːse*/*obeːsity*
(exception to shortening), or *compel*/*compulsive* (morphological exception). For
a phonological exception to occur, the ranking IO-F >> PHON must hold. If a
process is 'automatic'—i.e. exceptionless—then the opposite ranking must
uniquely hold, again precluding both types of NDEB. Hence both: exclusions
from non-derived environments; and exceptions (within derived environments),
require the ranking IO-F >> PHON, whence their coextensiveness.[26] From the

---

[26] Given this characterization of 'non-automatic', the further restriction to neutralizing processes
would in fact seem redundant. It is indeed redundant in the present system, which does not contem-
plate a category of non-neutralizing effects (requiring PHON >> IO-F) which are non-automatic, i.e.
with exceptions (since that would entail IO-F >> PHON). This category of effects is given in

present point of view, the descriptive adequacy of (49) is therefore not a surprise.

A major attempt to overcome the conceptual difficulty that (49) raises for rule systems was made in terms of the 'Strict Cycle Condition' (Mascaró 1976), a specific restriction on the mode of application of cyclic rules that would effectively exclude them from environments which are not 'derived' either in the morphological or the phonological sense. If the present proposal is correct, there can in fact be no correlation between 'cyclic' and NDEB effects, and the generalization captured by ascribing both effects to 'cyclic' rules would have to be spurious. The reason is that, as we have seen, cyclic effects result from the ranking OO-F >> PHON >> IO-F, while NDEB effects reflect just the opposite ranking IO-F >> PHON >> OO-F.[27] Note for instance that English vowel reduction, which yields the noted cyclic effect of *cond*[*e*]*nsation*, gives no indication of failing in underived environments. See Kiparsky's (1993) discussion of other cases showing lack of correlation between the two properties.

The next influential attempt was made by Kiparsky (1982) in terms of the 'Elsewhere Condition' (EC), which stipulates disjunctive ordering between rules whose environments of application stand in a subset-to-superset relation. In such cases, the more specific rule (applying to the subset of environments) has priority, and the more general rule will apply only disjunctively—i.e. to the complementary subset. Kiparsky proposed to reduce NDEB to EC by postulating that there is an 'identity rule' that applies to underived lexical items, e.g. *i:vory*. Any phonological rule whose structural description is met by the bare lexical item—like tri-syllabic shortening—would enter into the general-to-specific relation targeted by EC, and would thus be blocked by the disjunctive ordering thus imposed, the (item-specific) identity rule being the more specific of the two.

Kiparsky's (1973a) four-way classification, contrasting with the three-way classification given in (18) above. I leave this issue open.

[27] This is a simplification, since diagnostics for cyclicity of rules are not exhausted by the consistency or preservation effects of Section 1.2 (*cond*[*e*]*nsation*, etc.). Another diagnostic is simply multiple application of a rule through the derivation—an ordering paradox without the cycle (see Kenstowicz 1994: 205f. for an illustration of this type of case). In OT, this type of effect (like other rule-ordering paradoxes) is subsumed under the general parallel character of the theory. As with the cyclic effects considered in the text, this effect too should bear no correlation with NDEB.

Note as well that, aside from its utilization as an account of NDEB effects, 'strict' cyclicity effects have, at least in the more general case, a trivial account in the present system. Such effects are illustrated by the Catalan paradigm in (i) (Kenstowicz 1994: 206–8, from Mascaró 1976):

(i)   a.   ruínə 'ruin'   b.   ruin-ós 'ruinous'   c.   ruinus-ísim 'very ruinous'

Catalan reduces unstressed post-vocalic high vowels to glides. Assuming a cyclic account of the non reduction in (b) (reduction precedes removal of the earlier stress), the question is why should reduction fail again on the next cycle in (c), the answer to which would be strict cyclicity (the environment of application of the rule is fully contained within an earlier cycle). On the present approach, the cyclic effect in (b) is attributed to the ranking OO-F >> PHON as usual. Non-reduction in (c) follows from the same ranking. Hence 'strict cyclicity' trivially reduces to invariant ranking (although the full set of facts handled by Mascaró's original analysis would require further discussion).

The account proposed above bears considerable similarity to the EC account, confirming the correctness of Kiparsky's early insights, but shares none of its problems. As Prince and Smolensky (1993: 106–8) note, 'elsewhere' effects are an automatic consequence of violable constraints—an inference that they refer to as 'Pāṇini's theorem'. In a constraint hierarchy C-SPEC >> C-GEN, where C-SPEC is the more specific constraint and C-GEN is the more general one, the effects of the former will be observable whenever it is applicable, and those of the latter elsewhere. Should the opposite rank hold, the 'elsewhere' effect will simply not obtain (as if there was a single constraint or rule applying). No particular condition needs to be stipulated, as it does when a rule—not an inherently violable device—needs to be turned off. In the above account, the relevant hierarchy is IO-F >> PHON. The first constraint will be satisfied whenever applicable, as in the initial portion of Finnish *tilas-i*, or English *i:vory*, and the second elsewhere, as in the final portion of *tilas-i* or English *div*[*i*]*nity*, both derived environments lacking an active input. IO-F (the specific constraint) is the counterpart to Kiparsky's identity rule. But, while IO-F constraints are an essential component of OT architecture, 'identity' rules are specific artefacts in the rule-based theory. The basic empirical observation is that the identity of underived lexical items competes, sometimes successfully, with the principles that calculate sound structure in general. Competition presupposes some comparability of character. In OT, such comparability is given by the fact that calculations involve evaluation of alternative representations. Underived lexical items can compete because they constitute candidate representations. In a system in which the calculations are derivational, underived lexical items have no basis for competing unless one takes the extraordinary step of converting them into types of derivations via 'identity' rules.[28]

In sum, among previous accounts of NDEB, the Revised Alternation Condition (RAC) characterization is substantially correct, but only descriptive, while the Strict Cyclicity characterization does not seem empirically correct. NDEB is clearly an 'elsewhere' effect, but both the 'Elsewhere Condition' and the 'identity rules' required in a rule-based framework are specific stipulations. The account proposed above gives essentially the effects of the RAC; it correctly predicts that cyclic and NDEB effects should not be coextensive, and it gives the correct 'elsewhere' effects by the simple virtues of constraint ranking. As for the account of NDEB given in Kiparsky (1993), we have found that it is correct modulo certain modifications, but insufficient for environments which are derived only morphologically.

1.4.4   *The Status of Affixes*

Outer affixes do not generally behave like derived environments. This is particu-

---

[28] Insistence on the totally representational character of lexical organization has been a long-standing theme in the work of J. Bybee.

larly clear from English vowel shortening, as noted in PES: 232. Shortening applies multiply to stem vowels: *fI:nI:te/in-fInIte*, but does not apply to outer affixes. Items like *satIr-I:ze, oxYd-I:ze, sallv-A:te* have shortened stem vowels but long affixal ones. Affixes shorten their vowels when embedded, as in *organ-Iz-ation, articul-At-ory*. This fact is not predictable from stress, as shown by *mètamórph-I:ze*, where there is no stress on the long vowel. The opposite dissociation, stress on a short vowel, can be shown indirectly, by noting that in *còntradíct-ory*, a heavy syllable before -*ory* receives stress. Hence, in *artícul-Atòry*, there would be stress on the capitalized vowel if there were no shortening, but shortening occurs nonetheless. In PES, which simply stipulates GENERALIZED SHORTENING (23) above, the restriction of shortening to affixed (rather than affix-containing) environments is simply part of the stipulation. The resilience of outer affixes to allomorphy is more general, however. As noted in Burzio (1998), Italian lacks unstressed allomorphs of participial affixes -*út-, -ít-* in outer-most position, so that preservation of stem stress from the infinitives in (50a) is either impossible or possible only via syncopated suppletive forms of the affixes, as in (50b). In embedded position, however, unstressed -*it-* shows up, as in (50c).

(50)   a. *bátt-ere* 'beat'   b. *batt-út-o* 'beaten'   c. *bàtt-it-óre* 'beater'
       vínc-ere 'win'   *vín-t-o* 'won'   *vìnc-it-óre* 'winner'

The anti-allomorphy of outer affixes is at play as well in cases like *titán-ic* as noted in (20) above, where the metrical consistency of the affix prevails over that of the stem, which would give **títan-ic* instead (PES: 302–4).

Outer affixes may thus seem to behave like non-derived items, subject to IO-F rather than OO-F. Without UR, this view is not expressible, however, since—as discussed in Section 1.3 above—for affixes we take the active input to be present on one occurrence of the affix only (indeterminately which one), the other occurrences being held faithful to the former by OO-F. We therefore need to postulate that outer affixes are subject to a higher-ranked version of OO-F than stems. There is independent reason favouring this view. First, there are other distinctions requiring different ranking of OO-F constraints. As noted earlier and discussed in PES, 10.4, and in Benua (1997), 'level 1' and 'level 2' affixes appear to impose OO-F constraints of different rank on their stems. Second, there is reason to view identity effects as having a self-sustaining character. Items that satisfy OO-F constraints in some ways (semantically/segmentally/metrically) turn out to be relatively more faithful in others as well (PES: 276, 307f), suggesting that the ranking of OO-F constraints is in a sense 'self-adjusting'. The fact that OO-F is relevant to both morphology and phonology would just be an instance of this: morphological relatedness, a relatively course-grained type of similarity, seems coextensive with the application of phonologically relevant OO-F constraints, imposing finer-grained identity. Now since outer affixes (at least suffixes) are major determinants of semantic structure, at least by contributing specification of syntactic category, we should indeed expect on the above reasoning that instances of the same affix will collectively stand in a relation of relatively high-ranked OO-F. This view is supported by the fact that category shift makes outer affixes behave as if they were embedded—witness noun/adjective *altern-Ate*, with a short *A* compared with the verb *altern-A:te* (PES: 294f). As noted in Burzio (1998), this is quite similar to how Italian unstressed participial *-it-* shows up in nominalizations like *vínc-it-a* 'a winning' comparably to the embedded *-it-* of (50c) above, and in contrast to the impossible participle **vínc-it-o*. The interpretation of this is that the shift in category puts semantic distance between these and the main occurrences of the affixes, causing OO-F constraints to self-demote.

Beside morphological embedding and change of category, another set of circumstances can force affixes into allomorphy, related to the allomorphy of the stems. When satisfaction of OO-F in stem and affix are mutually exclusive, the affix appears to prevail (as in *titán-ic*) if the class of stems affected is relatively small. When that class is large, the stem prevails, forcing the affix into allomorphy instead. As argued in PES: 302f, suffix consistency prevails in *titán-ic* because, for reasons related to its syllabic structure, *-ic* cannot guarantee metrical consistency of the stem for all of its stems. In, for instance, *linguíst-ic*, or *carcinogén-ic*, there is no metrical parse of the suffix: *-i)cφ* or *-icφ*), that would yield preservation of the stress of *línguist* or *carcínogen*. In contrast, there is always a viable parse with *-ist*, as in *a(mérica)(n-ìstφ)*, or *propa(gánd-is)t*. So *-ist* seems to accept metrical allomorphy because this benefits the totality of its stems (stress 'neutrality'). In contrast, *-ic* seems to be metrically invariant because only a subset of its stems would benefit from its allomorphy. This situation is also similar to the fact that 'regressive' voicing assimilation induced by an affix, as in *wi[v]es*, *le[f]t*, occurs in a small class of items, while with the larger class assimilation is progressive, affecting the affix instead (*dog[z]*, etc.). This behaviour can be addressed by considerations similar to those invoked in the discussion of Restrained Input (19) above, specifically by supposing that the ranking of OO-F for any given class is tied to the number of cases that satisfy it within that class (hence causing patterns which are already stronger to prevail further). In the case of items suffixed with *-ist*, massive satisfaction of stem OO-F is inherently possible for the reasons just described. As a result, we may assume it is possible for the rank of stem-OO-F to rise above that of suffix-OO-F, thus forcing the suffix into allomorphy.[29] In contrast, in the case of *-ic*, the number of satisfactions of stem-OO-F is inherently capped by the inability of *-ic* to integrate into some of the stem metrical parses, hence leaving suffix-OO-F undominated, yielding stress-shifting *ti(tán-icφ)*, rather than stress-preserving **(títan-i)cφ*. One may

---

[29] The ranking 'Stem consistency >> Affix consistency' of PES (57), p.254, will now refer to this set of circumstances (massive satisfaction of stem consistency). The opposite ranking holds otherwise, as in the text.

object here that if a suffix like *-ist* maintained a fixed parse, then there would also be maximal satisfaction, and hence maximal ranking, of OO-F, this time for the suffix, raising the question of why this situation should not arise instead. The answer would seem to be that not only is the number of satisfactions relevant but (again, as in the discussion of Restrained Input (19)) also the number of violations. By keeping a single metrical parse, *-ist* would force a large number of stems to undergo independent allomorphies. On the other hand, all of these can be eliminated in one fell swoop by introducing a single allomorph of the suffix. The conclusion is thus that optimization is global.

In sum, the fact that allomorphy often affects affixes rather than stems follows from global optimization. By means of just a few allomorphs a suffix can often spare from allomorphy a large number of stems. On the other hand, the fact that allomorphy sometimes affects stems rather than affixes reflects the fact that affixes are inherently more anti-allomorphic, which also accounts for the fact that they do not generally behave like other morphologically-'derived' environments.

1.5 Conclusion

In a theory of morpho-phonology that uses Output-to-Output correspondence within OT, two important facts that formerly required specific provisions reduce to the simple effect of constraint ranking which Prince and Smolensky call 'Pāṇini's theorem'. In OT, a constraint will be violated and hence appear to be blocked over the domain of constraints that dominate it. Both 'cyclic' effects and NDEB are instances of such apparent blocking of phonological constraints.

Cyclic effects reduce to domination of phonological constraints by OO-F constraints, the blocking thus occurring over derived environments. NDEB similarly reduces to domination of phonological constraints by IO-F constraints, the blocking here occurring over underived environments. Each of these two accounts presupposes calculation of morphologically-derived forms via OO-F constraints rather than via UR. The account of cyclic effects makes UR unnecessary since OO-F constraints are sufficient. In contrast, the account of one class of NDEB makes non-existence of UR necessary. We have seen that if there was a UR, pairs like *diviːne/divinity* would have a common input /diviːn/ by definition of UR, leaving no explanation why a phonology which abhors long vowels should prevail in one case but not in the other.

Beside NDEB, the present approach has dealt with various forms of irregularity by permitting morphologically complex forms to have active inputs independent of their bases. Specifically, I have proposed that such input is involved in the following cases: (i) contrasts like *blásphemous/desíːrous*, where the rest of the grammar would be indeterminate; (ii) phonological irregulars like *obeːsity*; and (iii) morphological irregulars like *compuls-ive*. Many other irregularities of this sort exist, like *syllabify/syllabifiC-ation*, *problem/problemAT-ic*, *horizon/horizonT-al*,

president/presidentI-a, habit/habitU-al, rabbi/rabbiNic, where the capitalized portions in each case are missing from the corresponding bases. Bound stems, as in
STUPEND-ous are clearly just one end point in the scale of morphological irregularity: the stem is here totally missing and for that reason needs to be given in the
input for the affixed form. In addition, and similarly, semantic irregularity can
also be attributed to an independent input for a derived form, as in *regrett-able*,
which does not have the expected meaning of 'something that *can* be regretted'
(but rather means '. . . that *should* be regretted'); or as in *electric-ity*, which does
not refer to 'the condition of being electric'. All of these cases call for some input
independent of the one of their bases, and (except for *obe:sity*, which is consistent
with its base) invoke the ranking in (51), which thus appears to be the hallmark
of Latinate-type or 'level 1' affixation in English.[30]

(51) **'Level 1' grammar:** IO-F >> OO-F

Yet another characteristic of level 1 affixation is its relatively low productivity.
For instance, in contrast to *parent/parent-al* one does not find the parallel *stu-
dent/*student-al* or many other conceivable formations. Evidently, level 1 items
are partly memorized even when they are fully regular, like *parent-al*. Assuming
that active input is the formal characterization of memory, items like *parental*
would be associated with a minimal amount of active input to express their
existence. Non-existent items like *studental* would have no such input. Under
the ranking in (51) this would now correctly result in no output. The cluster of
properties that the above discussion is thus able to deal with is summarized
in (52).

(52) **'Level 1' properties:**
   a. NDEB
   b. (i)   morphological irregularity/bound stems *compUlS-ive/*
                                                      STUPEND-ous
        (ii) phonological irregularity   *obe:s-ity*
        (iii) semantic irregularity   *electric-ity*
        (iv) low productivity   **student-al*

If the above discussion is correct, the properties in (52a, b) respectively
instantiate each of the two logical possibilities created by the demise of the traditional UR: active input present in a base but not shared by its morphological
derivatives, as in our account of NDEB (52a); and active input in a morphological derivative independent of that of its base, as in the account proposed for
each of (52bi–iv).

   While the ranking in (51) thus seems to hold, recall that the effects of the

---

[30] Note, however, that the 'cyclic' effects attested with level-1 lexicon and discussed in Section 1.2
will need to be partly reinterpreted, since the ranking OO-F >> PHON >> IO-F attributed to those
effects superficially contradicts the one in (51).

input nonetheless need to be restrained, since the level-1 lexicon is still considerably regular—a problem that was adressed in Section 1.3.2 above. Yet the correctness of the ranking in (51) is further underscored by the fact that the 'level 2' affixes (like *-ness, -less, -ful, -ed, -ing*) simultaneously reverse all of the properties in (52), a difference that would follow if the level 2 grammar involved the ranking opposite that of (51), as argued in Benua (1997), Burzio (1997), a conclusion that was partly anticipated in PES: 10.4.5.

1.6 References

Alderete, J. (1995). 'Faithfulness to prosodic heads'. Ms, U.Mass., Amherst.

—— J. Beckman, L. Benua, A. Gnanadesikan, J. McCarthy, and S. Urbanczyk (1996). 'Reduplication and segmental unmarkedness'. Ms, U.Mass, Amherst.

Anderson, S. R. (1969). *West Scandinavian Vowel Systems and the Ordering of Phonological Rules*. PhD dissertation, MIT.

Aronoff, M. (1976). *Word Formation in Generative Grammar*. Cambridge, MA, MIT Press.

—— (1994). *Morphology By Itself*. Cambridge, MA, MIT Press.

Beckman, J. (1996). *Positional Faithfulness*, PhD dissertation, U.Mass, Amherst.

—— L. Walsh Dickey, and S. Urbanczyk (eds) (1995). *University of Massachusetts Occasional Papers in Linguistics 18: Papers in Optimality Theory*. Amherst, MA, GLSA.

Benua, L. (1995). 'Identity effects in morphological truncation'. In Beckman *et al.* (eds).

—— (1997). *Transderivational Identity: Phonological Relations between Words*, PhD dissertation, U.Mass, Amherst.

Borowsky, T. (1993). 'On the word level'. In S. Hargus and E. Kaisse (eds), 199–234.

Buckley, E. (1995). 'Cyclicity as correspondence'. Talk presented at the Tilburg University Conference on the Derivational Residue in Phonology.

Burzio, L. (1991). 'On the metrical unity of Latinate affixes'. In G. Westphal, B. Ao, and H. R. Chae (eds), *Proceedings of the Eighth Eastern States Conference on Linguistics*, Department of Linguistics, Ohio State University. Reprinted in *Rivista di Grammatica Generativa* 16, 1–27. Revised version in H. Campos and P. M. Kempchinsky (eds), (1995). *Evolution and Revolution in Linguistic Theory: Essays in Honor of Carlos Otero*. Washington, DC, Georgetown University Press.

—— (1992). 'Principles in phonology'. In E. Fava (ed.), *Proceedings of the XVII Meeting on Generative Grammar* (Trieste, February 22–24, 1991), 97–119. Turin, Rosenberg & Sellier.

—— (1993). 'English stress, vowel length and modularity'. *Journal of Linguistics* 29.2, 359–418.

—— (1994a). *Principles of English Stress*. Cambridge, Cambridge University Press.

—— (1994b). 'Metrical consistency'. In E. S. Ristad (ed.), *Language Computations*, American Mathematical Society, Providence RI.

—— (1996). 'Surface constraints versus underlying representation'. In Durand and Laks (eds).

—— (1997). 'Strength in numbers'. In V. Miglio and B. Morén (eds), *University of Maryland Working Papers in Linguistics 5* (1997): *Selected phonology papers from H-O-T 97*, 27–52.

—— (1998). 'Multiple correspondence', *Lingua* 103, 79–109.

Burzio, L. and E. DiFabio (1994). 'Accentual stability'. In M. Mazzola (ed.), *Issues and Theory in Romance Linguistics* (LSRL XXIII). Washington, DC, Georgetown University Press.

Bybee, J. L. (1988). 'Morphology as lexical organization'. In Hammond and Noonan (eds).

—— (1995). 'Regular morphology and the lexicon'. *Language and Cognitive Processes* 10 (5), 425–55.

Chomsky, N. and M. Halle (1968). *The Sound Pattern of English*. New York, Harper & Row.

Chung, S. (1983). 'Transderivational relationships in Chamorro phonology'. *Language* 59, 35–66.

Cole, J, (1995). 'The cycle in phonology'. In J. Goldsmith (ed.), *The Handbook of Phonological Theory*. Oxford, B. Blackwell, 72–113.

Duanmu, San (1997). 'Recursive constraint evaluation in Optimality Theory: Evidence from cyclic compounds in Shanghai', *Natural Language and Linguistic Theory* 15.3, 465–508.

Durand, J. and B. Laks (eds) (1996). *Current Trends in Phonology: Models and Methods*. Salford, Manchester, University of Salford Publications.

Giegerich, H. (1985). *Metrical Phonology and Phonological Structure: German and English*. Cambridge, Cambridge University Press.

Hammond, M. and M. Noonan (eds), (1988). *Theoretical Morphology*. San Diego, CA, Academic Press.

Hualde, J. (1989). 'The Strict-Cycle Condition and noncyclic rules'. *Linguistic Inquiry* 20, 675–80.

Inkelas, S. and C. O. Orgun (1995). 'Level ordering and economy in the lexical phonology of Turkish'. *Language* 71.4, 763–93.

Itô, J. (1990). 'Prosodic minimality in Japanese'. *Syntax Research Center, Cowell College, UCSC, Technical Report SRC-90–04*.

—— and A. Mester (1997). 'The ga-gyo variation in Japanese phonology'. In I. Roca (ed.), *Derivations and Constraints in Phonology*. Oxford, Oxford University Press, 419–62.

Hargus, S. and E. Kaisse (eds) (1993). *Phonetics and Phonology 4: Studies in Lexical Phonology*. San Diego, Academic Press.

Iverson, G. and D. Wheeler (1988). 'Blocking and the elsewhere condition'. In Hammond and Noonan (eds), 325–38.

Kager, R. (1989). *A Metrical Theory of Stress and Destressing in English and Dutch*. Dordrecht, Foris.

—— (1993). 'Consequences of catalexis'. In H. van der Hulst and J. van de Weijer (eds), *Leiden in Last. HIL Phonology Papers I*. The Hague, Holland Academic Graphics, 269–98.

—— H. van der Hulst, and W. Zonneveld (eds) (1999). *The Prosody-Morphology Interface*. Cambridge, Cambridge University Press.

Kenstowicz, M. (1994). *Phonology in Generative Grammar*. Cambridge, MA, Blackwell.

—— (1996). 'Base-identity and uniform exponence: alternatives to cyclicity'. In Durand and Laks (eds), 363–93.

Kiparsky, P. (1973a). 'Abstractness, opacity and global rules'. In O. Fujimura (ed.), *Three Dimensions of Linguistic Theory*. Tokyo, TEC, 57–86.

—— (1973b). 'Elsewhere in phonology'. In S. R. Anderson and P. Kiparsky (eds), *A Festschrift for Morris Halle*. New York, Holt, Rinehart & Winston.

—— (1982). 'From cyclic phonology to lexical phonology'. In H. van der Hulst and N. Smith (eds), *The Structure of Phonological Representations (Part I)*, 131–75. Dordrecht, Foris.

—— (1991). 'Catalexis'. Ms, Stanford.

—— (1993). 'Blocking in non-derived environments'. In Hargus and Kaisse (eds), 277–313.

Kirchner, R. (1995). 'Contrastiveness is an epiphenomenon of constraint ranking'. In BLS Proceedings.

Kisseberth, C. (1972). 'On derivative properties of phonological rules'. In M. Brame (ed.), *Contribution to Generative Phonology*. Austin, University of Texas Press.

Lamontagne, G. (1996). 'Relativized Contiguity, Part I: Contiguity and Syllable Prosody,' ROA-150.

McCarthy, J. (1995). 'Extensions of faithfulness: Rotuman revisited'. Ms, U.Mass, Amherst.

—— and A. Prince (1994). 'The Emergence of the unmarked: optimality in prosodic morphology'. In M. Gonzàlez (ed.), *Proceedings of the North East Linguistic Society* 24. Amherst, MA, GSLA, 333–79.

—— —— (1995). 'Faithfulness and reduplicative identity'. In Beckman *et al.* (eds).

—— (1999) 'Faithfulness and reduplicative identity'. In Kager *et al.* (eds), 218–309.

Mascaró, J. (1976). *Catalan Phonology and the Phonological Cycle*. PhD Dissertation, MIT. Reproduced (1978) by the Indiana University Linguistics Club, Bloomington.

Padgett, J. (1997). 'Perceptual distance of contrast: Vowel height and nasality'. In R. Walker, M. Katayama, and D. Karvonen (eds), *Phonology at Santa Cruz*, vol. 5.

Pater, J. (1999) 'Austronesian nasal substitution and other NC effects'. In Kager *et al.* (eds), 310–43.

Poser, W. (1993). 'Are strict cycle effects derivable?' In Hargus and Kaisse (eds), 277–313.

Prince, A. and P. Smolensky (1993). *Optimality Theory: Constraint Interaction in Generative Grammar*. Ms, Rutgers University, New Brunswick, and University of Colorado, Boulder. To appear, MIT Press.

Rosenthall, S. (1994). *Vowel/Glide Alternations in a Theory of Constraint Interaction*. PhD dissertation, U.Mass, Amherst.

Rubach, J. (1984). *Cyclic and Lexical Phonology: The Structure of Polish*. Dordrecht, Foris.

Smolensky, P. (1995). 'On the internal structure of the constraint component CON of UG'. Handout, UCLA lecture 4 July 1995.

—— (1997). 'Constraint interaction in generative grammar II: Local conjunction'. Paper presented at the Hopkins Optimality Theory Workshop/University of Maryland Mayfest 1997, 8–12 May 1997.

2

Gradient Well-Formedness in Optimality Theory[1]

Bruce P. Hayes

2.1 The Gradience Problem

Virtually every generative linguist has had the following experience: a given linguistic entity (sentence, novel word, pronunciation) is presented to a native speaker and judged to be neither fully well-formed nor fully unacceptable. In such instances, consultants often say things like 'I *guess* I could say that,' 'It's all right but not perfect,' 'It's pretty bad but not completely out,' and the like.

Such judgements often get reified: the data are sorted into grammatical and ungrammatical categories, and an analysis is developed in which the rules or principles generate all and only the grammatical outcomes. This procedure is controversial, as Schütze's (1996) comprehensive review points out. Critics of generative grammar might take the existence of gradient well-formedness judgements as an indication that the entire enterprise is misconceived: that discrete 'categories,' 'rules,' and 'constraints' are just illusions suffered by the linguist. In this eliminativist view, gradient well-formedness judgements constitute evidence that generative linguistics must be replaced by something very different, something much 'fuzzier.'

Other scholars, also reviewed by Schütze, have maintained that well-formedness really is categorical (surface appearances to the contrary), and that gradience is merely the result of performance factors that obscure the judgement process. However, while such factors certainly do exist, much of the patterning of gradient judgements is based on authentic structural aspects of the linguistic material being judged. This makes it unlikely that it could be described as mere performance (see Schütze 1996: 63–4; and 2.3.1.4 below).

A third possibility—the one advocated here—is to claim that gradient well-formedness judgements are on the whole authentic: abstracting away appropri-

[1] Many thanks to Osamu Fujimura, Carlos Gussenhoven, Janet Pierrehumbert, and Richard Sproat for critical commentary and suggestions during the preparation of this article. None is responsible for errors or shortcomings.

ately from performance factors, carefully elicited gradient judgements really do reflect the internalized knowledge of the native speaker. What has been lacking, in this view, is the right theoretical tools to model grammars that can generate outputs with varying degrees of well-formedness.

My specific suggestion is that within Optimality Theory (Prince and Smolensky 1993) it is possible to devise such grammars. The modification in the theory that is needed is strikingly minor, and is quite independent of the choice of formal representations and constraints used in the grammar.

The actual proposal has been briefly presented in Hayes and MacEachern (1998). The material that article deals with is perhaps somewhat peripheral, being drawn from the theory of metrics, particularly the part of the theory concerned with rhythmic form. The goal of the present article is to show that the approach we adopted can be extended to a strictly linguistic example. I will also attempt to increase the plausibility of the proposal by offering a rationale, based on language learning, for why gradient well-formedness exists and why it occurs in particular areas.

2.2 The Proposal

I will go through the proposal in a series of steps, each one a closer approximation to the final version.

2.2.1 *Free Ranking*

Consider first the issue of free variation, where a single input yields multiple outputs. A commonly adopted approach to free variation in Optimality Theory is to suppose that certain pairs of constraints may be *ranked freely*. Each variant outcome is obtained by fixing the free rankings of the grammar in a particular way.[2] In this view, a grammar is not a monolithic ranking, generating a single set of outputs, but a set of rankings, of which some are obligatory and some are free. If one examines the full set of possible total constraint rankings for such a grammar, it will be found that the set of 'subgrammars' thus defined will collectively generate all and only the forms permitted in the language, including all the free variants.[3]

2.2.2 *Strictness Bands*

It will be useful in what follows to consider rankings not as simple arrangements of constraint pairs but rather as the result of the constraints' each taking on a

---

[2] A nice example of the empirical effectiveness of the free-ranking approach may be found in Davidson and Noyer (1997).

[3] One should add that, in any real-life grammar, it will turn out that there are quite a few pairwise rankings that simply don't matter. They may without harm be considered free (vacuous free ranking), or they may be assigned a ranking arbitrarily: the same outcomes will be observed.

range of values on an abstract continuum. This is a concept explored independently by Boersma (this volume). We can speak of each constraint possessing a
strictness band, and depict the bands graphically as follows:

(1)

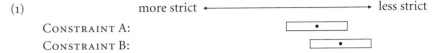

Within each band, I have given a *selection point*, which is defined as the particular value of strictness taken on by a constraint on a given speaking occasion. It
can be seen that as long as the strictness bands of two constraints overlap, then
both rankings of the two constraints will be available for the generation of outputs. In (1), the selection points are such that on the particular speaking occasion involved, outputs will be generated that respect a ranking of CONSTRAINT
A over CONSTRAINT B. Likewise, on other occasions the selection points could
require a ranking of B over A:

(2)

We may further suppose that in speech *perception*, the listener may explore the
strictness bands until a set of selection points is found that appropriately
matches the phonetic form to a suitable underlying phonological representation
(for discussion see Boersma 1997).

Where bands fail to overlap, the width of the bands is of course vacuous,
since the ranking that results will be the same no matter where the selection
points fall.

It is easy to imagine extensions of the strictness band notion beyond just
accounting for optionality. Suppose, for instance, that we adopt the assumption
that on any given speaking occasion the selection of a strictness value within a
band is made at random. In such cases, the *relative frequency* of output forms
will vary according to the width and relative position of the bands. The issue of
modeling text frequencies is discussed further in Boersma (this volume) and
below in Section 2.5.2.

2.2.3 *Fringes*

The actual problem at hand—gradient well-formedness—can be treated by
further amplifying the strictness-band idea. Let us suppose that, at least in the
crucial cases, the range of a constraint is not firmly delimited. Formally, we can
model this idea by positing *fringes*: at the edge of a constraint's strictness band,
we add special blocks labeled with traditional well-formedness diacritics such as
'?' and '??'. Selection points may occur within a fringe, but only at the cost of

the degree of ill-formedness indicated. For instance, the sample diagram in (3):

(3) CONSTRAINT A: [   ]
     CONSTRAINT B: [??|?|]
     CONSTRAINT C: [   ]

can be interpreted as follows: (a) Ordinarily, Constraint B is *outranked* by Constraints A and C. (b) However, it is *somewhat possible* for B to outrank C. This will occur if the selection point for B occurs quite close to the left edge of its '?' fringe, and the selection point for C occurs quite close to the right edge of its strictness band as a whole. Forms that can be generated only with this ranking are intuited to be mildly ill-formed (?). (c) It is only *marginally possible* for B to outrank A. This will occur if the selection point for B occurs close to the left edge of its '??' fringe, and that for A close to the right edge of its strictness band. Forms that can be generated only with this ranking are intuited to be considerably ill-formed, though they are not completely excluded (??).[4]

As for where the fringes come from: I conjecture that they arise as part of the acquisition process, in cases where the input data do not suffice to establish firmly what the upper or lower bounds of a constraint's strictness band are. This is discussed further in Section 2.4 below.

How do we evaluate the well-formedness of a given linguistic entity under the proposed model? I assume that in judging a form, a consultant will normally assign it *the highest rating possible* under the grammar. Thus, suppose a given form emerges from the grammar in two ways: (a) with '?' attached, using a choice of strictness values that employs a '?' fringe of one of the strictness bands; (b) perfectly, using a choice of strictness values that is drawn solely from the central (non-fringe) portions of the bands. This is illustrated below:

(4) a. CONSTRAINT A: [•   ]
         CONSTRAINT B: [??|•?|]

     b. CONSTRAINT A: [•   ]
         CONSTRAINT B: [??| ? | •   ]

---

[4] Carlos Gussenhoven sensibly notes that it is unlikely that strictness ranges involve discrete boundaries between '?', '??', and '*'; it seems more likely that the fringes are themselves gradient in the ill-formedness they impose. Thus, what one wants is not a set of discrete blocks, but rather a continuous, hump-shaped function. The x-axis of this function would be the constraint strictness continuum, and the y-axis would depict 'goodness' values.

Despite this, throughout the discussion below I will continue to assume an artificial categorization into discrete '?' and '??' fringes. It will be seen that this idealization greatly facilitates analysis. Moreover, I believe the idealization is harmless. In scientific modeling, step functions are frequently used to approximate continuous functions, provided the 'grain' imposed by the steps is innocuously fine. The '?' and '??' blocs used here can be regarded as a suitable approximation to a continuous 'goodness' function, because the data that would be needed to distinguish the predictions of the continuous function from the stepwise approximation would be far more refined than what is available here.

I assume that consultants normally avoid 'perverse' parsings of the input like (4a), which assign it some degree of ill-formedness, when there exist alternative selection points (4b) that generate the form as perfect.

The proposal here is strongly reminiscent of Schütze's (1996: 172, 189) view of the grammaticality judgement process. Schütze suggests that when consultants judge marginal forms, 'constraints [can] be selectively relaxed when an initial parse fail[s]. Once a parse [is] eventually found this way, . . . the nature and degree of constraint relaxation [is] reflected in their ungrammaticality ratings.' The difference here, following the general approach of OT, is that constraints *per se* are not relaxed, but rather their mutual rankings.

This is the proposal. In the remainder of this chapter, I will try to provide some empirical support for it with a case study, worked out under the assumptions just made. I will then address some general issues that the proposal raises.

2.3 Case Study: English Light and Dark /l/

From time to time I have pondered the distribution of the light and dark allophones of /l/ in my idiolect of American English. I have usually found the judgements difficult to make and rather gradient in character. Thus the light-versus-dark /l/ problem seemed a reasonable area to take on as a case study.

2.3.1 *The /l/ Data*

Below, I give what I take to be crucial background facts, followed by the results of a survey of well-formedness judgements.

2.3.1.1 The phonetics of /l/

The phonetic quality of /l/ in English dialects varies to a startling degree, as I have discovered by eliciting forms from speakers from different countries and regions. However, most dialects include some kind of distinction between 'light' and 'dark' /l/. In my own speech, which I find to be similar to that of many other Americans in the relevant respects, both light and dark /l/ are rather velarized (back tongue-body position). This has been noticed previously for American dialects by Wells (1982: 490). The light allophone [l] is less backed than the dark, and has obligatory tongue-blade contact in the denti-alveolar region. Dark [ɫ] is 'backer'; and in the more casual speech registers, if it is not prevocalic, it can lose its tongue-blade contact entirely, becoming a kind of high back vocoid with lateral tongue-body compression.[5]

A phonetic matter that is important here is the highly noticeable allophony found on vowels that precede dark [ɫ]. In my own speech, such vowels are

---

[5] In various dialects such as Cockney (Wells 1982) or Adelaide Australian (Borowsky and Horvath 1997), the dark /l/ can lose its laterality entirely, becoming a simple back vowel. This phenomenon does not occur, I believe, in the American varieties studied here.

backed, receive a schwa off-glide if front or high, and are otherwise monophthongized. /ɑ/ is slightly rounded; and the 'true diphthongs' /aɪ, aʊ, ɔɪ/ get schwa off-glides. The chart in (5) gives a survey; related observations may be found in Wells (1982: 487).

(5)

Default quality	Example	Pre-[ɫ] Allophone	Example
[i:]	*tree* [tɹi:]	[iə]	*feel* [fiəɫ]
[ɪ]	*fit* [fɪt]	[ɪə]	*fill* [fɪəɫ][6]
[e͡ɪ]	*pay* [pe͡ɪ]	[eə]	*pail* [peəɫ]
[ɛ]	*set* [sɛt]	[ɛə]	*sell* [sɛ͡əɫ][6]
[æ]	*pat* [pæt]	[aə]	*pal* [paəɫ]
[u͡u]	*do* [du͡u]	[uə]	*fool* [fuəɫ]
[o͡ʊ]	*foe* [fo͡ʊ]	[o:]	*foal* [fo:ɫ]
[ʊ]	*put* [pʊt]	[ʊ͡ə]	*pull* [pʊ͡əɫ][6]
[ʌ]	*but* [bʌt]	[ʌ]	*dull* [dʌɫ]
[ɔ͡ə]	*saw* [sɔ͡ə]	[ɔ]	*Saul* [sɔɫ]
[ɑ]	*Pa* [pɑ]	[ɒ]	*all* [ɒɫ]
[a͡ɪ]	*tie* [ta͡ɪ]	[a͡ɪə]	*tile* [ta͡ɪəɫ]
[a͡ʊ]	*cow* [ka͡ʊ]	[a͡ʊə]	*cowl* [ka͡ʊəɫ]
[ɔ͡ɪ]	*boy* [bɔ͡ɪ]	[ɔ͡ɪə]	*boil* [bɔ͡ɪəɫ]

The most careful phonetic study yet done of backness in English /l/ was carried out by Sproat and Fujimura (1993), who gathered X-ray microbeam data. An important claim that Sproat and Fujimura make is that there is no categorical distinction between light and dark /l/ in English, only a phonetic continuum. This claim strikes me as controversial. In particular, the data Sproat and Fujimura gathered did not include the most crucial cases for demonstrating categories, namely those cited below under (14). Inspection of the data plots in their article suggests, to me at least, that there are two analytical possibilities that remain tenable: (a) an outright phonetic continuum, as Sproat and Fujimura propose, or (b) two phonetic categories that are partly obscured by free variation and near-neutralizing lenition. It is the latter interpretation that will be adopted here, because it appears to be necessary to adopt this assumption in order to give a coherent account of the Paradigm Uniformity effects noted below.

2.3.1.2 A survey of well-formedness judgements

After exploring the pattern of /l/ allophony using just my own intuitions, I attempted to obtain higher-quality data by conducting an organized survey of ten

---

[6] A caution regarding [ɪ͡ə], [ɛ͡ə], and [ʊ͡ə]: like their corresponding default allophones, these nuclei are short, and the diphthongization is not nearly as perceptible for them as it is for other vowels.

native speakers of American English.[7] All of my consultants were volunteers and were known to me; half were linguists and half were not. Because subsequent statistical testing showed no essential differences between the two groups,[8] the results are pooled below. Each consultant was presented with 17 words, sometimes placed in a particular sentence context to make the meaning clear. Each word contained an /l/, and was pronounced by the author in two ways, with light [l] and dark [ɫ]. The consultants were asked to rate *both* pronunciations on an integer scale ranging from 1 to 7, from 1 designating 'sounds just right, perfectly normal in my dialect of English' to 7 designating 'sounds awful, I would never say it that way.' In addition, the consultants were invited, if it seemed appropriate, to check boxes labeled as follows: '*casual*: to the extent that it's acceptable, it's acceptable in casual speech only'; and '*formal*: to the extent that it's acceptable, it's acceptable in formal, careful speech only.'

On the whole, the consultants found the task somewhat difficult, and the variance in their responses was rather high. The view taken here is that *in any individual instance* the judgements were indeed subject to apparently random influences. However, when averaged over all the consultants, the results formed a quite coherent pattern.[9] I will report the results of the survey interspersed below amid a general, structurally-oriented description of the facts.

2.3.1.3 Data pattern

In *pretonic* position (that is, immediately before a stressed vowel) it seems utterly obligatory to produce a light [l]. Representative examples, as I would pronounce them, are the following:

(6)   **Pretonic: Obligatory Light [l]**
        light ['laɪt], *Lee* ['liː], *Lou* ['luː], *aloud* [ə'laʊd], *balloon* [bə'luːn], *apply* [ə'plaɪ]

This is likewise true for word-initial /l/ when the following vowel is stressless:

(7)   **Word-Initial Pre-Atonic: Obligatory Light [l]**
        Lamarck [lə'mɑɹk], *Louanne* [lu'æn]

---

[7] I discovered, somewhat late in the process, that there is recent literature that provides valuable guidance to linguists who conduct such surveys: Schütze (1996), Bard, Robertson, and Sorace (1996), and Cowart (1997). Much of what I have done here could have been done better by following the prescriptions of these works. All of the survey data may be downloaded from the author's Website at http://www.humnet.ucla.edu/linguistics/people/hayes.

[8] Here are the results of a factorial ANOVA test. For well-formedness judgements, there was no significant main effect of the linguist/non-linguist difference (Fisher's PLSD post-hoc test: p = .501), nor a significant interaction between type of word tested and linguist status (p = .891). For judgements of casualness, there was a small main effect (linguists tended to judge the forms overall as more casual, p = .019), but no significant interaction between word type and linguist status (p = .528).

[9] Cowart (1997: Ch. 2) provides an interesting review and defense of the use of such data patterns in judgement experiments.

If any of the forms of (6) or (7) is pronounced with dark [ɫ] instead, the result sounds laughable, like a phonetic exercise.

This is my own judgement, but it is clearly supported by the results of the survey, which included the words *light* and *Louanne*, ranked on the 1–7 scale. The crucial numbers given are the mean of the judgement of all ten consultants. The column labeled 'σ' gives the standard deviation, the accepted measure for describing how much the consultants differed from one another.

(8)	Word	with [l]		with [ɫ]	
		mean	σ	mean	σ
	light	1.30	0.48	6.10	1.10
	Louanne	1.10	0.32	5.55	1.74
	average for both words	1.20	0.41	5.83	1.44

There is also an environment where dark [ɫ] is just as obligatory: preconsonantal and prepausal position.

(9) **Preconsonantal: Obligatory Dark [ɫ]**
    fault ['fɒɫt], *help* ['hɛəɫp], *shelter* ['ʃɛəɫtɚ]
(10) **Prepausal: Obligatory Dark [ɫ]**
    feel ['fiəɫ], *whole* ['hoːɫ]

Here, too, the substitution of the wrong allophone (light [l]) produces, I think, a comic effect; in this case, a rather cruel one of mocking a foreign speaker whose native language has only light [l]. The data from the ten consultants is summarized in (11).

(11)	Word	with [l]		with [ɫ]	
		mean	σ	mean	σ
	bell	6.60	0.97	1.20	0.42
	help	6.60	0.97	1.05	0.16
	average	6.60	0.94	1.12	0.32

The next environment to consider is intervocalic pre-atonic position. This environment, sometimes called 'ambisyllabic', yields special allophones for quite a few English consonants. For /l/ in the target dialect, it evokes free variation between light and dark:

(12) **Intervocalic Pre-Atonic: Free Variation**
    Greeley ['griːli, 'griəɫi]
    Bailey ['beɪli, 'beəɫi]
    mellow ['mɛlou, 'mɛəɫou]
    Hayley ['heɪli, 'heəɫi]
    Mailer ['meɪlɚ, 'meəɫɚ]

The consultant survey examined four such words, and in all found fair acceptability for both variants, the light one being slightly preferred:

(13)

Word	with [l]		with [ɬ]	
	mean	σ	mean	σ
(*Norman*) *Mailer*	2.00	1.33	2.00	1.33
Hayley (*Mills*)	1.55	0.96	3.05	1.83
(*Horace*) *Greeley*	1.80	1.32	2.70	1.77
(*Mayor*) *Daley*	2.25	1.48	2.80	1.62
average	1.90	1.26	2.64	1.63

The realization of intervocalic pre-atonic /l/ is also influenced by morphology. Suppose first that the /l/ is the first segment of a suffix. Here, the preference is rather strongly shifted to a light [l], and I will mark the dark [ɬ] forms with a question mark:

(14)   **Suffix-initial: light acceptable, dark ?**
  free-ly   ['friːli], ?['friə̯ɬi]
  dai-ly   ['deɪli], ?['deə̯ɬi]
  gray-ling ['ɡɹeɪlɪŋ], ?['ɡɹeə̯ɬɪŋ]
  eye-let   ['aɪlət], ?['aɪə̯ɬət]

The forms examined in the survey were:

(15)

Word	with [l]		with [ɬ]	
	mean	σ	mean	σ
gray-ling[10]	1.39	0.49	3.17	2.32
gai-ly	1.45	0.76	3.65	2.14
free-ly	1.85	1.25	3.20	1.81
average	1.57	0.87	3.34	2.03

Contrariwise, supposing that a vowel-initial suffix is added to a stem ending in /l/, the form with dark [ɬ] is preferred, and the light [l] form deserves the ?:

(16)   **Stem-final before vowel-initial suffix: dark acceptable, light?**
  (*touchy-*)'*feel-y*   ['fiə̯ɬi], ?['fiːli]
  heal-ing   ['hiə̯ɬɪŋ], ?['hiːlɪŋ]
  mail-er 'one who mails' ['meə̯ɬɚ], ?['meɪlɚ]

These are the forms tested with the consultants:

---

[10] To assist intuitions of morphological relatedness, this was elicited in the frame: 'A grayling is a kind of trout with a gray color'. The words *mail-er* and *hail-y* were elucidated with similar frames.

(17)

Word	with [l]		with [ɫ]	
	mean	σ	mean	σ
mail-er	2.80	2.20	2.00	1.41
hail-y	4.00	1.80	1.56	1.01
gale-y	3.39	2.42	2.28	1.86
(*touchy-*)*feel-y*	2.00	1.49	2.20	1.87
average	3.01	2.06	2.01	1.54

Such influences of morphology have been observed before in other dialects: see Wells (1982: 312–13) for vernacular London English, Simpson (1980) for Australian English, and Gimson (1970: 202) for Standard British (RP) in a limited (postatonic) environment.

Stem-final /l/ can also become prevocalic when the stem precedes a vowel-initial word, as in *mail it*. The result here seems to be an exaggerated version of the preceding case: the /l/ 'wants' quite strongly to be dark. This preference appeared in the single such form checked in the consultant survey:

(18)

Word	with [l]:		with [ɫ]	
	mean	σ	mean	σ
mail it	4.40	1.71	1.10	0.32

One remaining word was elicited in the survey: *antler*, as an example of postconsonantal, pre-atonic /l/. The consultants strongly preferred light [l], but I was surprised by the relatively high level of acceptability of the dark [ɫ] variant:

(19)

Word	with [l]		with [ɫ]	
	mean	σ	mean	σ
antler	1.40	0.70	3.55	1.54

The relevant contrast here is with *Louanne* above, where the /l/ is likewise pre-atonic and non-post-vocalic, but the judgement of the dark variant is far harsher (3.55 versus 5.55—a difference that is highly significant statistically). For now, I will leave *antler* aside, taking it up again in Section 2.3.2.6.

We can now turn to the most crucial aspect of the survey: the demonstration that the differences in judgement between the various categories are not just the result of random fluctuations (which admittedly are present in abundance) but are an authentic effect of the underlying structural differences. To show this, I reduced the judgements for each datum (i.e. each individual word elicited from each individual consultant) to a single number, namely the light [l] judgement value subtracted from the dark [ɫ] value. The higher this number is, the greater the preference for light [l], with the overall range going from –6 to +6. Gathering all such numbers for the different categories of cases, I then carried out an ANOVA test, using the Fisher's PLSD post-hoc test for significance. This establishes the probability p that the difference in values could have been obtained by accident, given the amount of random variation present. Here are the results:

(20) Word set   Average   Significance
                                        difference
                                        score

    a. *light, Louanne*   4.62   p < .0001
    b. *gray-ling, gai-ly, free-ly*   1.78   p = .0527
    c. *Mailer, Hayley, Greeley, Daley*   0.74   p = .0006
    d. *mail-er, hail-y, gale-y, feel-y*   −0.97   p = .0031
    e. *mail it*   −3.30   p = .0021
    f. *mail, help*   −5.47

It can be seen that all the results but one are highly significant statistically, and that the remaining one is near-significant. Keeping the near-significant outcome as a case on which further checking should be done, I will assume for present purposes that all differences given here should be accounted for in an adequate analysis.[11]

To keep the size of the problem under control, I will further reduce the numerical data of the survey to the traditional categories '✔', '?', '??', and '*'. The categories assigned, with the survey numbers used to justify them, are given below:

(21)   As light   As dark

    light, Louanne   ✔ (1.20)   *   (5.83)
    gray-ling, gai-ly, free-ly   ✔ (1.57)   ?   (3.34)
    Mailer, Hayley, Greeley, Daley   ✔ (1.90)   ✔ (2.64)
    mail-er, hail-y, gale-y, feel-y   ?   (3.01)   ✔ (2.01)
    mail it   ?? (4.40)   ✔ (1.10)
    bell, help   *   (6.60)   ✔ (1.12)

In principle, one might analyse more finely, but given the uncertainties and high standard deviations, it seemed advisable to work with a fairly coarse well-formedness grid.

2.3.1.4 The 'performance' issue

Before going on to the analysis of these data, I wish first to address a crucial potential objection mentioned above. Suppose that linguistic well-formedness

---

[11] Some further statistics: for non-adjacent categories on the scale of (20), all comparisons came out significant; p < .0001. Further, of the word-to-word comparisons *within* groups, only one came out significant, namely *feel-y* versus *hail-y* (p = .0137). This suggests that most of the relevant structural differences have probably been located.

    The individual consultants gave so few judgements that few subject-internal results reached significance, but the profiles of individual subjects tend to resemble (20).

really is an all-or-nothing matter, but that the judgements we get are filtered through various performance mechanisms. It is the performance mechanisms, not the grammar itself, which results in the gradient intuitions. If this is so, then it is not legitimate to attempt to analyse the gradient data of (21)—rather, we should be reducing them (somehow) to two categories and developing a model of the judgement process itself to account for the numbers observed.

A problem with this view, as Schütze (1996: 64) has pointed out, is that patterns of gradient well-formedness often seem to be driven by the very same principles that govern absolute well-formedness. This holds true, for instance, for the phenomena under discussion here. Thus, for RP British English, Gimson (1970) and Wells (1982) report a data pattern that is reminiscent of what is described above, with gravitation of light and dark /l/ to pre-and post-vocalic positions and certain morphological effects similar to what we have seen. But there is also an important difference: RP does not allow dark [ł] in words like *free-ly* or *gray-ling* at all.[12] This categorical prohibition is rather likely to be based on the same principles that govern the subtler intermediate judgement of the American speakers.

I conclude that the proposed attribution of gradient well-formedness judgements to performance mechanisms would be uninsightful. Whatever 'performance' mechanisms we adopted would look startlingly like the grammatical mechanisms that account for non-gradient judgements. For this reason I will assume that the competence model itself should generate gradient judgements, and will now turn to the task of accounting for the data in (21).

2.3.2 *Analysis*

2.3.2.1 Constraints

Following traditional views in phonetics, we can plausibly attribute the variation in /l/ to conflicting principles based on articulation and perception. The loss or diminution of alveolar closure in dark [ł] seems fairly plainly a case of *lenition*, a process widely thought to be grounded in the conservation of articulatory effort.[13] I state the relevant constraint as follows:

(22)   /l/ is Dark

This leaves open exactly what 'darkness' is in English. Roughly, it should be characterized as involving a lenited, delayed, or absent tongue blade closure. Often, in compensation, there is an especially backed tongue body position.

A defect of the formulation in (22) is that it is categorical, not gradient. The expression of a constraint that would require darkness in /l/ in gradient fashion would require further theoretical development that goes beyond the scope of this

---

[12] Thanks to Peter Ladefoged, a native speaker, for confirming this judgement.
[13] See Kirchner (1998) for extended discussion of constraints covering lenition.

chapter. I believe the central point at hand can be made, however, with the artificially categorized constraint given here.

The other constraints on /l/ are perceptual in origin, and are more subtle in character. An important finding of Sproat and Fujimura's (1993) X-ray microbeam study is that English dark [ɫ] is *temporally asymmetrical*: it begins with a tongue body backing gesture and then in most cases continues with the blade-raising gesture. In light [l], the blade raising gesture is invariable and robust, and often comes somewhat earlier than the tongue body backing gesture. Sproat and Fujimura's findings tie into a recent proposal made by Steriade (1997), who studies the phonotactics of temporally-asymmetrical segments such as aspirated and pre-aspirated stops, ejectives, preglottalized sonorants, and (surprisingly) retroflexes. Her general finding is that if the acoustic cues for a particular consonant lie on one side of the consonant, then there is a very strong tendency for phonologies to require that side of the consonant to be vowel-adjacent. Aspirated stops are thus often limited to prevocalic position, pre-aspirated stops to postvocalic position.

Applying Steriade's principle to the present case, one would expect that languages would be likely to limit dark [ɫ] to postvocalic position. It is plain that [ɫ] imposes a massive degree of coarticulation on the preceding vowel, as is attested in the allophone chart of (5). Plausibly, this coarticulation plays a major role in rendering dark [ɫ] identifiable. If dark [ɫ] were allowed to occur nonpostvocalically, it would be harder to detect, and would in particular risk being confused with /w/, to which it is acoustically similar. Thus in Steriade's general view, there is good support for a constraint of the following character:

(23)   DARK [ɫ] IS POSTVOCALIC

Let us now consider the opposite side of the /l/, namely its articulatory release. Observations of prevocalic [l] on spectrograms show an important effect of the more-robust tongue blade gesture: at release, it produces a rapid amplitude rise and vivid formant shifts. These plausibly would form strong cues to the presence of prevocalic light [l]. The expenditure of articulatory effort in forming a light [l] is thus most effective in this context. The grammatical reflex of these considerations is postulated to be the following:

(24)   PREVOCALIC /l/ IS LIGHT

Somewhat more tentatively, I further conjecture that a *stressed* vowel forms the best acoustic backdrop for the formant transitions created in a light /l/. It is certainly true that stressed vowels license another important temporally-asymmetrical class of sounds in English, namely the aspirated stops, so this seems a plausible assumption. This leads to the similar, but generally stricter, constraint:

(25)   PRETONIC /l/ IS LIGHT

The informal predicates 'light', 'pretonic', and 'prevocalic' used here should be assumed to have suitable expressions in a formalized theory. The exact formulation chosen is non-crucial to present purposes.

In some of the data—cases (14) and (16)—the presence of a morpheme boundary before or after the /l/ is crucial. For these I will assume constraints that limit alternation among surface allomorphs, of the type propounded by McCarthy and Prince (1995), Benua (1995), Kenstowicz (1996, 1997), Steriade (1996), Burzio (1997), and others. Referring to these as Paradigm Uniformity constraints, I state the relevant such constraint here, in schematic form:

(26)   PARADIGM UNIFORMITY
       'Morphologically-derived forms may not deviate from their bases in
       Property X.'

Let us leave aside for a moment the issue of what Property X is in the present case. What is crucial is that in (say) *touchy-feel-y*, surface [ˈfi͡əɬi] possesses very much the same phonetic form as that observed in the base form *feel* [ˈfi͡əɬ]. This is not the case in the imperfect rival form ?[ˈfiːli]. Similarly, in *freely* [ˈfɹiːli], the segments show very much the same phonetic quality that one observes in related forms like *free* [ˈfɹiː] and *barely* [ˈbɛɹli]; this is not so in the imperfect rival ?[ˈfɹi͡əɬi].

Imitation of base forms by derived forms is commonplace in phonology, and has in pre-OT approaches been analysed with notions like cyclicity and word-internal boundaries (Chomsky and Halle 1968). It is not surprising that we should find them at work in /l/ allophony.

Let us now try to specify the identity of Property X, the property that is being conserved across the paradigm. At first glance, it looks as if X might be /l/ darkness itself: the dark /l/ of *feel* [ˈfi͡əɬ] must thus be carried over into the derived form *feel-y*. However, for forms like *freely* with /l/-initial suffixes, this view is more dubious since the suffix *-ly* has no isolation form that could serve as the light [l] base.

A more perspicuous analytic path would be to impose Paradigm Uniformity on *the quality of the stem vowel*, which as noted in (5), is always quite different before dark [ɬ] from elsewhere. Under this view, the diphthongized vowel of *feel* ([ˈfi͡əɬ]) is carried over into *touchy-feel-y* ([ˈfi͡əɬi]), and the non-diphthongized vowel of *free* [ˈfɹiː] is carried over into *freely* ([ˈfɹiːli]).

For this to work, the system must include undominated constraints specifying the appropriate match-up of light and dark /l/ with the vowel allophones that go with them, as noted above in (5). This will exclude any candidates like *[ˈfi͡əli] or *[ˈfiːɬi]. Because the exact formulation of these constraints is not crucial, I will not attempt it here.[14]

---

[14] Carlos Gussenhoven raises the important question of whether a phonological constraint can refer to surface vowel allophones before [ɬ], which may be coarticulatory in origin. There are two possibilities here: (a) as Gussenhoven suggests, the pre-[ɬ] allophones might be truly phonological, derived perhaps by feature spreading; (b) Paradigm Uniformity has access at least in some degree to phonetic representation, as Steriade (1996) has suggested.

Summing up, I will assume that in the present case Paradigm Uniformity requires morphologically-derived forms to possess the vowel quality of their bases, and that this indirectly regulates the distribution of light and dark /l/.

There is one further elaboration needed for the Paradigm Uniformity phenomena seen here. Consider that both *mail-er* ([ɫ, ʔl]) and *mail it* [ɫ, ??l] involve Paradigm Uniformity effects, with carry-over of the obligatory dark [ɫ] of *mail* into larger morphosyntactic constructions. But the effect is *stronger* in the phrasal construction than in the suffixed form: specifically, light [l] gets a '??' (consultant average 4.40) in *mail it* but only a '?' (= 3.01) in *mailer*. Why should this be so?

It is commonly observed that phonological alternation tends to be inhibited in relatively larger phonological domains. This typological observation has been translated into various theoretical approaches in various ways. So, for example, in one version of Lexical Phonology (Kiparsky 1985: 87), rules are held to be gradually 'turned off' as one reaches later levels of the grammar. Similarly, hierarchies of boundaries (McCawley 1968) or 'P-structure' (Selkirk 1981) are set up to permit less rule application (and thus less alternation) at higher levels.

In the present approach, employing Optimality Theory and Paradigm Uniformity, an appropriate implementation of this idea would be to suppose that the Paradigm Uniformity constraints are *a priori* stricter for higher levels—for example, stricter in phrases than in words. For the case at hand we can suppose that there are separate constraints of Paradigm Uniformity for phrasal versus morphological contexts, with the former ranked within UG as necessarily stricter than the latter. Thus:

(27)   PARADIGM UNIFORMITY(VOWEL QUALITY, PHRASAL)   >>
(28)   PARADIGM UNIFORMITY (VOWEL QUALITY, MORPHOLOGICAL)

With this distinction in place, we now have the constraints that will be needed to derive the correct outcomes. The constraints are listed below with the abbreviations that will be used.

(29)	/l/ IS DARK	/l/ IS DARK
	DARK [ɫ] IS POSTVOCALIC	[ɫ] IS /V___
	PREVOCALIC /l/ IS LIGHT	PREVOCALIC: [l]
	PRETONIC /l/ IS LIGHT	PRETONIC: [l]
	PARADIGM UNIFORMITY(VOWEL QUALITY, PHRASAL)	PU(PHRASAL)
	PARADIGM UNIFORMITY (V QUALITY, MORPHOLOGICAL)	PU(MORPHOL)

What I have tried to argue in this section is that each constraint is *principled*, being grounded either in general concepts of phonetically driven phonology or in widely attested typological patterns of paradigmatic alternation.

2.3.2.2 Generating one set of outcomes

For purposes of presentation only, let us temporarily commit the methodological sin of overidealization, and generate an invariant set of outcomes, with no free variation and no gradient well-formedness. These reified outcomes may be schematized as follows: [l] in *light* (pretonic position), *Louanne* (initial position), *Greeley* (medial pre-atonic) and *freely* (suffix-initial), and [ɫ] in *bell* (prepausal), *help* (preconsonantal), *feel-y* (stem-final before suffix), and *mail it* (word-final before vowel-initial word). To generate these outcomes it suffices to rank the two PARADIGM UNIFORMITY constraints over PREVOCALIC /l/ IS LIGHT, with the latter dominating /l/ IS DARK. The outcomes emerge as follows:

(30)	PRETONIC: [l]	[ɫ] IS /V___	PU(PHRASAL)	PU(MORPHOL)	PREVOCALIC: [l]	/l/ IS DARK
☞ a. light ['laɪt]						*
*['ɫaɪt]	*!	*			*	
☞ b. Louanne [lu'æn]						*
*[ɫu'æn]		*!			*	
☞ c. gray-ling ['gɹeɪ-lɪŋ]						*
*['gɹeə-ɫɪŋ]				*!	*	
☞ d. Greeley ['gɹi:li]						*
*['gɹiəɫi]					*!	
☞ e. mail-er ['meɪɫ-ɚ]					*	
*['meɪl-ɚ]				*!		*
☞ f. mail it ['meɪɫ it]					*	
*['meɪl it]			*!			*
☞ g. help ['hɛəɫp]						
*['hɛlp]						*!

Discussion of this tableau is slightly tricky because some of the rankings turn out to be crucial only later on, when we cover free variation and gradient well-formedness. Tentatively, we can say the following.

- Light [l] in (30d) *Greeley* is forced by the dominance of PREVOCALIC /l/ IS LIGHT over the lenition constraint /l/ IS DARK.
- Light [l] in (30a) *light* shows the same effect, though as it happens the light outcome here is forced by higher-ranking constraints as well: PRETONIC /l/ IS LIGHT and DARK [ɫ] IS POSTVOCALIC.
- Light [l] in *Louanne* (30b) also follows from PREVOCALIC /l/ IS LIGHT >> /l/ IS DARK, but again the high-ranking DARK [ɫ] IS POSTVOCALIC also suffices to rule out the dark [ɫ] candidate.

- The same thing is true for (30c) *gray-ling*, where the higher-ranked constraint is PARADIGM UNIFORMITY (VOWEL QUALITY, MORPHOLOGICAL).
- In (30g) *help* (similarly *bell*), the constraint violations are in a subset relation, so no matter what ranking is adopted, dark [ɫ] will win.
- The cases with the greatest interest here are (30e, f) *mail-er* and *mail it*. In these, the PARADIGM UNIFORMITY constraints (morphological and phrasal, respectively) force the appearance of dark [ɫ], despite the appearance of the /l/ in prevocalic position. The morphological base that drives both PU constraints is *mail*, which itself receives obligatory dark [ɫ] for the same reasons as *help*.

2.3.2.3 Accounting for free variation

Moving onward from this preliminary sketch toward a more accurate model, we can next account for the fact that monomorphemic forms with intervocalic pre-atonic /l/ (e.g. *Greeley*) show free variation.

To do this, let us assume that PREVOCALIC /l/ IS LIGHT and /l/ IS DARK are ranked freely. This means that all outputs derived under the tableau of (30),

(31)	PRETONIC: [l]	[ɫ] IS /V__	PU(PHRASAL)	PU(MORPHOL)	/l/ IS DARK	PREVOCALIC: [l]
☞ a. light ['laɪt]					*	
*['ɫaɪt]	*!	*				*
☞ b. Louanne [lu'æn]					*	
*[ɫu'æn]		*!				*
☞ c. gray-ling ['gɹeɪ-lɪŋ]					*	
*['gɹeə-ɫɪŋ]				*!		*
☞ d. Greeley ['gɹiəɫi]						*
*['gɹiːli]					*!	
☞ e. mail-er ['meəl-ɚ]						*
*['meɪl-ɚ]				*!	*	
☞ f. mail it ['meəɫ it]						*
*['meɪl it]			*!		*	
☞ g. help ['heəɫp]						
*['hɛlp]					*!	

where PREVOCALIC /l/ IS LIGHT outranks /l/ IS DARK, will still be obtainable, but in addition we will obtain whatever outcomes derive from the opposite ranking, as shown in (31).

As it happens, the only outcome that is altered under the new ranking is that for monomorphemic *Greeley* (31d), which now comes out with a dark [ɫ], since the lenitional constraint /l/ IS DARK outranks PREVOCALIC /l/ IS LIGHT. In all other instances, switching these two constraints makes no difference to the outcome: either a higher-ranking constraint has already decided the issue (*light*, *Louanne, gray-ling, feel-y*), or the loser has a superset of the violations of the winner (*help*), so that no reranking would ever make a difference.

Two further ranking arguments emerge from tableau (31):

- It can be seen that the continued appearance of light [l] in (31b) *Louanne* justifies the invariant ranking DARK [ɫ] IS POSTVOCALIC >> /l/ IS DARK, a ranking which could not be justified in the previous tableau.
- Likewise, the continued appearance of light [l] in (31c) *gray-ling* follows from the invariant ranking PU(MORPHOL) >> /l/ IS DARK.

2.3.2.4 The analysis in strictness bands

Recall from above that in the present proposal, free constraint rankings result from overlapping strictness bands. We can translate the analysis so far into a strictness band approach. It suffices here to assign the two constraints PREVOCALIC /l/ IS LIGHT and /l/ IS DARK to overlapping bands at the bottom of the scale, with all other constraints assigned to a group at the top of the scale. There must be no overlap of the two groups.

(32)   more strict ⟵─────────────────⟶ less strict

PRETONIC: [l]	▭
[ɫ] IS /V_	▭
PU(PHRASAL)	▭
PU(MORPHOL)	▭
PREVOCALIC: [l]		▭
/l/ IS DARK		▭

As it happens, the overlaps in the strictness bands are non-crucial in all cases except for the two laxest constraints. For the four strict constraints, the data considered so far would be compatible with many other arrangements as well. These could include, for instance, point-like strictness values, with zero widths.

2.3.2.5 Accounting for gradient well-formedness

Let us now take the final step in developing the full analysis—namely accounting for the gradient well-formedness of certain forms. To start, recall the cases that yielded intermediate well-formedness judgements in the consultant survey.

- Forms like *gray-ling* tend to preserve the pure, uncoarticulated quality of the stem vowel ([ẽɪ̃] of *gray* ['gɹẽɪ̃]), rather than adopting the altered, backed qual-ity ([ẽə̃]) that is elsewhere found before dark [ɫ]. The fact that the constraints (unstated here) which correlate vowel quality and /l/ darkness are undom-inated means that *gray-ling* prefers light [l]: ['gɹẽɪ̃lɪŋ], ?['gɹẽə̃ɫɪŋ].

- Forms like *mail-er* tend to preserve the dark [ɫ] and coarticulated vowel qual-ity of their bases; ['mẽə̃ɫɚ] is thus preferred over ?['mẽɪ̃lɚ], because of the base form *mail* ['mẽə̃ɫ].
- Forms like *mail it* work exactly the same way, only the judgement is strong; thus ['mẽə̃ɫ it], ??['mẽɪ̃l ɨt].

The basic approach to be followed here is like this. The two constraints which drive the appearance of light and dark /l/ in the crucial context (intervocalic, pre-atonic) are Prevocalic /l/ is Light and /l/ is Dark. These two opposed constraints are ranked freely, as is demonstrated by the variation in mono-morphemic forms like *Greeley*. But in suffixed forms, neither constraint is quite 'strong' enough to override the Paradigm Uniformity constraints that enforce light and dark /l/ based on what appears in the isolation stem.

But thus far we have considered only fringeless constraints. Once fringes are added in, greater descriptive accuracy becomes possible. Let us suppose that the *fringes* of Prevocalic /l/ is Light and /l/ is Dark, unlike their central ranges, extend upward into the areas occupied by the Paradigm Uniformity con-straints. If this is so, it becomes possible to analyse the gradient well-formedness judgements. The specific arrangements of bands and fringes required are:

- Only the upper '?' fringe of Prevocalic /l/ is Light, and not its central region, extends high enough to permit rankings in which Prevocalic /l/ is Light dominates Paradigm Uniformity (Vowel Quality, Morpho-logical). This means that forms crucially derived with this ranking (specifi-cally, *mai*[l]-*er* and similar cases) will receive a '?' under the analysis.
- Likewise, only the upper '?' fringe of /l/ is Dark, and not its central region, extends high enough to permit rankings in which /l/ is Dark dominates Par-adigm Uniformity (Vowel Quality, Morphological). This means that forms crucially derived with this ranking (specifically, *gray*-[ɫ]*ing* and similar cases) will also receive a ?.
- Only the upper '??' fringe of Prevocalic /l/ is Light (not its central region, nor even its '?' fringe) extends high enough to permit rankings in which Prevocalic /l/ is Light dominates Paradigm Uniformity (Vowel Quality, Phrasal). It is for this reason that ??*mai*[l] *it* receives its highly marginal status.

A further comment. The fact that one need use only the '?' fringe of Prevocalic /l/ is Light to rank it above Paradigm Uniformity (Vowel Quality, Morphological), but the '??' fringe to rank it above Paradigm Uniformity (Vowel Quality, Phrasal), is unlikely to be an accident. It will be recalled that, by a general and well-attested (but so far unexplained) principle of phonology, phrasal paradigm uniformity is always ranked more highly than morphological paradigm uniformity;[15] it is thus always apparently 'harder' for a given constraint to outrank a phrasal paradigm constraint than to outrank a morphological one. It is in the light of this general background that we should not be surprised to see ??*mai*[l] *it* receive worse judgements than ?*mai*[l]*er*.

Summing up this preview: the intermediately well-formed cases are posited to receive this status because they force the ranking of the basic constraints favoring light and dark /l/ into regions where they can dominate the relevant Paradigm Uniformity constraints. Such rankings require the use of the '?' and '??' fringes. To make the analysis fully explicit, the full set of strictness bands and fringes posited here is:

(33)

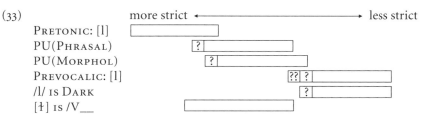

To obtain predictions about well-formedness from these bands and fringes in a rigorous way takes a bit of work. First, one must determine the *pairwise rankings* that result from the strictness bands, including those that are free rankings, or which arise when selection points occupy fringes. Because six constraints give rise to 15 pairwise rankings, the following is an exhaustive list:

(34)   a. Ranking is **irrelevant** because there are no empirical consequences:
PRETONIC: [l] w.r.t. [ł] IS / V___   (Both exclude [ł].)
PRETONIC: [l] w.r.t. PREVOCALIC: [l] (Both exclude [ł].)
[ł] IS / V___ w.r.t. PREVOCALIC: [l] (Both exclude [ł].)
[ł] IS / V___ w.r.t. PU(MORPHOL)   (No bases are required to start with [ł].)
[ł] IS / V___ w.r.t. PU(PHRASAL)   (No bases are required to start with [ł].)
PU(MORPHOL) w.r.t. PU(PHRASAL)   (Constraints apply in disjoint domains.)

   b. Ranking is *free*, because central ranges of strictness bands overlap:
PREVOCALIC: [l] w.r.t. /l/ IS DARK: *Gree*[l,ł]*ey*, etc.

   c. Ranking shown is possible only by placing a selection point within the '?' fringes of a constraint (opposite ranking is freely available):
PREVOCALIC: [l] >> PU(MORPHOL): mai[?l, ł]*er*, etc.
/l/ IS DARK >> PU(MORPHOL): gray-[l, ?ł]*ing*, etc.

---

[15] I assume that this holds true for any particular choice of selection points, not necessarily for the bands themselves.

d. Ranking shown is possible only by placing a selection point within the '??' fringes of a constraint (opposite ranking is freely available):
PREVOCALIC: [l] >> PU(PHRASAL): mai[??l, ł] *it*, etc.

e. Ranking is *obligatory*, because strictness bands fail to overlap even in the fringes:
[ł] is / V___ >> /l/ is DARK: [l,*ł]*ouanne*, etc. (but see below, Section 2.3.2.6)

f. Ranking **cannot be determined** with data given (see Section 2.3.2.6 for discussion):
PRETONIC: [l] w.r.t. /l/ is DARK
PRETONIC: [l] w.r.t. PU(MORPHOL)
PRETONIC: [l] w.r.t. PU(PHRASAL)
/l/ is DARK w.r.t PU(PHRASAL)

Once these specific rankings have been established, one can assign '*', '??', and '?' by means of a careful search. For each pairing of input form and output candidate, one seeks to find: (a) if *any* choice of selection points within the bands yields a grammar in which the output candidate defeats all rivals and is thus generated; (b) if so, which choice minimizes the use of '??' fringes and '?' fringes, in that order of priority. I assume that the rating given by consultants will generally correspond to the best available choice of strictness points.

Carrying out this check is rather tedious, and I will not recapitulate here the work that was done, other than to record in a footnote an algorithm that eases the task.[16] The relevant tableaus may be downloaded from the Web site listed at

---

[16] (a) Define *R* as the set of constraint rankings assumed at any particular stage of computation to be obligatory. To begin, examine the strictness bands of the constraints and set *R* equal to the cases where a ranking *always* holds, even when the selection points are permitted to occur within '??' and '?' strictness bands (these are the rankings that result from total non-overlap).

(b) For each possible output *O*, determine whether *O* can be derived from its input (that is, whether *O* wins the standard OT competition among rivals for output status) under at least one constraint ranking that is consistent with the rankings of *R*. If *O* cannot be so derived, assign it '*'.

(c) Add to *R* all pairwise constraint rankings that are possible only when a selection point occupies a '??' fringe. Repeat step (b), but this time, if an output *O* cannot be derived, assign it ??. All outputs assigned '*' earlier on keep their '*' status.

(d) Add to *R* all pairwise constraint rankings that are possible only when a selection point occupies a '?' fringe. Repeat step (c), this time assigning '?' to all nongenerated outputs. (As before, all outputs assigned '*' or '??' earlier on keep their status.)

(e) Assign fully well-formed status to all outputs that can be generated at stage (d).
This procedure will duly sort the outputs into those which cannot be derived at all, those which can be derived only by using the '??' strictness fringes, those which can be derived only by using the '?' strictness fringes, and those which can be derived using just the central strictness bands.
What makes the procedure workable is factorial typology software, which finds all outcomes of the constraint set at each stage, as the rankings are gradually tightened. Factorial typology software exists in forms prepared by Raymond and Hogan (1993) and by the author (available from the website listed in footnote 7.

the end of footnote 7. From the tableaus it can be shown that the result that emerges is indeed what I had originally aimed at in the analysis—namely:

(35)   as light   as dark

light, Louanne	✔	*
gray-ling, gai-ly, free-ly	✔	?
Mailer, Hayley, Greeley, Daley	✔	✔
mail-er, hail-y, gale-y, feel-y	?	✔
mail it	??	✔
bell, help	*	✔

To summarize the various cases:

- It is indeed possible to generate *?gray-*[ɫ]*ing*, *?mai*[l]*-er*, and *??mai*[l] *it*, but only by placing a selection point within the '?' fringe of /l/ is DARK, the '?' fringe of PREVOCALIC /l/ is LIGHT, and the '??' fringe of PREVOCALIC /l/ is LIGHT, respectively.
- The essentially free variation between *Gree*[l]*ey* and *Gree*[ɫ]*ey* works just as it did in (30) and (31) above.
- In *light*, the strict domination of /l/ is DARK by PRETONIC /l/ is LIGHT forces a '*' for the dark [ɫ] candidate.
- Likewise, complete ill-formedness for dark [ɫ] in *Louanne* is guaranteed by strict domination of /l/ is DARK by DARK /l/ is POSTVOCALIC.[17]
- *Bell* and *help* receive obligatory dark [ɫ]'s because there is no constraint in the system that would force light ones.

In the last of these cases, it is striking that the constraint forcing dark outcomes is one of the two weakest in the system, namely /l/ is DARK. Yet the intuition that light-[l] *bell* or *help* is ill-formed is very strong—a point verified by the consultants. This demonstrates, if demonstration were needed, that the 'lowness' in the tableaux at which a form is excluded has nothing to do with its degree of well-formedness.

2.3.2.6 Residual cases

There are a few cases that require additional discussion. None of these bears on the critical cases (of the *Greeley*, *gray-ling*, and *mail-er* classes) on which the treatment of gradient well-formedness rests.

(a) The data obtained from the consultant survey did not establish the ranking of PRETONIC /l/ is LIGHT with PU(MORPHOL). This ranking hinges on the well-formedness of words like *sty'listic* (from *style* [staɪəɫ]) or *'alcoho,lism* (from *alcohol* ['æɫkə,hɒɫ]). If such words tolerate light and dark /l/ equally, then these two constraints should overlap in their central ranges; but if light

---

[17] See Section 2.3.2.6 for further discussion of this form, however.

[l] is preferred, then the lower end of Pretonic /l/ is Light should overlap only with the upper '?' fringe of PU(Morphol). In laying out the
strictness bands of (33), I made the latter assumption, based on my own
judgement.
(b) Again guessing from my own intuitions, I conjecture that forms such as
mail it ??[mēīl ɪt], with phonological alternation between contextual [mēīl]
and the isolation form [mēəɫ], occur only before clitic pronouns. Forms
where the alternation crosses a large phonological juncture, like *mail Italian*
(*books*) *['mēīlə'tāəɫjən . . .], seem inconceivable to me. It thus seems likely
that there is a still stricter PU constraint that likewise forbids alternation,
but is limited to higher levels of phonological juncture, such as the Phonological Phrase (Selkirk 1981; Nespor and Vogel 1986; Hayes 1989). This constraint is plausibly undominated.
(c) Forms like *allow*, with medial pretonic /l/, were not included in the survey,
but relying on my own judgement I suspect that they would emerge with
obligatory light [l]. This outcome is derived in the present grammar by
having Pretonic /l/ is Light fully outrank /l/ is Dark.
(d) A difficulty for the analysis is the surprisingly high acceptability of dark [ɫ]
in *antler*, as determined in the survey (value: 3.55). This is considerably
better than the 5.55 awarded to dark-[ɫ] *Louanne*, and the difference is indeed statistically significant. But the two words have virtually identical /l/
environments: non-postvocalic, pre-atonic with no Paradigm Uniformity
effects.

I see two possible ways around the problem. First, it may be that the survey data
for *Louanne* were unreliable: Sproat and Fujimura (1993) collected a couple of
tokens of '*Likkovsky*', analogous to *Louanne*, with surprisingly dark /l/ (see their
data for speaker CS, p.302). I think it likely that my own renditions of *Louanne*
and *antler*, in performing the survey, were distorted towards a really grotesquely
dark [ɫ] in *Louanne* and only a moderately dark one in *antler*.[18] This naturally
would have skewed the results. If this is right, then we should adjust the ranking
of Dark /l/ is Postvocalic downward slightly, so that it overlaps the upward
'?' or '??' fringes of /l/ is Dark. This would let in both *ant*[ɫ]*er* and [ɫ]*ouanne*
on a '?' or '??' basis.

A second possibility is that more careful study would prove that dark-[ɫ]
Louanne really is worse than dark-[ɫ] *antler*. If this is so, a possibility to consider

---

[18] This is less of a problem for the really crucial cases of the *Greeley*, *mail-er*, and *gray-ling* classes,
because for these a technique was available to achieve more natural pronunciations. Specifically, I
pronounced light and dark /l/ by aiming at a *different word*, where necessary, from what the consultant was listening for. Thus, for example, to say *Greeley* with guaranteed light /l/ I thought to myself
'*gree-ly*: in a manner which is *gree*'; and to say it with a guaranteed dark [ɫ] I thought to myself
'*greel-y*: covered with *greel*'. In contrast, saying *Louanne* with a dark [ɫ] was much harder to do
naturally, and felt much more like a phonetic exercise.

is that stem-initial position calls for allophones that are especially salient acousti-cally, as Kohler (1990: 88) suggests. That something like this is right is also indi-cated by phonological work (Steriade 1993; Beckman 1995, 1997; Casali 1996) showing that stem-initial position favors particularly high-ranked faithfulness constraints; the same might well be true for salient allophones.

None of these questions is resolvable with the data presently gathered. How-ever, for the crucial cases demonstrating gradient well-formedness (see the pre-ceding section), the data and analysis seem rather more secure.

2.3.2.7 Variation in the consultants' intuitions

So far, I have simply pooled the opinions of my ten consultants, as if there were no difference in their opinions. For one case, however, it appears that there may have been a genuine split in their behavior.

Under the analysis proposed here, the judgement that one gives for forms like *mail-er* is logically independent of the judgement one gives for forms like *gray-ling*: light [l] will be tolerated in *mail-er* to the extent that one is able to rank PREVOCALIC /l/ IS LIGHT over PU(MORPHOL); whereas dark [ɫ] will be toler-ated in *gray-ling* to the extent that one is able to rank /l/ IS DARK over PU(MORPHOL).

My own judgement, or at least the one I brought to the project originally, is that *gray-[ɫ]ing* with dark [ɫ] is considerably worse than *mai[l]-er* with light [l]. In fact I would rate *gray-[ɫ]ing* as '??' and *mai[l]-er* as '?'. That this is not an isolated intuition is borne out by the consultants' individual judgements on the *gray-ling* and *mail-er* classes of forms. Here, we find two groups: one which agrees with me in finding *mai[l]-er* forms better than *gray-[ɫ]ing* forms, and one which goes in the opposite direction:

(36) a. *mai[l]-er* etc. better than *gray-[ɫ]ing* etc.

	Average for *mai[l]-er* words	Average for *gray-[ɫ]ing* words
DP	2.17	2.67
FC	2.67	4.00
KH	1.50	4.33
MS	3.00	4.33
PH	2.50	3.67

b. *gray-[ɫ]ing* etc. better than *mai[l]-er* etc.

	Average for *mai[l]-er* words	Average for *gray-[ɫ]ing* words
MP	4.75	3.33
MG	1.75	1.00
VA	4.75	4.00

The remaining two consultants ranked the two classes about equally.

It is straightforward to model these cases. As an application of the method described in footnote 16 has verified, a grammar that gives a '??' instead of a '?' to *gray-*[ɫ]*ing* etc.—as in (36a)—can be obtained by slightly lowering the range of /l/ is DARK, so that only its '??' fringe overlaps the range of PU(MORPHOL); and a grammar that gives a '??' instead of a '?' to *mai*[l]-*er* etc. can be obtained with an analogous weakening of PREVOCALIC /l/ is LIGHT. These detail adjustments for particular dialects can be seen below:

(37)   more strict ←————————————→ less strict

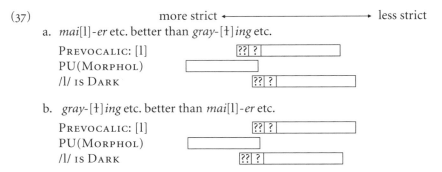

a. *mai*[l]-*er* etc. better than *gray-*[ɫ]*ing* etc.

   PREVOCALIC: [l]
   PU(MORPHOL)
   /l/ is DARK

b. *gray-*[ɫ]*ing* etc. better than *mai*[l]-*er* etc.

   PREVOCALIC: [l]
   PU(MORPHOL)
   /l/ is DARK

One would expect such grammars also in principle to differ on how they treat other forms as well—and indeed, the subjects that preferred (say) *gray-*[l]*ing* to *gray-*[ɫ]*ing* also tended to prefer *Gree*[l]*ey* to *Gree*[ɫ]*ey*, and so on.[19]

2.3.2.8 Judgements of speech style

Recall that the questionnaire given to the consultants permitted them to judge the casualness' or 'formality' of individual examples. They often had some difficulty in doing this, and not all tried to make such judgements. Nevertheless, a pattern did emerge in the judgements: in general, it is the output with *light* [l] that is felt to be formal relative to the one with dark [ɫ]. This result was statistically significant: testing the full set of judgements of light [l] against the full set of judgements of dark [ɫ], and treating a consultant's check mark in the 'casual' box as −1 and a check mark in the 'formal' box as 1 (with no check being counted as 0), we find means of .07 for light [l] as against −.11 for dark [ɫ]. This difference is shown to be statistically significant (p = .0002) by a Fisher's PLSD test. The difference emerged primarily in the *Greeley* and *gray-ling* word classes.[20]

I believe that the association of light [l] with formality, and dark [ɫ] with casualness, is not random but reflects the nature of the constraints themselves.

[19] For instance, across consultants there is a positive correlation between how the *gray-ling* forms and the *Greeley* forms were judged; for the statistic (dark judgements – light judgements) used above, r^2 = .638. Other relevant correlations were weaker but mostly positive.

[20] It seems likely that government of variation by speech style is only possible where both variants are reasonably well-formed; consultants thus did not have strong opinions about casualness in words like *light* or *help* where there was really only one option available in the first place.

Recall that, where variation is possible, light [l] reflects relatively high ranking of the constraint PREVOCALIC /l/ IS LIGHT, while dark [ɫ] reflects relatively high ranking of /l/ IS DARK. Recall further (from Section 2.3.2.1) that both of these constraints are grounded in phonetic principles: /l/ IS DARK is a lenitional constraint: its teleology is speaker-centered, involving the maximization of articulatory ease. PREVOCALIC /l/ IS LIGHT is grounded in speech perception, calling forth an articulation that will render /l/ more identifiable for the listener (in a context where the more costly articulation will be more effective).

As phoneticians have suggested (Kohler 1990; Lindblom 1990), formal speech is characteristically listener-centered speech, aimed at constructing a maximally-decodable acoustic signal, whereas casual speech is speaker-centered, aimed at specifying an articulatory program that is easy to execute. Within the approach established here, it is easy to imagine the grammatical reflex of these strategies: in formal speech, the selection point for PREVOCALIC /l/ IS LIGHT will be chosen from the upper part of its range, and the selection point for /l/ IS DARK will be chosen from the lower part. In casual speech, exactly the opposite will tend to occur.

Assuming that these speaker strategies are also decodable to some extent by listeners, we obtain the outlines of how the consultants might have judged casualness versus formality: hearing [l] or [ɫ], they tacitly deduced the rankings that were needed to obtain it, figured out the relative positions of the selection points that yielded these rankings, then obtained the casualness/formality ratings based on the selection points.

The upshot is that the strictness bands appear to possess some internal structure, with different ends annotated (following general principles of speaker-oriented and listener-oriented speech) for formal versus casual register. [21]

2.4 The Origin of Gradient Well-Formedness[22]

An issue only briefly mentioned thus far is where gradient well-formedness intuitions come from: specifically, the problem of language acquisition for gradient well-formedness.

There are two primary sources of linguistic knowledge on which the language-acquiring child can draw: the *a priori* principles of Universal Grammar, and the ambient data. If there are cases where UG principles firmly dictate an outcome, the judgement the learner acquires by adulthood will surely be quite firm. Like-

---

[21] There is one further data puzzle here: if significant formality effects appeared in the *gray-ling* and *Greeley* classes, why did such effects not appear in the phonetically similar *mail-er* class? I suspect that there may have been a conflict present with regard to what should be counted as 'formal': a light [l] renders the /l/ phoneme more identifiable, but a dark [ɫ] renders the morphological structure clearer; each factor is in principle helpful to the listener.

[22] This section presents several views that have been arrived at independently by Paul Boersma (1997).

wise, where the relevant phenomenon is not at all innately driven but the ambient data are very robust, there is also good reason to think that the judgements will be firm. For instance, the morphological principle specifying *-ing* suffixation in the formation of English present participles is utterly exceptionless in the input data for English. Accordingly, it seems inconceivable that the present participle of a hypothetical verb like *blick* could be anything other than *blicking*.

The place to look for the origin of gradient judgements, I believe, is in the remaining set of cases, where (as far as we can tell) no principle of UG forces the outcome, and the data for acquisition are sparse. Here are some examples:

- The present example: light and dark /l/ clearly participate in massive free variation, with the data further obscured by the variable phonetic realization of both categories (Sproat and Fujimura 1993). It seems very likely that the input data for most English learners do not suffice to establish firm rankings of /l/ is Dark and Prevocalic /l/ is Light with respect to the Paradigm Uniformity constraints.
- In a pilot study, I have found it possible at least tentatively to model gradient well-formedness judgements for a corpus of novel deverbal Latinate *-able* adjectives (like ?*obfuscable*, from *obfuscate*) currently under study by Donca Steriade. The judgements here are blatantly gradient, a fact that plausibly reflects the extreme sparseness of input data for what is a quite learned and unusual process of word formation.
- More generally, examination of the literature on theoretical syntax reveals a research strategy that is constantly leading to cases with gradient judgements: syntacticians consistently try to push the study of a given syntactic phenomenon into all contexts where it occurs or could logically be imagined to occur. Thus, for example, *Wh-* extraction for a given language is tested for all syntactic environments in which a noun phrase is ever permitted. This is good scientific strategy, since it gives us data of the fullest possible scope. However, the very act of pushing a phenomenon to its limits is often what leads to gradient well-formedness judgements. As before, I conjecture that the cases involved here are precisely those in which the combined effects of UG and input data do *not* suffice to establish a clear pattern of well-formedness. That is, the sentences that syntacticians ask are often so unusual that they correspond to areas in which the data given to the child did not suffice to create categorical well-formedness judgements.

If the view taken here is right, the way to gain insight into gradient well-formedness is to examine what language learning would look like in the difficult areas; namely, those with sparse data and no inviolable UG principles to help. Along these lines, let us consider one promising approach to learning within OT.

2.4.1 *The Tesar/Smolensky Ranking Algorithm*

Tesar and Smolensky (1993, 1996) have devised an algorithm, called Constraint

Demotion, which given (a) a set of well-formed outputs of a grammar, (b) a set of ill-formed rival candidates for each input, and (c) a set of constraints, will locate a ranking for the constraints that derives all and only the well-formed outputs. The algorithm is proved always to succeed, provided that such a ranking exists. Further, it is very efficient, working in quadratic time.

I believe that this algorithm is a good first step toward an ultimate formal theory of language learning. However, one should also understand its limitations. Most saliently, the algorithm cannot learn any grammar that generates free variation. The reason is that it is founded on the crucial assumption that if [A] is the output deriving from the underlying form /A/, then any other form [A'] distinct from [A] must be ill-formed. The algorithm uses the putative ill-formedness of [A'] as negative evidence, forcing the demotion of constraints that would select [A'] as the output instead of [A].

My own judgement is that it is unlikely that we will ever find a language in which the grammar does not generate free variation. This view is based on my experience in working with consultants, reading grammars, and studying the work of sociolinguists. If I am right, the inability of the Constraint Demotion algorithm to learn free variation must be considered a quite general failure, not an isolated difficulty.

What do we want a learner to do when it meets with free variation? Plausibly, it should do what OT analysts currently do—namely to posit a small stratum of crucially freely-ranked constraints. The size of the freely-ranked stratum should be as small as possible, so that it confines the variation to the cases that are justified by the data and does not overgenerate.

2.4.2 *Robust Algorithms and Their Consequences for Gradience*

There is one other characteristic that an improved constraint-ranking algorithm ought to have: robustness in the face of noisy input data. Consider, for example, a speech error collected by Joseph Stemberger (1983: 32):

(38)   *in a first floor [dl]orm–dorm room

Stemberger claims, based on his own error corpus, that cases that violate legal English segment sequencing occur with 'a reasonable frequency'. It is thus easy to imagine a form like (38) being uttered in the presence of a small child who is still in the process of learning the English segment-sequencing system. Taken at face value, the datum given is a clear invitation to the child to rerank the relevant Faithfulness constraints above whatever markedness constraint it is that forbids initial [dl]. But to my knowledge, all adult native speakers of English immediately recognize *dlorm* as impossible. The occasional hearing of a phonotactically-illegal sequence from speech errors during childhood does not prevent language-learners from developing an appropriate sense of phonotactic well-formedness by the time they have become adults.

From this we can conclude the following: the child learning language must consider *all* the data that he or she hears on a provisional basis. Only a reasonably healthy dosage of [dl] forms should ever induce him or her to consider a constraint ranking that would permit [dl] as a legal word onset.

One way to implement such a scheme would be to have input data adjust the rankings of constraints *incrementally*: hearing a datum that would imply a novel ranking leads the ranker to make a modest adjustment, only slightly advancing the fringes and central domains of the relevant constraints.[23] Plausibly, under such a regime, the hearing just once or twice in childhood of [dl] would not suffice to adjust the relevant constraint rankings to the point where [dl] emerged as well-formed in the adult grammar.

From this perspective, I think it is clear why gradient well-formedness intuitions might arise where input data are sparse or otherwise uninformative: an incremental learner would never get enough data to eliminate the fringes that it set up as tentative hypotheses.

A practical conclusion of this section is that computational linguists now have a major opportunity to contribute to progress in learning theory. The development of algorithms that do what the Tesar/Smolensky algorithm does, but with variable and sparse input data, would be a very significant advance, and justifies, I believe, a serious research effort.[24]

2.5 Conclusions: Advantages of Analysing Gradiently

To conclude, I will discuss some possible virtues of the proposal made here.

2.5.1 *Conservatism*

First, from the viewpoint of mainstream Optimality Theory the proposal is rather conservative, because all previous forms of constraint ranking are compatible with it. The kinds of rankings posited in earlier Optimality-theoretic work may be seen as a subset (indeed, a very important subset) of the rankings countenanced here. This was shown above under (32) and (33): to the existing inventory of invariant rankings (non-overlapping bands along the strictness continuum) and free ranking (overlapping strictness bands), the present proposal adds only the fringes. Constraints that overlap only in their fringes are assumed to have a strongly preferred, but not quite obligatory, ranking. It is easy to imagine a large grammar in which quite a few of the constraints have non-overlapping ranges, corresponding to empirical domains in which free variation is lacking and intuitions are robust.

---

[23] It seems likely, as Janet Pierrehumbert has pointed out to me, that fringes and central domains are adjusted *together*. In this view, fringes are a predictable adjunct to every constraint, rather than being learned separately.

[24] Since originally writing the above paragraph I have encountered the algorithm of Boersma (1997; this volume), which aspires to exactly the goals I have stated. We are currently submitting to the algorithm a number of empirical tests intended to assess its capacities as thoroughly as possible.

The upshot is that nothing in the current Optimality Theory literature is incompatible with what has been suggested here. For linguists who think that Optimality Theory has led to considerably deepened understanding of linguistic phenomena (and I am among them), this is an important point.

The conservatism of the present proposal may be contrasted with the view that gradient judgements imply 'gradient principles' or 'gradient representations', a view taken for instance by Ross (1972).[25] My own tentative view is that such an approach is unlikely to be fruitful: a gradient representation must be gradient in all contexts in which it appears, which is likely to make it hard to analyse those particular cases in which well-formedness judgements come out completely clear. In contrast, the more flexible mechanism of gradient constraint ranking can easily generate gradient outcomes in some cases and clear outcomes in others, as was shown here.

2.5.2 *Text Frequencies*

As noted above in Section 2.3.2.4, fine-tuning of the constraint ranking bands allows us to make predictions about the relative frequencies with which rival output types are used. Hayes and MacEachern (1998) have been able to do this in some detail for a problem in metrics (quatrain types), in which the data matched for textual frequency was a corpus of 1000 Appalachian folk song quatrains; see also Boersma (1997; this volume) for further frequency modeling.[26]

2.5.3 *Generality*

A further advantage that could be asserted for the present approach is that it deals with gradient well-formedness in a completely general way, one intimately tied up with the structure of the theory itself; rather than involving post hoc additions to the theory in particular areas. The pervasiveness of gradient well-formedness judgements in language suggests that a fully general approach is likely to be the correct one.

2.5.4 *Coda: Why This is Worth Trying*

To assert a commonplace: there is little point in analysing overidealized data (here: sorted into '✔' and '*') if you possess a theory that permits you to analyse accurate data. Suppose that some particular principles can be deployed with categorial ranking to analyse a particular data set, reified into '✔' and '*' catego-

---

[25] 'A number of phenomena . . . suggest that the traditional distinction between verbs, adjectives, and nouns—a distinction which is commonly thought of as discrete—should be modified. I will postulate, instead of a fixed, discrete inventory of syntactic categories, a quasi-continuum . . .' (Ross 1972: 316)

[26] Anttila (1997) models the frequency of certain unusual Finnish inflected forms in an amazingly simple way, simply by counting the number of grammars (under free ranking) that generate each output. At least for the case of English quatrain structure, it appears that it may be difficult to get Anttila's idea to generalize to other data.

ries—e.g. as in (30) above—and that the same principles can be more subtly deployed under the scheme laid out here to capture the full range of judgements. It would seem that in the latter case the principles at stake have passed a stricter empirical test.

This is a nontrivial result, because there is good evidence that at present linguistics is *not difficult enough*. Specifically, there are usually multiple theoretical approaches to a given problem that work reasonably well. The task of sorting them out is unlikely to succeed unless we submit all approaches to the most stringent empirical testing available.

To conclude, I will cite a rather disarming quotation from Pesetsky (1997: 151), whose view concerning one particular aspect of linguistic research seems quite pertinent here. I have harmlessly altered a couple of words to maximize relevance:

A useful tactic when considering novel ideas is to look–not for problems that have already received satisfying solutions–but for problems that are largely unsolved. This is not as easy as it sounds. One learns to live with one's unsolved problems, and with time one becomes so used to the unsolved that it almost comes to look solved . . . Attempts to deal with [the particular question Pesetsky is discussing] in the traditional program of [linguistic] theory have been fairly unsuccessful, and [linguists] have become used to the unsuccessful proposals that are popular.'

Gradient well-formedness may be one of the most pervasive overlooked-but-unsolved problems in linguistics. The proposal made here is presented in hopes that it may help bring this problem back into the light and, perhaps, serve as the key to solving it.

2.6 References

Anttila, A. (1997). 'Deriving variation from grammar'. Hinskens, van Hout, and Wetzels (eds), 35–68. ROA-63

Bard, E. G., D. Robertson, and A. Sorace (1996). 'Magnitude estimation of linguistic acceptability'. *Language 72*, 32–68.

Beckman, J. (1995). 'Shona height harmony: markedness and positional identity'. In Beckman *et al.* (eds), 53–75.

—— (1997). *Positional Faithfulness*. PhD dissertation, U.Mass, Amherst. ROA-234.

—— L. Walsh Dickey, and S. Urbanczyk (eds) (1995), *Papers in Optimality Theory, University of Massachusetts Occasional Papers* 18.

Benua, L. (1995). 'Identity effects in morphological truncation'. In Beckman *et al.* (eds), 77–136. ROA-74

Boersma, P. (1997). 'How we learn variation, optionality, and probability'. ROA-221

Borowsky, T. and B. Horvath (1997). 'L-vocalization in Australian English'. In Hinskens, van Hout, and Wetzels (eds), 101–23.

Burzio, L. (1997). 'Multiple correspondence'. Paper read at the BCN Workshop on Conflicting Constraints, Groningen.

Casali, R. F. (1996). *Resolving Hiatus*. PhD dissertation, Los Angeles, CA, UCLA.

Chomsky, N. and M. Halle (1968). *The Sound Pattern of English*. New York, Harper & Row.

Cowart, W. (1997). *Experimental Syntax: Applying Objective Methods to Sentence Judgments*. Thousand Oaks, CA, SAGE Publications.

Davidson, L. and R. Noyer (1997). 'Loan phonology in Huave: nativization and the ranking of Faithfulness constraints'. In B. Agbayani and S.-W. Tang (eds), *Proceedings of the Fifteenth West Coast Conference on Formal Linguistics*. Stanford, CA, Center for the Study of Language and Information, 65–79.

Gimson, A. C. (1970). *An Introduction to the Pronunciation of English* (2nd ed.). New York, St. Martin's Press.

Hardcastle, W. J. and A. Marchal (eds) (1990), *Speech Production and Speech Modelling*. Dordrecht, Kluwer.

Hayes, B. (1989). 'The prosodic hierarchy in meter'. In P. Kiparsky and G. Youmans (eds), *Rhythm and Meter*. Orlando, FL, Academic Press, 201–60.

—— and M. MacEachern (1998). 'Quatrain form in English folk verse'. *Language* 64, 473–507.

Hinskens, F., R. van Hout, and W. L. Wetzels (eds) (1997), *Variation, Change and Phonological Theory*. Amsterdam and Philadelphia, John Benjamins.

Kenstowicz, M. (1996). 'Base identity and Uniform Exponence: Alternatives to cyclicity'. In J. Durand and B. Laks (eds), *Current Trends in Phonology: Models and Methods*, Vol. 1. Salford, Manchester, University of Salford Press, 363–93. ROA-103.

—— (1997). 'Uniform Exponence: Exemplification and extension'. Paper read at the 1997 Johns Hopkins University workshop on Optimality Theory.

Kiparsky, P. (1985). 'Some consequences of Lexical Phonology'. *Phonology Yearbook* 2, 85–138.

Kirchner, R. (1998). *An Effort-Based Approach to Consonant Lenition*. PhD dissertation. UCLA, Los Angeles, CA.

Kohler, K. J. (1990). 'Segmental reduction in connected speech in German: phonological facts and phonetic explanations'. In Hardcastle and Marchal (eds), 69–92.

Lindblom, Björn (1990). 'Explaining phonetic variation: a sketch of the H&H theory'. In Hardcastle and Marchal (eds), 403–39.

McCarthy, J. and A. S. Prince (1995). 'Faithfulness and reduplicative identity'. In Beckman *et al.* (eds), 249–384. ROA-60.

McCawley, J. D. (1968). *The Phonological Component of a Grammar of Japanese*. The Hague, Mouton.

Nespor, M. and I. Vogel (1986). *Prosodic Phonology*. Dordrecht, Foris.

Pesetsky, D. (1997). 'OT and syntax: movement and pronunciation'. In D. Archangeli and D. T. Langendoen (eds), *Optimality Theory: An Overview*. Oxford, Blackwell, 134–70.

Prince, A. S. and P. Smolensky (1993). 'Optimality Theory: Constraint interaction in Generative Grammar'. Ms., Rutgers University and University of Colorado. To appear: Cambridge, MA: MIT Press.

Raymond, W. and A. Hogan (1993). 'The Optimality interpreter'. ROA-130.

Ross, J. R. (1972). 'The category squish: Endstation Hauptwort'. *Chicago Linguistic Society* 8, 316–28.

Schütze, C. T. (1996). *The Empirical Base of Linguistics: Grammaticality Judgments and Linguistic Methodology*. Chicago, University of Chicago Press.

Selkirk, E. O. (1980). 'Prosodic domains in phonology: Sanskrit revisited'. In M. Aronoff and M.-L. Kean (eds), *Juncture*. Saratoga, CA, Anima Libri.

Simpson, J. (1980). 'Cyclic syllabification and a first cycle rule of vowel-rounding in some dialects of Australian English'. Ms., Dept. of Linguistics and Philosophy, MIT.

Sproat, R. and O. Fujimura (1993). 'Allophonic variation in English /l/ and its implications for phonetic implementation'. *Journal of Phonetics* 21, 291–311.

Stemberger, J. P. (1983). 'Speech errors and theoretical phonology: a review'. Paper distributed by the Indiana University Linguistics Club, Bloomington, IN.

Steriade, D. (1993). 'Positional neutralization'. Talk presented at NELS 24, U.Mass, Amherst.

—— (1996). 'Paradigm Uniformity and the phonetics-phonology boundary'. Paper presented at the Fifth Conference in Laboratory Phonology, Northwestern University, Evanston, IL.

Steriade, D. (1997). 'Phonetics in phonology: the case of laryngeal neutralization'. Ms., Dept. of Linguistics, UCLA, Los Angeles, CA.

Tesar, B. B. and P. Smolensky (1993). 'The learnability of Optimality Theory: An algorithm and some basic complexity results'. ROA-2.

—— —— (1996). 'Learnability in Optimality Theory'. ROA-110.

Wells, J. C. (1982). *Accents of English* (in three volumes), Cambridge, Cambridge University Press.

3

Stem Stress and Peak Correspondence in Dutch[1]

René Kager

3.1 Introduction

3.1.1 *Background*

It is a well-known observation that morphologically complex words 'inherit' phonological properties of their stems. Famous examples involve trans-derivational preservation of stress, which is involved in the analysis of secondary stress in English (Chomsky and Halle 1968), syncope in Palestinian Arabic (Brame 1974) and diphthongization in Spanish (Harris 1983). This chapter deals with the preservation of stem stress in Dutch complex words. Before addressing this specific topic, I will sketch the theoretical background of this chapter, which involves a number of issues in the interaction of phonology and morphology.

The question of how 'transderivational' relationships come about has captured the attention of many linguists:

Q1: How do phonological properties of simplex forms carry over to morphologically complex forms?

In derivational theory (Chomsky and Halle 1968; Kiparsky 1982) the answer to this question involved the *cycle*: phonological rules apply to successively larger morphological domains. Cyclicity correctly predicts that a phonological property which is introduced on a smaller morphological domain is carried over to a larger domain. The cycle embodies the claim that phonological properties of derived words are *literally derived* from those of simpler words.

A major question that occupied cyclic phonologists is that of the definition of cyclic rule *domains*. Or, to put it more neutrally:

[1] An earlier version of this chapter was presented at the Germanic Prosody Workshop, University of Tromsø, March 22–23, 1996. It has benefited from discussions with the participants of this workshop, especially Carlos Gussenhoven, Mike Hammond, John McCarthy, and Curt Rice, as well as from later comments by Nine Elenbaas, Wim Zonneveld and two anonymous reviewers. As usual, all responsibility for errors is mine. Research for this chapter was sponsored by the Royal Dutch Academy of Sciences (KNAW).

Q2: What morphological domains can be transderivationally related?

It was proposed already by Brame (1974) that cycled substrings must occur as independent *words*. In contrast to free stems, (bound) roots are not cyclic domains (cf. Kiparsky 1982). Evidence for this asymmetry between bound roots and stems came from various languages, such as Spanish (Harris 1983), Palestinian Arabic (Brame 1974), Warlpiri (Kiparsky 1988), and Malayalam (Mohanan 1989). The observation that only free stems are cyclic domains is a cornerstone of the theory of Prosodic Lexical Phonology (Inkelas 1989), according to which phonological rules apply within prosodic domains.

The third major question is related to the interface of phonology and morphology. It has been observed (for example Strauss 1983 on English) that affixation may be sensitive to *derived* phonological properties of its base, such as the stress pattern. The question arises how morphological operations may have access to effects of phonological rules applying to their sub-parts. Or, to state it more generally:

Q3: How can derived phonological properties of stems affect stem-based affixation?

In the Cyclic Theory of Chomsky and Halle (1968), all morphology was assumed to precede the phonology, incorrectly predicting that phonology-sensitive morphology may not occur. Lexical Phonology (Kiparsky 1982) allows for such situations by *interleaving* morphology and phonology. Phonological rules on the stem cycle precede affixation rules creating outer cyclic domains, hence their effects are 'accessible' to such affixation rules.

Standard Optimality Theory (Prince and Smolensky 1993, McCarthy and Prince 1993) cannot appeal to derivational cyclicity to capture transderivational relationships, since it is in essence a non-derivational theory.[2] Instead it has been proposed by various authors (Burzio 1994, McCarthy 1995, Benua 1995) that there exists a *direct* 'surface-to-surface' dependence of morphologically complex words on their bases.[3] This relation is called 'identity' and it is an embodiment of a more general 'correspondence' relation between morphologically related forms (including as subcases the relations between stem and affixed form, input and output, and base and reduplicant, McCarthy and Prince 1999). Output-to-output identity is enforced by sets of constraints which require that elements in one member of a pair must be identical to elements in the other member of the pair. As constraints generally are, identity constraints are violable, but violation

[2] Orgun (1994, 1996) has developed a declarative (*sign-based*) theory of the phonology-morphology interface that accounts for both cyclic and noncyclic effects, and is compatible with OT. It is certainly possible that the analysis presented in this chapter can be restated equally well in Orgun's theory, an option that I will leave open for future research.

[3] Output-to-output correspondence can be seen as a manifestation of the traditional linguistic notion of paradigm regularity, developed as a formal part of grammar.

must be minimal. This means that any divergence of a complex word as compared to its 'base' must be forced by some superordinate constraint of structural well-formedness.

The answers given by (non-derivational) Correspondence Theory to the three major questions stated above are significantly different from those of (derivational) Cyclic Theory. First, as we have already seen, the derivational notion of cycle is abandoned in favor of surface identity. Correspondence Theory predicts that only *surface* properties are transferrable from morphologically simple words to complex words. In contrast, Cyclic Theory does not make this prediction, since surface forms play no special role in this theory, as compared to forms in intermediate stages of the derivation. Second, Correspondence Theory *predicts* that only properties of free stems (and not those of bound roots) can be inherited by complex words, since free stems (but not bound roots) are output forms. In contrast, the status of stems as cyclic domains must be *stipulated* under Cyclic Theory. Third, with respect to the sensitivity of affixation to 'derived' phonological properties, Correspondence Theory predicts that this should be the case, under the assumption of *parallelism*—phonological and morphological constraints are ranked together in a single hierarchy. One might argue that parallelism is the counterpart of the 'interleaving' of morphological and phonological rules in the derivational model of Lexical Phonology. However, parallel Correspondence Theory predicts a broader kind of sensitivity of morphology to phonology than is possible under interleaving Lexical Phonology. While interleaving restricts phonological sensitivity of affixation to properties that are present in the stem 'before' the affixation, the parallel model allows for sensitivity to the full range of output properties of the base-plus-affix combination (Kager 1996). This predicts that affixation may be blocked as a way of avoiding specific surface configurations.

In this chapter I will argue that Correspondence Theory is correct in all three respects, on the basis of an analysis of the interaction of stress and 'stem-based' affixation in Dutch. The main conclusions will be (i) that preservation of stress under 'stress-neutral' affixation is due to output-to-output identity, rather than to 'cyclicity'; (ii) that 'stress-shifting' affixes are formally on a par with affixes that impose a 'stress condition' on their base, in the sense that 'stress shift' and 'stress conditions' are both strategies toward the same surface target; and (iii) that affix distribution and stress behaviour of different classes of affix are related in a way that cannot be captured in Lexical Phonology, while it follows naturally from parallel interactions of phonological and morphological constraints.

3.1.2 *Stem Stress and Correspondence Theory*

Germanic languages such as Dutch, English, and German have word-based stress systems which place the stress peak on a stem syllable rather than on a suffix syllable. Consider the example below from Dutch, where the vertical lines indicate corresponding stress peaks:

(1)   [ánder]   'other'
                           |
                     [ver- [ánder]]   'alter'
                           |
                  [[ver- [ánder]] -lijk]   'alterable'
                           |
              [on- [[ver- [ánder]] -lijk]]   'unalterable'
                           |
          [[on- [[ver- [ánder]] -lijk]] -heid]   'unalterability'

This stem stress principle is usually referred to as 'stress-neutrality' of affixes. This reflects the observation that word-based affixes typically preserve the stress peak of the base: they cannot be stressed themselves, nor do they 'shift' the stress to another stem syllable.

This state of affairs changes under compounding, where multiple stems contribute their stress peaks to the construction: only one of these can be selected as the peak of the whole, which necessarily involves the loss of the other peaks:

(2)   [hánd] [dóek]   'hand', 'cloth'
                  |
          [bád] [[hánd]-[doek]]   'bath', 'towel'
            |
       [[bád]-[[hand]-[doek]]]   'bath towel'

The same languages also have affixes which impose stress conditions on their bases, requiring the affix to be *adjacent to the stress peak* (main stress) of the word, which it must directly precede or directly follow. Affixal stress conditions go under different names in the literature (stress shift, stress attraction, stress sensitivity), reflecting the fact that conditions take effect with different degrees of forcefulness. Two common situations are:

Stress shift: The affix 'actively' imposes its stress condition by 'shifting' the stress of the base. An example is the Dutch adjectival suffix *-ig*, which shifts the stress peak of its compound base to the syllable directly preceding the suffix:

(3)   [nóod] [lót]   'distress', 'fortune'

          [[nóod]-[lot]]   'fate'

        [[[nood]-[lót]]-ig]   'fatal'

Correspondence of stress peaks between the derived form and its 'direct ancestor' base is broken here. But an indirect correspondence relationship still holds between the peak of the derived form and one of the stems (*lot*) that is the base-of-the-base.

Stress-blocking: The affix 'passively' imposes its stress condition by selecting bases that fulfill it: bases with final stress in case of a suffix, and bases with initial stress in case of a prefix. If the base fails to meet the stress condition, then the affix simply fails to adjoin: it is 'stress-blocked'. A suffixal example is (again) Dutch *-ig*, which imposes a condition of final stress on morphologically simplex bases (Trommelen and Zonneveld 1989):

(4)   a.   [moerás]   'marsh'   b.   [pías]   'clown'
           | |
      [[moerás] -ig] 'marshy'   *[[pías] -ig] 'clownish'

Again peak correspondence is strictly enforced. Note that the suffix *-ig*, which shifts the stress peak in compound bases (3), is unable to shift stress in simplex bases (although there are a handful of exceptions, which will be discussed). A prefixal example is the German participular prefix *ge-*, which requires a verbal base with initial stress, e.g. *ge-ság-t* 'said', as opposed to (**ge-*)*studíer-t* 'studied'.

This chapter aims at modelling 'stress peak identity', stress-shifts, and stress-blocking as interactions of hierarchically-ranked and violable constraints, on theoretical assumptions of Optimality Theory. This model attributes the situations in (1–4) to interactions of four types of constraints, requiring (a) that outputs preserve the stress peaks of their bases (this is minimally violated under compounding and stress shift); (b) that stress peaks correspond to stress peaks in their bases (which is not violable in Dutch word-based affixation); (c) that specific affixes must occur adjacent to the stress peak (which triggers stress shifts); and (d) that outputs contain all affixes that are given in their inputs (which is violated under stress-blocking). That affixation depends on the prosodic shape of the derived word represents evidence for a *parallel* model of the phonology-morphology interface (rather than a *serial* model that interleaves phonology and morphology through level-ordering). I will show that this parallel model also accounts for linear ordering restrictions among word-based affixes, again on the basis of peak correspondence.

   This analysis is embedded in theoretical assumptions of Correspondence Theory (McCarthy and Prince 1999). At the heart of this theory is the idea that linguistic outputs reflect a competition of two types of constraints: first, *well-formedness* constraints, which enforce pure phonological 'markedness', and second, *identity* constraints, which enforce identity between corresponding elements. The notion of *correspondence* is defined between pairs of elements in different strings, for example input and output:

(5)   *I/O correspondence:*
      'Given two strings S_1 and S_2, *correspondence* is a relation $\mathfrak{R}$ from the elements of S_1 to those of S_2. Segments α (an element of an input string S_1) and β (an element of an output string S_2) are referred to as *correspondents* of one another when $\alpha\mathfrak{R}\beta$.'

Correspondence constraints may require outputs to be 'faithful' to their inputs in various ways. The three main types of constraints that have been proposed thus far are:

(6)   a. *Dependence*: Every element of S_2 has a correspondent in S_1.
       b. *Maximality*: Every element of S_1 has a correspondent in S_2.
       c. *Identity*(γF): Let α be a segment in S_1 and β be its correspondent in S_2. If α is [γF], then β is [γF].

The original motivation for Correspondence Theory was to express parallelisms between 'input-output' faithfulness on the one hand, and 'base-output' identity in reduplication on the other hand (McCarthy and Prince 1999). Recently, correspondence has been extended to relationships between two output strings (none of which involves reduplication) (Burzio 1994; McCarthy 1995; Benua 1995). The relevant constraints require identity between the output form and its 'base': the word from which the output is morphologically 'derived'. In a non-derivational model, a 'base' can be characterized as a fully prosodized, independently occurring *word*, which is also *compositionally related* to the output (Kager, forthcoming). In particular, the morphological and semantic features of the base must be a proper subset of those of the output. This definition predicts that an output may have more than one base—for example under compounding (7a), as well as in the case of affixed forms of which the 'direct' base is itself affixed (7b):

(7)   a. Output [[hánd]-[doek]]   b. Output [[ver-[ánder]]-lijk]
          Base   [hánd],[dóek]   Base   [ver-[ánder]], [ánder]

From here on I will refer to the 'base-of-the-base' as an 'indirect' base.

   Benua (1995) observes that English words derived by Class 2 affixes tend to display the phonological properties of their bases, even when they fail to meet the conditions under which these properties normally arise (Borowsky 1993). 'Over-application' of word-based phonology points to the conclusion (Benua 1995: 59) that: 'Class 2 affixation is derived through an O/O correspondence with the unaffixed word'. One of Benua's examples is the neutralization of lax front /æ/ and tense front /ɛ/ into [ɛ] in closed syllables, which is typical of New York and Philadelphia dialects of English: e.g. *pass* [pɛs], but *passive* [pæ.sɪv]. In the present participle *passing* [pɛ.sɪŋ], the same vowel [ɛ] appears as in its base form. Thus æ-Tensing 'over-applies' to *passing*, which itself fails to meet the syllabic context, since the relevant vowel appears in an open syllable. This over-application is attributed to pressure to maintain phonological identity between morphologically-related forms:

(8)   *B/A-Identity* (**B**=Base, **A**=Affixed form)

                  [pɛs] — [pɛ.sɪŋ]
    I/O-Faith |
                  /pæs/ (cf. *passive*)

'Application' of tensing in the base form shows that the constraint banning [æ] from closed syllables dominates another constraint against tense low vowels such as [ɛ]. The latter is also dominated by a B/A-identity constraint requiring identity between the affixed form and the base with respect to the feature [tense].

The proposal of this chapter is to extend Base-Output identity to *stress peaks* in the derived word and its base. The location of the stress peaks in the base must be preserved in the derived word, due to PK-MAX (B/O).[4] And conversely, the stress peak of the derived word must match some stress peak in the base, due to PK-DEP (O/B).

(9)   a. PK-MAX (B/O)
      Let α be a segment in B and β be its correspondent in O.
      If α is the stress peak of B, then β is the stress peak of O.

      b. PK-DEP (O/B)
      Let α be a segment in O and β be its correspondent in B.
      If α is the stress peak of O, then β is the stress peak of B.

These constraints express logically distinct requirements, even if (independent constraints require that) every word must have a unique stress peak. I assume that PK-MAX is violated by every base peak which is not preserved in the derived word. Conversely, a violation of PK-DEP occurs when the peak in the derived word fails to match any peak in any base. The distinction becomes empirically relevant in the case of a derived word which has multiple bases—for example, in compounds. Here PK-DEP may be easily satisfied (the compound peak has only to correspond to a peak of *some* base). However, PK-MAX is clearly violated in compounds under the requirement that outputs must have *unique* stress peaks. Violation of PK-MAX necessarily follows since only one base (out of two or more that make up the compound) can preserve its stress peak in the output. We will come across cases where this becomes relevant.

This pair of 'peak correspondence' constraints is related to the pair below, both due to Alderete (1995), who was the first to extend correspondence relationships to stress:

(10)   a. HD-DEP (I/O)
       The output prosodic head must have a correspondent in the input.
       b. HD-MAX (I/O)
       The input prosodic head must have a correspondent in the output.

HD-DEP (I/O) is violated by stressed epenthetic vowels (equating the notions *prosodic head* and *stress peak*), while HD-MAX (I/O) is violated by deletion of any vowel that is stressed in the input. Two important differences between

---

[4] Compare the use of the reduplicative identity constraint MAXIMISE in Kenstowicz (1995: 415), militating against divergences in the stress peaks of base and reduplicant.

Alderete's constraints in (10) and those of (9) are the following. First, Alderete's constraints require Input-Output identity, rather than Base-Output identity. A second, more important difference is that Alderete's constraints do not require correspondence of peaks between two strings, but only that the segment that is the peak of one string has another segment (not necessarily a peak) in the other string.

This chapter is organized as follows. Section 3.2 addresses the phenomenon of stem stress in Dutch, covering various morphological constructions. This results in a basic model that is tested for more complex constructions in subsequent sections. First, Section 3.3 concentrates on complex derived forms based on 'stress-neutral' adjectival suffixes, and demonstrates that the basic model of Section 3.2 accounts for their complete stress behaviour. Next, 'stress-shifting' adjectival affixes are discussed in Section 3.4. I will show that a simple extension of the basic model by an affix-specific stress requirement accounts for both stress shifts and stress-blocking. In particular, this will result in a generalized analysis of stress shift and stress-blocking. Finally, Section 3.5 summarizes the argument, and compares the analysis to level-ordered models.

3.2 Stem Stress in Affixed Forms and Compounds

The types of Dutch morphology that I discuss in this chapter are all 'word-based'. This notion requires some clarification vis-à-vis the standard bifurcation of Dutch morphology into Class-1 and Class-2 morphology, and related lexical levels. Various criteria in the literature support such a distinction. Words derived by Class-1 affixes behave phonotactically (in terms of syllable structure and stress) as simplex words (Trommelen and Zonneveld 1989). Closely related to their phonotactic dependence, Class-1 affixes freely adjoin to roots, and require no independent words as their bases.[5] In contrast, a requirement of *word-size* bases is evident for Class-2 morphology, and that is what I focus on in this chapter.

Word-based morphology in Dutch includes stress-neutral affixation (e.g. *-heid* in 1), compounding (e.g. *bad-hand-doek* in 2), and stress-shifting affixation (e.g. *-ig* in 3). Based on both accentual and distributional evidence, Trommelen and Zonneveld (1989) have argued that stress-shifting affixation is situated on a separate lexical level (Level 2) before stress-neutral affixation and compounding (Level 3).[6] Their model will be discussed later in this chapter. However, I do not accept this prior distinction into Level 2 and Level 3, and start from the simpler assumption that all word-based morphology belongs to a single class. Finer distinctions between 'stress-shifting' and 'stress-neutral' affixation are to be attributed to affix-specific stress conditions.

---

[5] The question of how to account for the stress properties of Class-1 affixes will be postponed to Section 3.7.   [6] Together with inflection, which I do not discuss.

Word-based suffixes in Dutch belong to either of two lexical categories: nouns and adjectives.[7] Words derived by these suffixes have stem stress,[8] as is shown by the choice of nominal suffixes in (11) and adjectival suffixes in (12):

(11) a. wáar-heid   'truth'   wáar   'true'
      b. wándel-ing   'walk'   wándel 'go for a walk'
      c. téken-aar   'draughtsman'   téken 'draw'
      d. spél-er   'player'   spéel 'play'
      e. vríend-schap 'friendship'   vríend 'friend'
      f.ríjk-dom   'wealth'   ríjk   'rich'

(12) a. wás-baar   'washable'   wás   'wash'
      b. éer-zaam   'honourable'   éer   'honour'
      c. wérk-loos   'unemployed'   wérk   'work'
      d. róod-achtig 'reddish'   róod   'red'
      e. kóorts-ig   'feverish'   kóorts 'fever'
      f. vróuw-elijk 'female'   vróuw 'woman'

Word-based prefixes occur in various lexical categories, although only verbal prefixes (and a single nominal prefix) are category-changing (van Beurden 1987). Again, the stem is stressed rather than the affix:[9]

(13) a.i ver-wáter 'water down'   wáter 'water'
      a.ii ont-hárd 'soften' (of water) hárd 'hard'
      b.i ge-lách   'laughter'   lách 'laugh'

Summarizing, we have found that affixed words are characterized by 'stem stress'. The explanation for stem stress that I develop below is based on the observation that stems (but not affixes) occur as independent prosodic words. Stem stress reflects a Base-Output correspondence constraint requiring that stress

---

[7] Putting aside the improductive verbal suffix -*ig* (e.g. *stenig* 'to stone', *reinig* 'to clean').

[8] Stress-shifting -*ig* and -*lijk* will be dealt with in Section 3.4. Four stressed nominal suffixes occur which are arguably word-based. Two are feminine suffixes, -*in* (*koningín* 'queen') and -*es* (*prinsés* 'princess'), while the other two are unproductive suffixes, -*ij* (*voogdíj* 'custody') and -*erij* (*loteríj* 'lottery'). These suffixes require brute-force accentuation, presumably by input specification plus top-ranking peak faithfulness.

[9] Four nominal prefixes are consistently stressed, apparently counter-exemplifying the stem stress principle:

(i)   a. ón-zin   'nonsense'   ón-mens   'brute'
      b. wán-klank   'dissonance'   wán-orde   'chaos'
      c. wéer-slag   'repercussion'   wéer-zin   'repugnance'
      d. óer-kreet   'primordial cry' óer-mens   'primitive man'

I attribute obligatory stress on these prefixes to their special semantics. The prefixes *on-*, *wan-*, and *weer-* share a distinctly negative-meaning aspect. Negation is linked to its stress peak status by some undominated constraint. Finally, the case of *oer-* is slightly less clear, but it may have enough independent semantics ('primordial') to be signalled accentually.

peaks of the base be preserved in the output. This is Pk-Max (B/O), stated above in (9a).

Pk-Max(B/O) is a *violable* constraint; to find this out, we must turn to compounds. Compounds of lexical categories other than adjective (nouns in 14a, verbs in 14b) carry the stress peak on the leftmost stem:

(14) a.i [klém-toon] 'accent'   a.iii [[hánd-doek]-rek]$_N$ 'towel rack'
      a.ii [kráak-been] 'cartilage' a.iv [bád-[hand-doek]]$_N$ 'bath towel'
      b.i [ráng-schik] 'rank'
      b.ii [snél-wandel] 'race walk'

The fact that compounds have a *single* stress peak (rather than two, or more) diagnoses a violation of Pk-Max (B/O), which requires that the stress peaks of every base be preserved in the output. The question is: what causes this violation? I attribute the fact that compounds have a unique stress peak to a general constraint ruling out multiple peaks:[10]

(15) Uni-Pk
      Words must have a unique stress peak.

In order to take effect, this constraint must dominate Pk-Max (B/O).

If compounds are limited to a single peak, what determines the choice of base peak? All we need is a general constraint requiring initial stress (Prince and Smolensky 1993).

(16) Leftmost
      Align (PrWd, L, peak, L).

Violations of this constraint will be counted by numbers of syllables from the right edge.

We are now in a position to rank all three constraints that have been introduced so far:

(17) Uni-Pk >> Pk-Max (B/O) >> Leftmost

That Leftmost must be dominated by both other constraints can be seen in tableau (18) of a prefixed verb. The prefix yields the stress peak to the stem, even though it is 'leftmost' in the word. Both candidates (18b-c) that satisfy Leftmost are ruled out by the dominating constraints Uni-Pk and Pk-Max (B/O):

---

[10] This constraint is violable under highly specific conditions in Dutch, which are not fully understood yet, but appear to be semantic in origin. For example, adjectival compounds consisting of a head adjective preceded by a modifier of degree can be double-peaked—e.g. *réuze-léuk* 'dead funny', *bére-stérk* 'strong as a bear'.

(18)	Input: {ont-, hard} Base: [hárd]	Uni-Pk	Pk-Max(B/O)	Leftmost
☞ a. [ont-hárd]				*
b. [ónt-hard]			*!	
c. [ónt-hárd]		*!		

The ranking Uni-Pk >> Pk-Max (B/O) is motivated by tableau (19) of a compound verb. Two bases submit their peak for preservation in the output. But only one can become the output peak because Uni-Pk rules out multiple peaks (19c). Both remaining candidates (19a–b) have a single violation of Pk-Max, and are evaluated thus as 'equally ill-formed' by this constraint. Naturally evaluation is passed on to Leftmost, which selects (19b):

(19)	Input: {rang, schik} Base: [ráng], [schík]	Uni-Pk	Pk- Max(B/O)	Leftmost
a. [rang-schík]			*	*!
☞ b. [ráng-schik]			*	
c. [ráng-schík]		*!		

As a necessary step up to the discussion of adjectival affixes in the next section, we must become acquainted with the stress pattern of adjectival compounds. Examples in (20) show that the position of the stress peak in compounds is sensitive to lexical category. In contrast to nominal and verbal compounds (14), the peak is now on the *rightmost* stem (Visch 1989, Trommelen and Zonneveld 1989):[11]

(20)   a. lood-vríj 'unleaded'   d. vuur-vást 'heat-proof'
       b. water-dícht 'waterproof'   e. kleur-écht 'colour-fast'
       c. rood-wit-bláuw 'red-white-and-blue' (the Dutch flag)

I assume that the location of the stress peak is due to the following constraint, a category-specific mirror-image version of Leftmost, which makes the maximally simple requirement that the stress peak in adjectives is 'rightmost':

(21)   Adj-Pk
       Align (Adjective, R, peak, R).

It will be clear that Adj-Pk dominates Leftmost. In sum, we now have the ranking:

---

[11] A class of complex adjectives (which are superficially adjectival compounds) have left peaks—e.g. *zée-ziek* 'sea-sick', *zín-vol* 'meaningful', *kléur-rijk* 'colourful'. Backhuys (1989) and Booij (1995) observe that the righthand constituents occur independently (*ziek* 'sick', *vol* 'full', *rijk* 'rich'), but that they are better analysed as adjectival suffixes, since their lexical meaning has faded. That is, we analyse these morphemes on a par with adjectival affixes such as *-baar* and *-loos*.

(22)   UNI-PK >> PK-MAX(B/A) >> ADJ-PK >> LEFTMOST

In adjectival compounds, violation of PK-MAX cannot be avoided, since UNI-PK rules out any multiple-peaked candidates (23d). Right-hind location of the peak is due to ADJ-PK:

(23) Input: {[róod], [wít], [bláuw]}	UNI-PK	PK-MAX	ADJ-PK	LEFTMOST
☞ a. [rood-wit-bláuw]		**		**
b. [rood-wít-blauw]		**	*!	*
c. [róod-wit-blauw]		**	*!*	
d. [róod-wít-bláuw]	*!			

Presence of ADJ-PK fails to change the previous evaluation of suffixed adjectives since the option of righthand stress is effectively ruled out by higher-ranking PK-MAX:

(24) Input: {[wás], -baar}	UNI-PK	PK-MAX	ADJ-PK	LEFTMOST
☞ a. [wás-baar]			*	
b. [was-báar]		*!		*

The interesting question now arises as to which stress patterns emerge when compounding and adjectival suffixation combine in a single construction (e.g. synthetic compounds). That is, will the stress peak of the compound base be preserved ('stress-neutrality'), or will it be shifted to the rightmost stem ('stress-attraction')? This question will be taken up in Section 3.3.

3.3 'Stress-Neutral' Adjectival Suffixes

The discussion below will adduce more evidence for the role of peak correspondence in the stress patterns of morphologically comples adjectives. This discussion incorporates various generalizations on the stress behaviour of adjectival affixes that were stated by Trommelen and Zonneveld (1989). However, I argue that the parallel OT model of the morphology-phonology interface captures these generalizations more straightforwardly than the 'multi-layered' serial interface of rule-based theory (assumed by Trommelen and Zonneveld).

The class of 'stress-neutral' adjectival suffixes in Dutch includes the following six:

(25)   *-baar, -zaam, -end, -loos, -achtig, -s*

Trommelen and Zonneveld (1989) argue that the genuine diagnostic for the stress behaviour of these suffixes is provided by constructions in which they combine with two stems into a suffixed compound. We should be careful to distinguish (i) suffixation to an independently existing compound (cf. 26) from (ii) synthetic compounding, in which the pair of stems to which the suffix is adjoined fails to occur as an independent compound (cf. 27). These two constructions have different stress patterns, which is of course what we are interested in.

Let us begin with the first type of construction: suffixed compounds. Here the stress peak coincides with the peak of the embedded compound. A compound base may be a verb (26a), or a noun (26b):

(26) a.i   [[ráng-schik]-baar]   'rankable'   [ráng-schik]   'rank'
     a.ii   [[ráad-pleeg]-baar]   'consultable'   [ráad-pleeg]   'consult'
     a.iii [[húis-vest]-baar]   'lodgeable'   [húis-vest]   'lodge'
     a.iv   [[hánd-haaf]-baar]   'maintainable   [hánd-haaf]   'maintain'

     b.i   [[be-klém-toon]-baar]   'accentable'   [klém-toon]   'accent'
     b.ii   [[méren-deel]-s]   'for the greater   [méren-deel]   'majority'
                                      part'
     b.iii [[stád-houder]-loos]   'without a gover-   [stád-houder]   'governor'
                                      nor'
     b.iv   [[kráak-been]-achtig]   'cartilaginous'   [kráak-been]   'cartilage'

This is clearly 'stress-neutral' affixation, preserving the stress peak of the compound base.

In synthetic compounds (which contain two independent words plus a suffix), the rightmost stem (a verb in 27a, or a noun in 27b) is stressed.

(27) a.i   [[zelf]-[réd]-zaam]   'self-supportive'   [zélf] 'self', [réd] 'support'
     a.ii   [[zelf]-[wérk]-zaam]   'automatic'   [zélf] 'self', [wérk] 'operate'
     a.iii [[goed]-[lách]-s]   'fond of laughing' [góed] 'good', [lách] 'laugh'
     a.iiv [[diep]-[gráv]-end]   'penetrating'   [díep] 'deep', [gráaf] 'dig'
     b.i   [[gelijk]-[vlóer]-s]   'on the ground   [gelíjk] 'equal', [vlóer], 'floor'
                                      floor'
     b.ii   [[bloot]-[vóet]-s]   'bare-footed'   [blóot] 'bare', [vóet] 'foot'
     b.iii [[buiten]-[áard]-s]   'extraterrestrial' [búiten] 'outside', [áarde]
                                                         'earth'

Trommelen and Zonneveld (1989) state the correct generalisation about these forms: that the 'right-stem-strong' stress pattern of synthetic compounds is directly related to the general right-strong stress pattern of bare adjectival compounds (20). So no specific stress shift rule is involved in the pattern of synthetic compounds.

As will be clear from a comparison of (26) and (27), the morphological differences between these constructions are reflected in their stress behaviour. In fact, all the ingredients for a full explanation are readily available from the discussion in the previous section.

The suffixed compound [[ráng-schik]-baar] in (26a) preserves the stress peak of its compound base [ráng-schik]. This compound, in its turn, has a dual base, the pair {[ráng], [schík]}, each of which has its own stress peak. Maximally one of these stress peaks can be preserved as the peak of the compound, because of UNI-PK. The choice is made for the left peak by LEFTMOST. (Recall that the compound [ráng-schik] is verbal.)

(28)   a. [ráng], [schík]   (*indirect bases*)   b. [zélf], [réd]   (*direct bases*)

　　　　　　│

　　　　[ráng - schik]   (*direct base*)

　　　　　│

　　　[[ráng - schik] -baar]　　　　　　　　　　[[zelf - réd] -zaam]

In contrast, the synthetic compound [[zelf-réd]-zaam] in (21b) has a direct dual base, the pair {[zélf], [réd]}, of which it preserves only one peak.

First consider tableau (29), which shows the suffixed compound *rángschikbaar*. The definition of 'base' that I proposed earlier predicts that the direct base (*rángschik*), as well as both of its indirect bases (*ráng, schík*), may cause violations of PK-MAX. (This is not yet crucial in tableau (29) because the direct base is sufficient for the evaluation, but it will become important later on.) The evaluation proceeds as follows. Candidate (29a) has a violation of PK-MAX that is due to the non-preservation of the stress peak of the indirect base [schík]. Candidate (29b) has two violations because it is unfaithful to two stress peaks: that of its direct base [ráng-schik], and that of its indirect base [ráng]. Finally, candidate (29c) is unfaithful to all three stress peaks. By gradient evaluation, PK-MAX selects (29a) as the optimal candidate before ADJ-PK even gets a chance to enter the evaluation.

(29)　　I: {rang, schik, -baar} B: [ráng-schik], [ráng], [schík]	UNI-PK	PK-MAX	ADJ-PK	LEFTMOST
☞ a. [[ráng-schik]-baar]		*	**	
b. [[rang-schík]-baar]		**!	*	*
c. [[rang-schik]-báar]		**!*		**
d. [[ráng-schík]-baar]	*!		*	

Now compare tableau (30), which features a synthetic compound. Synthetic compounds crucially lack a compound base in which the stress peak could have been relevant to PK-MAX. Candidates (30a–b) are therefore evaluated as equal by PK-MAX, both being unfaithful to one of both stress peaks in the dual base. The evaluation is passed on to the next-lower constraint in the hierarchy, ADJ-PK, which decides in favour of (30a).

(30) I: {zelf, red, -zaam} B: [zélf], [réd]	Uni-Pk	Pk-Max	Adj-Pk	Leftmost
a. [[zélf]-[red]-zaam]		*	**!	
☞ b. [[zelf]-[réd]-zaam]		*	*	*
c. [[zelf]-[red]-záam]		**!		**
d. [[zélf]-[réd]-zaam]	*!		*	

In sum, adjectival synthetic compounds reflect a combination of the 'stem stress pattern' and the 'adjectival compound pattern', with the stress peak located on the rightmost stem.

So far I have referred to the adjectival suffixes under discussion as 'stress-neutral'. However, this terminology is not uncontroversial. Many analysts before Trommelen and Zonneveld (1989) have actually claimed that suffixes such as -*baar*, -*zaam*, and -*end* are 'stress-shifting' because of the stress patterns of constructions in which they adjoin to 'separable' verbs:

(31)   a.i [[aan]-[tóon]-baar] 'demonstrable'   áan-toon 'demonstrate'
       a.ii [[waar]-[néem]-baar] 'perceptible'   wáar-neem 'perceive'

       b.i [[op]-[mérk]-zaam]   'attentive'   óp-merk   'notice'
       b.ii [[mede]-[déel]-zaam] 'communicative' méde-deel 'communicate'

       c.i [[op]-[wínd]-end]   'exciting'   óp-wind   'excite'
       c.ii [[in]-[léid]-end]   'introductory'   ín-leid   'introduce'

The alleged 'stress-shifting' behaviour is based on the stress patterns of separable verbs in a phrasal context, where the *particle* is stressed. Separable verbs display a strong-weak stress pattern in subordinate clauses (32a.i), where both parts may be separated by an infinitival marker (32a.ii) or an auxiliary verb (32a.iii). Second, a weak-strong pattern occurs in main clauses (32b), where the distance between the verbal part (in verb-second position) and the particle (stranded in clause-final position) is unbounded (Koster 1975):

(32)   a.i   . . . dat ik áan toon 'that I demonstrate'
       a.ii . . . áan te tonen   'to demonstrate'
       a.iii . . . áan zal tonen   'will demonstrate'

       b.   (ik) toon ('t) áan   '(I) demonstrate (it)'

Particle stress is not reducible to compound stress, which is restricted to word units that are joined both morphologically and phonologically. Trommelen and Zonneveld (1989) argue that particle stress is *phrasal*, following the general stress pattern of VP (in which objects and other arguments are stressed, rather than verbs). This important insight paves the way for an analysis of -*baar* suffixations of separable verbs (31) which no longer involves 'stress attraction', but which runs parallel to that of synthetic compounds (30).

In my analysis, this insight is translated as follows. The *phrasal* nature of the stress pattern of separable verb renders it 'invisible' to PK-MAX, which accesses lexical prosodic units only. Note that if separable verbs were prosodic units in the lexicon, their separability would be a complete mystery, since syntax cannot undo Prosodic Word status. I therefore assume that separable verbs enjoy a status of lexical units only in a morphosyntactic sense, and crucially not in a prosodic sense. Accordingly, separable verbs are prosodically analysed as dual bases, and their derivations as synthetic compounds.

We have not yet considered the behaviour of stress-neutral adjectival affixes with respect to bases which consist of a single suffixed word. Nothing happens here that we do not already expect: the generalization of stress-neutrality that we reached earlier still holds, and the stress peak in the derived word corresponds to that of the base:

(33) a. [[wáar-heid]-loos]   'truthless'   wáar-heid   'truth'
     b. [[be-wég-ing]-loos]   'motionless'   be-wég-ing   'motion'
     c. [[ver-wáar-loos]-baar] 'neglectable' ver-wáar-loos 'neglect'

A tableau of *wáarheidloos* is given in (34). It is a straightforward demonstration of stem stress—that is, the domination of ADJ-PK by PK-MAX:

(34) I: {waar, -heid, -loos} B: [wáar-heid], [wáar]	UNI-PK	PK-MAX	ADJ-PK	LEFTMOST
a. [[wáar-heid]-loos]			**	
☞ b. [[waar-héid]-loos]		*!*	*	*
c. [[waar-heid]-lóos]		*!*		**
d. [[wáar-héid]-loos]	*!		*	

Next, consider adjectival compounds suffixed by a nominal suffix. The compound's stress peak is preserved in the affixed form (data from Trommelen and Zonneveld 1989: 186):

(35) a. [[gast-vríj]-heid]   'hospitability'   gast-vríj   'hospitable'
     b. [[vak-bekwáam]-heid] 'professional skill' vak-bekwáam 'skillful'

This stress preservation follows from the current model:

(36) I: {gast, vrij, -heid} B: [gast-vríj], [gást], [vríj]	UNI-PK	PK-MAX	ADJ-PK	LEFTMOST
☞ a. [[gast-vríj]-heid]		*	*	*
b. [[gást-vrij]-heid]		**!	**	
c. [[gast-vrij]-héid]		**!		*
d. [[gást-vríj]-heid]	*!		*	

So far we have not paid attention to affixations of polysyllabic bases, which in level-ordering models provide the main diagnostic of stress behaviour of affixes. Not surprisingly, we find that the adjectival suffixes under discussion are strictly 'stress-neutral'. The stress peak in the affixed word coincides with that of the polysyllabic base:

(37) a. scháduw-loos   'shadowless'   scháduw   'shadow'
      b. bránie-achtig   'swanky'   bránie   'tumult'
      c. Énschedee-s   'from Enschede'   Énschede   (place name)
      d. ver-ántwoord-baar 'accountable'   ver-ántwoord 'account'
      e. árbeid-zaam[12]   'laborious'   árbeid   'labour'

Again, this follows straightforwardly from the current model:

(38) I: {schaduw, -loos} B: [scháduw]	Uni-Pk	Pk-Max	Adj-Pk	Leftmost
☞ a. [[scháduw]-loos]			**	
b. [[schadúw]-loos]		*!	*	*
c. [[schaduw]-lóos]		*!		**

To summarize: stem stress is due to Pk-Max, a correspondence constraint which dominates the category-specific stress constraint Adj-Pk, as well as Leftmost. Moreover, pre-stressing in adjectical suffixation is restricted to forms that have 'dual' bases, hence two input stress peaks. Genuine cases of 'stress-shift' will be considered in the next Section.

3.4 'Stress-Shifting' Adjectival Suffixes

Dutch has a pair of adjectival suffixes, -*ig* and -*lijk*,[13] that induce stress shifts in their bases. The morphological distribution of these affixes is governed by restrictions which previous researchers (Trommelen and Zonneveld 1989, and others) have attempted to derive from the layered lexicon. However, such attempts were seriously hampered by an ordering paradox.

The central observation that stood at the basis of all layer-lexicon analyses of stress-shifting suffixes is that they may only occur 'inside' stress-neutral suffixes:[14]

(39) a. [[méns-elijk]-heid] 'humanity'   méns-elijk 'human'
      b. [[zóet-ig]-heid]   'sweeties'   zóet-ig   'ratger sweet'

---

[12] The form *herbérg-zaam* 'hospitable' (from *hérberg*, 'tavern') is the single counter-example to stress neutrality.

[13] The suffix -*lijk* [lək] has an allomorph -*elijk* [ələk] of which the distribution is governed by segmental conditions that are irrelevant to the present discussion.

[14] Observe that all examples involve nominal -*heid*. This is the only derivational suffix that is productive with adjectival bases.

Conversely, stress-shifting suffixes never occur 'outside' stress-neutral suffixes, regardless of whether the stress peak of the base is shifted to the stress-neutral affix:

(40) a. *[[waar-héid]-elijk]   'truthful'   wáar-heid   'truth'
      b. *[[zénuw-achtig]-lijk] 'somewhat nervous' zénuw-   'nervous'
                                                     achtig
      c. *[[waarde-lóos]-ig]   'somewhat worthless' wáarde-loos 'worthless'
      d. *[[was-báar]-ig]   'somewhat washable'   wás-baar   'washable'

So far this distribution perfectly matches a two-layered lexicon model which has stem stress and 'stress-shifting' affixation at an earlier level than compound stress and 'stress-neutral' affixation (as proposed by Trommelen and Zonneveld 1989, to which I will return below).

The ranking paradox arises when we find that stress-shifting adjectival affixes freely occur outside compounds, where they shift the stress peak of the compound base:

(41) a.i   [[nood-lót]-ig]   'fatal'   nóod-lot   'fate'
      a.ii [[mis-dáad]-ig]   'criminal'   mís-daad   'crime'
      a.iii [[voor-béeld]-ig]   'examplary'   vóor-beeld 'example'

      b.i   [[werk-wóord]-elijk] 'verbal'   wérk-woord 'verb'
      b.ii [[grond-wét]-elijk] 'constitutional' grónd-wet   'constitution'
      b.iii [[ogen-blík]-elijk] 'instantly'   ógen-blik   'instant'

These are not merely exceptions: this list can be extended with dozens of similar cases. It has been observed by Trommelen and Zonneveld (1989: 190) that the compounds which form bases of -*ig* and-*lijk* affixation have lexicalized semantics (many are abstract nouns), and are typically non-recursive. Accordingly, they propose a lexical model in which compounds of this type are situated at an earlier level than recursive compounding:

(42)   Level 1 underived words (and Class-1 affixation)
                         ↓
       Level 2 -*ig*, -*lijk*, early compounds
                         ↓
       Level 3 stress-neutral (Class-2) affixation, compounds

However, by applying the same criteria of lexicalized (abstract-noun) semantics and non-recursivity, the *affixed* forms in (43), should also qualify as 'early' formations. They might thus be expected to be suitable bases for -*ig* and-*lijk* affixation, which is incorrect:

(43)   a.i   [schóon-heid] 'beauty' schóon 'clean' *[[schoon-heid]-ig]
       a.ii [éen-heid]   'unity'   éen   'one'   *[[een-heid]-ig]

| b.i [hóud-ing] | 'attitude' | hóud | 'hold' | *[[houd-ing]-lijk][15] |
| b.ii [dwál-ing] | 'error' | dwáal | 'wander' | *[[dwal-ing]-lijk] |

Lexicalized abstract nouns based on *-heid* and *-ing* are abundant in Dutch morphology, but none allows *-ig* or-*lijk* affixation.[16] One may, as is always possible, stipulate some property of compounding in (42) which the affixes in (43) lack in order to 'explain' the difference in stress conditions. But as far as I can see, this would amount to a purely diacritic marking. The single relevant *overt* property that the suffixes lack, but the righthand members have, is that the latter occur as independent words. This will explain differences in stress conditions between compounding and 'stress-neutral' suffixation without any additional assumptions.

I will present an analysis of these data which does not rely on the assumption that stress-neutral and stress-shifting suffixes belong to different lexical layers. Instead, I simply assume that both kinds of suffixes are word-based. It then follows that stress-shifting suffixes {*-ig, -lijk*}, like any word-based affix, may freely adjoin to compound bases. The question can now be restated: what blocks stress-shifting suffixes after bases that contain stress-neutral suffixes? Intuitively, the solution must take into account the important fact that stress-shifting suffixes differ from stress-neutral ones in one crucial aspect: they must immediately follow the stress peak of the word. An affix-to-peak alignment constraint expresses this:[17]

(44)   SFX-TO-PK
       Align ({*-ig, -elijk*}, L, stress peak, R).
       'The left edge of affixes {*-ig, -elijk*} coincides with the right edge of the stress peak.'

SFX-TO-PK dominates the correspondence constraint PK-MAX (requiring that stress peaks of bases are preserved in the output). This is why we find stress shift in compound bases. But why is a stress shift to an unstressed suffix excluded?

---

[15] Or perhaps **hóudinklijk*, by analogy to *koning* 'king' (simplex)–*koninklijk* 'royal'.

[16] The only stress-neutral affix that consistently allows *-lijk* affixation is *-schap*:

(i) *vríend* 'friend'   *vríend-schap* 'friendship'   *vriendscháp-elijk* 'friendly'
(ii) *lánd* 'land'   *lánd-schap* 'landscape'   *landscháp-elijk* 'of the landscape'

These data are problematic to both the layered-lexicon model and the correspondence model which is advocated here. (The word *schap* 'industrial board' is only vaguely related to the suffix in a semantic sense.)

[17] Alternatively, pre-accenting behaviour of these suffixes might be encoded in inputs by pre-specification in the weak position of a trochee, in combination with a constraint that enforces lexical feet (Inkelas 1999). However, we will see later in the discussion of prefixes that a mirror-image constraint of (44) is required, which would require iambic feet. Since evidence for iambic feet is totally lacking in Dutch, general considerations have lead me to use constraints rather than pre-specification. However, the issue may not have been settled yet.

The intuitive idea is that shift to the second half of a compound base is allowed because it occurs an an independent word. In contrast, suffixes do not occur independently. We can formalize this idea by requiring that a derived word's stress peak should match a peak of some of its composing morphemes. This constraint is PK-DEP, repeated from (9b):

(45)   PK-DEP (O/B)
        Let α be a segment in O and β be its correspondent in B.
        If α is the stress peak of O, then β is the stress peak of B.

As shown in (46a), a compound base offers a 'landing site' for the stress peak even when this is shifted: it is the righthand element of the compound, itself a prosodically independent word with its own stress peak. This correspondence relationship holds between the output and its indirect base [lót], rather than its direct base [nóod-lot]. In contrast, no such 'landing site' occurs in suffixed bases, since the suffix is by definition prosodically dependent, and thus has no stress peak. See (46b):

(46)   a.   [nóod] [lót]   b.   [wáar]
              | | |
             [nóod -lot]   [wáar-heid]
                      |
            [[nood -lót] -ig]   *[[waar-héid]-ig]

I therefore propose that the notion 'base' is *transitive*. More formally, if B is the direct base of an output form O, and B′ is the direct base of B, then B′ is also *indirectly* the base of O.

Let us now turn to the mechanism of stress-induced blocking. I will use a mechanism of morphological blocking which was introduced by Prince and Smolensky (1993). Among the logically possible outputs of the Generator component (GEN) is the 'null parse' Ø, which is equal to no analysis of the input at all. This 'null parse' may be selected as the optimal output—that is, preferred over non-zero outputs—when the violation of some constraint C is avoided even at the cost of unfaithfulness to the input morphology. The null parse implies a violation of the constraint M-MAX (47), a correspondence version of M-PARSE in Prince and Smolensky (1993: 49):

(47)   M-MAX (I/O)
        'Every morpheme in the input has a correspondent in the output'.

Affix-blocking constitutes a violation of M-MAX, the morphological null parse. Observe that both SFX-TO-PK and PK-DEP must dominate M-MAX since the null parse Ø is preferred over both outputs in (48a–b):

(48)   a.   Ø > *[[waar-héid]-ig] PK-DEP >> M-MAX
        b.   Ø > *[[wáar-heid]-ig] SFX-TO-PK >> M-MAX

Regardless of whether stress is shifted (48a) or not (48b), any morphologically faithful output must violate some constraint whose violation is avoided by the grammar at all costs—even when this means silence.

The total ranking accounting for all effects of stress neutrality, stress shift, and affix-blocking that have been discussed so far is:

(49) UNI-PK, SFX-TO-PK, PK-DEP >> M-MAX >> PK-MAX >> ADJ-PK
>> LEFTMOST

I have now introduced the relevant constraints, and argued for their ranking. This exposition will now be completed by tableaus of both crucial cases. First, tableau (50) of an affixed compound shows shows that M-MAX dominates PK-MAX, ADJ-PK, and LEFTMOST. There is a narrow win of candidate (50a), which violates PK-MAX, over its main competitor (50d), the null-parse candidate, which violates M-MAX. This tableau shows that M-MAX >> PK-MAX:[18]

(50)	I: {nood, lot, -ig} B: [nóod-lot], [nóod], [lót]	UNI- PK	SFX- TO-PK	PK- DEP	M- MAX	PK- MAX	ADJ- PK	LEFT- MOST
☞	a. [[nood-lót]-ig]					**	*	*
	b. [[nóod-lot]-ig]		*!			*	**	
	c. [[nóod-lót]-ig]	*!					*	
	d. Ø				*!			

Tableau (51) shows an unsuccessful attempt to provide a non-null output form for an input containing a suffixed noun *waarheid*, and the suffix -*ig*. This produces evidence for the ranking UNI-PK, SFX-TO-PK, PK-DEP >> M-MAX. The optimal candidate is the null parse (51d), which is impeccable with respect to all constraints, except to M-MAX. However, all possible non-null competitors (51a–c) violate some high-ranked constraint.

(51)	I: {waar, -heid, -ig} B: [wáar-heid], [wáar]	UNI- PK	SFX- TO-PK	PK- DEP	M- MAX	PK- MAX	ADJ- PK	LEFT- MOST
	a. [[waar-héid]-ig]			*!		**	*	*
	b. [[wáar-heid]-ig]		*!				**	
	c. [[wáar-héid]-ig]	*!					*	
☞	d. Ø				*			

Crucially, the null parse (51c) does not violate any of the peak correspondence

---

[18] Although it is not crucial here, I assume that the null parse incurs no violation of PK-MAX since it has no phonological content.

constraints (in particular, Pκ-Dep) since it has no correspondence relation with the base.

We correctly predict that stress-shifting suffixes may freely adjoin to 'dual' bases in synthetic compounds (52a), as well as to separable verbs (52b), with prestressing behaviour in both cases:

(52) a.i [[los]-[líp]-ig]   'loose-tongued'   los 'loose'   lip 'lip'
      a.ii [[groot]-[schál]-ig]   'on a big scale' groot 'big'   schaal 'scale'
      a.iii [[hand]-[tást]-elijk] 'palpable'   hand 'hand'   tast 'touch'
      a.iv [[klaar]-[blíjk]-elijk] 'evident'   klaar 'clear' blijk 'appear'

      b.i [[in]-[háal]-ig]   'greedy'   in-haal   'fetch in'
      b.ii [[na]-[láat]-ig]   'neglectful'   na-laat   'omit'
      b.iii [[op]-[mérk]-elijk]   'remarkable'   op-merk   'remark'
      b.iv [[aan]-[hóud]-elijk]   'sustained'   aan-houd   'keep on'

The only difference with affixed compounds (*noodlottig*, etc.) is that the 'landing site' for a stress peak happens to be available in a direct base. But by transitivity of the notion 'base', this makes no difference to Pκ-Dep. The three different situations are portrayed in (53):

(53) Affixed form: [[nood-lót]-ig] [[waar-héid]-ig] [[los]-[líp]-ig]
      Direct base(s):   [nóod-lot]   [wáar-heid]   [lós], [líp]
      Indirect base(s): [nóod], [lót]   [wáar]
      Pκ-Dep: satisfied in IB violated   satisfied in DB

We also correctly predict a second environment in which 'stress-shifting' affixes are blocked. While stress-shifting affixes should freely adjoin to a morphologically simplex base that ends in a stressed syllable (54), the same affixes should be blocked with simplex bases that end in an unstressed syllable (55).

(54) a.i huméur   'temper'   huméur-ig   'moody'
      a.ii veníjn   'venom'   veníjn-ig   'venomous'
      a.iii schandáal 'scandal'   schandál-ig   'scandalous'
      a.iv moerás   'marsh'   moeráss-ig   'marshy'
      a.v pietlút   'niggler'   pietlútt-ig   'niggling'
      a.vi kolóm   'column'   (twee-) kolómm-ig   '(two-)columned'

      b.i paradíjs   'paradise'   paradíjs-elijk   'paradisiacal'
      b.ii natúur   'nature'   natúur-lijk   'naturally', natural'
      b.iii fatsóen   'decency'   fatsóen-lijk   'decent'
      b.iv publíek   'public'   publíek-elijk   'publicly'
      b.v recént   'recent'   recént-elijk   'recently'
      b.vi triomfánt   'triumphant' triomfánt-elijk   'triumphantly'

(55) a.i ménthol   'menthol'   *mentholl-ig   'menthol-like'
      a.ii cháos   'chaos'   *chaoss-ig   'chaotic'
      a.iii Sódom   'Sodom'   *Sodomm-ig   'Sodom-like'

b.i	pélgrim	'pilgrim'	*pelgrimm-elijk	'pilgrim-like'
b.ii	sátan	'Satan'	*satann-elijk	'satanic'
b.iii	júnior	'junior'	*júnior-lijk	'junior-like'

The stress-blocking context (55) was first observed by Trommelen and Zonneveld (1989), who note that it does not follow from a layered lexical model: 'It is unclear to us why these suffixes impose this requirement. There have been times in phonology when such a situation was referred to as a "conspiracy", with reference to work by Kisseberth (1970); however, naming some phenomenon does not amount to explaining it.' (Trommelen and Zonneveld 1989: 189; my translation). In a constraint-based OT analysis, the nature of the 'conspiracy' is evident: the pre-stressing condition of these suffixes is respected at all costs, and so is the constraint that the stressed syllable must have a stressed correspondent in the base.

The pattern is simply predicted by the current ranking—the unstressed final syllable of the base is no proper landing site for the derived word's stress peak—while preserving the base stress peak fatally violates SFX-TO-PK:

(56)	I: {menthol, -ig} B: [ménthol]	UNI-PK	SFX-TO-PK	PK-DEP	M-MAX	PK-MAX	ADJ-PK	LEFT-MOST
	a. [[menthól]-ig]			*!	*	*	*	
	b. [[ménthol]-ig]		*!				**	
☞	c. Ø				*			

Examples presented earlier in (37) show that stress-neutral suffixes are freely allowed with bases of this stress type—e.g. *ménthol-achtig* 'menthol-like'. The null parse can be successfully avoided in this case since SFX-TO-PK is vacuously satisfied here, so that a candidate is available that satisfies both SFX-TO-PK and M-MAX.

Summarizing, we have connected 'stress-shifting' and 'affix-blocking' behaviour of suffixes. The generalization that this model captures is that any suffix that shifts the stress peak in compound bases also imposes a stress condition on simplex bases, while any suffix that fails to shift the stress peak in compound bases also fails to impose a stress condition on simplex bases.

The generalization that *-ig* and *-lijk* are blocked in context (47) seems hampered by a set of observations, which I will now discuss. Firstly, *-ig* and *-lijk* freely adjoin to bases in which the second syllable contains schwa:

(57) a.i váder-lijk 'paternal' b.i módder-ig 'muddy'
      a.ii ádel-lijk 'noble' b.ii rímpel-ig 'wrinkled'
      a.iii ópen-lijk 'public'

Actually these data only confirm a generalization that was stated by Kager and Zonneveld (1986) and Kager (1989), that schwa in final syllables behaves 'as if not there' for prosody (for syllable phonotactics as well as word stress). If we assume that schwa is denied a grid position by some undominated constraint (which also explains schwa's stresslessness), then the current statement of SFX-TO-PK suffices: the suffixes in (57) are linearly adjacent to the stress peak *as defined on the grid*.

Secondly, a number of stress-shifting cases occur. A small set of words ending in a 'superheavy' syllable (CvvC or CvCC) allows for stress shift under *-ig* and *-lijk* affixation:

(58) a.i   ármoede   'poverty'   armóed-ig   'poor'
      a.ii   víjand   'enemy'   vijánd-ig   'hostile'

      b.i   ámbacht   'handicraft'   ambácht-elijk   'craftsmanly'
      b.ii   bísschop   'bishop'   bisschópp-elijk 'episcopal'
      b.iii víjand   'enemy'   vijánd-elijk   'enemy' (adj.)
      b.iv   líchaam   'body'   lichám-elijk   'bodily'
      b.v   májesteit 'majesty'   majestéit-elijk 'majestic'
      b.vi   ver-ántwoord 'account'   verantwóord-elijk 'responsible'

These words display compound behaviour, precisely matching their historical origins. There is no reason to consider them to be compounds in present-day Dutch, however. A tentative analysis may be based on stress allomorphy, e.g. {víjand ~ vijánd}. The proper allomorph (in nominals versus adjectival derivations) would then be automatically selected by the ranking ADJ-PK >> LEFTMOST. An allomorph analysis is supported by a second tiny group of shifting cases, where shift to the final syllable is accompanied by vowel lengthening (historically a result of open syllable lengthening):

(59) a. hértog [ɔ] 'duke'   hertóg-elijk [oː] 'ducal'
      b. mótor [ɔ] 'motor'   motór-ig   [oː] 'of a motor'

This vowel-lengthening has become completely unproductive in present-day Dutch, which is why it requires an allomorph analysis on independent grounds.[19]

This completes the analysis of 'peak-dependent' suffixation, which I summarize in the next section.

3.5 A Summary of the Analysis

Table (60) summarizes empirical findings with respect to the two classes of suffix:

---

[19] In the case of words ending in - *or*, this allomorphy is present at the level of a (semi-)suffix, e.g. singular-plural alternations *dóctor ~ doctóren*, *senátor ~ senatóren*, etc. Note that the end-stressed allomorph is selected when an unstressed suffix follows, while the initial-stressed allomorph is the isolation form. Booij (1998) argues that this is a case of phonologically conditioned allomorphy (cf. Kager 1996), which has a word-final trochee (the Dutch stress foot) as its target.

(60)

	Base		Affixed form		
	Type	Pattern	-ig, -elijk	-baar, -zaam, -end, -s	
a.i	Underived	[SW]	blocked	neutral	[SW]-sfx
a.ii	Suffixed	[S-W]	blocked	neutral	[SW]-sfx
a.iii	Compound	[[S][W]]	shifting [WS]-sfx	neutral	[SW]-sfx
b.i	Two words	[S] [S]	pre-stress [WS]-sfx	pre-stress	[WS]-sfx
b.ii	Separable V	[S] [W]	shifting [WS]-sfx	shifting	[WS]-sfx

Findings are explained by my analysis as follows. First, all adjectival suffixes place stress on a stem syllable, rather than a suffixal syllable, due to high-ranked PK-DEP (B/A). Second, all outputs of 'dual' bases follow the General Adjectival Pattern (UNI-PK >> PK-DEP (B/A) >> ADJ-PK). Third, both types of suffixes differ only in outputs of single bases. More precisely, 'neutral' suffixes consistently respect the stress peak of the base, whereas 'shifting' suffixes stress the immediately preceding syllable, except when this has no stressed correspondent in the base: then the output is blocked. These possibilities are accounted for by the following sub-rankings:

(61) a. Shift: SFX-TO-PK, M-MAX >> PK-MAX
      b. Neutrality: PK-MAX >> ADJ-PK
      c. Blocking: SFX-TO-PK, PK-DEP >> M-MAX
      d. Pre-stressing: PK-DEP >> ADJ-PK

These sub-rankings are part of the integrated ranking (62), repeated from (49):

(62) UNI-PK, SFX-TO-PK, PK-DEP >> M-MAX >> PK-MAX >> ADJ-PK
      >> LEFTMOST

The following table ranks the constraints by pairs, and gives the relevant candidates:

(63) a.i   PK-DEP >> ADJ-PK   *wásbaar*   > *wasbáar*
      a.ii PK-DEP >> M-MAX   Ø   > *waarhéidig*
      b.i   SFX-TO-PK >> PK-MAX   *noodlóttig*   > *nóodlottig*
      b.ii SFX-TO-PK >> LEFTMOST *noodlóttig*   > Ø
      b.ii SFX-TO-PK >> M-MAX   Ø   > *schóonheidig*
      c.i   M-MAX >> PK-MAX   *noodlóttig*   > Ø
      c.ii M-MAX >> LEFTMOST   *noodlóttig*   > *nóodlottig*
      d.   PK-MAX >> ADJ-PK   *rángschikbaar* > *rangschíkbaar*
      e.   ADJ-PK >> LEFTMOST   *zelfrédzaam*   > *zélfredzaam*

The final section draws general conclusions, and also presents a detailed comparison of the correspondence model and the layered-lexicon models.

3.6 Conclusions

I have argued that the preservation of stem stress in affixed forms is an effect of output-to-output identity, rather than of the derivational (cyclic) preservation of stress. In this analysis a crucial role is played by a set of correspondence constraints requiring 'identity' between a derived word and its morphological base, with respect to the position of the stress peak. The assumption that only output forms (free stems) are involved in a stress correspondence relation explains a number of behavioral differences between stems and stem-based affixes: the fact that affixes 'reject' stress in favour of stems, the fact that stress shifts apply inside compounds (but not inside affixed words), and the fact that stem-based affixation (but not compounding) may be blocked by stems with non-final stress. A Lexical Phonology model is not able to relate these properties in the same way as the correspondence analysis does. To back up this point, both types of analyses will now be compared.

I will now build the theoretical argument for the 'parallel' morphology-phonology interface of OT over the 'serial' level-ordered interface of Lexical Phonology (*LP*). In LP, phonology and morphology communicate by interleaving morphological and phonological rules in a layered structure. For example, let us assume a two-layered model of the Dutch lexicon in which word-based shifting suffixes (-*ig, -elijk*) are adjoined at Level 1 (the level at which root-based affixation takes place), while 'stress-neutral' suffixes (-*baar, -loos*, etc.) adjoin at Level 2:

(64)   Morphology   Phonology

       Level-1 -*ig*, etc.   Stem stress rule
       Level-2 -*baar*, etc., compounding   Adjectival and compound stress rule

On the phonological side of the model are the following stress rules:

(65)   a. Stem stress rule (L1):   'Place the stress peak on the penult'[20]
        b. Compound stress rule (L2):   In $[X–Y]_{N,V}$ place the peak on [X].
        c. Adjectival stress rule (L2): In $[X–Y]_A$ place the peak on [Y].

This model provides immediate explanations for three observations. First, the preservation of stress peaks by neutral (L2) suffixes in both simplex and compound bases (e.g. *scháduw-loos, ráng-schik-baar*). Second, the distributional restriction that L2 suffixes must occur inside L1 suffixes (e.g. **schoon-heid-ig*). Third, the stress shift induced by L1 suffixes in simplex bases (e.g. *vijánd-ig*), which follows from the stem stress rule. (Recall that such cases are rare.)

However, this level-based model runs into two problems, one empirical and another conceptual. The empirical problem is that it fails to explain why word-based L1 suffixes may occur outside compounding (*nood-lótt-ig*). Whatever solution is adopted (such that the output of L2 can be fed back into L1) immediately runs into the problem that Level-2 suffixed words are, incorrectly, predicted to undergo L1 affixation as well (**schoon-heid-ig*). The conceptual problem is that

---

[20] This statement of the stem stress rule is grossly simplified, but it suffices for present purposes.

this model fails to relate two morphological blocking effects attested in word-based L1 suffixes: blocking after L2 suffixes and that after simplex bases that have initial stress (*menthol-ig*). The first blocking is attributed to level-ordering, while the second must be due to affixal stress conditions. The two-layered model thus fails to relate two properties of stress-shifting L1 suffixes which the peak correspondence analysis manages to unify: their pre-accenting condition on simplex bases, and their stress-shifting behaviour with compound bases.

Up to this point I have made no claims regarding 'genuine' Class-1 affixation. Dutch, like English and German, has a class of affixes (mostly of Romance origin) that prosodically integrate with their morphological bases, and with respect to stress behave fully like simplex words. For example, Class-1 affixes ending in a *superheavy syllable* (containing a long vowel plus consonant, Kager 1989, Trommelen and Zonneveld 1989) are regularly stressed:

(66) a. rad-éer   'erase'
      b. stabil-itéit 'stability'   (*stabíel* 'stable')

Such affixes, unlike word-based affixes, can take roots as their base (66a). If the base is an independently-occurring word, its stress properties are simply over-ruled (66b). This mode of affixation is clearly not stem-based, since its stress properties are completely different. The question is: what causes this difference between both types of affixation? Although I will not offer a complete analysis of Class-1 affixation, I will make suggestions for a model that does not use level-ordering but instead works on the assumption that Class-I affixes are elements adjoining to *roots*, rather than stems (Selkirk 1982). Whereas word-based affixes (67a) produce a nested, *recursive* stem-bracketing, root-based structures are non-recursive at the stem-level:

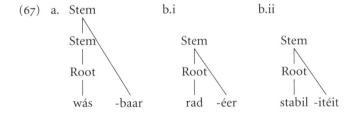

(67) a. Stem   b.i   b.ii

If stem-stress (67a) is indeed a correspondence effect between stems restricted to word-based affixation, as have argued in previous sections, then it is correctly predicted that root-based affixation (67b.i–ii) does not exhibit stress-preservation effects. The analytic problem which must be solved is: what forces affixation to the root even when a stem (an independent word) is available for affixation? To state it differently, how exclude a recursive stem analysis for *stabiliteit* (66b)? I attribute this to a constraint militating against self-embedded stem structure modelled after non-recursivity constraints on prosodic categories (Selkirk 1995,

Truckenbrodt 1995). This morphological non-recursivity constraint must be to some extent affix-specific:

(68) NonRec$_{Stem}$
No Stem (affixed by *-eer, -iteit*, etc.) immediately dominates a Stem.

When undominated, this constraint prohibits specified affixes from adjoining to a Stem-size base, which have no other choice but adjoin to a Root-size base. In the case of *stabiliteit* this goes at the expense of violating a constraint Stem-Max which requires that the Stem property of the base be respected.

(69) I: {stabiel, -iteit} B: [$_{Stem}$ stabíel]	NonRec$_{PWd}$-*iteit*	Stem-Max
a. [$_{Stem}$ [$_{Stem}$ stabíl] -iteit]	*!	
☞ b. [$_{Stem}$ stabil -itéit]		*!

No stem-size constituent [$_{Stem}$ stabíel] occurs in the optimal output analysis (69b). I assume that Output-to-Output correspondence constraints can only affect cases in which there is total morphological isomorphy between Base and Output (that is, both of the potentially related morphemes must be stems).

To wind up, let us return to the three general questions with respect to the phonology-morphology interface that were raised in the introduction. The first question, of how to model the transfer of phonological properties of simplex forms to complex forms, can now be answered as follows. Transfer involves violable constraints, enforcing identity between pairs of morphologically-related output forms. For example, the identity constraints that figured in the analysis of stem-based stress in Dutch enforce identity of stress peaks in a derived word and its base. Secondly, the question of which types of morphological domains are involved in transderivational relationships is answered as follows. Only properties of freely-occurring stems are carried over transderivationally, since identity constraints inherently involve pairs of output forms. Thirdly, it is predicted that 'derived' phonological properties of stems affect their potential for further affixation ('blocking'). This is due to parallelism, the interaction of phonological and morphological constraints in a single constraint hierarchy.

3.7 References

Alderete, J. (1995). 'Faithfulness to prosodic heads'. Paper presented at the Tilburg Conference on *The Derivational Residue in Phonology*, 5–6 October 1995.

Backhuys, K.-J. (1989). 'Adjectival compounds in Dutch.' In H. Bennis and A. van Kemenade (eds), *Linguistics in the Netherlands 1989*. Dordrecht, Foris, 1–10.

Beckman, J., L. Walsh Dickey, and S. Urbanczyk (eds) (1995), University of Massachusetts Occasional Papers in Linguistics 18: *Papers in Optimality Theory*. Amherst, MA: Graduate Linguistic Student Association.

Benua, L. (1995). 'Identity effects in morphological truncation.' In Beckman *et al.* (eds), 77–136.

Beurden, L. van (1987). 'Playing level with Dutch morphology.' In F. Beukema and P. Coopmans (eds), *Linguistics in the Netherlands 1987*, Dordrecht, Foris, 21–30.

Booij, G. E. (1995). *The Phonology of Dutch*. Oxford, Oxford University Press.

—— (1998). 'Phonological output constraints in morphology'. In W. Kehrein and R. Wiese (eds), *Phonology and Morphology of the Germanic Languages*. Tübingen, Max Niemeyer Verlag, 143–63.

Borowsky, T. (1993). 'On the word-level.' In S. Hargus and E. Kaisse (eds), *Studies in Lexical Phonology*. San Diego, Academic Press, 199–234.

Brame, M. (1974). 'The cycle in phonology', *Linguistic Inquiry* 5, 39–60.

Burzio, L. (1994). *Principles of English Stress*. Cambridge, Cambridge University Press.

Chomsky, N. and M. Halle (1968). *The Sound Pattern of English*. New York: Harper & Row.

Haas, W. de (1990). 'De notie "Stress Minimalizatie" en klemtoonaantrekking'. *Spektator* 20, 245–72.

Harris, J. (1983). *Syllable Structure and Stress in Spanish: A Nonlinear Analysis*. Cambridge, MA, MIT Press.

Inkelas, S. (1989). *Prosodic Constituency in the Lexicon*. Unpublished doctoral dissertation, Stanford University.

—— (1999), 'Exceptional stress attracting suffixes in Turkish: Representations vs. the grammar'. In R. Kager, H. van der Hulst, and W. Zonneveld (eds), 134–87.

Kager, R. (1989). *A Metrical Theory of Stress and Destressing in English and Dutch*. Dordrecht, Foris.

—— (1996). 'On affix allomorphy and syllable counting'. In U. Kleinhenz (ed.), *Interfaces in Phonology* [Studia Grammatica 41]. Berlin, Akademie Verlag, 155–70.

—— (forthcoming). 'Surface opacity of metrical structure in Optimality Theory'. To appear in B. Hermans and M. van Oostendorp (eds), *The Derivational Residue in Phonology*. Amsterdam and Philadelphia, John Benjamins.

—— and W. Zonneveld (1986). 'Schwa, syllables, and extrametricality in Dutch'. *Linguistic Review* 5, 197–221.

—— H. van der Hulst, and W. Zonneveld (eds) (1999), *The Prosody Morphology Interface*. Cambridge, Cambridge University Press.

Kenstowicz, M. (1995). 'Cyclic vs. non-cyclic constraint evaluation'. *Phonology* 12, 397–436.

Kiparsky, P. (1982). 'From cyclic phonology to Lexical Phonology.' In H. van der Hulst and N. Smith (eds), *The Structure of Phonological Representations, vol. 1*. Dordrecht, Foris, 131–75.

—— (1988). 'Vowel harmony as delinking'. Ms, Stanford University.

Kisseberth, C. W. (1970). 'On the functional unity of phonological rules'. *Linguistic Inquiry* 1, 291–306.

Koster, J. (1975). 'Dutch as an SOV language'. *Linguistic Analysis* 1, 111–36.

McCarthy, J. (1995). 'Extensions of faithfulness: Rotuman revisited'. Ms, U.Mass, Amherst.

—— and A. Prince (1993). *Prosodic Morphology I: Constraint Interaction and Satisfaction*. Ms, U.Mass, Amherst, and Rutgers University.

—— —— (1999). 'Faithfulness and identity in Prosodic Morphology'. In Kager, van der Hulst, and Zonneveld (eds), 218–309.

Mohanan, T. (1989). 'Syllable structure in Malayalam', *Linguistic Inquiry* 22, 315–44.

Orgun, O. C. (1994). 'Monotonic cyclicity and Optimality Theory.' In M. Gonzàlez (ed.) *Proceedings of the Northeastern Linguistic Society* 24, 461–74.

—— (1996). *Sign-Based Morphology and Phonology: With Special Attention to Optimality Theory.* PhD dissertation, University of California, Berkeley.

Prince, A. and P. Smolensky (1993). 'Optimality Theory: Constraint interaction in Generative Grammar'. Ms, Rutgers University and University of Colorado, Boulder.

Selkirk, E. (1982). *The Syntax of Words.* Cambridge, MA, MIT Press.

—— (1995). 'The prosodic structure of function words.' In Beckman *et al.* (eds), 439–69.

Strauss, S. (1983). 'Stress assignment as morphological adjustment in English'. *Linguistic Analysis* 11, 419–27.

Trommelen, M. and W. Zonneveld (1989). *Klemtoon en Metrische Fonologie.* Muiderberg, Coutinho.

—— —— (1990). 'Klemtoonaantrekking bestaat niet'. *Spektator* 19, 265–93.

Truckenbrodt, H. (1995). *Phonological Phrases: Their Relation to Syntax, Focus, and Prominence.* PhD dissertation, MIT.

Visch, E. (1989). *A Metrical Theory of Rhythmic Stress Phenomena.* Dordrecht, Foris.

4

Faithfulness and Prosodic Circumscription[1]

John J. McCarthy

4.1 Introduction

Faithfulness constraints have been an essential part of Optimality Theory (OT) since its inception (Prince and Smolensky 1991, 1993), but the form and function of faithfulness constraints have evolved. McCarthy and Prince (1995a) propose that faithfulness constraints are formalized within a Correspondence Theory of relations between representations. Correspondence Theory permits the statement of constraints demanding faithfulness to diverse linguistic entities, such as features, segments, and prosodic constituents. Furthermore, it generalizes faithfulness from its original role, comparing underlying and surface forms, to similar but distinct linguistic relations, such as comparing a stem to its reduplicative copy.

Here, I will focus on *prosodic* faithfulness constraints. Studies of lexical stress systems and the like provide abundant evidence for constraints requiring that underlying prosodic structure (such as metrical feet) be faithfully preserved on the surface. The goal of this chapter is to show how prosodic faithfulness constraints shed light on a different set of phenomena—those that have been attributed to *operational prosodic circumscription* (McCarthy and Prince 1990a).

Yidiɲ reduplication, as shown in (1), is a typical case:

[1] I am grateful to John Alderete, Katy Carlson, Paul de Lacy, Caroline Jones, Ania Łubowicz, Lisa Selkirk, Jennifer Smith, and two anonymous reviewers for comments on this article, and to audiences at the University of Maryland (especially Luigi Burzio, Diamandis Gafos, Linda Lombardi, and Paul Smolensky), at the University of Tromsø (especially Patrik Bye, Mike Hammond, René Kager, Ove Lorentz, and Curt Rice), at the 1997 LSA Summer Institute (especially Tivoli Majors and Eric Baković), and at a 1997 HIL course in Amsterdam (especially Harry van der Hulst, Helga Humbert, Claartje Levelt, Michael Redford, Nancy Ritter, Grażyna Rowicka, Norval Smith, and Laura Walsh Dickey). Thanks also to Armin Mester for his long-ago reactions to a draft of another paper that contained some of this material, to Alan Prince for many helpful remarks along the way, and especially to Laura Benua for extensive discussion of the theory and its applications. This work was supported by the National Science Foundation under grant SBR–9420424.

(1)   Yidiɲ Reduplication (Dixon 1977; Nash 1979; Marantz 1982; McCarthy
and Prince 1990a; Spring 1990)

Singular   Plural

[mula]$_{Ft}$ ri   mula-[mula]$_{Ft}$ ri   'initiated man'
[tʲukar]$_{Ft}$ pa   tʲukar-[tʲukar]$_{Ft}$ pa-n   'unsettled mind'

The choice of how much to reduplicate depends on the foot structure of the
base. In the second example, but not in the first, *r* is copied because it is part
of the base-initial foot. In the operational circumscription model of McCarthy
and Prince (1990a), this dependency is expressed by a succession of derivational
steps: the initial foot of the base is parsed out by a circumscription operation,
and then the parsed-out constituent, rather than the whole base, undergoes
reduplicative copying. Below, I argue that Yidiɲ is better analysed in terms of
prosodic faithfulness: the foot structure of the reduplicative copy must faithfully
match the foot structure of the base. Similar arguments are presented for other
phenomena attributed to operational circumscription.

An approach based on prosodic faithfulness enjoys several conceptual advantages over operational circumscription. Most importantly, prosodic faithfulness
constraints are independently motivated, but operational circumscription is not.
The results obtained here therefore support the reductionist goals of McCarthy
and Prince (1994b): to achieve a more explanatory theory of Prosodic Morphology (PM) by eliminating all PM-specific devices like circumscription, templates,
or reduplicative copying. There is also significant convergence with the results
of other work on PM within OT. A close parallel can be found in Itô, Kitagawa,
and Mester's (1996) study of the Japanese *zuuja-go* secret language, which
strongly resembles classic circumscriptional cases like Yidiɲ. Farther afield, these
results also converge with the proposal to eliminate other types of circumscription, such as infixation, discussed below in Section 4.2. The overall picture, then,
is one in which there is no role for operational prosodic circumscription in
linguistic theory, its descriptive effects having been usurped by mechanisms that
enjoy strong independent support.

The organization of this article is as follows. In Section 4.2, I introduce the
operational circumscription model of McCarthy and Prince (1990a). Section 4.3
presents and illustrates the premises of Optimality Theory and Correspondence
Theory that are essential to my proposal; and Sections 4.4 and 4.5 apply them
to two distinct types of circumscriptional phenomena. Section 4.6 concludes the
article with an overview of the results.

4.2 Operational Prosodic Circumscription

Operational prosodic circumscription is based on a factoring function $\Phi(C, E, B)$ which returns the prosodic constituent C standing at edge E of a base form

B (McCarthy and Prince 1990a).[2] The factors of *B* given by Φ can be notated as *B*:Φ for the part that satisfies the (*C*, *E*) conditions, called the kernel, and *B*/Φ for the residue, the complement of *B*:Φ within *B*. These terms are combined in the following equation, where '*' gives the relation (normally left- or right-concatenation) that holds between the factors:

(2)   Factoring of *B* by Φ
       $B = B{:}\Phi \ * \ B/\Phi$

The key idea of operational circumscription is that a morphological operation can target one of the factors in (2) instead of *B* as a whole. If the kernel, the *B*:Φ factor, is the target of the morphological operation, then we have *positive prosodic circumscription*. If the residue, the *B*/Φ factor, is targeted, then we have *negative prosodic circumscription*.

   The Yidiɲ example in (1) is a typical case of positive prosodic circumscription. The foot standing at the left edge of *B* is the factor returned by $\Phi(Ft, Left, B)$. This foot is subject to a morphological operation of reduplicative copying, so the foot structure of the base determines whether a consonant is copied at the juncture of the second and third syllables.

   In general, this means that the result of applying a morphological operation to *B* under positive prosodic circumscription is the result of applying that operation to just the kernel:

(3)   Definition of Operation Applying under Positive Prosodic Circumscription
       $O{:}\Phi(B) = O(B{:}\Phi) \ * \ B/\Phi$

Paraphrastically, to apply *O* to *B* under positive prosodic circumscription is to apply *O* to the kernel, *B*:Φ, concatenating the result with *B*/Φ in the same way ('*') that *B*:Φ concatenates with the residue *B*/Φ in the base *B*. In effect, the relation '*' puts the pieces back together, combining the transformed *B*:Φ factor with the intact *B*/Φ factor. The following derivations show how the system plays out in Yidiɲ, letting *O*:Φ stand for the morphological operation of reduplication applied under positive prosodic circumscription:

(4)   Application of positive prosodic circumscription to Yidiɲ

   a.   i. $O{:}\Phi([\text{múla}]_{Ft}\ ri)$ $= O([\text{múla}]_{Ft}\ ri{:}\Phi) \ * \ [\text{múla}]_{Ft}\ ri/\Phi$
        ii. $= O([\text{múla}]_{Ft}) \ * \ ri$
        iii. $= [\text{múla}]_{Ft}\ [\text{múla}]_{Ft} \ * \ ri$
        iv. $= [\text{múla}]_{Ft}\ [\text{múla}]_{Ft}\ ri$

[2] Other work on operational circumscription includes Broselow and McCarthy (1983), Crowhurst (1994), Itô, Kitagawa, and Mester (1992), Lombardi and McCarthy (1991), McCarthy and Prince (1990a), and Mester (1990). For a comprehensive list of references see McCarthy and Prince (1995b).

  b.   i. O:Φ([tʲúkar]_Ft pan) = O([tʲúkar]_Ft pan:Φ) * [tʲúkar]_Ft pan/Φ
      ii.   = O([tʲúkar]_Ft) * pan
      iii.   = [tʲúkar]_Ft [tʲúkar]_Ft * pan
      iv.   = [tʲúkar]_Ft [tʲúkar]_Ft pan

Step (i) shows the basic factoring, with the terms simplified in step (ii). At step
(iii), the copy operation *O* has applied to the Φ-delimited factor, and the terms
are reassembled in step (iv).

The main feature of positive prosodic circumscription, then, is that a morphological operation is applied to some prosodic constituent within a base instead
of being applied to the whole base. In this way the morphological operation can
show sensitivity to the prosodic structure of its input. Such sensitivity is not
typical of reduplication (Moravcsik 1978; Marantz 1982); compare Lardil *parel-*
pareli, with copying of the *l* even though it is not part of the initial foot. According to McCarthy and Prince (1990a), Yidiɲ and Lardil differ precisely on this
dimension: Yidiɲ reduplicates modulo foot circumscription, while Lardil
reduplicates without the intervention of circumscription.

In Section 4.4, I discuss cases like Yidiɲ that come under the rubric of *picking*
prosodic circumscription.[3] In picking mode, positive prosodic circumscription
picks out a prosodic constituent C, such as a foot, that is already present in the
basic form. I will argue that a superior account of these systems is available in
an Optimality-theoretic grammar that includes prosodic faithfulness constraints
referring to C. These constraints require that certain properties of C be conserved in related forms, leading to a variety of effects that have been previously
identified with the prosodic circumscription mechanism operating in its picking
mode.

In Section 4.5, I analyse an instance of *parsing* prosodic circumscription: the
Arabic broken plural. In operational terms, parsing-mode prosodic circumscription imposes an analysis in terms of a constituent C when no such constituent
is already available, because the form being analysed lacks one (either entirely
or at the designated edge). For example, in the McCarthy and Prince (1990a)
analysis of Arabic, circumscription parses out an initial trochaic foot from any
stem, even a basically iambic one like *jaziir(+at)*. The result is that the prosodic
structure of the original form is disregarded, even to the point of splitting a
syllable: *B*:Φ = *jazi*, *B*/Φ = *ir*.

Here I will reject this treatment entirely, showing that a radically different
account of these systems is available, based on a proper understanding of faithfulness to moras and autosegmental associations. Details differ, but the core of
this proposal recalls some of the insights obtained by Samek-Lodovici (1992,
1993) in analysing Choctaw. Indeed, the account given here for Arabic generalizes straightforwardly to the Choctaw material.

---

[3] The parsing/picking classification and terminology come from McCarthy and Prince (1991).

In the end, these developments lead to the elimination of a special mechanism for *positive* prosodic circumscription.[4] This follows and extends a result already securely established in the OT literature: the elimination of any special mechanism for *negative* prosodic circumscription (Prince and Smolensky 1991, 1993; McCarthy and Prince 1993ab). In negative prosodic circumscription, a morphological operation targets the residue B/Φ rather than the kernel $B{:}\Phi$. Thus, negative prosodic circumscription is a kind of extrametricality: a prosodic constituent at some edge is parsed out and the remainder of the word counts as the base for some morphological (or phonological) operation.[5]

Negative prosodic circumscription is often invoked to deal with infixation phenomena like that in Timugon Murut (5):

(5) Infixation in Timugon Murut (Prentice 1971; McCarthy and Prince 1993a, b)

    a. Data

bulud	bu-bulud	'hill'/'ridge'
limo	li-limo	'five'/'about five'
ulampoy	u-la-lampoy	no gloss
abalan	a-ba-balan	'bathes'/'often bathes'
ompodon	om-po-podon	'flatter'/'always flatter'

    b. Circumscriptional Analysis

        Φ(Onsetless Syllable, Left), O = Prefix σ_μ (reduplicative prefix)

$$
\begin{aligned}
O/\Phi(\text{ompodon}) &= O(\text{ompodon}/\Phi) * \text{ompodon}{:}\Phi \\
&= O(\text{podon}) * \text{om} \\
&= \text{popodon} * \text{om} \\
&= \text{ompopodon}
\end{aligned}
$$

The kernel of circumscription is an initial onsetless syllable, if any. It is stripped away, and the reduplicative morpheme is a simple prefix to the residue. From this perspective, infixes are just ordinary prefixes (or suffixes) attached to a base that has been modified by prior negative circumscription.

Though it is surely correct to regard this infix as basically a prefix, the implementation of this idea in circumscriptional terms is deeply flawed. One problem is that the onsetless syllable must be regarded as a type of prosodic constituent so it can be called on as an argument of Φ. Another, more serious problem is

---

  [4] A third type of positive prosodic circumscription is not considered here because it has already been addressed in the OT literature. This is prosodic subcategorization, where a morpheme is prefixed or suffixed to a prosodic constituent (typically the foot, as in Ulwa and Samoan). These subcategorizational effects are attributed to alignment constraints by McCarthy and Prince (1993a: Ch. 7, 1993b), building on Broselow and McCarthy (1983).

  [5] McCarthy and Prince (1990a) also discuss a third type of prosodic circumscription, in which the Φ function is used to select only those bases meeting a particular prosodic criterion. See Kager (1996) and Hargus and Tuttle (1997) for recent discussion from an OT perspective.

that only *reduplicative* infixes are located after an initial onsetless syllable (McCarthy and Prince 1993a, b). Circumscription entirely divorces the nature of Φ from the nature of the morphological operation *O*, and so it cannot explain observed correlations between them. These observations reveal significant failures of the theory of negative circumscription as applied to infixation. They support the investigation of alternatives within OT.

Two key insights underlie the OT approach to infixation developed by Prince and Smolensky and extended by McCarthy and Prince. One, inherited from the circumscriptional treatment, is the idea that infixes are inherently prefixes (or suffixes) which have been minimally displaced from peripheral position by some outside force. Formally, this means that there are constraints of the Alignment family demanding initial (resp. final) placement of prefixes (resp. suffixes). The other factor, the 'outside force' demanding non-peripheral affixation, is a higher-ranking constraint of the syllabic markedness family, such as ONSET (Itô 1989). The following ranking argument shows the crucial constraint interaction.

(6) ONSET >> ALIGN-RED in Timugon Murut		
/RED+ulampoy/	ONSET	ALIGN-RED
a. *u*-u-lam-poy	** !	
☞ b. u-la-lam-poy	*	u

This ranking asserts that the reduplicative affix is located as far to the left as possible (ALIGN-RED), subject to the requirement that it contribute no onsetless syllables (ONSET).

Obviously, no special PM-specific mechanism of negative circumscription is necessary in such cases. The analysis of Timugon Murut is constructed out of the very stuff of phonological and morphological theory: constraints on syllabic markedness, which are independently needed for language typology; constraints asserting prefixality of these affixes, which any analysis requires in some form or other; and the ranking between the two constraint types, which derives from the notion of factorial typology, central to OT. Furthermore, the role of syllable markedness in forcing infixation provides an explanation for why only *reduplicative* infixes are placed after an initial onsetless syllable (McCarthy and Prince 1993a). Operational circumscription offers no illumination of this point, nor can it hope to, since it does nothing more than stipulate the locus of infixation independent of any properties of the form of the infix itself.

For these and other reasons, the mechanism of negative circumscription no longer has a place in current thinking about Prosodic Morphology or prosody generally.[6] Positive circumscription must stand or fall on its own merits; no

---

[6] In prosody generally, the notion of extrametricality, which is another type of negative circumscription, has been much transformed in OT works like Prince and Smolensky (1993) and Hung (1994).

crutch of negative circumscription is available to prop it up. Here I will argue that positive circumscription should be eliminated from linguistic theory as well. In its place, the analyses here call on independently motivated constraints demanding faithfulness to prosodic structure or prosodic roles. This new view brings out a range of connections and explanations that are superior to those of the operational model, with its (ultimately misconceived) positive/negative symmetry.

4.3 Prosodic Faithfulness

In Optimality Theory (Prince and Smolensky 1991, 1993), each grammar is a ranking of the constraints of Universal Grammar. These include the markedness constraints, which militate against structural elaboration of various kinds, and the antagonistic faithfulness constraints, which demand identity of linguistically related forms.

Faithfulness constraints are formulated under Correspondence Theory (McCarthy and Prince 1993a, 1995a), which posits the following general relation between linguistic forms:

(7) Correspondence
     Given two linguistic forms S_1 and S_2 standing to one another as input and output, base and reduplicant, etc., correspondence is a relation $\Re$ between any subset of elements of S_1 and S_2. Any element α of S_1 and any element β of S_2 are correspondents of one another if $\alpha \Re \beta$.

Each candidate S_2 comes equipped with a correspondence relation which shows how it is the same as or different from S_1. When full explicitness is necessary in a particular example, the correspondence relation is shown by coindexation of correspondent elements in S_1 and S_2.

In addition to this very general idea, common to all implementations of Correspondence Theory, I also adopt certain additional assumptions, as specific answers to the following questions:

 (i) What elements of S_1 and S_2 are related by $\Re$?
 (ii) What kinds of linguistic forms stand in correspondence with one another? That is, how are S_1 and S_2 related independently of $\Re$?
(iii) What are the faithfulness constraints?

I will take each of these questions in turn. The responses I give are not intended to be exhaustive but rather to supply a working framework that is sufficient for present purposes.

What elements of S_1 and S_2 are related by $\Re$?
If an element stands in correspondence, then it may receive faithful treatment independent of any other elements of the representation. At a minimum, then, correspondence is a relation between segments. Whether or not features stand

in correspondence is a subject of current discussion, irrelevant to our concerns here. Of the various prosodic units, the clearest case can be made for correspondence between moras, to account for the broad class of compensatory lengthening phenomena. Below (Section 4.5) I will also present evidence for moraic correspondence based on the analysis of the parsing type of prosodic circumscription. On the other hand, there appears to be no justification for setting up direct correspondence relations among feet or syllables. Instead, faithfulness to feet and perhaps syllables[7] is indirect, mediated by the edge or head segments that make up those constituents. In this implementation of correspondence, then, moras are reified as segment-like entities, but other aspects of prosodic structure are not.

What kinds of linguistic forms are related by correspondence?
Correspondence Theory was originally conceived as a relation between the base and its reduplicative copy, called the reduplicant (McCarthy and Prince 1993a). The many parallels between exactness of base-reduplicant (B-R) matching and faithfulness of input-output matching led McCarthy and Prince (1995a) to extend correspondence to the familiar input-output (I-O) faithfulness relation. Benua (1995, 1997) argues that morphologically-related output forms must also stand in a transderivational correspondence relation (dubbed O-O, for output-output), to account for phenomena that have previously been attributed to mechanisms like the cycle or strata.[8] A given candidate form, then, may simultaneously have several distinct correspondence relations—with its underlying input, with some related base word, and between reduplicated parts. Separate, and therefore separately rankable, faithfulness constraints on each correspondence relation negotiate the demands of faithfulness in the I-O, B-R, and O-O dimensions, which may compete with each other and with markedness constraints.

What are the faithfulness constraints?
Various constraints of Universal Grammar demand completeness of correspondence or identity of correspondent elements under various conditions. Among them are the anti-deletion faithfulness constraint MAX-*seg* and its symmetric anti-epenthesis counterpart DEP-*seg*.

---

[7] Syllabic faithfulness presents significant difficulties. If there are input-output syllabic faithfulness constraints, then some languages would be expected to contrast monomorphemic *pa.ta* with *pat.a*, by ranking syllabic faithfulness above ONSET and NO-CODA. Notoriously, such contrasts are never observed. Likewise, a base-reduplicant syllabic faithfulness constraint, through domination of MAX$_{BR}$, would be capable of enforcing syllable-copying reduplication, a pattern that is also unknown (Moravcsik 1978; Marantz 1982; McCarthy and Prince 1986, 1990a). On the other hand, syllabic faithfulness is surely necessary in output-output relations, to account for such well-known contrasts as *night-rate/nitrate* or *lightening /lightning*. Clearly, there is an interesting research problem here.

[8] For further discussion of O-O correspondence and related approaches, see Archangeli (1996), Buckley (to appear), Burzio (1994a, b, 1996, 1997), Bybee (1985), Crosswhite (1996), Kager (to appear), Kenstowicz (1996), Kraska-Szlenk (1995), Orgun (1994, 1996), and Pater (1995).

(8) MAX-*seg*

Every segment in S_1 has a correspondent in S_2. (S_1 and S_2 stand to one another as in (7) above.)

(9) DEP-*seg*

Every segment in S_2 has a correspondent in S_1.

Other constraints militate against segment coalescence or splitting, metathesis, and featural change (McCarthy and Prince 1995a). Names of particular constraints also include the correspondence relation involved, so MAX-seg_{IO} and MAX-seg_{OO} are distinguished.

Of particular importance in the current context are *prosodic* faithfulness constraints. Three types of prosodic faithfulness constraints will be called upon in the course of this work:

- constraints demanding the conservation of autosegmental association.
- constraints demanding conservation of prosodic constituents *per se*
- constraints demanding faithfulness to the edges or heads of prosodic constituents

Constraints demanding the conservation of autosegmental association.
There is a faithfulness cost to altering autosegmental associations by spreading or delinking. Universal Grammar must therefore include faithfulness constraints which have the effect of conserving autosegmental association. There are thus constraints militating against spreading and delinking, with separate constraints for each pair of associated autosegmental tiers. (For instance, the constraint against tone spreading is different from the constraint against place spreading.) From these considerations, we obtain two families of constraints that, respectively, prohibit gain and loss of autosegmental associations:

(10) NO-SPREAD(τ, ς)

Let τ_i and ς_j stand for elements on distinct autosegmental tiers in two related phonological representations S_1 and S_2, where

τ_1 and $\varsigma_1 \in S_1$,
τ_2 and $\varsigma_2 \in S_2$,
$\tau_1 \Re \tau_2$, and
$\varsigma_1 \Re \varsigma_2$,
if τ_2 is associated with ς_2,
then τ_1 is associated with ς_1.

(11) NO-DELINK(τ, ς)

Let τ_i and ς_j stand for elements on distinct autosegmental tiers in two related phonological representations S_1 and S_2, where

τ_1 and $\varsigma_1 \in S_1$,
τ_2 and $\varsigma_2 \in S_2$,

$\tau_{_1}\Re\tau_{_2}$, and
$\varsigma_{_1}\Re\varsigma_{_2}$,
if $\tau_{_1}$ is associated with $\varsigma_{_1}$,
then $\tau_{_2}$ is associated with $\varsigma_{_2}$.

The various antecedent conditions limit the relevance of these constraints to situations where τ and ς are present in both $S_{_1}$ and $S_{_2}$. If either τ or ς is added or inserted, I assume, the concomitant changes in association lines do not transgress these constraints. It is an empirical question whether this detail of formulation is correct, but it is a reasonable first guess.

Some relevant examples: the (σ, *tone*) versions of both these constraints are violated in the Kikuyu tone shift process (Clements and Ford 1979); the ([aspirated], *seg*) versions of both are violated in forms undergoing Grassmann's Law in Sanskrit (Whitney 1924). Below, in Section 4.5, which deals with prosodic circumscription of the parsing variety, we will see a role for the (μ, *seg*) versions.

Constraints demanding conservation of prosodic constituents per se.
As I noted above, phenomena like compensatory lengthening show that moras are subject to faithfulness requirements independent of the segments that sponsor them. This fact justifies including moras in the scope of the correspondence relation $\Re$, as is necessary for well-definition of the constraints MAX-μ and DEP-μ:

(12)   MAX-μ
Every mora in $S_{_1}$ has a correspondent in $S_{_2}$.

(13)   DEP-μ
Every mora in $S_{_2}$ has a correspondent in $S_{_1}$.

These constraints will be important in Section 4.5, when parsing-mode circumscription is discussed.

Constraints demanding faithfulness to the edges or heads of prosodic constituents.
There is nothing like compensatory lengthening at foot level. That is, there are no effects of conservation of feet independent of the segments that make them up. Yet there are surely foot-faithfulness constraints, as the existence of lexical stress systems and other phenomena prove.[9] The key to the difference is this: foot faithfulness is never direct; it is always mediated by segments bearing head or edge roles in the foot.[10]

Rather than MAX and DEP, then, constraints of the Anchoring family (successors to Alignment) are responsible for foot faithfulness. Details of formalization

---

[9] Works discussing prosodic faithfulness include Alderete (1996, to appear), Beckman (1997), Burzio (1994ab), Bye (1996), Inkelas (1999), Itô, Kitagawa, and Mester (1996), Kenstowicz (1994, 1996), McCarthy (1996), and Pater (1995).

[10] In this respect, foot faithfulness is analogous to featural faithfulness in the IDENT sense rather than the MAX sense. (On this distinction, see McCarthy and Prince (1995a).)

are treated in Appendix (4.7); for present purposes, the following will suffice:

(14)   ANCHOR-POS (Foot, Foot, P)
         where P is one of {Initial, Final, Head}
             If ς_1, Foot$_1$ ∈ S$_1$,
                   ς_2, Foot$_2$ ∈ S$_2$,
                   $\varsigma_1\Re\varsigma_2$, and
                   ς_1 stands in position P of Foot$_1$,
             then ς_2 stands in position P of Foot$_2$.

By anchoring foot to foot, this constraint demands that the S$_1$→S$_2$ mapping conserve the prosodic position—foot-initial, foot-final, or foot-head—of any corresponding segment.

Below, I argue that ANCHOR-POS(Ft, Ft, Initial/Final/Head) goes far toward eliminating the need for operational prosodic circumscription. For example, the pattern of reduplication in Yidiɲ (1) is determined by undominated ANCHOR-POS$_{BR}$(Ft, Ft, F)—any foot-final segment in the reduplicative base must correspond to a foot-final segment in the reduplicative copy. This constraint makes exactly the right distinction: ANCHOR-POS$_{BR}$(Ft, Ft, F) is satisfied by [mula$_4$]$_{Ft}$-[mula$_4$]$_{Ft}$ ri but not by the failed candidate *[mula$_4$r$_5$]$_{Ft}$-[mula$_4$]$_{Ft}$ ri. This is clearly a reasonable idea: similarity between base and reduplicant is improved if they have similar foot structure. It is also a simple idea: it is nothing more than a straightforward application of familiar Alignment notions combined with equally familiar faithfulness notions. And it is an idea with ample independent support, since such constraints are also required to enforce faithfulness to lexical prosody in the input→output mapping (Alderete 1996; Bye 1996; Inkelas, to appear; Itô, Kitagawa, and Mester 1996; McCarthy 1996; Pater 1995).[11] Yet, as I will now show, this idea is sufficient to account for a range of prosodic circumscription phenomena of the picking type.

4.4 Prosodic Circumscription as Prosodic Anchoring

Operational prosodic circumscription in the picking mode locates a prosodic constituent (typically a foot) at one edge of a form and then performs a morphological operation on it, such as reduplication or mapping to a template. Here, I will examine several systems that have been analysed in these terms.

---

[11] The idea that prosodic structure may be present in underlying representations is a frequent cause of anxiety, because it seems to run afoul of the assumption in underspecification theory that only unpredictable information can be present lexically. This assumption, though, plays no role in OT, which instead hypothesizes richness of the base (Prince and Smolensky 1993): there are no language-particular restrictions on underlying forms. (Richness of the base is essential to OT's solution for conspiracies or the duplication problem (Kisseberth 1970; Kenstowicz and Kisseberth 1977).) The predictability of prosodic structure in some language is an indication of low-ranking prosodic faithfulness constraints, not underspecification.

I will show that empirically equivalent and explanatorily superior accounts can be obtained by calling on prosodic faithfulness constraints of the form ANCHOR-POS(Ft, Ft, Initial/Final/Head), as proposed in Section 4.3. The cases I discuss include reduplication in Yidiɲ and mapping to a template in Rotuman and Cupeño. (Yet another case, reduplication in Makassarese, is addressed in McCarthy and Prince (1994a, b) and McCarthy (1997).[12] I conclude this section by summing up the results and arguing that prosodic faithfulness theory constitutes a conceptual advance over operational circumscription theory.

The most straightforward example comes from reduplication in the Australian language Yidiɲ. Recall the following contrast, which shows how foot structure plays a role in determining the well-formedness of the Yidiɲ reduplicant:

(15) Yidiɲ reduplication
    a. [mula₄]-[mula₄]ri   vs. *[mular₅]-[mula₄]ri
    b. [tʲukar₅]-[tʲukar₅]pa-n vs. *[tʲuka₄]-[tʲukar₅]pa-n

In (a), the initial foot of the base is *mula*, and the reduplicant consists of a copy of that foot. Likewise, in (b) the foot *tʲukar* is copied. No condition on the reduplicant alone can account for this distinction; rather, it is a matter of matching the foot structure of the reduplicant with the foot structure of the base.

The operative high-ranking constraint here is ANCHOR-POS$_{BR}$(Ft, Ft, Final), which requires that the base→reduplicant mapping preserve a segment's status as foot-final. This matching of prosodic structures is obtained even at the expense of more complete reduplication of the base's segments, as the following ranking argument proves:

(16) Ranking Argument: ANCHOR-POS$_{BR}$(Ft, Ft, Final) >> MAX-*seg*$_{BR}$		
Candidates	ANCHOR-POS$_{BR}$(Ft, Ft, F)	MAX-*seg*$_{BR}$
☞ a. [mula₄]-[mula₄]ri		**
b. [mular₅]-[mula₄]ri	* !	*

This candidate-comparison shows that prosodic and segmental faithfulness are both relevant factors in base-reduplicant matching—though only segmental faithfulness is widely recognized as such. Candidate (b) achieves more complete copying than (a) does, but it is not optimal, because the foot-to-foot match is imperfect. Here, prosodic faithfulness takes precedence, through ranking, over segmental faithfulness. A special circumscription operation plays no role; rather, the circumscriptional effect is simply a matter of base-reduplicant identity.

---

[12] Other studies of circumscriptional phenomena within OT include Avery and Lamontagne (1995), Benua (1995), Crowhurst (1997), de Lacy (1996), Downing (1998a, b), Hung (1992), Itô, Kitagawa, and Mester (1996), Kager (1996), McCarthy (1996), Prince and Smolensky (1991, 1993), and Samek-Lodovici (1992, 1993).

An important detail remains: what about the candidate [múla]ri-[múla]ri, which fully satisfies both ANCHOR-POS$_{BR}$(Ft, Ft, F) and MAX-*seg* $_{BR}$? The ill-formedness of this candidate is a typical templatic effect, independent of circumscription proper: [múla]ri- is too big as a reduplicant, since Yidiɲ limits the reduplicant to a single foot, which is the minimal word of Yidiɲ. Generalized Template Theory (GTT) (McCarthy and Prince 1994a, b, 1999; Urbanczyk 1995, 1996a, b; Itô, Kitagawa, and Mester 1996; Gafos 1996, 1998; Downing 1998a, b, 1999; Spaelti 1997) asserts that prosodic-morphological templates are not free-standing constraints or entities,[13] but rather are consequences of particular rankings of constraints that are independently motivated. (This conception of templates also furthers the self-annihilatory goal of Prosodic Morphology mentioned in Section 4.1.) The Yidiɲ minimal-word template can be analysed in the same way as Diyari is handled by McCarthy and Prince (1994a, b). The minimal word is the most harmonic type of prosodic word: it contains a foot which is properly aligned at both edges and it contains no stray syllables. Thus, through domination of MAX-*seg* $_{BR}$, constraints on foot alignment and syllable parsing ensure the disyllabicity of the Yidiɲ reduplicant and rule out candidates like [múla]ri-[múla]ri.

Yidiɲ is perhaps the best-known example of operational circumscription, and it yields readily to reanalysis in terms of Anchoring. Two other cases of operational positive circumscription involve mapping *B*:Φ to a template: the formation of the 'incomplete phase' (a kind of morphological category) in Rotuman and the habilitative in Cupeño. The Rotuman phenomenon is exemplified in (17):

(17)   Phase in Rotuman (Churchward 1940)
        Complete   Incomplete
    a. Deletion
        to.ki.ri   to.kir   'to roll'
        ti.ʔu   tiʔ   'big'
        mo.se   mös   'to sleep'

    b. Metathesis
        se.se.va   se.seav   'erroneous'
        pu.re   puer   'to rule'
        pa.ro.fi.ta pa.ro.fiat 'prophet'

    c. Diphthong formation
        pu.pu.i   pu.pui   'floor'
        ke.u   keu   'to push'
        jo.se.u.a   jo.se.ua   'Joshua'

---

[13] The impossibility of positing a templatic morpheme consisting of a free-standing foot follows from the assumption made in Section 4.3 that feet (and syllables) do not stand in correspondence, so foot-faithfulness is always mediated by segments. An underlying foot with no segments is invisible to the faithfulness theory, and so by the logic of Stampean occultation (Prince and Smolensky 1993) it plays no useful role in the lexicon. Effectively, it does not exist.

  d. No formal distinction of phase
     rī   rī   'house'
     si.kā   si.kā   'cigar'

In (a), the incomplete phase is formed by dropping the final vowel, leaving a final heavy CVC syllable. (Syllable boundaries are indicated by '.'.) In (b), the result is also a final heavy syllable, achieved in this case by metathesizing the final CV sequence to yield a diphthongal CVVC syllable. Case (c) shows how a final heterosyllabic V.V sequence is syllabified as tautosyllabic in the incomplete phase, producing a final CVV syllable. Finally, case (d) consists of words with final long vowels, which do not alternate in phase. The choice of how to form the incomplete phase is fully determined by the phonological properties of the complete phase; the relevant factors include whether the complete phase ends in VCV or VV, the quality of the vowels involved, and other considerations (Churchward 1940; McCarthy 1996).

  Stress in Rotuman falls on the penultimate mora, so stress is on the penultimate syllable in *pa.ro.fi.ta* and on the final heavy syllable in *pa.ro.fiat*. The foot type in Rotuman is thus the moraic trochee (Hayes 1987; McCarthy and Prince 1986), which consists of exactly two moras, grouped into two light syllables or a single heavy syllable: pa.ro.[fi.ta]$_{Ft}$, pa.ro.[fiat]$_{Ft}$. Indeed, a consistent finding is that incomplete-phase words end in a monosyllabic foot—a single heavy syllable parsed as a bimoraic trochee. This generalization cross-cuts the differences among (17a–d).

  Schematically, the foot structure of corresponding complete and incomplete phase forms is this:

(18)   Complete   Incomplete
     a. to.[kí.ri]   to.[kír]
        [tí.ʔu]   [tíʔ]

     b. se.[sé.va]   se.[séav]
        [pú.re]   [púer]
        pu.[pú.i]   pu.[púi]
        [ké.u]   [kéu]

     d. [rí]   [rí]
        si.[ká]   si.[ká]

The relevance of prosodic circumscription to Rotuman is now apparent. There is a templatic requirement on the incomplete phase: it must end in a monosyllabic foot (i.e. a heavy syllable).[14] But this template is imposed only on the seg

---

[14] Under GTT, the requirement that the Rotuman incomplete phase end in a monosyllabic foot must be understood in terms of some independently necessary constraint of Universal Grammar. There are two likely possibilities. One is that the templatic requirement of Rotuman is enforced by the same constraint that is responsible for neutralization of weight distinctions word-finally in many

ments belonging to the corresponding (usually disyllabic) foot of the complete phase. Syllables outside that foot are not involved in the phase alternation.

In terms of the operational theory of circumscription in McCarthy and Prince (1990a), this phenomenon requires circumscription of the final foot by $\Phi(Ft, Right)$ followed by an operation O mapping $B{:}\Phi$ onto a monosyllabic foot template:

(19)   Operational circumscription applied to Rotuman

   i. $O{:}\Phi(\text{to}[\text{kíri}]_{Ft})$ $= O(\text{to}[\text{kíri}]_{Ft}{:}\Phi) \,^{*}\, \text{to}[\text{kíri}]_{Ft}/\Phi$

   ii. $= O([\text{kíri}]_{Ft}) \,^{*}\, \text{to}$

   iii. $= [\text{kír}]_{Ft} \,^{*}\, \text{to}$

   iv. $= \text{to}.[\text{kír}]_{Ft}$

At step (iii), the circumscribed foot is mapped onto a heavy-syllable template, in this case transforming it into a CVC syllable by deleting the final vowel. In other cases there is metathesis, formation of a diphthong, and so on, as was noted above.

These observations readily lend themselves to an analysis in terms of prosodic faithfulness. The foot of the incomplete phase is a transformed version of the foot in the corresponding complete phase, reliably retaining some properties of that foot (its left edge and head) and often altering others (its right edge). Hence, the constraints ANCHOR-POS(Ft, Ft, Initial) and ANCHOR-POS(Ft, Ft, Head) are undominated. In contrast, the constraint ANCHOR-POS(Ft, Ft, Final) is low-ranking; it is violated systematically in deleting and metathesizing cases like (18a, b). These constraints hold over the O-O correspondence relation, the transderivational correspondence relation between the output form of the complete phase and the output form of the incomplete phase, in accordance with the general program of Benua (1995 1997).[15] Similarity in foot structure between the complete phase and the incomplete phase is a consequence of obedience to these constraints.

The effects of the high-ranking ANCHOR-POS constraints are most apparent in candidates like the following:

(20)   Some Plausible But Failed Incomplete Phase Candidates
    a. Complete Phase   b. Incomplete Phase
       $[\text{r}_1\text{á}_2.\text{k}_3\text{o}_4]$ $[\text{r}_1\text{á}_2\text{k}_3]$ vs. failed candidate $^{*}\text{r}_1\text{a}_2.[\text{ó}_4\text{k}_3]$
       he.$[\text{l}_3\text{é}_4.?_5\text{u}_6]$ he.$[\text{l}_3\text{é}_4?_5]$ vs. failed candidate *he.$\text{l}_3\text{e}_4.[\text{ú}_6?_5]$

Were it not for ANCHOR-POS, the failed candidates in (b) would be more harmonic than the actual output forms. The reason—all other constraints are, for independent reasons discussed in McCarthy (1996), ranked in a way that favours the failed candidates.

---

languages (McCarthy 1996). Another is a constraint demanding word-final stress—also a common typological option (Pater 1996).

[15] Segmental evidence for the O-O relation in Rotuman is presented by McCarthy (1996).

- The form he.[lé?] violates Max-*seg* and obeys Onset, while *he.le.[ú?] obeys Max-*seg* and violates Onset. But we can establish independently that Max-*seg* >> Onset because onsetless syllables are abundantly attested in Rotuman.[16]
- The form he.[lé?] also obeys Linearity (no metathesis), while *he.le.[ú?] violates Linearity. But we can show independently that Max-*seg* >> Linearity because metathesis is preferred to deletion in incomplete-phase formation. Deletion occurs only when metathesis is impossible because the resulting diphthong would violate a congeries of undominated constraints requiring that diphthongs in closed syllables be light and that light diphthongs rise in sonority.[17]

Therefore we cannot appeal to Linearity or Onset to explain the ill-formedness of *he.le.[ú?].

Rather, what distinguishes the failed candidate *he.le.[ú?] from the actual output he.[lé?] is the O-O prosodic faithfulness Anchor-Pos$_{OO}$:

(21) Anchor-Pos$_{OO}$(Ft, Ft, Initial) >> Max-*seg*$_{OO}$		
com. ph. = he.[l$_3$é$_4$.?$_5$u$_6$]	Anchor-Pos$_{OO}$(Ft, Ft, Initial)	Max-*seg*$_{OO}$
☞ a. he.[l$_3$é$_4$?$_5$]		*
b. he.l$_3$e$_4$.[ú$_6$?$_5$]	* !	

The incomplete phase form in (21a) is more faithful to the prosody of the corresponding complete phase than its competitor in (21b) is, because in (21a) the foot-initial segments of the complete phase and incomplete phase match.[18]

The ranking in (21) is the core of the circumscriptional effect in Rotuman. Like the Yidiɲ ranking in (16), which it closely resembles, (21) prizes prosodic similarity over segmental similarity. No special mechanism of circumscription is needed since the matching of foot structure is obtained by faithfulness constraints no different in kind from those that enforce segmental similarity between the phases.

Another case of circumscription with template-mapping comes from the formation of the habilitative verb in the Uto-Aztecan language Cupeño. When the verb root is consonant-final, the habilitative is constructed by a complex pattern of reduplication.[19]

---

[16] Epenthesis is out of the picture because Dep-*seg* is undominated.

[17] For this reason, we need not concern ourselves with candidates like *he.[leu?]. Though they achieve satisfactory prosodic faithfulness, they violate undominated constraints by including a falling-sonority diphthong in a closed syllable.

[18] The constraint Anchor-Pos$_{OO}$(Ft, Ft, Head) could also have been adduced in (21), with identical results. Forms like he.[lé.u?] or he.[lé].u? might be expected to fare better than *either* candidate considered in (21), since they violate neither Anchor-Pos nor Max-*seg*. But they do so by positing metrical structures that are never attested in Rotuman: a light-heavy trochee in he.[lé.u?] and an unaligned foot in he.[lé].u?. Undominated constraints foreclose both options.

[19] I am indebted to John Alderete for his detailed comments on the Cupeño material.

(22)   Cupeño Habilitative (Hill 1970; McCarthy 1979, 1984; McCarthy and
       Prince 1990a; Crowhurst 1994)

	Simple Stem	Habilitative	
a.	čál	čá*ʔaʔ*al	'husk'
	tə́w	tə́*ʔəʔ*əw	'see'
	həlʸə́p	həlʸə́*ʔəʔ*əp	'hiccup'
	kəláw	kəlá*ʔaʔ*aw	'gather wood'
	ʔatís	ʔatí*ʔiʔ*is	'sneeze'
b.	páčik	páči*ʔí*k	'leach acorns'
	čáŋnəw	čáŋnə*ʔə*w	'be angry'
	čəkúkʷilʸ	čəkúkʷi*ʔí*lʸ	'joke'
c.	pínəʔwəx	pínəʔwəx	'sing enemy songs'
	xáləyəw	xáləyəw	'fall'

With oxytone (i.e. end-stressed) roots (22a), the habilitative adds two syllables
(italicized) to the simple stem. Each added syllable consists of a *ʔ* onset and a
copy of the preceding vowel. The root-final consonant remains in place, with the
reduplicative action occurring to its left. With paroxytone roots (22b), the
habilitative adds a single syllable, which likewise has a *ʔ* onset and a copy of the
last vowel. With proparoxytone roots (22c), the habilitative and the simple stem
are identical.

  Hill (1970) is responsible for a key insight that all subsequent accounts have
tried to refine: the habilitative is based on a target of having two post-stress
syllables, and this target is achieved by copying the last vowel as many times as
necessary. (The *ʔ* is provided as a default onset, in conformity with a regular
pattern of the language.) This core idea has been implemented in various ways:

• McCarthy (1979, 1984): mapping to a template with variable and fixed portions. The template is Xόσσ. The variable X licenses the pretonic material, if
  any, and the όσσ sequence determines the shape of the rest of the habilitative.
• McCarthy and Prince (1990a): positive prosodic circumscription and mapping
  to a fixed template. Every stem is assumed to end with a left-headed foot of
  one to three syllables: [čál]$_{Ft}$, ʔa[tís]$_{Ft}$, [páčik]$_{Ft}$, [pínəʔwəx]$_{Ft}$. This foot is circumscribed by Φ(Ft, Right), and the B:Φ portion is mapped onto a template
  consisting of the maximal expansion of this foot, a dactyl [όσσ]$_{Ft}$.
• Crowhurst (1994): negative prosodic circumscription and mapping to a fixed
  template. Every stem is argued to begin with an iambic foot of one or two
  syllables (modulo final-consonant extrametricality): [čá]$_{Ft}$l, [pá]$_{Ft}$čik, [kəlá]$_{Ft}$w,
  [čəkú]$_{Ft}$kʷilʸ. This foot is circumscribed by Φ(Ft, Left), and the B/Φ portion
  is mapped onto a template consisting of a binary foot, [σσ]$_{Ft}$.

Though they differ in many ways, these previous accounts have one important
property in common: they all take special precautions to ensure that the
habilitative template affects only the post-tonic portion of the verb. From the

stressed vowel leftward, pre-tonically, the habilitative is identical to the simple stem. This is an obvious circumcircumscriptional effect. In McCarthy and Prince's analysis, the pre-tonic string is *hors de combat* because it is outside the scope of positive circumscription. And in Crowhurst's analysis, the pre-tonic string is segregated out (together with the stressed syllable) by negative circumscription.

In operational approaches like these, circumscription is necessary to protect the pre-tonic string from being affected by the template. But Optimality Theory offers another way of protecting it: directly, by faithfulness constraints, which have no counterpart in operational theories. If we rely on Crowhurst's well-motivated claim that Cupeño feet are iambic,[20] then it is apparent that the habilitative contains a (mostly) faithful reproduction of the initial foot of the basic stem:

(23)   Prosodic Faithfulness in the Cupeño Habilitative

        Simple Stem   Habilitative

    a. [č$_1$á$_2$l]   [č$_1$á$_2$][ʔaʔal]

        [kəl$_3$á$_4$w]   [kəl$_3$á$_4$][ʔaʔaw]

        [ʔat$_3$í$_4$s]   [ʔat$_3$í$_4$][ʔiʔis]

    b. [p$_1$á$_2$]čik   [p$_1$á$_2$][čiʔik]

        [čək$_3$ú$_4$]k^{w}il^y [čək$_3$ú$_4$][k^{w}iʔil^y]

    c. [p$_1$í$_2$]naʔwəx [p$_1$í$_2$][naʔwəx]

The left-aligned, mono- or disyllabic foot of the basic stem is preserved unchanged in the habilitative, except for displacement of the stem-final consonant in (a). The habilitative is otherwise dramatically different from the basic stem since it adds a second, disyllabic foot. By virtue of high-ranking prosodic faithfulness constraints, the disyllabic foot template added in the habilitative is not permitted to disrupt the foot inherited from the basic stem. What circumscription does indirectly, prosodic faithfulness does directly, and it does so without the liabilities that circumscription brings, such as the duplication of effort that will be made apparent below in (26).

This is the essential element of the analysis of Cupeño. It is nothing but a straightforward application of the same ideas called on in Yidiɲ and Rotuman. As the co-indexation of correspondent elements in (23) shows, the segments of the stressed syllable in the simple stem stand in correspondence with segments

---

[20] Crowhurst observes that Cupeño roots are regularly stressed on the first or second syllable—the choice is lexically determined. She therefore proposes that roots are provided lexically with a left-aligned mono- or disyllabic iambic foot. (See Alderete (1996) for a detailed discussion of the system in OT terms.) This analysis supports the idea that the native foot type is binary and iambic, just as in Crowhurst's assumed simple stem forms and habilitative template.

in the stressed syllable in the habilitative. Thus, ANCHOR-POS(Ft, Ft, Head) is unviolated and undominated.[21]

A particularly striking effect of ANCHOR-POS can be observed from its inter-action with the anti-epenthesis constraint DEP-*seg*. The habilitative $[kəl_3á_4]$ [ʔaʔaw] has a total of two epenthetic syllables containing four epenthetic seg-ments, the two default ʔ's and the two copied a's. Now compare this form to the failed candidate *$[kə][l_3a_4ʔaw]$, which avoids epenthesizing an entire syllable by moving stress onto the initial syllable. The problem with this candidate does not lie with prosody per se—compare the prosodically identical form $[č_1á_2]$ [ʔaʔal]. Rather, what's wrong with *$[kə][l_3a_4ʔaw]$ is that it is prosodically unfaithful to the simple stem $[k_1əl_3á_4w]$, because the segments of the head syllable in the sim-ple stem do not stand in correspondence with segments in the head syllable of the habilitative. The following tableau completes the argument:

(24) ANCHOR-POS(Ft, Ft, Head) >> DEP-*seg*		
$[k_1ə_2l_3á_4w]$	ANCHOR-POS(Ft, Ft, Head)	DEP-*seg*[22]
☞ a. $[k_1ə_2l_3á_4][ʔaʔaw]$		****
b. $[k_1ə_2][l_3a_4ʔaw]$	* !	**

This ranking argument emphasizes that prosodic faithfulness in the stem→ habilitative mapping may be purchased at a cost in segmental faithfulness, such as epenthesis.

We have seen, then, that the segments of the foot-heading or stressed syllable must stand in correspondence in the stem and habilitative. Foot-finally, though, a mismatch is possible. ANCHOR-POS(Ft, Ft, Final) is violated by the habilitative of oxytone stems, as can be seen from (23a). The responsible constraint here is a different kind of Anchoring—one that is more in the nature of classic MCat-PCat alignment effects. Specifically, ANCHOR-POS(Stem, Word, Final) must dominate ANCHOR-POS(Ft, Ft, Final), as the following tableau shows:

(25) ANCHOR-POS(Stem, Word, Final) >> ANCHOR-POS(Ft, Ft, Final)		
$[č_1á_2l_3]$	ANCHOR-POS (Stem, Wd, Final)	ANCHOR-POS (Ft, Ft, Head)
☞ a. $[č_1á_2]$ $[ʔaʔal_3]$		*
b. $[č_1á_2l_3]$ $[ʔaʔa]$	* !	

---

[21] Equivalently, starting from the observation that the foot-initial segment in the simple stem stands in correspondence with a foot-initial segment in the habilitative, we could assert that ANCHOR-POS(Ft, Ft, Initial) is undominated.

[22] The violation marks for DEP-*seg* are here presented under the assumption that the added vowels in e.g. kəláʔaʔaw have epenthetic root nodes (though their place nodes are supplied by autosegmental spreading). Alternative assumptions are possible and certainly compatible with the argument made here. (I am indebted to Ania Łubowicz for a question on this point.)

Absolutely perfect foot-faithfulness is thus not always achieved—it suffers when it would run afoul of right-edge stem alignment. Effects like this, here attributed to ANCHOR-POS(Stem, Wd, Final), are familiar from the literature on Alignment constraints (and earlier from extrametricality-based approaches like Crowhurst's). For example, the constraints dubbed ALIGN-L and ALIGN-R have very similar edge-preserving consequences in the phonologies of Axininca Campa and Lardil.[23]

To sum up, undominated ANCHOR-POS(Ft, Ft, Head) accounts for the inertia of the stem-initial foot in forming the habilitative. The habilitative template must be satisfied without altering the headedness or segmental contents of the initial foot (except for the stem-final consonant, which is controlled by ANCHOR-POS(Stem, Word, Final)).

In Crowhurst's (1994) analysis, by comparison, inertia of the initial foot is a matter of negative circumscription. Here is how she derives the habilitative of some representative oxytone and paroxytone roots:

(26)   Negative circumscription in Cupeño (simplified from Crowhurst 1994: 17)
    a. Basic stem
        [pá]$_{Ft}$ čik   [kə láw]$_{Ft}$

    b. Final consonant extrametricality: B/Φ(C, Right)
        [pá]$_{Ft}$ či ⟨k⟩   [kə lá]$_{Ft}$ ⟨w⟩

    c. Negative prosodic circumscription of initial foot: Φ(Ft, Left)
        ⟨[pá]$_{Ft}$⟩ či ⟨k⟩   ⟨[kə lá]$_{Ft}$⟩ ⟨w⟩

    d. Left-to-right mapping of B/Φ to [σσ]$_{Ft}$ tEmplate
        ⟨[pá]$_{Ft}$⟩ [či σ]$_{Ft}$ ⟨k⟩   ⟨[kə lá]$_{Ft}$⟩ [σσ] ⟨w⟩

    e. Spreading from B/Φ to Satisfy [σσ]$_{Ft}$ Template
        ⟨[pá]$_{Ft}$⟩ [či ʔi]$_{Ft}$ ⟨k⟩   *No change*

    f. Restore B:Φ portion and proceed again with spreading step (e)
        [pá]$_{Ft}$ [či ʔi]$_{Ft}$ ⟨k⟩   [kə lá]$_{Ft}$ [ʔa ʔa]$_{Ft}$ ⟨w⟩

    g. Restore extrametrical consonant
        [pá]$_{Ft}$ [či ʔik]$_{Ft}$ [kə lá]$_{Ft}$ [ʔa ʔaw]$_{Ft}$

Inactivity of the initial foot is obtained by negative circumscription at step (c). In this way, the initial foot and its contents are temporarily removed from consideration, leaving template satisfaction to any post-tonic segments in steps (d) and (e).

This is the main idea of the circumscriptional analysis, but it is buttressed by an auxiliary assumption that renders the overall package somewhat less

---

[23] Caroline Jones points out that the candidate *[čal$_{3}$]ʔaʔal$_{3}$, with doubling of the *l*, is anchored in both dimensions simultaneously. Candidates like this, with long-distance consonant gemination, are not just less harmonic but in all likelihood impossible. For relevant discussion, see Clements and Hume (1995) and Gafos (1996, 1999).

attractive. With oxytones like *kəláw*, consonant extrametricality and negative circumscription leave no visible segments whatsoever, and so there is nothing to map onto the template at steps (d) and (e). This is the reason for step (f), which attempts vowel spreading again after the negatively circumscribed material has been restored. The problem revealed here is that operational circumscription goes too far—it has a protective effect on the initial foot, as desired, but it also has the undesirable consequence of rendering the contents of the initial foot entirely inaccessible to phonological manipulation. Merely copying the stressed vowel does no violence to the initial foot, but negative circumscription, over-protectively, bans even that. In contrast, the prosodic faithfulness constraints require only that the initial foot be preserved intact; they say nothing about processes, such as vowel copying, that do not and can not affect the initial foot. A significant complication in the circumscriptional analysis is thus avoided.

Having sketched an analysis of Cupeño based on prosodic faithfulness and having presented some reasons to prefer it to alternatives, I now need to clear up a few remaining details. The matters to be addressed are these:

- The stem→habilitative correspondence relation.
- The nature of the template.
- The choice of epenthetic material.

The correspondence relation

In Cupeño, many roots have lexical stress, nearly always on the first or second syllable. Except in compounds, the lexical stress of roots emerges faithfully on the surface by virtue of high-ranking I-O prosodic faithfulness constraints (Alderete 1996). For instance, surface [kəláw] is derived from underlying /[kəláw]/, with faithful preservation of the underlying foot structure. This leads to a question: in tableaux like (24), is ANCHOR-POS enforcing prosodic faithfulness on the I→O mapping (/[kəláw]/→[kəlá][ʔaʔaw]) or the O→O mapping [kəláw]→[kəlá][ʔaʔaw]?

Decisive evidence comes from roots that are underlyingly unaccented. Unaccented roots can be distinguished by the fact that they are unstressed in the presence of an accented affix; otherwise, accented roots take precedence over accented affixes. (See Alderete (1996) for discussion and analysis.) By this criterion, the root /təw/ 'see' is unaccented, though it receives default initial stress, surfacing as [tə́w] when not in the presence of an accented affix. Significantly, the habilitative of /təw/→[tə́w] is [tə́][ʔəʔəw]—just like the habilitative [čá][ʔaʔal] from the accented root /[čál]/→[čál]. Unaccented and accented roots, which are distinct in the input but identical in the output, form their habilitatives in exactly the same way. This fact proves that prosodic faithfulness is enforced on an O-O correspondence relation between the output form of the simple stem and the output form of the habilitative, and the constraint involved should properly be called ANCHOR-POS$_{OO}$(Ft, Ft, Head).

The template

The habilitative consists of two feet. The first, which is mono- or disyllabic, is faithfully inherited from the simple stem. The second, which is always disyllabic, is added in response to some constraints of which the force is limited to the habilitative. Under GTT we must locate those constraints of Universal Grammar which explain why the added foot is disyllabic and why it is added at all.

The added foot is disyllabic to satisfy FT-BIN, foot binarity (Prince 1980; McCarthy and Prince 1986; Hayes 1995), which demands that all feet be disyllabic (or bimoraic, in quantity-sensitive systems). True, FT-BIN is little honored in Cupeño, since faithful treatment of lexically specified feet takes precedence (Crowhurst 1994; Alderete 1996). But the added foot of the habilitative has no faithfulness commitments to honor; it is created *ex nihilo*. By the logic of emergence of the unmarked (McCarthy and Prince 1994a), novel structures that have no faithfulness commitments will satisfy markedness constraints that inherited structures, bound by faithfulness, routinely violate. The added foot in the habilitative is binary because binary feet are good, by FT-BIN.

The overall structure of the habilitative is bipodal. This is reminiscent of *zuuja-go* secret language forms in Japanese. Itô, Kitagawa, and Mester (1996) propose that *zuuja-go* bipodality is an effect of NON-FINALITY, which requires that the head foot be foot-wise non-final (i.e. be followed by another foot). The same idea can be recruited in Cupeño: the head foot, which has an overt stress, is rendered non-final in the habilitative by supplying another foot to follow it. The situation is much like the placement of main stress in English, except that it is limited to a specific morphological category instead of extending to the whole language.

Epenthesis

The choice of epenthetic material for added syllables in the habilitative is also a consequence of emergence of the unmarked. The onset is the default ʔ, which satisfies markedness constraints that other consonants violate. The nucleus is filled by epenthesizing a root node and spreading a place node from the preceding vowel. Beckman (1995) and Alderete *et al.* (1999) propose that spreading is favoured for markedness reasons, because markedness is evaluated on autosegmental units rather than their individual segmental projections.

In principle, the same result could have been achieved by spreading a consonant and inserting a default vowel, yielding *čáčəčəl, or by spreading both vowel and consonant, yielding *čáčačal. These outcomes seem impossible not merely in Cupeño but universally. The property that unites them in impossibility is the spreading of a consonant across a vowel. Arguably, this is not met with in any language. (For relevant discussion, see Clements and Hume (1995) and Gafos (1996, 1999).)

To sum up, I have argued that inertia of the stem-initial foot in forming the Cupeño habilitative is a consequence of high-ranking prosodic faithfulness constraints. This account is superior to a circumscriptional analysis because the latter goes too far, making the initial foot entirely invisible to the phonology, even though visibility for copying purposes is required. The comparison between prosodic faithfulness and operational circumscription is unusually direct and probative in Cupeño, offering strong support for the overall program pursued here.

In this section, I have shown how ANCHOR-POS constraints, which require forms to match in specific aspects of prosodic constituency, take on much of the descriptive burden of operational prosodic circumscription. From this perspective, circumscriptional phenomena are seen in terms of prosodic faithfulness rather than successive steps of constituent parsing, performing an operation on that constituent, and then putting the pieces back together.

   The approach based on Anchoring appears to be at least as successful empirically as the operational circumscription model. As far as explanation goes, it is surely superior, since it accounts without special pleading for the case of Cupeño, for which there is no fully satisfactory operational analysis. More broadly, the connection made between circumscriptional phenomena and faithfulness reveals a truth that the operational model obscured—that circumscription is really a matter of ensuring particular kinds of prosodic similarity between reduplicant and base or within partial paradigms. This account thus brings with it interesting connections to the theory and practice of faithfulness—connections that the more parochial notion of operational prosodic circumscription cannot provide. In the end, then, these results support the ultimate goal of the theory of Prosodic Morphology since they lead to the elimination of the PM-specific device for picking-mode prosodic circumscription in favour of faithfulness constraints, which are surely independently necessary in OT.

4.5 Prosodic Circumscription as Moraic Faithfulness: The Arabic Broken Plural

We turn now to prosodic circumscription in the parsing mode, of which the Arabic broken plural (McCarthy and Prince 1990a) is the classic exemplar. In the Φ-parsing stage, a foot is extracted from the base even at the expense of disrupting any pre-existing prosodic analysis; in the limit, even individual syllables may be split up. Subsequent events then proceed just as they do in the simpler picking-mode cases. The Arabic plural, like the similar Choctaw phenomenon (Lombardi and McCarthy 1991; Hung 1992; Samek-Lodovici 1992, 1993), calls on the full power of a serial derivation in the operational model, and it therefore presents a particular challenge to the constraint-based theory advocated here. The approach taken here to Arabic is inspired by Samek-Lodovici's work on Choctaw, though of course details are different.

   The data of interest—the iambic plural and diminutive pattern—are as follows:

(27)   Arabic Iambic Broken Plural and Diminutive

	Sg.	Pl.	Dim.	
a.	CvCC singular nouns			
	nafs	nufuus	nufays-at	'soul'
	qidħ	qidaaħ	qudayħ	'arrow'
	ħukm	ʔaħkaam	ħukaym	'judgement'
b.	CvCvC singular nouns			
	ʔasad	ʔusuud	ʔusayd	'lion'
	rajul	rijaal	rujayl	'man'
	ʕinab	ʔaʕnaab	ʕunayb	'grape'
c.	CvCvvC+at singular nouns			
	saħaab+at	saħaaʔib	suħayyib	'cloud'
	jaziir+at	jazaaʔir	juzayyir	'island'
	kariim+at	karaaʔim	kurayyim	'noble'
	ħaluub+at	ħalaaʔib	ħulayyib	'milch-camel'
d.	CvvCvC+at singular nouns			
	faakih+at	fawaakih	fuwaykih	'fruit'
	ʔaanis+at	ʔawaanis	ʔuwaynis	'cheerfulness'
e.	CvvCv(v)C singular nouns			
	xaatam	xawaatim	xuwaytim	'signet-ring'
	jaamuus	jawaamiis	juwaymiis	'buffalo'
f.	CvCCv(v)C singular nouns			
	jundub	janaadib	junaydib	'locust'
	sulṭaan	salaaṭiin	sulayṭiin	'sultan'

In keeping with the overall aims of this chapter, I will focus here on the principal motivation for circumscription: the relation between the prosodic structure of the singular noun and its plural or diminutive. There are many details to be considered in a full account; see McCarthy and Prince (1990a).

The core of the operational analysis of Arabic is circumscription of a bimoraic sequence—the foot type known as a moraic trochee—at the left edge of the singular stem. Thus the circumscriptional operation is $\Phi(\mathrm{Ft}_{\mu\mu}, \mathrm{Left})$. Typically, Arabic stems do not begin with such a foot, and sometimes they begin with a light-heavy sequence that cannot be matched with a bimoraic foot. But prosodic circumscription in the parsing mode has no regard for such niceties. Its force may be particularly observed in cases like (28d), where the $B{:}\Phi$ portion does not even correspond to a whole number of syllables in the singular stem:

(28)   Formal treatment circumscriptionally

	Sg.	B Φ	B/Φ	Pl.	Dim.
a.	nafs	naf	s	nufuus	nufays-at
	ʔasad	ʔasa	d	ʔusuud	ʔusayd

b.	jundub	jun	dub	janaadib	junaydib
	sulṭaan	sul	ṭaan	salaaṭiin	sulayṭiin
c.	xaatam	xaa	tam	xawaatim	xuwaytim
	jaamuus	jaa	muus	jawaamiis	juwaymiis
d.	saḥaab-at	saḥa	ab	saḥaaʔib	suḥayyib
	jaziir-at	jazi	ir	jazaaʔir	juzayyir
e.	kuttaab	kut	taab	kataatiib	kutaytiib
	jilbaab	jil	baab	jalaabiib	julaybiib

Once the *B*:Φ portion has been extracted, it is mapped onto a light-heavy iambic foot template. The form is then reassembled and adjustments are made in the vocalism (which will not be considered further here).

Operational circumscription lays claim to three principal descriptive results in the analysis of Arabic. First, circumscription protects the *B*/Φ portion from alteration by the template. That effect is clearest in the contrast between *jundub/janaadib* and *sulṭaan/salaaṭiin* (28b)—the weight of the final syllable is preserved in the mapping from singular to plural, despite the havoc the iambic template wreaks on the rest of the form. More subtly, the protected *B*/Φ factor consists of a syllable fragment like *ab* in *saḥaab+at* (28d), and this fragment is preserved (with an epenthetic onset) in the corresponding plural *saḥaaʔib*. Second, there is a more abstract effect of circumscription that can be seen from a contrast in the distribution of epenthetic consonants in (28c, d). In *xaatam/xawaatim*, the circumscribed portion *xaa* contains just a single root consonant, *x*, so the templatic portion *xawaa* is supplied with an epenthetic consonant *w*.[24] But in *saḥaab+at/saḥaaʔib*, the circumscribed portion *saḥa* contains two root consonants, and then the epenthetic consonant appears in the *B*/Φ portion. Third, circumscription gives a principled account of why plural/diminutive formation conserves spreading of a root consonant, as in (28e)—even to the point of swapping local spreading for long-distance (*kuttaab* → *kataatiib*).

Here I will argue that these empirical consequences of operational circumscription can also be obtained from prosodic faithfulness constraints in OT. The preservation of the weight of the final syllable is a typical prosodic faithfulness effect—a consequence of high-ranking MAX-μ and DEP-μ. The contrast in position of the epenthetic consonant—*xawaatim* versus *saḥaaʔib*—and the conservation of consonantal spreading are also a matter of faithfulness, but in this case it is faithfulness to autosegmental associations. Both are effects of preserving corresponding segment-to-mora linkage—that is, they are anti-spreading, anti-delinking faithfulness effects of the type that are commonplace in tone systems. In this way, the peculiarities of Arabic plural formation are derived from the activ-

---

[24] The choice between epenthetic *ʔ* in *saḥaaʔib* and epenthetic *w* in *xawaatim* is made on phonological grounds—see McCarthy and Prince (1990a).

ity of universal constraints rather than a parochial mechanism of circumscription.

Before these results can be ratified, though, it is necessary to develop a fuller picture of the prosodic structure and the correspondence relations in the singular → plural/diminutive mapping. As I noted above (Section 4.3), both moras and segments stand in correspondence. As a notational convenience, superscripted indices will be used for the mora-to-mora correspondence relation and subscripted indices for the segment-to-segment correspondence relation. The *jundub* → *janaadib* mapping can be characterized as follows:[25]

(29)   *jundub* → *janaadib* correspondence relations

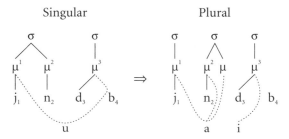

These representations reflects several assumptions I am making to simplify the discussion:

- Onsets are linked to the nuclear mora, forming CV moraic sequences (Hyman 1985; Itô 1986, 1989; Zec 1988; etc.).
- Final consonants are extrametrical, not participating in the prosody of the stem as a whole (as in McCarthy and Prince 1990a, b).
- The 'added' mora in *janaadib* appears at the end of the second syllable. In (29), this mora is shown without a superscript, since it lacks a correspondent in the singular.[26] In the diminutive, this mora has an attached *y*: *junaydib*.
- Because vowel melodies are prescribed for the plural and diminutive, the vowels of *jundub* and *janaadib* are not in correspondence with one another (and so are shown without subscripts).

These assumptions are not absolutely indispensable, but they (especially the first) greatly simplify the working-out of the proposal.

For compactness, tree structures like (29) can be folded into a single string combining super-and subscripts, with the ligature connecting shared CV moras. In this way, we obtain the following summary of the correspondence relations holding between singulars and plurals:

---

[25] In order to maintain the closest possible parallel to the McCarthy and Prince (1990a) analysis, I continue to assume that Arabic has CV tier segregation. But compare footnote 23.

[26] If the added mora of the plural is an affix though, as suggested below, it does have a correspondent in the input.

(30)   Singular → Plural Correspondence Relations

    a. nafs/nufuus

$$\widehat{n_1a}{}^1\ f_3{}^2\ s_4 \qquad\Rightarrow\qquad \widehat{n_1u}{}^1\ \widehat{f_3u}{}^2{:}\ s_4$$

    b. ʔasad/ʔusuud

$$\widehat{ʔ_1a}{}^1\widehat{s_3a}{}^2d_5 \qquad\Rightarrow\qquad \widehat{ʔ_1u}{}^1\ \widehat{s_3u}{}^2{:}\ d_5$$

    c. jundub/janaadib

$$\widehat{j_1u}{}^1\ n_3{}^2\ \widehat{d_4u}{}^3\,b_6 \qquad\Rightarrow\qquad \widehat{j_1a}{}^1\ \widehat{n_3a}{}^2{:}\ \widehat{d_4i}{}^3\,b_6$$

    d. sulṭaan/salaaṭiin

$$\widehat{s_1u}{}^1\ l_3{}^2\ \widehat{ṭ_4a}{}^{3}{:}^4\,n_6 \qquad\Rightarrow\qquad \widehat{s_1a}{}^1\ \widehat{l_3a}{}^2{:}\ \widehat{ṭ_4i}{}^{3}{:}^4\,n_6$$

    e. xaatam/xawaatim

$$\widehat{x_1a}{}^{1}{:}^2\ \widehat{t_3a}{}^3\,m_5 \qquad\Rightarrow\qquad \widehat{x_1a}{}^1\ \widehat{wa}{}^2{:}\ \widehat{t_3i}{}^3\,m_5$$

    f. jaamuus/jawaamiis

$$\widehat{j_1a}{}^{1}{:}^2\widehat{m_3u}{}^{3}{:}^4s_5 \qquad\Rightarrow\qquad \widehat{j_1a}{}^1\ \widehat{wa}{}^2{:}\ \widehat{m_3i}{}^{3}{:}^4\,s_5$$

    g. jaziir(+at)/jazaaʔir

$$\widehat{j_1a}{}^1\ \widehat{z_3i}{}^{2}{:}^3\,r_5 \qquad\Rightarrow\qquad \widehat{j_1a}{}^1\ \widehat{z_3a}{}^2{:}\ \widehat{ʔi}{}^3\,r_5$$

With these preliminaries out of the way, the goal of the analysis can now be described exactly: to characterize the mapping in (30) in terms of a hierarchy of universal constraints, with a focus on faithfulness.

The mapping in (30) is along the O-O dimension of correspondence, since the connection is between output forms of singular and plural, rather than between the output plural and the underlying consonantal root (McCarthy and Prince 1990a). Two kinds of faithfulness constraints are relevant to this mapping: faithfulness to the elements standing in correspondence (segments and moras), and faithfulness to the autosegmental association relations between these elements. Faithfulness to segments and moras is a matter of obedience to constraints like MAX-*seg*, DEP-*seg*, MAX-μ, and DEP-μ. Faithfulness to autosegmental association involves obeying NO-DELINK and NO-SPREAD (see Section 4.3 above). In Arabic, the autosegmental associations of interest are between segments and moras in a representation like (29). The constraints demanding conservation of these associations are therefore NO-DELINK(μ, *seg*) and NO-SPREAD(μ, *seg*). These constraints, which must in any case be part of Universal Grammar, help to explain the properties of the Arabic plural.

One of the main descriptive results claimed for the operational circumscription model is conservation of the final syllable's weight (see (30c, d, e, f)). From the perspective of OT, this is just faithfulness to moras in the singular→plural mapping. MAX-μ_{OO} is undominated in Arabic; DEP-μ_{OO} is violated only by virtue of the the added mora (an affix) in the plural. In short, failed candidates like *janaadiib* (for *jundub/janaadib*) or *salaaṭin* (for *sulṭaan/salaaṭiin*) present no difficulties; they are straightforward consequences of the high-ranking μ-faithfulness constraints.

Another descriptive result claimed for the operational model is its account of the distribution of epenthetic consonants in the plural. It can be seen by comparing (30e, f) to (30g)—the singulars differ only in the locus of the bimoraic syllable relative to the second root consonant, and this somehow translates into a difference in placement of the epenthetic consonant in the plural. To put the matter in terms of candidate selection, it is necessary to explain why the plural of *xaatam* is *xawaatim* and not **xataaʔim* and likewise why the plural of *jaziir+at* is *jazaaʔir* and not **jawaazir*.

The representations in (31) show how this contrast plays out in the singular/plural O-O correspondence relation:

(31)   Correspondence relations in *xataam → xawaatim, *xataaʔim*

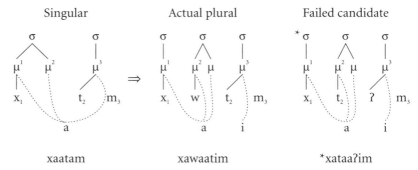

Singular	Actual plural	Failed candidate
xaatam	xawaatim	*xataaʔim

The problem with the failed candidate is that it has undergone a kind of reassociation or 'flop' process relative to the singular: correspondence-wise, t_2 of the failed candidate is linked to a different mora from that in the singular. This is a violation of No-Delink$_{OO}$(μ, *seg*) and No-Spread$_{OO}$(μ, *seg*), which militate against loss and gain of association lines, respectively. All of the interesting cases in (30e–g) can be subsumed under this rubric. Here they are, with the epenthetic consonant indicated by C and the locus of flop italicized:

(32)   Role of No-Delink$_{OO}$(μ, *seg*) and/or No-Spread$_{OO}$(μ, *seg*)

        Singular   Plural   Failed Plural Candidate

    e. xaatam/xawaatim

        $\widehat{x_1a}^{1}{:}^2\ \widehat{t_3a}^3\ m_5$ $\widehat{x_1a}^1\ \widehat{Ca}^2{:}\ \widehat{t_3i}^3\ m_5$ $^*\widehat{x_1a}^1\ \widehat{t_3a}^2{:}\ \widehat{Ci}^3\ m_5$

    f. jaamuus/jawaamiis

        $\widehat{j_1a}^1{:}^2\widehat{m_3u}^3{:}^4s_5$ $\widehat{j_1a}^1\ \widehat{Ca}^2{:}\ \widehat{m_3i}^3{:}^4\ s_5$ $^*\widehat{j_1a}^1\ \widehat{m_3a}^2{:}\ \widehat{Ci}^3{:}^4\ s_5$

    g. jaziir(+at)/jazaaʔir

        $\widehat{j_1a}^1\ \widehat{z_3i}^2{:}^3\ r_5$ $\widehat{j_1a}^1\ \widehat{z_3a}^2{:}\ \widehat{Ci}^3\ r_5$ $^*\widehat{j_1a}^1\ \widehat{Ca}^2{:}\ \widehat{z_3i}^3\ r_5$

The paired successful and failed candidates in (32) differ only in the placement of the epenthetic consonant; they do not differ in any respect that is relevant to the other constraints, such as moraic or segmental faithfulness. This means that No-Delink$_{OO}$(μ, *seg*) and/or No-Spread$_{OO}$(μ, *seg*) will settle the matter in favour of the actual output form no matter how they are ranked. In this way, we explain the second main empirical result claimed by the operational model: the complex dependency between the distribution of light and heavy syllables in the singular and the distribution of epenthetic consonants in the plural.

The third main descriptive result that the operational model obtains in Arabic involves the conservation of consonantal spreading. Formation of the plural and diminutive preserves consonantal spreading from the singular, even when original geminates must become long-distance linked structures:

(33) Effect of consonantal spreading in operational circumscription

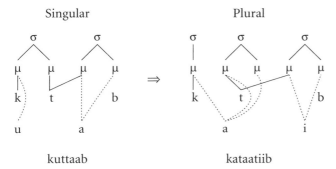

In these spreading configurations, a single consonant occupies more than one syllabic position, either locally or long-distance. Since segmental correspondence is a relation between root-nodes, there is just one root-node *t* in the singular in (33) standing in correspondence with just one root-node *t* in the plural:

(34) O-O correspondence relations in spreading configurations

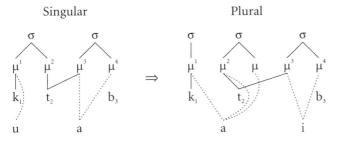

(35) Principal Cases of Spreading in Singular/Plural Pairs

  Singular   Plural
a. *baSS/buSuus* (common, productive, N > 100)
   $\widehat{b_1a}^1$ S_3^2 S_3 $\widehat{b_1u}^1$ $\widehat{S_3u}^2$: S_3
b. *jilbaab/jalaabiib* (uncommon, N < 30)
   $\widehat{j_1i}^1$ l_3^2 $\widehat{b_4a}^{3:4}$ b_4 $\widehat{j_1a}^1$ $\widehat{l_3a}^2$: $\widehat{b_4i}^{3:4}$ b_4

c. *kuttaab/kataatiib* (common, productive, N > 100)
$\widehat{k_1}u^1 \; t_3^{\,2} \; \widehat{t_3}a^{3\text{:}4} \; b_5$ $\widehat{k_1}a^1 \; \widehat{t_3}a^{2}\text{:} \; \widehat{t_1}i^{3\text{:}4} \; b_5$

d. *tinniin/tanaaniin* (rare, N < 5)
$\widehat{t_1}i^{\,1} \; n_3^{\,2} \; \widehat{n_3}i^{3\text{:}4} \; n_3$ $\widehat{t_1}a^1 \; \widehat{n_3}a^{2}\text{:} \; \widehat{n_3}i^{3\text{:}4} \; n_3$

This conservation of autosegmental spreading in the singular→plural mapping follows from the μ-faithfulness constraints No-Delink$_{OO}$(μ, *seg*) and No-Spread$_{OO}$(μ, *seg*). The former ensures that spreading in the singular is maintained in the plural. The latter, by dominating Dep-*seg*$_{OO}$, accounts for the fact that spreading is not normally an option in onset-filling situations.[27] Compare:

(36) Spreading in singular $\Rightarrow$ spreading—not epenthesis—in plural

> *kuttaab*   *kataatiib*
> $k_1 \, u^1 \, t_3^{\,2} \, t_3 \, a^{3\text{:}4} \, b_5$ $k_1 \, a^1 \, t_3 \, a^2\text{:} \, t_3 \, i^{3\text{:}4} \, b_5$ (with preservation of spread *t*)
>   *$k_1 \, a^1 \, t_3 \, a^2\text{:} \, ?\, i^{3\text{:}4} \, b_5$ (with epenthetic *ʔ*)

(37) No spreading in singular $\Rightarrow$ epenthesis—not spreading—in plural

> a. *xaatam*   *xawaatim*
> $x_1 \, a^{1\text{:}2} \, t_3 \, a^3 \, m_5$ $x_1 \, a^1 \, w \, a^2\text{:} \, t_3 \, i^3 \, m_5$ (with epenthetic *w*)
>   *$x_1 \, a^1 \, t_3 \, a^2\text{:} \, t_3 \, i^3 \, m_5$ (with spreading of root-medial *t*)
>   *$x_1 \, a^1 \, t_3 \, a^2\text{:} \, m_5 \, i^3 \, m_5$ (with spreading of root-final *m*)
>
> b. *jaziir(+at)*   *jazaaʔir*
> $j_1 \, a^1 \, z_3 \, i^{2\text{:}3} \, r_5$ $j_1 \, a^1 \, z_3 \, a^2\text{:} \, ?\, i^3 \, r_5$ (with epenthetic *ʔ*)
>   *$j_1 \, a^1 \, z_3 \, a^2\text{:} \, z_3 \, i^3 \, r_5$ (with spreading of root-medial *z*)
>   *$j_1 \, a^1 \, z_3 \, a^2\text{:} \, r_5 \, i^3 \, r_5$ (with spreading of root-final *r*)

The competition between the actual output and any of the failed candidates in (37) is sufficient to prove that No-Spread$_{OO}$(μ, *seg*) >> Dep-*seg*$_{OO}$. This ranking ensures that spreading is dispreferred in onset-filling situations. But when spreading is already present in the basic form, it is preserved in the plural, because of No-Delink$_{OO}$(μ, *seg*).

I began this section by pointing out three main analytic results obtained by applying operational circumscription to Arabic: conservation of the weight of the final syllable in certain singular→plural/diminutive mappings; the complex relation between the weight of syllables in the singular and the position of epenthetic consonants in the plural/diminutive; and the conservation of consonantal spreading in all singular→plural/diminutive mappings. I have argued that each of these phenomena can be equally well understood within a correspondence-based approach to prosodic faithfulness. Conservation of weight is

---

[27] A few nouns—about 10, all of them C*ii*CaaC—show onset-filling spreading in the singular→plural mapping: *diinaar* → *danaaniir* 'dinar (unit of currency)'.

simply a matter of satisfying DEP-μ and MAX-μ; the other two results follow from the associational faithfulness constraints NO-DELINK$_{OO}$(μ, *seg*) and NO-SPREAD$_{OO}$(μ, *seg*). Unlike parsing-mode prosodic circumscription, which appears to have no applicability beyond a narrow range of cases like Arabic, all of these constraints are independently motivated. Indeed, they would appear to be essential aspects of phonological theory, with obvious ties to other types of faithfulness constraints.

I have not offered a complete account of the Arabic plural and diminutive in this brief sketch, but I have disposed of the principal arguments for operational circumscription. Before concluding, though, I should say something about the templatic morphology of the plural and diminutive. In the operational approach, the template is an iambic (light-heavy) foot to which *B*:Φ is mapped. In contrast, I have proceeded under the assumption that a mora (with a *y* in the diminutive) is infixed into a particular position in the stem. The locus of infixation can be seen in the following list or in (30) above:

(38)   Locus of added mora (and *y*) in plural and diminutive

	Singular	Plural	Diminutive
a.	nafs	nufu*u*s	nufa*y*s
b.	ʔasad	ʔusu*u*d	ʔusa*y*d
c.	jundub	jana*a*dib	juna*y*dib
d.	sulṭaan	sula*a*ṭiin	sula*yṭ*iin
e.	xaatam	xawa*a*tim	xuwa*y*tim
f.	jaamuus	jawa*a*miis	juwa*y*miis
g.	jaziir(+at)	jaza*a*ʔir	juza*yy*ir

The added mora appears in a consistent position: at the end of the second syllable.

The logic of infixation in OT (see Section 4.2) is that infixes are normal (peripheral) affixes forced to non-peripheral position by high-ranking constraints. Here, I propose that the responsible constraints are members of the positional faithfulness family identified by Beckman (1995, 1997). The theory of positional faithfulness asserts that some positions are privileged to receive special faithfulness treatment. Among the positions so privileged are stem-initial and stem-final syllables. If faithfulness to stem-initial and stem-final syllables is high-ranking, then the μ-affix, though formally a suffix, will be forced into into a stem-medial syllable. With disyllabic stems there is no medial syllable, of course;[28] in that case, faithfulness to the stem-initial syllable takes precedence over faithfulness to the stem-final syllable, following a pattern that is widely observed cross-

---

[28] This then raises the possibility of singular→plural mappings like *nafs*→*nafaʔis, to force the affixal mora into medial position. In general, though, Arabic prohibits stem-forms consisting of three light syllables (McCarthy and Prince 1990b).

linguistically. The point, then, is that there is a plausible affixational analysis to replace the templatic one of the operational theory.

4.6 Conclusion

The theory of Prosodic Morphology is concerned with explaining the properties of phenomena like template-mapping, infixation, and reduplication. In Prosodic Morphology, and in the field generally, the goal of explanation is advanced when local stipulations and parochial mechanisms are replaced by principles of broad applicability. This chapter pursues that goal in relation to phenomena coming under the purview of operational prosodic circumscription.

Though it has achieved some significant descriptive and analytic successes, operational prosodic circumscription includes much that is local and parochial and therefore incompatible with explanation. Research in Optimality Theory, however, has already led to significant improvements in our understanding of one circumscriptional phenomenon, infixation. Infixation (Section 4.2) is now understood in a much more revealing way as a consequence of the interaction of syllable-structure constraints with affixal alignment constraints. Both of these constraint types have ample support outside the narrow domain of infixation, and so they supply the kind of independent support that is essential to further development of any theory. These results in the study of infixation show what can be achieved by re-casting the central idea of Prosodic Morphology—to understand morphological phenomena in terms of independently motivated principles of prosody—within the OT framework.

This chapter continues that research program by addressing a different body of cases that had also been analysed in terms of operational circumscription. These include morphological processes of foot reduplication and circumscriptional template-mapping. I have argued that all can be better understood as effects of prosodic faithfulness constraints, which demand preservation of the location of foot or syllable edges or heads, of moras, or of mora-segment associations. Prosodic faithfulness is by no means peculiar or special—rather, it is part of the very stuff of phonology in OT, essential to dealing with facts as diverse as lexical stress, compensatory lengthening, and tone shift. To the extent that they are correct, then, these results carry us further toward the ultimate aim of Prosodic Morphology: to explain all relevant data in terms of the interaction of independently-motivated constraints of prosody, morphology, and their interface.

Appendix: Anchoring Constraints

The original Alignment constraints were defined within the PARSE/FILL/Containment-based model of Prince and Smolensky (1991, 1993), which posits a single output representation containing information about underlying morphological structure and surface prosodic structure. They require coincidence of the edges of prosodic and/or morphological constituents within the output structure:

(39) Generalized alignment (McCarthy and Prince 1993b)

Align(Cat1, Edge1, Cat2, Edge2) = $_{def}$

$\forall$ Cat1 $\exists$ Cat2 such that Edge1 of Cat1 and Edge2 of Cat2 coincide.

where

Cat1, Cat2 $\in$ PCat $\cup$ GCat
Edge1, Edge2 $\in$ {Right, Left}.

In Correspondence Theory, which allows direct reference to the input (or other related representation), Anchoring replaces Alignment in some applications:[29]

(40) {RIGHT, LEFT}-ANCHOR(S_1, S_2) (McCarthy and Prince 1995a: 372)

Any element at the designated periphery of S_1 has a correspondent at the designated periphery of S_2.

Let *Edge*(X, {R, L}) = the element standing at the *Edge* = {R, L} of X.
RIGHT-ANCHOR . If x = Edge(S_1, R) and y = Edge(S_2, R) then x$\Re$y.
LEFT-ANCHOR. Likewise, *mutatis mutandis*.

Starting from the basic schema in (40), I will present several refinements here based on more recent developments.[30]

First, in accordance with a standard move in the Alignment literature (McCarthy and Prince 1993b; Pierrehumbert 1994), Anchoring is extended to include identity of constituent heads as well as edges. This is important in Section 4.4, where it is shown that circumscriptional effects can involve faithfulness to foot-head position.

Second, following Benua (1997) and Gafos (1997), I assume the existence of distinct but symmetric Anchoring constraints from S_1 to S_2 and from S_2 to S_1. This move parallels an established symmetry in Correspondence Theory: e.g. between MAX and DEP or between I-CONTIG 'no skipping (maintain contiguity of input string)' and O-CONTIG 'no intrusion (maintain contiguity of output string)'. The Anchoring constraints distinguished in this way can be referred to as I-ANCHOR and O-ANCHOR.

Third, also following a proposal by Benua (1997)—(which is itself based on

---

[29] Alignment in the sense of McCarthy and Prince (1993b) and Anchoring in the sense of McCarthy and Prince (1995a) differ in two respects. First, Alignment can have a subcategorizational effect, by demanding coincidence of different edges of the two constituents. The Anchoring schema does not include that possibility. Second, Alignment can demand the coincidence of edges of two constituents which are present only in the output, such as ALIGN(Ft, L, PrWd, L). Anchoring does not generalize to these cases unless it is assumed that the correspondence relation is reflexive.

[30] Another refinement: Zoll (1996) and Gafos (1997) develop a distinction between categorical and gradient senses of Anchoring/Alignment. This distinction does not appear to be relevant to the analysis of prosodic circumscription and so I will not address it here.

positional faithfulness and allied notions in Beckman (1995, 1997) and Alderete (to appear)—I assume a distinction between two senses of Anchoring:

- ANCHOR-POS is satisfied when a segment's position as constituent-initial, -final, or -head is conserved under correspondence
- ANCHOR-SEG is positional faithfulness *per se*, conserving the segment itself standing in the designated position.

As Benua points out, the Alignment theory fuses these two notions into a single constraint-type, but the richer Correspondence framework allows them to be treated separately, and, she argues, they must be.

Crossing the I-ANCHOR/O-ANCHOR distinction with the ANCHOR-POS/ANCHOR-SEG distinction gives four main types of Anchoring constraints. Within each constraint type, a particular constraint token must also specify the constituents involved, the type of correspondence relation between them (I-O, B-R, O-O), and the position P anchored to (initial, final, head).

The ANCHOR-POS constraints produce the kinds of prosodic faithfulness effects that replace operational prosodic circumscription:

(41) Anchoring as alignment and prosodic faithfulness: ANCHOR-POS

    a. I-ANCHOR-POS (Cat_1, Cat_2, P)

      If $\varsigma_1, Cat_1 \in S_1,$

           $\varsigma_2, Cat_2 \in S_2,$

           $\varsigma_1 \Re \varsigma_2,$ and

           ς_1 stands in position P of $Cat_1,$

      then ς_2 stands in position P of $Cat_2.$

    b. O-ANCHOR-POS (Cat_1, Cat_2, P)

      If $\varsigma_1, Cat_1 \in S_1,$

           $\varsigma_2, Cat_2 \in S_2,$

           $\varsigma_1 \Re \varsigma_2,$ and

           ς_2 stands in position P of $Cat_2,$

      then ς_1 stands in position P of $Cat_1.$

When $Cat_1 = Cat_2$, we have prosodic faithfulness *per se*: for instance, I-ANCHOR-POS$_{IO}$(Ft, Ft, Head) says that the locus of stress must not change in the input→output mapping. Constraints of this type are important in lexical stress systems and in the analysis of prosodic circumscription. When $Cat_1 = $ Base and $Cat_2 = $ Reduplicant, we have a typical Base-Reduplicant Anchoring effect of the type explored in McCarthy and Prince (1993b: Ch. 5), Alderete *et al.* (1999), and Gafos (1997). When $Cat_1 = $ Stem and $Cat_2 = \sigma$, I-ANCHOR-POS subsumes the effects of classic (MCat, PCat) alignment, demanding that every stem-edge coincide with a syllable-edge.

The ANCHOR-POS constraints, because of the antecedent conditions in (41), are irrelevant when a segment is deleted or inserted at the designated edge. But deletion or insertion at edges—that is, positional faithfulness in Beckman's (1997) sense—is regulated by Anchoring constraints of the other type, ANCHOR-SEG. I-ANCHOR-SEG is a position-specific MAX constraint; O-ANCHOR-SEG is a position-specific DEP constraint.[31]

(42)   Anchoring as positional faithfulness: ANCHOR-SEG

   a. I-ANCHOR-SEG (Cat, P)

      If ς_1, Cat $\in$ S_1,

            ς_2 $\in$ S_2, and

            ς_1 stands in position P of Cat,

      then there exists ς_2 such that $\varsigma_1 \Re \varsigma_2$.

   b. O-ANCHOR-SEG (Cat, P)

      If ς_1 $\in$ S_1,

            ς_2, Cat $\in$ S_2, and

            ς_2 stands in position P of Cat,

      then there exists ς_1 such that $\varsigma_1 \Re \varsigma_2$.

When Cat is a prosodic category, these are prosodically-sensitive faithfulness constraints. When Cat is a morphological category, they express resistance of, say, stem-edges to epenthesis or deletion. In this way, ANCHOR-SEG and ANCHOR-POS separate the faithfulness and parsing consequences of (MCat, PCat) alignment, in a way that Correspondence Theory permits but its Containment-based predecessor did not.

4.7 References

Alderete, J. (1996). 'Prosodic faithfulness in Cupeño'. Ms, U.Mass, Amherst. ROA-253.

—— (to appear). 'Faithfulness to prosodic heads'. In Hermans and van Oostendorp (eds).

—— J. Beckman, L. Benua, A. Gnanadesikan, J. McCarthy, and S. Urbanczyk (1999). 'Reduplication with fixed segmentism'. *Linguistic Inquiry* 30, 327–64.

Archangeli, D. (1996). 'Output identity and Javanese vowels'. Handout of talk presented at the third annual meeting of the Austronesian Formal Linguistic Association, UCLA.

Avery, P. and G. Lamontagne (1995). 'Infixation ⟨and metathesis⟩ in Tagalog'. Handout of talk presented at the annual meeting of the Canadian Linguistic Association.

Beckman, J. (1995). 'Shona height harmony: markedness and positional identity'. In Beckman *et al.* (eds), 53–76.

Beckman, J. (1997). *Positional Faithfulness*. PhD thesis, U.Mass, Amherst.

—— L. Walsh Dickey, and S. Urbanczyk (eds), University of Massachusetts occasional papers 18: *Papers in Optimality Theory*. Amherst, MA: GLSA.

Benua, L. (1995). 'Identity effects in morphological truncation'. In Beckman *et al.* (eds), 88–136. ROA-74.

---

[31] A full account of positional faithfulness will also require IDENT-like constraints that militate against featural alteration in edges or heads. See Beckman (1997).

Benua, L. (1997). *Transderivational Identity: Phonological Relations Between Words.* PhD thesis, U.Mass, Amherst.

Broselow, E. and J. McCarthy (1983). 'A theory of internal reduplication'. *The Linguistic Review* 3, 25–88.

Buckley, E. (to appear). 'Uniformity in extended paradigms'. In Hermans and van Oostendorp (eds).

Burzio, L. (1994a). *Principles of English Stress.* Cambridge, Cambridge University Press.

—— (1994b). 'Metrical consistency'. In E. Ristad (ed.), *Language Computations.* Providence, RI, American Mathematical Society, 93–126.

—— (1996). 'Surface constraints versus underlying representation'. In J. Durand and B. Laks (eds), 123–42.

—— (1997). 'Strength in numbers'. In V. Miglio and B. Morén (eds), *University of Maryland Working Papers in Linguistics* 5. *Selected Phonology Papers from the Hopkins Optimality Theory Workshop* 1997. College Park, Maryland, 27–52.

Bybee, J. (1985). *Morphology: A study of the relation between meaning and form.* Amsterdam, John Benjamins.

Bye, P. (1996). 'Correspondence in the prosodic hierarchy and the grid: Case studies in overlength and level stress'. Cand. Philol. Thesis, Institut for Språk og Litteratur, University of Tromsø.

Churchward, C. M. (1940). *Rotuman Grammar and Dictionary.* Sydney, Australasia Medical Publishing Company. [Reprinted New York, AMS Press, 1978.]

Clements, G. N. and K. Ford (1979). 'Kikuyu tone shift and its synchronic consequences'. *Linguistic Inquiry* 10, 179-210.

—— and E. Hume (1995). 'The internal organization of speech sounds'. In J. Goldsmith (ed.), 245–306.

Crosswhite, K. (1996). 'A non-cyclic approach to Chamorro cyclicity'. Handout of talk presented at the third annual meeting of the Austronesian Formal Linguistic Association, UCLA.

Crowhurst, M. (1994). 'Foot extrametricality and template mapping in Cupeño'. *Natural Language and Linguistic Theory* 12, 177–201.

—— (1997). 'Coda conditions and Um infixation in Toba Batak'. Ms, University of North Carolina, Chapel Hill.

de Lacy, P. (1996). 'Circumscription revisited: An analysis of Maori reduplication'. Ms, University of Auckland. ROA-133.

Dixon, R. M. W. (1977). *A Grammar of Yidiɲ.* Cambridge, Cambridge University Press.

Downing, L. J. (1998a). 'Prosodic misalignment and reduplication'. In G. Booij and J. van Marle (eds), *Yearbook of Morphology 1997.* Dordrecht, Kluwer, 83–120.

—— (1998b). 'On the prosodic misalignment of onsetless syllables'. *Natural Language and Linguistic Theory* 16, 1–52.

—— (1999). 'Verbal reduplication in three Bantu languages'. In Kager, van der Hulst, and Zonneveld (eds), 62–89.

Durand, J. and B. Laks (eds) (1996). *Current Trends in Phonology: Models and Methods.* Salford, Manchester, University of Salford Press.

Gafos, A. (1996). *The Articulatory Basis of Locality in Phonology.* PhD thesis, The Johns Hopkins University.

—— (1997). 'The two faces of anchoring'. Ms, U.Mass, Amherst.

—— (1998). 'Eliminating long-distance consonantal spreading'. *Natural Language and Linguistic Theory* 16, 223–278.

Goldsmith, J. (ed.) (1995). *The Handbook of Phonological Theory*. Oxford, Basil Blackwell.

Hargus, S. and S. G. Tuttle (1997). 'Augmentation as affixation in Athabaskan languages'. *Phonology* 14, 177–220.

Hayes, B. (1987). 'A revised parametric metrical theory'. In J. McDonough and B. Plunkett (eds), *Proceedings of NELS 17*, Amherst: GLSA, University of Massachusetts, 274–89.

—— (1995). *Metrical Stress Theory: Principles and case studies*. Chicago, University of Chicago Press.

Hermans, B. and M. van Oostendorp (eds) (to appear), *The Derivational Residue in Phonology*. Amsterdam and Philadelphia, John Benjamins.

Hill, J. H. (1970). 'A peeking rule in Cupeño'. *Linguistic Inquiry* 1, 534–39.

Hung, H. (1992). 'Relativized suffixation in Choctaw: A constraint-based analysis of the verb grade system'. Ms, Brandeis University.

—— (1994). *The Rhythmic and Prosodic Organization of Edge Constituents*. PhD thesis, Brandeis University. ROA-24.

Hyman, L. (1985). *A Theory of Phonological Weight*. Dordrecht, Foris.

Inkelas, S. (1999). 'Exceptional stress-attracting suffixes in Turkish: Representation vs. the grammar'. In Kager, van der Hulst, and Zonneveld (eds).

Itô, J. (1986). *Syllable theory in prosodic phonology*. PhD thesis, U.Mass, Amherst.

—— (1989). 'A prosodic theory of epenthesis'. *Natural Language and Linguistic Theory* 7, 217–60.

—— Y. Kitagawa, and R. A. Mester (1992). 'Prosodic type preservation in Japanese: Evidence from *zuuja-go*'. SRC–92–05, Syntax Research Center, University of California, Santa Cruz.

—— —— —— (1996). 'Prosodic faithfulness and correspondence: Evidence from a Japanese argot'. *Journal of East Asian Linguistics* 5, 217–94. ROA-146.

Kager, R. (1996). 'On affix allomorphy and syllable counting'. In U. Kleinhenz (ed.), *Interfaces in Phonology*. Berlin, Akademie Verlag, 155–71.

—— (to appear). 'Surface opacity of metrical structure in Optimality Theory'. In Hermans and van Oostendorp (eds).

—— H. van der Hulst, and W. Zonneveld (eds) (1999). *The Prosody-Morphology Interface*. Cambridge, Cambridge University Press.

Kenstowicz, M. (1994). 'Cyclic vs. non-cyclic constraint evaluation'. *MIT Working Papers in Linguistics* 21, 11–42.

—— (1996). 'Base-identity and uniform exponence: alternatives to cyclicity'. In J. Durand and B. Laks (eds), 363–93.

—— and C. Kisseberth (1977). *Topics in Phonological Theory*. New York, Academic Press.

Kisseberth, C. (1970). 'On the functional unity of phonological rules'. *Linguistic Inquiry* 1, 291–306.

Kraska-Szlenk, I. (1995). *The phonology of stress in Polish*. PhD thesis, University of Illinois.

Lombardi, L. and J. McCarthy (1991). 'Prosodic circumscription in Choctaw morphology'. *Phonology* 8, 37–71.

McCarthy, J. (1979). *Formal Problems in Semitic Phonology and Morphology*. PhD thesis, MIT.

McCarthy, J. (1984). 'Prosodic organization in morphology'. In M. Aronoff and R. Oehrle (eds), *Language Sound Structure*. Cambridge, MA, MIT Press, 299–317.

—— (1996). 'Extensions of faithfulness: Rotuman revisited'. Ms, U.Mass, Amherst. ROA-110.

—— (1997). 'Prosodic morphology in Optimality Theory'. Handout packet from LSA Summer Institute and Holland Institute of Linguistics Courses.

—— and A. Prince (1986). *Prosodic morphology*. Ms, U.Mass, Amherst, and Brandeis University. [Revised and reissued (November, 1996) as *Prosodic Morphology 1986*. RuCCS TR-32, Rutgers Center for Cognitive Science.]

—— —— (1990a). 'Foot and word in prosodic morphology: The Arabic broken plurals'. *Natural Language and Linguistic Theory* 8, 209–82.

—— —— (1990b). 'Prosodic morphology and templatic morphology'. In M. Eid and J. McCarthy (eds), *Perspectives on Arabic Linguistics: Papers from the second symposium*. Amsterdam, John Benjamins, 1–54.

—— —— (1991). 'Linguistics 240: prosodic morphology'. Lectures and handouts from 1991 LSA Linguistic Institute Course, University of California, Santa Cruz.

—— —— (1993a). 'Prosodic morphology I: Constraint interaction and satisfaction'. Ms, U.Mass, Amherst, and Rutgers University. [To appear, MIT Press.]

—— —— (1993b). 'Generalized alignment'. In G. Booij and J. van Marle (eds), *Yearbook of Morphology 1993*. Dordrecht, Kluwer, 79–153.

—— —— (1994a). 'The emergence of the unmarked: optimality in prosodic morphology'. In *Proceedings of NELS 24*, Amherst: GLSA, University of Massachusetts, 333–79.

—— —— (1994b). 'Prosodic morphology: An overview'. Talks presented at the OTS/HIL Workshop on Prosodic Morphology, University of Utrecht.

—— —— (1995a). 'Faithfulness and reduplicative identity'. In Beckman *et al.* (eds), 249–384. ROA-60.

—— —— (1995b). 'Prosodic morphology'. In J. Goldsmith (ed.), 318–66.

—— —— (1999). 'Faithfulness and identity in prosodic morphology'. In Kager, van der Hulst, and Zonneveld (eds), 218–309.

Marantz, A. (1982). 'Re reduplication'. *Linguistic Inquiry* 13, 435–82.

Mester, R. A. (1990). 'Patterns of truncation'. *Linguistic Inquiry* 21, 478–85.

Moravcsik, E. (1978). 'Reduplicative constructions'. In J. Greenberg, C. Ferguson, and E. Moravcsik (eds), *Universals of Human Language 3: Word Structure*. Stanford, Stanford University Press, 297–334.

Nash, D. (1979). 'Yidinʸ stress: a metrical account'. *Cunyforum* 7/8, 112–30.

Orgun, C. O. (1994). 'Monotonic cyclicity and Optimality Theory'. In *Proceedings of NELS 24*. Amherst: GLSA, University of Massachusetts, 461–74. ROA-123.

—— (1996). *Sign-Based Morphology and Phonology With Special Attention to Optimality Theory*. PhD thesis, University of California, Berkeley. ROA-171.

Pater, J. (1995). 'On the non-uniformity of weight-to-stress and stress preservation effects in English'. Ms, McGill University.

—— (1996). 'Restricting quantity sensitivity by respecting alignment'. Handout of talk presented at WECOL 96, University of California, Santa Cruz.

Pierrehumbert, J. (1994). 'Alignment and prosodic heads'. In *Proceedings of the Eastern States Conference on Formal Linguistics*. Cornell University, Linguistics Graduate Student Association.

Prentice, D. J. (1971). *The Murut Languages of Sabah.* Pacific Linguistics, Series C, no. 18. Canberra, Australian National University.

Prince, A. (1980). 'A metrical theory for Estonian quantity'. *Linguistic Inquiry* 11, 511–62.

—— and P. Smolensky (1991). 'Linguistics 247: Notes on connectionism and harmony theory in linguistics'. Technical Report CU–CS–533–91. Department of Computer Science, University of Colorado, Boulder.

—— (1993). 'Optimality Theory: constraint interaction in generative grammar'. Ms, Rutgers University, New Brunswick, and University of Colorado, Boulder. [To appear, MIT Press.]

Samek-Lodovici, V. (1992). 'Universal constraints and morphological gemination: A crosslinguistic study'. Ms, Brandeis University.

—— (1993). 'A unified analysis of crosslinguistic morphological gemination'. In P. Ackema and M. Schoorlemmer (eds), *Proceedings of CONSOLE I.* The Hague, Holland Academic Graphics, 265–83.

Spaelti, P. (1997). *Dimensions of Variation in Multi-Pattern Reduplication.* PhD thesis, University of California, Santa Cruz.

Spring, C. (1990). *Implications of Axininca Campa for Prosodic Morphology and Reduplication.* PhD thesis, University of Arizona, Tucson.

Urbanczyk, S. (1995). 'Double reduplications in parallel'. In Beckman *et al.* (eds), 499–532. ROA-73.

—— (1996a). 'Morphological templates in reduplication'. In *Proceedings of NELS 26.* Amherst: GLSA, University of Massachusetts.

—— (1996b). *Patterns of Reduplication in Lushootseed.* PhD thesis, U.Mass, Amherst.

Whitney, W. (1924) *Sanskrit Grammar.* Leipzig. Repr. 1977 Delhi, Motilal Banarsidass.

Zec, D. (1988). *Sonority Constraints on Prosodic Structure.* PhD thesis, Stanford University.

Zoll, C. (1996). *Parsing Below the Segment in a Constraint Based Framework.* PhD thesis, University of California, Berkeley. ROA-143.

PART TWO

Phonology: Segmental Phonology

5

Loan Phonology: Perception, Salience, the Lexicon and OT

Haike Jacobs and Carlos Gussenhoven

5.1 Introduction

Unless they are treated as exceptions, loanwords whose phonological stucture does not fit into the phonology of the borrowing language need to be adapted to it. Rule-based accounts of the adaptation (or 'nativisation') of loanwords are typically confronted with the duplication problem (Kenstowicz and Kisseberth 1977: 136). This situation arises when a rule needs to be added to the grammar which duplicates a morpheme structure constraint, of which the sole function is to adapt loanwords to the native phonological system. As has been argued by Yip (1993), a constraint-based theory like Optimality Theory (OT) does not have to add extra rules to account for the nativisation of loan words. Rather, the adaptation ought to follow from the constraint ranking of the borrowing language.

This chapter readdresses this question and is organized as follows. In Section 5.2, we will discuss Silverman's rule-based account of loanword phonology in Cantonese and Yip's argument that a constraint-based model in contrast to a rule-based theory does not have to add extra rules but can make the nativisation simply follow as an automatic consequence of the constraint hierarchy of the language. Following Silverman, Yip distinguishes two levels: a Perceptual and an Operative level. In Section 5.3, we will go one step further and claim that the Perceptual level can entirely be dispensed with and that the constraint hierarchy alone suffices to deal adequately with loanword phonology.

An important claim that we will make is that what counts as an input to the phonological grammar of the borrowing language is not an unanalysed acoustic pattern but a universally defined, fully specified phonological representation, which is identical to what counts as an input to the phonological grammar of a child acquiring his or her language. We thus dispense with the notion of 'phonetic salience', appealed to by Silverman and Yip to explain the exclusion of certain segments from the nativised loans. The difference between child phonology and loan phonology is to be located in what Smolensky (1996) has called the Constraint Demotion algorithm, which is active in child phonology but is not, or is only marginally, active in loan phonology. It will be argued that the fact that Constraint Demotion does not play a role in loan phonology has important consequences for the underlying representation of loanwords. Finally, Section 5.4 summarizes the main conclusions.

5.2 Loanword Phonology: Rule-Based Versus Constraint-Based

5.2.1 *Silverman (1992)*

Silverman (1992) has advanced a rule-based account of loanword phonology in which a distinction is made between two levels: a Perceptual level and an Operative level. At the Perceptual level, the input, which according to Silverman (1992: 289) consists 'solely of a superficial acoustic signal, lacking all phonological representation' is interpreted as a string of native segments, in conformity with the Perceptual Uniformity Hypothesis in (1) (cf. Silverman 1992: 297, 325).

(1)   Perceptual Uniformity Hypothesis

At the Perceptual Level, the native segment inventory constrains segmental representation in a uniform fashion, regardless of string position.

Caveat: input whose acoustic phonetic properties cannot be discerned due to its presence in an impoverished context (a context to be determined on a language-specific basis) is not supplied [a] representation.

Some examples from Cantonese in (2) will make this clear.

(2)   **Input**   **Perceptual level**
       sharp   [sap]
       shaft   [saf]
       soda   [sota]
       size   [says]
       cheese   [tsis]

Silverman's assumption is that because Cantonese has only a single coronal fricative, the differences between [s], [z], [ʃ] and [ʒ] are not perceived by Cantonese speakers, and all four sibilants are replaced by the Cantonese segment [s]. Similarly, Cantonese does not have any voiced obstruents, which means that the difference between [d] and [t], for instance, is not perceived. Hence, [d] in *soda* is represented as [t].

   In addition to the translation of foreign segments into native segments, there are two further elements in Silverman's treatment that contribute to the phonological shape of of the loanword: phonological rules and a pre-grammatical evaluation of the phonetic salience of the segments in the foreign word.

   First, we discuss the rules, which constitute the Operative level. Here, Syllable

Structure Constraints hold, and to satisfy these in the case of Cantonese, a phonological process (peculiar to that level of loanword phonology) of occlusivation
will apply to fricatives and affricates that have been assigned a coda position. In
Cantonese, the only possible codas are [-cont] segments and the glides [j] and
[w]. The occlusivation rule Silverman proposes is given in (3).

(3)   Occlusivisation C → [–cont] / ____]_σ

The rule in (3) will change loans such as *shaft* as in (4).

(4)   Input   *shaft*

       Perceptual level   [saf]
       Operative level   [sap]

Unlike [f], [s] in coda position does not undergo (3), i.e. does not lead to [t].
Instead, regardless of its original identity in the lending language, [s] is subject
to a rule of vowel epenthesis, given in (6).

(5)   Input   *tips*   *waste*   *bus*

       Perceptual level   [tips]   [ways]   [pas]
       Operative level   [tipsi]   [waysi]   [pasi]

(6)   Epenthesis Ø → V/ s]_σ ____

The question arises as to why the data in (4) and (5) are treated differently. Yip
(1990) suggests that occlusivisation primarily applies to coda continuants when
they are followed by a stop, and that a process of segment merger which preserves the place of articulation of the fricative and the manner of articulation of
the stop should be postulated to account for [ft] → [p]. Yip also notes that
fricatives in non-branching codas normally undergo epenthesis, as in *bus*→[pasi]
(*[pat]). However, given that *waste* becomes [weysi] and not *[weyt], it seems
unlikely that the branching coda is of any relevance. Rather, it seems that a
distinction between [s] and [f] has to be made. In Silverman's account, this
difference can be accounted for by ordering Epenthesis (6) before Occlusivisation (3). If Occlusivisation were to apply first, [s] would become [t].

  The second additonal element in the process of loanword adaptation is illustrated by the treatment of final consonants in a cluster. If the final consonant
is [t], as in *lift*, *shaft* and *waste*, it is not realised in Cantonese, whereas if it is
[s], as in *tips*, it is realised as an onset consonant. Given that both [t] and [s]
are part of the Cantonese segment inventory, both segments must be perceivable
by Cantonese speakers in Silverman's view. Silverman (1992: 325) accounts for
this difference by relying on a notion of phonetic salience, given as the caveat
in (1). Essentially, this boils down to the assumption that postconsonantal [s] in
these examples is above some level of phonetic salience for Cantonese speakers,
but that postconsonantal [t] is not. The latter consonant is thus not included in
the representation at the Perceptual level.

In summary, Silverman's analysis of English loans in Cantonese rests on three assumptions. First, before the grammar is called into action, segments of which the phonetic salience falls below some language-specific cut-off point are excluded, even though they are part of the borrowing language's segment inventory. Second, the analysis requires a level of representation, the Perceptual level, which acts as a filter on what is to be processed by the rules of loanword phonology. It adjusts the feature configurations of any segments that do pass the salience test, but that do not occur as such in Cantonese, so as to bring them in line with segments that do form part of the Cantonese inventory. Third, ordered rules must be postulated that are specific to loanword phonology. In fact, Silverman stresses that because of the highly constrained nature of the Cantonese morphophonology, the need for segmental rules is virtually non-existent, and therefore all segmental processes are to be relegated to the loanword phonology. This illustrates quite dramatically that a rule-based analysis will typically run into the duplication problem (Kenstowicz and Kisseberth 1977: 136), the point also stressed by Yip (1993). That is, a rule-based theory can account for loanword phonology, if rules are added to the grammar which duplicate morpheme structure constraints.

5.2.2 *Yip (1993)*

Yip (1993) claims that a constraint-based theory can account for loanword adaptations without extra machinery. More specifically, she claims that the adaptation follows as an automatic consequence of the constraint hierarchy that is independently needed to describe the phonology of the language. The phonological scan, she claims, is nothing more than 'the set of ranked constraints independently needed for the native vocabulary'. In other words, the first objection—that of the duplication problem—is met in her approach. However, Yip follows Silverman's division of the loanword phonology into two scans, a perceptual and a phonological one. This has the consequence that the filtering out of ill-formed segments is not accounted for in her OT analysis. Yip also follows Silverman's suggestion that relative salience plays a role in loanword phonology and proposes to that end a somewhat modified PARSE constraint (viz. PARSE(salient)). This constraint will see to it that, in the case of Cantonese, [s] will always be parsed; that other consonants, like liquids, will be parsed depending on the context; while post-consonantal stops are not parsed at all. We illustrate this with the Cantonese adaptation of English *bus*. Tableau (7), from Yip (1993: 284), illustrates the constraints involved. OK-σ is a blanket constraint that inspects the syllabic well-formedness of the output candidate, Faithfulness demands that the underlying form is not altered (i.e. does not lose or gain segments), MinWd requires the output candidate to be bisyllabic, and Fill, apparently partly duplicating Faithfulness, avoids inserted segments. Recall that □ indicates an inserted segment, and ⟨ ⟩ embrace a deleted segment.

(7) /bʌs/	OK-σ	Faithful	MinWd	Parse (salient)	Fill
pas.	*!		*		
☞ pa.s□		*			*
pa.⟨s⟩		*	*!	*	

With examples like (7), Yip shows that the constraints she uses are independently needed in the language. Hence, there is no need for a rule like Epenthesis (6); rather, the adaptation of coda [s] in *bus* follows as an automatic consequence of the independently-needed constraint hierarchy. The effect of the perceptual scan can be observed in (7) in that the feature [+voice] is not perceived at all in the context of [-son] by Cantonese speakers, there being no voiced obstruents in Cantonese, and that as a result both the input form and the output form have a voiceless initial [p] (Yip 1993: 266-8). And the disappearance of [t] in words like *lift* is dealt with by allowing Parse(salient) to be satisfied when [t] is not parsed, and violated when it is.

Yip's point that, in OT, adaptations can be described with the same grammar that is needed for the language anyway is obviously very important, and we fully subscribe to it in general terms. However, her adherence to Silverman's Perceptual Uniformity Principle (1), which says that the perception of segments in the input depends on their presence in the segment inventory of the borrowing language, is less well motivated. There is no evidence that people cannot in general perceive segmental contrasts that do not occur in their own language. For example, her position leads to the unlikely conclusion that speakers of German or Dutch do, but Cantonese speakers do not, perceive voice contrasts in obstruents in word-final position, even though they are neutralized in both languages. Since in Dutch, voiced and voiceless obstruents are contrastive in onset position, their Perceptual representation of an English loanword like [klʌb] *club* would contain a [b], which is subsequently rejected in favour of [p], whereas the Cantonese speaker would perceive a [p] right from the start. This language-specific conception of perception leads to even less probable positions in the case of languages with small segment inventories, like Hawaiian (Elbert and Pukui 1979). Yip's theory predicts that speakers of this language are incapable of perceiving the difference between [s] and [k], since their language does not have this opposition. This is difficult to reconcile with the common finding that language users appear to be capable of perceiving non-native segments with evident ease, and not infrequently incorporate new sounds into their phonological inventories as 'marginal' phonemes.

Likewise, by adhering to the notion of phonetic salience, Yip is forced to take the improbable view that salience is determined on a language-specific basis. While for Cantonese speakers the phonetic salience of post-consonantal stops falls below the required perceptual threshold, speakers of Dutch, in which the phonological form of the English loanword *lift* is [lɪft], have apparently no trouble hearing them. Once more, to give a more extreme example, Hawaiian English does not parse [s] in initial consonant clusters in English loans. Yip's theory will have it that the pre-consonantal [s] is salient for the speakers of many languages but not for speakers of Hawaiian. In addition, it is not immediately clear how the same set of PARSE(salient) constraints can create these language-specific effects, or, if they can, how this subgrammar is prevented from (partly) duplicating the regular constraint hierarchy. In the next section, we will argue that Yip's model must be taken one step further—one which will allow us to get rid of the problems related to salience and the perceptual scan.

5.3 Loanword Phonology: OT All the Way

In our discussion we will attempt to separate the isues involved. First, we deal with the question of what the representation of the loanword is when it is first processed by the grammar. Second, we recapitulate Prince and Smolensky's treatment of (native) segment inventories in OT. Next, we show how that treatment can be applied to the adaptation of foreign segments to native segments without the need for extra machinery beyond that required for characterizing the native segment inventory. Fourth, we will discuss the consequences of Constraint Demotion's not being active in loan phonology for the underlying representation of loanwords. Fifth, we show how phonetic salience can be dispensed with in an OT analysis.

5.3.1 *The Issue of the Input*

Instead of Silverman's (1992) assumption that the input to the Perceptual parse is an unanalysed acoustic signal, we propose that language users analyse speech signals in terms of a universal phonological vocabulary, which is of course much larger than the subset that is incorporated in their native language. Under this view, both Dutch and Cantonese speakers perceive the final [t] in *lift*, but only speakers of Dutch allow it to survive the demands of their constraint grammar. Similarly, speakers of both Cantonese and Dutch allow *club* to enter their phonology as an input form with [b], but reject the parsing of [+voice] for slightly different reasons: Dutch cannot tolerate it in the coda, and Cantonese cannot tolerate it at all.

A comparison with first-language acquisition will be useful. What we propose is essentially the way perception works in child language as viewed by Smolensky (1996), who argues that during the earlier stages of first-language acquisition children analyse the input, an overt form, with the same constraint hierarchy that they use for production. Paradoxically, even if production leads to only one possible output, say [ta], for all underlying forms, an overt input form like [kæt] will be faithfully analysed as /kæt/, and—in the ideal case of an efficient child language learner—be stored as such as the underlying form. The paradox that pronounced forms obey the phonological markedness constraints, while perceived forms apparently flout these constraints and instead obey the faithfulness constraints, is solved by the fact that perceived forms and pronounced forms face different classes of competitors. While in production [kæt] competes with [ta], [ka], [skæti], etc. to lose to [ta], as shown in (7), in perception [kæt] has no competitors at all, since the form is given as an overt form. The game now is to find the best underlying form: the competition is thus between /ta/, /ka/, /kæt/, /skæti/, etc. In (8), we see that the phonological markedness constraints judge all instances of the overt form [kæt] as equally bad, and the faithfulness constraints can thus decide the winner: /kæt/, which will be stored in the lexicon (or recognized if it was already there).

(7) Input forms	Output forms	Markedness	Faithfulness
/kæt/	[kæt]	*!	
☞ /kæt/	[ta]		***
/kæt/	[skæti]	*!	**

(8) Input forms	Output forms	Markedness	Faithfulness
☞ /kæt/	[kæt]	*	
/ta/	[kæt]	*	*!**
/skæti/	[kæt]	*	*!*

Language acquistion can now be seen in terms of the demotion of phonological markedness constraints: whenever the structural description that results as optimal in the perception parse is less harmonic than the output of that structural description by the production parse (as is the case in (7) and (8)), relevant constraints are demoted by the Constraint Demotion algorithm (cf. Tesar and Smolensky 1995) to make the perception parse the more harmonic. Accordingly, production will become more faithful. The important difference between first-language acquisition and loan phonology, then, is that Constraint Demotion does not (usually) take place in the latter. As a result, the constraint hierarchy will not be adapted to make production conform to the perception, causing the drastic structural changes that we often see in loans. The consequences for the underlying representations of loanwords will be discussed below.

5.3.2 *Characterizing the Native Segment Inventory*

By way of prelude to our discussion of how segmental adjustments in loans are accounted for in OT we briefly recapitulate the way Prince and Smolensky (1993) characterize native segments inventories. The example they give happens not to be particularly suitable for loanword adaptations, but the emphasis here is on the mechanics. They describe segment inventories as resulting from the interaction of faithfulness constraints (PARSE and FILL) and anti-association constraints that forbid the parsing of segmental material to the feature tree. In Yidiɲ, palatalisation occurs as a secondary articulation on the coronal consonants [d,n], which thus contrast with [dʸ,nʸ]; however, there are no palatalised versions of the simplex labials and velars [b,g,m,ŋ]. In order to express universal markedness differences in place of articulation, Prince and Smolensky assume the harmony scale in (9a), according to which the association of an articulator Coronal to a place node is more harmonic (less marked) than the association of any other articulator, like Labial. The assumption is that (9a) is true both for consonantal articulations, i.e. associations to C-Place, and vocalic associations, i.e. associations to V-Place, which latter associations create secondary articulations when combined in the same segment with C-Place associations (Clements 1993). The harmony scale (9a) translates into the constraint hierachy (9b), which ranks 'anti-association constraints' forbidding unmarked articulations below those forbidding marked articulations.

(9)   a.   Coronal unmarkedness: harmony scale: PL/Cor > PL/Lab
       b.   Coronal unmarkedness: dominance hierarchy: *PL/Lab >> *PL/Cor

The crucial constraints that are needed by the side of (9b) are given in (10) and (11).

(10)   PARSE(feature): An input feature must be parsed

(11)   FILL(place): A place node must not be empty

The constraints in (9b), (10), and (11) can of course be violated and will lead to different outputs depending on the way they are ranked. In (12), an example of an input like [dʸ] is given. The notation Cor' indicates a feature which should associate to a V-Place node, i.e. a secondary articulation.

(12) {PL,Cor,Cor'}	*PL/Lab	PARSE(feat)	*PL/Cor	*[f'
☞ a. [Cor Cor']			* *	
b. [Cor' Cor]			* *	*!
c. [Cor]⟨Cor'⟩	*!		*	
d. [Cor']⟨Cor⟩	*!		*	*
e. []⟨Cor Cor'⟩	*!*			

Before discussing the interactions of the first four constraints, we clarify the difference between candidates (a) and (b). The input {PL,Cor,Cor'} in (12) lists the place node, plus two as yet unassociated features Cor and Cor'. In order to distinguish labialised coronals ([dʷ]) from palatalised labials [bʸ]), Prince and Smolensky assume that features that characterize secondary articulations come with a marker for secondary articulation, f'. Constraint *[f', given in (13), would ensure that an input {PL,Lab,Cor'} ends up as [bʸ], instead of leaving the interpretation as [bʸ] and [dʷ] undecided. Although in our example the issue is vacuous (since both features are coronal), constraint *[f will select candidate (a) in preference to candidate (b). (Square brackets indicate the parsing of a feature into C-Place and V-Place, respectively.)

(13)   *[f′ : f′ (secondary articulator) must not be parsed as the primary one

Tableau (12) shows that because PARSE(feature) is ranked above *PL/Cor, candidate (a) is favoured over candidate (e), in which neither feature is parsed, and over candidates (c) and (d), in which one feature is left unparsed.

In order to ban palatalised labials, the constraint *PL/Lab is ranked above PARSE(feature), as shown in (14), where the input is {PL,Lab,Cor′}. The candidate that best satisfies the constraints is (c), in which {Cor′} is parsed in C-Place, leading to [d]. (The Yidiɲ inventory does not include voiceless plosives.) The association of the secondary articulator Cor as the primary one (a violation of the lowest constraint) avoids a violation of one of the two topmost constraints. Without going into all the details it is clear that the relative ranking of the constraints PARSE and the anti-association constraints adequately provides a description of the segment inventory of Yidiɲ.

(14) {PL,Lab,Cor′}	*PL/Lab	PARSE(feat)	*PL/Cor	*[f′
a. [Lab Cor′]	*!		*	
b. [Lab]⟨Cor′⟩	*!	*		
☞ c. [Cor′]⟨Lab⟩		*	*	*
d. []⟨Lab,Cor′⟩		*!*		

Finally, in order to prevent the favouring of an empty place node over the parsing of at least one feature in inputs without {Cor}, FILL(place) must dominate *PL/Lab, as shown in (15).

(15) {PL,Lab,Lab′}	FILL(place)	*PL/Lab	PARSE(feat)	*PL/Cor	*[f′
a. [Lab Lab′]		*!*			
☞ b. [Lab]⟨Lab′⟩		*	*		
c. []⟨Lab Lab′⟩	*!				

As said before, the predictions that this particular set of data and assumptions makes in the context of loan phonology, such that an input [pʸ] should turn up as [d] in Yidiɲ loans, are not at issue here.

5.3.3 Segmental Adaptations in Loan Phonology

We now turn to a demonstration that the Perceptual level argued for by Silverman and Yip can be dispensed with on the basis of the adaptation of French front rounded vowels in Mauritian Creole (MC). In (16), we give the vowel inventory of MC, which lacks front rounded vowels. The vowel inventory of French, which does contain front rounded vowels, is given in (17).

(16) MC vowel system   i   u
                           e   o
                              a

(17) French vowel system i   y   u
                           e   ø   o
                           ɛ   œ   a   ɔ

French loans containing front rounded vowels are adapted in MC with front unrounded vowels. By the logic of the Perceptual Hypothesis (1), Silverman and Yip would claim that the contrast is simply undetectable for MC speakers, who are believed to perceive front rounded vowels as front unrounded vowels. Our own assumption is that the structural description resulting from the perception parse of a front rounded vowel is that of a front rounded vowel, and since the form has no competitors, it will be stored as such in the lexicon. In the production parse, an input form containing the front rounded vowel is evaluated by the constraint hierarchy of MC so as to produce a front unrounded vowel. The existence of front rounded vowels in French means that both coronal and dorsal vowels may have a labial articulation. We will assume that if vowels have a double articulation, the two articulations are unordered. We also assume the following anti-association constraints, which specifically hold for the association of articulators to the V-Place node in the feature geometry (cf. Clements 1993, Jacobs 1998): *V-Place/Lab, *V-Place/Cor, *V-Place/Dor, *V-Place/Dor-Lab, *V-Place/Cor-Lab, *V-Place/Dor-Cor. In addition, there are the familiar constraints PARSE (feature) and FILL(place). Depending on the relative ranking of these constraints, different vowel segment inventories will result. The ranking that must be assumed for French is given in (18).

(18) Vowel articulation ranking in French
      FILL(Place) >> *V-Place/Dor-Cor, *V-Place/Lab >> PARSE(feature) >>
      *V-Place/Cor, *V-Place/Dor, *V-Place/ Cor-Lab, *V-Place/Lab-Dor.

The effect of this ranking is of course that in French only vowels will surface that have either a Cor ([i,e,ɛ]), a Dor ([a]), a Cor-Lab ([y,ø,œ]) or a Dor-Lab ([u,o,ɔ]) articulation. All other possible articulations for vowels will be excluded by the relative ranking of the constraint PARSE(feature) with the anti-association constraints. For MC, the only possible complex articulation for vowels is Lab-Dor (back, rounded vowels). Therefore, the MC ranking is minimally different from (18) in that *PL/Cor,Lab must rank above PARSE(feature), as shown in (19).

(19) Vowel articulation ranking in MC

      FILL(Pl) >> *V-Pl/Dor-Cor, *V-Pl/Cor-Lab, *V-Pl/Lab >>
      PARSE(feature) >> *V-Pl/Cor, *V-Pl/Dor, *V-Pl/Lab-Dor.

The correct prediction is of course that for an input form containing both a Cor and Lab articulation, as in French loans with front rounded vowels, like *plumeau* [ply'mo] 'duster' and *cheveux* [ʃə'vø] 'hair', the optimal output is a plain coronal vowel, as in MC *plimo* [plimo] and *seve* [seve], respectively.

(20) {V-Pl, Lab,Cor}	FILL(Place)	*V/Dor-Cor, *V/Cor-Lab, *V/Lab	PARSE(f)	*V/Lab-Dor	*V-/Cor	*V-/Dor
a. [Cor, Lab]		*!				
b. ⟨Cor⟩[Lab]		*!		*		
c. [ ]⟨Cor, Lab⟩	*!			* *		
☞ d. [Cor]⟨Lab⟩				*		*

In this section we have seen that the Perceptual level can be dispensed with in loan phonology. There is one single constraint hierarchy, which has different effects in production and perception. In the next section we will consider the consequences of the fact that Constraint Demotion is no longer active.

5.3.4 *The Underlying Representation of Loanwords*

If foreign inputs are faithfully parsed, are they also faithfully stored in the lexicon, in the way that first-language learners store new native inputs? When speakers are aware of the fact that they are dealing with a loanword, this may indeed well be the case, but of course loanwords often are restructured, and stored in an adapted shape in the lexicon.[1] In Optimality Theory, such restructuring follows as an automatic consequence of the organization of the grammar. To return to the example of Yidiɲ, the optimal output form of an input form containing {Lab, Cor'}, as shown in (14), only has a Cor-articulation. In other words, an input containing only {Cor} yields the same output as an input containing a complex articulation {Lab, Cor'}. Similarly, as shown in tableau (15), an input {Lab, Lab'} will yield the same output as an input {Lab}. It is improbable, however, that the underlying forms of any language will actually instantiate

---

[1] Valdman (1973) reports the reaction by a Haitian Creole-speaking maid who attended evening literacy classes to her teacher's pronunciation of *oeuf* 'egg' as [ze]: she decided to leave the class. Although she herself pronounced it that way, she was aware that her bilingual employers realised it as [zø]. In terms of the discussion here, this nicely illustrates that the structural description arrived at in the perception parse indeed contains the front rounded vowel, which, however, leaves the production parse as unrounded. The fact that not all lexical items are adapted at once can be illustrated with the two forms [plym] 'pen', 'feather' and [plim] 'feather', both from French [plym] *plume* 'pen', 'feather', as distinguished by some speakers.

this baroque range of theoretically possible inputs. Prince and Smolensky (1993: 192) therefore propose the Lexicon Optimization Principle, according to which only one of the many theoretically possible underlying forms leading to equivalent outputs will be stored, the one that incurs the fewest violation marks during the evaluation: 'The items in the Yidiɲ lexicon will not be filled with detritus like feature sets {PL, Cor, Lab'} or {PL, Lab, Lab'}. Since the former surfaces just like {PL, Cor} and the latter just like {PL, Lab}, and since the parses associated with these simpler inputs avoids the marks *PARSE(feature) incurred by the more complex counterparts, the needlessly complex inputs will never be chosen for underlying forms by the Yidiɲ learner'.

Tableau (21) makes the point explicit for MC. An input with only {V-Pl, Cor} will of course, given the hierarchy in (19), yield the same phonetic output as the input form {V-Pl, Cor, Lab} in (20). Compared to the optimal output candidate in (20), the optimal output candidate in (21) has one violation mark less, and will therefore be selected as the actual input by the language learner to be used whenever the word is pronounced.

(21) {V-Pl, Cor}	FILL(V-Place)	*V-Pl/Dor-Cor, *V-Pl/Cor-Lab, *V-Pl/Lab	PARSE(f)	*V-Pl/Lab-Cor, *V-Pl/Dor, *V-Pl/Cor
[ ]⟨Cor⟩	*!			
☞　[Cor]				*

The difference between first-language acquisition and loan phonology is thus that in child phonology Constraint Demotion will optimize harmony by changing the hierarchy, while in loan phonology Lexicon Optimization will optimize harmony by changing the lexical representations. Put differently, in loan phonology it is the production parse that wins and creates changes in the lexicon, whereas in child phonology it is the comprehension/perception parse that wins and creates changes in the constraint hierarchy. We schematize the entire process from the foreign word to the adapted underlying representation in (22).

A question that remains to be answered is whether OT can handle alternative solutions to the adaptation problem. For instance, what if there were a language which is identical to MC except that it turns front rounded vowels into back rounded vowels instead of to front rounded ones? Tunica is apparently an example of a language that borrowed French rounded front vowels as back rounded vowels (Haas 1947). Haas provides only a handful of examples, among which is *déjeuner*, pronounced as [tesuni]. The situation in Haitian Creole (Valdman 1973) is slightly more complicated. Words like *brûler* [bryle] and *adieu* [adjø] are realized as [bule] and [adjo]. Other words, like *mur* and *(les) yeux* are realised with front vowels, [mi] and [ze]. The adaptation of front rounded as back rounded vowels, instead of front unrounded ones, occurred at an earlier stage of Haitian Creole. The question arises how cases like Tunica and

(22)

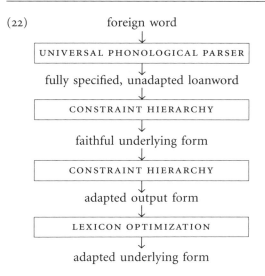

foreign word
↓
| UNIVERSAL PHONOLOGICAL PARSER |
↓
fully specified, unadapted loanword
↓
| CONSTRAINT HIERARCHY |
↓
faithful underlying form
↓
| CONSTRAINT HIERARCHY |
↓
adapted output form
↓
| LEXICON OPTIMIZATION |
↓
adapted underlying form

older Haitian Creole should be dealt with.

In (23), which is a copy of (20) with the ranking of *V/Lab-Dor and *V/Cor inverted and the output candidate (e) added, we see that the reversal of two constraints produces the desired effect. The interesting thing is that in the absence of the evidence of loans, it would not have been possible to decide how the constraints *V/Lab-Dor and *V/Cor are ranked. Loanword phonology, much in the same way as reduplicative morphology (cf. McCarthy and Prince 1993), can thus provide evidence of how these otherwise seemingly unranked constraints are in fact ranked. The appearance of [o] for [ø] in older Haitian Creole or of [e] for [ø] in MC may thus be seen as another instance of the 'emergence of the unmarked' (McCarthy and Prince 1994).

(23) {V-Pl,Lab,Cor}	FILL(Place)	*V/Dor-Cor, *V/Cor-Lab, *V/Lab	PARSE(f)	*V/Cor	*V-/Dor-Lab	*V-/Dor
a. [Cor, Lab]		*!				
b. ⟨Cor⟩[Lab]		*!	*			
c. []⟨Cor, Lab⟩	*!		* *			
d. [Cor]⟨Lab⟩			*	*!		
☞ e. [Dor, Lab]			*		*	

Tableau (23) simply says that back rounded vowels are less marked than front vowels. Statistically, this is unexpected—reranking in line with (17) is to be expected and indeed is what happened in the evolution of Haitian Creole. Tableau (24) shows that the implication of the constraint hierarchy in (23) is not that an ordinary coronal vowel is turned into a dorsal one.

(24) {V-Pl,Cor}	Fᵢₗₗ(Place)	*V/Dor-Cor, *V/Cor-Lab, *V/Lab	Pᴀʀsᴇ(f)	*V/Cor	*V/Dor-Lab	*V/Dor
☞ [Cor]				*		
[Dor]			*!			*

5.3.5 *Dealing With Nonsalient Segments*

Lastly, we turn to the question of the non-salient sounds in the input, which according to Silverman and Yip fail to get a hearing, so to speak, because they fall below some threshold of phonetic salience and are excluded by means of a pre-grammatical weeding of the input. There is no doubt that these nonsalient segments will indeed be phonetically nonsalient to speakers of languages that do not accommodate them. However, the fact that this nonsalience is apparently language-specific, as in the example of the English segments that are nonsalient for the purposes of Cantonese, but are readily accommodated in Dutch, suggests that their fate is determined by the grammar. The crucial prediction is that underlying forms are not treated differently from structural representations that arise from the parsing of foreign words. Concretely, the prediction is that a hypothetical underlying form /lipt/ in Cantonese should not be treated differently from a hypothetical /lipt/ which results from the parsing of the English word *lipped*. Because of the virtual absence of phonological adjustments in the native vocabulary, this prediction cannot be tested in the case of Cantonese, but it would be a trivial matter to give numerous examples illustrating this point. Importantly, the postulation of a constraint Pᴀʀsᴇ(salient), as proposed by Yip (1993), does not make this prediction.

Having said this, it is not immediately obvious how the non-parsing of [t] in *lift* should be accounted for. Since Cantonese disyllabic words contain stop-stop sequences, such as [syt.ka] 'cigar', we cannot rely on sonority-based constraints to exclude forms like *[lip.ti] for *lift*. A specific anti-association constraint forbidding the parsing of stem-final, postconsonantal plosives must then exist. Presumably, such a constraint is part of a range of constraints in the CᴏᴅᴀCᴏɴᴅɪᴛɪᴏɴ family, within which different languages choose different cutoff points (cf. English, which allows stop-[t] codas, but not stop-[k] or stop-[p] codas, etc.).

(25)   *Ct: Do not parse stemfinal, postconsonantal stops

Moreover, in order to be able to account for the different treatment of coda-[f] and coda-[s] in Cantonese, we will refine Yip's Faithfulness by making use of Correspondence Theory (McCarthy and Prince 1995). In Correspondence Theory, input-output faithfulness, or I-O Faithfulness, is divided into a number of constraints. MAX-IO (every segment of the input has a correspondent in the output) and DEP-IO (every segment of the output has a correspondent in the input) are constraints which prohibit deletion and insertion, and replace PARSE(segment) and FILL, respectively, while IDENT(f) (corresponding segment in the output is identical in feature with segment in the input) replaces PARSE(feature).

Just as in the case of Mauritian Creole and Yidiɲ, we will assume that every segment of a language is defined by an appropriate ranking of faithfulness constraints and anti-association constraints. This is illustrated for the voiced/voiceless obstruents in Cantonese in (26). In order to exclude voiced obstruents, we have to rank IDENT(+voice) for obstruents lower than the anti-association constraint for [+voice] for obstruents.

(26) /bʌs/	OK-σ	MAX-IO	DEP-IO	MinWd	*−son +voice	IDENT (−son +voice)
[pas]	*!			*		* *
[bas]	*!			*	*	*
☞ [pa.si]			*			* *
[ba.si]			*		*!	*
[ba⟨s⟩]		*!		*	*	
[pa⟨s⟩]		*!		*		o

Let us now show how the different treatment of coda-[f] and coda-[s] in Cantonese can be accounted for. In (28) and (29) we will take as examples *waste* and *lift* and assume, contrary to Yip (1993: 275) and Silverman (1992: 325), that [t] is present in the input. It is not some language-specific notion of saliency that will take care of not parsing post-consonantal [t], but the high-ranking of constraint (25). Also, in order to make sure that an input [s] is parsed, but not an input [f]—or, put differently, why we get [wei.si], but not [li.fi]—we have to revise the ranking of the IDENT constraints for [f] and [s]. Instead of listing the features defining [f] and [s], respectively (we follow Yip in assuming that the feature [strident] can only be present in coronal fricatives), we will simply refer to these constraints as IDENT(f) and IDENT(s). In order to obtain [lip] rather than [lit] as the optimal ouput for underlying

/lɪft/, we assume the two constraints in (27), which state that [p] is a better coda than [t].

(27)   *V-t >> *V-p

It should be noticed that in both tableaus (28) and (29) we have omitted purely for considerations of space the constraint MinWd. Its ranking, right below DEP-IO, does not affect the outcome.

(28) /lɪft/	OK-σ	Id(s)	*Ct	Max-IO	Id(t)	*V-t	Dep-IO	Id(p)	*V-p	Id(f)
☞ [lip⟨t⟩]				*					*	*
[lif⟨t⟩]	*!			*						
[li⟨f⟩t]				*		*!				
[li.f⟨t⟩i]				*			*!			
[lip.ti]			*!				*		*	*
[lift]	*!			*						
[lipt]			*!							*
[li.p⟨t⟩i]				*			*!			*

(29) /weist/	OK-σ	Id(s)	*Ct	Max-IO	Id(t)	*V-t	Dep-IO	Id(p)	*V-p	Id(f)
☞ [wei.s⟨t⟩i]				*			*			
[weist]	*!		*							
[weis⟨t⟩]	*!			*						
[wei⟨s⟩t]				*		*!				
[weit⟨t⟩]		*!		*		*				

Finally, it is shown in (30) that a monosyllabic input /kæt/ will still lead to an optimal output [kæt] and not [kæp] given that ID(t) is higher ranked than *V-t.

(30) /kæt/	OK-σ	Id(s)	*Ct	Max-IO	Id(t)	*V-t	Dep-IO	Id(p)	*V-p	Id(f)
☞ [kæt]						*				
[kæp]					*!				*	

It is interesting to note that Yip mentions vowel epenthesis as a possibility for the preservation of coda [f]. Besides /lift/ → [lip], /soft/ may become [sofu]. The analysis presented here can quite elegantly describe this possibility by allowing the constraint IDENT(f) to be optionally ranked: either as in (28) or higher, next to IDENT(s), as illustrated in (31).

(31) /soft/	OK-σ	Id(f)	Id(s)	*Ct	Max-IO	Id(t)	*V-t	Dep-IO	Id(p)	*V-p
[sop⟨t⟩]		*!			*					*
[sof⟨t⟩]	*!				*					
[so⟨f⟩t]					*		*!			
☞ [so.f⟨t⟩u]					*			*		
[sop.tu]		*!		*				*		*
[soft]	*!			*						
[sopt]		*!		*						
[so.p⟨t⟩u]		*!			*			*		

5.4 Summary

Loan phonology is not a separate component of the grammar. Phonological adjustments that are made by the borrowing language must be accounted for by the same constraint hierarchy that characterizes the native phonology. A crucial issue in loan phonology concerns the nature of the input to the grammar. We have argued that it is incorrect to claim, as does Silverman (1992), that prior to the processing of foreign words by the native grammar, the segments of the word are vetted for phonetic salience. Neither is it the case that the input consists of a raw acoustic signal. The language user's universal segment parser will assign a phonological representation to the foreign word in the same way that the language-learning child assigns a phonological representation to the words of his or her native language (even though he or she might not be able to pronounce it even remotely faithfully). In the case of the loanword adopter, this representation may, and typically will, include segmental and phonotactic configurations that are ill-formed in his or her own language. Upon production, the language's constraint hierarchy will cause the form to be adjusted to the native grammar in the same way that any native underlying form would. Integration of the loanword in the native vocabulary is achieved by Lexicon Optimization, which will cause the distance between the underlying form and the surface form to be minimized in favour of the produced, adjusted form.

   We have argued that Yip's OT account of loanword phonology, which follows Silverman (1992) in including a Perceptual parse which causes all non-native segments to be replaced with native segments, is incorrect. Again, the native grammar characterizes what a well-formed segment is, and that same grammar must see to it that any incoming segment that violates it is 'replaced' with one that does not. In fact, loanword phonology can in some cases reveal rankings in the grammar that for the purposes of the native phonology are not crucially ranked.

5.5 References

Clements, G. N. (1993). 'Lieu d'articulation des consonnes et voyelles: une théorie unifiée'. In B. Laks and A. Rialland (eds), *Architecture des représentations phonologiques.* Paris, CNRS, 101–45.

Elbert, H. S. and M. K. Pukui (1979). *Hawaiian Grammar.* Honolulu, University of Hawaiian Press.

Haas, M. (1947). 'Some French loanwords in Tunica.' Reprinted in *Language, Culture and History.* Essays by M. Haas, selected and introduced by A. S. Dil. Stanford, Stanford University Press, 1978, 89–92.

Jacobs, H. (1998). 'Changement linguistique: optimalité et articulation secondaire'. In P. Sauzet (ed.), *Proceedings of Langues et Grammaire II et III.* Paris.

Kenstowicz, M. and C. Kisseberth (1977). *Topics in Phonological Theory.* New York, Academic Press.

McCarthy, J. and A. Prince (1994). 'The emergence of the unmarked: optimality in prosodic morphology.' *NELS* 24, Amherst, GSLA, 333–79.

—— —— (1995). 'Faithfulness and reduplicative identity'. In J. Beckman, L. Walsh Dickey, and S. Urbanczyk (eds), University of Massachusetts occasional papers 18: *Papers in Optimality Theory.* Amherst, MA, GLSA.

Paradis, C. (1996). 'The inadequacy of filters and faithfulness in loanword adaptation'. In J. Durand and B. Laks (eds), *Current Trends in Phonology.* Salford, Manchester, University of Salford Press.

Prince, A. and P. Smolensky (1993). *Optimality Theory: Constraint Interaction in Generative Grammar.* Technical Report #2, Rutgers University.

Silverman, D. (1992). 'Multiple scansions in loanword phonology: Evidence from Cantonese'. *Phonology* 9, 289–328.

Smolensky, P. (1996). 'On the comprehension/production dilemma in child language', *Linguistic Inquiry* 27, 720–31.

Tesar, B. and P. Smolensky (1995). 'The learnability of Optimality Theory', *WCCFL* 13, 122–37.

Yip, M. (1988). 'The obligatory contour principle and phonological rules: A loss of identity'. *Linguistic Inquiry* 19, 65–100.

—— (1990). 'The phonology of Cantonese loanwords: evidence for unmarked settings for prosodic parameters'. In J. Packard (ed.), *New directions in Chinese Linguistics.* Dordrecht, Kluwer.

—— (1993). 'Cantonese loanword phonology and Optimality Theory'. *Journal of East Asian Linguistics* 2, 261–91.

Valdman, A. (1973). 'Some aspects of decreolization in Creole French'. In T. Sebeok (ed.), *Diachronic, Areal, and Typological Linguistics.* Current Trends in Linguistics, vol. 11. The Hague and Paris, Mouton.

6

Derivational Residue: Hidden Rules in Optimality Theory

Darlene LaCharité and Carole Paradis

6.1 Introduction

Optimality Theory (OT) (following McCarthy and Prince 1993; Prince and Smolensky 1993) has focused on the identification and articulation of ranked phonological constraints by test-driving phonological phenomena from a variety of languages through selected subsets of those constraints. OT's goal has been to account for phonological generalizations within languages, and for differences among languages, using universal surface constraints that are prioritized on a language-specific basis, instead of using rules, derivations and intermediate representations, as in Chomsky and Halle (1968) (henceforth SPE).

There is now general agreement that shifting the focus from rules to constraints has been remarkably successful. Perhaps because of that success, some of OT's proponents have concluded that OT has replaced rules with ranked constraints entirely. For example, when comparing OT with phonotactic and repair theories, including Harmonic Phonology (following Goldsmith 1989; Goldsmith and Larson 1990; Wiltshire 1992; Goldsmith 1993; etc.) and the Theory of Constraints and Repair Strategies (henceforth TCRS) (following Paradis 1988a, 1988b, 1990; LaCharité and Paradis 1993; etc.), Prince and Smolensky (1993: 203), two of OT's principal architects, imply that the results of rules are achieved in OT solely through the interaction of violable constraints. Itô *et al.* (1995: 578) say explicitly that in OT 'there are no rules or repair strategies, and no serial derivation'. Yip (1993: 2) asserts that an OT account of onsets in Cantonese, which rests on ranked, violable constraints, render[s] rules 'unnecessary'. Archangeli (1997: 27) sums up the prevailing view when she says that in OT, 'there simply is no rule component at all'. Hammond (1995: 6) elaborates on the idea that OT is rule-free: after claiming that in OT 'rules are virtually gone . . .' he goes on to say that 'The change performed by rules is factored out into *a single operation* [our emphasis] termed GEN'. This clearly suggests that GEN is functionally very different from, and considerably simpler than, rules. Yet there is no explanation or exploration of that assumption, either in Hammond's paper or elsewhere. In fact, virtually all research in OT to date has glossed over the inner workings of GEN, upon which OT's claim to rule replacement crucially relies.

Our present purpose is to examine whether ranked constraints have indeed made rules redundant, by considering whether and how rules are circumvented within OT. We maintain that when the generation, as well as the evaluation, of candidates is considered, GEN might well be regarded as the new incarnation of rules, and although processes are not overtly discussed and are no longer central to phonological theory, they are not redundant in OT. The claim that OT has done away with rules obscures what is really a revised view of phonological rules, particularly with respect to their relationship to constraints in phonological theory, since in OT rules do not apply in response to constraint violations— i.e. they are not repair strategies. Nonetheless, this revision of the role of rules in OT, through GEN, represents not a fundamental change in our view of what a rule accomplishes—which is to relate one level of representation to another—but a continuation of the steady decline in the status and role of arbitrary rules that has been taking place for over two decades.

We will show explicitly, using mainly examples from the adaptation of borrowings, that to generate an optimal candidate, GEN, sometimes with the help of the post-phonological interpretive component, effects the operations to which rules had been reduced prior to the advent of OT. Even under the most restrictive view of GEN, it must be relied upon to insert content, as well as structure, and to delete at least structure. However, we are not suggesting that proponents of OT, most particularly McCarthy and Prince, are unaware of the extent of GEN's powers to alter the input. For although GEN's capacities and limitations are generally implied or, at most, briefly stated, rather than being argued for or even demonstrated, they are nonetheless intended, intrinsic aspects of OT.[1] The idea behind this lack of argumentation or demonstration is OT's belief that what GEN does (i.e. insert content and structure and delete at least structure) is relatively unimportant, or beside the point, because OT places such a heavy burden of phonological explanation on the constraint system.

While we agree with OT's general view of the balance of power between rules and constraints, the fact remains that as long as OT retains GEN in its current conception, it is a procedural theory. To wit, OT is based on the assumption of a representation, which comprises the input to GEN, which can be modified by the addition or deletion of any amount of content or structure, to create a set of potential output forms, which OT calls candidates. The actual surface form is simply the particular output of GEN which best satisfies the constraint hierarchy.

As just hinted, a notable feature of OT, that distinguishes it from either Harmonic Phonology or TCRS is that GEN effects the changes to the input prior to encountering the constraints, rather than as a response to the constraints.

---

[1] There have been proposals (e.g. Golston 1997) which would reduce or even gut GEN, but such views have not yet been incorporated into what Golston refers to as 'Standard OT'.

However, this does not strike us as grounds for discounting the changes that occur. The point, it seems to us, is that they occur at all. Indeed, we see this as a fundamental paradox in OT: it repudiates the notions of being procedural or derivational, but it nonetheless relies on the operations that defined rules to transform an input form into an output surface form.

The remainder of the chapter is organized in the following way: Section 6.2 provides a brief overview of the form and function of SPE-type rules. We discuss how and why the form of rules changed during the course of the 1980s, as well as how and why defined limits were set on their power. We also consider the emergence of constraints and how they came to occupy a pre-eminent, if generally non-formal, place in generative phonological theory. A summary of these discussions is provided in 6.2.3.

In Section 6.3 we turn to OT and its handling of the traditional rule functions of insertion and deletion of content and structure, applying these notions to the adaptation of French loanwords in Fula. Loanword adaptation is then used to demonstrate the insufficiency of parsing and non-parsing, the mechanisms first employed by OT in lieu of insertion and deletion of content and structure. Section 6.4 takes up the issue of recent innovations to GEN under Correspondence Theory. The conclusion is presented in Section 6.5.

6.2 The Decline of SPE-Type Rules

Claiming victory over SPE-type context rules, in the 1990s, might be like claiming victory over a retired, if not quite dead, horse, because generative phonologists had been doing without SPE-type rules for some time before constraint-based theories, and more recently OT, made their debut. In this section we will briefly sketch the decline of SPE phonological rules and their replacement by rules which, although they still effect the input-change-output cycle inherent in relating one level of representation to another, are less powerful, though more principled, more restricted, and considerably more general in nature than SPE rules. In addition, these more principled rules are, in some frameworks at least, functionally motivated rather than being arbitrary, as in SPE.

The core purpose of a phonological rule has always been to relate one level of representation to another. They have been used to model changes in, and alternations among, phonological representations. That view of their task has often been made explicit, as these representative statements indicate:

The phonological system of a language is comprised of two parts, representations and relations between representations [i.e. rules].   (Archangeli and Pulleyblank 1994: 283)

Formal rules characterize how underlying and surface representations are related. (Archangeli and Pulleyblank 1994: 285)

The phonological rules, then, make up the phonological component of the grammar, and their function is to convert the UR [underlying representation] of any utterance into its corresponding PR [phonetic representation] . . .   (Kenstowicz and Kisseberth 1979: 32)

The two representations [underlying and surface] are systematically related by phonological rules that delete, insert, or change sounds in precise contexts.   (Kenstowicz 1994: 7)

. . . phonologists have couched alternations in terms of a process applying to one type of representation to derive another representation.   (Spencer 1996: 45)

As some of these statements might suggest, the debates spawned by research into phonological rules came to focus primarily on identifying the levels that were to be related, and on what a rule could and could not do to relate one level of phonological representation to another.

In early generative phonology (following SPE), the specific job of rules was to assign a phonetic representation to the syntactic surface structure. More important than this view of their specific task was the assumption that the phonological component was synonymous with the system of rules. For some time after their introduction within generative phonology, rules constituted the only available explanation for phonological changes and alternations: a given alternation occurred because the language had a rule to that effect. For example, the fact that, in English, the vowel /i/ is realized as [j] in a word like *companion* was attributed to the rule in (1) (SPE: 87):

$$(1) \quad i \rightarrow j / \begin{bmatrix} \text{dental} \\ C \end{bmatrix} + \underline{\quad} V$$

The basic assumption of the early generative view was that, in relating one level of representation to another, rules were capturing the phonological generalizations of the language. The rules were seen not only to express the 'how' of phonological phenomena in a language, but also to stand intrinsically for the 'why' of those phenomena.

6.2.1 *Generalizing and Limiting SPE-Type Rules*

As research into the identification and elaboration of phonological rules proceeded, phonologists became increasingly aware of the need to shift their focus away from the rules to the phonological representations. That is to say, the nature of the input and the output, not just the processes to which they submitted, came to assume greater importance. Very soon theories of representation not only augmented rule-based models but took priority, as indicated by the familiar slogan 'if the representations are right, then the rules will follow' (McCarthy 1988: 84). In a broader perspective, the shift in focus from rules to representations led to a revised view of where the real generalizations in phonology lay. Autosegmental phonology and feature geometry, in particular, were motivated by the view that representations rather than rules were the bread and butter of phonology. During the 1980s this conviction launched a research program within those frameworks that led to a radical revision of rule form and a drastic curtailment of what was widely acknowledged to be the excessive power of SPE-type rules. More specifically, as a result of work within autosegmental phonology and feature geometry, phonological rules were reduced to basic operations of insertion or deletion, mostly of association lines (Archangeli and Pulleyblank 1986; see also McCarthy 1988 and Goldsmith 1995 for an overview). Nasal place assimilation provides a good illustration of the changes in rules that occurred. Under SPE's approach, nasal place assimilation is expressed by the following rule (McCarthy 1988: 86) which basically states that a nasal takes on whatever values for the features [coronal], [anterior] and [back] are possessed by the following consonant:

(2)   Place assimilation in SPE

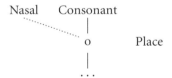

$$[+\text{nasal}] \rightarrow \begin{bmatrix} \alpha \text{ coronal} \\ \beta \text{ anterior} \\ \gamma \text{ back} \end{bmatrix} / \underline{\quad} \begin{bmatrix} \alpha \text{ coronal} \\ \beta \text{ anterior} \\ \gamma \text{ back} \end{bmatrix} \quad \text{where } \alpha, \beta, \gamma \text{ are variables over } + \text{ and } -$$

Among other deficiencies of this approach, the formalism offers no insights into why the language, indeed many languages, have this process, as opposed to other processes that are formally conceivable, though unusual or even unheard of.

In contrast, feature geometry reduces the rule of nasal place assimilation to the insertion of an association line, as shown in (3):

(3)   Place assimilation in feature geometry (McCarthy 1988: 87)

Nasal   Consonant

o   Place

. . .

In addition to streamlining the rule of nasal assimilation, feature geometry was able to offer a deeper level of explanation for the process than SPE. Recall that in SPE the rule, in and of itself, is the inherent reason for change, and there is no formal explanation for why a language has a particular rule. Within the framework of feature geometry, a deeper level of explanation is integrated into the expression of the rule. To return to the example of nasal place assimilation, it was hypothesized to occur because dental/alveolar nasals lack place features of their own. The (widespread, if not totally universal) lack of place features for anterior coronals inclines them to assimilate in place to a following segment specified for place (cf. Paradis and Prunet 1991 for an overview of the special properties of coronals and their relationship to coronal underspecification).

As just mentioned, by focusing on representations and pursuing theories of autosegmental phonology and feature geometry, phonologists addressed a serious deficiency of SPE-type rules—namely, that one could formulate rules expressing all kinds of unlikely, or even impossible, phonological changes. To provide just one example of how focusing on representations led to limiting the power of rules, feature geometry made it difficult, if not altogether impossible, to insert or delete arbitrary groups of features. Only a single feature, or a group of features dominated by a common node could function together in a rule. This advance, alone, radically reduced the power of rules. Even the rule-based approach of Archangeli and Pulleyblank (1986; 1994), which argued 'that rules vary independently of representations: [and that] taking care of the representations is not enough' (1994: 283) permitted only rules that could be defined by four parameters: 'function', 'type', 'direction' and 'iteration'. Although that approach allowed rules to include statements of context, direction and iterativity, it still curtailed how rules could effect their work, allowing them only to insert or delete structure (e.g. an association line) or content (e.g. a feature).

6.2.2 *Rules Versus Constraints*

Investigation into rules and rule systems convinced generative phonologists that their efforts would be better spent building models of phonological representations, rather than rules. However, the research also confirmed that rules very often produced an output that conformed to an obvious phonological preference in the language (cf. LaCharité and Paradis 1993 for a detailed synopsis of the emergence of constraints in generative phonology). Already in 1970, Kisseberth showed how different phonological rules of Yawelmani, including both consonant deletion and vowel epenthesis rules, took, as input, forms that violated Yawelmani prohibitions against word-final and triliteral consonant clusters, and conspired to yield outputs that respected them.

Although it was some time before constraints were given a formal place in our phonological models—TCRS, introduced by Paradis (1987), was the first constraint-based model—constraints came increasingly to be seen as providing a better answer to the question of why languages exhibit phonological changes and alternations. The notion of constraints suggested that alternations or phonological changes occur not simply because a language has particular rules but because it has a preference for representations of a particular phonological shape. That is, a language has constraints favoring certain representations and disallowing others. For example, Yawelmani requires that syllables conform to the shape V, CV, VC or CVC (Kenstowicz 1994: 254). The application of a rule thus serves to ensure conformity to a universal or language-specific phonological constraint. The reliance on constraints intensified among those working within the frameworks of autosegmental phonology and feature geometry, both of which came to enjoy widespread acceptance among generative phonologists.

In addition to offering an explanation for why certain processes occur within a language, constraints were often called upon to explain the non-occurrence of a generally expected process. Rendaku, a phenomenon in Japanese, provides a familiar concrete example. As shown in (4), the initial obstruent of a word is voiced when the word is the second member of a compound (Kenstowicz 1994: 162):

(4)   *iro* 'color' + * kami* 'paper' → *origami* 'colored paper'

However, as seen in (5), the initial obstruent is not voiced if there is already a voiced obstruent, here *z*, within the word.

(5)   *kami* 'divine' + *kazi* 'wind' → *kamikazi* 'divine wind' (**kamigazi)

This was explained as avoiding a violation of the Obligatory Contour Principle (OCP), an independently attested constraint prohibiting adjacent identical featural specifications (in this case, [+voice]).

(6)   k a z i   *g a z i
        | | \
    [+voice]   [+voice] [+voice]

Yip (1988) provided an in-depth analysis of both the triggering and blocking effects of the OCP and she observed that having rules that thus serve constraints allowed a large class of rules to 'be stated as context-free insertion and deletion rules' and rendered alpha notation unnecessary (Yip 1988: 65). In this way, focusing on constraints led to a further erosion of traditional phonological rules.

At least two constraint-based theories that predate OT—i.e. TCRS and Harmonic Phonology—crucially incorporated context-free rules that were, in essence, responses to constraints and/or well-formedness conditions. In TCRS, context-free rules are called Repair Strategies. Their express function is to transform input representations that are deficient with respect to the requirements of particular constraints into output representations that meet the well-formedness criteria established by those constraints. They do so by inserting or deleting content or structure. In other words, the 'rules' of TCRS are processes which are a) operationally restricted (according to the limits imposed on rules by autosegmental phonology and feature geometry) and b) context-free, since they are motivated entirely by constraints which include both principles (universal constraints) and parameter settings (language-specific answers to universal options). Indeed, repair strategies have very little to do with the language-specific contextual rules of SPE.

6.2.3 *Summary*

To sum up, the traditional view that the phonological generalizations of a language lay in language-specific context rules and rule systems was superseded by the view that the real generalizations lay in the output or, more precisely, in the restrictions and preferences that outputs and output alternations revealed. To the extent that rules functioned to bring about a particular condition in their outputs, they came to be regarded as mechanisms for enforcing conformity to constraints, rather than as a driving force in and of themselves.

The focus on phonological representations led to much stricter limits on the power and form of phonological rules, while the focus on constraints led to a revised view of the *raison d'être* for rules, and to the removal of their statements of context. Even before constraint-based frameworks received formal articulation, three fundamental and interrelated changes took place in generative phonology: (1) our view of the phonological component implicitly broadened to include constraints, as well as rules; (2) the burden of explanation for phonological change steadily shifted from rules to representations to constraints; and (3) the importance of rules was successively downgraded.

By the end of the 1980s, the glory days of phonological rules had definitely passed, and it was rare to find SPE-type rules used anywhere outside introductory courses in generative phonology. Yet throughout these changes, which saw fundamental alterations in their form, a severe curtailment of their power, and a precipitous decline in their status, the basic function of rules—noncontextual as well as contextual—went essentially unchanged and unchallenged: they remained a mechanism for relating one level of phonological representation to another.

6.3 OT and the Insertion and Deletion of Content and Structure

The general aim of this section is to show how GEN is used to accomplish what was previously handled by rules—i.e. relate one level of representation to another through the insertion and deletion of content and structure. We will see how, under the most restrictive view of GEN that has been taken in standard OT, GEN achieves the effects of insertion (6.3.1) and deletion (6.3.2). In 6.3.3 we will show how these mechanisms apply to loanword adaptation where the focus of insertion and deletion is generally at the featural level rather than the segmental as in the cases used to introduce and refine OT. In 6.3.4 it will be shown that GEN must perform the traditional rule functions of insertion of content as well as structure, and deletion of structure; it cannot achieve the desired results simply through parsing and unparsing.

6.3.1 *Insertion of Structure and Content*

In the earliest days of OT, GEN's function was to create candidates primarily via the insertion of structure. The effect of inserting content was achieved through the collaboration of a post-phonological phonetic component.[2] The implication was that GEN inserted structure, while the post-phonological phonetic compo-

---

[2] This suggested that OT, like Declarative Phonology, was monotonic, a suggestion which is now clearly insupportable since early assumptions that GEN is restricted to adding structure have been abandoned.

nent inserted any actual content. To illustrate how this was conceived to work, we will look briefly at reduplication in Axininca Campa, which McCarthy and Prince (1993) use to introduce OT.[3] Both segment insertions and deletions are apparent in Axininca Campa (cf. McCarthy and Prince 1993: ch. 5), but at this point we consider only insertion.

Axininca Campa verbal reduplication basically involves suffixation of a copy of the stem (e.g. -*kawosi* 'cut' *noŋkawosi-kawosi* 'cut more and more'). However, a reduplicated verb must be minimally disyllabic, so if a monosyllabic verb reduplicates, the output contains an epenthetic vowel—designated *V*—both in the root and in the reduplicant. This is seen in (4).

(4)   Axininca Campa verbal reduplication (McCarthy and Prince 1993: 65)

    Base   *Reduplication*

    kow   kowV-kowV-waitaki   'search'

From the perspective of OT, 'An epenthetic structure is a simply licit syllable form that contains *structure* [our emphasis] not motivated by the presence of a segment [. . . and] the site of epenthesis is an empty syllabic position that arises during the course of syllabification' (Prince and Smolensky 1993: 24). Thus, in the reduplication of monosyllabic verbs in Axininca Campa, GEN must insert nuclear structure (and appropriate suprastructure) that is not present in the input: 'The phonetic value of the epenthetic item [designated V] is filled in by post-phonological interpretive principles that read the output of the level of structure we are concerned with' (*ibid.*). In the early versions of OT, content is thus supplied 'non-phonologically' to the structure inserted 'phonologically' by GEN. In the cases used to introduce and illustrate the theory's operating principles, GEN is often required to effect epenthesis, so we take it as uncontroversial that GEN carries out this one function previously attributed to rules, the insertion of structure.

6.3.2 *The Deletion of Content*

The effects of deletion are achieved in OT through non-parsing of content or structure by GEN, and subsequent failure to realize unparsed material by the phonetic implementation mechanism. The following example from the prefixal morphology of Axininca Campa (McCarthy and Prince 1993: ch. 3) again serves to illustrate how deletion was handled in a version of OT that allowed GEN relatively little operational power. In Axininca Campa, ill-formed syllables result-

---

[3] McCarthy and Prince (1993) assume the widely accepted view of reduplication, that a reduplicative morpheme is an element of the input, designated RED, whose precise phonological form is underarticulated and thus dependent on that of the element to which it is affixed. Reduplication has provided fertile soil for OT; many crucial aspects—such as whether reduplication is total or partial, suffixal or prefixal, whether elements are inserted or deleted—are attributed to the ranking of particular constraints.

ing from V+V or C+C sequences are avoided in the output forms, as shown in (5).

(5)   *Input*   *Optimal candidate*   *Phonetic output*
  a. ir-saik-i   i(r)saiki   isaiki   'will sit'
  b. no-ana-ni   n(o)anani   nanani   'my black dye'

In (5), the candidates that satisfy the constraints against V+V or C+C sequences leave *r* and *o*, respectively, unparsed. It is by virtue of leaving these segments unparsed that these candidates best satisfy the constraint hierarchy and are submitted for phonetic implementation. Because *r* and *o* are unlinked to higher prosodic structure, they are phonetically deleted. OT maintained that input material was not actually deleted, but if it is left unlinked, it cannot be realized phonetically.

6.3.3 *Applying Parsing and Non-Parsing to Loanword Adaptation*

McCarthy and Prince (1993) and Prince and Smolensky (1993) focus on the parsing and non-parsing of whole segments and segmental positions, but loanword adaptation can be used to illustrate these operations at the level of distinctive features. If we take the position that loanword adaptation is phonological (Hyman 1970; Prunet 1990; etc.), which has most recently been extensively argued by Paradis and LaCharité (1996, 1997),[4] an unadapted loanword (the word as it occurs in its language of origin) and an adapted loanword (the word as it occurs in the borrowing language) would constitute in standard OT, respectively, input to, and output of GEN that are directly observable.

Borrowings are particularly interesting for two reasons. First, the nature of loanword input does not have to be hypothesized to the extent that native word input often does. Second, an unadapted loanword often contains what are, from the point of view of the borrowing language, infelicitous feature combinations and structures. That is to say, in their original state, loanwords are often an affront to the structural and segmental constraints of the borrowing language. It is for this reason that loanwords are, whenever necessary, adapted through the apparent addition or substraction of features and/or structure. Of particular interest about loanwords is that, irrespective of the particular choice of features assumed for segments, and of one's position on various issues, such as whether input representations in OT are underspecified or not, whether features are binary or monovalent, etc., the fact remains that the optimal candidate for a loanword is often quite unfaithful to the input.[5]

---

[4] These authors show that the borrowers and adapters are bilinguals—the term being taken in its broad sense—and provide arguments against the phonetic stance supported by Silverman (1992), for instance.

[5] Prince and Smolensky (1993) propose that learners infer input forms that, by-and-large, reflect surface constraint preferences. Violations of faithfulness in underlying native forms are therefore expected to be much less usual than in borrowed words.

Put another way, an adapted loanword must incur violations of faithfulness constraints in order to satisfy what are obviously more highly-ranked segmental and structural constraints of the borrowing language. Informally characterized, faithfulness constraints require that output form, in this case the adapted loanword, contain all and only the material of the input form, in this case the unadapted loanword.[6]

Let us now consider in more detail how the adaptation of loanwords would have been handled in early versions of OT, which considered GEN capable only of inserting structure and leaving material unparsed. Recall that OT considered that the 'input to the grammar is a string of root nodes each with a set of (unassociated) features. The output is an optimal parse in which these features are associated to root nodes (with the root nodes associated to syllable position nodes, and so on up the prosodic hierarchy)' (Prince and Smolensky 1993: 180). This meant that GEN assembled the featural input into segments and the constraints of the borrowing language were responsible for selecting the candidate that represented the best assemblage. Consider how this works in the case of the French word *marchandise* [marʃãdiz] 'merchandise', which is borrowed into Fula as [marsanⁿdis]. Fula is a West African language that has neither the alveopalatal fricatives nor the nasal vowels that occur in French. Of particular focus here are the adaptations of the alveopalatal fricative [ʃ] and the following nasal vowel [ã], neither of which are licit segments in Fula. Let us assume, for the sake of illustration, that the constraints barring these segments are those in (6a) and (6b):

(6)   a. *[ʃ]: *[+continuant] [−anterior]
         b. *[ã]: *[−consonantal] [+nasal]

The constraint in (6a) is intended to indicate that the co-occurrence of the features [+continuant] and [−anterior] is prohibited in Fula. The constraint in (6b) indicates that nasal cannot occur on vowels. By virtue of containing the alveopalatal strident [ʃ] and the nasal vowel [ã], the unadapted loan violates these Fula constraints. The fact that the word is adapted indicates that these structural constraints are higher-ranked than the faithfulness constraints which would have the segments remain unchanged.

From an OT perspective, GEN creates from the input a set of candidates. The ranked constraints of Fula will select that candidate which it deems best. Let us consider what it means to come up with the optimal candidate for a word which, in its unadapted state, is an unacceptable surface form in Fula. In this case, the optimal candidate, [marsanⁿdis] is created by, among other things, parsing the feature [+continuant] and leaving the feature [−anterior], which co-occurs with [+continuant] in the input, unparsed, as shown in (7).

---

[6] Under Correspondence Theory, the material is further required to serve the same prosodic functions in input and output.

(7)   ʃ   → s
                          |
     [+cont] [−ant]   [+cont] [−ant]

Because [−anterior] is not parsed (i.e. linked to a root node and higher prosodic structure), it is stray-erased at the phonetic level. In this way the deletion of features, as well as of segments and segmental positions, is effected through non-parsing by GEN and subsequent stray erasure at the level of phonetic implementation.

In the case of the nasal vowel, the feature [+nasal] is parsed in the output, but instead of being linked to the vowel, as it is in French, it is linked to both an epenthesized coda consonant and to the following onset consonant, to produce the optimal output form [marsan^{n}dis]. This is illustrated in (8) (for clarity, articulated syllable structure is used and the epenthesized coda is underlined):

(8)

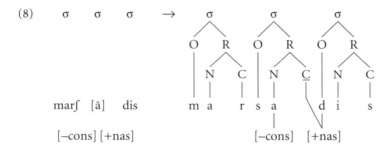

By linking [+nasal] to an epenthesized coda consonant, GEN produces an adaptation that meets the requirements of Fula's constraint hierarchy. Those features not present in the input, and which remain underspecified in the output of GEN—for instance the coronal place of articulation features for the epenthesized coda nasal—are filled in phonetically.

6.3.4 *The Insufficiency of Parsing and Non-Parsing*

We have just seen that GEN may leave individual features unparsed for postphonological stray erasure in the same way that it leaves whole segments unparsed, to be stray-erased by the phonetic implementation component. We have also seen that just as GEN inserts consonant and vowel slots to be filled in by default features phonetically, so it may insert consonant or vowel slots to host features that are differently distributed in the unadapted loanword. In short, to the limited extent that we have pursued the topic, loanword adaptation does not seem to tax OT, or to require any additional assumptions. Even if GEN is restricted to parsing and non-parsing, it appears equal to the task of loanword adaptation.

However, a deeper look at the adaptation of loanwords reveals that such a restricted view of GEN is untenable. In addition to leaving features and segments unparsed, or linking them in different ways than occurs in the unadapted loan-word surface form, GEN must also be able to insert content and to delete structure. We consider, first, the insertion of content by GEN. The possibility that GEN might be required to insert content, as well as structure, was clearly enter-tained by Prince and Smolensky (1993: 103) who acknowledge that 'perhaps, for example, the set of candidates issued by GEN should include actual featural and segmental insertions, as well as new association lines'. Loanword adaption shows this to be the case. Consider the adaptation of **v* that occurs in French loan-words borrowed into Fula, which lacks voiced fricatives, and which adapts those that occur in French borrowings. Examples are given in (9a), along with exam-ples of **z* and **ʒ* adaptation in (9b).

(9)   a.   The adaptation of **v* in Fula loanwords

	Adaptation	French			Fula	
i.	v → w	avocat	[avɔka]	→	[awɔka]	'lawyer'
		civil	[sivil]	→	[siwil]	'civil'
ii.	v → b	avion	[avjɔ̃]	→	[abijɔn]	'airplane'
		livre	[livr]	→	[liː bar]	'book'
iii.	v → f	élève	[elɛv]	→	[ɛlɛf]	'student'
		mouvement	[muvmã]	→	[mufmaŋ]	'movement'

b.   The adaptation of **z* and **ʒ* in Fula

	Adaptation	French			Fula	
i.	z → s	kerosene	[kerozɛn]	→	[kerosɛn]	'kerosene'
		télévision	[televizjõ]	→	[tɛlɛfisjoŋ]	'television'
ii.	ʒ → s	barrage	[baraʒ]	→	[baras]	'dam'
		chambre	[ʃãbr]	→	[samᵐburu]	'room'

Both the absence of voiced fricatives in Fula words and their adaptation in loanwords (cf. 9b) suggest an undominated phonological constraint against the co-occurrence of [+cont] and [+voice], the feature combination assumed to define voiced fricatives.[7] *A priori*, an optimal output of GEN may not contain the infelicitous feature combination or it will not satisfy the constraint. To produce a candidate that satisfies this highly-ranked constraint, GEN might leave either feature, [+continuant] or [+voice], unparsed. Failure to parse a feature ulti-mately allows the non-phonological interpretive component to supply redundant and default features (McCarthy and Prince 1993: 24), in some cases replacing the feature value of the input. For instance, in the case of **v*, if [+voice] were left

---

[7] The relevant Fula constraint cannot be as specific as *[+strident] [+voice] because it must also account for the adaptation of [v] (cf. 9a). It has been shown (Lahiri and Evers 1991; Shaw 1991; LaCharité 1993; Rubach 1994; Steriade 1994) that [strident] is a coronal dependent, and [v] and [f] cannot be considered coronal.

unparsed, the interpretive insertion of [–voice] would yield adaptation to [f]; if [+continuant] were left unparsed, the interpretive insertion of [–continuant] would yield adaptation to [b]. Both of these attested adaptations are schematized in (10):

(10)   Input to GEN:

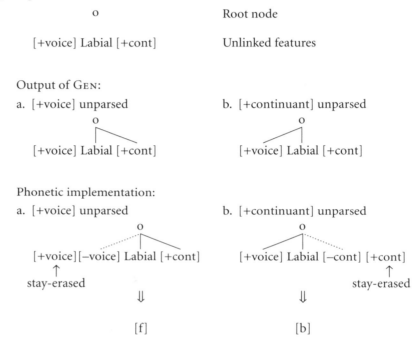

o   Root node

[+voice] Labial [+cont]   Unlinked features

Output of GEN:
a. [+voice] unparsed   b. [+continuant] unparsed
   o   o

   [+voice] Labial [+cont]   [+voice] Labial [+cont]

Phonetic implementation:
a. [+voice] unparsed   b. [+continuant] unparsed
   o   o

   [+voice] [–voice] Labial [+cont]   [+voice] Labial [–cont] [+cont]
   ↑   ↑
   stay-erased   stay-erased
                    ⇓   ⇓

                    [f]   [b]

However, although both the adaptation of French *v* to *b* and *f* in Fula are well attested, neither is Fula's preferred adaptation. In our data, [v] is adapted to [b] in only 14 cases out of 81, i.e. in 17.3 per cent of the cases; [v] is adapted to [f] in only 5 cases out of 81, i.e. in 6.2 per cent of the cases. As in many other languages, *v* in Fula is usually adapted to *w*, as in the examples in (9ai). In our database, this occurs in 62 cases out of 81, i.e. 76.5 per cent of the cases.[8] Adaptation of [v] to [w] shows that GEN must insert content; we cannot assume that it inserts structure that is supplied with content only post-phonologically. Specifically, glides are both [+voice] and [+continuant], by virtue of the fact that they are [+sonorant]. This suggests that in the adaptation of *v* to *w*, [+sonorant] is added to [+continuant] and [+voice] to license the otherwise unacceptable com-

---

[8] The remainder of the cases involve metathesis (9 cases, i.e. 9.1 per cent) and deletions (9 cases, i.e. 9.1 per cent), which occur under predictable phonological conditions (Paradis and LaCharité 1997).

bination. However, unlike insertion of the redundant values [–voice] and [–continuant], which produce surface [f] and [b], respectively, [+sonorant]—which can by no means be considered a redundant or default feature in the cases at hand—must obligatorily be inserted by GEN. If GEN did not insert [+sonorant], the candidate could not be selected because it would not satisfy the constraint *[+continuant] [+voice]. In other words, the winning candidate can only be the winning candidate if it satisfies this constraint (among others, of course).

We point out that issues of underspecification are beside the point here. That is to say, the fact that the output of GEN is more than minimally or contrastively specified—since it bears both [+sonorant] and, redundantly, [+voice]—poses no problem for OT, which does not rely on underspecification to anywhere near the extent that previous generative theories have done (cf. Inkelas 1994; Itô *et al.* 1995). Although the preceding discussion of epenthesis in Axininca Campa indicated that the interpretive component adds redundant and default feature values, OT does not necessarily bar such features and feature combinations from occurring earlier. Thus, the fact that GEN inserts [+sonorant], which is in this instance redundant, to the feature combination [+continuant] [+voice] to create an optimal candidate from French loanword input containing *v* is not an issue from the point of view of underspecification. It does show, though, that GEN inserts not only structure but content as well.

One might be committed to maintaining a non-procedural view of GEN in which GEN only parses or leaves unparsed, and is unable to insert content not present in the input. From this perspective, an alternative might be considered which relies on candidate outputs where either [+voice] or [+continuant], or both, are simply left unparsed. Then, [+sonorant] insertion (like [–voice] or [–continuant] insertion that produce adaptation to *f* or *b*, respectively) is left to the phonetic interpretive component. As with the *f* and *b* cases illustrated in (10), such outputs of GEN could then be selected as optimal because they would not really instantiate the offending feature combination. However, any such analysis faces a significant problem: there is no principled means for ensuring the phonetic insertion of [+sonorant], as opposed to some other feature. For instance, why would a labial, in a consonant position, which emerged from GEN without continuant or voicing specifications, be interpreted as a glide? In other words, if the optimal candidate emerged from GEN with neither [+voice] nor [+continuant] parsed, why would the segment not be interpreted as a more prototypical consonant, such as a voiceless labial stop? Even if the labial emerged with [+voice] parsed, why would the segment not be interpreted as a voiced labial stop, rather than as a glide? If the emergent candidate contained the features Labial and [+continuant], why would that not be interpreted as a voiceless labial fricative, rather than as a sonorant? In short, no matter which feature we choose to leave unlinked in order to avoid a fatal constraint violation, [+sonorant] is a very unlikely feature to be inserted as a default or redundant value for a consonant. We conclude that [+sonorant] must be inserted by GEN.

Now let us reconsider deletion by GEN. By handling deletion via the mechanism of unparsing, OT implied that GEN did not delete association lines. However, the adaptation of loanwords again shows that this restrictive view of GEN does not work. GEN must be able to delink—that is, to delete structure, as well as insert it. Although segments in inputs may be 'unassembled', McCarthy and Prince (1993: 21) contend that 'Vowels, long or short, come with moraic structure attached in the lexicon . . .'. Therefore, if vowels in loanwords are shortened or consonantalized, to produce an optimal candidate, then GEN must have delinked the vowel from its mora. In fact, McCarthy and Prince (*ibid.*) allude to this possibility when they say that 'underlying vowel length distinctions are represented by lexical mora specifications, so they must be present (though not necessarily realized) in all candidate forms . . .'. Examples of delinking of vowels from their moras are provided by French loanwords borrowed into Kinyarwanda.

(11)   *French*   *Kinyarwanda*
    a. coin   [kwɛ̃]   → [kʷe]   'corner'
    b. cuisine [kɥizin] → [kʷuwizine] 'kitchen'
    c. François [frãswa] → [faraⁿskʷa] 'François'

In each of these examples, part of a diphthong becomes part of an onset (cf. e.g. Kaye and Lowenstamm 1984 for a discussion of diphthongs in French and arguments). That is to say, in adaptation, a moraic glide becomes a non-moraic on-glide. Let us consider French [frãswa] 'François'. Because [wa] is a diphthong in French, [w] must be linked to a mora. However, both diphthongs and nuclear segment sequences are unacceptable in Kinyarwanda, and must be adapted. In the examples in (11), we see that, in the Kinyarwanda adaptations of these French loanwords, [w] labializes the preceding consonant, indicating that it is linked to the onset, clearly a non-moraic consonant position.[9] This means that [w] must delink from its mora. In cases where the moraic glide cannot become an on-glide, as with onset fricatives, which cannot be labialized, not only is the glide delinked from its mora but it is totally lost, as shown by the examples in (12).

(12)   *French*   *Kinyarwanda*
    a. essuie-main [esɥimɛ̃] → [esume] *[esʷume] 'handtowel'
    b. voiture   [vwatyr] → [ivatiiri] *[ivʷatiiri] 'car'

We thus conclude that GEN must be able to delete structure and that a restricted view of GEN, which limits it to adding structure, is untenable.

Again, if one were dedicated to keeping a more restricted view of GEN, one might seek refuge in the position that [w]'s mora is simply unrealized, as op-

---

[9] Although complex consonants—like labialized and palatalized consonants—are permitted in Kinyarwanda, complex (i.e. branching) onsets, codas or nuclei (except for long vowels) are not.

posed to having [w] actually delink from the mora. Given the fact that [w]—if not its mora and moraic link—can be realized (as the on-glide of a labialized consonant), this would be suspicious. Moreover, other adaptations of diphthongs show that this view cannot be uniformly maintained. Kinyarwanda contrasts long and short vowels, and in many cases, the abdication of the mora by [w] leads to lengthening of the following vowel, especially in non-word-final position. In other words, the free mora is used, although not by [w], which clearly shows that [w] has been delinked from the mora to which it was attached at the level of underlying representation. Some examples are given in (13):

(13)   *French*   *Kinyarwanda*
      a. boîte   [bwat]   → βʷaate   'box'
      b. laboratoire   [labɔratwar]   → raβoratkʷaari   'laboratory'
      c. mouchoir   [muʃwar]   → muʃkʷaara   'handkerchief'
      d. passoire   [paswar]   → paskʷaari   'strainer'
      e. quadragésime   [kwadraʒezim] → kʷaadaraʒeezima 'quadragesima'

The changes exemplified in (13) are particularly reminiscent of the delinking and spreading operations that were so characteristic of autosegmental phonology and feature geometry. We conclude that such loanword adaptations show that GEN is capable of delinking and spreading features, or more to the present point, that GEN can delink features as well as simply leave them unparsed.

To summarize, OT as it was first conceived by McCarthy and Prince (1993) and Prince and Smolensky (1993) allowed for the insertion of content and structure and the deletion of content and structure, though not in the conventional manner of rules. In OT, primary responsibility for inserting structure rests with GEN, which creates a candidate set for assessment by ranked constraints. The primary means of effecting deletion was through failure to parse particular material, leading to its phonetic deletion. However, applying OT to loanword adaptation shows that the desired effects cannot be achieved simply through parsing or failing to parse. GEN's operations are shown to include at least those in (14):

(14)   The functions of GEN
                              Insert   *Delete*
        GEN   *Content*   yes   no (claim)[10]
               Structure   yes   yes

Both the insertion of content (cf. the discussion of adaptation of French [v] to [w] in Fula, via the insertion of [+sonorant] in 6.3.4) and the deletion of structure (as just shown by the cases where French diphthongs are delinked from one of their moras in Kinyarwanda adaptations) cast doubt on the claim that OT is non-procedural, and that the relation between input and output is

---

[10] That material is unparsed, as opposed to being phonologically deleted, is simply a claim made by OT. It has not, as far as we are aware, been argued for anywhere in the OT literature.

'straightforwardly monotonic' (Prince and Smolensky 1993: 25). Monotonicity depends crucially on the idea that GEN in effect just provides different possible ways of looking at the input—that it simply interprets the input, so to speak. If GEN actively creates output candidates by inserting content, and more especially, by effectively deleting content through the erasure of structure, then the relation between input and output cannot be considered either monotonic or non-procedural.

6.4 Lifting the Restrictions on GEN

OT has undergone a recent important refinement, referred to as Correspondence Theory, which has had an impact on the characterization of GEN (cf. McCarthy 1995). The purpose of this section is to provide a brief look at the main changes to OT under Correspondence Theory in order to show that they do not obviate the point that we raise here, which is that GEN is a procedural component. Indeed, under Correspondence Theory, GEN is more procedural, not less so.

The crux of the change to OT under Correspondence Theory is that faithfulness is achieved somewhat differently. The faithfulness constraints Parse and Fill have given way to a more articulated, more powerful and more general class of what are now called correspondence constraints. One difference between the implementation of faithfulness using Parse and Fill and the implementation of faithfulness in Correspondence Theory is that in the latter, constraints press not only for substantive identity between input and output, as the faithfulness constraints Parse and Fill do, but they further require that segmental content in each member of the pair serve the same prosodic function. For example, a segment that functions, in the input, as the nucleus of a syllable is required by the (relevant) correspondence constraint to function as the nucleus of a syllable in the output. Thus, delinking a segment from the nucleus and relinking it to the onset, as occurs in the Kinyarwanda adaptations shown in (11), is a violation of the correspondence relation, even though the segmental material is otherwise unaltered.

Another difference between faithfulness and correspondence is that the correspondence relation governs not only the underlying and surface pair, as the faithfulness constraints were conceived to do, but surface alternations as well. For instance, McCarthy (1995) shows how correspondence constraints govern the incomplete and complete phase forms in Rotuman, both of which are surface forms. However, this proposal does not have a bearing on the point being made here, mainly because no loanword that undergoes adaptation could be related to its unadapted counterpart in this way. In other words, an unadapted loan containing illicit segments or structures is an unacceptable surface form in the borrowing language. To be a surface form, it must be adapted, which means that it must pass through GEN. The pertinent question remains, then, whether GEN is any less procedural under Correspondence Theory. We suggest that it is not.

In fact, under Correspondence Theory, GEN is much less restricted in its operation than it was initially conceived to be, and OT no longer maintains that GEN is restricted to effecting changes between input and output solely through parsing and non-parsing. The current position is that 'GEN is quite creative, being able to add, delete, or rearrange things without restriction' (Archangeli 1997: 14). Lifting the restrictions on GEN is partly attributable to the fact that as research into the identification and articulation of constraints has continued in OT, the need to restrict GEN's operations to parsing and non-parsing has been rendered unnecessary because the constraint system has emerged strong enough to deal with whatever GEN might come up with. However, the restrictions on GEN have not been relaxed solely because they are unnecessary; they have necessarily been lifted. In early OT, GEN was governed by three principles, one of which was Containment. Containment required the input to be contained in every output, something that is at odds with the notion of deletion (cf. McCarthy and Prince 1993: 20). However, Containment is not only unnecessary under assumptions of Correspondence Theory, it restricts constraint ranking in ways that contradict actual outcomes (see, for example, McCarthy 1995: 13) and is thus antithetical to Correspondence Theory. So Containment has been abandoned, and along with it, the restriction of GEN's operations to parsing and non-parsing. The net result is that while OT would formerly have resisted the idea that GEN inserts and deletes content and structure, OT under Correspondence Theory openly accepts that it does. Therefore, if GEN was already procedural in early versions of OT, there can be no doubt that it is equally if not more procedural now.

6.5 Conclusion

Prior to the emergence of formal constraint-based theories, the power and role of phonological rules had already been seriously eroded. In a *de facto* sense, if not always formally, the power of rules has been limited to inserting or deleting content or structure (see Section 6.2.1). Rules were increasingly treated not as an explanation for phonological changes and alternations but as the servants of phonological constraints, wherein the real explanations were seen to lie (see Section 6.2.2). When rules ensure conformity to constraints, they are also context-free.

OT is a highly articulated effort to account for phonological regularities in a language in terms of constraints, rather than rules. Indeed, OT is billed as a rule-free alternative to derivational constraint-based theories (Prince and Smolensky 1993: 5) such as TCRS and Harmonic Phonology, which indeed resort to 'rules'. The rules they resort to, though, are universal and rely on a violated (universal or universally-based) constraint to provide context, and their power is limited to insertion/deletion of content/structure. TCRS terms such operations 'repairs', but OT considers them rules, which is often misleading. This view is obvious in Roca (1997: 14), who, noting the seminal difference between OT and TCRS, points to the latter's use of rules. The reliance versus non-reliance on repair is thus considered to be a defining point of difference between OT and TCRS. OT's basic claim might well be characterized as 'take care of the constraints and the rules become unnecessary'. However, given the revolutionary nature of OT's position, it is crucial to probe the mechanisms by which disposition of phonological rules is to be accomplished. It is insufficient to simply claim that 'GEN . . . generates for any given input a large space of candidate analyses by freely exercising the basic structural resources of the representational theory. The idea is that the desired output lies somewhere in this space . . .' (Prince and Smolensky 1993: 5).

As noted in the introduction, OT researchers have thus far been preoccupied with the selection of one candidate from a field of potential output representations, not with the operations behind the provision of candidates. Because of that, OT has been able to maintain—speciously, we think—that it has done away with rules. However, if in order to generate that field of candidates, or even one optimal candidate, GEN, even in its most restricted conception, must have the power to insert content as well as structure, and to delete structure, then we must conclude that, contrary to its claims, OT does indeed rely on rules, as well as constraints. GEN might then be seen to be a cover-term for the most recent incarnation of the phonology's rule component.

Archangeli (1997: x) likens OT's task to that of a fisherman who turns his attention away from designing the ideal net to designing the ideal separator, in order to weed out whatever undesirables his imperfect net admits. While the analogy is enlightening, there is a crucial difference that we feel cannot be overlooked: the fisherman's net gathers what is already in the environment, whereas GEN actually creates the undesirables which the separator must subsequently deselect. Surely the idea that GEN is able to insert or delete any amount of content or structure casts doubt on the ideas that GEN constitutes *a single operation* (cf. Hammond 1995: 6), that 'There are no rules or repair strategies, and no serial derivation', (cf. Itô, Mester and Padgett 1995: 578), that an OT account render[s] rules 'unnecessary' (Yip 1993: 2), or that GEN really dispenses with the structural change of rules (Prince and Smolensky 1993: 5). OT cannot disavow the use of repair while depending on the operations that define repair (it would be trivial, and dishonest, to reject the mechanism but not the operations that define it). If our interpretations of loanword adaptations within OT are correct, or even if they are to be meaningfully challenged, we must seriously question the idea that GEN functions in a radically different way from the way that rules do.

Regardless of the fact that OT has profitably shifted its focus from the procedures expressed by rules to the constraints and, more important, to constraint systems, the fact remains that if GEN is a rule component by another name, then one of OT's basic claims is compromised. Roca (1997: 33) says that OT can claim a formal advantage over derivational constraint-based theories such as TCRS and Harmonic Phonology, insofar as OT does not need rules. If, as we suggest here, this is not the case, then this formal advantage is lost and the real difference between OT and other derivational constraint-based theories may be seen to lie in its view of the relationship between rules and phonological constraints.

6.6 References

Archangeli, D. (1997). 'Optimality Theory: An introduction to linguistics in the 1990s'. In D. Archangeli and D. T. Langendoen (eds), *Optimality Theory: An Overview*. Malden, MA, Blackwell Publishers, 1–32.

—— and D. Pulleyblank (1986). 'The structure and content of phonological representations'. Ms, University of Arizona at Tucson and University of British Columbia, Vancouver.

—— —— (1994). *Grounded Phonology*. Cambridge, MA, MIT Press.

Chomsky, N. and M. Halle (1968). *The Sound Pattern of English*. New York, Harper & Row.

Goldsmith, J. (1989). 'Autosegmental licensing, inalterability, and harmonic rule application'. In C. Wiltshire, R. Graczyk, and B. Music (eds), *Proceedings of the 25th Annual Meeting of the Chicago Linguistic Society*, 1. Chicago, Chicago Linguistic Society, 145–56.

—— (1993). 'Harmonic phonology'. In J. Goldsmith (ed.), *The Last Phonological Rule*. Chicago, University of Chicago Press, 21–60.

—— (ed.) (1995). *The Handbook of Phonological Theory*. Cambridge, MA, Blackwell Publishers.

—— and G. Larson (1990). 'Local modeling and syllabification'. In M. Ziolkowski, M. Noske, and K. Deaton (eds), *Proceedings of the 26th Annual Regional Meeting of the Chicago Linguistic Society*, 1. Chicago, Chicago Linguistic Society, 129–41.

Golston, C. (1997). 'Direct Optimality Theory: Representation as pure markedness'. *Language 74*, 713–48.

Hammond, M. (1995). 'There is No Lexicon!'. Ms, University of Arizona at Tucson. ROA-20.

Hyman, L. (1970). 'The role of borrowings in the justification of phonological grammars'. *Studies in African Linguistics 1*, 1–48.

Inkelas, S. (1994). 'The consequences of optimization for underspecification'. Ms, University of California at Berkeley.

Itô, J., A. Mester, and J. Padgett (1995). 'NC: licensing and underspecification in Optimality Theory'. *Linguistic Inquiry 26*, 571–613. ROA-38.

Kaye, J. and J. Lowenstamm (1984). 'De la syllabicité'. In F. Dell, D. Hirst, and J.-R. Vergnaud (eds), *Forme Sonore du Langage*. Paris, Hermann, 123–161.

Kenstowicz, M. (1994). *Phonology in Generative Grammar*. Cambridge, MA, Blackwell Publishers.

—— and C. Kisseberth (1979). *Generative Phonology: Description and Theory*. New York, Academic Press.

Kisseberth, C. (1970). 'On the functional unity of phonological rules'. *Linguistic Inquiry* 1, 291–306.

LaCharité, D. (1993). *The Internal Structure of Affricates*. PhD thesis, University of Ottawa.

—— and C. Paradis (1993). 'Introduction: The emergence of constraints in generative phonology and a comparison of three current constraint-based models'. In C. Paradis and D. LaCharité (eds), *Constraint-Based Theories in Multilinear Phonology*. *Canadian Journal of Linguistics* 38(2), 127–53.

Lahiri, A. and V. Evers (1991). 'Palatalization and coronality'. In C. Paradis and J.-F. Prunet (eds), *The Special Status of Coronals: Internal and External Evidence*. San Diego, Academic Press, 79–100.

McCarthy, J. (1988). 'Feature geometry and dependency: A review'. *Phonetica* 43, 84–108.

—— (1995). 'Faithfulness in prosodic morphology and phonology: Rotuman revisited'. Ms, U.Mass. ROA-110.

—— and A. Prince (1993). 'Prosodic morphology I: Constraint interaction and satisfaction'. Ms, U.Mass. and Rutgers University.

Paradis, C. (1987).'Explanations for constraint violations'. MIT Linguistics Colloquium, Massachusetts Institute of Technology, Cambridge, MA, December.

—— (1988a). 'On constraints and repair strategies'. *The Linguistic Review* 6, 71–97.

—— (1988b). 'Towards a theory of constraint violations'. *McGill Working Papers in Linguistics* 5(1), 1–43.

—— (1990). 'Focus in Gere configurational constraints'. In J. Hutchison and V. Manfredi (eds), *Current Approaches to African Linguistics* 7. Dordrecht, Foris, 53–62.

—— and D. LaCharité (1996). 'Saving and cost in loanword adaptation: Predictions of the TCRS-phonological model'. *McGill Working Papers in Linguistics* 11, 46–84.

—— —— (1997). 'Preservation and minimality in loanword adaptation'. *Journal of Linguistics* 33, 379–430.

—— and J.-F. Prunet (eds) (1991). *The Special Status of Coronals: Internal and External Evidence*. Phonetics and Phonology 2. San Diego, Academic Press.

Prince, A. and P. Smolensky (1993). 'Optimality Theory: Constraint interaction in generative grammar'. *RUCCs Technical Report #2*, Rutgers University for Cognitive Science at Piscataway [to appear, Cambridge, MA, MIT Press].

—— (1990). 'The origin and interpretation of French loans in Carrier'. *International Journal of American Linguistics* 56, 484–502.

Roca, I. (1997). 'Derivations or constraints, or derivations and constraints?' In I. Roca (ed.), *Derivations and Constraints in Phonology*. Oxford, Oxford University Press, 3–41.

Rubach, Jerzy (1994). 'Affricates as strident stops in Polish'. *Linguistic Inquiry* 25, 119–43.

Shaw, P. (1991). 'Consonant harmony systems: The special status of coronal harmony'. In C. Paradis and J.-F. Prunet (eds), 125–57.

Silverman, D. (1992). 'Multiple scansions in loanword phonology: Evidence from Cantonese'. *Phonology* 9, 289–328.

Spencer, A. (1996). *Phonology: Theory and Description*. Oxford, Blackwell Publishers.

Steriade, D. (1994). 'Complex onsets as single segments: The Mazateco pattern'. In J. Cole and C. Kisseberth (eds), *Perspectives in Phonology*, 51. Stanford, California, Center for the Study of Language and Information, 203–91.

Wiltshire, C. (1992). *Syllabification and Rule Application in Harmonic Phonology*. PhD thesis, University of Chicago.

Yip, M. (1988). 'The obligatory contour principle and phonological rules: A loss of identity'. *Linguistic Inquiry* 19, 65–100.

—— (1993). 'Phonological constraints, optimality and phonetic realization in Cantonese'. Ms, University of California at Los Angeles.

7

Dependency Theory Meets OT: A Proposal for a New Approach to Segmental Structure[1]

Norval Smith

7.1 Introduction

It used to be suggested that the question of phonological segmental structure was orthogonal to Optimality Theory (OT). In other words, it was claimed that from the point of view of OT there was no particular reason to prefer one theory of segmental structure to another—OT could as it were be used together with any segmental theory with equal facility. More recently, a consensus seems to have emerged that the point of view that segmental structure is somehow not the concern of OT cannot be maintained, as discussions on the Optimality List during 1997 have concluded.

Optimality Theory represents probably the most important paradigm change in linguistics—not just in phonology—since the publication of Chomsky's *Syntactic Structures*. As a theory of the relationship between input and output structures it is not obvious why, while being relevant for higher levels of phonological organization, such as the syllable and the foot, it should not have relevance for segmental structure. And in addition, more and more phonologists are coming to realize that the prosodic and segmental aspects of phonology are inextricably linked to each other, most obviously at the level of syllable structure—for a recent example of this, compare Bolognesi (1998).

In my contribution to this volume I will attempt to set out why I think that

[1] I am indebted to the Netherlands Organization for Scientific Research (NWO) and the Faculty of Arts of the University of Amsterdam for jointly providing a travel grant which enabled me to visit the Department of Linguistics of the University of Massachusetts in connection with research on syllable structure.

I am very grateful to Toni Borowsky, Colin Ewen, John McCarthy, Jaye Padgett, Douglas Pulleyblank, Marcel van de Dikken, Jeroen van de Weijer, Sophie van Besouw and an anonymous reviewer, for comments on (parts of) this chapter, and/or assistance with particular concepts. The responsibility for all errors of fact or interpretation remains mine.

I am also grateful to John McCarthy, Ellen Woolford, Toni Borowsky, Mohammed Guerssel, John Kingston, Lisa Selkirk and others of the U.Mass linguistics community for various kinds of interaction and logistical assistance.

the particular view of segmental theory to which I adhere—a version of Dependency Phonology—represents a good candidate for the theory of segmental structure to be combined with OT. Obviously many 'segmental' constraints have already been proposed, in particular within the feature geometry approach, but this version of the DP model of segmental structure would seem to have certain advantages over other segmental approaches, not least because of the more inclusive nature of (the smaller number of) the features in this model.

7.2 Features in OT

There are a limited number of general discussions of the nature of segmental structure within OT, or in reaction to it. In general, many workers in the field have continued to use some version of the pre-existing feature geometry model, in particular that developed by Sagey (1986).

Archangeli and Pulleyblank (1994), and Pulleyblank (1997) discuss constraints (Grounded Conditions) relating segmental features, while Padgett (1995, 1997) has indicated problems with the strict interpretation of the feature geometry model.

7.2.1 *Pulleyblank's Grounded Conditions*

An examination of Pulleyblank (1995) implies that he recognizes the following partial feature hierarchy:

(1)   Partial feature geometry from Pulleyblank (1995)

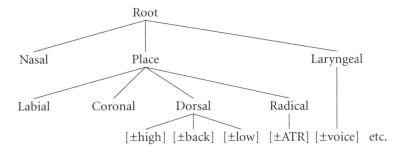

Although this structure does not in itself imply any particular radical revision as compared to pre-existing feature geometry models, Pulleyblank has addressed himself in recent years to the questions of the relationships holding between various pairs of features (cf. Pulleyblank 1997; Pulleyblank, Ping, Leitch and Ọla 1995). Many of these relationships are first discussed in his joint work with Archangeli (Archangeli and Pulleyblank 1994, hereafter AP).

This is the type of relationship he refers to as the Paradigmatic Constraint (Pulleyblank 1997), which expresses segment-internal restrictions on the combination of features. And as will be seen in Section 7.4, some relationships between vocalic features indicated by AP coincide with those claimed to exist in van der Hulst (1988a, b), Smith (1988) and van der Hulst and Smith (1989, 1990) working on segmental structure in Dependency Phonology terms.

Featural relationships that require to be stated by (Archangeli and) Pulley-blank, but which fall out naturally in DP include the following. These relationships are self-explanatory in DP terms since the pairs of features involved turn out to be instantiations of the same feature in each case (cf. Section 7.4.4.4).

(2)   Constraints on the interaction of ATR and Front
    i. ATR/FR: [+ATR] implies [–back]   (AP p.175: 'ATR/BK')
    ii. FR/ATR: [–back] implies [+ATR]   (AP p.151: 'BK/ATR')

(3)   Constraints on the interaction of RTR and Low
    i. RTR/LO: [–ATR] implies [+low]   (AP p.150: 'RTR/LO')
    ii. LO/RTR: [+low] implies [–ATR]   (AP p.148: 'LO/ATR')

(4)   Constraints on the interaction of Back and Round
    i. RD/BK: [+round] implies [+back] (inferred from AP p.61: 'RD/BK')
    ii. BK/RD: [+back] implies [+round] (Stevens *et al.* 1986)

These relationships comprise only a small subset of the constraints that can be derived from AP and subsequent work by Pulleyblank. However, the nature of this article does not allow for a full-scale discussion of parallels and differences between our proposals.

7.2.2 *Padgett's Feature Class Theory*

Padgett (1995) introduces the notion of the Feature Class Theory. Whereas the work of the first feature geometrists (e.g. Clements 1985) concentrated on establishing the geometry of segments by having recourse to evidence showing class behaviour in assimilation processes, Padgett draws attention to cases of *partial class behaviour*, or cases where not all the features that usually behave as natural classes in fact do so in certain assimilatory processes.This led him to posit abstract Feature Classes without geometrical consequences (Padgett 1995, 1997). The geometry of segments becomes maximally simple, without any intermediate hierarchical structure.

Note that the original feature geometry proposal was primarily based on evidence from *partial* assimilations. Complete or total assimilations, and assimilations in terms of one feature are of little diagnostic value for this purpose—for or against. Padgett requires to demonstrate cases where subsets of the assimilations defined by the intermediate nodes of feature geometry are involved. For example in a case where a node dominates three features (all utilized contrastively in the language in question), only two are involved in some assimilation. The reason for this is that an assimilation in terms of a single feature could simply be handled as assimilation of a terminal feature. It is not obvious, however, that Padgett succeeds in making his point in all the cases he discusses. In the face of a similar argument by Cahill and Parkinson (1997), Padgett (1997) disagrees, and remarks that cases of the two-out-of-three type are difficult to find. Padgett then requires the additional stipulation that single-feature assimilations do not exist as a type, and that only feature class assimilations occur (in interaction with the constraint hierarchy). This he expresses as follows:

(5)   Assumption of Privilege

Within the full set of features, a limited number of universal and (according to many) phonetically-motivated subsets are distinguished. Reference by rules to just these subsets is made simple (with the help of implementational assumptions of some kind)

This in my opinion begs the question. However, he manages to come up with some promising evidence in favour of his position, so I will ignore his Assumption of Privilege in the further discussion.

I will discuss two cases of partial class behaviour mentioned by Padgett (1997) in support of his approach. The first is taken from Kɔɔni nasal place assimilation, and the second from Turkic vowel harmony.

7.2.2.1 Kɔɔni nasal place assimilation

In Kɔɔni (Cahill 1995), nasal place assimilation applies normally except preceding complex labial-velar stops. Assimilation is total across words, but partial within words (including compounds). Within words nasal assimilation only applies in respect of the feature [dorsal] and not in respect of the feature [labial]. Note that this is a strong piece of evidence for Padgett's position as [labial] is otherwise normally involved in nasal assimilation. As Padgett says (1997: 29) the only way to characterize this kind of assimilation as a constraint in the feature geometry approach is to make reference both to the Place node and the individual features it dominates. So Cahill and Parkinson (1997) give the following constraint:

(6)   ALIGNPLACE:

All features from the Place constituent are realized on both a consonant and an immediately preceding nasal.

This allows them to refer to the Place node at the same time as its constituent features. On the one hand they are then able to generalize over Place and at the same time make use of the interaction between the above constraint and a higher-ranked *COMPLEXSEGMENT, which prevents the assimilation of both features when the following consonant is a labial-velar. As Padgett remarks, this is using feature geometry as if it was Feature Class Theory.

7.2.2.2 Turkic vowel harmony

This example is more tendentious. I will ignore the fact that while Palatal Harmony (PH) is very similar across the various languages, Labial Harmony (LH) takes a different form in practically every language of the Turkic languages it occurs in, inasmuch as this could well be explained in terms of various constraints against rounding particular (classes of) vowels. One problem is, however, that in some Turkic languages LH is completely absent. When it is present, though, PH is always present as well. But this dependence of LH on PH is not characteristic of all languages. A number of Kwa languages, such as Igbo (Carrell 1970), have LH but no PH. These facts are not easy to explain if only Feature Class assimilations are possible, as it is not obvious why there is no full PH in such cases, because it is apparently much less restricted in the languages in which it occurs than LH which, as far as I know, rarely occurs in a 'perfect' form.

7.2.2.3 Final observations on Padgett

Padgett makes the point that whereas he sees no need for intermediate hierarchical nodes in segmental structure, his Feature Class approach would still be applicable if they were present. I am of the opinion that Padgett's work indicates at the very least a need for a much more precise definition of what is meant by a feature hierarchy. If one node dominates another, what precisely is implied?

One might remark that Padgett's very feature classes imply a hierarchy in any case:

(7)   Place $=_{def}$ Pharyngeal $\cup$ Oral
       Oral $=_{def}$ Labial $\cup$ Coronal $\cup$ Dorsal $\cup$ VPlace   (Padgett 1997: 10)

Here, for instance, it is obvious that there is a hierarchical relationship between the Feature Class 'Place' and the Feature Class 'Oral', in that the first contains the second.

Furthermore, Padgett has not not given any indication of what proportion of the cases we get partial class behaviour in. The more frequent such cases are, the more persuasive his reasoning that the geometry should be simplified becomes.

While his proposals would have less influence on the approach proposed in this article, because of the less elaborate nature of the hierarchical relationships involved, the problems he points out would be applicable in some of cases of place assimilation at least.[2]

7.3 Dutch Dependency Phonology

In this chapter I will espouse a variant of the DP model utilizing certain insights of Smith *et al.* (1991) and Humbert (1995). I follow Smith *et al.* (1991) as to the general set of features employed, although I introduce a number of architectural

---

[2] Not however in the case of nasal assimilation to labial-velar stops. These are expressed in my system in terms of a complex structure involving two separate stop structures, each with its own Place node.

modifications here. I follow Humbert in particular in that all Place features are assumed to be dominated by all Manner features, while Laryngeal features such as Aspiration and Glottalizaton are assumed to be represented in terms of degenerate segments (see Section 7.2.2.2).

In previous work by van der Hulst and Smith (1989, 1990), van der Hulst (1988a, b), and Smith (1988), the idea was mooted that the same place features could be employed with different but related meanings, provided that they were allowed to occupy different positions (in terms of geometry) in segmental structure. Firstly, the primary place features received different interpretations in terms of whether vowel articulations or consonant articulations were involved. Secondly, advantage was taken of the availability of head and dependent configurations within Dependency Phonology to introduce additional differentiation in the interpretation of place features. In this way it proved possible to provide a unified account of distinct articulatory types which displayed significant acoustic agreement.

It also proved possible to express all possible place distinctions with the help of three place features [A, I, U]. The use of these labels hails back to early work in Dependency Phonology (Anderson and Jones 1972). Note that these three features have a certain resemblance to the acoustically defined place features in Jakobson, Fant and Halle (1952, 1965)—[compact] being equivalent to [A] and [diffuse], its opposite, to [I] and [U]; and [acute] to [I] and [grave], its opposite, to [U] and [A]. [A, I, U] are also utilized,[3] although only as vowel features, in a variety of other approaches—in Particle Theory (Schane 1984), in Government Phonology (Kaye, Lowenstamm and Vergnaud 1985), and in the work of Rennison (1986).

I will build on Smith *et al.* (1991) and Humbert (1995) in developing further the basic Manner superstructure of the segment. As observed by Smith *et al.* (1991) the Manner aspect of articulations appears to be the most significant characteristic of a segment. So if we consider, say, a labial stop, the fact that it is a stop seems to be more important than the fact that it is a labial. Consider also the typical phonological process affecting Place. These operate only in the context of some Manner type. On the other hand, processes affecting Manner typically do not take account of Place. Consider, for example, the well-known process turning voiced stops into fricatives in Spanish. It is for this reason all the more surprising that Manner has received such a disparate and diffuse treatment for such a long time from so many researchers working within the framework of feature geometry (cf. Sagey 1986; Padgett 1991; Halle 1992 and others, and Government Phonology (cf. Harris and Lindsey 1995). The lead provided by Clements (1985) in recognizing a Manner node was never followed up. One reason was presumably the disparate nature of the features dominated by the Manner node.

---

[3] With variations as to their precise theoretical status.

Once again, note that in Dependency Phonology the status of Manner has been consistently recognized since Anderson and Jones (1972).

There has been, I think, a general reluctance among many generative phonologists to abandon completely the feature set introduced in SPE (Chomsky and Halle 1968). Despite assertions to the contrary these features seem largely to have been based on articulatory phonetic categories. The low-level nature of some of these features concealed rather than revealed certain aspects of phonological patterning. For some phonological processes involving Place the result was less satisfactory, less explanatory, in some respects than the picture obtained with the previously dominant system—that of Jakobson, Fant and Halle (1952, 1965) (henceforth JFH)—which worked with explicitly acoustically-based features. As a reaction to certain problems, some phonologists felt it necessary to reintroduce some of the JFH features again as extra 'cover' features. Compare Hyman (1973) on [grave], for example.

7.3.1 *Smith* et al. *(1991)*

The primary status of Manner was recognized by Smith *et al.* (1991) by representing the segment as a dependency structure with Manner as head, and the Laryngeal and Place nodes as dependents. This is obviously modeled on Clements (1985).

(8)   The segment according to Smith *et al.* (1991)

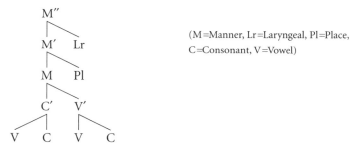

(M=Manner, Lr=Laryngeal, Pl=Place, C=Consonant, V=Vowel)

So for instance a stop appeared in terms of this model as follows:

(9)   Stop

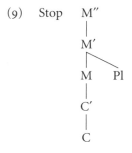

The possibility of C′ dominating V, or V′ dominating C meant, however, that the structures were illegitimate as the X′-structures they were intended to be.

7.3.2 Humbert's Model

7.3.2.1 Humbert's treatment of manner

Humbert (1995) represents the above-mentioned primacy of Manner more effectively in terms of the direct dominance of Place by Manner, rather than by representing Place as a complement in X′ terms (as in 10).

(10)   manner component (C, V)

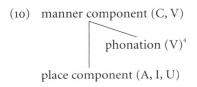

As stated above, a similar geometry will be utilized in this article.

7.3.2.2 Humbert's treatment of Laryngeal aspects

The Laryngeal aspects of aspiration and glottalization were represented by Humbert respectively in terms of degenerate (placeless) fricative ([h]) and stop ([ʔ]) structures. These stand in a complex segment relationship to the segments thus modified.

(11)   /f′/

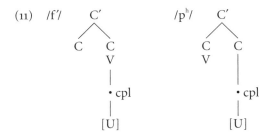

So the first segment represents a labial ([U]) fricative (^C_V) forming a complex segment together with a degenerate stop (C). The second segment represents a labial ([U]) stop (C) forming a complex segment together with a degenerate fricative (^C_V).

I modify this representation of laryngeal features to the extent that I make the degenerate segment a *dependent* of the fully specified segment. Contrary to

---

[4] In obstruents only.

Humbert I treat voice[5] on a par with aspiration and glottalization—in terms of a dependent degenerate vowel.

7.4 The Present Model

The present system, like that of Smith *et al.* (1991) and Humbert (1995), operates with two manner features [C, V] and three place features [A, I, U]. Different is the recognition here of the special status of sibilants (partly similar to the proposal in Anderson and Ewen (1987)), and concomitantly, the recognition that the basic Place distinctions among coronals are largely concerned with various different sibilant types, and should in fact be formally restricted to these, at least in structural terms. It is necessary also, I think, to introduce a three-level structure in the manner portion of the segment instead of Humbert's one or two levels,[6] in order to distinguish fully among the different manners of articulation. Additionally, the relationship among the Place Features has been slightly modified in comparison with previous work by van der Hulst and Smith (1990), van der Hulst (1988a) and Smith (1988).[7]

Finally, as I have stated above, it becomes possible to state various constraints more naturally in terms of the particular feature system adopted here. All constraints require basically to fulfil what I refer to as the condition of Functionality. In other words, all constraints have to be functional, either in terms of phonetic motivation ('grounding' in terms of Archangeli and Pulleyblank 1994), perceptual factors, faithfulness of input-output relations, a well-formed (prosodic) phonological organization, cognitive factors, or the like. Language-particular or crazy conditions are to be excluded in principle (see also Smith 1997).

For a class of constraints referring to 'grounded' Place relationships, the two features involved can now be regarded as different instantiations of the same feature. The claim is then that we do not have two features sharing some phonetic aspect but just simply the same phonological feature.

7.4.1 *Segmental Architecture*

I would like first to re-examine some aspects of Manner. I will do this against the backdrop of the basic syllable type—CV—concentrating my attention on the ONSET position. The uncontroversial assumption will be made that the Optimal onset consonant is the stop. The simplest syllable type occurring in the languages of the world is the CV-syllable—basically the Onset-Nucleus syllable.

---

[5] Humbert also expresses nasalization in terms of a degenerate nasal combined with whatever other articulation is involved. This seems a reasonable hypothesis.

[6] Humbert's two-level representations of Manner—used to characterize fricatives and nasals—are referred to by her as 'complex', by which she means that the two levels are not separately accessible for phonological processes, but are only referenceable as unitary objects.

[7] Specifically, the head-dependent relationship of round and back has been reversed.

Among the systems of this type evidenced are systems where the only possible consonants are stops. By the Subset Principle it can be assumed that the unmarked consonant is in fact the stop. That this is the case is obvious also from its nature as the segment type most distinct from the vowel, involving as it does maximum closure in the vocal tract as against maximum openness for vowels. It is also the consonant-type where the different place manifestations are maximally distinct from each other perceptually. Any kind of modification, whether it be voicing, nasality, or continuancy, will reduce the distinctiveness of the various place manifestations.

The basic architecture of segments is assumed to be as follows:

(12)   M″[C/V] ([C] = obstruent;   [V] = sonorant)

         |

         M′ [C/V] ([C] = non-continu- [V] = continuant)
                   ant;

         |

         M [C/V] ([C] = constrictive; [V] = non-constric-
                   tive)[8]

         |

    [Place features] (Place features = [A, I, U])

    (M = Manner; [C, V] = Manner features)

In other words, there are assumed to be three relevant levels of structure in the Manner[9] specification of segments. At each of these levels the relevant Manner node must be specified as being [C] or [V], in order to define a valid segment.

I regard the most important distinction to be that between obstruent and sonorant. What is the basis for this decision? For instance, obstruents allow of a distinction between voiceless and voiced; sonorants do not. The cases where such a distinction has been claimed to exist actually seem to refer, as is usually recognized, to a distinction between aspirated and non-aspirated sonorants.[10]

All combinations occur except for M″[C]–M′[V]–M [V], which is excluded because of the impossibility of non-constrictive obstruents (or obstruent vowels).[11]

Note that these three distinctions—obstruent/sonorant, noncontinuant/continuant, and constrictive/nonconstrictive—correspond to no fewer than seven separate features distinguished in some versions of the feature geometry model.

---

[8] This is more or less equivalent to the traditional difference between consonantal and vocalic articulations

[9] Note that the M″, M′, and M nodes of this model do not correspond to those of Smith *et al.* (1991).

[10] Languages seem to vary in fact as to whether Aspirated Sonorants are voiced or voiceless. A simple illustration of this can be found in Scottish English where the aspirated 'wh' is variously [hʷ] or [ɦʷ]. I know of no language contrasting the voiceless and voiced variants.

[11] Syllabic obstruents occur of course, but that is quite a different matter.

I regard all these as variants of the two features [C] and [V], further distinguishing them thus in terms of three hierarchical levels.

The reader might argue that I have really only replaced seven features with six, and that anyway, at least one distinction between features in the feature geometry model appears to be redundant, giving us six against six. My reply to this would be that I have introduced three important improvements. Firstly, Manner is treated in a unified fashion, different from the 'distributed' treatment it receives in the standard feature geometry model. Secondly, in this model various 'consonantal' aspects are associated in terms of C-ness, while various 'vocalic' aspects are associated in terms of V-ness. Thirdly, and most important, Manner is assigned the primacy it merits. Manner is, as I have argued, just more important an aspect of a sound than Place or laryngeal mode.[12] In addition the six or seven features used by Feature Geometrists may potentially involve 12 or 14 binary-valued specifications, while the DP Manner features are crucially single-valued.

The various different Manners of articulation are distinguished in my version of the DP model as follows:

(13)

	M″: obstruent: [C] sonorant: [V]	M′: noncontinuant: [C] continuant: [V]	M: constrictive: [C] nonconstrict.: [V]
stop	[C]	[C]	[C]
fricative[13]	[C]	[V]	[C]
nasal	[V]	[C]	[C]
liquid	[V]	[V]	[C]
glide/vowel	[V]	[V]	[V]

These compare to the following feature specifications in a typical Feature geometry approach:

(14)

	cons	son	nas	cont	strid	dist	lat
stop	+	−	−	−	−	$\pm$	
fricative	+	−	$\pm$	+	$\pm$	+	+
nasal	+	+	+	−	−	$\pm$	
liquid	+	+	$\pm$	+	−	$\pm$	+
glide	−	+	$\pm$	+	−	+	$\pm$

Irrelevant features have been blocked out. In terms of the version of feature geometry presented in Halle (1995), which can be considered to be representa-

---

[12] In fact laryngeal distinctions are treated here as Manner distinctions following Humbert (1995).

[13] I will shortly introduce a distinction between different types of fricatives.

tive, [consonantal] and [sonorant] would be located on the root node itself; [continuant], [strident] and [lateral] would be daughters of the root node; [nasal] is located under the Soft Palate node; while [distributed] is located under the Coronal place node. In other words, there is neither a single Manner node, nor are the various 'manner' features treated in any uniform way.

7.4.2 Onsets

The basic constraint—ONSET—in terms of which #CV-structures are preferred to #V-structures is not sufficient to express all the well-formedness aspects of onsets. We need to employ a more subtle set of constraints to express the fact that some kinds of onset are better than others. This should state, as I have just said, that Stop-Vowel syllables are Optimal. These are the first to develop in phonological acquisition, and, as we have seen in some languages, are the only possible type. Cf. the Togarao dialect of the Rotokas language (Firchow and Firchow 1969), where there are only six consonant phonemes /p, t, k, b, d, g/,[14] and all syllables are open.

7.4.2.1 The Stop as unmarked onset

The optimal syllable is the stop-vowel syllable—i.e. that with the maximum sonority gradient.

I will utilize here Levin's X-bar model to represent syllabic structure (1984). For a more detailed discussion of a recent model of syllable structure utilizing this X-bar notation, I refer the reader to Smith (1999):

(15)

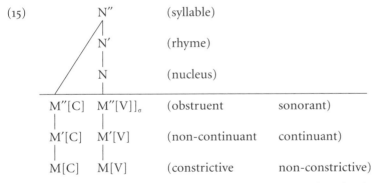

In terms of the architecture defined above, a stop onset has the feature [C] at each level of Manner structure.

By utilizing the C/V values given in the above table, the various compromises between the two extremes of stop (the non-syllabic *par excellence*) and vowel (the syllabic *par excellence*) can be described.

---

[14] Firchow and Firchow give the inventory as /p, t, k, b, ř, g/. In fact all three voiced phonemes possess stop, continuant, and nasal allophones.

In these terms the sonority hierarchy can be interpreted as a derived multi-dimensional hierarchy—defined by the C/V values and the hierarchical relationships among the various instantiations of the C/V relationship.

Any other combination of manners than Stop-Vowel will result in a less optimal syllable type. The stop-vowel syllable is the only type observable in every language. Why is this the optimal syllable? Some articulatory and perceptual phonetic reasons have already been given. The answer formalized in terms of our theoretical approach is that it is the only type of syllable that displays the structure 'CV' at every level of Manner structure. This means that at every level a 'sonority' difference is defined. Any other combination of onset and nucleus will involve departures from the ideal combination of CV at one or more levels.

Three CV-constraints corresponding to the three levels of manner structure are now available to express the deviations from the optimal (voiceless) stop-vowel syllable:

(16)   a. ONSETTEMPLATE-(CV)″   The obstruent-sonorant template
        b. ONSETTEMPLATE-(CV)′   The noncontinuant-continuant template
        c. ONSETTEMPLATE-(CV)°   The constrictive-nonconstrictive template

I will show below that it is in fact unnecessary to have three separate constraints, and that the same effects may be derived in a more general way. However, for ease of exposition I will continue for the moment with the idea of a family of three CV-constraints.

7.4.2.2 The (semi)vowel onset

Now let us look at the other extreme—a syllable with a semi-vowel onset. This will exhibit a violation of the optimal CV-pattern at no less than three levels of structure.

(17)

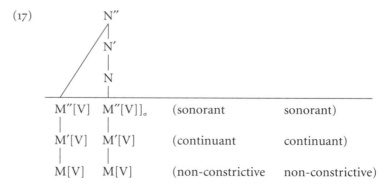

A semi-vowel is of course nothing else than a vowel in a non-nuclear position—nothing else in particular requires to be said about them.

Semi-vowels are subject to frequent alteration as we might expect, for instance by various 'Fortition' processes that act to replace them with some kind of more

Optimal consonant-like articulation. Compare the fortition effects visible in the reflexes of Latin /j/ in Italian and French.

(18)   Fortition effects in reflexes of Latin /j/

Latin		French		Italian	
maiorem	/j/	majeure	/ʒ/	maggiore	/ddʒ/
Iohannem	/j/	Jean	/ʒ/	Giovanni	/ddʒ/
iocum	/j/	jeu	/ʒ/	gioco	/ddʒ/

Here Italian (and Old French) display a development to an affricate. Modern Standard French has replaced the affricate by a fricative. The corresponding back glide did not, however, develop in French and Italian further than a fricative.

(19)   Fortition effects in reflexes of Latin /w/

Latin		French		Italian	
vivere	/w/	vivre	/v/	vivere	/v/
viginti	/w/	vingt	/v/	venti	/v/
vendere	/w/	vendre	/v/	vendere	/v/

In the light of the above characterization of consonant-types, these changes in the structure of semi-vowel onsets are completely comprehensible—leading to less undesirable syllable structure, or to fewer violations of syllabic constraints.

7.4.2.3 Compromises between Stop and (Semi-)Vowel

Note that intermediate consonantal types—involving nasal or liquid onsets—will involve less violation of the ideal syllable structure than those with a glide onset. These types involve various compromises between a maximally closed vocal tract and a maximally open vocal tract. The different articulatory types met with among the various types of liquid articulation do not seem to have much phonological relevance except for the lateral-rhotic distinction, on which more later (see the section on nasals and liquids—Section 7.3.4.1.). In particular the numerous different types of rhotic articulation do not seem in general to be distinctive as far as Place is concerned. This can be seen from a consideration of the various types of /r/-sound in several European languages. To take English dialects as an example, we find at least a postalveolar approximant, an alveolar tap, an alveolar trill, a retroflex approximant, and a uvular approximant, all functioning as the rhotic in different forms of the language. And similar conditions pertain in the case of other languages.

To take the apparently less sonorous nasal to start with, this will display the following structure:

(20)

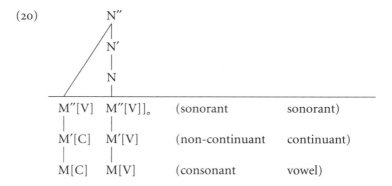

M″[V]	M″[V]]ₒ	(sonorant	sonorant)
M′[C]	M′[V]	(non-continuant	continuant)
M[C]	M[V]	(consonant	vowel)

This will involve one violation of a constraint of the ONSETTEMPLATE-CV family as compared with the optimal stop-vowel structure.

The corresponding structure for a liquid will look like this:

(21)

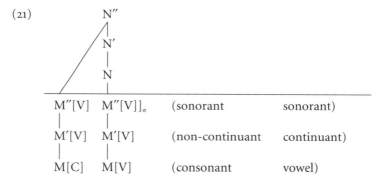

M″[V]	M″[V]]ₒ	(sonorant	sonorant)
M′[V]	M′[V]	(non-continuant	continuant)
M[C]	M[V]	(consonant	vowel)

This—because of the greater sonority of the onset—will involve two violations of the ONSETTEMPLATE-CV constraint(s) rather than one.

I will return to the question of the difference between laterals and rhotics below.

7.4.2.4 Sibilant and non-sibilant fricatives

Anderson and Ewen (1987) regard sibilants as having an optimal status in comparison to other fricatives. They regard other (Non-sibilant) fricatives as possessing a dependent stop aspect. I will however regard non-sibilant fricatives primarily as stops, but stops modified by a dependent fricative aspect, for the following reasons.

• Non-sibilant fricatives have basically the same (or fewer) possibilities of place of articulation as do the prototypical stop types. I regard place of articulation as providing an important diagnostic for Manner of articulation. So in (some forms of) English[15] we have voiceless stops /p, t, k/, and at the same basic places of articulation, the Non-sibilant fricatives /f, θ, x/.

- Conversely, most affricates are sibilant in nature—that is, they have basically the same (or fewer) possibilities of place of articulation as do the sibilant fricatives. Compare English with two voiceless sibilants /s, ʃ/, and a single voiceless affricate /ʧ/. Or Bžedukh with five voiceless sibilants /s, ɕ, ɕʷ, ʃː, ʃʲː/[16] and four types of affricate /tsː, tɕʷː, ʧː, ʧʲː/, corresponding in place of articulation to four of the five sibilant places of articulation. For these reasons I consider both non-sibilant fricative (23) and sibilant affricate articulation (24) types to be secondary in nature, and therefore more complex than the basic segment types.

(22) **Fricative:**   M″[C]–M′[C]–M [C][17]
                     \M′[V]–M [C]

(23) **Affricate:**   M″[C]–M′[V]–M [C]
                     \M′[C]–M [C]

In other words a fricative is a stop *as regards place of articulation*, with *continuant consonantal modification*. Similarly an affricate is a sibilant (fricative) *as regards place of articulation*, with *non-continuant consonantal modification*.

At this juncture the reader might point out that there are also labial and dorsal affricates. We will argue that most of the infrequent 'phonological' cases of such segments involve additional factors, such as a geminate-type nature, which they clearly have in Zurich German for example (van Riemsdijk and Smith 1973). This allows them to be represented as stop-fricative complexes.

In other cases only low-level phonetic affrication is involved, such as when the phonological uvular 'stop' in some language is in fact phonetically a uvular affricate. For instance, compare the heavy affrication of uvular stops in Kabardian (Kuipers 1960), the affrication of the plain uvular stop in Iraqw (Mous 1992), and the affrication of the voiceless uvular stop /q/ in Nez Perce (Aoki 1970). In some languages all voiceless stops are to some extent affricated. For instance, compare the affrication of all voiceless stops in broad Cockney (Sivertsen 1960), and the light affrication of most pre-vocalic voiceless stops in Kabardian (Kuipers 1960). In such cases there is absolutely no phonological reason for indicating the merely phonetic affrication. However, there is a small residue of cases where non-sibilant affricates must be recognized. Conceivably a treatment as contour segments would be possible in these cases. Our conclusion is that only sibilant affricates may be true affricates, in our sense of stopped fricatives.

---

[15] At the present day, largely restricted to Scottish and Irish forms of English, as well as in certain obsolescent dialects spoken in northern England.

[16] The latter two are geminates, but this does not affect the point at issue.

[17] Note that whether a dependent structure is represented to the left or to the right of its head is purely for typographical convenience.

This is a conclusion related to that of LaCharité (1993) that only (strident) coronal affricates pattern with (strident) fricatives.

An examination of Maddieson (1984: 35, 45) demonstrates that the relative complexity assigned by my version of the DP model to these various types of obstruent is in accord with their relative frequencies in the sample of the world's languages examined by the Maddieson.

(24)

	Sibilant	Non-sibilant
Non-continuant	tʃ 141	p 263
Continuant	s 266	f 135

These figures are very striking. Taking non-continuants first, we note that roughly twice as many languages have non-sibilants as have sibilants—in other words twice as many languages have stops as have the most frequent affricate /tʃ/. Turning to continuants, we note that roughly twice as many languages have the most frequent sibilant /s/ as have the most frequent non-sibilant /f/. Turning then to sibilants, we note that roughly twice as many languages have continuants as have non-continuants (affricates). Turning finally to non-sibilants, we note that roughly twice as many languages have (non-sibilant) non-continuants as have (non-sibilant) continuants.

So sibilants are much more frequent than other types of fricatives. The two basic types of obstruent are then those printed in bold type in the table.

The choice to represent sibilants as the basic fricative type, justified by the above statistical evidence, will enable us to represent Place distinctions in sibilants (in general the extra place distinctions found specifically among coronal sounds) in terms of the basic A-I-U set of place features.

A sibilant onset will result in a structure like the following:

(25)

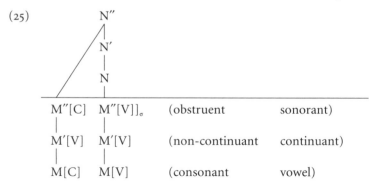

This will also exhibit a single violation of the ONSETTEMPLATE-(CV)′ constraint. What advantage is gained from separating sibilants from other fricatives, by assigning them the status of prototypical fricatives? Note that we achieve a way of expressing the implicational universal of consonant-systems that if a language has one fricative then it will be a sibilant. Other fricatives are rarer, and it is significant that in very many cases they can be identified as the result of diachronic or synchronic lenition-processes that have applied to the corresponding stops.

Note also that I have chosen to hardcode the phonological typological universals discussed above directly in the geometry of segmental structure. Do we not additionally require constraints of the form 'A continuant obstruent is a sibilant'? Note that because of the decisions I have made above regarding the geometrical representation of fricatives, sibilant fricatives will be preferred over non-sibilant fricatives, all other things being equal, by the constraint *COMPLEX(SEGMENT) which will be discussed further in the next section. This constraint forbids branching structure in segment geometry. And non-sibilant fricatives involve branching under the M″[C]-node, while sibilant fricatives do not.

For the above-mentioned reason we will regard non-sibilant fricatives structurally as derived stops—a kind of 'fricativized' stop.

(26)   Stop onset   Fricative onset   Sibilant onset

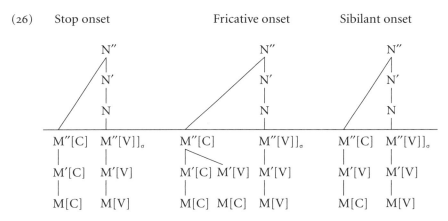

Observe that in terms of these structures, the sibilant onset case will display one violation of the ONSETTEMPLATE-CV′ constraint. The non-sibilant onset will also display one violation, as it seems only reasonable to calculate such violations only in terms of the head or major Manner articulation involved in the structure. The basic Manner of an articulation is determined by its head. Any dependent structures will only introduce minor modifications, and thus should not affect the situation as regards violations of the ONSETTEMPLATE-CV′ constraint. However, the (non-sibilant) fricative structure will also have two violations of a constraint against complex segments, which we may call *COMPLEX (SEGMENT). There are two violations because the extra structure involves two extra nodes.

(27) *COMPLEX(SEGMENT):
      Dependent nodes are prohibited. [Count one violation for each extra node.]

This will then reflect the relative infrequency of non-sibilant fricatives vis-à-vis their sibilant counterparts.

It is conceivable that *COMPLEX(SEGMENT) represents a whole family of constraints. It might be the case that the level in structure at which branching occurs is relevant. At the moment I do not regard this as necessary, preferring to count one violation for each node in a dependent branch. This penalizes branchings at higher levels more than those at lower levels because in general, the higher the level the branching occurs at, the more nodes there will be involved in the dependent branch.

Note that expressing (non-sibilant) fricatives as fricativized stops, as compared with (sibilant) fricatives, allows us to represent affricates as stopped sibilants, as discussed above, in contrast to ordinary stops.

(28)   Sibilant   Affricate

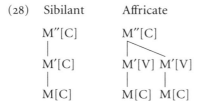

What advantages does this have? Note that (sibilant) affricates exhibit the typical behaviour of sibilants. They observe sibilant harmony, for example, in languages that possess this. They (partly) share the same places of articulation. Also in respect of other phonological phenomena associated with sibilants, affricates exhibit sibilant-like behaviour. In English, for instance, the palato-alveolar affricate exhibits the same epenthesis behaviour as the alveolar and palato-alveolar sibilants in plural formation, possessive formation, 3rd-person-singular verb inflection, and *is*-cliticization.

Similarly to the above case of the non-sibilant fricative, this structure will involve violations of *COMPLEX(SEGMENT).

7.4.3 *Paradigmatic Constraints, and their Interaction with Syntagmatic Constraints*

All other things being equal the Projections M″[C]–M′[C]–M[C] (stop) and M″[V]–M′[V]–M[V] (vowel) will be preferred over other segment types. Other segment types may of course be preferred because of faithfulness to lexical representations, or because of syntagmatic factors other than the single case of the Onset-Nucleus patterns which we employed to discuss the representation of different Manner types. Otherwise, one of these two unmarked types will appear. For instance, epenthetic segments may be expected to be either a glottal stop [ʔ] or an unmarked vowel [ə] or [i] (depending on the vowel system of the language concerned). This is an illustration of what is referred to as the 'emergence of the unmarked' (McCarthy and Prince 1994).

This can easily be expressed in terms of a constraint:

(29)   M-PROJECTION: A node M° is dominated by nodes which agree with
it in terms of features

That is: an M[C]-node is dominated by nodes M′[C] and M″[C]; and an M[V]-node by nodes M′[V] and M″[V].

Now we can see that the three syntagmatic syllable structure constraints mentioned above—ONSETTEMPLATE-(CV)′ (the obstruent-sonorant template), ONSETTEMPLATE-(CV)′ (the non–continuant-continuant template), and ONSETTEMPLATE-(CV)° (the constrictive-nonconstrictive template), whose function is to express deviations from the optimal (voiceless) stop-vowel syllable —are in fact partly redundant. They can be derived from the combination of M-PROJECTION and a more general ONSETTEMPLATE-CV constraint stating that the head of N″ is M[V], and the dependent of N″ is M[C].

As well as leading to a more general result, this approach circumvents the problems caused by the non-existence of the factorial typology[18] effects that might be expected if the three above-mentioned syntagmatic constraints really existed. In other words, the intervention of faithfulness constraints between the various ONSETTEMPLATE-(CV) constraints would potentially produce strange effects.

7.4.4 *The Interaction of Manner and Place*

The basic Place of articulation of consonants or vowels is determined by the head. I will claim that there are basically three primary dimensions of Place among the various different Manner types. As we have suggested above, the different manners define different primary distinctions of place. The basic place distinctions met with among stops are labial (U), coronal (I) and dorsal (A).

Among sibilants we have indicated above that the basic place distinctions are assumed to be the various subdivisions of *coronal*, such as *apical, laminal* and *retroflex*. This is an empirical fact, of course, not a theoretical pronouncement. The reason this is so is to be found in articulatory phonetics. The production of all sibilants involves the formation of a longitudinal channel in the front part of the tongue. All articulations involving the front part of the tongue are of course coronal, but not all coronal articulations involve channelling in the tongue. Because the front of the tongue is not primarily involved in the articulation of labial or dorsal fricatives, no sibilants are possible among these.

Among the vowels we will shortly see that we can distinguish between the primary place features front (I), back (U) and low (A), and the secondary place features RTR (A), ATR (I) and round (U).

It is only complete manner structures, as I have said above, which are assumed to dominate place features. This implies that secondary articulations involve complex segments with two complete manner structures. For instance, a labialized coronal stop will have to be represented as a stop with a coronal

---

[18] This problem was pointed out by the anonymous reviewer.

articulation, associated with a (full) dependent vowel with a labial articulation.

7.4.4.1 Nasals and liquids

Missing in the above list are two manner types belonging to the class of sonorant consonants—nasals and liquids. These differ in their relationship to place.

A few languages have only coronal nasals—such as Tlingit, Chipewyan, Wichita, Yuchi and Southern Nambiquara (Maddieson 1984). The vast majority have, however, basically one of two options: (a) a labial and a coronal nasal, or (b) the basic 'stop' places of articulation—labial, coronal and dorsal—as well as other possibilities paralleled in the stop system of the language concerned. This suggests that, in terms of the Subset Principle, nasals do not basically require to distinguish place of articulation, but that they can do so *secondarily*, and of course usually do.

In cases where languages have only a single nasal segment, I would claim that we have instantiations of the so-called nasal glide. Another view of this—taken by Humbert (1995), for example—is that nasal glides can never surface as such, but require therapeutic measures in order to manifest themselves phonetically, such as attaching to vowels to become nasalized vowels, or attaching to consonants giving prenasalized segments. I will assume, however, that a language with only a single nasal—normally [n], but sometimes [ŋ] in coda position—in fact possesses such a nasal glide.

Nasals explicitly distinguished in terms of place will receive a different explanation. They will be represented as complex structures with dependent stops.

(30)   M″[V]
        ┌──────┐
    M″[V] M″[C]
      │   │
    M′[C] M′[C]
      │   │
    M[C]   M[C]

The labial, alveolar and velar nasals will then be represented as follows:

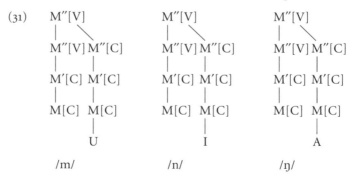

(31)   M″[V]   M″[V]   M″[V]
        │   \   │   \   │   \
    M″[V] M″[C]   M″[V] M″[C]   M″[V] M″[C]
      │   │   │   │   │   │
    M′[C] M′[C]   M′[C] M′[C]   M′[C] M′[C]
      │   │   │   │   │   │
    M[C]   M[C]   M[C]   M[C]   M[C]   M[C]
             │   │   │
             U   I   A

        /m/   /n/   /ŋ/

In other words these structures represent nasals, modified respectively by dependent labial, coronal and dorsal stop articulations. Note that labial nasals may display a different mode of behaviour as compared to coronal nasals, even when they occur in the same phonological system. For instance, the labial nasals[19] exhibit stop-like behaviour in the Goidelic languages (the various stages of Irish, Scottish Gaelic and Manx) in that they lenite to (voiced) fricatives, while in contrast the coronal nasals behave more like sonorants, as they lenite to lax counterparts, just as the laterals and rhotics do.[20]

(32)   Goidelic lenition patterns

	Place	Basic	Lenited
Labial	nasal	m, m^y	v, v^y
	voiced stop	b, b^y	v, v^y
	voiceless stop	p, p^y	f, f^y
Coronal	nasal	N, N^{y}[21]	n, n^y
	lateral	L, L^y	l, l^y
	rhotic	R, R^y	r, r^y

I conclude then that, while the coronal nasal(s) represent nasal glides, the labial nasals in Gaelic are indeed complex structures, showing a closer relationship to stops in their phonological behaviour.

I have mentioned three types of nasal system so far. The first type has one (coronal or velar[22]) nasal. I have interpreted this as an (underlying) placeless nasal—a so-called Nasal Glide. The second type has a set of nasals closely mimicking the place distinctions found with stops. I assume that these nasals are all (complex) nasals to be represented with dependent stops containing the relevant place information. The third type is very frequent, and has only labials and coronal nasals. If the Goidelic languages are typical, what we find here may be an (underlying) placeless nasal (realized as coronal), and an explicit complex labial nasal. This possibility requires further research.

Note that we require to account for two so far unexplained facts. Firstly that nasals 'like' to have Place, although they don't require to have it (underlyingly at least). This is evidenced by the tendency to mimic the stop system as far as Place is concerned. Another illustration of this is the frequent tendency, pointed out in Humbert (1995) for nasals to 'snatch' Place features—as in nasal assimilation. Secondly, and this is in a sense the other side of the coin,

---

[19] Irish Gaelic has two labial nasals (palatalized and non-palatalized) while Scottish Gaelic has only one, in the surface phonology at least.

[20] In fact, the full set of coronal sonorants is not found in all dialects (at least phonetically), there having been frequent cases of mergers.

[21] The tradition in Goidelic studies is to represent the non-lenited sonorants with capital letters. The original phonetic characteristics involved differences in place of articulation and, in non-initial positions at least, a geminate nature.

[22] This possibility exists only in coda position.

there are so few languages with only a single (underlyingly placeless) nasal.

These facts can be accommodated by the constraint NASALPLACE.

(33)   NASALPLACE:
       Nasals must have Place.

So, on the one hand we have the place-free structural representation of nasals, and on the other hand two constraints that are of relevance—NASALPLACE and *COMPLEX(SEGMENT). In terms of nasals, these constraints conflict in their implications, while the place-free structure of nasals is of course in conflict with the assumptions of NASALPLACE.

Let us now examine assimilated nasal clusters for a moment. These may be represented as follows:

(34)

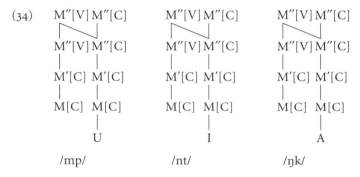

Note that all that the fact of assimilating a placeless nasal to a (placed) stop involves is the addition of an association line. I will assume that the mere projection of extra head nodes—M″[C] and M″[V]—in order to allow the expression of the dependency relations between the two segments comes at no additional cost. Also, I take it that we have no complex segments here—there are two head structures present—so that no violation of *COMPLEX will be involved. We have inserted an association line, but the only constraint violated would be DEPASS, which forbids the creation of new associations. This explains the relative ease with which we get nasal assimilation, even in languages with no underlying 'complex' nasals.

I will now address the problem of liquids. Unlike nasals, liquids are never distinguished in terms of the major consonantal (i.e. 'stop') places of articulation. There are two types of liquid: laterals and rhotics. Laterals are virtually always coronal phonetically, but this fact is irrelevant in the sense that there is never a contrast with labial or dorsal. Dorsal (velar) liquids supposedly occur in some New Guinea languages, but their behaviour is claimed by Levin (1988) to be not so much that expected of dorsals but rather that expected of coronals. Those languages that do distinguish laterals in terms of place do so either in terms of the 'sibilant' place distinctions such as laminal and retroflex, or the 'vowel' distinctions such as palatalized or rounded.

Rhotics are formed, as we noted above, at different places of articulation—dental, alveolar, postalveolar, retroflex, palatal-velar, uvular, etc.—but these distinctions are once again never relevant as such as place distinctions. The options appear to be restricted to coronal—the most frequent type, and the less frequent dorsals. These coronal and dorsal places of articulation again never function as relevant phonological distinctions between two rhotics. What phonological distinctions are found in terms of place are basically those of vocalic place.[23]

This leads us to the consideration that laterals—which have a more radical constriction—are more related to sibilants in some fashion, inasmuch as they may display the same types of place distinctions, while rhotics may only display vocalic place distinctions. Can we then not draw the following proportion?

(35) Place types available for the various types of sonorant consonant[24]

Manner type	stop $M''[C]$–$M'[C]$–$M[C]$	sibilant $M''[C]$–$M'[V]$–$M[C]$	vowel/glide $M''[V]$–$M'[V]$–$M[V]$
Place types available:	**stop** (sibilant) (vowel)	**sibilant** (vowel)	**vowel**
Manner type	nasal $M''[V]$–$M'[C]$–$M[C]$	lateral $M''[V]$–$M'[V]$–$M[C]$	rhotic $M''[V]$–$M'[V]$–$M[C]$
Place types available:	(stop) (sibilant) (vowel)	(sibilant) (vowel)	(vowel)

Bold type characterizes the native (Head) feature interpretations; bracketing characterizes feature interpretations only present in Dependent structures.

What I mean by these proportions is that the main place-of-articulation distinctions of stops are precisely those most typical of stops—not unsurprisingly. However, in addition, stops may also exhibit place distinctions typical of sibilants (the various coronal subtypes), and those typical of vowels (palatalized, labialized, etc.). Similarly, the main articulatory distinctions of sibilants are precisely those of sibilants. Additionally, sibilants of course may also display distinctions typical of vowels.

Note that the primary place features associated with the first three types—those indicated in bold type—are directly dominated by the manner structure. The other place types are represented in terms of dependent structures.

To judge from the phonological inventories encountered in the languages of

[23] At this point the reader will protest that there are languages with retroflex rhotics in contrast with alveolar rhotics, such as many Australian languages. However, in these cases, it is generally assumed in the literature that these retroflex segments are in fact glides.

[24] This table in effect also defines the different types of dependent structures allowed with the various head types.

the world, laterals sometimes possess the same coronal distinctions which I have suggested are basic to sibilants: laminal, apical, retroflex, etc. Rhotics do not seem to have the same (phonological) possibilities, despite the fact that a subset of these distinctions may be present phonetically. They do however utilize the familiar vocalic secondary articulations, such as palatalized and labialized, which are also available for laterals, of course.

I conclude that laterals and rhotics differ in that laterals involve a dependent sibilant structure:

(36)

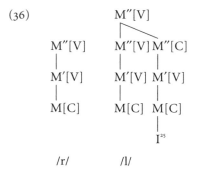

In this way the intuition that laterals are somehow more 'consonantal' than rhotics can also be captured.

7.4.4.2 (Secondary) Place in stops

Stops will have the primary place features [U, I, A] as defined in Smith (1988).

(37)   [U] is labial [I] is coronal [A] is dorsal

Besides these primary distinctions, all other (secondary) types involve combinations with dependent segment structures as I have stated:

(38)

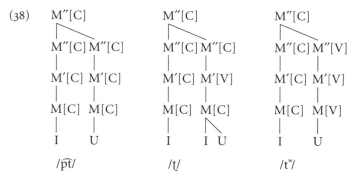

---

[25] The expression of place in sibilants will be examined below. Note that stating that laterals have a dependent coronal place would explain why laterals are more consistently coronal in their place than rhotics.

Simultaneous stop-stop and stop-fricative articulations (not phonologically distinguished in any language) will be represented in terms of two stop structures, one of which is assumed to be dependent on the other. Sub-types of coronals which mirror the place types of sibilants, such as retroflex coronals, will be represented as coronal stop segments, with a secondary sibilant articulation. A retroflex segment is illustrated here. And coronals with secondary (vocalic) articulations, such as labialization, will be represented as stops with a secondary vowel articulation.

7.4.4.3 Place in sibilants

Sibilants will all have the primary place feature [I]. Languages with more than one sibilant type will also have sibilants involving dependent [U/A].

(39) [U] is retroflex

  [A] refers to articulations involving retraction. This can be interpreted in two ways. An articulation either involves retraction of the front part of the tongue (i.e. the active articulator) or involves a locus further back on the palatal arch (i.e. the passive articulator). For instance, if an apical and a laminal articulation contrast at the *same* closure location, then the apical will be the more retracted of the two[26] (i.e. [A]). Where different (phonetic) locations of closure represent the only difference between two articulations, the one that is located further back will be referred to as [A].

An abiding aspect of sibilants, then, is their coronality. So while we can refer uniquely to the class of sibilants in terms of their manner structure, it will also be necessary to be able to refer to them as coronals, in that there are also phenomena applying to all coronals including sibilants. For an example, take coronal harmony in certain Athabascan languages, such as Tahltan (Shaw 1991).

Some basic types of sibilant are illustrated below:

(40)

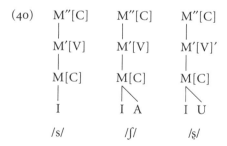

As I have just said, all sibilants are marked explicitly as coronals. The common-

---

[26] Note that by 'retraction' we mean that the tongue as a whole is further back in the oral cavity, not that the contact is made further back on the tongue.

est place types are indicated with secondary place features—there are only two possibilities, assuming we want to exclude:

(40)   M[C]

I   I

as ill-formed.[27]

The first (and simplest) structure represents the most frequent sibilant /s/. The second represents the laminal palato-alveolar /ʃ/. The feature [A] represents a (non-palatalized) distinctively alveolar or retracted articulation. The feature [U] indicates a retroflex articulation.

The justification for representing retroflex sounds with the feature [U] is that these involve a perceptually 'hollow' component. This must be distinguished from a purely velarized secondary articulation, which would be indicated by a dependent vocalic articulation involving a back vowel (also represented by the feature [U]). However it seems fairly clear that retroflex consonants have a phonological relationship to backness. Compare the case of Kodagu (Schiffman 1975), for instance, which has a process backing /i, e/ to [ɨ, ʌ] before retroflex consonants, presumably for perceptual rather than articulatory reasons.

Note that the IPA symbols used by the authors of language descriptions are not always sufficient guide in this context. Some sounds indicated by /ʃ/ which are more clearly palatal in articulation—conceivably better indicated by the symbol [ɕ]—would best be represented as:

(42)   M″[C]

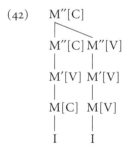

M″[C] M″[V]
  | |
M′[V] M′[V]
  | |
M[C]   M[V]
  | |
  I   I

that is to say, as a palatalized /s/. The Scottish Gaelic /ʃ/ is a sound of this type—or at least it is in some dialects, as is the sound symbolized the same way in Dutch and spelt *sj* (cf. the description of this sound in Collins and Mees 1981).

7.4.4.4 An exemplification: Basque

The question now arises of how complex coronal systems of stops and nasals are to be represented. I will first turn to a consideration of the case of Basque (cf.

---

[27] I will assume that a Place node can only dominate a single example of each Place feature.

van der Hulst and Smith 1990). The details of this case are taken from Saltarelli (1988). Basque basically distinguishes five types of coronal articulation (in Basque orthography):

(43) apico-dental   (stops + nasal)   t   [t̪]
      lamino-alveolar   (affricate + fricative)   tz   [ts]
      apico-alveolar   (affricate, fricative + liquids)   ts   [ts̠]
      lamino-postalveolar   (affricate + fricative)   tx   [tɕ]
      (pre-)dorso-palatal   (stops + nasal + liquid)   tt   [tʸ]

Here the stops are unproblematic in our terms, these being the only non-sibilants. The apico-dental is represented as a plain coronal, while the dorso-palatal can be represented as a palatalized coronal.

One phonological process which might have a bearing on the representation of the other sounds is a limited process of affective consonantism, resulting mostly in articulations of a palatal nature. The affective counterpart of the dentals is the dorso-palatals, which I would represent as modified with a dependent vocalic articulation with the place feature [I] (as in 45)). The affective counterpart of both types of alveolar is represented by the lamino-postalveolar series. I will represent this as a palatalized sibilant affricate articulation.

(44)   Non-affective   Affective

      apico-dental   t d [t̪ d̪]   tt dd [tʸ dʸ]   (pre-)dorso-palatal
      lamino-alveolar   tz   [ts]   tx   [tɕ]   lamino-postalveolar
      apico-alveolar   ts   [ts̠]   tx   [tɕ]   lamino-postalveolar

The question that remains to be decided is the representation of the two alveolar sibilant types. One obvious possibility is to say that the laminal segment represents the basic sibilant affricate in Basque, while the apical variety—presumably retracted in articulation—might be assigned the dependent feature [A].

This leaves us with the obvious problem of just how the lamino-postalveolar is to be represented. One avenue of approach is to assume that this is an affricate segment similar in place of articulation to the above-mentioned Scottish Gaelic /ʃ/, probably more accurately represented as [ɕ].

The five types of articulation would then be represented as follows:

(45)

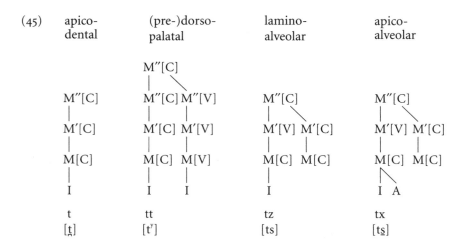

	apico- dental	(pre-)dorso- palatal	lamino- alveolar	apico- alveolar

lamino-
postalveolar

Why is [tɕ] chosen as the affective form of [ts] and not for instance [tsʸ] or [tʃʸ], a more retracted articulation in terms of the active articulator? Let us see whether this is amenable to an OT explanation.

(46)

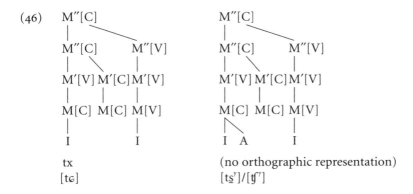

The second structure represents the putative affective candidate derived by palatalizing the underlying apico-alveolar *ts*. Consider the following tableau.

(43) /ts̪ʸ/	Recover-ability	*Complex	Max(A)
[ts] (lamino-alveolar)	*!	**	*
[ts̺] (apico-alveolar)	*!	***	
☞ [tɕ] (lamino-postalveolar)		*****	*
[ts̺ʸ] (palatalized apico-alveolar)		******!	

RECOVERABILITY is a constraint stated against the non-recoverability of morphological material. It is undesirable to delete morphemes completely without trace (see Chomsky 1965: 222). In this case the morpheme consists of a floating feature [I].

(48) RECOVERABILITY:
Do not delete all the phonological material of a morpheme.

The correct result is obtained quite simply. The affective marking must be maintained—otherwise the form would not be identifiable as an affective. The least complex derived affective form is then selected. Additional constraints will be required to ensure the survival of complex underlying forms like the apico-alveolars when not modified by the affective morpheme, but this does not seem to be problematic.

7.4.5 *Place in Vowels*

7.4.5.1 Absolute place

The set of place features is as we have stated above [A,I,U]. Directly dominated by a vocalic structure this will give us, respectively, a low vowel, a front (palatal) vowel, and a back (velar) vowel. In other words, each of these features introduces a(n absolute) partition of the vowel space into two regions:

(49)   Partitions of the Vowel Space

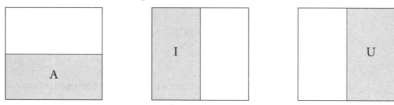

We will refer to vowel features in head position—that is, directly dominated by the head manner structure—as absolute or primary features.

Note that I do not postulate a feature high. The absence of low will imply a high interpretation, so front alone will result in /i/, a (high) front vowel, while back alone will result in /u/, a (high) back vowel. Normally this last will also be round, inasmuch as non-low back vowels are normally round, giving /u/. The main function of rounding in vowel systems of a triangular nature appears to be to enhance the backness aspect (cf. Stevens *et al.* 1986). So the rounding of back vowels increases the perceived difference between back vowels and their front counterparts.

The lack of a feature corresponding to [high] is an empirical question. This position was inspired by the belief that for every Place feature utilized in vowel systems there should be a corresponding type of vowel harmony occurring in languages. Obviously front-harmony is an example of a very frequent type. The existence of low harmony can also be argued for. Potential cases of high harmony seem to be rather rare, leading me to the tentative conclusion that these apparent cases of high harmony may be accountable for in other ways. The reader is quite entitled to observe at this point that cases of back harmony are also not very frequent in the literature. However, this point should be seen in relation to the increased importance in this feature system that is given to back vis-à-vis round. It is not clear that some cases of what has been assumed to be round harmony in the literature do not in fact represent cases of back harmony.

Note that rounding is by no means an essential phonetic aspect of non-low back vowels. What is usually referred to as /u/ is in fact unrounded, or weakly rounded in a number of languages such as Japanese and Nez Perce (Aoki 1970), for example.

The three features [A, I, U] give us the three simplex vowels:

(50)

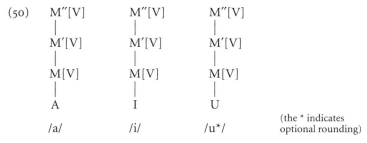

(the * indicates
optional rounding)

The combination of A with I, or U, gives us:

(51)

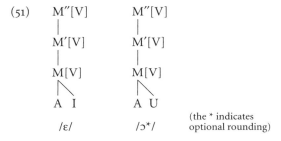

(the * indicates
optional rounding)

These will be the first choice for additional vowels, on the not unreasonable assumption that A—the feature that typifies the most open, and therefore the most vowel-like vowel—is preferred as head over the other features. We can formulate this in terms of the following constraint:

(52)   AHEAD-M [V]:
'[A] is head of a vowel structure.'

The dispreferred head-dependency relationship gives us the next two vowels:

(53)

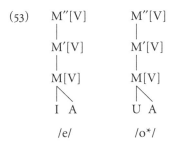

Note that this might appear to be in conflict with the generality of five systems which are described with the help of the phonetic symbols /e, o/. As Maddieson (1984) observes, however, the precise meaning of /e, o/ is frequently not precisely phonetically defined in descriptions of languages.

Note that the four mid vowels will fall under the ambit of *COMPLEX, giving a single violation in each case.

The combination of I and U with each other will give:

(54)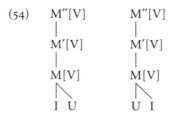

What will be the meaning of these structures? The first will be a backed front vowel, and the second will be a fronted back vowel. What do these expressions

really mean? Note that in the case of A̖ I, we have two overlapping sectors of the vowel space:

(55)   The meaning of [AI]

In the case of I̖ U, however, we have a different situation. Here we have adjacent non-overlapping sectors.

(56)   The meaning of [IU] and [UI]

The vowels denoted as combinations of I and U can only be located, in some sense, at the border of the two sectors. Because it does not contain A, the vowel concerned must be a high Vowel—/ɨ/. Note that we cannot make a distinction between IU and UI in the same way we can between AI and IA. Because the A-sector and the I-sector overlap, we can distinguish between a vowel where the A is dominant (i.e. head), and one where the I is dominant. In the case of IU and UI, however, the difference, while phonetically meaningless, is potentially phonologically meaningful. And we are of course interested in phonology here, rather than phonetics.

(57)   The meanings of [IA] and [AI]

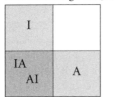

Note that an A vowel will normally be lower than an AI or AU vowel, because I and U are inherently non-low. The system also allows for a distinction between IUA and AIU. So we get the following vowels from these basic sections.

(58)   I   IU   U
          IA   IUA   UA
             AI AIU AU
                A

So, in addition to the triangular 3-, 5-, and 7-vowel systems, we also get parallel systems with the addition of corresponding central vowels, i.e. 4-, 7-, and 10-vowel systems.

7.4.5.2 Vowels and Optimal syllables

In van der Hulst (1994) high vowels are described as having a consonantal aspect, indicated explicitly by the occurrence of C-elements in their structure referring to the labial or palatal coloration of /u/ or /i/ respectively (cf. also Bolognesi 1998). This is a move I do not wish to make, preferring to regard these aspects of vowel structure in Place terms.

However, the intuition that vowels with low vowels make better (more Optimal) syllables must be represented somehow. Compare the following tableau, taking as input a velar stop followed by a placeless vowel. The constraints that seem to be relevant are at least AHEAD-V, *COMPLEX, DEP-IO, and *EMPTY. These may be defined as follows:

(59)   AHEAD-M [V]   [A] is head of a vowel structure (see 53) above).

          *COMPLEX (SEGMENT)   Branching in segmental structure is not allowed (see 28) above).

          DEP-IO   Do not insert segments. This is a constraint family.

          *EMPTY (PLACE)   Placeless segments are disallowed.[28]

---

[28] Assuming the manner is such that Place is possible

Assuming that, all other things being equal, the constraints are unranked—and the non-relevance of constraints forbidding the occurrence of particular phonological features—we get the following tableau.

The Optimal vowel

(60) kV	AHEAD-M[V]	*COMPLEX	DEP-IO	*EMPTY
ki	*		*	
ku	*		*	
ke	*	*	*	
ko	*	*	*	
kɛ		*	*	
kɔ		*	*	
☞ ka			*	
kə	*			*

From this evaluation it is clear that, for any given onset combined with a placeless nucleus, the optimal result will involve an /a/.

The fact that I do not treat high vowels as involving consonantal aspects is therefore compensated for by the assumption of the existence of the constraint AHEAD-M[V].

7.4.5.3 Relative Place

It is also possible to have the same three features, [A,I,U], as terminal nodes to a dependent V-element.

(45)   M″[V]
        | \
        M″[V] M″[V]
        | |
        M′[V] M′[V]
        | |
        M[V]   M[V]
        | |
        x   y

As features of such a dependent M [V]-structure however, these features have a different type of meaning. Clearly the interpretation of such secondary features cannot proceed in absolute terms. I interpret these as relative features with the following interpretations:

(62)   [A]: (More) constricted pharyngeal cavity (i.e. Retracted Tongue Root/ RTR)

[I]:   (More) constricted oral cavity (i.e. Advanced Tongue Root/ATR or expanded Pharynx)

[U]:   (More) constricted labial cavity (i.e. Rounded)

An example of a vowel system making extensive use of both pharyngealized and rounded vowels is the Turkic language Tofalar (Rassadin 1978).

(63)

Plain		Rounded		Pharyngeal		Round and Phar.	
i	ɯ	y	u	i̤	ɯ̤	y̤	ṳ
e	a	ø	ơ	e̤	a̤	ø̤	o̤

7.4.5.4 Types of vowel harmony

Ideally any theory of vowel place should allow any feature, or instantiation of a feature, to determine its own type of vowel harmony. In other words we would then expect to find six types of harmony utilizing vowel features.

(64)   Primary or absolute harmony

Low harmony:	Primary [A]	or A¹-harmony
Front harmony:	Primary [I]	or I¹-harmony
Back harmony:	Primary [U]	or U¹-harmony

Secondary or relative harmony

RTR harmony:	Secondary [A]	or A²-harmony
ATR harmony:	Secondary [I]	or I²-harmony
Rounding harmony:	Secondary [U]	or U²-harmony

What limits would we expect to find on the combinations of possible types of harmony? Because harmony involves outputs with vowels with added features, and each of the features [A], [I], and [U] can appear in two possible configurations, it would appear reasonable not to allow the Primary and Secondary harmony types involving the same feature to occur. In fact there is no uncontroversial recorded instance of the combinations of low and RTR harmony, of front and ATR harmony, or of back and rounding harmony. In other words A¹ and A²-harmonies should not occur together, and neither should I¹ and I²-harmonies, nor U¹ and U²-harmonies. A good reason why this should not be allowed is the frequent analysis of vowel harmony as involving floating features. There is of course no *a priori* way of knowing whether a floating feature should attach to a head structure or to a dependent structure. This restriction has to be built into GEN if it is unviolable.

  That this restriction is possible to state depends directly of course on the use of the same features with different phonetic instantiations as Primary and secondary features.

7.4.5.5 The relationship between primary and secondary vocalic features

In addition the claim made in van der Hulst and Smith (1990) that the primary and secondary vocalic features are directly related should be expressed in terms of constraints:

(65) [Back] > [Round] = HEAD-U¹ > U²   (Stevens *et al.* 1986)
      [Round] > [Back] = U² > HEAD-U¹   (AP p.61: 'RD/BK')

This pair of relationships is relatively uncontroversial. [Round] is interpreted by Stevens *et al.* (1986) as an enhancement of [Back].

(66) [Low] > [RTR] = HEAD-A¹ > A²   (AP p.148: 'LO/ATR')
      [RTR] > [Low] = A² > HEAD-A¹   (AP p.150: 'RTR/LO')

This pair of relationships is also uncontroversial.

(67) [Front] > [ATR] = HEAD-I¹ > I²   (AP p.151: 'BK/ATR')
      [ATR] > [Front] = I² > HEAD-I¹   (AP p.175: 'ATR/BK')

The second constraint is seen in operation by the frequent cases where in African languages /e/ acts as the ATR counterpart of /a/ in vowel-systems lacking the true [ATR] counterpart /ə/.

The first constraint, while certainly more controversial, could be claimed to be relevant in systems like those forms of Mongolian which contrast ATR /u/ and non-ATR /ʊ/, but only have a single high front vowel /i/ (Svantesson 1985). Archangeli and Pulleyblank (1994) quote the similar cases of the Edoid languages Epie and Ibilo.

7.4.5.6 A final word on the interaction of Manner and Place

The following interpretations of Place features have been discussed for the different Manners:

(68) Manner-sensitive interpretations of Place features

Stop	Sibilant (coronal)	Vowel (primary)	Vowel (secondary)
A [dorsal]	IA 'retracted'	A [low]	A [RTR]
I [coronal]	I 'normal'	I [front]	I [ATR]
U [labial]	IU 'retroflex'	U [back]	U [round]

So, the only two Manner types that may be combined freely with Place features are the two extreme types—stops (M″[C]–M′[C]–M[C]) and Vowels (M″[V]–M′[V]–M[V]). Mixed types in terms of [C/V] feature assignments are restricted as far as this is concerned. In fact the only case where the head structure is combinable with Place features at all is the sibilant, where the head feature [I] (coronal) is always present. This type is the only other case apart from the stop where the M′ feature is [C]. Mixed types with the M′ feature as [V] never have a head dominating a Place feature.[29]

---

[29] I am indebted to the anonymous reviewer for the observation that projections involving a mixture of [C] and [V] features were restricted as to the Place features occurring with them.

7.4.6 *The Interaction of Consonantal and Vocalic Place Features*

Now that I have covered the various features I wish to recognize, I would like to present an example illustrating relationships between consonantal and vocalic uses of Place features.

7.4.6.1 An example: The development of the PIE labiovelars in Ancient Greek

In the oldest form of Greek known to us, archaic Mycenean Greek of *ca* 1100 BC, the Proto-Indo-European labiovelars—a series of rounded velars—were, it is assumed, still realized as a separate series of sounds. They are represented by different syllabic symbols from the other stop series: labials, dentals and velars. There seems little reason to assume that they were anything other than labialized velars, as they were at a much later date in Latin, for example.

However, this state of affairs was not preserved in any of the numerous attested dialects of Classical Greek. The dialects with the simplest relationship to the Mycenean situation, as far as the labio-velars are concerned, were those usually termed the Aeolic dialects, of which Lesbian, Boeotian and Thessalian are the most prominent representatives.

(69)   Reflexes of Indo-European /k^w/ in some ancient Greek dialects

IE	k^{w}i k^{w}e k^{w}a k^{w}o k^{w}u
Mycaenian	k^{w}i k^{w}e k^{w}a k^{w}o
Aeolic	pi pe pa po ku
Ionic	ti te pa po ku

7.4.6.2 The Aeolic developments

The labiovelar or labialized velar appears in Aeolic as /p/ in all situations except before [u] where it is realized as /k/. Let us first examine the context preceding /u/.

/k^{w}u/ in Aeolic Greek dialects

(70) /k$_1^w$$_2u_3$/	*CompSeg	Max[U]-V(2)	Ident (Seg)	Max-IO	SharePlace-[I]
a. k^{w}u 1,2,3	!*				
b. ku 1,3		!*	*	*	
☞ c. ku 1,23			*		
d. pu 12,3		!*	*		
e. pu 4,3		!*	*	**	
f. kpu 1,2,3	!*	*	*		
g. wu 2,3			*	!*	

Secondarily articulated outputs will be disfavoured by the highly-ranked *COM-PLEXSEGMENT. The next ranked constraint, MAX[U]–V (2), favours maintenance of the secondary vocalic [U]-feature in the Output. Note that having [U] present as a consonantal feature, as in candidate d, will not help

The introduction of correspondence theory as an improvement to Optimality Theory has introduced a certain lack of precision as regards the nature of the correspondence that is required between segments. I assume that correspondence cannot exist between segments which do not have any features in common. It is clear however that absolute identity is also not required. In some sense we want to be able to say that [p] corresponds to /kʷ/. However, it still seems necessary to have a constraint which penalizes *any* deviation from the underlying form. The constraint IDENT(SEG)[30] does precisely this.

The following constraint, MAX-IO, does not look at the detail of the features—all that counts is whether the elements of the input correspond with those in the output, ignoring splits, mergers, and switches of position. In order to qualify as a realistic output, segments which are assumed to be merged in the ouput must be *justified* in some sense.

The OCP constraint, SHAREPLACE-[I], is not relevant in the above evaluation.

/kʷi/ in Aeolic Greek dialects

(71) /$k_1^w{}_2i_3$/	*COMPSEG	MAX[U]-V(2)	IDENT (SEG)	MAX-IO	SHAREPLACE-[I]
a. kʷi 1,2,3	!*				*
b. ki 1,3		*	*	!*	*
☞ c. pi 12,3		*	*		*
d. ti 13,3		*	*	!*	
e. ti 4,3		*	*	*!*	*
f. ti 3		*	*	*!*	*

The basic difference between the two tableaus is that there is no candidate [k_1i_{23}] available. There is no way that [i] can realistically correspond to the secondary vocalic segment [ʷ]. I assume that such candidates will not in fact be produced by GEN.

7.4.6.3 The Ionic and Doric developments

The developments preceding [u, o, a, C] are the same—the difference appears with the vowels [i, e]. What I assume has happened here is the re-ordering of SHAREPLACE-[I] above MAX-IO. Note that it cannot be assumed that the Ionic and Doric dialects went through a stage at which they were identical to

---

[30] Note that a constraint on the identity of features (IDENT(F)) no longer guarantees the identity of segments in a model in which the same feature may appear in more than one place.

Aeolic. In other words we can be sure that the development was not /kʷi/ > /pi/ > [ti]. If this had been the case, inherited /pi/ would have appeared as [ti] too, which does not of course happen.

/kʷi/ in Ionic/Doric Greek dialects

(72) /k₁ʷ₂i₃/		*CompSeg	Max[U]-V(2)	Ident(Seg)	SharePlace-[I]	Max-IO
	a. kʷi 1,2,3	!*				
	b. ki 1,3		*	*	!*	*
	c. pi 12,3		*	*	!*	
☞	d. ti 13,3		*	*		*
	e. ti 4,3		*	*	!*	**
	f. ti 3		*	*		*!*

How does this tableau differ from any other sequence of a voiceless stop and /i/? Compare the corresponding tableau for /pi/.

/pi/ in Ionic/Doric Greek dialects

(73) /p₁i₂/		*CompSeg	Max[U]-V(2)	Ident(Seg)	SharePlace-[I]	Max-IO
	a. ki 3,2			!*	*	*
☞	b. pi 1,2				*	
	c. ti 4,2			!*	*	*
	d. ti 2			!*		*

In this case IDENT(SEG) penalizes any deviation from the underlying /pi/. Candidate d.[ti] may be preferred in terms of the OCP constraint SHAREPLACE-[I], but this latter constraint is lower-ranked.

In (72) the difference is that the input form /kʷi/ violates the high-ranked constraint *COMPSEG. Therefore it cannot surface as the optimal form. Because the underlying form is thus blocked, SHAREPLACE-[I] makes the choice among the various non-complex possibilities.

There is obviously more to be said on the question of the developments of the Indo-European labio-velars in ancient Greek. I think however that OT, combined with the DP approach to segments, offers some interesting new perspectives on the topic.

7.5 Conclusion

This chapter has attempted to provide a summary account of how a DP-type approach to segmental structure can be used within an Optimality Theory framework.

Obviously, given the limitations of space involved, I have been able to do no more than scratch the surface of the possibilities offered by the DP approach to segmental structure. Not to mention the numerous problems it undoubtedly raises. I am however convinced of the benefits of a reductionist approach to Place and Manner features, and hope to have demonstrated some idea of the potential of this.

A frequently-heard criticism of much work in DP is that while demonstrating the possibilities of new approaches to segmental structure, it does not get much further than dealing with static inventories. This chapter suffers to some extent from the same problems but has been able to examine at least a few actual phonological phenomena as well.

7.6 References

Anderson, J. M. and C. J. Ewen (1987). *Principles of Dependency Phonology*. Cambridge, Cambridge University Press.

—— and C. Jones (1972). 'Three these concerning phonological representations'. *Edinburgh University Working Papers in Linguistics* 1, 72–104.

Aoki, H. (1970). *Nez Perce Grammar*. Berkeley, University of California Press.

Archangeli, D. and D. Pulleyblank (1994). *Grounded Phonology*. Cambridge, MA, MIT Press.

Bolognesi, R. (1998). *The Phonology of Campidanian Sardinian*. The Hague, Holland Academic Graphics.

Cahill, M. (1995). 'Nasal assimilation and labiovelar geometry'. Paper presented at ACAL 26.

—— and F. Parkinson (1997). 'Partial class behavior and feature geometry: remarks on Feature Class Theory'. *Proceedings of the North East Linguistics Society* 27. Amherst, MA, GLSA, Department of Linguistics, U.Mass.

Carrell, P. L. (1970). *A Transformational Grammar of Igbo*. Cambridge, Cambridge University Press.

Chomsky, N. (1957). *Syntactic Structures*. The Hague, Mouton.

—— (1965). *Aspects of the Theory of Syntax*. Cambridge, MA, MIT Press.

—— and M. Halle (1968). *The Sound Pattern of English*. New York, Harper & Row.

Clements, G. N. (1985). 'The geometry of phonological features'. *Phonology Yearbook* 2, 225–52.

Collins, B. and I. Mees (1981). *The Sounds of English and Dutch*. The Hague, Leiden University Press.

Cook, T. L. (1985). 'An integrated phonology of Efik'. DLitt dissertation, University of Amsterdam.

Durand, J. and F. Katamba (eds), *Frontiers in Phonology: Atoms, Structures, Derivations*. London, Longman.

Firchow, I. and J. Firchow (1969). 'An abbreviated phoneme inventory'. *Anthropological Linguistics* 11, 271–6.

Halle, M. (1995). 'Feature geometry and feature spreading'. *Linguistic Inquiry* 26, 1–46.

Harris, J. and G. Lindsey (1995). 'The elements of phonological representation'. In Durand and Katamba (eds), 34–79.

van der Hulst, H. (1988a). 'The geometry of vocalic features'. In H. van der Hulst and N. S. H. Smith (eds), *Features, Segmental Structure and Harmony Processes* (Part II). Dordrecht, Foris, 77–125.

—— (1988b). 'The dual interpretation of |i|, |u| and |a|'. NELS 18, 208–22.

—— (1994). 'Radical CV phonology'. In S. Shore and N. Vilkuna (eds), *SKY 1994: Yearbook of the Linguistics Association of Finland*. Helsinki, 23–56.

—— (1995). 'Radical CV phonology: the categorial gesture'. In Durand and Katamba (eds), 80–116.

—— and N. S. H. Smith (1989). 'The structure of (complex) consonants'. Paper presented at the MIT conference on Feature and Underspecification Theories (7–9 October 1989).

—— —— (1990). 'Components for vowels and consonants'. Ms, Universities of Leiden and Amsterdam.

Humbert, H. (1995). *Phonological segments*. The Hague, Holland Academic Graphics.

Hyman, L. (1973). 'The feature [grave] in phonological theory'. *Journal of Phonetics* 1, 329–37.

Jakobson, R., C. G. M. Fant, and M. Halle (1952). 'Preliminaries to speech analysis: The distinctive features and their correlates'. Cambridge, MA, MIT Acoustics Laboratories Technical Report, no. 13.

—— —— —— (1965). *Preliminaries to Speech Analysis: The Distinctive Features and Their Correlates*. Cambridge, MA, MIT Press.

Kaye, J., J. Lowenstanmm, and J. R. Vergnaud (1985). 'The internal structure of phonological elements: A theory of charm and government'. *Phonology Yearbook* 2, 305–28.

Kuipers, A. H. (1960). *Phoneme and Morpheme in Kabardian*. The Hague, Mouton.

LaCharité, D. (1993). *The Internal Structure of Affricates*. PhD dissertation, University of Ottawa.

Ladefoged, P. (1968). *A Phonetic Study of West African Languages*. Cambridge, Cambridge University Press.

Levin, J. (1984). 'Conditions on syllable structure and categories in Klamath phonology'. *WCCFL* 3.

—— (1988). 'A place for lateral in the feature geometry'. Ms, University of Texas at Austin.

Maddieson, I. (1984). *Patterns of Sounds*. Cambridge, Cambridge University Press.

McCarthy, J. and A. Prince (1994). 'The Emergence of the Unmarked'. In M. Gonzàlez (ed.), *NELS 24: Proceedings of [the 1993 meeting of] the Northeastern Linguistic Society*, vol. 2. Amherst, MA, GLSA, 333–79.

Mous, M. (1992). *A Grammar of Iraqw*. PhD dissertation, University of Leiden.

Padgett, J. (1991). *Stricture in Feature Geometry*. PhD dissertation, U.Mass at Amherst.

—— (1995). 'Feature classes'. In J. N. Beckman, L. Walsh Dickey, and S. Urbanczyk (eds), *Papers in Optimality Theory* (= University of Massachusetts Occasional Papers 18). Amherst, MA, GLSA, U.Mass, 385–420.

—— (1997). 'On the characterization of feature classes in phonology'. Ms, University of California at Santa Cruz.

Pulleyblank, D. (1995). 'Feature geometry and underspecification'. In Durand and Katamba (eds), 3-33.

—— (1997). 'Optimality Theory and Features'. In D. Archangeli and D. T. Langendoen (eds), *Optimality Theory: An Overview*. Oxford, Blackwell Publishers, 59–101.

Pulleyblank, D., J.-K. Ping, M. Leitch, and O. Ola (1995). 'Typological variation through constraint rankings: Low vowels in tongue root harmony'. In *Proceedings of the Arizona Phonology Conference: Workshop on Features in Optimality Theory*. Tucson, University of Arizona.

Rassadin, V. I. (1978). *Morfologija tofalarskogo jazyka v sravnitel' nom osveščenii*. Moscow.

Rennison, J. (1986). 'On tridirectional feature systems for vowels'. In J. Durand (ed.), *Dependency and Non-Linear Phonology*. London, Croom Helm, 281–303.

van Riemsdijk, H. C. and N. S. H. Smith (1973). 'Zur Instabilität komplexer Segmente'. In A. P. ten Cate and P. Jordens (eds), *Linguistische Perspektiven: Referate des VII Linguistischen Kolloquiums* (= *Linguistische Arbeiten* 5). Tübingen, Niemeyer, 293–304.

Sagey, E. (1986). *The Representation of Features and Relations in Nonlinear Phonology*. PhD dissertation, MIT.

Saltarelli, M. (1988). *Basque*. London, Croom Helm.

Schane, S. (1984). 'The fundamentals of particle phonology'. *Phonology Yearbook* 1, 129–55.

Schiffman, H. F. (1975). 'On the ternary contrast in Dravidian coronal stops'. In H. F. Schiffman and C. M. Eastman (eds), *Dravidian Phonological Systems*. Seattle, Institute for Comparative and Foreign Area Studies, University of Washington.

Shaw, P. A. (1991). 'Consonant harmony systems: The special status of coronal harmony'. In C. Paradis and J.-F. Prunet (eds), *Phonetics and Phonology: The Special Status of Coronals*. San Diego, Academic Press, 125–57.

Sivertsen, E. (1960). *Cockney Phonology*. Oslo, Oslo University Press.

Smith, N. S. H. (1988). 'Consonant place features'. In H. van der Hulst and N. S. H. Smith (eds), *Features, Segmental Structure and Harmony Processes* (Part I). Dordrecht, Foris, 209–35.

—— (1997). 'Shrinking and hopping vowels in Northern Cape York: Minimally different systems'. In F. Hinskens, R. van Hout and L. Wetzels (eds), *Variation, Change and Phonological Theory*. Amsterdam and Philadelphia, John Benjamins, 267–302.

—— (1999). 'A preliminary account of some aspects of Leurbost Gaelic syllable structure'. In H. van der Hulst and N. Ritter (eds), *The Syllable: Views and Ideas*. Berlin: Mouton-de Gruyter, 577–630.

—— M. Beers, R. Bod, R. Bolognesi, H. Humbert and F. van der Leeuw (1991). 'Lenition in a Sardinian dialect'. In P. M. Bertinetto, M. Kenstowicz and M. Loporcaro (eds), *Certamen Phonologicum II*. Turin, Rosenberg and Sellier, 309–28.

Stevens, K. N., S. J. Keyser and H. Kawasaki (1986). 'Toward a phonetic and phonological investigation of redundant features'. In J. Perkell and D. H. Klatt (eds), *Symposium on Invariance and Variability of Speech Processes*. Hillsdale, NJ, Erlbaum.

Svantesson, J.-O. (1985). 'Vowel harmony shift in Mongolian'. *Lingua* 67, 283–327.

Welmers, W. E., (1973). *African Language Structures*. Berkeley, University of California Press.

PART THREE
Syntax

8

Absolute Ungrammaticality[1]

Peter Ackema and Ad Neeleman

8.1 Introduction

Given the principles of optimality theory, there should be a grammatical output for every input. After all, of the possible outputs corresponding to a particular input, the one that is the most harmonic with respect to a set of ranked universal constraints is grammatical by definition. Nonetheless, it appears to be a rather obvious fact that certain constructions have no realization at all in some, or even all, languages. How is this possible, then?

Given the structure of the grammar in optimality theory, several types of solutions have been proposed for this problem. An Optimality-theoretic grammar consists of two components: a device GEN that generates all possible structural realizations of a particular input and a function EVAL that selects out of this candidate set the structure that is optimal. One possibility therefore is to argue that there are restrictions on GEN such that certain constructions never enter into competition.[2] It is also possible that two candidates score equally on all constraints but one. In that case, the candidate that wins out on this particular constraint will block the other candidate under any constraint ranking. In the terminology of Prince and Smolensky 1993, this is expressed by saying that the latter is harmonically bound by the former. A third possibility is that certain constructions cannot be realized because the lexicon of the language in question lacks the crucial morphemes. Finally, it is possible that under some constraint rankings the optimal candidate is the so-called null parse, that is, a candidate that does not realize any of the information contained in the input (cf. Prince and Smolensky 1993). This means that in the relevant language there is in fact an instantiation of the apparently ungrammatical construction, but one which is silent. These solutions to absolute ungrammaticality have been developed to

[1] For various reasons, we would like to thank Damir Cavar, Cathal Doherty, René Kager, Henk van Riemsdijk, Maaike Schoorlemmer, Sten Vikner, Frank Wijnen, two anonymous reviewers and the editors of this volume.

[2] One may think of universal conditions on well-formed structure (X-bar theory, Subjacency, etc.) and universal conditions on interpretability like the θ-Criterion and the ban on vacuous quantification.

some extent in the phonological literature, but in general the problem still requires considerable attention.[3]

In this paper, we will discuss some cases of absolute ungrammaticality in syntax. The above-mentioned solutions are all valid, but they apply to different instantiations of the general problem of absolute ungrammaticality. The first two (restrictions on GEN and candidates being harmonically bound) apply to different cases of universal ungrammaticality. We will not go into restrictions imposed by GEN here; a case of harmonic boundedness is discussed in Section 8.6. Our main focus will be on constructions that are not universally impossible, but are absent in some languages while present in others. As we will argue in Sections 3–5, a number of such cases must be explained by means of the null parse.

A solution of language-specific ineffability that makes use of underparsing in syntax was first proposed by Legendre *et al.* (1998). Their approach differs from the one we will propose below in that Legendre *et al.* do not employ the null parse, but rather allow partially underparsed structures to enter into competition. We will briefly discuss the differences between these approaches in Section 8.7.

8.2 The Null Parse and Parse Constraints

Obviously, the question of which structures enter into competition with one another, that is, the exact definition of the candidate set, is very important in optimality-theoretic calculations. In syntax, the issue is complicated by the fact that the targeted semantic representation seems to be relevant for this definition. There seems to be something of a consensus in the literature to the effect that only candidates projected from the same set of lexical heads (the numeration) and targeting the same semantic representation should compete with each other. This is not only argued for in optimality-theoretic literature (see, for instance, Grimshaw 1997, Samek-Lodovici 1996 and Ackema and Neeleman 1998a), but also in literature from other frameworks in which competition between structures plays a crucial role (see, for instance, Golan 1993; Reinhart 1995 and Fox 1995). More specifically, following Grimshaw, we assume that what competing candidates must have in common is:

(1)   a. a lexical head and its argument structure
      b. an assignment of lexical heads to its arguments
      c. equivalent semantics, including specifications of features such as *Wh*, tense, etc.

The consequence of this definition is that candidates do not need to consist of exactly the same words in order to compete. They may differ in function words

[3] For discussion in phonology see Prince and Smolensky 1993, McCarthy and Prince 1993 and, for some problems, Orgun and Sprouse 1996.

(and hence functional structure), as long as the same semantic representation is obtained.[4]

If semantic equivalence is part of the definition of candidate set, it must be established when two candidates can be said to be semantically equivalent. Consider, in this respect, the notion of underparsing. If a structure is projected, GEN may, in some candidates, not realize part of the numeration. In many cases, however, this gives rise to a candidate whose semantics are different from those candidates in which the entire numeration is realized. Given a numeration like (2a), it will be clear that realizing or not realizing *Mary* affects the interpretation considerably. Hence, (2b) and (2c) are not in the same candidate set and neither can rule out the other.

(2)   a.   {I, see, Mary}
      b.   I see Mary
      c.   I see

The condition of semantic equivalence thus has the consequence that within one candidate set, underparsing of contentful elements is blocked.

There is one exception to this, however. If nothing of the numeration is realized, a candidate is obtained that has no syntactic structure at all. This candidate, the so-called null parse, consequently is not fed into the interpretational component (or, if it is, it does not receive any interpretation). It is an open issue which implications the condition of interpretational equivalence has for candidates that do not have an interpretation in the first place. We interpret the condition such that it removes from the candidate set those candidates that have a interpretation which deviates from that of the other candidates. Since the null parse does not have an interpretation it cannot have a deviating interpretation either. It is therefore never affected by the condition of semantic equivalence. Hence, every candidate set contains the null parse.

The null parse hardly violates any constraints. Since most constraints define structural wellformedness, a candidate without structure vacuously satisfies them. This raises the question why the null parse is not always optimal.

The answer, of course, is that there are constraints which require the realization of certain elements of the numeration. These belong to a family of constraints, usually referred to as Parse (Prince and Smolensky 1993). Whereas it is successful on the other constraints, the null parse violates the Parse constraint.

---

[4] Since using different lexical words will usually result in different semantics, one may wonder if it is not possible to abandon the requirement of identical numerations altogether (see Broekhuis and Dekkers, this volume). We will not discuss this issue here, but some potential problems should be noted. For example, idioms (*kick the bucket*) would compete with semantically equivalent non-idiomatic expressions (*die*). So would syntactic and morphological realizations of the same argument structure (*driver of trucks* versus *truck driver*). Since such expressions coexist, while they differ almost certainly in their evaluation (given their completely different structures), some notion of numeration seems necessary.

As remarked, Parse is not a monolithic constraint. Rather, there are various constraints that 'protect' specific elements in the numeration. As we will illustrate below, instantiations of the general constraint include Parse-Passive and PARSE-*Wh*. However, it is unlikely that a constraint like Parse-*John* exists. In other words, not every imaginable instantiation of the Parse constraint occurs. We propose that Parse may only refer to specific morphological features of elements in the numeration and not to their lexical semantic content, for instance.

Note that this does not mean that elements like *John* can be left unparsed without repercussions. As we have just argued, omission of such content words alters the semantics of the candidate and hence puts it outside the relevant candidate set. In fact, one cannot possibly express the semantics of an element like *John* without parsing it.

Let us now return to the main issue of this paper: absolute ungrammaticality. The null parse's membership in every candidate set is relevant for this issue, because the low ranking of the parse constraint(s) can lead to the absence of certain structures in a language. As Prince and Smolensky (1993: 176) remark, '[. . .] it is clear that assigning null structure to an input is one means a grammar may use to prevent certain structures from appearing in the output. The null parse is a possible candidate which must always be considered and which may well be optimal for certain particularly problematic inputs.'

The general form of the argument is as follows. Consider the interaction of PARSE-F (where F is some morphological feature) with some CONSTRAINT X, and suppose there are only two candidates: the null parse and a candidate C that parses F but violates CONSTRAINT X. Under such conditions, the ranking of PARSE-F with respect to CONSTRAINT X determines whether candidate C or the null parse will be selected as optimal. Low ranking of PARSE-F has the consequence that a language will lack C:

(3) Input with feature F	CONSTRAINT X	PARSE-F
Candidate C	*!	
☞ 0		*

In this way, language-specific ineffability can be explained. We will illustrate this with some concrete cases in the next sections. (A morphophonological application of this idea is discussed by Kager, this volume).

8.3 Multiple *Wh*-Questions

In many languages, questions can be formed that contain more than one *Wh*-word, as in the English example in (4).

(4)   Who saw what?

There is cross-linguistic variation in the distribution of the *Wh*-words and the verb in such multiple questions (for discussion see Ackema and Neeleman 1998a). What we are concerned with here is how languages can be dealt with in which no pattern at all exists for multiple questions. Irish is of this type, as shown by McCloskey (1979: 56, 71). It allows simple questions like (5a), but multiple questions like (5b–b') are ungrammatical.

(5)   a.   Cén   rothar aL   ghoud an garda?
           Which bicycle COMP *stole   the policeman*

      b. *Cé   aL   rinne caidé?
           Who COMP *did   what*

      b'. *Cé   caidé aL   rinne?
           Who what COMP *did*

Given the argument of Section 8.2, if the ungrammaticality of (5b–b') is to be ascribed to the null parse being the optimal output for a multiple question in Irish, there must be a constraint that is violated in multiple questions and that interacts with a member of the family of Parse constraints. The Parse constraint that is relevant in questions is PARSE-*Wh* (*Wh* being a feature that is morphologically identifiable). The other constraint that is relevant is Grimshaw's (1997) constraint that requires operators to appear in a specifier position (OP-SPEC). Simplifying things considerably, let us assume that *Wh*-operators can only satisfy this constraint if they appear in a suitable, i.e. [+*Wh*], specifier position. Furthermore, let us adopt the standard assumption that sentences contain only one specifier position that can be [+*Wh*], namely spec-CP.

Consider now sentences containing more than one *Wh*-operator. OP-SPEC requires all these operators to be in spec-CP. However, due to limitations on specifiers, in practice only one *Wh* can be moved there.[5] This means that in a multiple question OP-SPEC is always violated, except by the null parse (which does not contain any *Wh*-operator). If PARSE-*Wh* is outranked by OP-SPEC, the null parse will therefore be optimal. This explains the absence of multiple questions in a language like Irish:

(6) Irish multiple questions	OP-SPEC	PARSE-*Wh*
[CP *Wh* C [VP . . . *Wh*]]	*!	
☞ 0		*

In a simple question, OP-SPEC is satisfied by *Wh*-movement to spec-CP. The

---

[5] This is not contradicted by those languages in which all *Wh*s are fronted, since even in those cases that the *Wh*s form a cluster in spec-CP, only one *Wh* will be the actual specifier of CP, with the others adjoined to it (cf. Rudin 1988). It is plausible that elements adjoined to a specifier do not satisfy OP-SPEC, since they do not occupy a specifier, but rather an adjunct position.

resulting candidate therefore is to be preferred over the null parse, since it does not violate PARSE-*Wh*. Hence, Irish does have simple questions:

(7) Irish simple questions	OP-SPEC	PARSE-*Wh*
☞ [_CP_ *Wh* C [_VP_ . . .]]		
0		*!

If PARSE-*Wh* outranks OP-SPEC, the English pattern results, with both simple and multiple *Wh*-questions.

Recall that partial underparsing usually expels the resulting candidate from the relevant candidate set. This is the case here as well. A candidate in which only one *Wh*-operator is realized of a numeration containing more than one such operator cannot receive an interpretation as a multiple question. It therefore falls outside the relevant candidate set.

Obviously, the above analysis is a simplification, since OP-SPEC alone cannot explain the various patterns of question formation in those languages that do have multiple questions. We refer to Ackema and Neeleman (1998a) for discussion of this issue.

If we consider the line of argumentation developed in this section, a general issue arises concerning the interaction of parse constraints with other parse constraints. Suppose that a constraint Parse-X dominates OP-SPEC in a language like Irish (where OP-SPEC dominates PARSE-*Wh*). Then, a multiple question would be parsed after all if, apart from the *Wh*-features, the input also contains the feature X. Thus, we predict that certain features will not be realized, unless they happen to cooccur with certain other features. Some of the interactions thus predicted seem to be improbable, however, a complication to which we will return in Section 8.8.

8.4 Passive

In the previous section we discussed a case where a Parse constraint interacts with one other constraint. In this section we will turn to a slightly more complicated situation, namely one in which a Parse constraint crucially interacts with two other constraints. We will show that, as a result, the construction under discussion need not be either absent or present in a language. It may, in some languages, surface only if the input meets certain conditions (namely if the verb is transitive). The construction under discussion is the passive.[6]

A fundamental property of passives is that the external θ-role of the verb is no longer available for the subject position and that, as a consequence of this, the subject position is nonthematic. Let us consider which syntactic constraints are relevant for such an input.

---

[6] This section is based on Ackema and Neeleman (1998b).

Ackema and Neeleman: *Absolute Ungrammaticality*   285

The first is the Epp. This constraint says that inherently predicative categories like VP must have a subject. The notion of subject can be defined in terms of local A-binding (cf. Williams 1994). Hence, the Epp is satisfied if a co-indexed referential category c-commands VP.

(8)   Epp
      VP must be A-bound

Following Marantz (1992) and others, we assume that this condition is the trigger for A-movement if no category is base-generated in subject position.[7]

Next to A-movement, expletive insertion is often argued to save a structure from violating the Epp. If the expletive has an associate, this is correct: the expletive inherits the referential index of its associate and can hence bind VP. If there is no associate, however, the expletive has no referential index and thus is not a potential binder. This means, crucially, that impersonal passives as in (9) violate the Epp.

(9)   a. Er   wordt gedanst (Dutch)
          there is   danced

      b. Es wurde getanzt (German)
          It was   danced

In fact, it has been argued before that impersonal passives are subjectless sentences. Siewierska (1984) points out that in most languages with impersonal passives no expletive is inserted.[8] In those languages which do have an expletive in impersonal passives, this element is inserted for other reasons than to satisfy the Epp. This is straightforwardly shown by the fact that in German the expletive appears only to satisfy the V2 constraint. It occurs exclusively in first position in main clauses. Whenever some element is topicalized or when the V2 constraint does not play a role (namely in embedded clauses), insertion is prohibited.[9]

---

[7] Strictly speaking, the formulation of the Epp in (8) cannot be correct, since in some constructions an underlying object can be promoted to subject without A-movement (although A-movement is always a possibility). Examples are nominative-dative inversion in the Germanic OV-languages (cf. Den Besten 1985, Weerman 1989) and the possibility that the argument of an unaccusative verb remains in situ in pro-drop languages like Italian (cf. Rizzi 1982, Belletti 1988). It would take us too far afield to discuss this issue here, but it must have one of two implications. Either constructions in which A-movement is optional must invoke violations of Stay in any case, or Stay only excludes promotion of the object to subject in languages where movement is required for this—that is, VO-languages without Italian-style pro drop.

[8] We assume that empty expletives do not exist; see Weerman (1989), Samek-Lodovici (1996) and Picallo (1996).

[9] The distribution of expletives in Dutch impersonal passives is largely identical to that in German. Again, expletive insertion is only obligatory when the V2 constraint must be satisfied through it. The difference with German is that the expletive appears optionally in embedded clauses and in clauses with topicalization. See Bennis (1986) for analysis.

So, the E pp plays a role in passive formation in that it requires NP raising. Given that movement can hence be involved in passives, another very general constraint comes into play, namely the constraint Stay, which forbids movement (cf. Grimshaw 1997).

(10)   Stay
    Do not move

Here, we will follow Grimshaw in interpreting this constraint such that it is violated whenever a trace occurs in the structure. The result is that, in case of simple object-to-subject raising, it is violated once.[10]

Finally, in the explanation of why passives can be absolutely ungrammatical in some languages, a Parse constraint must be involved. As noted in Section 8.2, members of the Parse family in syntax must mention some morphologically identifiable feature. In the case at hand, the constraint has the following instantiation:

(11)   Parse-Passive
    Parse passive morphology

Passive morphology is relevant for the interpretation of a sentence, since the verb's external θ-role is assigned to it (cf. Jaeggli 1986, Baker *et al.* 1989). The result is that, although the syntactic subject position is nonthematic in passive, the verb's external θ-role is still syntactically 'active'; it can, for instance, act as controller of an embedded PRO subject. This means that if the passive morphology is not parsed, a construction will result that has an interpretation that deviates from the semantics of a passive. Hence, it is removed from the candidate set. The only candidate that violates (11) and is in the relevant candidate set is the null parse, which belongs to every candidate set.

Let us now consider how these constraints explain the absence of (certain) passives in some languages. As noted by Siewierska (1984: 23), 'there is no doubt that the passive is not a language universal.' There are many languages in which it is not attested at all, either with transitive or with intransitive verbs. Examples mentioned by Siewierska are Tongan, Samoan and Hungarian.[11]

It should be clear after the last section how the complete absence of passives

---

[10] In other work we have interpreted Stay as requiring movement chains to have a minimal length, so the longer the movement, the more violations of Stay (see Ackema and Neeleman 1998a, b). This explains locality effects with both A- and A′-movement. It would have no consequences if we were to interpret Stay in this way as well in the present paper, but for reasons of exposition we leave out the extra violations of Stay this would incur.

[11] This is not to say that in some of these languages there are no constructions in which the verb's external θ-role is suppressed. However, if this θ-role is not assigned to passive morphology, but rather not present in syntax at all (due to some presyntactic procedure), the relevant construction does not qualify as a member of the candidate set for passives. There also are languages in which the absence of passive is only apparent, because passive morphology may not have an overt reflex. Such languages have constructions with all characteristics of passives (for instance, an agentive *by*-phrase is possible), but without an overt morphological marker. Examples may be Acehnese and Mandarin Chinese; see Spencer (1991: 243–4) and references cited there.

in these languages should be accounted for: the null parse must be the optimal output for any passive input. Note that the null parse vacuously satisfies both the Epp and Stay. It does not contain a VP, which would need a subject, nor does it involve movement. Hence, if Parse-Passive is outranked by these two constraints, the null parse blocks any candidate that violates one of these, and any parsed passive does exactly that.

First, consider what happens if the input contains a passivized intransitive and the Epp outranks Parse-Passive. With an intransitive there are only two relevant candidates: an impersonal passive and the null parse. The impersonal passive violates the Epp (since it is a subjectless structure), but not Parse-Passive. The null parse violates Parse-Passive, but not the Epp. Therefore, if satisfying the Epp is more important than satisfying Parse-Passive, the null parse wins:

(12) passive intransitive	Epp	Parse-Passive
___ V-pass	*!	
☞ 0		*

In the case of a transitive, three candidates must be considered: the null parse, an impersonal passive and a personal passive derived by promotion of the object. If, in addition to the Epp, Stay also dominates Parse-Passive, the language in question will also lack passives of transitives. The impersonal passive is suboptimal because it fatally violates the Epp. The personal passive fatally violates Stay since there is movement of an argument to subject position. This leaves the null parse as the optimal candidate. In (13) this is illustrated for one of the two rankings with the relevant characteristic.

(13) passive transitive	Stay	Epp	Parse-Passive
DP$_i$ V-pass t$_i$	*!		
___ V-pass DP		*!	
☞ 0			*

In case Parse-Passive outranks both the Epp and Stay, the language obviously has passives of both transitives and intransitives. The mutual ranking between Stay and the Epp then determines whether a personal or an impersonal passive is derived from a transitive (see Ackema and Neeleman 1998b for further discussion).

An interesting situation arises when Parse-Passive is situated between the other two constraints. The ranking Stay >> Parse-Passive >> Epp has the same effects as the ranking Parse-Passive >> Stay >> Epp: it constitutes a grammar that produces impersonal passives of both transitives and intransitives. But the ranking Epp >> Parse-Passive >> Stay has an effect we have not encountered thus far: it constitutes a grammar in which passives are derived from some inputs but not from others.

As we have seen in (12), the null parse is optimal for a passivized intransitive if the EPP outranks PARSE-Passive. However, given the ranking just mentioned, in which PARSE-Passive dominates STAY, a passive *is* derived from a transitive input. In that case, both the EPP and PARSE-Passive can be satisfied at the cost of violating STAY. The result is a personal passive:

(14) passive transitive	EPP	PARSE-Passive	STAY
☞ DP$_i$ V-PASS t$_i$			*
__ V-PASS DP	*!		
o		*!	

Of course, this type of language exists. English has personal passives of transitives, but no (impersonal) passives of intransitives:

(15)   a. The house was painted yesterday
      b. *There was danced yesterday

The fatal character of EPP violations in English contrasts with the existence of impersonal passives in other languages, as in (9). This situation illustrates that the EPP (and other principles) must be parametrized in theories that do not allow for constraint violation. The consequence is that all sentences of a language must have a subject, or none need to have one. This is unattractive, however, since the EPP does seem to be valid in other constructions in the relevant languages. In particular, it accounts for the fact that, if an underlying object is present in a passive, it must be promoted to subject. German, for example, does not have impersonal passives of transitives:

(16)   a. *Gestern   ist [$_{VP}$ uns geschlagen worden]
        yesterday is   us   hit   been

      b. Gestern   sind wir$_i$ [$_{VP}$ t$_i$ geschlagen worden]
        yesterday are   we   hit   been

This is exactly the type of situation expected in optimality theory. The EPP, like other constraints, is universal. It is present in every grammar, including that of German. However, its effects can only be observed if higher ranked constraints allow this. So, a constraint can have its effects in some constructions while being overruled in others.

    To conclude this section, a brief remark on optionality. As a reviewer points out, there are languages in which more than one of the patterns of passive formation discussed above occurs. Spencer (1991: 240), for instance, observes that in Ukrainian both a personal and an impersonal passive can be derived from a transitive verb. As the reviewer suggests, this may follow from equal ranking of STAY and EPP (provided that PARSE-Passive is ranked highest). Under one interpretation of equal ranking, both the candidate that is optimal given the ranking PARSE-Pass >> STAY >> EPP and the candidate that is optimal given the ranking PARSE-Pass >> EPP>> STAY are grammatical. For a discussion of potential problems with equal ranking, see Tesar and Smolensky 1998.

8.5 Imperfect Periphrastic Passives

As we have illustrated in the previous section, optimality theory allows certain peculiarities of the lexicon of a language to be derived from its grammar (see also Prince and Smolensky 1993 and Grimshaw 1997). The fact that certain languages lack passive morphology is not a consequence of an accidental gap in their lexicon. Instead, this gap follows from how the constraints are ranked. Under certain rankings a morpheme, even if it were part of the lexicon of the language, will never be realized. Therefore, it will not be part of the actual lexicon of the language, although, for the sake of the discussion, we may assume that it is part of its 'virtual' lexicon.

In this section we will show that a similar line of argumentation can be applied to languages that lack the auxiliaries needed to form nonperfect passives and nonpassive perfects. The consequence is that such languages only have perfect periphrastic passives.

A language of this type is Russian. Apart from the synthetic *sja*-passive, Russian has a periphrastic passive construction with a past participle. This construction is necessarily perfect, as shown by Kiparsky (1963), Schoorlemmer (1995) and others.[12]

(17) a. *Naš dom byl stroen   izvestnym arxitektorom
         our house was built (by) famous   architect

      b. *Kryša byla kryta   otcom
         roof   was covered (by) father

(18) a. Naš dom byl po-stroen
         our house was PF-built

      b. Zdanie bylo s-neseno
         building was PF-pulled-down

Similar data can be found in Irish and Hindi. So, what is missing in these languages are correlates of the Dutch examples in (19a–b); only the correlate of (19c) exists.

---

[12] In this section, we use 'perfect' to refer to perfect tense rather than to perfective aspect. Thus, we follow Schoorlemmer's (1995: 274) conclusion that 'Russian participial passives act like a form of perfect tense, which lacks an active counterpart'. Note, however, that in Russian there is a correlation between perfect tense and perfective aspect in that perfect tense is limited to sentences with an aspectually perfective verb (Schoorlemmer 1995, ch. 4). Hence, Russian participial passives are also necessarily perfective in the aspectual sense. Schoorlemmer (1995: 280–2) notes that some authors allow a few lexically restricted exceptions to this pattern. According to Schoorlemmer, these examples are a result of formal instruction and do not belong to the core grammar.

(19) a. Het huis   werd gebouwd door Rem Koolhaas (nonperfect passive)
          the house was   built   by   Rem Koolhaas

      b. Rem Koolhaas heeft het huis   gebouwd (perfect nonpassive)
          Rem Koolhaas has   the house built
          'Rem Koolhaas has built the house'

      c. Het huis   is gebouwd door Rem Koolhaas (perfect passive)
          the house is built   by   Rem Koolhaas
          'the house has been built by Rem Koolhaas'

It might be argued that the absence of nonperfect passives and nonpassive perfects is caused by the absence of two auxiliaries that are used in other languages
to form the relevant constructions. The problem with this line of argumentation
lies in the fact that two accidental gaps in the lexicon must be assumed. However, to the best of our knowledge, there are no languages that lack periphrastic
nonperfect passives but have periphrastic nonpassive perfects, or vice versa. Languages either lack both (and only have a periphrastic perfect passive) or have
both (next to the periphrastic perfect passive).

This can be explained under the following assumptions. For a start, there is
only one verbal past participle, which is both perfect and passive in nature. This
is an assumption that can be motivated independently, as we will now explain.
The forms of the perfect and the passive participle are one and the same in
languages using a periphrastic construction for both perfect and passive. In
languages that do not use participial constructions, perfect and passive morphology are usually distinct. This fact makes it implausible that the almost
exceptionless morphological covarience of passive and perfect participles is coincidental. Therefore, various recent syntactic analyses of periphrastic perfects are
based on the idea that the participle used in this construction is identical in all
respects to the passive participle (see Haider 1984, Hoekstra 1986, Kayne 1993
and Ackema 1999).

The assumption that the verbal past participle is both perfect and passive in
nature is supported by the observation that in a language like Dutch, where
passive and perfect do not necessarily coincide (see 19), participial constructions
lacking an auxiliary must be interpreted as having both properties mentioned.
Examples include prenominally and absolutively used participles:[13]

---

[13] Constructions with a prenominal participle of an unaccusative (like *de gestorven man* 'the died
man') seem to be counter-examples to the claim that such constructions are (perfect) passives. However, the crucial property of passives for the analysis in this section is the absence of an external
θ-role, indicated below by the feature $[-\theta_{ext}]$. Unaccusative verbs already have this property of their
own. (Below we will provide an explanation for why next to *de gestorven man* 'the died man' it is
impossible to say *de man wordt gestorven* 'the man is died'.)

   Another potential counterexample is the Italian absolute construction in (i), which, according to
Giorgi and Pianesi (1991: 20), has an active perfect reading. However, it may well be a passive perfect.
The impression that it is active may be caused by the fact that the unrealized agent of the passive

(20) a. de door Piet geslagen man
         the by   Piet hit   man
         'the man that has been hit by Pete'

      b. door het noodweer overvallen kwam Piet drijfnat   thuis
         by   the storm   surprised came Pete soaking-wet home
         'having been caught in a storm, Pete came home soaking wet'

We conclude that in a periphrastic construction, the past participle has both perfect and passive properties.

What also plays an important role in periphrastic constructions is the notion of relativized head. As argued by Grimshaw (1991) and Williams (1994), a head will project a feature throughout an extended projection, unless there is a higher head specified differently for that feature. In a periphrastic construction, the extended projection contains two verbal heads: the auxiliary and the participle. Since the past participle is both perfect and passive, feature projection from the participle is blocked in case the auxiliary is either nonperfect or nonpassive.

By 'nonpassive' we mean that the auxiliary is unergative and assigns an external θ-role that is covalued with the external θ-role of the base verb of the participle (see Haider 1984, Hoekstra 1986 and Ackema 1999 for detailed argumentation). Although projection is not literally blocked here (since 'passive' and 'nonpassive' in this sense are not features), this is an instance of the same process: a higher head overrules the properties of a lower head. The participial morphology absorbs the external θ-role, whereas the auxiliary adds a covalued one again. Below we will refer to this informally by using the notation '$[+/-\theta_{ext}]$', and treat it as a feature for ease of exposition.

The two cases in which an auxiliary changes the properties induced by the participle are illustrated in (21) (a nonperfect passive) and (22) (an active perfect).

(21)

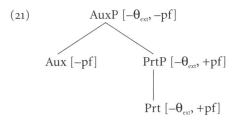

AuxP $[-\theta_{ext}, -pf]$

Aux $[-pf]$ PrtP $[-\theta_{ext}, +pf]$

Prt $[-\theta_{ext}, +pf]$

---

is interpreted as 'Maria' here (the friends were greeted by Maria). This interpretation is presumably due to pragmatic considerations, since a situation in which Maria leaves her friends after they have been greeted strongly suggests that Maria greeted them.

(i) Salutati gli amici, Maria parti
    greeted the friends, Mary left

(22)

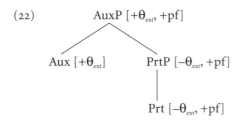

It is plausible that there is a constraint against changing properties of a projection line. The properties of each head in an extended projection must match those of the top node:

(23)   Project
       The head(s) of an extended projection and its top node may not have opposite values for a feature

The interaction of this constraint with the PARSE-Passive constraint introduced in Section 8.4 explains the difference between languages like Russian and languages like Dutch. In Dutch, PROJECT is ranked below PARSE-Passive. This means that, if the input contains a past participle, it will be parsed even if it also contains an auxiliary with opposite feature specification; see (24). Hence, (19a–b) occur as well as (19c).

(24) aux [–f], participle [+f]	PARSE-Passive	PROJECT
☞ [$_{AuxP}$ Aux [$_{PrtP}$ Prt]]		*
o	*!	

Note that PARSE-Passive requires passive morphology to be parsed. We have already argued that passive morphology is identical to perfect morphology in periphrastic constructions. Consequently, PARSE-Passive also requires the realization of the periphrastic perfect.

If the constraints are ranked the other way around, the only periphrastic construction that is allowed is the one where the feature specification of the auxiliary does not conflict with the main verb's properties. This is the perfect passive:

(25) aux [$-\theta_{ext}$, +pf], prt [$-\theta_{ext}$, +pf]	PROJECT	PARSE-Passive
☞ [$_{AuxP}$ Aux [$_{PrtP}$ Prt]]		
o		*!

Periphrastic active perfects or periphrastic nonperfect passives cannot surface, however. In both cases, one of the features of the auxiliary ([$+\theta_{ext}$] in the first case, [–pf] in the second) conflicts with a property of the participle:[14]

---

[14] A reviewer remarks that Russian does not only lack auxiliary *have* but possessive *have* as well. This might be an argument in favour of the hypothesis that the absence of *have* is an accidental

(26) aux [−f], prt [+f]	PROJECT	PARSE-Passive
[$_\text{AuxP}$ Aux [$_\text{PrtP}$ Prt]]	*!	
☞ 0		*

To conclude, a construction can be ruled out in a particular language if there is a crucial interaction between a Parse constraint and some constraint(s) that define structural wellformedness. Thus language-specific ineffability can be understood. In the next section we will turn to constructions that are universally impossible. We will develop the analysis of this section further, showing that some combinations of participles and auxiliaries are harmonically bound by constructions without an auxiliary and therefore do not occur at all.

8.6 Superfluous Auxiliaries

Some interesting further predictions concerning participial constructions can be made, given our earlier definition of candidate sets (see (1)). Recall that, according to this definition, constructions with different choices of function words and inflection compete as long as they target the same semantics. This implies that a construction with an auxiliary and a participle is in the same candidate set as one with an active main verb if (and only if) they target the same semantics.

From this, it follows that, universally, constructions are ruled out in which the addition of an auxiliary to a participle yields exactly the same feature set as the main verb would have in its nonparticipial form. This is because the construction with the auxiliary violates Project, whereas the construction with the main verb only obviously does not. In this way, (27a) blocks (27b).

(27)   a. dat Jan$_i$ t$_i$ valt
             that John   falls

        b. *dat Jan$_i$ t$_i$ wordt gevallen
            that John   is   fallen

The unaccusative main verb in (27a) has the properties [$-\theta_\text{ext}$, $-$pf]. The participle of the main verb in (27b) has the properties [$-\theta_\text{ext}$, $+$pf]. These are overruled by the features of the auxiliary, however, which yields a [$-\theta_\text{ext}$, $-$pf] structure

lexical gap. However, it does not seem to be a universal property of languages that if auxiliary *have* is lacking, possessive *have* is lacking as well. In Latin, like in Russian, there is no verbal participial construction with auxiliary *have*, but there is a possessive verb *habere*. Similar facts hold in Lithuanian and Serbo-Croatian (Maaike Schoorlemmer, p.c.).

  Nevertheless, there may be a connection between absence of possessive *have* and a relatively high ranking of the PROJECT constraint (which is, as explained in the main text, required to rule out auxiliary *have*). If there is only one verb *have*, this must be specified as [+perf] in all its usages. In a nonperfect possessive construction, the [+perf] feature may not percolate, in obvious violation of PROJECT. Hence, the interaction of Project and some Parse constraint which wants *have* to be parsed would determine whether or not possessive *have* will surface.

again. The periphrastic structure induces a violation of Project, and will there-fore score worse than the nonperiphrastic one, irrespective of how Project is ranked. In (28), the columns of the constraints above Project are shaded, as well as those below it, in order to indicate their irrelevance; the two candidates will not score differently here.

(28) V $[-\theta_{ext}, -pf]$	. . .	PROJECT	. . .
☞ V $[-\theta_{ext}, -pf]$	. . .		. . .
Aux $[-\theta_{ext}, -pf]$, prt $[-\theta_{ext}, +pf]$	. . .	*!	. . .

Note that a sentence like (29b), derived from an unergative, is not in the same candidate set as (29a). In (29a), the subject is assigned the main verb's external θ-role; in (29b) no θ-role can be assigned to it: both the participle and the aux-iliary are $[-\theta_{ext}]$ (*worden* is a $[-\theta_{ext}]$ auxiliary in Dutch; it occurs in passives). Although in this case the periphrastic construction is not blocked by its nonparticipial counterpart, it is uninterpretable since it contains a referential argument without a θ-role. This, then, is an instance of absolute ungrammatical-ity induced by an inviolable principle (the θ-Criterion), that is, a principle which can be assumed to be part of GEN.

(29)   a.   Jan   werkt
           John works

       b. *Jan   wordt gewerkt
           John is   worked

The fact that participial constructions can be harmonically bound because of a PROJECT violation also explains why no nonperfect counterpart of the auxil-iary *have* exists. This would be an auxiliary with the properties $[+\theta_{ext}, -pf]$. Suppose the participle of an unergative or transitive verb is combined with this hypothetical auxiliary. In that case, PROJECT is violated because the $[-\theta_{ext}]$ property of the participle is overruled. However, the $[+\theta_{ext}, -pf]$ properties of the whole construction can also be realized by simply using the main verb in its finite form. Thus, the hypothetical periphrastic construction is blocked:

(30) V $[+\theta_{ext}, -pf]$	. . .	PROJECT	. . .
☞ V $[+\theta_{ext}, -pf]$	. . .		. . .
Aux $[+\theta_{ext}, -pf]$, prt $[-\theta_{ext}, +pf]$	. . .	*!*	. . .

A similar argument can be made for unaccusatives. In many languages unaccusatives cannot be combined with a $[+\theta_{ext}]$ auxiliary in the first place. In some languages, however, the perfect of an unaccusative is formed with $[+\theta_{ext}]$ *have* (see Ackema 1996 for discussion of the difference between the two types of language). Even so, a nonperfect counterpart of *have* is still impossible, also with the participle of an unaccusative. This is because Project is violated as a result of the [–pf] feature of the auxiliary, whereas the properties of the input can also be realized by the main verb in its finite form without violating Project.

One may wonder now why auxiliaries are ever used. Either they induce violations of Project (as in (19a–b)/(24)) or they double the information encoded by the participle (as in the perfect passive, see (25)). The reason that they do in fact exist lies in morphological restrictions that make it impossible to attach more than one inflectional marker to a single verb in certain languages. In order to create a perfect or passive in such languages, an auxiliary must be inserted. This hosts the finite (or nonfinite) inflection that cannot be carried by a main verb already carrying passive or perfect inflection (cf. Drijkoningen 1989, Ouhalla 1991 for analysis).[15]

8.7 Partial Underparsing

In Sections 8.2–5 we have argued that underparsing can be responsible for the absence of certain constructions in a language. A similar position is taken in Legendre *et al.* (1998). The way in which the idea is developed there is different, however. Legendre *et al.* argue that the input of GEN consists of a target semantics and a numeration, comparable to what is usually assumed. However, the optimal candidate need not have the target semantics, since the 'sameness of semantics' demand on candidate sets (see Section 8.2) is abandoned. It is replaced by a violable (faithfulness) constraint that has the effect that the semantics of a candidate must be as close as possible to the intended semantics.

Absolute ungrammaticality, as in the case of multiple questions in Irish (see Section 8.3), then is explained as follows. There are constraints that are violated in the candidates that fully realize the input of a multiple question, but not in candidates in which only one *Wh* is realized. Consequently, if PARSE-*Wh* (the relevant faithfulness constraint here) is ranked below these constraints, the optimal candidate for a multiple question is actually a simple question.

If the definition of candidate set argued for above is adopted, this line of argumentation is impossible. If one or more of the *Wh*s in the input are not realized, the candidate will not have the semantics of a multiple question. Therefore, it cannot be in the candidate set for multiple questions either. Only a candidate with no semantics, the null parse, competes with candidates with a particular semantics.

---

[15] A reviewer poses the question of why *do* is never used in periphrastic constructions. The first thing to note in this respect is that, no matter what verb is used as auxiliary, PROJECT must always be violated in active perfects and nonperfect passives. The properties of these constructions differ from those of the participle, so they can only be derived at the cost of a PROJECT violation. Inserting *do* therefore makes no difference. The fact that there is no free alternation between the relevant auxiliaries and *do* suggests that *do* has the wrong feature specification to function as auxiliary in a participial construction. This would follow if it is specified as $[+\theta_{ext}, -perf]$ (as just argued in the main text, an auxiliary with such a specification will never occur in a periphrastic passive or perfect, since it always invokes fatal violations).

The difference between these approaches lies in the interpretation of constraints like PARSE-*Wh*. We interpret it such that some particular, morphologically identifiable, element in the numeration must occur in the output. Legendre *et al.* interpret it as a constraint that requires faithfulness to the target semantics, which includes the semantics of *Wh*-phrases. PARSE-*Wh* then is an essentially semantic constraint, which is evaluated in a hierarchy containing syntactic constraints such as *ADJOIN ('Do not adjoin').

This is a possible approach, of course, but one which we think is not very attractive for conceptual reasons. It has the consequence that the autonomy of syntax must be relinquished, since syntactic and semantic constraints are evaluated on a par. Another problem concerns the determination of what the optimal candidate is. Considering multiple questions again, there seem to be various options.

First, it is conceivable that all *Wh*s occur in the structure, but that only one is interpreted as such. Obviously, this is not what one would wish, since the absence of structures with more than one *Wh* in a language like Irish would remain unexplained.[16]

Second, it might be that not interpreting a *Wh* implies that it cannot be inserted in the structure. This would predict, however, that a sentence like *who destroyed* would be the optimal candidate for an input that expresses 'who destroyed what'. However, it is not the case that obligatory argument positions in questions need not be realized in Irish.

Third, the underparsed *Wh* might be realized as another element, for instance as an indefinite quantifier. This option agrees with the facts, since sentences like *who destroyed something* can very well be grammatical in languages that lack multiple questions. The consequence is that one must now assume that if a feature is removed from a *Wh*-word another word results, not only semantically but also phonologically. However, there is no plausible phonological relation between the Irish counterparts of *something* and *what* (Cathal Doherty, p.c.). Alternatively, if *something* is not related at all to the *Wh*-word it stands in for, the condition on equal numerations for candidates must be relinquished, since then *who saw what* and *who saw something* with underparsed *what* have different numerations. Giving up this condition probably leads to new problems, however (see footnote 4).

Of course, partial underparsing as such is not disallowed. And in some cases, the resulting candidate *will* compete with fully parsed ones, namely if the semantics is not affected by omitting lexical material. This may be the correct analysis for, for instance, pro-drop in languages like Italian (cf. Samek-Lodovici 1996).

If the semantics does change, the resulting structure will end up in a different candidate set. In that candidate set, it can in principle be optimal. As a consequence, it is possible that the numeration of an optimal candidate contains a

---

[16] Note that *Wh*s that are not interpreted as such cannot violate syntactic constraints on *Wh*-positioning.

number of superfluous elements that remain unparsed. This has no empirical consequences, however. Let a structure acb be the optimal candidate that expresses semantics S and that is projected from a numeration containing the elements a, b and c. Obviously, the same semantics can be expressed by projecting from a numeration containing the elements a, b, c and d and not parsing d. Since the numeration is different we are in a different candidate set now, but the optimal candidate will again be acb. So, a distinction can be made between the minimal numeration of a sentence and irrelevant extensions of this numeration.

8.8 The Non-Interaction of Parse Constraints

An issue that was introduced in Section 8.3 and that still needs to be addressed concerns the interaction of parse constraints with other parse constraints. Suppose that there are two parse constraints, PARSE-F and PARSE-G. Suppose, furthermore that there is some other CONSTRAINT X that dominates PARSE-F and which is violated by candidates containing the feature F, with the effect that the null parse wins (see (3), repeated here as (31)).

(31) Input with feature F	CONSTRAINT X	PARSE-F
Candidate C	*!	
☞ o		*

However, if PARSE-G dominates CONSTRAINT X, it is predicted that inputs containing both features F and G will be structurally realized by some candidate C′:

(32) Input with features F and G	PARSE-G	CONSTRAINT X	PARSE-F
☞ Candidate C′		*	
o	*!		*

So, interaction of parse constraints leads to situations in which inputs containing a particular feature are realized only if they also contain some particular other feature.

It is unclear to us to which extent situations of this type exist in syntax, but if we consider the parse constraints adopted in this chapter, some undesirable predictions seem to be made. For instance, languages could exist in which multiple questions do not exist, except in passive sentences (namely languages with a ranking PARSE-Passive >> OP-SPEC >> PARSE-Wh). Similarly, there could be languages that do not have passives, except in questions. We presume that such languages do not exist. In that case, parse constraints must not interact. In the remainder of this section, we will sketch an organization of grammar from which this follows. We will conclude with some speculations on the special status of parse constraints in the grammar.

In optimality theory, a grammar is a total ranking of universal constraints. The usual view of selection of the optimal candidate is that there is a single procedure of evaluation, in which all constraints are considered.[17] We propose that this is true, except for parse constraints. Per evaluation procedure only one parse constraint is included in the ranking. The total process of evaluation then consists of a series of evaluations each involving one parse constraint. The output of one such evaluation is the input for the next, with the effect that if the null parse is optimal in one evaluation, it will also be the optimal output of the total procedure. Hence, the cases of absolute ungrammaticality discussed in this paper are unaffected by the presence of features that are subject to other parse constraints.

Let us illustrate this organization of grammar. Consider our abstract example in tableaux (31) and (32) above. Suppose that the language has the following ranking of constraints:

(33)   . . . >> Parse-G >> . . . >> Constraint X >> . . . >> Parse-F >>
        . . .

Since there are two parse constraints in (33), the evaluation procedure will consist of two cycles, in which the candidates are evaluated against the following two rankings respectively.

(34)   a. . . . >> Parse-G >> . . . >> Constraint X >> . . .
        b. . . . >> Constraint X >> . . . >> Parse-F >> . . .

Although it does not matter which of the parse constraints is taken into consideration first, let us for the sake of concreteness assume that it is Parse-G. In that case, the candidate that comes out as optimal in the first evaluation cycle is some candidate C:

(35) Input with features F and G	. . .	Parse-G	. . .	Constraint X	. . .
☞ Candidate C				*	
O		*!			

This entails that the input for the next evaluation cycle is the set of features and lexical items realized by candidate C (including a specified semantics). This input is fed once more into Gen and the resulting candidates are now evaluated against the ranking in (34b), with the result that the null parse comes out as optimal:

(36) Input with features F and G	. . .	Constraint X	. . .	Parse-F	. . .
Candidate C		*!			
☞ O				*	

[17] That is, there is a single procedure of evaluation per grammatical component (phonology, syntax, etc.).

The result of the overall evaluation procedure, then, is the null parse. Note that the same result is obtained if the order of the evaluation cycles is reversed. In that case, the first cycle would be as in (36). The optimal candidate in this cycle has no features (it is the null parse). The consequence is that the input for the next cycle has no features either, so that only the null parse will be considered. The subsequent evaluation is trivial:

(37) Input without features	...	Parse-G	...	Constraint X	...
☞ 0					

In sum, if parse constraints are evaluated on separate cycles, they will not interact, with the consequence that if it is optimal in a language not to parse some feature, this does not depend on the presence of other features.

Let us conclude with some speculations on why parse constraints are special: why are they evaluated differently from other constraints? What sets parse constraints apart from other constraints is that they alone relate to specific elements from the lexicon. Parse constraints alone check whether elements in the input appear in the syntactic structure. For every constraint it is possible to check for violations by considering the candidate as such; only parse constraints require that the input for Gen is considered as well.

So, in order to evaluate parse constraints, one must start out from the input and then consider whether the relevant elements from the input are realized in the various candidates. One can do so in two ways: by considering the realization of the entire input at once, or by considering the realization of one element in the input at a time. If the latter option is correct, the fact that parse constraints are evaluated in cycles follows. For each morphological element the corresponding parse constraint is relevant but the other ones are not.

The question then is which factors favour the second mode of evaluation (checking of violation of parse constraints per feature) over the first one (checking of violation of parse constraints for the entire input at once). Perhaps the difference between the two can be characterized as follows: in the first mode of evaluation a complicated task is performed once, whereas in the second one a simple task is performed a number of times. (Of course, the total number of comparisons between features in the input and the various candidates is the same in both cases). If in general multiple performance of a simple task is preferred over single performance of a more complicated task, the proposed evaluation procedure for parse constraints is indeed preferred.[18]

---

[18] There might be a relation with the work of Sternberg (1966, 1975). Sternberg argues that if subjects are asked to compare a test item with a set of elements stored in short-term memory, they do so in a serial manner (per element in short-term memory), rather than in a parallel one (for all elements in short-term memory at once). Although the similarity with the situation described in the main text is clear, it is not obvious whether Sternberg's conclusion carry over directly.

8.9 References

Ackema, P. (1996). 'Case-features and changes in auxiliary selection in unaccusative perfects'. Ms, Utrecht University.

Ackema, P. (1999). *Issues in Morposyntax*. Amsterdam and Philadelphia, John Benjamins.

—— and A. Neeleman (1998a). 'Optimal questions'. *Natural Language and Linguistic Theory* 16, 443–90.

—— —— (1998b). 'Conflict resolution in passive formation'. *Lingua* 104, 13–29.

Baker, M., K. Johnson, and I. Roberts (1989). 'Passive arguments raised'. *Linguistic Inquiry* 20, 219–51.

Belletti, A. (1988). 'The case of unaccusatives'. *Linguistic Inquiry* 19, 1–34.

Bennis, H. (1986). *Gaps and Dummies*. Dordrecht, Foris.

Besten, H. den (1985). 'The ergative hypothesis and free word order in Dutch and German'. In J. Toman (ed.), *Studies in German Grammar*. Dordrecht, Foris, 23–64.

Drijkoningen, F. (1989). *The Syntax of Verbal Affixation*. Tübingen, Niemeyer.

Fox, D. (1995). 'Economy and scope'. *Natural Language Semantics* 3, 283–341.

Giorgi, A. and F. Pianesi (1991). 'Toward a syntax of temporal representations'. *Probus* 3, 1–27.

Golan, Y. (1993). 'Node crossing economy, superiority and d-linking'. Ms, Tel Aviv University.

Grimshaw, J. (1991). 'Extended projection'. Ms, Brandeis University.

—— (1997). 'Projection, heads, and optimality'. *Linguistic Inquiry* 28, 373–422.

Haider, H. (1984). 'Was zu haben ist und was zu sein hat'. *Papiere zur Linguistik* 30, 23–36.

Hoekstra, T. (1986). 'Passives and participles'. In F. Beukema and A. Hulk (eds), *Linguistics in the Netherlands 1986*. Dordrecht, Foris, 95–104.

Jaeggli, O. (1986). 'Passive'. *Linguistic Inquiry* 17, 587–622.

Kayne, R. (1993). 'Toward a modular theory of auxiliary selection'. *Studia Linguistica* 47, 3–31.

Kiparsky, V. (1963). *Russische Historische Grammatik II: Die Entwicklung des Formensystems*. Heidelberg, Winter.

Legendre, G., P. Smolensky, and C. Wilson (1998). 'When is less more?' Ms, Johns Hopkins University. In P. Barbosa *et al.* (eds), *Is the best good enough?* MIT Press/MITWPL.

McCarthy, J. and A. Prince (1993). 'Prosodic morphology I'. Ms, University of Massachusetts at Amherst/Rutgers University.

McCloskey, J. (1979). *Transformational Syntax and Model Theoretic Semantics*. Dordrecht, Reidel.

Marantz, A. (1992). 'Case and licensing'. In *Proceedings of ESCOL 1991*, 234–53. Ohio State University.

Orgun, O. and R. Sprouse (1996). 'When the best isn't good enough'. Paper presented at WECOL 1996, University of California at Santa Cruz.

Ouhalla, J. (1991). *Functional Categories and Parametric Variation*. London, Routledge.

Picallo, M. C. (1997). 'On the Extended Projection Principle and null expletive subjects'. Ms, Universitat Autònoma de Barcelona.

Prince, A. and P. Smolensky (1993). 'Optimality Theory'. Ms, Rutgers University/University of Colorado at Boulder.

Reinhart, T. (1995). '*Wh*-in-situ in the framework of the Minimalist Program'. Ms, Utrecht University.

Rizzi, L. (1982). *Issues in Italian Syntax*. Dordrecht, Foris.

Rudin, C. (1988). 'On multiple questions and multiple *Wh* fronting'. *Natural Language and Linguistic Theory* 6, 445–501.

Samek-Lodovici, V. (1996). *Constraints on Subjects: An Optimality Theoretic Analysis*. PhD thesis, Rutgers University.

Schoorlemmer, M. (1995). *Participial Passive and Aspect in Russian*. PhD thesis, Utrecht University.

Siewierska, A. (1984). *The Passive: A Comparative Linguistic Analysis*. London, Croom Helm.

Spencer, A. (1991). *Morphological Theory*. Oxford, Blackwell.

Sternberg, S. (1966). 'High-speed scanning in human memory'. *Science* 153, 652–4.

—— (1975). 'Memory scanning: new findings and current controversies'. *Quarterly Journal of Experimental Psychology* 27, 1–32.

Tesar, B. and P. Smolensky (1998). 'The learnability of Optimality Theory'. *Linguistic Inquiry* 29, 229–68.

Weerman, F. (1989). *The V2 Conspiracy*. Dordrecht, Foris.

Williams, E. (1994). *Thematic Structure in Syntax*. Cambridge, MA, MIT Press.

9

Towards an Optimal Account of Second-Position Phenomena[1]

Stephen R. Anderson

9.1 Introduction

One of the early classics in generative grammar, published in the same year as Chomsky's *Syntactic Structures*, was a paper by Morris Halle (1957) 'In Defense of the Number Two'. The present chapter might be seen as a further attempt to substantiate the linguistic significance of 'two', this time in the ordinal sense of 'second' rather than that of binarity.

A variety of recent analyses have attempted to claim, in effect, that the appearance of a notion of 'second position' in the descriptive statement of several natural language regularities is actually an artifact, that the real generalizations in each case refer to something else, and that the connection with second position is coincidental. I will argue, in contrast, that a number of effects are indeed related in a fundamental and unitary way to the notion of second position. The most appropriate way to capture these regularities appears to be in terms of a system of interacting constraints of the type envisioned in Optimality Theory, referring to the organization of a 'post-Spell Out' level of syntactic structure such as PF.

In the syntactic literature of the past hundred years and more, there are two principal places where the notion of 'second position' seems to figure. Although the phenomena in question are at least superficially rather heterogeneous, one's curiosity is naturally aroused as to whether there might be some generalization that would unite them. What is involved, basically, is the question of whether there is any connection between the placement of certain clitics immediately

[1] The work represented here was supported in part by grant number SBR–9514682 from the US National Science Foundation to Yale University. This paper has benefited from comments received when earlier versions were presented to audiences at MIT, the University of Washington, CUNY, Stanford, and the University of Maryland. I am especially grateful to the members of my seminar on clitics at Yale during 1996–97: David Harrison, Lizanne Kaiser, Matt Richardson and Jennifer VanLoon. Their comments and criticisms, as well as those of Joost Dekkers specifically for this volume, have been very helpful.

after an initial element (of their clause, or in some instances, of a phrase to which they are relevant) and the well known requirement in several languages (the most discussed cases being Germanic, but also including several others) that the finite verb come in second position in e.g. German declarative main clauses.

Do these facts have anything to do with one another? Jakob Wackernagel, with whose name the placement of clitics in second position is commonly associated, certainly thought so. In his widely cited (but perhaps less widely read) discussion of the clitic facts, Wackernagel (1892) explicitly argued that Verb-Second in Germanic could be derived from the same principles as those governing second-position clitics in the classical languages. Let us recall that for Wackernagel, the class of 'clitics'[2] was precisely that of 'unstressed words'. The bulk of his paper is devoted to a demonstration that in Proto Indo-European (PIE), these clitics appeared in second position, as illustrated by the following Homeric Greek example.[3]

(1)   polees-**te-min** ērēsanto hippēes phoreein
       many-and-it prayed   riders   carry
       'And many riders prayed to carry it' (*Iliad* 4.143)

Facts such as the accentless nature of finite main verbs in Sanskrit and the consistent regressive accentuation of finite verbs in Greek led Wackernagel to the conclusion that finite verbs in PIE were unaccented, a conclusion which is still accepted today by most Indo-Europeanists. But in that case, by virtue of its lack of accent, the PIE finite verb was by definition a member of the class of clitics, and thus should behave in the same way as other clitics: in particular, it ought to be attracted to the same, second position within the clause. On this basis, Wackernagel argued that the Verb-Second phenomenon in modern German should be regarded as the reflex of this original clitic status.

Taken literally, Wackernagel's analysis seems rather unpersuasive as an account of the synchronic syntax of modern German (or other Germanic Verb-Second languages). For one thing, German lacks second-position clitics, and thus there is no wider class for the Verb's behavior to be derived from; and for another, German main verbs bear stress, and thus would not be candidates (in Wackernagel's terms) for clitic status in any event. Recall, of course, that Wackernagel intended his account to be taken diachronically, such that the potential unity of the two phenomena is not essentially compromised by these facts about German. Even in a diachronic sense, however, Wackernagel's account of Verb-Second has not gained many adherents. Germanic Verb-Second appears to

---

[2] To be more accurate, *enclitics* and *proclitics*: the modern generalization to a class of *clitics* is a rather recent terminological innovation.

[3] Clitics in this and subsequent examples appear in bold type, separated from their phonological 'hosts' by a hyphen. This convention is purely typographical, and is not intended to make any claims about boundary elements or other aspects of their phonology beyond their incorporation into a phonological word with the host.

be historically a relatively recent innovation, not dating to a stage for which second-position clitics can be reconstructed. Kiparsky (1995: 159) argues that Germanic poetry based on alliteration (and thus implying stress on alliterating words, including finite verbs) 'was certainly flourishing around the time Verb-Second word order gained ground in the Germanic languages'. Although other work (Eythórsson 1996) suggests that Verb-Second actually appears much earlier in Germanic than Kiparsky's account assumes, a diachronic connection with second-position clitics has not seemed very appealing.

The question remains, however, of whether there is anything that the phenomena of second-position clitics and second-position finite verbs have in common beyond mere descriptive appearance. In order to determine whether there is anything deeper that relates these facts to one another, we need to equip ourselves with a concrete theory of clitics, and then ask whether that theory extends in a natural way to encompass Verb-Second. In Section 9.2 below, I will summarize a particular view of clitics which suggests they (or at least the relevant ones among them) should be regarded as analogues at the phrase level of morphological affixation in words. Section 9.3 supports that conclusion by demonstrating that the descriptive regularities governing the placement of (especially second position) clitics are ones that fall outside the scope of syntactic formulation. Section 9.4 then addresses the issue of how clitic placement is to be described, and after considering other alternatives, proposes a system based on the notions of Optimality Theory. Section 9.5 discusses the differentiation in these terms of various notions of 'second position'. Section 9.6 then returns to the question of Verb Second, and argues that the system developed for clitics provides an appropriate account for the position of the verb in Verb-Second languages. Section 9.7 draws some general conclusions about the architecture of linguistic description.

9.2 A View of Clitics

We begin by noting that the notion of a 'clitic' actually conflates two rather different kinds of behavior. On the one hand, in what we can think of as 'traditional' (by which I mean pre-generative) grammatical usage, such as Wackernagel's, a clitic is a linguistic element that 'leans' on another word. That is, clitics are classically construed as elements that are phonologically (especially accentually) dependent on an adjacent word. On the other hand, in the usage of many syntacticians, a clitic is a member of a class of (typically pronominal) forms whose placement is unusual or unique in terms of the syntax of corresponding non-clitic elements. The paradigmatic exemplars of clitics in this sense are the non-subject pronominals of, e.g., French or Spanish.

These two senses were usefully disentangled in a classic paper by Arnold Zwicky (1977), where a distinction was introduced between *simple* clitics and *special* clitics. The former are the phonologically dependent elements, while the latter are the syntactically unusual ones. One interpretation of Zwicky's distinction (that of e.g. Anderson 1992) sees in simple clitics a class of elements that are 'prosodically deficient', in the specific sense that they lack some of the higher-level prosodic organization (assignment to a phonological word, for example) that characterizes other words in their language. As a result of this lack of structure, they must necessarily be incorporated into some adjacent element of an appropriate prosodic type, resulting in their 'leaning' on that element and thus exhibiting the characteristic phonological dependency.

Special clitics, in contrast, are not actually lexically autonomous linguistic elements at all, but rather should be seen as the morphology of phrases (cf. Anderson 1992, 1993, 1995, 1996). Functional (and in some cases, substantive) properties of phrases can be realized by affixes (as well as certain 'non-concatenative' markers) added to phrases, just as the functional content of words is reflected by the inflectional (and derivational) markers they bear. The apparently unusual placement of clitics within their phrase then, does not result from strictly syntactic mechanisms (special or otherwise), but rather from essentially *morphological* processes.

This view, then, results in two distinct parameters that characterize the overall class of 'clitics': (a) prosodic deficiency; and (b) special placement by morphological, rather than syntactic, means. These are independent of one another, since we can have prosodically full elements with special placement as well as prosodically deficient elements with no special syntax. These latter, of course, are Zwicky's simple clitics, such as the English reduced auxiliaries spelled *'s* (= *is, has*).[4] In most cases, special clitics are also prosodically deficient elements, just as most (but not all) word-level affixation consists in the addition of elements lacking independent stress or other properties of higher-level prosodic structure. Just as some inflectional affixes may demonstrate independent stress or other word-like properties, though, so some special clitics (e.g., Italian *loro*; cf. Nespor 1994) may fail to be simple clitics, establishing the independence of these two dimensions.

While the phonological dimension of cliticization has interesting and important properties and consequences, it is the regularities underlying the placement of special clitics that concern us here. Descriptively, we can identify (following a substantial literature, summarized in Anderson 1992) a limited set of positional possibilities for special clitics. With reference to the phrase that contains them, and whose properties they reflect, these may appear initially, or finally; post-initially (second position) or (perhaps) prefinally; or preceding or following the head of the phrase. With the exception of pre-final (penultimate position) clitics, these are fairly robustly attested in the world's languages.

---

[4] A long research literature makes it clear that the special properties of English reduced finite auxiliaries are not confined to their prosody: see Wilder (1997) for a recent summary. Nonetheless, it seems clear that the possible positions in which these elements appear constitute a proper subset of the positions in which corresponding full forms can be found; and at least one dimension of their behavior follows from their reduced prosody, as suggested here. We leave a fuller account of the syntactic conditions on the occurence of these forms to another time and place.

When we look at these positional possibilities for (special) clitics, they seem strikingly analogous to those for affixes inside words, where we find essentially the same range of placement options relative to the word in which they appear (as well as other similarities, such as rigid ordering). The parallel extends to such details as the relatively tenuous attestation of pre-final infixes, comparable to the situation with respect to pre-final special clitics. The theory of A-Morphous Morphology (Anderson 1992, 1993) takes this analogy seriously, and proposes to generalize this result by treating special clitics not as lexical items inserted and moved around within the syntax, but rather as phonological material inserted (like affixes) into the phonological content of a phrase.

Special clitics, then, are elements that fall under the general theory of morphological form. They are formal markers within phrases that express (a) the phrase's properties (the content of its functional categories, more or less), or (b) modifications to the semantics, discourse properties, etc. of the phrase.[5] The precise character of the mechanisms responsible for placing both clitics and word-level affixes should follow from these considerations, and it is to this matter that we now turn.

9.3 Can the Syntax be Responsible for the Placement of Clitics?

The common view among syntacticians (who have long tended toward this kind of imperialism, especially *vis à vis* morphologists) is of course that special clitics are 'special' in that they undergo particular processes in the syntax. That is, special clitics occupy the position in sentence structure that they do by virtue of rules of the syntax—just different rules (in part) from those applicable to non-clitics.

In evaluating this position, what we want is evidence as to whether the kinds of regularity that turn up with respect to special clitics are such as to fall, at least potentially, within the independently motivated capacities of the syntactic computational system. For those purposes, evidence from clitics that are located in phrase-peripheral positions (i.e. initial or final clitics) is unlikely to be probative, because virtually any sort of mechanism one can imagine should be able to accommodate these positions. Much more interesting, however, are examples of clitics that are located in second position, and it is these cases that will principally occupy us in this section.

How does a syntactic account yield the result that clitics occur systematically in the second position within a given phrasal domain? Essentially, there are two such mechanisms that have been proposed. On the one hand, the clitic might

---

[5] This latter possibility provides a clitic analogue to derivational morphology: see Kaiser (1997b) for an analysis of a Korean construction that makes crucial use of this notion. Our focus below will be primarily on 'inflectional' clitics, so the properties of such elements will not play a role in this discussion.

be generated in (or moved to) a structural position within the phrase where it will be preceded by exactly one other element. The standard form of such an analysis is to assume the placement of clitics in the position of the functional head of the relevant phrase, on the assumption that exactly one other constituent will consistently precede this position, to wit the occupant of the specifier position with respect to that head.

A second way to secure the result that clitics follow exactly one element within their phrase is to position them at the left edge; and then to require that exactly one other constituent move to their left. This movement might be an instance of adjunction to the phrasal category; or it might consist in the filling of some structurally characterized position (that of 'Topic', for example). In any event, the clitics will now be in second position because they are preceded by exactly this pre-posed constituent.

Both of these approaches appeal to quite standard syntactic mechanisms, though of course the details (such as the motivations for the various movements involved) remain to be filled in. The two have in common, however, a pair of predictions that make it possible to test the adequacy of such accounts. First, each of these analytic lines relies on the claim that the clitics occupy some specific, designated position in syntactic structure; and secondly, each has the consequence that the clitics will be preceded by exactly one syntactic constituent. When we explore the facts surrounding second-position clitic placement in a variety of languages, however, we find that neither of these expectations is actually met in the general case.

Taking up the second of these matters first, we can examine the constituent-hood of the material preceding second-position clitics. It is interesting to observe that, although Wackernagel's name is routinely invoked in connection with the observation that clitics often follow exactly one constituent within their clause (or phrase), Wackernagel himself thought of 'his' position as 'after the first word', rather than 'after the first constituent'. His discussion was primarily focused on the facts of Homeric Greek and Vedic Sanskrit, languages in which extensive scrambling suggests that virtually any (non-clitic) word can be a syntactically movable constituent, thus obscuring the difference between these two notions. In other ancient Indo-European languages, however, scrambling is considerably less free, and we can better distinguish words from phrases.

In Hittite (Garrett 1990), for example, word order is generally quite fixed. Members of a set of clitics[6] appear consistently in second position within the clause. The applicable notion of 'second position' is quite consistently 'after the first word', even when that involves placement internal to a constituent which would never be broken up through scrambling or syntactic movement.

---

[6] This clitic cluster was rather more extensively elaborated at some stages in the long history of Hittite than others, but its placement with respect to the rest of the sentence was consistent over time.

(2) a. kun-**wa-za**   DUMU-an da nu-**kan** É.ŠÀ-ni   anda it . . .
this-QUOT-REFL *baby*-ACC *take* CONN-DIR *house*-LOC *in*   *go* . . .
'Take this baby and go into the house . . .' (KUB XXIV 7 IV 45–6)

b. nepisas-**as-sta**   ^DIŠKUR-unni   āssus   ēsta
heaven-GEN-*he*-PTC *Weather-God*-DAT *dear*-NOM *he-was*
'He was dear to the Weather-God of Heaven' (StBoT 18.2)

c. Lupakkin-**ma-kan**   Uzalman-**na** INA Amka paraa naista
Lupakkis-QUOT-PTC *Uzalaas-and into Amka forth he-sent*
'He sent L. and U. forth to Amka' (JCS 10, p. 94, *apud* Golston 1991)

In example (2a) above, the clitics immediately follow a Noun Phrase-initial demonstrative. In example (2b), the clitics appear between a genitive modifier and
the Noun it modifies, while in example (2c) the clitics follow the first of two
conjoined elements. In none of these cases is the material preceding the clitic an
independently movable constituent within the grammar of Hittite.

The best-known example of a language in which it is a single word rather
than a single syntactic constituent that precedes second-position clitics is of
course Serbo-Croatian. Browne (1974) was the first work (in the generative literature) to point out that, for at least some speakers, *either* the first word *or* the
first constituent could define the location of second-position clitics, as in the
following examples.

(3) a. Moja -**će** mladja sestra doći u utorak
my   FUT *younger sister come on Tuesday*
'My younger sister will come on Tuesday'

b. Moja mladja sestra -**će** doći u utorak
my   younger sister FUT *come on Tuesday*
'My younger sister will come on Tuesday'

c. Lav -**je** Tolstoi veliki ruski   pisac
Leo is Tolstoi great Russian writer
'Leo Tolstoi is a great Russian writer'

d. Lav Tolstoi -**je** veliki ruski   pisac
Leo Tolstoi is great Russian writer
'Leo Tolstoi is a great Russian writer'

A massive subsequent literature has discussed the details of these facts, and it is
clear that speakers vary considerably (perhaps, but not necessarily, along otherwise motivated dialect lines) in their acceptance of sentences with clitics located
after exactly one (non-constituent) word. What is clear, however, is that for at
least some speakers, in at least some constructions, this placement is possible;
and that when it occurs, it involves locating the clitic after material that does
not constitute a syntactically motivated constituent of the clause.

Facts of the sort just reviewed militate against accounts that derive second position for clitics from their placement in such a way as to be preceded by exactly one phrasal position (whether this is a specifier, an adjoined phrase, or some designated position such as 'Topic'), because the preceding material is not a phrasal unit. Syntactic accounts that treat second position as essentially epiphenomenal are also challenged by the observation that the structural position in which clitics must appear cannot in some cases be characterized in a unitary way.

An argument to this effect is provided by Željko Bošković (1995), who shows (in the context of an account based on syntactic mechanisms for clitic placement) that there is no consistent structural position for Serbo-Croatian clitics. Bošković assumes, along with most of the literature, that sentence structure in these languages is straightforwardly right-branching, and thus that when an element A precedes another element B in sentences, the structural position of A is higher in the tree than that of B. On this basis, the sentences in (4) show us the position of VP adverbs relative to that of sentence Adverbs, since fronted participles may move to a position that precedes that of VP-adverbs, but not sentence adverbs:

(4)   a. Jovan -je   potpuno zaboravio Petra
          Jovan AUX *completely forgotten   Petar*
          'Jovan completely forgot Petar'

     b. Jovan -je   zaboravio$_i$ potpuno [t$_i$] Petra
          Jovan AUX *forgotten   completely   Petar*
          'Jovan forgot Petar completely'

     c. Jovan -je   nesumnjivo istukao Petra
          Jovan AUX *undoubtedly beaten Petar*
          'Jovan undoubtedly beat Petar'

     d. *Jovan -je   istukao$_i$ nesumnjivo [t$_i$] Petra
          Jovan AUX *beaten   undoubtedly   Petar*
          *'Jovan beat Petar undoubtedly'

Note that in all of these examples, the clitic (-je) precedes both sentential and VP adverbs. Assuming that clitics occupy a consistent structural position, this position must thus be higher than that of either variety of Adverb—in particular, it must be higher than that of sentence adverbs. But participles can precede (and thus occupy a position higher than) clitics, so long as they do not also precede sentence adverbs—an apparent contradiction:

(5)   a. Predstavili -smo -mu -je mudro juče
          introduced AUX *him her wisely yesterday*
          '(We) introduced her to him in a wise manner yesterday'

b. Jovan -je   pravilno odgovorio Mariji
   Jovan AUX *correctly answered   Marija*
   either 'Jovan gave Marija a correct answer'
   or 'Jovan did the right thing in answering Marija'

c. Odgovorio$_i$ -je   pravilno [t$_i$] Mariji
   answered AUX *correctly   Marija*
   only '(He) answered Marija correctly'
   not '(He) was correct to answer Marija'

The problem disappears if we assume that while VP-adverbs and sentential adverbs may occupy consistent positions with respect to one another, and participles may precede one (but not the other), the position of clitics is simply 'after the first element of the sentence', without regard to the hierarchical position in phrase structure this may entail.

In work based on premises closely similar to those of this chapter, Legendre develops a set of arguments for Bulgarian (Legendre this volume) and Romanian (Legendre 1997b) leading to the same conclusion. In each of these languages, the assumption that clitics are attracted to a position with a consistent structural characterization (e.g., a particular functional head) leads to a host of complications, unwarranted assumptions and otherwise unmotivated movements.[7] For Serbo-Croatian, on the other hand, the assumption that the clitics are located in second position (regardless of the way that might be described in terms of hierarchically organized phrase structure) is clear and straightforward. The only complication is the choice between an initial word (prosodically characterized) and an initial phrase as occupying the first position, a matter that will be addressed below.

Most of the discussion of second-position clitic placement has focused on cases in which the clitics at issue have the clause as their domain. This is not the only possibility, however. In several languages, we find clitics that occupy second position within a nominal expression.[8] The structural properties of these clitics are quite parallel to those of clausal second-position elements, and the problems they pose for a syntactic account of their positioning are at least as significant.

The best known cases of second position nominal clitics are the definite determiner elements found in a number of Balkan languages, including Albanian,[9] Bulgarian, Macedonian, and Romanian. These appear after the first word of the relevant NP, regardless of the function of that word, as in the examples in (6) from Macedonian.

---

[7] In addition, Legendre (1997a) details arguments showing that in these systems the clitic elements are syntactically 'inert', as opposed to corresponding non-clitics.

[8] Except where the issue of a DP analysis of such expressions is explicitly at issue, I will simply refer to these as NPs, without necessarily presupposing a specific stand on what their head may be.

[9] See Harrison (1997) for an account of NP clitics in Albanian along the lines suggested below.

(6) a. luǵe-**vo**
people+the
'the people'

b. gostoljubivi-**ve**   luǵe
hospitable[PL]+*the people*
'the hospitable people'

c. naši-**ve**   gostoljubivi   luǵe
our[PL]+*the hospitable*[PL] *people*
'our hospitable people'

A syntactic analysis of the placement of these determiners is offered by Tomić (1996), who proposes to derive e.g. (6c) as follows. Assuming that the expressions in (6) are DP's, the clitic element (-vo/-ve) is generated as the D° head of the DP, with the rest of the phrase's content in a NP that is the complement of this element. The first word of this NP then raises to the Spec position of the DP, thus coming to precede the clitic article.

In terms of widespread assumptions about syntax, this analysis poses some problems. First, we note that the element that raises to Spec$_{DP}$ position consists of a single word, rather than a syntactic constituent of arbitrary size. This suggests that the movement in question must be of a head; but the Spec position within a phrase is generally considered to be a phrasal position, not a head position. The movement posited by Tomić, then, must be of a head to a phrasal position, which is not well formed.[10]

A further problem arises when we attempt to account for why the movement should take place at all. As Tomić puts it, the movement is driven by the fact that the clitic requires an element to its left to which it can attach. Putting aside the issue of why a preceding phrase cannot satisfy this requirement (as indeed it can in some languages: see the discussion of Kwakw'ala immediately below), we can note that this is inconsistent with the assumptions of current work in the Minimalist Program. In that framework, movement must always take place to satisfy the requirements of the element that moves ('Greed'), rather than those of some other element of the structure. It must thus be the clitic, not its host, that undergoes movement, and we would then be confronted with a problematic instance of lowering.

---

[10] On the other hand, Tomić also notes that when an otherwise phrase-initial adjective is preceded by an adverbial or PP modifier, the article clitic attaches to the adjective, not to the first word. In exactly that case, but no other, the movement involved would have to be that of a phrase, not a head. The target position for movement thus does not have a consistent characterization as head or phrasal, and the type of movement involved is problematic. On the account to be offered below, in contrast, this distribution is straightforwardly accounted for: the clitic attempts to position itself as far to the left as possible within the phrase. Words cannot be broken up, so the leftmost position that is accessible in general is after the first word. If we add the condition that modified AdjPs also cannot be broken up, a phrase beginning with such a modifier will have the clitic following it.

A full account of the Balkan determiner clitics involves a number of additional features as well, but the basic regularity is quite similar to that which we saw above for clausal clitics in e.g. Hittite: the clitic element appears immediately after the first word of the phrase that constitutes its scope. Such a regularity, based on the (prosodic, phonological) notion of a 'word' rather than the (syntactic) notion of a phrase, is not the sort for which syntactic mechanisms are appropriate.

Similar conclusions can be drawn from the properties of another system of second-position NP-internal clitics, those of Kwakw'ala (cf. Anderson 1984). In this language, determiner elements are structurally complex. Every NP is preceded by an element which indicates case, deictic status, definiteness, and possibly a possessor. This is a clitic whose position is straightforward (it appears at the left edge of the phrase to which it relates), but whose phonological attachment is unusual, in that it attaches to the rightmost element of the preceding phrase, a fact which has made these clitics a standard example in the literature of the independence of phonology and syntax in clitic placement. More interesting for our purposes, however, is the fact that in certain deictic categories there is an additional overt element which attaches to the end of the first word in the NP, as illustrated in (7). In these examples, the NP-initial element is indicated as 'DET$_1$,' and the second-position element as 'DET$_2$.'

(7) a. məx'id-**ida** 'walas-**i** bəg^{w}anəm-**x̣a** gənanəm
    hit-DET$_1$ *big*-DET$_2$ *man*-OBJ[DET$_1$] *child*
    'The big man hit the child'

  b. *(*vs.*) məx'id-**ida** bəg^{w}anəm-**a**-x̣a gənanəm
    hit-DET$_1$ *man*-DET$_2$-OBJ[DET$_1$] *child*
    'The man hit the child'

  c. le næ'nak^w la-**x̣es** həs-**aq** guk^{w}a
    AUX *goes home to-self's*[DET$_1$] *own*-DET$_2$ *house*
    'She goes home to her own house'

Since the functional content of the 'DET$_1$,' and 'DET$_2$,' elements in Kwakw'ala NP's is quite intermixed, there is no plausible analysis of these facts as involving two discrete head positions, one of which is followed by the rest of the NP (or DP) and the other of which undergoes movement into a preceding specifier (or other) position. In addition, the motivation for such a movement would be even more problematic in this case, since the 'DET$_2$,' element would always be preceded by material to which it could attach phonologically even if no movement took place. We must conclude that these elements are simply placed in second position (that is, following the first word) within the NP by mechanisms which it is hard to see as fundamentally those of the syntax.

A further reason to doubt that the syntax is responsible for the placement of special clitics (second position or others) comes from the following consideration. Whatever it is that determines clitic placement also determines the order among clitics, relative to one another. Now if this is a fundamentally syntactic mechanism, we ought to find that the ordering within sequences of clitics is coherent in terms of syntactically relevant factors, such as the relative scope of functional categories, etc. At least since the work of Perlmutter (1971), however, we have known that this is not in general the case. While clitic sequences may largely follow some syntactically coherent principle (e.g., direct object clitics preceding indirect object clitics, etc.), there are nearly always a few syntactically unexplained deviations from this regularity. Two such examples—one quite well known and the other less so—are given in (8).

(8)   French: dative/accusative *me* 1SG, *te* 2SG, *se* '3 reflexive', *nous* 1PL, *vous* 2PL < 3rd person accusative *le, la, les* < 3rd person dative *lui, leur* < (adverbial) *y* < (partitive) *en*
        Hittite (following Friederich 1974; Hoffner 1986): Sentence connectives < quotative (*-wa(r)-*) < dative/accusative plural < 3rd person nominative, accusative singular < 1st, 2nd person dative/accusative singular, 3rd person dative singular < reflexive (*-z(a)-*) < local, aspectual particles

In each of these cases we can see that some functionally unitary classes (indirect objects, datives, etc.) are not consistently ordered with respect to others; while some functionally heterogeneous classes of clitics have a consistent place in the ordering.

An even more dramatic example of syntactically incoherent ordering is apparently furnished by Sanskrit, where second-position clitics can be shown (cf. Insler 1997) to follow a sequence determined by a small set of entirely phonological conditions. The conditions at issue are also applicable to the sequence of items in compounds and various fixed collocations. They are similar to the sort of conditions studied by Ross, Bolinger and others on preferred orders in English. These are chiefly 'shorter before longer', otherwise 'V-initial before C-initial', otherwise by the vowel of the first syllable (where $i/e > \breve{u}/o > r > \bar{a} > a$) and otherwise 'prosodically lighter before heavier'. Syntactic categories seem to play no role in determining the required sequence.

For a variety of reasons, then, I conclude that syntactic accounts of clitic placement (and specifically, of the basis of 'second-position' phenomena in clitic systems) are not appropriate (or, in general, adequate). For that reason, taken together with the substantive parallels between clitics and the morphology of words referred to above, it seems worthwhile to explore an account of special clitics as the 'morphology' of phrases. We go on in the following section to consider the formal mechanisms that might underlie such an analysis.

9.4 Clitic Ordering and Optimality

Suppose, then, that clitics are not syntactically autonomous elements comparable to the words and phrases that constitute phrase markers, but rather the morphological markers of the properties of phrases. In that case, their introduction into sentences (and more generally, phrases) is not an instance of lexical insertion but rather the overt manifestation of a phrasal analog to a Word Formation Rule. At least in the inflectional domain,[11] such a rule modifies the PF shape of a phrase on the basis of its functional content. I assume (cf. Anderson 1992) that principles generalizing notions such as 'feature percolation' and 'Agreement' construct a morphosyntactic representation for a phrase, a representation of its phrasal properties that includes most of the content of what are often treated as structurally autonomous heads of functional categories. Rules of phrasal morphology refer to this representation and modify the shape of the phrase in a way precisely analogous to the way Word Formation Rules modify the shape of a word on the basis of its morphosyntactic representation.

I thus assume that clitics are the overt realization of material that is part of the featural content of the node dominating the phrase.[12] Most of this analysis could, however, be translated into other terms: the featural content of a node such as IP, in a system based on articulated structures with independent functional heads for tense, agreement, etc. might be taken to mean 'the content of functional categories dominated by IP' without loss of generality.

A fundamental issue arises immediately for this theory of clitics from the fact that a single phrase may contain more than one clitic associated with the 'same' (e.g., second) position. In such a case, what ensures that the clitics will appear in the right sequence in the surface form? If clitics are (the surface manifestation of) rules, an obvious possibility is to relate linear order of clitics to order of application of rules. But some apparently minor mechanical problems that follow from that assumption suggest a somewhat different view. Sometimes the shape of a clitic depends on that of another clitic which follows it, and which (on an analysis where surface sequence is the reflection of the order of application of rules) would have to be introduced later in the descriptive sequence. In Serbo-Croatian, for example the feminine singular accusative clitic, normally *je*, is pronounced *ju* when another clitic with the shape *je* occurs after it. This is not due to any general phonological rule of the language, but is rather a fact specific to this particular clitic. Since the conditioning environment for the change of *je* to *ju* would (on the view we are examining) only be introduced after the affected element, however, there is a difficulty in the statement of the relevant variation.

This example is by no means isolated. In Italian, for example, the clitics *mi*,

[11] See footnote 5 above.

[12] E.g., in the case of clitics associated with a clause, the content of S (or IP), or with CP. In the discussion below, I will generally assume much flatter structures, with much less functional articulation, than has become general in the syntactic literature. Attributing functional content to phrases directly, rather than to hierarchically structured heads, has a number of advantages, but I will not defend these overall assumptions here. A tendency away from the elaborate functional structures of recent years can be discerned in recent work such as that of Chomsky (1995: ch. 4), Williams (1994), Bresnan, Grimshaw and others.

ti, si, ci, vi are replaced by *me, te, se, ce, ve* when they come immediately before *ne, lo, la, li, le*. In the same environment, *gli* and *le* are both replaced by *glie*. These changes, again, are part of the idiosyncratic 'allomorphy' of the clitics involved, but their statement requires reference to an element that would only be introduced by a rule following[13] the one introducing the affected clitic.

These examples, involving clitic introduction rules that would apparently have to look ahead, could be avoided if in fact the clitics were introduced simultaneously, rather than one at a time. In that case, they would all be simultaneously 'co-present', and presumably available to condition one another's form. This suggests part of the character of an analysis that could replace the one based on rule ordering.

Another problem is presented by the fact that, in several languages, the same sequence(s) of clitics can appear either preceding or following an anchor point, depending on various environmental factors. In such an instance, if surface order derives from sequence of application, we would expect the sequences preceding and following a comparable anchor to be mirror-images of each other, resulting from a simple change of 'precedes' to 'follows' in the content of the rule. In virtually every case, however, the linear order of a sequence of clitics remains the same regardless of whether the sequence as a whole precedes or follows the anchor point.

Italian pronominal clitics, for example, precede the finite verb in a fixed order, but follow non-finite verbs and imperatives (in the same sequence). E.g., *me-lo-dice* 'he tells me it', but *dicendo-me-lo* 'saying it to me', *dir-me-lo* '(to) say it to me', *dimmelo* 'tell me it!' Pronominal and auxiliary clitics in Macedonian appear in a rigid sequence before finite verbs (which themselves appear in second position: cf. Legendre 1997a), but (in the same sequence) after non-finite verbs or the imperative:

(9) a. Ne -bi -me -go dal
         NEG AUX *me it   gave*
         'He wouldn't give it to me'

     b. Dajte   -mi -go
         give (IMPER) *me it*
         'give it to me!'

     c. nosejḱi -mi -go
         bringing me it
         bringing it to me . . .

---

[13] In both the Serbo-Croatian and the Italian examples, it might be asked why the clitics should be introduced from left to right, rather than from right to left. The reasons are related to the theory of how clitic positions are anchored, and will not be explored here; suffice it to say that parallel examples with the opposite orientation could be presented against introducing the clitics in the opposite order.

In Bulgarian the facts are quite similar to those of Macedonian, but clitics (except *šte, ne, li*, which are subject to slightly different conditions: cf. Legendre, this volume) also follow the finite verb when this is sentence initial:

(10)   a.   Ivančo -**mi** -**go** pokaza
            Ivancho me   it   showed
            'Ivancho showed it to me'
        b.   Pokaza -**mi** -**go** Ivančo
            showed me   it   Ivancho
            'Ivancho showed it to me'

Bulgarian clitics also follow the same classes of verbs as those mentioned for Macedonian noted above.

Because the same ordering is maintained in these cases regardless of the relation of the entire clitic sequence to its anchor point, they too argue for a view of clitic introduction other than that provided by a set of sequentially ordered rules applying one at a time. An alternative view that offers remedies for the problems just noted is suggested by analyses of the sort associated with Optimality Theory (OT—cf. Prince and Smolensky 1993). Without necessarily adopting all of the assumptions that have come to characterize OT as a theory of PF relations, we can draw on some of its leading ideas in ways that seem particularly relevant to the analysis of clitic sequences. Prominent among these is a greatly reduced reliance on sequential derivation as a mechanism for reconstructing left-right relations within phonological representations. Instead of introducing, e.g., affixes within a word one at a time such that each new prefix comes to precede the ones already introduced, etc., OT descriptions associate a number of affixes with a form simultaneously, such that their surface order results from a kind of competition regulated by the relative priority of element-specific constraints.

Such a view has the advantage that, as we have seen above for clitics, all of the comparable material within a domain may be treated as co-present at its introduction. Descriptive order reflects the ranking of element-specific constraints, not the sequence in which the elements are introduced. Relative ordering results from the fact that a number of elements all want to be located in the same position, but the demands of some outweigh those of others. For example, suppose a number of affixes all want to be prefixes. That means that for each of them, there is a constraint to the effect that it should be at the left edge of the word. Since these constraints are ranked, however, one will outweigh another. The one with the highest rank will actually be an initial prefix; the next-highest-ranked will occupy a position as close to the left as possible: i.e., that of the second prefix, etc.

Such an analysis would allow us to resolve the other problem that arose with respect to clitic ordering, namely the invariance of internal order within the clitic sequence regardless of where that sequence appears relative to an anchor. That is because the relative ranking of constraints specifying the position of individual elements remains the same regardless of how those constraints are ranked with respect to some other constraint. As we will see below, this is exactly what is necessary to allow the same clitic sequence to be anchored in different ways in different environments.

In Section 9.2 above, we gave a descriptive characterization of the positions in which special clitics appear, which are entirely parallel to those in which affixes appear in words. In Anderson (1992) this typology was taken to specify the structural changes of a set of Word (and by natural extension, Phrase) Formation Rules: such rules make a specified phonological modification (such as the introduction of affixal material) within a specified domain; with reference to the initial, final, or head element of that domain; and either preceding or following the designated element. How are we to translate that derivationally oriented description into a more representational framework based on the OT assumptions we have just been considering?

Let us take Word (and Phrase) Formation rules to associate phonological material with a domain, without specifying where within that domain it is to be realized, with that being determined by constraints specific to the individual elements. Assume there is a family of constraints EDGEMOST(e,E,D), each of which says the element e should appear as close to the edge E (Left or Right) of the domain D as possible. Analogous constraints EDGEMOST(e,L,D) and EDGEMOST(e,R,D) say e should be at the left or right edge of D. A given clitic/affix is characterized as a prefix or as a suffix, depending on whether EDGEMOST(cl_i,L,D) dominates EDGEMOST(cl_i,R,D) or *vice versa*. The descriptive order of two clitics cl_i and cl_j, both prefixes or both suffixes, is determined by the dominance relation that obtains between their corresponding EDGEMOST constraints.

Post-initial infixes and second-position clitics can now be described by saying that the element in question (a) should be as close as possible to the left edge of its domain (a word or a syntactic constituent); but (b) should not be absolutely initial. To achieve this, let us assume a constraint family NON-INITIAL(e,D) that says the element e should not be initial within a domain D.[14] To characterize a clitic (or affix) cl_i as 'second position' on this view, what we want to say is that NON-INITIAL(cl_i,D) dominates EDGEMOST(cl_i,L,D). That means the clitic/affix will go as far to the left of D as possible without actually becoming initial: i.e., it will appear in second position within D.

In some instances, second position effects result from factors other than the prominence of NON-INITIAL(cl_j) constraints, since the phonology will do the right work without the need to invoke additional requirements. Consider Warlpiri, for example. In this language, auxiliary clitics are located in either first or second position within the clause, according to the principle in (11):

---

[14] Both the NON-INITIAL family and the EDGEMOST constraint family must be relativized to a given domain, but we will sometimes omit reference to this domain in the constraint formulations below, where it is either obvious or not directly relevant.

(11)   a. When the base of the auxiliary is monosyllabic (or Ø), the auxiliary
           follows the first word of the sentence.
        b. When the base of the auxiliary is disyllabic, the auxiliary can appear
           either initially or in second position.

The fact that the phonological shape of the base determines its position suggests
that the phonology is implicated in this effect, rather than its being a consequence of element-specific constraints.

To account for this distribution, we can note that the 'minimal word' in
Warlpiri, as in many languages, is disyllabic. An element containing fewer than
two syllables presumably cannot be independently footed within the phonology,
and thus must be treated as prosodically deficient. Let us assume that Stray
Adjunction[15] in Warlpiri always operates leftward. In order to be incorporated
into prosodic structure, then, an unfooted auxiliary base will have to be preceded by some other material. This, of course, will affect all bases with fewer
than two syllables, which are intrinsically incapable of being footed independently. When we say that auxiliary bases are subject to EDGEMOST(cl_i,L,S), the
furthest to the left that they can go is after the first word, if they are to be
footed. That accounts for their appearance in second position.

We can note that, according to Simpson (1991), even 'small' auxiliary bases
can appear in sentence-initial position, provided the sentence in question is
preceded closely in discourse by other material. In that event, the auxiliary attaches phonologically to the final word of the preceding sentence. In this case, it
is quite clear that the relevant requirement on the base is not that it be noninitial within its clause but that it attach to preceding material within a phonological phrase (or some other relevant domain). Where a larger domain is available for the (leftward) operation of Stray Adjunction, a sentence-initial auxiliary
base can still satisfy phonetic Full Interpretation.

Disyllabic bases, unlike shorter ones, contain enough material to constitute
a foot (and thus a word) on their own. Suppose we say that these bases have
two variants: one where the potential foot constitutes a phonological word, and
one where it does not. If we choose the prosodically autonomous form, then
EDGEMOST(cl_i,L,S) will locate it in initial position. If we choose the prosodically
weak alternant, EDGEMOST(cl_i,L,S) will give us second position just as for short
bases. Such lexical optionality is quite comparable to the fact that English *is* and
has have both full forms (/ɪz/ and /hæz/, respectively) and a simple clitic,
prosodically deficient variant (/z/ in both cases).

Such an account may be available for many languages, but it is unlikely to

---

[15] 'Stray Adjunction' refers to the partially language-specific principle(s) governing the way in
which prosodically-deficient material is incorporated into an adjacent prosodic constituent in order
to render it pronounceable with respect to a principle of Full Phonetic Interpretation. As such, it
subsumes the effects achieved in some theories of clitics by clitic-specific directionality of phonological attachment, a degree of lexical idiosyncrasy that seems unnecessary.

work for all. For instance, some second-position clitics are not prosodically deficient, in which case there is no phonological reason why they could not be initial:
it is simply a fact that they must satisfy NON-INITIAL(cl$_i$,D). In some languages,
some clitics appear in second position, but other (prosodically weak) clitics are
allowed to appear initially (e.g., Bulgarian *ne, šte* as opposed to others: cf
Legendre, this volume). In such a language, Stray Adjunction must in principle
be able to operate in either direction. The need to satisfy Full Interpretation could
thus be met in inital as well as second position, but the clitics are still required
to be non-initial. These arguments show that we cannot replace the constraint
NON-INITIAL(cl$_i$,D) entirely by appealing to phonological requirements.

Note that, unless we assume a 'Non-Final' analog of NON-INITIAL(e), the
present account has no mechanism for (and thus implicitly excludes) penultimate-
position clitics and affixes, one of the types that have figured in discussions such
as those of Klavans (1985) and Anderson 1992. The extent to which real examples
of these categories exist, however, is quite tenuous. It is entirely possible that it
was the apparent symmetry of the earlier system that impelled us to seek them;
within the present system, their absence follows without further stipulation
(though of course real, secure examples might force a revision that would accommodate this possibility). In any event, 'penultimate' or 'pre-final' position seems
about as marginal in clitic systems as in morphology, which re-inforces in a way
the decision to treat them as parts of the same grammatical domain.

Apart from languages like Warlpiri, where phonology is partly responsible for
the effect, we have effectively equated the notion that an element e appears in
second position within a domain D with the claim that the constraint
EDGEMOST(e,L,D) is highly-ranked within the overall hierarchy of constraints
governing PF in the relevant language, and NON-INITIAL(e,D)[16] even more so.
These two constraint families thus provide us with a rather parsimonious apparatus for characterizing exactly the three robustly-attested varieties of special
clitic. Two other types, pre-head and post-head clitics, do not require additional
apparatus, but rather reflect a different parametrization of the domain within
which clitics are introduced, as we will note below.

9.5 The Nature of 'Second Position'

As we saw above in discussing Serbo-Croatian, the notion of 'second position'
is subject to a certain amount of variation as to what occupies the related first

---

[16] Note that the relevant domain D to which these constraints are relevant is the same. Some
'second position' phenomena are somewhat more complex, however: Richardson (1997) suggests that
in Czech, second-position clitics are subject to EDGEMOST(e,L,IP) but are required to be NON-
INITIAL(e,CP). Since the left edges of IP and CP generally coincide in main clauses, this difference
only shows up when other material, such as certain topicalized elements, is part of CP but external
to IP.

position, and we must now ask how that variation is to be reconstructed within the OT-based theory under consideration. In particular, how are we to describe the difference between languages (or even constructions) in which a second-position element is preceded by a syntactic phrase, as opposed to those in which it is preceded by a single word?

Suppose we assume that in the derivation of the form of phrases, there is a high-ranking constraint (INTEGRITY(Word)) to the effect that a word may not be interrupted by phonological material that is not a part of that word. In virtually all languages,[17] this constraint is undominated. As a result, there will always be at least one phonological word between a second-position clitic and the left edge of the phrase, since the only way there could be less would be by violating either INTEGRITY(Word) or NON-INITIAL(cl$_p$,D), both of which (*ex hypothesi*) dominate EDGEMOST(cl$_p$,L,D). But given EDGEMOST(cl$_p$,L,D), the only way there could be more than one word before the clitic would be if some other higher-ranking constraint required it.

We can now describe cases where 'second position' means 'after the first phrase' by generalizing the notion of INTEGRITY to a constraint family: INTEGRITY(C), where C ranges over prosodic and syntactic category types. The basic instantiation of this notion is where C=Word, but other instances of the same family involve syntactic phrasal categories. Where C=XP, the effect is to require that phrases not contain elements that are not members of that phrase. INTEGRITY(Word) and INTEGRITY(XP) are obviously instances of the same family: constraints to the effect that material cannot be properly contained within a domain unless it represents a member or element of that domain.

In some languages, some phrasal types may be more 'permeable' than others. The literature on Serbo-Croatian suggests that in this language, speakers vary considerably as to what constructions can be interrupted by clitics when they appear sentence initially (cf Anderson 1996 and references cited there). In that case, certain instances of INTEGRITY(XP) would be highly ranked (e.g., the case where XP consists of a noun governing a following genitive), while the more general constraint would be ranked lower than EDGEMOST(e,L) constraints applicable to various second-position clitics. Another example is supplied by determiner clitics within the Macedonian or Bulgarian NP: these clitics generally follow exactly a single word at the left edge of their phrase, but when the NP begins with an adjective that has a preceding modifier, the clitic does not interrupt this phrase. Thus, compare the (Macedonian) examples in (6) above with those in (12), cited from Tomić (1996):

---

[17] The most notable *prima facie* exception to this generalization is Pashto: cf Tegey (1977), van der Leeuw (1995) and references cited there. Other authors, however (e.g. Roberts 1996) have argued that the constructions in which clitics appear to be located within a word in this language are actually internally complex so that they do not really violate INTEGRITY(Word).

(12)   a.   mošne rasprostraneta-**ta** upotreba
            very   widespread+the   use
            'the very widespread use'
       b.   so   maka dobiena-**ta**   stipendia
            with pain   obtained+the scholarship
            'the painfully obtained scholarship'

These facts indicate that in these languages, INTEGRITY(AdjP) is ranked above the clitic leftmost constraints.

Now suppose that where INTEGRITY(XP) is relevant, it is, like INTEG-RITY(Word), effectively undominated. In that case, the earliest that 'second position' can come is after the first phrasal daughter of the containing phrase, and so that is exactly where second-position clitics will be found. The difference between cases where clitics appear after the first word and those where they appear after the first phrase (either in general, or of a specifiable type), then, comes down to the question of where INTEGRITY(XP) constraints are ranked. We assume that INTEGRITY(Word) is essentially always undominated, but only if INTEGRITY(XP) is dominated by EDGEMOST(cl$_i$,L,D) constraints for the various clitics can their desire to get to the left violate phrasal (though still not word) integrity if necessary.

The apparatus developed to this point, involving the constraint families EDGEMOST, NON-INITIAL, and INTEGRITY, suffice to describe clitics (or affixes) located initially, finally, or in second position; and we have suggested above that the further possibility of pre-final elements may well be illusory. The remaining possibility for clitics, first raised in Kaisse (1985) and incorporated into the theory of Anderson (1992), is that of clitics located with respect to a phrase's (possibly non-peripheral) head.

Where clitics are located with respect to the head of a phrase, instead of treating this as the result of some other mechanism, we can accommodate it in terms of the relevant domain D within which the clitics are placed. That is, we say that they are actually placed (by the same constraints as those just discussed) within a domain circumscribed to contain only the head (e.g., V).[18]

In cases such as those of object clitics in the Romance languages, clitics are introduced within a domain circumscribed to the head verb—typically, the finite verb that also bears the properties of tense and (subject) agreement within the clause. They are then subject to constraints of the form EDGEMOST(cl,L,V) within that domain, ranked in such a way as to yield the observed order.

But now we are in a position to describe the cases where the clitic cluster appears sometimes before the verb (as when the verb is finite) and sometimes

---

[18] Note that this syntactic domain is not to be identified with the word that might otherwise be its only content: thus a clitic placed within the domain V, otherwise occupied only by a single word which is the lexical verb inserted there, is not the same as a morphological affix of the verb itself.

after the verb (when the verb is an imperative, or non-finite, etc.). All we have to say is that in languages like Italian, additional, even higher-ranking constraints require that imperatives (and such non-finite forms as are relevant) are constrained to appear at the left edge of the same (or an including) domain, and these constraints outrank the EDGEMOST(e,L,V) constraints applicable to the clitics. We thus derive the difference between the finite and the non-finite case as a single additional constraint on the non-finite form; while with the derivational theory there is no such simple and direct solution.

We can also accommodate the facts of European Portuguese, where the preverbal clitics become post-verbal when the finite verb is initial in IP:[19]

(13) a. Ninguem **o**-viu
          no-one   him–saw
          'No one saw him'

     b. Viu-**o**   o   João
          saw–him ART John
          'John saw him'

In such a case we say that the clitics are constrained not to occur sentence initially: that is, that the applicable Leftmost constraints (EDGEMOST(cl_i,L,V)) are themselves dominated by Non-Initial constraints (NON-INITIAL(cl_i,CP)). What is interesting about this situation is the fact that the domains within which the clitics (a) attract to the left and and (b) must be non-initial are distinct. In discussions of the Romance languages, this requirement that clitics follow a verb that is initial within IP (or in some cases, CP) while otherwise preceding the main (or finite) verb is known as the 'Tobler-Mussafia Law'. As is evident, our account extends straightforwardly to this variant of the second-position placement of clitics.

Notice that in cases where some constraint requiring e.g. non-finite verbs to be initial in their local domain dominates the corresponding leftmost constraints for clitics, the relative order of the EDGEMOST(cl_i,L) constraints is not affected. The internal order of the clitic sequence, therefore, remains invariant in all of these cases, as we saw above is necessary.

We have now provided a formal theory of clitics within an OT-like framework. This approach treats the introduction and placement of clitics as essentially a PF phenomenon, akin to morphology rather than to syntactic movement. On this view, the appearance of clitics in (several distinguishable variants of) second position is not an epiphenomenon, but rather results from the interac-

---

[19] As discussed by Barbosa (1996), several types of pre-verbal NP's as well as adverbs should be regarded as preposed and adjoined to IP within CP in Portuguese. As a result, the choice of whether clitics precede or follow the verb appears to depend on factors such as the referentiality of the subject, but in fact what is at stake is the requirement that referential (though not non-referential) subjects regularly move to this position, leaving the verb initial within its IP.

tion of constraints specifying their PF position: specifically, the interaction of
EDGEMOST(cl_i,L,D_x) and NON-INITIAL(cl_i,D_y) within the same domain (where
$x = y$) or different domains (where $x \neq y$). We now return, in the following section, to the issue of whether this notion of 'second position' can be unified with
the principles necessary to an understanding of the Verb-Second phenomenon.

9.6 Back to Verb-Second

The central issue in the recent literature on verb movement, and Verb-Second
in particular, is that of the motivation for such movement. That is, the location
in which the verb originates and the target position to which it moves are typically clear, at least within a particular view of clause structure, and what must
be elucidated is the principle that requires the dislocation in question.

A major theme in recent syntax is the notion that movement is forced by
'morphological' considerations. Theories invoking 'morphologically based movement' are not generally very closely related to a theory of morphology, however,
because the connection between the required movement and the concrete details
of word formation is often quite obscure or even contradictory. Rather than
movement being an integral part of the way words are to be constructed, the
image is sometimes more like that of a scavenger hunt in which the grammar
has scattered inflectionally relevant features here and there within the structure,
and it is a word's (or a constituent's) task to visit all of these places and reassure
itself that its features are exactly those that are called for. The actual workings
of morphology hardly come into play, if at all. Perhaps, however, movement in
some instances is based on more centrally morphological concerns than the need
to check features.

If clitics are introduced into the PF forms of phrases by a generalization of
essentially morphological mechanisms, and find their position within the representation through a system of hierarchically-ranked violable constraints, as
we proposed in Section 9.4 above, is there any relation between the notion of
'second position' as it relates to clitics and the principle(s) governing Verb-
Second, as Wackernagel proposed? Ignoring the conditions under which Verb-
Second is found,[20] the descriptive generalization which defines Verb-Second is
the following:

(14)   The verb which is marked for the tense, mood and agreement properties
         of a clause appears immediately after the first constituent of the clause.

That is, the formal markers of a clause's relational properties (a subset, perhaps,

---

[20] Thus, in German, Verb-Second characterizes declarative main clauses, while (most) subordinate
clauses are Verb-Final; across the Scandinavian languages, Verb-Second is found in clauses of all
types; etc. There are certainly interesting issues involved in distinguishing the Verb-Second environments of a language from others, as an abundant literature attests, but we ignore those matters here.

of its functional categories) appear as morphology on a verb that is placed immediately after the the first element of the clause in terms of its syntactic analysis.

This is not very different from the descriptive regularity governing second-position clitics: these, too, appear immediately after the first (non-'permeable') constituent of the clause. And there is a substantive analogy, as well: both finite main verbs and sentential clitics provide formal realizations for the content of a clause's functional categories in the form of inflectional features. From the present perspective, a Verb-Second language like, e.g., Icelandic differs from a second-position clitic language like Warlpiri in that the clause's grammatical features are realized by the inflectional form of the verb in Icelandic, but by phrasal affixes (the Auxiliary and agreement clitics) in Warlpiri.

Taking the analogy seriously, we ask how the descriptive regularity in (14) could be translated into the theoretical framework in which clitic placement has found its expression—or, in other words, how to express (14) in terms of ranked, violable constraints. In fact, we can characterize the position of the verb in a Verb-Second structure by saying that the locus of realization of tense, aspect, agreement, etc. is constrained as in (15), with these constraints outranking others relevant to clause internal word order.

(15)   a. NON-INITIAL(V_{fin},S)
        b. EDGEMOST(V_{fin},L,S)

A language that expresses the functional content of a clause (tense and various forms of Agreement) through a system of clitics in second position obviously contains a virtually identical constraint ranking, except that the constraints in question refer to clitics rather than inflected verbs as the exponents of the relevant properties. In the Verb-Second case, a high ranking for the constraints in (15) expresses the requirement that unless some even higher-ranking consideration intervenes, structures in which the finite verb is in second position are to be preferred to candidate structures in which it appears elsewhere.

What is the role of these constraints in the grammar? How, that is, do they participate in ensuring that the generalization in (14) holds? For the sake of argument, I assume that the framework within which an answer is to be sought involves the assumption that the finite verb in German main clauses moves from its underlying clause final position to one following the initial constituent of the clause. Commonly, this is assumed to be movement from a position I[21] to that of C, where C is itself preceded by a single phrasal position (Spec$_{CP}$). In the syntactic literature of the past 10 years or so, a derivation of Verb-Second clauses

---

[21] The initial movement of the verb from its base position to I simply reflects the fact that this verb bears inflection. On a view such as that of Anderson (1992) where functional content propagates as features, rather than constituting a head of its own, this movement is unnecessary.

something like that indicated in the phrase marker below has thus come to be widely accepted.

(16)

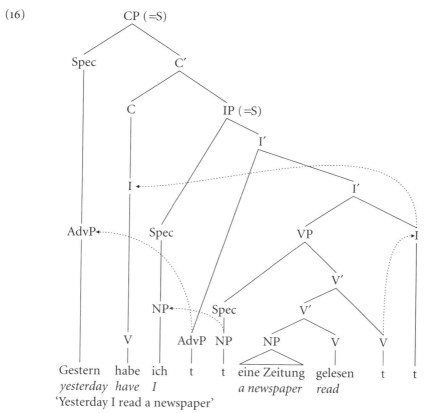

Gestern habe ich t t eine Zeitung gelesen t t
yesterday have I *a newspaper read*
'Yesterday I read a newspaper'

By no means all of the details of this derivation are crucial: what is important to understand is the movement of the inflected verb, represented here as going from I (the locus of inflectional properties) to C. Does such movement take place because of some property of the C position itself? Attempts to force this movement, for instance by positing some feature-checking relation between the positions Spec_CP and the verb in C, or by requiring C to be lexically filled, etc., amount to camouflaged language-particular stipulations of the requirement 'Move I to C'. The movement remains, accordingly, without independent motivation.

The suggestion of the present analysis is that it is not a need to check some hypothetical feature(s) that drives the placement of the verb, but rather the requirement that it be in second position. The verb moves from I to C (or whatever positions are involved) because (a) this movement is syntactically possible, and violates no constraints of the syntactic computational system; and (b) the

structures that result have fewer violations of the constraints in (15) than structures in which this movement has not taken place, and in which the verb is thus
farther from the left edge of the sentence. The movement of the inflectionally
marked (finite) verb into second position is thus forced by constraints on PF
representations that are nearly identical with those that obtain in a language that
realizes the functional content of a clause through phrasal affixation (special
clitics) in second position.

Note that the theory of Verb-Second presented here does not *per se* deny
that this involves movement of the verb into C (though it is neutral with respect
to whether this is the correct structural characterization of its target position).
This account simply proposes that the reason for such movement is to get the
verb to be in second position, rather than to check a feature or to fill C. The
thrust of the proposal concerns the motivation for the movement, not its
mechanics.

If this view is on the right track, we might expect to find cases where the
effect of the Verb-Second constraints (15) can be seen, but where the position
occupied by the verb in derived structure is not uniform (apart from the fact
that it follows the first element of the clause). This would be quite analogous to
the evidence we discussed above that second-position clitics do not in general
occupy a single, consistent position in the hierarchical structure of clauses (apart
from the fact that they are always preceded by exactly one other element). In
fact, that seems to be the case in Icelandic. Icelandic exhibits Verb-Second in
both main and subordinate clauses, as shown in (17)

(17) a. Jón harmar að þessa bók skuli ég hafa lesið
          John regrets   that this   book shall I   have read
          'John regrets that I have read this book'

      b. Ég veit   að það hefur enginn lesið bókina
          I   know that there has   no one read the book
          'I know that no one has read the book'

These examples above show that the finite verb (printed in bold in these
sentences) may follow (a) the subject; (b) a preposed, topicalized XP; or (c) an
expletive such as *það*. In addition, there is also a further possibility illustrated
in (18):

(18) a. Ég hélt   að kysst hefðu hana margir stúdentar
          I   thought that kissed had   her   many   students
          'I thought that many students had kissed her'

      b. *Ég hélt   að hana kysst hefðu margir stúdentar
          I   thought that her   kissed had   many   students
          'I thought that many students had kissed her'

Example (18a) illustrates the application of 'stylistic fronting', a construction with well-established and distinctive characteristics (Maling 1980; Jónsson 1991; Holmberg 1997a), quite separate from Topicalization. It involves the movement to a position before the inflected verb of a single word (participle, negative *ekki*, or certain adverbs).[22] Example (18b) shows that stylistic fronting cannot take place when the verb is otherwise non-initial in its clause: such a movement would of course produce a violation of Verb-Second.

There are several points to note about this construction: (a) As opposed to Topicalization, stylistic fronting involves no special emphasis, foregrounding, or other pragmatic effect; (b) stylistic fronting involves the movement of a single word, not a phrase, and thus must be an instance of head movement rather than of phrasal movement, with a head position rather than a phrasal position as its target;[23] and (c) stylistic fronting is possible exactly if the subject position is not overtly occupied (as in impersonals, or as a consequence of extraction, postposing, etc.—the 'subject gap condition' described by Maling).

(19)   a.   i.   Honum mætti standa á sama, hvað sagt væri   um   hann
                 to him   would be the same   what said would be about him
                 'It would be all the same to him, what was said about him'

       ii.   Honum mætti standa á sama, hvað sagt hefði Hjördís um   hann
             to him   would be the same   what said had   Hjördís about him
             'It would be all the same to him, what H. had said about him'

       b.   i.   Hann er sá eini, sem ekki er líklegur til að koma
                 he   is the only that not is likely to   come
                 'He is the only one that is not likely to come'

       ii.   Hún spurði, hvort   líklegur væri   hann til að koma
             she asked   whether likely   would be he   to   come
             'She asked whether he would be likely to come'

       c.   i.   þetta er bærinn, þar sem fæddir eru margir frægir Íslendingar
                 this is the town where   born   are many famous Icelanders
                 'This is the town where many famous Icelanders were born'

---

[22] Examples have occasionally been cited in the literature (cf. Holmberg 1997a) in which a PP or NP appears to have undergone stylistic fronting. Significantly, these cases mostly involve determinerless one-word NP's with abstract reference, or a single-word NP together with a phonologically short preposition (e.g., *í Oslo* 'in Oslo'). If such fronted units are in fact analysed as single words, as seems plausible, they are potentially compatible with the account offered here. Clearly phrasal NPs are at best marginally attested in stylistic fronting constructions: I assume that they can ultimately be analysed in some other way, perhaps as topicalized elements.

[23] Holmberg (1997b) discusses several cases cross-linguistically in which a head has apparently moved into a Spec position. This is therefore a possibility countenanced by at least some syntacticians, though the resultant weakening of the structure preserving nature of movement operations is obviously to be avoided if possible.

    ii. þetta er bréfið,   sem ekki skrifaði Helgi
       this is the letter that not wrote Helgi
    'This is the letter that Helgi didn't write'

In each of the pairs in (19), the second sentence is bad because stylistic fronting has applied in the presence of an overt subject, while the first sentence of each pair illustrates the possibility of applying the rule when the subject is not in its base position.

    Analyses of stylistic fronting in the existing literature have generally fallen into two classes. Some, such as Maling (1980) have assumed that the fronted element actually moves to the subject position. This gives a natural account of the relation between the construction and the requirement of a subject gap, but requires us to say that a head moves to a phrasal position, a problematic assumption as noted above. The other possibility (Jónsson 1991) is to treat stylistic fronting as adjunction to the finite verb; but on that analysis, there is no longer any natural connection between such movement and the requirement of a gap in subject position. It seems reasonable to say that no satisfactory account of the structure and motivation of stylistic fronting constructions has yet emerged, despite the very considerable attention that has been paid to them.[24]

    Let us attempt to find a unified account of the basic properties of Icelandic constituent order as just sketched. The properties of ordinary clauses (as illustrated in (17)) argue that the base positions for the subject and for the verb must be preceded by a phrasal position, to which some phrase can move as an instance of topicalization. The properties of the stylistic fronting construction, on the other hand, indicate that there must also be a non-phrasal, head position preceding the base positions of subject and verb, a position which can serve as the target of this distinct movement. Let us then assume (as is general in the literature) that Icelandic has basic SVO order, and that clauses have the structure in (20):

(20)   [(XP) (X) [(Subject) [$_{VP}$ (Verb) . . .

'X' and 'XP' in (20) might be 'C' and 'Spec$_{CP}$', 'Top' and 'Spec$_{TopP}$', or something else, but nothing here hinges on the choice of one or another categorial analysis.

    We can now describe the Verb-Second phenomenon in Icelandic as follows. Tense/aspect and agreement are realized on the main verb (where they appear as its inflection). If we then rank NON-INITIAL(V_{fin},S) above EDGEMOST(V_{fin},L,S)[25] and both of these high in the hierarchy of constraints governing PF, this will

---

[24] I include the account of Holmberg (1997a) among those that do not really resolve the problems of stylistic fronting, though a discussion of the very different assumptions underlying Holmberg's analysis would take me much too far afield here.

[25] The domain of these constraints is simply left as 'S', without further commitment about the relevant structure. The domain within which Icelandic Verb-Second applies generally includes all of the main clause, and excludes an introductory complementizer in a subordinate clause.

force a preference for structures in which the finite verb appears immediately following the first constituent of the clause.

It will now be apparent that there are several diverse ways in which structures that are relatively optimal with respect to the Verb-Second constraint can be formed. First, if no phrase moves to the (topic) XP position in (20), and everything remains in its 'natural' base position, Verb-Second is satisfied without further movement. This avoids the claim that where nothing else is topicalized, the subject must move to topic position: the only motivation for that movement is the assumption that Verb-Second must consist in the movement of the verb to C (and thus, something else must always appear in $Spec_{CP}$). On the present account, Verb-Second can be satisfied without the sometimes counter-factual claim that subjects are always topical if nothing else is.

Secondly, some phrase may move from clause-internal position to the initial XP position in (20) where it is interpreted as a topic. In that case, if the subject remains in place, the finite verb must move to the X position in (20).

Thirdly, there may be no topicalized phrase in the topical XP position; if the finite verb precedes the subject (perhaps because this is indefinite, or has been postposed), an expletive (*það*) can be inserted in the initial X position to avoid a violation of NON-INITIAL(V_{fin},S), as in (21):

(21) það   eru margir frægir Íslendingar fæddir í þessum bæ
      EXPL *are many famous Icelanders   born in this   town*
      'There were many famous Icelanders born in this town'

As is well known, expletives in Icelandic appear only in clause-initial position, which is also the only position where they would be motivated under this analysis.

Finally, if no phrase moves to topic XP, but there is a gap in the subject position, 'stylistic fronting' can move a participle, or *ekki*, etc. to the initial X position. The relation between stylistic fronting and a subject gap follows from the fact that the former moves an element into a pre-subject position, where it would produce a violation of Verb-Second exactly if the subject were overt. The verb itself could not move to the left of such a filled subject position since the head position that would be the target of such movement is already filled by the stylistically fronted element.

What unites the position of the verb in all of these cases is not its configurational definition but rather the fact that in each instance, the verb is second in its clause. And of course, this is exactly the claim of an analysis on which Verb-Second results from a mechanism similar to that governing second-position clitics. The non-uniform nature of the structures in which Verb-Second is satisfied is quite comparable to the point made by Bošković (1995) (see Section 9.3. above) concerning the nature of second position in the placement of Serbo-Croatian clitics, and similar points made by Legendre in relation to the position of clitics in Bulgarian and Romanian.

There is one further issue to be resolved in connection with this analysis. If Verb-Second results from a 'morphological' imperative which is formally more or less the same as what governs second-position clitic placement, why do we never find languages in which the finite verb appears (at least as an option) immediately after the first *word* of its clause, rather than (uniformly) after an initial phrase? Why, that is, are certain initial phrases in some languages 'permeable' for the purpose of clitic placement, but the parallel possibility is never instantiated with respect to Verb-Second?

There is a straightforward answer to this: such placement of the finite verb is never found because the syntax cannot in general access this position. Clitics are placed by 'affixation' rules that modify the phonological shape of the form; it is thus possible for these rules to introduce material anywhere in the structure, subject only to the Integrity constraints. Verb-Second, on the other hand, is the result of syntactic movement, and the only structures the syntax provides for comparative evaluation by the constraint system are ones that instantiate well formed syntactic operations.

We assume that the computational system involves a subsystem which produces a set of formally possible structures, and a set of constraints on PF that choose the optimal one from among these various candidates. The former subsystem is usually referred to as 'GEN' in the OT literature, and we assume that it incorporates basic notions of syntactic well-formedness such that only structures conforming to fundamental principles (e.g., $\bar{X}$-theory) and involving syntactically possible movements are presented for comparative evaluation by the constraint system. Thus, the only structures that are available for evaluation at PF (with respect to constraints such as EDGEMOST(V_{fin},L,S) and NON-INITIAL(V_{fin},S)) are ones that are syntactically well-formed in terms of these general principles. Insofar as syntactic movement of the verb to a position after a sentence-initial word but internal to a larger containing phrase is disallowed by the general nature of movement, candidate structures of this sort are not found in the output of GEN, and thus no language preferring them could exist.

9.7 Conclusion

We see, then, that we can incorporate an OT-like view of the mechanisms determining appropriate surface forms into the overall picture developed in *A-Morphous Morphology*. We can treat clitics as described by essentially the same theoretical devices as affixes, thus preserving the generalization argued for in Anderson (1992) that a single theory is applicable both to words and to phrases. While Optimality Theory has primarily been employed in the description of phonological phenomena, its originators have stressed that its basic notions might well be applicable to a much broader range of facts in language. The present chapter suggests that this is indeed true, and that OT may well provide a better way to express the generalizations of a comprehensive theory of the morphology of words and phrases.

Essentially the same account extends naturally to the other principal class of 'second-position' phenomena in natural language, Verb-Second. What second-position clitics and Verb-Second have in common is the following: both reflect constraints requiring the grammatical properties of a phrase or clause—that is, the functional categorial content that is often treated as a separate structural head (I) or set of heads (T, Agr_s, Agr_o, etc.)—to be aligned as closely as possible with its left edge, without being absolutely initial. They differ, on the other hand, in that clitics are introduced by a phonological mechanism of affixation, while Verbs that inherit the functional properties of the clause they head are subject to movement by normal syntactic mechanisms.

The discovery that grammatical well-formedness involves an interplay of 'pure' syntactic principles with others of a more 'morphological' character may seem somewhat surprising. The descriptive burden of the syntactic system, on the view presented above, is distributed across (at least) two distinct parts of the grammar. On the one hand, a basic computational system describes a set of formally possible structures. Much of the burden of describing just which movements are not only possible but forced, however, falls not on this part of the grammar but rather on a system of hierarchically-ranked constraints that choose the 'best' from among a number of syntactically possible structures. These constraints refer to properties of PF, and are clearly integrated with principles that are a natural extension of those governing word formation.

The class of possible languages thus lies in the intersection of the morphological and the syntactic possibilities. In these terms, both the syntactic and the morphological principles can be stated with a very high degree of generality, leaving many apparent idiosyncrasies as matters of their interaction. And that, of course, is just the kind of result a modular approach to grammar is supposed to lead to.

The properties that constrain the range of structures produced by GEN have a kind of necessary and inviolable character, while those that choose the optimal output from among the formal possibilities are intrinsically contingent, violable, and hierarchical. Indeed, much discussion of principles such as 'greed', 'procrastinate', etc. in the recent syntactic literature attributes to them a kind of relative status: they rank one derivation with respect to another, rather than defining the very logical space within which derivations are carried out, as do principles such as those of X̄-theory or anaphoric binding. The division of labor between these two sorts of principle remains an empirical issue, of course, but the fundamental architecture of grammar that we assume here is not radically innovative.

It is not obvious that Wackernagel would recognize his original insight in the form in which this unification is achieved here, but the fact remains that his attempt to connect two prominent roles of the number 'two' in language was undoubtedly more appropriate than some subsequent writers have suggested.

9.8 References

Anderson, S. R. (1984). 'Kwakwala syntax and the Government-Binding theory'. In E.-D. Cook and D. B. Gerdts (eds), *The Syntax of Native American Languages*. [Syntax and Semantics 16]. New York, Academic Press, 21–75.

—— (1992). *A-Morphous Morphology*. Cambridge, Cambridge University Press.

—— (1993). 'Wackernagel's revenge: Clitics, morphology and the syntax of second position'. *Language* 69, 68–98.

—— (1995). 'Rules and constraints in describing the morphology of phrases'. *Proceedings of the Chicago Linguistic Society* 31 [Proceedings of the Parasession on Clitics, vol 2], 15–31.

—— (1996). 'How to put your clitics in their place'. *The Linguistic Review* 13, 165–91.

Barbosa, P. (1996). 'Clitic placement in European Portuguese and the position of subjects'. In Halpern and Zwicky (1996), 1–40.

Boškovic, Ž. (1995). 'Participle movement and second position clitics in Serbo-Croatian'. *Lingua* 96, 245–66.

Browne, W. (1974). 'On the problem of enclitic placement in Serbo-Croatian'. In R. D. Brecht and C. V. Chvany (eds), *Slavic Transformational Syntax*. *Michigan Slavic Materials* vol. 10. Ann Arbor, 36–52.

Chomsky, N. (1995). *The Minimalist Program*. Cambridge, MA, MIT Press.

Eythórsson, T. (1996). 'Functional categories, cliticization, and verb movement in the early Germanic languages'. In H. Thráinsson, S. D. Epstein, and S. Peter (eds), *Studies in Comparative Germanic Syntax*, vol. ii. Dordrecht, Kluwer, 109–39.

Friederich, J. (1974). *Hethitisches Elementarbuch I*. Heidelberg, Carl Winter.

Garrett, A. (1990). *The Syntax of Anatolian Pronominal Clitics*. Doctoral dissertation, Harvard University.

Golston, C. (1991). 'Clisis in Hittite'. Ms, UCLA.

Halle, M. (1957). 'In defense of the number two'. *Studies Presented to Joshua Whatmough on his 60th Birthday*. The Hague, Mouton, 65–72.

Halpern, A. L. and A. Zwicky (eds), (1996). 'Approaching second: Second position clitics and related phenomena'. *CSLI Publications*, Stanford, CA, Center for the Study of Language and Information.

Harrison, K. D. (1997). 'The morphology of special NP clitics: The definite article in Albanian'. In Kaiser (1997a).

Hoffner, Jr., H. A. (1986). 'Studies in Hittite grammar'. In H. A. Hoffner and G. M. Backman (eds), *Kaniššuwar: A Tribute to Hans A. Güterbock*. Number 23 in *Assyriological Studies*. Chicago, Oriental Institute, University of Chicago, 83–94.

Holmberg, A. (1997a). 'Scandinavian stylistic fronting: Movement of phonological features in the syntax'. *Working Papers in Scandinavian Syntax* 60, 82–124.

—— (1997b). 'The true nature of Holmberg's generalization'. *Proceedings of the North Eastern Linguistics Society*, vol. 27. Amherst, MA, GLSA, 203–17.

Insler, S. (1997). 'The phonological organization of the Rigvedic clitic chain'. In Kaiser (1997a), 75–88.

Jónsson, J. S. (1991). 'Stylistic fronting in Icelandic'. *Working Papers in Scandinavian Syntax* 48, 1–43.

Kaiser, L. (ed.) (1997a). 'Y.A.L.E. 1: Studies in the Morphosyntax of Clitics'. Dept. of Linguistics, Yale University.

—— (1997b). 'CPR for Korean type III nominalizations'. In S. Kuno *et al.* (eds), *Harvard Studies in Korean Linguistics*, vol. vii. Seoul, Hanshin Publishing Company. To appear.

Kaisse, E. M. (1985). *Connected Speech.* New York, Academic Press.

Kiparsky, P. (1995). 'Indo-European origins of Germanic syntax'. In A. Battye and I. Roberts (eds), *Clause Structure and Language Change.* Oxford, Oxford University Press, 140–69.

Klavans, J. L. (1985). 'The independence of syntax and phonology in cliticization'. *Language* 61, 95–120.

Legendre, G. (1997a). 'Macedonian clitics'. ESCOL '97, Yale University.

Legendre, G. (1997b). 'Optimal Romanian clitics: A cross-linguistic perspective'. *Technical Report JHU-CogSci-97-9*, Dept. of Cognitive Science, the Johns Hopkins University.

Maling, J. (1980). 'Inversion in embedded clauses in modern Icelandic'. *Íslenskt Mál* 2, 175–93.

Nespor, M. (1994). 'The phonology of clitic groups'. In L. Hellan and H. van Riemsdijk (eds), *Clitic Doubling and Clitic Groups*, vol. 5, ESF-Eurotyp Working Papers, 67–90.

Perlmutter, D. M. (1971). *Deep and Surface Structure Constraints in Syntax.* New York, Holt, Rinehart & Winston.

Prince, A. and P. Smolensky (1993). 'Optimality theory: Constraint interaction in generative grammar'. Ms, Rutgers University and University of Colorado.

Richardson, M. (1997). 'Czech clitics: 2P or not 2P, that is the question'. In Kaiser (1997a).

Roberts, T. (1996). 'The optimal second position in Pashto'. ROA-174.

Simpson, J. (1991). *Warlpiri Morpho-Syntax: A Lexicalist Approach* [*Studies in Natural Language and Linguistic Theory*]. Dordrecht, Kluwer Academic.

Tegey, H. (1977). *The Grammar of Clitics: Evidence from Pashto and Other Languages.* Doctoral dissertation, University of Illinois.

Tomić, O. M. (1996). 'The Balkan Slavic nominal clitics'. In Halpern and Zwicky (1996), 511–36.

van der Leeuw, F. (1995). 'Cliticization as alignment to morphological slots'. *Proceedings of the Chicago Linguistic Society* 31 [*Proceedings of the Parasession on Clitics*, vol. 2], 168–80.

Wackernagel, J. (1892). 'Über ein Gesetz der indogermanischen Wortstellung'. *Indogermanische Forschungen* 1, 333–436.

Wilder, C. (1997). 'English finite auxiliaries in syntax and phonology'. In J. R. Balck and V. Motapanyane (eds), *Clitics, Pronouns and Movement.* Amsterdam and Philadelphia, John Benjamins, 321–62.

Williams, E. S. (1994). *Thematic Structure in Syntax.* Cambridge, MA, MIT Press.

Zwicky, A. M. (1977). *On Clitics.* Indiana University Linguistics Club.

10

Optimal Syntax[1]

Joan Bresnan

10.1 Introduction

Most OT syntax work to date has taken the OUTPUT to consist of representational simulations of transformational derivations using chains and traces
(e.g. Grimshaw 1997; Legendre, Smolensky, and Wilson 1998; Grimshaw and
Samek-Lodovici 1998).[2] The purpose of these notes is to show that there may be
advantages, both conceptual and empirical, to adopting a more radically
nonderivational theory of GEN, based on a parallel correspondence theory of
syntactic structures.

Parallel correspondence theories are familiar in syntax from LFG (e.g. Bresnan
ed. 1982, Dalrymple *et al.* 1995), autolexical syntax (e.g. Sadock 1991), synchronous and unification-based tree adjoining grammars (e.g. Shieber and Shabes
1990; Vijay-Shanker and Joshi 1990), some work in the categorial tradition (e.g.
Oehrle 1981), and functional syntactic theories (e.g. Van Valin 1993). They are
widely adopted in contemporary non-derivational phonology, appearing in OT
phonology in the form of alignment and correspondence theories (McCarthy and
Prince 1993, 1995); and they have recently been advocated as the general architecture of Universal Grammar by Jackendoff (1996). However, they have not yet
been integrated with OT syntax. In what follows I will explore how OT fits together with a variant of parallel correspondence syntactic theory based on recent
work in LFG (Bresnan 1998 and references therein). Specifically I will develop an
imperfect correspondence approach to 'head movement' phenomena within OT,
and compare it to the framework of Grimshaw (1997), which assumes representations based on serial derivations or their chain-theoretic simulations.

In the example candidate structure of (1) (similar to those adopted in Grimshaw 1997), head movement has taken place in GEN, recorded by annotating

[1] For valuable comments on earlier versions of this work, I am grateful to Andrew Bredenkamp,
Edward Flemming, Jane Grimshaw, Dick Hudson, Scott Myers, Louisa Sadler, Ida Toivonen, Nigel
Vincent, Steve Wechsler, and a reviewer for the present volume, though they are not responsible for
my use of their comments.

[2] Notable exceptions include Legendre, Raymond, and Smolensky (1993), Aissen (1998), and Sells
(1997).

the extended X′ structure with a trace (*t*) index coindexed with the verb in I:

(1)

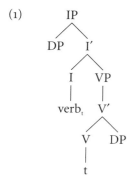

Those syntactic constraints which apply to the initial structure of a serial derivation, prior to movement, are applied to the substructure of the output which preserves information about the initial structure. For example, verbal valence (or θ-grid) requirements must apply to the structure in (1) by using the location of the trace *t* of the verb under V′ to satisfy the constraint, not the derived position of the verb under I, which would violate it (because valence satisfaction requires locality to the head). See Grimshaw's (1997) application of the θ-criterion for an example. In contrast, those syntactic constraints which apply to derived structures in a serial derivation, subsequent to movement, are applied only to the substructures of the output which do not express the relevant information about the initial structure. For example, a constraint that determines overt word order must not in general apply to the initial structures in transformational derivations, and so traces must be exempted from it (see for example Grimshaw's Case-Left constraint (1997: 406–7)). Thus, in general, different regions of a single tree structure are placed in correspondence through coindexing (trace) annotations, and are used to satisfy constraints that apply at different points in the serial derivation. The linking or correspondence mechanism across these different subregions of tree structure is the transformation.

Parallel correspondence theory provides a more general model of the same relations. Instead of co-indexing a single tree structure with itself, with different subtrees functioning as the domains of different sets of constraints, we co-index two parallel (synchronous, copresent) structures, a categorial structure and a feature structure in LFG, as illustrated in (2).[3] The cor-

---

[3] Here the attribute SPEC refers generally to the most prominent argument of verbal and nominal categories (the subject and possessor, respectively); the attribute COMPL refers to lexically selected complement arguments such as objects and predicate complements (OBJ and XCOMP in LFG). Other parallel structures are also included in the general theory: semantic structure, prosodic structure, information structure, etc., but I will limit discussion to c- and f-structures in what follows. See Choi (1999) for an analysis of the interactions of information structure and the syntax of scrambling in the present framework.

respondence between structures is indicated by co-indexing in this diagram:[4]

(2)   c-structure: f-structure:

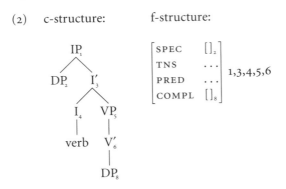

The correspondence function associates each c-structure node with a unique (but not necessarily distinct) f-structure, which is given a numerical subscript in this example. Thus the leftmost DP node is associated with the SPEC f-structure $[\ ]_2$, the rightmost DP node with the COMPL f-structure $[\ ]_8$, and the V and I nodes and their projections are all associated with the outermost f-structure, which bears the multiple subscripts 1, 2, 4, 5, 6. Note that in LFG (as in autolexical syntax) the correspondence mapping is imperfect (not being a one-to-one function from domain onto codomain), relates non-homogeneous structures, and so is formally non-transformational.

The categorial (c-)structure represents the variety of surface forms, showing the order of overt elements; the feature (f-)structure represents language-independent content, including the roles and functions of arguments and predicators, abstracting away from their linear order and constituency. This scheme eliminates the problem of stipulating which constraints apply to which points in the derivation, or to which types of constituents in the representational simulations of a derivation: moved or unmoved, projected or unprojected, null or overt, trace or non-trace. For example, because the f-structure lacks information about linear order, constraints on the overt positions of constituents must apply to c-structure; because the c-structure lacks information about predicate argument structure, constraints on valence satisfaction (e.g. Grimshaw's θ-criterion, which corresponds to LFG 's Completeness and Coherence conditions) apply to f-structure. Constraints also govern the correspondence between c- and f-structures.

Further results follow from imperfect correspondence. Because the mapping from tree to feature structure is many-to-one, for example, large regions of categorial structure, such as the entire verbal extended projection in (2) includ-

---

[4] See Kaplan (1995) for the formal Theory of Correspondence.

ing nodes 1 and 5, may be mapped into a single feature structure. This means that in principle the main predicator of a large structure (in (2) this is the verb) can appear overtly in any of the range of different categorial positions for heads that correspond to the same feature structure, while still ensuring satisfaction of its valence requirements. Which positions it actually appears in depends not on movement (the paired structures are generated without movement), but on *correspondence*, by principles discussed below. Correspondence constraints determine how lexical items correspond to categorial structure and how the categorial structure corresponds to the feature structure.

This approach to head movement phenomena, we will see, can explain the generalizations captured under the movement approach and its representational simulations based on chains. Yet it is not a notational variant of the movement approach; it is more general. While movement configurations co-index only one lexically-filled position with a chain of empty ones, imperfect correspondence allows for 'co-indexing' (formally, a correspondence mapping) between multiple lexically-filled positions. Phenomenologically, this means that information from the same feature structure may appear distributed across multiple lexical heads in the categorial structure. Such situations occur in many languages with multiple inflectional exponents of the same morphosyntactic category. For example, tense marking in the Australian language Wambaya (Nordlinger, 1998b) occurs simultaneously on both auxiliary (I) and main verb (V). In Wambaya, the tense values of a clause arise compositionally from the individual inflections on I and V which have overlapping values. Nordlinger and Bresnan (1996) show that the tense system exploits the general theory of imperfect correspondence outlined here, unifying information from different regions of the verbal extended projection.[5] Thus while the parallel correspondence approach can capture the valid generalizations modelled by movement, it also encompasses to the merger of information from multiple unmoved heads.

Another aspect of imperfect correspondence is that some feature structures may lack any correspondents in the syntactic tree: the correspondence mapping is 'into' but not 'onto'. The result is the existence of elements which have real functions in syntax but are not expressed as tree constituents: null arguments and other covert elements. The source of feature structures not represented by tree nodes can be the lexicon, the morphology, or the discourse context. A simple illustration is given in (3), showing a Chicheŵa verb under the analysis of Bresnan and Mchombo (1987) (modulo n. 3), and (4), showing an equivalent English clause. As (3) graphically illustrates, in Chicheŵa it is the subject and object morphology of the verbal head (represented by the prefixes *ndi-* and *mú-*) that specifies the pronominal content of the f-structure arguments.

---

[5] Niño (1995) analyses Finnish negation from this perspective.

(3)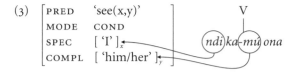

(4)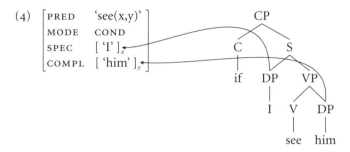

The theory that morphology and the lexicon construct complex feature structures independently of phrase structure has a long tradition within LFG (see Bresnan and Mchombo 1995 for references) and is being developed and exemplified in much recent work (e.g. Börjars, Vincent, and Chapman 1997; Nordlinger 1998a; Sadler 1997; Bresnan forthcoming; among others).

Thus in this approach the informational complexity of words may match that of large syntactic phrases without the need to assume that words are dependent on the principles of structural formation of syntactic phrases. Words may be functionally equivalent to phrases in the sense of corresponding to the same feature structures, yet they exhibit lexical integrity in the sense of being alternative forms of expression constructed from different elements and by different principles of combination (Bresnan and Mchombo 1995; Mohanan 1995; Börjars, Vincent, and Chapman 1997; Sells 1995). In a parallel correspondence theory of GEN, therefore, the same feature structure may correspond to candidate expressions arising independently from the morphology and syntax. The resulting competition can give rise to distributional patterns quite atypical of movement, as we will see.

10.2 Recasting Grimshaw's (1997) Framework

Let us now turn to the work on head movement in OT pioneered by Grimshaw (1997). While Grimshaw advances our understanding of the distribution of heads, there are some drawbacks to her transformational conception of GEN.

First, Grimshaw (1997) rather uncomfortably embeds the transformational framework within the OT framework. GEN includes a transformational derivation, alongside a means of base generating all transformationally derived structures. (In other words, for every transformationally derived candidate, there are isomorphic base-generated candidates with empty categories EC in place of all traces *t*.) Derivational information is preserved in the output by distinguishing multiple types of empty heads: *t* and [*e*], in addition to [∅] filled by a phonologically null morpheme (as in the SPEC of yes-no questions) and *e* (a category position being empty because the category is optional and is not present in the tree structure). Although these representational distinctions are widespread in much of contemporary syntax, they are reminiscent of the once widespread use of different types of abstract boundary symbols (+, $, etc.) in the segment strings of early generative phonology to encode junctures between higher-level (nonstring) structures such as morphemes or syllables. In effect, information about non-tree structures (semantic and functional) is being encoded into the syntactic tree. It works because the information projected from the other levels is real, but it is not naturally represented. One indication that this representation is not the most natural is that it requires numerous stipulations to be added to the constraints (such as exempting traces from directionality constraints, or heads in moved positions from the θ-criterion) to ensure their correct application as Grimshaw (1997: 408–9) does.

Secondly, Grimshaw's syntactic analysis of heads includes non-uniformities in the analysis of their morphological inflections. Grimshaw proposes (382) that 'in the English system inflection is morphologically associated with a V (i.e. it is lexically attached to a V head), whereas in French it is syntactically projected as head of a projection'. Surely it would be preferable to account for the different word order properties of English and French verbs without assuming that French inflections are syntactically reified as phrase structure heads while those of English are not. More generally, the syntactic analysis seems to accept the most anti-lexicalist syntactic accounts of inflectional morphology, cheek by jowl with lexicalist versions, the choice depending on the language.

Thirdly, the proposed universal constraint set raises questions of generality. The core constraints (OP-SPEC, OB-HD) reflect real or defensible syntactic generalizations (interrogative words tend to reside in prominent peripheral positions in phrase structure, modelled as SPEC of FP; subject-verb inversion is induced to provide heads for these projections which would otherwise lack them). Yet other constraints seem rather framework-internal, referring to specific mechanisms of the transformational GEN. Should we allow reference to derivational (or more generally GEN) mechanisms at all? Intuitively, constraints should be about linguistic substance, not mechanisms or operations. Thus if we can capture the same generalizations without mechanistic (framework internal) constraints, so much the better.

Finally, there is the question of the generality of the theory of structures. Grimshaw's theory is narrowly concerned with structural properties of English and a few closely-related European languages, and her choice of GEN reflects this. There is no way to capture the idea that morphology competes with syntax: morphologically complete words may carry information functionally equivalent to that carried by complex hierarchical phrase structures and may preempt or

be preempted by such structures. As we will see, such competition plays a hith-
erto unexplained role in English auxiliary inversion.

These considerations motivate work on a reanalysis of Grimshaw (1997), consistent with the aims of her (substantive) theory. I propose to do this by replacing her GEN with an LFG version (Bresnan, forthcoming) as an exploratory
exercise. The LFG version is well suited to this exploration because (i) it incorporates a lexicalized version of extended X′ theory (which closely matches
Grimshaw (1991, 1997)) as a typological option; (ii) it derives the effects and the
generalizations of head movement from general principles without any movements; (iii) it is completely compatible with a strong form of lexical integrity;
(iv) it permits both non-configurational and mixed configurational/non-confi-
gurational language types; (v) due to its parallel, correspondence-based architecture, it allows a coherent and explicit formulation of certain types of faithfulness
constraints in syntax that remain obscure under the derivational approach; and
(vi) it can explain distributional patterns that remain unaccountable under
movement theories and their simulations. I'll modestly call this version 'Optimal
Syntax' in what follows.

10.2.1   *The Input*

In OT the INPUT requires a more abstract characterization of lexical elements
and sentential constituents than the customary starting-point for a syntactic
derivation in most generative frameworks, which usually includes an enumeration of specific morphemes or language-particular lexical heads. For OT syntax
the INPUT must represent morphosyntactic content in a universal, language-
independent form. The role of the input is to provide a baseline against which
the universal candidate set of possible analyses is evaluated to determine the
optimal output. Which of the universally available candidates are optimal for a
given language depends only on the ranking of constraints, not on any language-
particular differences in input. (This is called the principle of 'richness of the
base'; see Smolensky (1996b) for recent discussion and references.) Thus a more
principled means of explaining language variation is required than simply stipulating morpholexical differences among languages.

Grimshaw says little about what the INPUT is in her theory: for a verbal extended projection it consists of a lexical head and its argument structure, an
assignment of lexical heads to its arguments, and 'a specification of associated
tense and aspect' (376). She gives the sole example input shown in (5):

(5)   see(x,y), x = John, y = who

Although Grimshaw uses English words to represent the lexical heads of the
input informally, it is evident that a more abstract characterization of the input
is required by the principle of richness of the base.

In Optimal Syntax the INPUT for a verbal extended projection will be a (possibly underspecified) feature structure representing some given morphosyntactic

content independently of its forms of expression. (5) would be replaced by (6), for example:

$$(6) \quad \begin{bmatrix} \text{PRED} & \text{`see(x,y)'} \\ \text{GF}_1 & \begin{bmatrix} \text{PRED} & \text{`NAMED-}\textit{John'} \\ \text{GEND} & \text{MASC} \\ \text{NUM} & \text{SG} \end{bmatrix}_x \\ \text{GF}_2 & \begin{bmatrix} \text{OP} & \text{Q} \\ \text{PRED} & \text{`PERSON'} \end{bmatrix}_y \\ \text{TNS} & \text{PAST} \end{bmatrix}$$

Exactly as in (5), (6) represents the relations of the lexical heads 'see', 'John' and 'who' to each other and specifies the clausal property of tense; unlike (5) (6) replaces the English-specific lexical heads with structured sets of abstract features representing their morphosyntactic content (insofar as it is systematic) in a language-independent format. Also unlike (5), (6) asserts that the main lexical head has the function of PRED(icator) and that 'John' and 'who' have under-specified (or generalized) grammatical functions GF.[6] The differences between (5) and (6) are mainly notational, but (6) has the advantage of belonging to a mathematically well-defined system that has been studied in formal, morphosyntactic, and computational domains. This makes it possible to effectively enumerate the harmonically-ordered candidate set for a given input, for example. The desirability of this more abstract conception of the morphosyntactic INPUT is further discussed and exemplified in Bresnan (1997a, b, c).

10.2.2 *The Candidate Set*

In OT, competing candidates are evaluated as structural analyses of the content specified by the input. For learnability the input must be recoverable from the output (Tesar and Smolensky 1998), either by being contained in the output (Prince and Smolensky 1993) or by being in correspondence with it (McCarthy and Prince 1995), and the output must also contain the overt data of linguistic perception. Thus the candidate set from which the output is selected is subject to seemingly conflicting requirements of being both highly abstract (to contain the language-independent input) and highly concrete and 'surfacy' (to contain the perceptible overt data).

For Grimshaw, the candidate set of analyses of the input consists of all extended projections (in the sense of Grimshaw (1991)) which conform to X′ theory.[7] All nodes are optionally absent from the output.[8] Hence, nodes may be

---

[6] The subscripts on GF in (6) are arbitrary; technically, each instance of the symbol 'GF' in (6) must be distinct to respect the functional uniqueness axiom on f-structures. Underspecification (or generalization) of attributes can be formalized using Johnson's (1988) model of attribute names as feature structures.

[7] The extended projections of VP include IP and CP; these are 'verbal extended projections'. DP is an extended nominal projection of NP.

omitted in the output trees in ways that would violate strict endocentricity in
X' theory. For example, a head X node may be omitted from an XP in the output.[9] These X' structures may be further annotated by indices [t, t_i, e_j, etc.] that
represent traces of movement transformations in GEN. Finally, though no reference is made to where or how Logical Form (LF) is generated or accessed in her
framework of assumptions, Grimshaw assumes (376) that 'competing candidates
have non-distinct logical forms', meaning minimally that they must be truth
functionally equivalent.

The version of X' theory Grimshaw adopts for her candidate set is very close
to that of recent work in LFG (e.g. Kroeger 1993; King 1995; Choi 1999; Nordlinger 1998a; Berman 1996, 1997; Austin and Bresnan 1996; Bresnan 1998, forthcoming; Sadler 1997; Sells 1998). Both functional projections (FP, short for CP,
IP, DP, etc.) and lexical projections (LP, short for NP, VP, AP, PP) are employed
in the theory of (endocentric) c-structures, and all c-structure nodes are optional,
unless required by general principles (such as Completeness and Coherence).[10]
The main differences are these. First, the extended X' theory of LFG is *lexicalized*,
in the sense that every syntactic category X represents a lexical class. In particular, functional categories such as I or C are specialized subclasses of (morphologically complete) words which have a syncategorematic role in the grammar (such
as marking subordination, clause type, or finiteness). Hence, nothing ever moves
to I or C; if there is overt evidence for an element occupying a special head position such as I or C, it is base-generated in I or C. Second, the extended X' theory
of LFG is *non-derivational*: the effects of movement in X' trees arise from the fact
that different c-structure positions may correspond to the same f-structure by
general principles of correspondence between parallel structures. In particular,
it follows from (7a–c) (from Bresnan, forthcoming) that verbal extended projections correspond to the same f-structures as their verbal heads:

(7)   a. Head principle:
          A c-structure head is an f-structure head.

       b. Co-head principle:
          A c-structure complement of a functional head is an f-structure co-
          head.

---

   [8] Cf. 'each node must be a good projection of a lower one, *if a lower one is present*' (376 [emphasis
added], 408).
   [9] An omitted head is not the same as an empty head X = [e] or a head filled by a phonologically
null morpheme X=[Ø]. An omitted head would vacuously satisfy Grimshaw's HD-LFT constraint,
while the empty heads would violate it. Similarly, a head filled by a null morpheme [Ø] would satisfy
OB-HD, while an omitted X or unfilled head e would violate it. Traces of head-movement behave
like null morphemes with respect to OB-HD but like omitted heads with respect to HD-LFT. See
Grimshaw (1997: 408–9).
   [10] Completeness requires that every argument required by a PRED(icator) be present in the
f-structure; Coherence requires that every function present in the f-structure be associated with a
PRED through identification as an argument or adjunct. See Kaplan and Bresnan 1995 [1982], Bresnan
and Mchombo (1987), Bresnan (forthcoming).

c. Complement principle:
    A c-structure complement of a lexical head is an f-structure comple-
    ment.

Translated into the LFG formalism (Dalrymple *et al.* (eds) 1995), (7a–c) can be
rendered as in (8a–c):[11]

(8)   a. Annotate projecting categories (e.g. X, X′) in c-structure with ↑ = ↓.
       b. Annotate nonprojecting categories in F′ with ↑ = ↓.
       c. Annotate nonprojecting categories (e.g. X″) in L′ with (↑ COMPL) = ↓.

These principles yield the effects of head movement. For example, in a structure
like (9), VP is mapped into the same f-structure as I by the head and co-head
principles (7a, b):

(9)

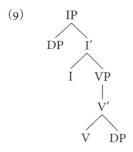

Further, V′ is mapped into the same f-structure as VP by (7a), and DP in V′ is
a COMPL by (7c). If I contains the main verb and V is omitted, the verb's PRED
will be satisified by the COMPL in f-structure. Thus the mapping between the
c-structure in (9), V omitted, and its parallel f-structure will look like (10),
where TNS and PRED are lexical and morphological features of the verb in I:

(10)

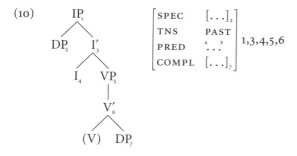

---

[11] The 'up' (↑) and 'down' (↓) arrows refer to the unique f-structures respectively associated by
correspondence to the mother and the annotated node. Hence '↑ = ↓' means that the f-structure of
the mother of the node so annotated is identical to the f-structure of the annotated node. This
equation has the effect that the feature structures of heads are merged with those of their projections,
an example of the many-to-one nature of the correspondence between c-structure and f-structure.
The equation '(↑ COMPL) = ↓' has the effect that the feature structure of the annotated node is
embedded within the COMPL function of the f-structure of the mother node.

The omission of V is preferred to postulating an empty V because the latter adds no additional information to the f-structure and therefore violates economy of expression (Bresnan 1998, forthcoming). For Grimshaw, base generation of 'movement' configurations like (10) violates the theta criterion, which (as in transformational grammar) is assumed to apply to X′ representations. For LFG, as we saw before, the effects of the theta criterion (satisfaction of the argument structure of the PRED) are obtained at f-structure, not c-structure. In (10), the PRED and its arguments (SPEC and COMPL) all lie within the same f-structure, where completeness and coherence obtain. It is this use of parallel, copresent structures which obviates the need for a serial derivation in capturing 'movement' generalizations.

The third departure of the extended X′ theory of recent LFG from that of Grimshaw (1997) is *typological*: the former includes non-endocentric categories and structures. In particular, S is universally available as an exocentric category having no fixed categorial head and projecting no higher category. (Thus, there is no category X such that $S = X^{max}$, and there is no S′.) S may dominate either configurational or non-configurational (flat) structures. In the latter instances, grammatical functions are determined not by the X′ configuration (as in 7a–c), but by the morphology (Simpson 1991; Austin and Bresnan 1996; Nordlinger 1998a). Configurational S consists of a subject constituent and an XP predicate, which is the f-structure head. A configurational 'internal-subject' language (e.g. Welsh according to Sproat 1985, Kroeger 1993, Sadler 1997) would have S under IP, and VP under S:

(11)

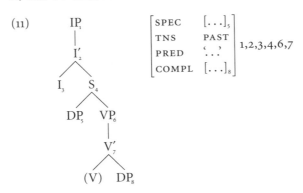

A non-configurational subject-internal language (e.g. Warlpiri according to Kroeger 1993, Austin and Bresnan 1996, following Simpson 1991, and Nordlinger 1998a) would have S under IP, but no VP:

(12)

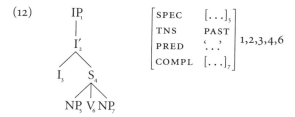

In fact, the main predicator in a Warlpiri sentence can be N; with N predicators, an auxiliary (and hence IP) is optional, yielding a fully non-configurational sentence structure S. The functions of the NPs in Warlpiri are determined by principles which associate GFs with case morphology rather than configurations (see Nordlinger 1998a and the references cited there).

Treating S as the category of the 'internal subject' solves a number of problems raised by the VP-internal subject hypothesis: if subject is SPEC of VP (as assumed by Grimshaw 1997), then the fact that V′ behaves syntactically like X^{max} is unexplained; if subject is instead adjoined to VP, then a stipulative disjunction is introduced into the definition of SPEC. Kroeger (1993) argues in favour of S and not VP as the category of the internal subject in Tagalog. In the present version of X′ theory, therefore, SPEC of LP is taken to be undefined and VP-internal subjects are actually S-internal subjects.

Note that syntactic evidence cited by Grimshaw (1997: 379) in favour of the VP-internal subject hypothesis in English already follows from the present theory. Because the VP under the above principles always corresponds to the same f-structure as its extended projection, *VP always has an internal subject in the f-structure.* The need to hypothesize a structural subject constituent in c-structure where none is ever overt is an artifact of the derivational representations assumed in movement frameworks.[12]

Under this conception of GEN, the candidates in Optimal Syntax will be multi-dimensional structures whose components correspond imperfectly. Each candidate is a quadruple consisting of a c-structure, an f-structure, a lexicalization function mapping preterminal nodes of the c-structure into instances of

---

[12] Burton and Grimshaw (1992) observe that the coordination of active and passive or unaccusative VPs (e.g *The criminal will be arrested and confess to the crime*) is inconsistent with movement theories of passive and unaccusative if the VP lacks an internal subject position: movement of an underlying object NP to a subject position external to the VP will violate across-the-board constraints on movement from conjunctions; movement to a subject position internal to the conjunct VP will solve the problem. This problem is an artifact of the derivational representational framework: correspondence theories of passives and unaccusatives (e.g. Bresnan and Zaenen 1990; Legendre, Raymond, and Smolensky 1993; Aissen 1998; Sells 1997), already capture these generalizations without movement, by assuming alternative correspondences between argument structures and syntactic functions or case arrays. For example, in the present framework, the f-structure of the VP already includes all of the information needed for the passive voice correspondence between a(rgument)-structure and syntactic functions.

the morpholexical inventory, and a correspondence function mapping each nonterminal node onto a unique (but not necessarily distinct) f-structure. (Other structures in parallel to c-structure and f-structure are disregarded here.)[13]

For a given input such as (13), the universal candidate set will include the (simplified) members illustrated in (14)–(17).[14]

(13)
$$\begin{bmatrix} \text{PRED} & \text{'see(x,y)'} \\ \text{GF}_1 & \begin{bmatrix} \text{PRED} & \text{'PRO'} \\ \text{PERS} & 1 \\ \text{NUM} & \text{SG} \end{bmatrix}_x \\ \text{GF}_2 & \begin{bmatrix} \text{PRED} & \text{'PRO'} \\ \text{PERS} & 3 \\ \text{NUM} & \text{SG} \\ \text{GEND} & \text{FEM} \end{bmatrix}_y \\ \text{TNS} & \text{PAST} \end{bmatrix}$$

Candidate (14) categorizes the finite main verb of English as I rather than V, as Grimshaw (1997) assumes for French (cf. also Netter and Kärcher 1986; Netter 1988; Meier 1992; Frank and Kärcher-Momma 1992; Kroeger 1993; King 1995; Niño 1997; Bresnan 1998, forthcoming; Sadler 1997; Berman and Frank 1996; and Berman 1996, 1997 for similar analyses within LFG).

(14)

$$\begin{bmatrix} \text{SPEC} & [\text{'I'}]_{x,2} \\ \text{TNS} & \text{PAST} \\ \text{PRED} & \text{'see(x,y)'} \\ \text{COMPL} & [\text{'her'}]_{y,6} \end{bmatrix} 1,3,4,5$$

Candidate (15) categorizes the finite main verb as V, as in English:

---

[13] On an alternative formalization (cf. Andrews and Manning 1999), the candidates would be trees annotated at the nodes with (partial) feature structures, either lexical or syntactically composed. The correspondence is then the annotation function. I will adhere to the classic LFG formalism here, but this alternative, with its affinities to Construction Grammar and HPSG, is also of interest and completely compatible with the Optimal Syntax framework.

[14] These candidates are simplified by omitting X′ c-structure nodes dominated by nonbranching XP, by omitting the contents of the morpholexical feature structures of the terminals in favour of labelling by their English orthographic names, and by abbreviating the contents of subsidiary feature structures in the global feature structure with quoted labels.

(15)

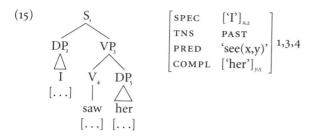

$$\begin{bmatrix} \text{SPEC} & [\text{`I'}]_{x,2} \\ \text{TNS} & \text{PAST} \\ \text{PRED} & \text{`see(x,y)'} \\ \text{COMPL} & [\text{`her'}]_{y,5} \end{bmatrix} 1,3,4$$

Candidate (16) categorizes the pronominal subject as a verbal inflection—a universally available structural type found in some languages (cf. Bresnan and Mchombo 1987; Demuth and Johnson 1989; Andrews 1990; Börjars, Vincent, and Chapman 1997; Nordlinger 1998a for a range of examples analyzed within LFG). In OT the absence of pronominally inflected verbs from the English inventory must be derived from the ranking of universal markedness constraints on categorization (as in Bresnan 1997a, b, c), rather than stipulated as a morpholexical feature of the language; it could in fact emerge as a variant structural possibility in English too (cf. Börjars and Chapman 1998).

(16)

$$\begin{array}{c} \text{VP}_1 \\ \diagup \diagdown \\ \text{V}_2 \qquad \text{DP}_3 \\ | \qquad \triangle \\ \text{I-saw} \quad \text{her} \\ [\dots] \quad [\dots] \end{array}$$

$$\begin{bmatrix} \text{SPEC} & [\text{`I'}]_x \\ \text{TNS} & \text{PAST} \\ \text{PRED} & \text{`see(x,y)'} \\ \text{COMPL} & [\text{`her'}]_{y,3} \end{bmatrix} 1,3,4$$

Candidate (17) categorizes the finite main verb as I and maps its co-head to S rather than VP, yielding an internal-subject construction as is found in Welsh and other Celtic languages (see Kroeger 1993; Bresnan, forthcoming; Sadler 1997 for an LFG analysis).

(17)

$$\begin{array}{c} \text{IP}_1 \\ \diagup \diagdown \\ \text{I}_2 \qquad \text{S}_3 \\ | \qquad \diagup \diagdown \\ \text{saw} \quad \text{DP}_4 \; \text{VP}_5 \\ [\dots] \quad \triangle \quad | \\ \quad \text{I} \quad \text{DP}_6 \\ \quad [\dots] \; \triangle \\ \quad \quad \text{her} \\ \quad \quad [\dots] \end{array}$$

$$\begin{bmatrix} \text{SPEC} & [\text{`I'}]_{x,4} \\ \text{TNS} & \text{PAST} \\ \text{PRED} & \text{`see(x,y)'} \\ \text{COMPL} & [\text{`her'}]_{y,6} \end{bmatrix} 1,2,3,5$$

Candidate (18) reflects the non-endocentric c- to f-structure correspondence found in non-configurational languages which use morpholexical specification of functions (see Simpson 1991; Austin and Bresnan 1996; Nordlinger 1998a for recent analyses in LFG):

(18)

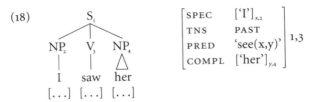

Being infinite, the universal candidate set includes many more realizations of the given content than are illustrated here, as well as many unfaithful candidates with different morphosyntactic content. It is the job of the constraint ranking to select those belonging to a given language.

In sum, where Grimshaw's (1997) candidate set has X′ structures which en-code transformational derivations of the input lexical heads by means of trace indices and which must match some unformalized LF, Optimal Syntax has a typologically richer set of lexicalized tree structures which are indexed to parallel feature structures and matched to the input under correspondence.

10.2.3 *Constraints*

On the conception of GEN developed here the INPUT simply represents language-independent morphosyntactic 'content' to be expressed with varying fidelity by the candidate morphosyntactic forms, which carry with them their own interpre-tations of that content (Bresnan 1997a,c). Faithfulness constraints ensure the expressibility of the input content in some possible output form. Correspondence constraints regulate the behaviour of the lexicalization function and the mapping from c-structure to f-structure. The optimal candidates represent a balancing of the priority each language gives to expressibility of the input, the uniformity of the form/content correspondences, and the markedness of the output.

Faithfulness constraints require the feature structure of the output to match the input, thus enforcing expressibility of the input content by some form of expres-sion that carries similar content. In the present study, we will simply assume the PARSE and FILL family of constraints from Prince and Smolensky (1993): for each morphosyntactic attribute such as NUM, PRED, and SPEC, there is a pair of constraints PARSE-ATTR and FILL-ATTR. Following Grimshaw (1996) we interpret PARSE-ATTR constraints to require input feature values to have identi-cal correspondents in the output, and FILL-ATTR constraints to require output features to have some value compatible with the input. An application of these constraints is given in Section 10.4.

Categorization constraints influence the lexical inventory of each language by regulating the association of preterminal categories with various types of featural content. (They are thus constraints on the correspondence between the c-structure and the terminal string produced by the lexicalization function.) For example, Grimshaw's No-Lex-Mvt constraint ('A lexical head cannot move' 374) is recast in the present framework as a constraint on categorization No-Lex-in-F: it assigns a mark to the lexicalization of a preterminal functional category by an inventory element having lexical content (which we model with the PRED attribute). Since constraints are violable, and may be overridden by higher-ranking constraints, this approach allows verbal content to be lexically inserted into a variety of more or less marked preterminal categories such as V, I, C, rather than invariantly inserted into V by definition and then moved by serial derivation to accord with observed distribution.

I will assume that the categorization constraints of English classify finite auxiliaries as belonging to a verbal functional category F (comprehending I and C as in Grimshaw (1991)), and all other finite verbs as belonging to a verbal lexical category V. Verb-raising languages (such as Russian (King 1995), Finnish (Niño 1997), Welsh (Kroeger 1993; Sadler 1997), or French as assumed by Grimshaw (1997)) would classify finite verbs as members of I, not V. Thus in Optimal Syntax English differs from verb-raising languages in the categorization of finite main verbs (as V or I), not in whether inflections are syntactic heads projecting their own syntactic category, and this difference in categorization can itself be derived from a constraint ranking difference (see below).

Correspondence constraints govern the possible correspondences between the multiple dimensions of the output. Optimal Syntax assumes flexible, imperfect correspondences between the parallel structures representing various linguistic dimensions. Because this approach is not widely familiar I will briefly outline here some of the types of correspondence constraints possible within this framework.[15]

Many of these constraints refer to 'prominence', which is defined by ordering relations on c-structure nodes (e.g. c-command), a(rgument)-structure roles (e.g. the thematic hierarchy), and f-structure functions (e.g. the functional hierarchy: TOP FOC SUBJ COMPL ADJUNCT). Syntactic functions are classified into argument/non-argument functions, distinguishing SUBJ and COMPL from the others, and discourse/nondiscourse functions, distinguishing the syntactic functions having special discourse prominence (the DF functions TOP, FOC, and SUBJ) from the rest (Bresnan 1998, forthcoming).[16] Where different prominence rela-

---

[15] These illustrative constraints are based on Bresnan and Zaenen (1990) (cf. Legendre, Raymond, and Smolensky 1993), Bresnan (1998, forthcoming), and much other recent work in LFG.

[16] Note that DF functions are *syntactic* functions subject to Completeness, Coherence, and Functional uniqueness, and are not to be equated with communicative functions in discourse, intonationally-marked information-packaging functions, and the like. DF may be compared to the highest clausal Ā-positions in derivational theories. Note also that the SUBJ function is the unique function which is both an argument function and a discourse function (DF).

tions correspond in such a way as to reinforce each other (prominence on one dimension matching prominence on another), we have instances of harmonic alignment in syntax (Aissen 1998).

(19) (I) A- to F-structure Correspondence
      (i) The most prominent a-structure argument corresponds to the most prominent (least oblique) syntactic argument function.
      (ii) The most affected a-structure argument corresponds to the most prominent syntactic argument function.
      (iii) Arguments correspond to the least prominent syntactic argument function.
      (iv) Completeness and Coherence (every function has a role and conversely).

   (II) C- to F-structure Correspondence: Endocentric Constraints
      (i) Heads correspond to heads.
            (A c-structure head is an f-structure head (7a).)
      (ii) LP complements correspond to complements.
            (The c-structure complement of a lexical category is an f-structure complement (7c).)
      (iii) FP complements do not correspond to complements.
            (The c-structure complement of a functional category is an f-structure co-head (7b).)
      (iv) Prominence in the functional hierarchy corresponds to prominence in c-structure.
            (The DF functions SUBJ, TOP, FOC are specifiers of functional categories FP.)

   (III) Morpho-functional Correspondence: Lexocentric Constraints
      (i) Obliqueness of case corresponds to obliqueness of function (lesser prominence of argument functions).
            (A nominative c-structure constituent is an f-structure SUBJ, an accusative c-structure constituent is an f-structure OBJ, etc.)
      (ii) Agreement corresponds to greater prominence of argument functions. (OBJ agrees only if SUBJ agrees, etc.)

Other constraints include analogues of Grimshaw's (1997) constraints discussed in detail in the next section, and a constraint on syntactic phrase structure requiring it to contribute nonredundant information to the f-structure. The latter constraint, proposed as a principle of LFG in Bresnan (1998, forthcoming), is variously referred to as a principle of functionality of structure or economy of expression: '*All syntactic phrase-structure nodes are optional and are not used unless required by independent principles*'. The principle favours morpholexical expression by penalizing phrasal nodes in favour of terminals and preterminals. Here we call it DON'T-PROJECT:

(20)   DON'T-PROJECT: Avoid phrase structure.

Note that the 'unless' clause and the stipulation of optionality in the LFG formulation are unnecessary in the Optimal Syntax version: the exceptions to the principle follow from whatever constraints dominate (20) in the constraint ranking; these will include, for example, the very highly-ranked Completeness and Coherence constraints (19)(I)(iv).

As a highly endocentric language, English ranks the endocentricity constraints (19)(II) higher than DON'T-PROJECT. This ranking will make outputs like (14), (15) and (17) more harmonic than (16) and (18).

In the next section I will translate Grimshaw's (1997) theory into the present framework of Optimal Syntax. I will focus just on constraints that correspond to Grimshaw's and assume the same constraint ranking that she does. Equivalents of several other constraints she hypothesizes will be added later.

10.3 Deriving Grimshaw's Results

Given the framework outlined in the preceding sections, it is not (too) difficult to derive Grimshaw's (1997) results. There are certain systematic differences between the two accounts to take note of, which generally stem from the more 'surfacy' X′ theory adopted in Optimal Syntax.

First, in what follows, wherever one of Grimshaw's output structures has a VP with an overt internal subject, we have S, distinct from IP. This is because VP is defined within our X′ theory to be a category that does not dominate a subject constituent (Bresnan 1982, forthcoming; Bresnan and Zaenen 1990; Kroeger 1993). C-structural subject positions appear only in SPEC of FP and S; SPEC of LP (for lexical categories XP, including VP) are undefined.

Second, wherever Grimshaw has an optimal structure containing a head-movement trace which prevents a violation of OB-HD, we have the structures lacking them. Such empty heads can of course be generated by GEN, but they are completely redundant, adding no information to the f-structure that is not already captured by the c- to f-structure correspondence constraints; Economy of Expression (DON'T-PROJECT) therefore renders them less harmonic than the same structures with the empty heads omitted (cf. Bresnan 1998). (Nevertheless, in displaying candidates in tableaus, we will sometimes use an *e* as Grimshaw does to disambiguate the intended structural analysis.)

Let us turn now to the problem of formulating OB-HD in our parallel correspondence framework. As observed in the preceding, there is not a perfect correspondence between the categorial (c-structure) head and the functional (f-structure) head. One case where c- and f-structure heads show imperfect correspondence, as we have seen, is S. Though S has no fixed categorial head from which it must be projected, it has an f-structure head, which provides its PRED attribute (this would be the XP in a configurational language, but could be a lexical category X in a non-configurational language (Simpson 1991; Kroeger 1993; Austin and Bresnan 1995; Nordlinger 1998a). Another case where correspondence of heads fails is in functional projections, because of the co-head principle (19)(II)(ii). Now consider the implications of this imperfect correspondence for the formulation of the obligatory head principle OB-HD:

(21)   OB-HD: every projected category (X', X'') has a lexically filled head.

Suppose we took a narrowly local categorial definition of 'head' in determining violations of OB-HD. Looking at a category X', we would ask: does it immediately dominate a lexically filled category X? 'Yes' would pass OB-HD; 'No' would incur a mark. But this is not equivalent in substance to what Grimshaw (1997) does. For Grimshaw, a violation of OB-HD is incurred if X' does not dominate a lexically filled category X *or the trace of a lexically filled category* (see footnote 9). Thus, Grimshaw crucially distinguishes examples like (22a) and (22b) (Tableau 1, 378):

(22)   a. $[_{CP}$ *what* e $[_{IP}$ DP *will* $[_{VP}$ *read* $[e]]]$
        b. $[_{CP}$ *what will* $[_{IP}$ DP e $[_{VP}$ *read* $[e]]]$

If the *e* in IP in (22b) is interpreted as a trace of verb movement, only (a) incurs a mark from OB-HD, because of Grimshaw's assumption that GEN allows only upward movements. Here we see a crucial point of dependence of Grimshaw's constraints on her derivational conception of GEN. OB-HD is violated in just those structures which lack a lexically filled head at some point in the transformational derivation; her disjunctive definition arises from the translation of this derivational generalization into a representational simulation with chains of co-indexed traces. How then should we define 'head' in a non-derivational version of this constraint?

It turns out that this question has already been addressed in LFG in other contexts (M. Jar, n.d.; Zaenen and Kaplan 1995: 221–2). Because of the imperfect correspondence between c-structure and f-structure, the head of a constituent cannot in general be fixed in a unique structural configuration (indeed, this is why variable head positioning can occur at all, within the present framework); but the head can be recovered from looking at the inverse image of the constituent's f-structure under the correspondence mapping. Within the inverse image of $\phi(C)$ (that is, within the set of constituents that are mapped into the same f-structure as C by ϕ) will be all of the constituents that contribute to C's f-structure. In the c-structure theory adopted here, this inverse image will contain the entire extended projection of a constituent, including all of the higher functional heads. One of these higher elements can be identified as the head of a locally headless phrasal category if it matches the categorial features of the latter (Jar, n.d.; Zaenen and Kaplan 1995: 221–2):[17]

(23)   X is the **extended head** of Y if X is the lowest node Z such that (i) Z corresponds to the same f-structure as Y, (ii) Z shares the categorial features of Y, and (iii) every node other than Y that dominates Z also dominates Y.

This definition allows the head to count as an extended head of its own category. Thus (23) is equivalent to saying that X is an extended head of Y if X is the categorial head of Y, or Y lacks a categorial head but X is the closest element higher up in the tree that looks and functions like a head. The inverted modal *will* in C position in (22b) is the extended head of C′ (assuming with Grimshaw (1991) that functional categories have lexical categorial features, verbal in this case). By (23), *will* is also an extended head of I′: first, through the correspondence constraints (19)(II)(i),(iii), *will* corresponds to the same f-structure as the I′; second, because modals are verbal functional heads F in English, occurring in both I and C (inverted) positions, *will* is of the same category type as I′; third, *will* occurs in the upwards extended projection of I′, IP, in that there is no category that dominates C and does not dominate I′, IP. In contrast, *will* in (22a) cannot be the extended head of C′, because IP dominates *will* and does not dominate CP. Finally, by (23iii), *will* in (22b) cannot be the extended head of V′ because though it meets conditions (i)–(iii), V is a lower node that meets the same conditions.

A rather different example of an extended head in this framework is the filler of a *Wh*-gap. In both (22a) and (22b) the gap EC corresponds to the same f-structure as the *Wh*-phrase head *what*, which has the correct category type and position to be an extended head of the [*e*].[18] Thus one way to think of an extended head is to imagine it as one of the parts of a discontinuous constituent in the c-structure that are put back together (unified) into a single f-structure.

Let us interpret 'head' in the OB-HD constraint to refer to 'extended head' in the sense just explained. We now get very close to Grimshaw's results. In fact, with this definition, we can state a parallel-correspondence version of STAY:

(24)   STAY: Categories dominate their extended heads.

This constraint is not equivalent to OB-HD (see above), because OB-HD specifies that the head (of a projecting category X′, X″) must be lexically filled; it does not say where the head is. STAY says where the head is.

---

[17] I have added the 'dominates' clause in (23) to restrict the inverse image to upwards regions of structure, corresponding to Grimshaw's assumptions and to the deeper generalization that variable head positioning, being marked, appears only in prominent positions of the tree. This result should be derived from the constraint theory itself, but is treated definitionally in the present exploratory study.

[18] Gaps are not uniformly represented by empty categories in the LFG framework. They arise only where there are no other means than phrase structure configuration for the identification of syntactic function (Bresnan 1998, forthcoming; Choi 1996; Berman 1999), and in some LFG frameworks they are absent altogether (Kaplan and Zaenen 1989).

Those of Grimshaw's constraints that make reference to 'heads' including traces of heads can now be reformulated in terms of 'extended head'. For example, Grimshaw assumes two constraints SUBJ and CASE which regulate the positions in which subjects can appear with respect to their heads (390). We can derive the substantive effects of such constraints as well, e.g.:

(25)   AGR: A subject and its predicate in c-structure agree. (i.e. A c-structure subject requires that its sister constituent have an agreeing extended head.)

This constraint usefully distinguishes between the following examples. In (26a, b) the subject *she* is sister to a VP whose head (hence, extended head) agrees in (a) and does not in (b).

(26)   a. *She* [$_{\text{VP}}$ *wants what*]?
       b. * *She* [$_{\text{VP}}$ *want*$_{\text{infin}}$ *what*]?

In (27a, b) the subject is now sister to an I′ whose extended head (the inverted auxiliary) agrees in (a) and does not in (b).

(27)   a. *What does* [$_{\text{IP}}$ *she* [$_{\text{VP}}$ *want*$_{\text{infin}}$]]?
       b. * *What do*$_{\text{infin}}$ [$_{\text{IP}}$ *she* [$_{\text{VP}}$ *wants*]]?

Here are the constraint rankings that will be operative in deriving Grimshaw's results, assuming the new definitions of OB-HD and STAY. Some of the constraints from the latter part of Grimshaw (1997), such as PURE-EP, aren't included, but fit in completely transparently. The constraint ranking follows Grimshaw (1997).

(28)   Constraint ranking (in descending order of dominance):
       CC   [Completeness and Coherence, as in (19)(II)(iv)]
       OP(-SPEC)   [defined below]
       *LEX-F   [defined below]
       OB-HD   [assuming definition of 'extended head' in (23)]
       AGR   [(25)]
       FULL(-INT)   [Full Interpretation; discussed below]
       STAY   [as in (24)]

Completeness and Coherence are assumed to be undominated. I will omit them from the following tables, and also *LEX-F until it comes into play.

This reconstrual of 'head' yields optimal structural analyses isomorphic to Grimshaw's, as we are now in a position to demonstrate.

10.3.1 *Matrix Interrogatives and Declaratives*

For the case of matrix interrogatives and declaratives shown in (29) (based on Grimshaw's (1)–(2), 377), Grimshaw's basic explanation is this: OP-SPEC requires that a *Wh*-operator be in a specifier position c-commanding the entire extended projection (379), Ob-Hd requires that the projection of this specifier have a lexically filled head, and both of these constraints outrank Stay, which penalizes movement. Hence, violating them is worse than displacing a constituent by movement.

(29)   a. They will read something.
　　　b. *Will they read something. (ungrammatical as declarative)
　　　c. What will they read?
　　　d. What they will read?

It follows that (29c) will be optimal among the interrogative candidates (29c–d), because even though it violates Stay twice compared the the single violation of (29d), it has both its *Wh*-operator in spec of CP and its CP head lexically filled by the auxiliary (unlike (29d)); the alternatives incur worse violations than the Stay violations incurred by the optimal candidate.[19] In declaratives, in contrast, no higher functional projection is needed because no operator is present and Op-Spec is vacuously satisfied. The violation of Stay then emerges to render auxiliary inversion (b) less harmonic and the uninverted structure (29a) optimal.

　　　An undesirable consequence of this analysis, on which Grimshaw (1997) is silent, is that an *in situ* question like (30) is not optimal compared to (c), because it violates Op-Spec; hence it is ungrammatical:

(30)   They will read what?

Yet of course the sentence is perfectly grammatical. How can this fact be explained given Grimshaw's logic? If (30) competes with (29c), it should always lose by violating Op-Spec. The answer, I believe, comes from considering the role of the input.

　　　Though they always compete against each other in the universal candidate set, matrix interrogatives and declaratives are both grammatical because they differ in content: each is more faithful to a different input, as illustrated by the respective inputs shown in (31a,b):

(31)　a.
$$\begin{bmatrix} \text{PRED} & \text{`read}(x,y)\text{'} \\ \text{GF}_1 & [\text{`they'}]_x \\ \text{GF}_2 & [\text{`what'}]_y \\ \text{TNS} & \text{FUT} \end{bmatrix}$$
　b.
$$\begin{bmatrix} \text{PRED} & \text{`read}(x,y)\text{'} \\ \text{GF}_1 & [\text{`they'}]_x \\ \text{GF}_2 & [\text{`something'}]_y \\ \text{TNS} & \text{FUT} \end{bmatrix}$$

Despite the fact that the matrix declarative (29a) incurs fewer violations than (29c) of the constraint Stay, its fatal defect in comparison to the interrogative candidate is unfaithfulness to the interrogative input (31a).

---

[19] A further piece of the argument is that a base-generated complementizer cannot fill the CP head position without violating another constraint formulated expressly against just this possibility (Hd-Lft, 408).

Now one might be tempted to consider the *in situ* question construction (30) simply to be an optional variant of the fronting question construction (29c), drawing on recent developments in the treatment of optionality in OT (as discussed in Bresnan (1997b): e.g. Anttila 1997, 1998; Boersma 1997). However, there is evidence that (29c) and (30) are not optional variants, but differ in content in some way. As shown in (32) a class of intensifiers is possible only with the fronted *Wh*-phrase (Brame 1978: 21–2):

(32)   a.   Who the hell/on earth/in the world/in God's name is he talking about?
        b.   He is talking about who (*the hell/*on earth/*in the world/*in God's name)?

These intensifiers are clearly constituents of the *Wh*-phrase; (33) shows that one can occur in each of two coordinated *Wh*-phrases:

(33)   How on earth and why in God's name did he do it?

Yet the intensifiers can only appear in the *Wh*-constituents when fronted. These facts suggest that some additional feature distinguishes the fronted and *in situ* *Wh*-question constituents, allowing for these intensifying expressions.

Following recent work on extraction constructions in LFG (Kroeger 1993; Bresnan 1998, forthcoming; Berman 1996, 1997), we can identify the feature as one of the DF functions. These are the most prominent functions on the functional hierarchy (FOC, TOP, SUBJ), and in endocentric languages they are generally associated with c-structure positions that iconically express this prominence, such as the SPEC of FP. See (19)(II)(iv). This gives us two distinct types of interrogative inputs, having the same content except for the additional attribute DF in (b), representing syntactic prominence of the interrogative constituents:

(34)   a.
$$
\begin{bmatrix}
\text{PRED} & \text{'read(x,y)'} \\
\text{GF}_1 & \text{['they']}_x \\
\text{GF}_2 & \text{['what']}_y \\
\text{TNS} & \text{FUT}
\end{bmatrix}
$$
b.
$$
\begin{bmatrix}
\text{PRED} & \text{'read(x,y)'} \\
\text{GF}_1 & \text{['they']}_x \\
\text{GF}_2 \longrightarrow & \text{['what']}_y \\
\text{DF} \nearrow & \\
\text{TNS} & \text{FUT}
\end{bmatrix}
$$

According to this analysis the two inputs differ in their morphosyntactic content, one specifying that the f-structure for *what* is syntactically marked for prominence (as a DF), the other not (intonational marking may be used instead). The fronted question (29) corresponds most faithfully to (b); the *in situ* type (30), to (a). We now interpret Grimshaw's OP-SPEC to require that an operator must be the value of a DF in the f-structure (as well as, possibly, the value of another GF). Faithfulness to the input must dominate OP-SPEC. Then for input (34a) the optimal candidate will be (30), because it will lack the DF attribute present in (29c), and fidelity to the input will mark the latter as less harmonic. This motivates our LFG-style interpretation of the constraint Op-Spec, which we adopt for concreteness in what follows.

For the input (b) the optimal candidate is illustrated in (35) (see (36)):

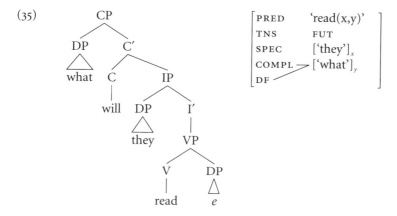

(35)

$$\begin{bmatrix} \text{PRED} & \text{'read(x,y)'} \\ \text{TNS} & \text{FUT} \\ \text{SPEC} & [\text{'they'}]_x \\ \text{COMPL} & [\text{'what'}]_y \\ \text{DF} & \end{bmatrix}$$

(36) Matrix interrogatives	Op-Spec	Ob-Hd	Agr	Full	Stay
i. [IP DP will [VP read what]]	*!				
ii. [CP e [IP DP will [VP read what]]]	*!	*			
iii. [CP what e [IP DP will [VP read [e]]]]		*!			*
☞ iv. [CP what will [IP DP e [VP read [e]]]]					**
v. [CP what will [S DP [VP read [e]]]]			*!		*

Grimshaw (1997) rules out candidate (i) by Op-Spec, and we have followed her analysis here for purposes of comparison; however, in the present framework the candidate also violates the even more highly ranked constraint of faithfulness to the input because it lacks the DF attribute discussed above. Notice that candidate (iii) and not (iv) violates Ob-Hd. This follows from the considerations just given concerning extended heads. Further, if we did not have the Agr constraint, then (v) would be optimal, because there is no Stay violation in generating *will* outside of S, as opposed to an empty-headed IP. Agr, however, rules out (v): the nonfinite verb in the VP of (v) is the extended head of its VP; since it does not agree with the subject (being an infinitive), there is a violation of Agr. Although Grimshaw does not include a structure like (v) in her candidate set in (Tableau 1, 378), she does in fact rule out an exactly equivalent structure, in which the modal *will* is base-generated in C position, with the subject internal to VP:

(37)   [_CP_ what will [_VP_ DP read t]]

This candidate is ruled out by her SUBJ and/or CASE conditions, which license subjects only in the right positions with respect to heads (see her definitions, 390). Our constraint that subjects agree with the extended heads of their sister predicates (25) has the same substantive effect.

Grimshaw's results on matrix declaratives (her examples (1a, b)) also follow straightforwardly from these constraints:

(38)   a. They will read some books.
        b. *Will they read some books. (ungrammatical as declarative)

The input is shown in (39):

(39)   INPUT = $\begin{bmatrix} \text{PRED} & \text{'read(x,y)'} \\ \text{GF}_1 & \text{['they']}_x \\ \text{GF}_2 & \text{['some books']}_y \\ \text{TNS} & \text{FUT} \end{bmatrix}$

A nonoptimal candidate ((iii) in (41)) is illustrated in (40):

(40)
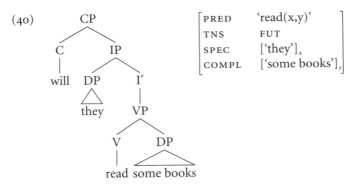

(41) Matrix declaratives		O_P	O_B-H_D	A_GR	F_ULL	S_TAY
☞	i. [_IP_ DP will [_VP_ read books]]					
	ii. [_CP_ e [_IP_ DP will [_VP_ read books]]]		*			
	iii. [_CP_ will [_IP_ DP e [_VP_ read books]]]					*
	iv. [_CP_ will [_S_ DP [_VP_ read books]]]			*		

Turning now to yes/no questions, while (38b) is ungrammatical for the declarative input in (39), it is grammatical for an appropriate interrogative input. What should this input be? Grimshaw's solution is to postulate a null operator in SPEC of CP (hedging in footnote 4 (380), however). This empty operator requires an FP which needs a head to avoid an O-HD violation, thus bringing about auxiliary inversion. We could adopt this approach, but there is some evidence that it is incorrect (Toivonen 1996). Moreover, such a null operator is a language-particular lexical solution: other languages may make use of overt yes/ no question markers (e.g. Russian *li*, Chicheŵa *kodí*) which can be classed with complementizers (a complementizer clitic in the case of Russian (King 1995)), and the same may be true cross-linguistically (cf. Grimshaw's n. 4). Thus, a better solution may be to let GEN universally treat C as the category carrying information about formally marked 'sentence types' such as interrogative (Sadock and Zwicky 1985). For purposes of these exploratory notes, I will assume that the verbal category C (that is, C filled by a verb) specifies a value for the attribute DF. Thus, *will*, like most English modals, belongs to the category F, comprising I and C; when generated in C by GEN, it carries an additional attribute $(\uparrow$ DF OP$) =$ Q, yielding the feature structure [DF [OP Q]].[20] The latter can be viewed as a property of all verbal members of C. Given this analysis, only inverted forms will be faithful to the input for a yes/no question.

I will pass over a demonstration of how Grimshaw's results with multiple *Wh*-questions are derived. As with the preceding examples, the present account is equivalent to hers because of the essential equivalence of both structural analyses and constraints.

10.3.2 *The Distribution of* Do

The present framework provides an interesting perspective on Grimshaw's explanation for the distribution of the English auxiliary verb *do*. The generalization Grimshaw wishes to capture—the rather delphic pronouncement '*do* is possible only where it is necessary' (381)—means, in effect, that *do* is used only where it fills specific functions. The functions, according to Grimshaw, are to satisfy her OB-HD and CASE constraints (meaning that it fills the head position required either by having a *Wh*-phrase in SPEC of CP or by having an IP above NegP required for the 'case' or agreement features that license the subject). To capture the fact that *do* is ungrammatical elsewhere, there must be a constraint that penalizes its presence, but is outranked by these constraints. Because the auxiliary *do* is commonly analyzed as a semantically empty carrier of tense inflections, one could simply propose that all semantically empty elements incur a mark, but Grimshaw relies elsewhere on the unmarked use of such elements (for example, in allowing the free variation of IP and CP propositional complements (her tableau (24))). Hence, she proposes a constraint of 'Full Interpretation' (FULL in our tableaus), which is intended to make the purely grammatical use of meaningful elements marked (in the OT sense).

The idea is that the auxiliary verb *do* is a use of the main verb *do* which does not 'parse' the lexical semantics ('lcs') of the main verb. It is unclear from her

---

[20] This is overly narrow, because inversions are used for other marked sentence types than questions. Presumably a fuller range of sentential operators is available.

account, however, exactly how this material is 'unparsed': is it present in the input? In the OT of Prince and Smolensky (1993) PARSE constraints enforce faithfulness to the input. Yet an input containing the main verb *do* (with its lcs waiting to be unparsed) together with the main verb it accompanies would be semantically incoherent, having two unintegrated semantic structures for a single predication. On the other hand, if *do* is introduced into the output by GEN as a kind of syntactic analogue to epenthesis (which seems to be what Grimshaw has in mind), how can its meaning be 'unparsed'? The role of lcs within derivational syntax has been to 'project' an argument structure and thence an initial X′ structure in the transformational derivation (e.g. Grimshaw 1990; Rappaport Hovav and Levin 1995). It is quite obscure how an unparsed lcs could project anything at all. Grimshaw's proposal seems to assume quite inexplicitly a very different view of how these structures are related: that in addition to the X′ structures there is a parallel level of representation containing the lcs, which is being 'parsed' in GEN. However, the serial derivational framework lacks an explicit correspondence theory of such parallel structures, and the same is true of Grimshaw's representational version. Since Grimshaw never states where 'lcs' (the lexical semantics) appears in this model, its role, like that of LF, remains inexplicit and is conveyed primarily by metaphorical appeals to phonology.

This unclarity can be removed by modelling the situation within an explicit parallel correspondence architecture of syntax. In the present framework, Grimshaw's 'lcs' can be modelled by the lexical PRED, her 'parsed' relation by the correspondence mapping between c-structure and f-structure, and her 'Full Interpretation' (FULL(-INT)) constraint by the FAITHFULNESS relation between the output f-structure and the input f-structure. This I will now demonstrate.

It is the lexical semantics which projects the a(rgument)-structure, and it is the a-structure which is the value of the PRED attribute. So in our terms the auxiliary verb *do* lacks a lexical PRED attribute. Grimshaw wishes to have the result that every time we use the auxiliary verb *do*, it creates a FULL(-INT) violation. In our terms, this means that it has an attribute (the 'unparsed' PRED) that does not correspond to the input. There is a simple way to model this idea formally in GEN in the present framework.

In this framework, words are modelled as sets of morpholexical constraints on parallel structures, as I remarked at the outset. Hence the correspondence between c-structure and f-structure at the word level is defined by the same formal system as the correspondence at the syntactic phrasal level. The parallel categorial and feature structures of a word like *did* can be represented as follows:

$$(42) \quad V_z \\ \quad | \\ \quad did \quad \begin{bmatrix} \text{TNS} & \text{PAST} \\ \text{PRED} & \text{`do}(x,\ldots)\text{'} \end{bmatrix}_z$$

The feature structure in (42) is the unification of the two simple feature structures in (43):

(43)   V_z $\begin{bmatrix} \text{TNS} & \text{PAST} \end{bmatrix}_z$
                       $\begin{bmatrix} \text{PRED} & \text{'do(x, ...)'} \end{bmatrix}_z$
        |
        did

Every f-structure is the unification of a set of such simple feature structures. What GEN does is integrate the partial c- and f-structures of words with those of phrasal configurations by fitting together the various pieces of the categorial structure and unifying the corresponding partial feature structures. All we need to do to model a failure to 'parse the lcs' is to let GEN set aside one of the simple lexical feature structures—specifically, the PRED feature. The result will be a *disconnected* f-structure, having some unused lexical attributes which were set aside by GEN:

(44)

The unused little f-structure indexed by * in (44) was set aside by GEN; it does not correspond to anything in the input (45):

(45)   INPUT = $\begin{bmatrix} \text{PRED} & \text{'say(x,y)'} \\ \text{GF}_1 & \text{['she']}_x \\ \text{GF}_2 & \text{['that']}_y \\ \text{TNS} & \text{PAST} \end{bmatrix}$

This lack of correspondence is a faithfulness violation, specifically a FILL-PRED violation.[21] Hence the supporting *do* will incur a mark which penalizes its pres-

---

[21] In terms of the formal solution algorithm of LFG (Kaplan and Bresnan 1995 [1982]; Bresnan, forthcoming), the correspondence between c-structure and f-structure at both the word and phrase level is defined using functional schemata that specify the functional attributes and relations of mother ('↑') and daughter ('↓') nodes. (For any node N annotated with a f-structure specification schema containing '↑' or '↓', '↑' designates the f-structure of the mother of N and '↓' the f-structure of the N.) The algorithm for defining the correspondence between parallel c- and f-structures involves instantiating these functional schemata with indices referring to the nodes of specific structures. Formally, we can say that an unparsed lexical feature is *uninstantiatable*. Specifically, let us represent an 'unparsed' lexical feature as one which instantiates '↑ ' with an arbitrary index unused in the correspondence mapping between c-structure and f-structure (the 'parse'); this index is '*' in the following illustration:

main verb *did*: (↑ PRED) = 'do(x, . . .)'   ⇒ aux verb *did*: (* PRED) = 'do(x, . . .)'
                  (↑ TNS) = PAST   (↑ TNS) = PAST

ence except where overriding constraints such as OB-HD or the need for affirmative emphasis (not discussed by Grimshaw (1997)) apply. This accounts for our next example set (= Grimshaw's (6), 383):[22]

(46)   a. She said that.
       b. *She did say that. (unstressed *did*)

(47) Matrix declaratives with and without *do*	OP	OB-HD	AGR	FULL	STAY
☞ i. [S DP [VP V that]]					
ii. [IP DP do [VP V that]]				*!	
iii. [IP e [S DP V that]]		*!			

The distribution of *do* with *wh* questions also follows straightforwardly from this analysis. Consider (48) (= Grimshaw's (7), 383), its input (49), and the outcome (50):

(48)   a. What did she say?
       b. *What she said?
       c. *What she did say?

(49)   INPUT = $\begin{bmatrix} \text{TNS} & \text{PAST} \\ \text{PRED} & \text{'say(x,y)'} \\ \text{GF}_1 & \text{['she']}_x \\ \text{GF}_2 & \text{['what']}_y \\ \text{DF} \end{bmatrix}$

(50) Matrix interrogatives with and without *do*	OP	OB-HD	AGR	FULL	STAY
☞ i. [CP wh do [IP DP e [VP V ec]]]				*	**
ii. [CP wh e [IP DP e [VP V ec]]]		*!			*
iii. [CP wh e [S DP [VP V ec]]]		*!			*
iv. [CP wh e [IP DP do [VP V ec]]]		*!			*

The examples so far are parallel to Grimshaw's both in structural descriptions

Then following exactly the same (LFG) correspondence algorithm used elsewhere in GEN, the disconnected f-structure shown in (44) results.

[22] Note that the S in candidates (i) and (iii) does not violate AGR, in contrast to candidate (v) of (36) and (iv) of (41). That is because the extended head of the subject in (i) and (iii), which is the main verb in (46), is finite, and can satisfy AGR.

for the optimal outputs and in the patterns of violation of the constraints. The same is true for the next set of examples (= Grimshaw's (8), 384). (51a) wins over (b, c) because the latter are penalized for unfaithfulness, having empty *do*:

(51)   a. What will she say?
       b. *What will she do say?
       c. *What does she will say?

The penalties for *do* accumulate, just as in Grimshaw's analysis, explaining (52) (= Grimshaw's (9), 384):

(52)   a. What did she say?
       b. *What did she do say?
       c. *What did she do do say?

We see, then, that the distribution of the auxiliary *do* can indeed be explained as a syntactic analogue of phonological epenthesis, which appears to be the intended substance of Grimshaw's proposal. *Do* arises as outlined above; it is hypothesized to be the element in the infinite candidate set that allows the most harmonic balancing of constraints, including both OB-HD and FULL. The unparsing of its semantically minimal PRED feature is a smaller violation of faithfulness than that incurred by unparsing the semantically richer PREDS of *shout, obfuscate*, or any other verb in the English lexicon.[23] By replacing Grimshaw's derivational GEN with an explicit parallel correspondence ('linking') theory of syntax, we can quite naturally model 'unparsing' as imperfect correspondence. No new rules or structures need be added to the framework; the possibility of syntactic epenthesis is (and always has been) intrinsic in the formal correspondence architecture of this syntactic framework.

10.3.3   *Main Verbs and* Do

The Optimal Syntax framework can obtain main verb inversion by re-ranking, just as Grimshaw does. To explain why only auxiliary verbs invert in English, as shown in (53) (= Grimshaw's (10), 385)—

(53)   a. *What said she?
       b. What did she say?

—Grimshaw adds a new constraint: NO-LEX-MVT, which marks movement of a lexical head. She does not define what counts as a 'lexical head' in language-

---

[23] Presumably other semantically minimal verbs, such as *be* or *have*, have other features that diminish faithfulness. There is some evidence (brought to my attention by Dick Hudson (p.c., 7 March 1997)) that other features may be involved even with *do*: some nonstandard dialects of English use different tense forms for main and auxiliary verb *do* (Cheshire 1978). There are also dialects of German that allow *tun* 'do' in Verb-Second position as an auxiliary to the main verb (Susanne Riehemann, p.c.). Further empirical investigation is needed.

independent terms, which is crucial for determining the typological validity of this constraint. It is clear that having semantic content is not sufficient to be a lexical head, because the English modals have this property, but are generated in I and not V. They are always 'functional heads' F in the sense of extended X′ theory and its functional projections (FP), and never lexical heads.

For the purposes of this exploratory demonstration, let us assume that a lexical head has a (parsed) lexical PRED attribute, and that modal auxiliaries carry semantic features of other types. (For example, we have tacitly represented the English modal verb *will* as carrying TNS = FUT.) Then we can recast Grimshaw's NO-LEX-MVT constraint in non-derivational terms as *a constraint on categorization*:

(54)   *LEX-F: No lexical heads in functional categories.

By ranking this constraint just where Grimshaw ranks her NO-LEX-MVT constraint, we can derive all of her results. For example, (53a, b) compare as follows:[24]

(55) Inversion of a main verb vs. presence of *do*	OP	*LEX-F	OB-HD	AGR	FULL	STAY
i. $[_{CP}$ wh V $[_S$ DP $[_{VP}$ e ec]]]		*!				**
☞ ii. $[_{CP}$ wh do $[_{IP}$ DP *e* $[_{VP}$V ec]]]					*	**
iii. $[_{CP}$ wh do $[_S$ DP $[_{VP}$ V ec]]]				*!		*

Under the re-ranking of *LEX-F, main verb inversion would result, exactly as in Grimshaw (386):

(56) Effect of re-ranking on verb/*do* inversion	OP	OB-HD	AGR	FULL	*LEX-F	STAY
☞ i. $[_{CP}$ wh V $[_S$ DP $[_{VP}$ *e* ec]]]					*	**
ii. $[_{CP}$ wh do $[_{IP}$ DP *e* $[_{VP}$V ec]]]				*!		**
iii. $[_{CP}$ wh do $[_S$ DP $[_{VP}$ V ec]]]			*!			*

We can now also capture Grimshaw's derivation of lexical gaps (such as the lack of an empty auxiliary *do*) from constraint ranking, since our account is (in substance) isomorphic with hers, for the range of data she considers.

10.3.4 Do *and* Wh-*subjects*

Grimshaw explains the interaction of *do* and *Wh*-subjects shown in (57)

---

[24] In both (i) and (iii) of (55) the verb V is the extended head of the VP sister to the subject. The fact that this V is finite in (i) but not in (iii) accounts for the difference in AGR violations.

(= Grimshaw's (13), 388) by letting the VP-internal subject count as a 'specifier position' for OP-SPEC:

(57) a. Who saw it?
      b. Who did see it? [unstressed *did*]

Since this SPEC of VP position is already a prominent SPEC position, according to Grimshaw, no CP and no head movement are needed, and we are more harmonic without them (because of FULL, which penalizes *do*).

The same result follows from our reformulation of OP-SPEC as requiring that an operator must be the value of a DF in the f-structure. By definition the subject function is one of the DF functions (Bresnan, forthcoming).[25] Grimshaw's results now follow:

(58) INPUT = $\begin{bmatrix} \text{DF} & \\ \text{GF}_1 & ['\text{who}']_x \\ \text{PRED} & '\text{say(x,y)}' \\ \text{GF}_2 & ['\text{it}']_y \\ \text{TNS} & \text{PAST} \end{bmatrix}$

(59) The position of subject *Wh*-phrases	OP	OB-HD	AGR	FULL	STAY
☞ i. [$_S$ wh [$_{VP}$ V it]]					
ii. [$_{CP}$ wh *e* [$_S$ [*e*] [$_{VP}$ V it]]]	*!				*
iii. [$_{CP}$ wh did [$_S$ [*e*] [$_{VP}$ V it]]]			*!	*	*
iv. [$_{IP}$ wh *e* [$_{VP}$ V it]]		*!	*		

10.3.5 *Negation and* Do

Grimshaw's analysis of negation assumes that Neg heads a functional projection in the phrase structure, and that a conspiracy of constraints and conditions causes it to appear below IP (or TP). By Grimshaw's CASE constraint, the subject must be licensed by appropriate agreement features, which Neg lacks. By her SUBJ constraint, the subject must appear in the SPEC of the highest 'I-related' head, of which Neg (but not C) is one. It follows Neg must be c-commanded by the agreeing verb and cannot c-command the subject. Thus Grimshaw's theory hypothesizes negation structures like (60). (This example also shows the trace of the subject raised successively from its VP-internal position, through SPEC of NegP, to SPEC of IP.)

---

[25] The SUBJ is universally optionally identified as the default TOP of the clause. See the discussion and references in Andrews (1985).

(60)

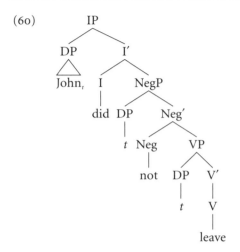

However, this proposal does not capture the fact that standard sentence negation *not* seems to form a constituent with the finite verbal auxiliary. Constituency is suggested by the possibility of constituent coordinators *both . . . and . . .* and *either . . . or . . .—*

(61)   a.   John either did or did not leave.
         b.   Mary both may not and must not come.
         c.   You either were not or are not included.

—and by the fact that this constituent has been lexicalized in the form of negative auxiliary verbs: *didn't, aren't, isn't, weren't*, etc. As shown by Zwicky and Pullum (1983), contracted *-n't* is an affix, not a clitic. These considerations suggest the alternative syntactic structure shown in (62):

(62)

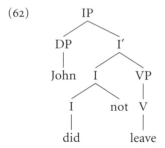

Here standard sentence negation *not* is adjoined to I. See Bresnan (1997b) for further evidence and discussion.

This alternative immediately accounts for the distributional facts about sentential negation *not* in finite clauses cited by Grimshaw (1997) (her examples (15)–(18), 390–1).

(63) a. *John not left.
      b. *Not John left.
      c. *John left not.
      d. John did not leave.

(64) a. Who did not leave?
      b. *Who not left?

Grimshaw considers an analysis similar to the above, but rejects it because *not* stands alone in subjunctive clauses in English, as shown in (65) (= Grimshaw's (19), 392):

(65) a. I insist that John not leave.
      b. *I insist that not John left.
      c. *I insist that John do not leave.
      d. *I insist that John leave not.

Kim and Sag (1996: 9) also point to examples where an adverb separates the finite auxiliary from *not* as evidence against adjoining *not* to the finite auxiliary:

(66) a. They will obviously not have time to change.
      b. You are usually not thinking about the problem.
      c. They are obviously not good citizens.

They propose instead that *not* selects a nonfinite VP in English (similar ideas are found in the analyses of Baker (1991), Ernst (1992), Warner (1993: 86), and Williams (1994)). This would offer an alternative account of the examples in (63)–(64). However, as Grimshaw (1997: 392) observes, the lexical specification for (non)finiteness seems arbitrary. Further, such an approach offers no explanation for examples like (67), which though they may be accepted as expressions of sentence negation in a formal style, are fully obsolete in the English of many speakers (except perhaps in contrastive uses):[26]

(67) a. %Did he not leave?
      b. %Is she not smart?

How can these problems be resolved? The possibilities for standard sentence negation that we see in English are instances of a much broader typological generalization (Payne 1985): across languages negation is realized as a *verbal category*—by means of negative lexical verbs, negative auxiliaries, negative verbal inflections, and negative particles adjoined to verbs or verb phrases. For example, negation may be expressed by full negative lexical verbs which take complements containing the lexical verb of the affirmative proposition being negated (see Unseth 1994 for a detailed example). Among languages which have invariant

---

[26] An example of this type is accepted without comment by Warner (1993: 86), so there may be variation in American and British usage.

negative particles for standard negation—like English *not* and Russian *ne*—the negative particle is most often adjacent to the verb, exactly as expressed by our adjunction analysis (62).[27] Thus it is reasonable to assume that the structure in (62) is one typological instantiation of a universal (and violable) constraint on categorization classifying standard sentence negation as a verbal category. But this candidate structure competes with others, including the expression of negation by means of a particle adjoined to a verb phrase rather than to a verb. Harmonically ranking the finite-auxiliary adjunction analysis above the VP adjunction analysis would explain why adjunction of *not* to VP in English emerges only in restricted circumstances when the finite auxiliary is unavailable, such in subjunctive complements (as in (65)), or when faithfulness to adverbial scope relations overrides the preference for adjunction to I (as in (66)).

Modern English adjoins *not* to a verbal category, but not to any verbal category. C and V are excluded, as shown by (68b and c), respectively:

(68)   a. He did not leave.
        b. *Did not he leave?
        c. *He left not.

In other words, *not* in modern English is 'I-related', as Grimshaw (1997) stipulates in her principle for interpreting her suBj constraint. Our alternative hypothesis is that *not* adjoins to I, not C. This can be viewed as a violable categorization constraint, one of a family of (re-rankable) constraints instantiating the universal verbal categorization of negation. (See Bresnan 1997b.) Note further that since the syntactic constituents of I never get moved to C in Optimal Syntax, *not* is never dragged with them, and since virtually all auxiliary verbs in English are categorized as F, occuring in both I and C, the lexically inflected negative auxiliaries are expected to belong to this class as well. Thus we easily explain the contrast between (69a, b):[28]

(69)   a. *Did not he leave?
        b. Didn't he leave?

In sum, we have adopted the categorization constraint in (70) as one instance of a family of constraints requiring negation to belong to a verbal category; in English it dominates constraints allowing the negative particle to adjoin to VP:

(70)   NEG-TO-I: A negative particle adjoins to I.

---

[27] According to King (1995), Russian *ne* 'not' also adjoins to I, and her work on cliticization and prosodic inversion in Slavic (King 1996) shows that this analysis can be uniformly maintained across a variety of Slavic languages that otherwise differ in word order.

[28] Warner (1993: 86, 250) presents examples like (69a) as grammatical, citing Quirk *et al.* (1985) who observe that 'some speakers accept' it as a 'rather formal' construction. He nevertheless finds the uncontracted negation in tags ungrammatical (*—did not he?*, *—is not she?*), an exception he attributes to 'weight ordering'.

In addition, we have assumed that finite auxiliaries in English are categorized as verbal functional heads; we need not formulate a separate constraint to this effect, however, since it would follow from interpreting *Lex-F (54) bidirectionally.

To see in detail how the present analysis works, consider the following pair of examples:

(71)   a. He did not leave.
       b. He didn't leave.

These examples illustrate an important feature of the parallel correspondence theory that I referred to at the outset: that lexical words may correspond to the same feature structures as syntactic phrases. Let us hypothesize the respective representations in (72) and (73) for *did* and *didn't* (ignoring the unparsed PRED attribute for present purposes). The attribute POL represents 'polarity', and is contributed morphologically by the negative affix to the form *didn't*. The category 'F' represents a verbal functional projection (I or C), allowing these auxiliaries to appear in both inverted and uninverted positions. The attribute [DF [OP Q]] is associated with the C instantiation of verbal F by the conditional constraint in (74), as in the discussion of yes/no questions above.

(72) F_i $\begin{bmatrix} TNS & PAST \end{bmatrix}_z$
         |
        did

(73) F_i $\begin{bmatrix} TNS & PAST \\ POL & NEG \end{bmatrix}_i$
         |
        didn't

(74) $C_i \Rightarrow \begin{bmatrix} DF & [QP\ Q] \end{bmatrix}_i$
         |
        verb

Observe that the lexical negative auxiliary *didn't* has exactly the same feature structure as the partial c-structure we hypothesize for analytic sentence negation:

(75) I_i $\begin{bmatrix} TNS & PAST \\ POL & NEG \end{bmatrix}_i$
        /\
       I   not
       |
      did

Thus we have both (77) and (78) in the near-optimal portion of the candidate set for the input (76):

(76)   INPUT =$\begin{bmatrix} \text{PRED} & \text{'leave(x)'} \\ \text{GF} & [\text{'he'}]_x \\ \text{POL} & \text{NEG} \\ \text{TNS} & \text{PAST} \end{bmatrix}$

(77)

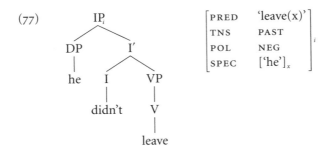

(78)

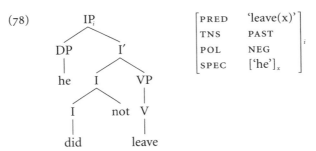

The feature-structure content of these two candidates is identical.[29] None of our constraints distinguish these candidates.[30] Hence, the candidates will fare identically with respect to EVAL, and both will in fact be optimal for the given input. (Possibly there are non-syntactic factors such as style or speech level that choose between these forms, but they are disregarded in this account of the syntax. They are equally marked by all of the constraints of interest here.)

To see why the yes/no interrogative counterparts (74a, b) of these declarative

[29] Some contracted negative modals differ in scope relations from uncontracted ones, and so would not be equivalent candidates. Unlike the present examples, these would be distinguished by faithfulness to different semantic inputs. See Bresnan (1997b).

[30] The constraint DON'T-PROJECT penalizes unnecessary use of phrase structure (nonterminal and non-preterminal) nodes, favouring lexical over structural expressions. However, it does not penalize (77) because the I immediately dominating *not* is a preterminal node. The constaint marks any c-structure node which does not immediately dominate a lexical element. Both instances of I in our *not* adjunction structures immediately dominate lexical elements.

alternants differ in grammaticality, it is necessary only to examine the following two respective structures for (74a, b):

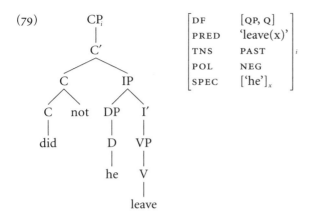

(79)

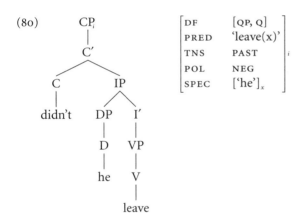

(80)

As with the declaratives, the feature structures are identical. The negatively inflected auxiliary *didn't* in (80) and the *did* in (79) both satisfy the bidirectional categorization constraint *LEX-F: they are functional heads in functional categories. In contrast, the analytic negative *did not* in (79) violates the categorization constraint NEG-TO-I (70), because *not* is adjoined to C, not I, and so incurs a fatal mark.

Now with this analysis, we can explain Grimshaw's example sets, the additional data showing constituency of *not* and I, and the alternation contrasts with inflected and analytic negatives, repeated here:

(81) a. He did not leave.
      b. He didn't leave.

(82)   a. *Did not he leave?
        b. Didn't he leave?

10.4 Evidence for Imperfect Correspondence

We have now seen how Grimshaw's derivationally-framed ideas can be translated into the Optimal Syntax framework without loss of generality and with some empirical and conceptual gains. The interest of this exercise, however, is not only in showing how Grimshaw's theory can be reconstructed in a truly non-derivational framework, but in discovering thereby a solution to an inversion problem that has resisted explanation in other terms.

As we observed above, most finite auxiliaries of English show regularity in occurring in I or C (inverted) position, as captured in (83) :

(83) $\text{verb}_{\text{aux,fin}} \in \text{F}$
        $\text{verb}_{\text{fin}} \in \text{V}$

This property in turn may be derived from the constraint rankings of *Lex-F, Full, and Ob-Hd, and the bidirectionality of *Lex-F, as discussed just below (70). Despite these regularities there are specific lexical elements in English that appear only in a restricted category. A well-known example is that *aren't* plays the role of the first person singular present negative form of *be* in some varieties of English which lack negative inflection of *am* in the paradigm of *be* (cf. Langendoen 1970; Hudson 1977; Dixon 1982; Gazdar *et al.* 1982; Kim and Sag 1996):

(84)   *aren't* $\in$ C [first person singular]

The asymmetry appears in (85):

(85)   a. Isn't she smart? ~ She isn't smart.
        b. Aren't you smart? ~ You aren't smart.
        c. Aren't I smart? ~ *I aren't smart.

Various hypotheses have been advanced about the sources of this gap in the inflectional paradigm of *be*. Some dialects of English have first person negative forms *amn't* or *ain't*, but these have been dropped from standard English, possibly as a result of phonological complexity (Dixon 1982 on *amn't*) or social stigmatization (*ain't*); see Bresnan (1997b) for further discussion. What is important to observe here is that the analytic form of negation (*not* adjoined to I) only partially fills this gap:

(86)   *Am not I smart? ~ I am not smart.

This fact follows from the analysis given in Section 10.3: *not* is categorized as an adjunct to I and there is no I-to-C movement; hence *not* cannot appear in inverted position.[31] That leaves just one cell in the paradigm to fill: the inverted (verbal C) position, and this is precisely the role of *aren't*, as shown in (84).

Such cases are an embarrassment to movement theories: in a case like (85c), for example, a 'moved' element fails to have a source position from which movement could have occurred. One might propose, following the style of work in the Minimalist Program, that there is some special feature carried by the particular form *aren't* in the first person singular that requires it to be checked in (and hence moved to) C.[32] But what feature could this be? One might respond that this could be whatever feature allows us to lexically categorize it as belonging to the restricted category C in our framework, as in (84) (see Kim and Sag (1996) for an example of this approach using the feature [+INV]). However, in the Optimal Syntax framework we need no such special lexical feature at all, as I will now demonstrate.

The most harmonic solution to an overall set of constraints on the expression of some input may force a lexicalization that is not perfectly faithful to the input but which is the best match available to the input within the paradigm. The use of *aren't* for the inverted first person singular appears to be such a case. The table in (87) shows that *are* is the least marked form in the present tense paradigm of *be* for expressing both number and person:[33]

(87)

	sg	pl
1	am	are
2	are	are
3	is	are

The corresponding negative paradigm is shown in (88); as remarked above, it is defective, lacking a negatively affixed form of *am*:

(88)

	sg	pl
1		aren't
2	aren't	aren't
3	isn't	aren't

Each of these verbal forms has a corresponding feature structure expressing tense, polarity, and the person and number of the subject. For example, the feature structure for *isn't* is illustrated in (89):

---

[31] In terms of the logic of markedness on OT, this categorization means that in English adjoining *not* to other categories than to I as standard sentence negation generally incurs more marks.

[32] A possibility suggested by Jane Grimshaw (p.c., 23 March 1996).

[33] The significance of this fact in the present context was pointed out to me by Jane Grimshaw (p.c., 23 Feb. 1996).

(89) F_i
       |
       isn't
$$\begin{bmatrix} \text{TNS} & \text{PAST} \\ \text{POL} & \text{NEG} \\ \text{SPEC} & \begin{bmatrix} \text{PERS} & 3 \\ \text{NUM} & \text{SG} \end{bmatrix} \end{bmatrix}_i$$

As discussed in Section 10.3, the analytic standard sentence negation form has an identical feature structure, but is shown adjoined to I in accordance with the categorization constraint NEG-TO-I:

(90) I_i
       /\
      I   not
      |
      is
$$\begin{bmatrix} \text{TNS} & \text{PAST} \\ \text{POL} & \text{NEG} \\ \text{SPEC} & \begin{bmatrix} \text{PERS} & 3 \\ \text{NUM} & \text{SG} \end{bmatrix} \end{bmatrix}_i$$

Thus, both the analytic and synthetic forms will be close competitors in the candidate set.

Now to represent the fact that *are* and *aren't* are unmarked members of their paradigms, we can assume that they simply lack feature values for person and number. This is represented by the feature structure in (91), which has valueless attributes PERS and NUM:[34]

(91) F_i
       |
       aren't
$$\begin{bmatrix} \text{TNS} & \text{PAST} \\ \text{POL} & \text{NEG} \\ \text{SPEC} & \begin{bmatrix} \text{PERS} \\ \text{NUM} \end{bmatrix} \end{bmatrix}_i$$

How do we interpret such unmarked features with respect to the input? Let us assume with Grimshaw (1996) that the input is fully specified for all features and that candidate forms may be partially specified. We further assume with Grimshaw that FILL penalizes any form which specifies a feature value that conflicts with the input, while PARSE penalizes any form that does not preserve the feature value of the input. FILL thus exempts partially specified forms from marks if they do not conflict with the input.

To explain in this framework why unmarked forms are preferred over marked forms, we must hypothesize that the FILL constraints dominate the PARSE constraints.[35] Finally, we model the accidental lexical gap for the first person singular

---

[34] Formally, the structure in (91) may be taken to represent the presence of the existential constraints ($\uparrow$ PERS) and ($\uparrow$ NUM) associated with this lexical form (Kaplan and Bresnan 1995 [1982]).

[35] The reverse ranking is also possible, as Grimshaw (1996) shows, though presumably rare. A parallel assumption under the different faithfulness framework of Smolensky (1996a, b) is that structural markedness constraints dominate the faithfulness constraints (which include PARSE but not

present negative form of *be* by a highly ranked constraint LEX (see Bresnan (1997a, b, c) for further discussion and other examples):

(92)   LEX: Structurally non-empty inventory elements must be lexically paired with phonological realizations.

English dialects having the forms *amn't* and *ain't* satisfy this constraint for inputs specifying the first person singular present negative, but Standard English violates it, having no such form.

The details of the analysis follow straightforwardly. We need only assume that the constraint against inverting *not* with the auxiliary (NEG-TO-I (70)) dominates the faithfulness constraints for person and number. Under these assumptions, analytic and synthetic forms will be close competitors. When there are specific forms matching the input, they will be optimal, as shown in tableaux (93) and (94). (Crucial constraint rankings are indicated by vertical bars. We abbreviate the input and candidate feature structures using Grimshaw's (1996) notation: angled brackets enclose a feature structure, features are represented by their values, and valueless or unmarked features by the feature name enclosed in parentheses.)

Negative third person singular input (declarative)

(93)	INPUT < neg 3 sg >		LEX	NEG-I	FILL	PARSE
☞	i. isn't	< neg 3 sg >				
☞	ii. is not	< neg 3 sg >				
	iii. aren't	< neg (P)(N) >				*!*
	iv. are not	< neg (P)(N) >				*!*
	v. am not	< neg 1 sg >			*!	*
	vi.	< neg 1 sg >	*!		*	*

Negative first person singular input (declarative)

(94)	INPUT < neg 1 sg >		LEX	NEG-I	FILL	PARSE
	i. isn't	< neg 3 sg >			*!	*
	ii. is not	< neg 3 sg >			*!	*
	iii. aren't	< neg (P)(N) >				*!*
	iv. are not	< neg (P)(N) >				*!*
☞	v. am not	< neg 1 sg >				
	vi.	< neg 1 sg >	*!			

FILL) in the initial state, though re-ranking can occur. See Bresnan (1997b, c) for further development of this alternative faithfulness framework in explaining the problem at hand.

Observe in (94) how the lexical gap for the first person negative is filled by the analytic form *am not*. When the most specified forms conflict with the input, the general forms will be optimal, as we expect:

Negative first person plural input (declarative)

(95) INPUT < neg 1 pl >	LEX	NEG-I	FILL	PARSE
i. isn't < neg 3 sg >			*!*	**
ii. is not < neg 3 sg >			*!*	**
☞ iii. aren't < neg (P)(N) >				**
☞ iv. are not < neg (P)(N) >				**
v. am not < neg 1 sg >		*!		*
vi. < neg 1 sg >	*!	*		*

Now in all these tableaus the analytic (*not*) forms are equally harmonic with the synthetic negative forms available as long as both are in I° (postsubject position). When inverted (in C° position), however, the analytic form will incur a mark by NEG-TO-I, and the synthetic form becomes more harmonic. This is fine in all cases except for the first person singular input, where a synthetic first person singular form is lacking (see (94)). The analytic form still cannot be used in this (inverted) case, which tells us that NEG-TO-I must outrank the PARSE constraints at least. In just this case, the optimal candidate becomes *aren't*:

Negative first person singular input (interrogative):

(96) INPUT < Q neg 1 sg >	LEX	NEG-I	FILL	PARSE
i. isn't < Q neg 3 sg >			*!	*
ii. is not < Q neg 3 sg >		*!	*	*
☞ iii. aren't < Q neg (P)(N) >				**
iv. are not < Q neg (P)(N) >		*!		**
v. am not < Q neg 1 sg >		*!		
vi. < Q neg 1 sg >	*!			

What we have demonstrated is that the appearance of *aren't* in the inverted position for the first person singular follows from its unmarked status for person and number in the verbal paradigm for *be*, given the strong constraint against using the analytic forms in inverted position. Its appearance in *only* the inverted position results from the competition by the more harmonic analytic form in the uninverted position.

The negative auxiliary inversion paradigm (85) is an embarrassment for the transformational theory of verb positioning, as noted above and originally observed by Gazdar *et al.* (1982), because there is no source for the moved form in its underlying position. However, the problem is a deeper one than has been recognized. The correct forms can easily be generated in a transformational framework which allows post-movement feature checking (such as the Minimalist Program). Suppose, for example, that the features shown in (97) are to be checked against derived positions; the feature INV is a special feature which must be checked in C (the inverted position):

$$(97) \quad \text{aren't:} \quad \begin{bmatrix} \text{P} & 1 \\ \text{N} & \text{SG} \\ \text{NEG} & + \\ \text{INV} & + \end{bmatrix}$$

Now the asymmetry follows straightforwardly. **I aren't smart* is bad because the feature INV cannot be checked in I°, although the person and number agreement features can successfully be checked; *Aren't I smart?* is good, because the checking for INV is now satisfied, and the agreement features were checked in I° along the derivational path to C°. Note, however, that this solution requires overspecification (filling in features for the general form). It thus becomes accidental that it is the *general* form that fills the paradigmatic gap under this approach, and then only where there is not a more faithful analytic form available. But this is not an accident. Asymmetries in the formal patterns of morphosyntax in other dialects of English and other languages reflect exactly the same factors of paradigmatic competition between alternative morphological and syntactic forms.[36]

10.5 Discussion

I have now shown that the effects that Grimshaw attributes to head movement in English (or to its representational simulations) can be captured in the Imperfect Correspondence theory without any loss of generalization, and that there are further effects—such as the asymmetric distribution of the first person negative auxiliary *be*—that only have an explanation under imperfect correspondence. Let us now step back and reconsider our original motivations for improving on Grimshaw's framework.

10.5.1 *Optimal Syntax and Derivationalism*

Despite the recent importation of functionalist concepts such as 'economy' into transformational theory, it continues to build upon the 1950s and 1960s technology of serial derivations by transformational rules. While the 1980s brought representational simulations of derivations with chains and traces, the 1990s Minimalist Program brings us squarely back to derivationalism (cf. Johnson and Lappin 1997; Jackendoff 1996). The core idea expressed by derivationalism in syntax is that there is an underlying perfect correspondence between roles, functions, and categories, which is distorted by transformational operations (such as

---

[36] See Bresnan (1997a, b, c) for further discussion and exemplification.

movements). The traces that annotate derived X′ trees are derivational records of this more perfect correspondence. It is the assumption of perfect correspondence that justifies encoding information about non-tree structures (semantic and functional) into the syntactic tree.

What Optimal Syntax makes evident is that syntactic 'movements' are nothing more than imperfect correspondences between different dimension of linguistic substance—roles, functions, and categories—modelled by the correspondence mappings of parallel structures. While it may be highly unmarked for these structures to correspond perfectly, the assumption that perfect correspondence is an inviolable core of Universal Grammar is conceptually unnecessary and empirically unwarranted (see Bresnan 1994, 1995, forthcoming). It also seems counter to the spirit of OT to express violations of universal constraints (such as correspondence) operationally and mechanistically.

10.5.2 *Optimal Syntax and Lexicalism*

As I remarked at the outset, Grimshaw's (1997) syntactic analysis of heads demands non-uniformities in the treatment of morphological inflections. On the basis of differing verb order properties in English and French, she treats the tense and agreement inflections of English as part of its lexical morphology, while she supposes that the tense and agreement inflections of French are syntactically projected as heads of a phrase structure category (IP, TP, AgrP, etc.) to be united with their verbal hosts by movement. From the point of view of either lexicalist or anti-lexicalist morphological theory, this is perhaps the worst of both worlds. Optimal Syntax is coherently lexicalist. In this framework, the c-structures of English and French are very similar, both languages having I and V as heads of IP and VP and both languages having lexically attached verbal inflections. The two languages differ in verbal categorization, French classing finite verbs as elements of the verbal functional categories F (subsuming I and C), English classing only finite auxiliaries as elements of verbal F:[37]

(98)   a. English: $\text{verb}_{\text{aux,fin}} \in \text{F}$
              $\text{verb}_{\text{fin}} \in \text{V}$
          b. French: $\text{verb}_{\text{fin}} \in \text{F}$

This difference in turn may be derived from alternative constraint rankings of *Lex-F, FULL, and OB-HD, as discussed in Section 10.3. The possibility of different verbal categorizations stems from the theory of functional projections F′ in Optimal Syntax, which allows imperfect correspondence in the positioning of heads in an extended verbal projection. Some lexicalist theories of syntax have denied the value of an extended X′ theory of functional categories, which they take to be inextricably associated with nonlexicalist derivational syntax (e.g.

---

[37] French may not be the most convincing example of a V-to-I language, compared to other languages, but I accept that analysis here for the sake of the argument.

Pollard and Sag 1994). Following recent work in LFG cited above, Optimal Syntax shows that something of value can be extricated from both lexicalism and extended X′ theory.[38]

However, there is an also an important sense in which the lexicalism of Optimal Syntax is qualified. While morphological and syntactic forms of expression are subject to different principles of formation, they correspond to the same types of feature structures under the parallel correspondence theory. It is for this reason that words and phrases may compete as candidate expressions of the same information. The functional equivalence of lexical morphology and syntax is crucial in our explanation of the English auxiliary inversion patterns, and explains many typologically varied ways in which morphology competes with syntax (see Bresnan 1997b, forthcoming; Nordlinger 1998a; and the references cited therein).

10.5.3 *Substance of Constraints*

Several of Grimshaw's (1997) constraints (e.g. STAY, NO-LEX-MVT) are formulated in terms of the theory-internal mechanism of movement. In the present framework of Optimal Syntax these have been generalized into constraints that make no reference to specific mechanisms of GEN. The substance of our STAY constraint (24), repeated here—

(99)   STAY: Categories dominate their extended heads.

—is about *endocentricity*. The constraint states that an element that functions as the head of XP is dominated by XP. Likewise, our version of NO-LEX-MVT is *LEX-F:

(100)   *LEX-F: No lexical heads in functional categories.

The substance of this constraint is about *categorization*. Lexical heads are those having descriptive content, which we have (approximately) modelled by having the PRED attribute. The constraint is that such descriptively contentful elements belong to lexical categories (e.g. V, N, etc.) and not functional categories (e.g. C, I, etc.). Languages which place lexical heads in special functional positions (e.g. Russian or possibly French) do so for overriding reasons.

10.5.4 *Generality of the Theory of Structures*

Although I have only hinted at the possibility (Section 1.3), I think that Optimal

---

[38] There are of course problems in giving a clear set of criteria for determining the extensions of the functional categories in a lexicalized X′-theory, but they are no different in principle from the problems of determining the extensions of the lexical categories V, N, A, P, etc., in the face of apparently gradient lexical classes. This problem is given a far more concrete empirical grounding in the present lexicalized version of the theory of functional categories, than it has in derivational frameworks. The use of imperfect correspondence and violable constraints may provide a new solution to problems of gradiance in categorization; see Hayes (this volume).

Syntax can gracefully generalize to language types which make greater use of morphology than X' configurations to express syntactic relations (see Bresnan 1998, forthcoming; Austin and Bresnan 1996; Choi 1999; Nordlinger 1998a; Sadler 1997; Sells 1995). Given the parallel-correspondence theory of structures, the crucial idea is that endocentricity is not an inviolable constraint, built into the very architecture of GEN, but just one among alternative form/content correspondence strategies for natural language. The importance of endocentricity in the optimal outputs of a language will vary with constraint rankings.

10.6 Conclusion

In Optimality Theory, as we have seen, a grammar consists of ranked constraints which are (i) universal and (ii) violable. Because OT *per se* is a theory of constraint interaction rather than a theory of substantive linguistic constraints, it is compatible with a wide range of substantive theoretical choices. (Some consider this an explanatory weakness of the framework, but it is also the source of its great integrative potential.) In phonology and to a lesser extent morphology, OT has led to a fundamental rethinking of the domain and to the widespread adoption of non-derivational theories. Syntax, in contrast, is still greatly influenced by the derivational frameworks advanced by Chomsky, and much of the initial work applying OT to syntax reflects this way of thinking by simulating derivational analyses. It is instructive to consider the history of architectural design, which shows that earlier designs, for example in bridge-building, persist long after the development of new materials with radically different engineering properties (e.g. steel compared to wood and stone). The purpose of these notes, then, has been simply to stimulate exploration of a wider imaginative space for syntactic analysis by combining the ideas of imperfect correspondence and violable constraints.

10.7 References

Aissen, J. (1998). 'Markedness and subject choice in optimality theory'. Revised version of paper presented at the Hopkins Optimality Theory Workshop/Maryland Mayfest 1997, Inner Harbor, Baltimore, 9–12 May 1997. To appear in *Natural Language and Linguistic Theory* and Legendre *et al.* (eds).

Andrews, A. D. (1985). 'The major functions of the noun phrase'. In Shopen (ed.), 62–154.

—— (1990). 'Unification and morphological blocking'. *Natural Language and Linguistic Theory* 8, 507–57.

—— and C. Manning (1999). *Complex Predicates and Information Spreading in LFG*. Stanford, CSLI Publications.

Anttila, A. (1997). *Variation in Finnish Phonology and Morphology*. PhD thesis, Stanford University.

—— (1998). 'Deriving variation from grammar'. In F. Hinskens, R. van Hout, and L. Wetzels (eds), *Variation, Change and Phonological Theory*. Amsterdam and Philadelphia, John Benjamins.

Austin, P. and J. Bresnan (1996). 'Non-configurationality in Australian aboriginal languages'. *Natural Language and Linguistic Theory* 14, 215–68.

Baker, L. (1991). 'The syntax of English *not*: the limits of core grammar'. *Linguistic Inquiry* 22, 387–429.

Baltin, M. and A. Kroch (eds) (1989). *Alternative Conceptions of Phrase Structure*. Chicago, Chicago University Press.

Barbosa, P., D. Fox, P. Hagstrom, M. McGinnis, and D. Pesetsky (eds) (1998). *Is the Best Good Enough?* Cambridge, MA, MIT Press and MIT Working Papers in Linguistics.

Beckman, J., L. Walsh Dickey, and S. Urbanczyk (eds). (1995). *Papers in Optimality Theory*. University of Massachusetts Occasional Papers 18. Amherst, MA, Graduate Linguistics Students Association.

Berman, J. (1996). 'Topicalization vs. left dislocation of sentential arguments in German'. In Butt and King (eds).

—— (1997). 'Empty categories in LFG'. In Butt and King (eds).

—— and A. Frank (1996). *Deutsche und französische syntax im formalismus der LFG*. Tübingen, May Niemeyer Verlag.

Boersma, P. (1997). 'How we learn variation, optionality, and probability'. *IFA Proceedings* 21, 43–58. ROA-221.

Börjars, K. and C. Chapman. (1998). 'Agreement and pro-drop in some dialects of English'. *Linguistics* 36, 71–9.

—— N. Vincent, and C. Chapman, C. (1997). 'Paradigms, periphrases and pronominal inflection: a feature-based account'. In Booij and van Marle (eds), 1–26.

Booij, G. and J. van Marle (eds) (1993). *The Yearbook of Morphology*. Dordrecht, Kluwer.

Brame, M. K. (1978). *Base-Generated Syntax*. Seattle, Noit Amrofer.

Bresnan, J. (ed.) (1982). *The Mental Representation of Grammatical Relations*. Cambridge, MA, MIT Press.

—— (1982). 'Control and Complementation.' *Linguistic Inquiry* 13, 343–434.

—— (1994). 'Locative inversion and the architecture of Universal Grammar'. *Language* 70, 72–131.

—— (1995). 'Category mismatches'. In A. Akinlabi (ed.), *Theoretical Approaches to African Languages*. Lawrenceville, NJ, Africa World Press, 19–46.

—— (1997a). 'The emergence of the unmarked pronoun: Chicheŵa pronominals in Optimality Theory'. To appear in *BLS* 23.

—— (1997b). 'Explaining morphosyntactic competition'. To appear in M. Baltin and C. Collins (eds), *Handbook of Contemporary Syntactic Theory*. Oxford, Blackwell.

—— (1997c). 'The emergence of the unmarked pronoun'. Paper presented at the Hopkins Optimality Theory Workshop, Inner Harbor, Baltimore, 9–12 May 1997. To appear in Legendre *et al.* (eds).

—— (1998). 'Morphology competes with syntax: explaining typological variation in weak crossover effects'. In Barbosa *et al.* (eds), 59–92.

—— Forthcoming. *Lexical-Functional Syntax*. Oxford, Blackwell.

—— and S. A. Mchombo (1987). 'Topic, pronoun, and agreement in Chicheŵa'. *Language* 68, 741–82.

—— (1995). 'The lexical integrity principle: evidence from Bantu'. *Natural Language and Linguistic Theory* 13, 181–252.

Bresnan, J. and Zaenen, A. (1990). 'Deep unaccusativity in LFG'. In K. Dziwirek, P. Farrell, and E. Mejías-Bikandi (eds), *Grammatical Relations: A Cross-Theoretical Perspective.* Stanford, CSLI Publications/SLA, 45–57.

Burton, S. and J. Grimshaw (1992). 'Coordination and VP-internal subjects'. *Linguistic Inquiry* 23, 305–13.

Butt, M. and T. H. King (eds) (1996). Proceedings of the LFG 96 conference, Rank Xerox, Grenoble, France, On-line, Stanford University: http://csli-publications.stanford.edu/LFG/1/lfg96.html.

—— (eds) (1997). Proceedings of the LFG 97 conference, University of California, San Diego. On-line, Stanford University: http://csli-publications.stanford.edu/LFG/2/lfg97.html.

—— (eds) (1998). *Proceedings of the LFG 98 Conference,* University of Queensland, Brisbane, On-line, Stanford University: http://csli-publications.stanford.edu/LFG/3/lfg98.html.

Cheshire, J. (1978). 'Present tense verbs in Reading English'. In P. Trudgill (ed.), *Sociolinguistic Patterns in British English.* London, Arnold, 52–68.

Choi, H.-W. (1999). *Optimizing Structure in Context: Scrambling and Information Structure.* Stanford, CSLI Publications.

Corbin, F. D. Goddard, and J.-M. Marandin (eds) (1997). *Empirical Issues in Formal Syntax and Semantics.* Berne, Peter Lang.

Dalrymple, M., R. M. Kaplan, J. T. Maxwell III, and A. Zaenen (eds) (1995). *Formal Issues in Lexical-Functional Grammar.* Stanford, CSLI Publications.

Demuth, K. and M. Johnson (1989). 'Interaction between discourse functions and agreement in Setawana'. *Journal of African Languages and Linguistics* 11, 21–35.

Dixon, R. M. W. (1982). 'Semantic neutralisation for phonological reasons'. In *Where have all the adjectives gone? and Other Essays in Semantics and Syntax.* Berlin, Mouton Publishers, 235–8.

Ernst, T. (1992). 'The phrase structure of English negation'. *The Linguistic Review* 9, 109–44.

Frank, Anette and Ursula Kärcher-Momma (1992). *Dokumentation zur Französischen Syntax im Formalismus der Lexical Functional Grammar (LFG).* Stuttgart, Institut für Maschinelle Sprachverarbeitung, University of Stuttgart.

Gazdar, G., G. K. Pullum, and I. A. Sag (1982). 'Auxiliaries and related phenomena in a restrictive theory of grammar'. *Language* 58, 591-638.

Grimshaw, J. (1990). *Argument Structure.* Cambridge, MA, MIT Press.

—— (1991). 'Extended projection'. Ms, Rutgers University.

—— (1996). 'Optimizing lexical choice: expletives and opaque clitics as cases of minimal violation'. Colloquium, Stanford University Department of Linguistics, 23 February 1996.

—— (1996). 'The best clitic: constraint conflict in morphosyntax'. To appear in L. Haegeman (ed.), *Handbook of Contemporary Syntactic Theory.* Dordrecht, Kluwer Academic Publishers.

—— (1997). 'Projection, heads, and optimality'. *Linguistic Inquiry* 28, 373–422.

—— and V. Samek-Lodovici (1998). 'Optimal subjects and subject universals'. In Barbosa *et al.* (eds), 193–219.

Hudson, R. (1977). 'The power of morphological rules'. *Lingua* 42, 73-89.

Jackendoff, R. (1996). *The Architecture of the Language Faculty.* Cambridge, MA, MIT Press.

Jar, M. (n.d.) 'Reconstituted X′ constituents in LFG'. Ms, Palo Alto, CA, Xerox Palo Alto Research Center.

Johnson, D. and S. Lappin (1997). 'A critique of the minimalist program'. *Linguistics and Philosophy* 20, 273–333.

Johnson, M. (1988). *Attribute-Value Logic and the Theory of Grammar*. Stanford, CSLI Publications.

Kaplan, R. M. (1995). 'The formal architecture of lexical-functional grammar'. In Dalrymple *et al.* (eds), 7–27.

—— and J. Bresnan (1995) [1982]. 'Lexical-functional grammar: a formal system for grammatical representation'. In Dalrymple *et al.* (eds), 29–130. [reprinted from Bresnan (ed.) (1982), 173–281.]

—— and A. Zaenen (1989). 'Long-distance dependencies, constituent structure, and functional uncertainty'. In Baltin and Kroch (eds), 17–42. [reprinted in Dalrymple *et al.* (eds), 137–65]

Kim, J.-B. and I. A. Sag (1996). 'French and English negation: a lexicalist alternative to head movement'. [On-line, Stanford University: http://hpsg.stanford.edu/hpsg/sag.html.]

King, T. H. (1995). *Configuring Topic and Focus in Russian*. Stanford, CSLI Publications.

—— (1996) 'Slavic clitics, long head movement, and prosodic inversion'. *Journal of Slavic Linguistics* 4, 274–311.

Kroeger, P. (1993). *Phrase Structure and Grammatical Relations in Tagalog*. Stanford, CSLI Publications.

Langendoen, D. T. (1970). *Essentials of English grammar*. New York, Holt, Rinehart, & Winston.

Legendre, G., J. Grimshaw, and S. Vikner (eds) (to appear). *Optimality-Theoretic Syntax*. Cambridge, MA, MIT Press.

—— P. Smolensky, and C. Wilson (1998). 'When is less more? faithfulness and minimal links in *Wh*-chains'. In Barbosa *et al.* (eds).

—— W. Raymond, and P. Smolensky (1993). 'An optimality-theoretic typology of case and grammatical voice systems'. *BLS* 19, 464–78.

—— C. Wilson, P. Smolensky, K. Homer, and W. Raymond (1995). 'Optimality and *wh* extraction'. In Beckman *et al.* (eds), 607–36.

McCarthy, J. J. and A. S. Prince (1993). 'Generalized alignment'. In Booij and van Marle (eds), 79–153.

—— —— (1995). 'Faithfulness and reduplicative identity'. In Beckman *et al.* (eds), 249–384.

Meier, J. (1992). *Eine Grammatik des Deutschen im Formalismus der Lexical Functional Grammar (LFG) unter Berücksichtigung funktionaler Kategorien*. Stuttgart, Institut für Maschinelle Sprachverarbeitung, University of Stuttgart.

Mohanan, T. (1995). 'Lexicality and wordhood: noun incorporation in Hindi'. *Natural Language and Linguistic Theory* 13, 75–134.

Netter, K. (1988). 'Syntactic aspects of LFG-based dialogue parsing'. Esprit Acord project 393, Deliverable Task 2.7(a). Stuttgart, Institut für Maschinelle Sprachverarbeitung, University of Stuttgart.

—— and U. Kärcher (1986). 'Documentation of the German grammar'. Esprit Acord project 393, Deliverable Task 1.4. Stuttgart, Institut für Maschinelle Sprachverarbeitung, University of Stuttgart.

Niño, M.-E. (1997). 'The multiple expression of inflectional information and grammatical architecture'. In Corbin *et al.* (eds), 127–47.

Nordlinger, R. (1998a). *Constructive Case: Dependent-Marking Non-Configurationality in Australia.* Stanford, CSLI Publications.

—— (1998b). *A Grammar of Wambaya.* Camberra, Pacific Linguistics.

—— and J. Bresnan (1996). 'Nonconfigurational tense in Wambaya'. In Butt and King (eds).

Oehrle, R. (1981). 'Lexical justification'. In J. Moortgat, H. van der Hulst, and T. Hoekstra (eds), *The Scope of Lexical Rules.* Dordrecht, Foris, 201–28.

Payne, J. R. (1985). 'Negation'. In Shopen (ed.), 197–242.

Pollard, C. and I. A. Sag (1994). *Head-Driven Phrase Structure Grammar.* Stanford and Chicago, CSLI Publications and University of Chicago Press.

Prince, A. S. and P. Smolensky (1993). 'Optimality Theory: Constraint interaction in generative grammar'. RuCCS Technical Report #2. Piscataway, NJ, Rutgers University Center for Cognitive Science.

Quirk, R., S. Greenbaum, G. Leech, and J. Svartvik (1985). *A Comprehensive Grammar of the English Language.* London: Longman.

Rappaport Hovav, M. and B. Levin (1995). 'The elasticity of verb meaning'. IATL 2: Proceedings of the tenth annual conference of the Israel association for Theoretical Linguistics and the Workshop on the syntax-semantics interface, 1995.

Sadler, L. (1997). 'Clitics and the structure-function mapping'. In Butt and King (eds).

Sadock, J. (1991). *Autolexical Syntax.* Chicago, University of Chicago Press.

—— and A. Zwicky (1985). 'Speech-act distinctions in syntax'. In Shopen (ed.), 155–196.

Sells, P. (1995). 'Korean and Japanese morphology from a lexical perspective'. *Linguistic Inquiry* 26, 277–325.

—— (1997). 'The typology of grammatical voice systems revisited'. Paper presented at the Hopkins Optimality Theory Workshop, Inner Harbor, Baltimore, 9–12 May (1997). To appear in Legendre *et al.* (eds).

—— (1998). 'Scandinavian clause structure and object shift'. In Butt and King (eds).

Shieber, S. (1986). *An Introduction to Unification Based Approaches to Grammar.* Stanford, CSLI Publications.

—— and Y. Schabes (1990). 'Synchronous tree adjdoining grammars'. Proceedings of the 13th international conference on computational linguistics (COLING '90). Helsinki.

Shopen, T. (ed.) (1985). *Language Typology and Syntactic Description.* Vol. I: Clause Structure. Cambridge, Cambridge University Press.

Simpson, J. (1991). *Warlpiri Morpho-Syntax: A Lexicalist Approach.* Dordrecht, Kluwer Academic Publishers.

Smolensky, P. (1996a). 'On the comprehension/production dilemma in child language'. *Linguistic Inquiry* 27, 720–731.

—— (1996b). 'The initial state and "richness of the base" in optimality theory'. Technical report JHU-CogSci-96-4, Department of Cognitive Science, Johns Hopkins University.

Sproat, R. (1985). 'Welsh syntax and VSO structure'. *Natural Language and Linguistic Theory* 2, 173–116.

Tesar, B. and P. Smolensky (1998). 'Learnability of optimality theory'. *Linguistic Inquiry* 29, 229–68.

Toivonen, I. (1996). 'On projection, heads and optimality in AAVE'. Stanford Syntax Seminar presentation, 11 March 1996.

Unseth, P. (1994). 'Verbal negation in Majang'. Paper presented at the 25th Annual Conference on African Linguistics 1994, Rutgers University.

Van Valin, R. D., Jr. (1993). 'A synopsis of role and reference grammar'. In R. D. Van Valin (ed.), *Advances in Role and Reference Grammar*. Amsterdam and Philadelphia, John Benjamins, 1–164.

Vijay-Shanker, K. and A. K. Joshi (1990). 'Unification-based tree adjoining grammars'. In J. Wedekin (ed.), *Unification-Based Grammars*. Cambridge, MA, MIT Press.

Warner, A. R. (1993). *English Auxiliaries. Structure and History*. Cambridge, Cambridge University Press.

Williams, E. (1994). *Thematic Structure in Syntax*. Cambridge, MA, MIT Press.

Zaenen, A. and R. M. Kaplan (1995). 'Formal devices for linguistic generalizations: West Germanic word order in LFG'. In Dalrymple *et al.* (eds), 215–39.

Zwicky, A. M. and G. K. Pullum (1983). 'Cliticization vs. inflection: English *n't. Language* 59, 502–13.

11

The Minimalist Program and Optimality Theory: Derivations and Evaluations[1]

Hans Broekhuis and Joost Dekkers

11.1 Introduction

Optimality Theory (OT) syntax is often considered to be an alternative to the Minimalist Program outlined in Chomsky (1995). This is by no means a necessary point of view. The very reason why OT syntax and the Minimalist Program are considered to be competitors may be invoked to reconcile the two approaches to syntax: OT deals with outputs, with representations, while the Minimalist Program is mainly concerned with derivations. In the present chapter, we will put forth reasons to assume that this complementarity should be exploited by combining the two frameworks.

Chomsky (1995) aims at constructing a syntactic system of the highest degree of explanatory adequacy i.e. he attempts to design the ultimate computational system for human language (C_{HL}). In pursuit of this goal, he proposes an extreme reduction of the descriptive apparatus, leaving many phenomena which received an account in earlier stages of the theory outside the scope of C_{HL} (cf. Chomsky 1995: 389, fn. 93). However, these phenomena must be accounted for in one way or another, if we want to prevent that a rise in explanatory adequacy goes at the expense of the descriptive adequacy of the system. Chomsky suggests that they should receive an account in the PF wing of the grammar, although he does not put forth a theory that can deal with these matters. We will show that OT syntax can fill this gap. More particularly, we will follow Pesetsky (to appear), who argues for an OT system taking LF representations as its Input.

[1] We would like to thank João Costa, Marcel den Dikken, as well as the audiences present at the GLOW Colloquium 1997 (Rabat), the HIL OT Workshop (University of Leiden), the Staff Seminar Grammatica-modellen (University of Tilburg), the ATW op vrijdag Colloquium (University of Amsterdam), and the Taalkundig Colloquium (University of Groningen) for suggestions, comments, and discussion.

The Generator of this OT system creates the relevant candidate set by applying the operation DELETE in a random fashion. This candidate set is subsequently evaluated with respect to a ranking of violable constraints. This enables Pesetsky to account for several filters proposed in the 1970s, such as the Doubly Filled COMP Filter and the *For-to* Filter.

In short, the merger of C_{HL} and OT syntax is advantageous from a Minimalist point of view: the syntactic OT module, taking the place of the aforementioned filters, acts as the interface between C_{HL} and the phonological component. But also OT syntax benefits from such a step: C_{HL} provides the OT system with the generative power it needs. It is of course a truism that a generative grammar needs to generate structure in an explicit manner, even if the generating device is not primarily responsible for the descriptive adequacy of the system as a whole, a consideration which has led many practitioners of OT to ignore the precise nature of the Generator.

This leads us to a model of syntax consisting of a generator, to be identified with Chomsky's C_{HL}, and a filtering device, which operates in the standard OT fashion. In Section 11.2, we will discuss one possible realization of this general idea, and take it as our point of departure. In Section 11.3, we will investigate finite relative clauses in English and (varieties of) Dutch, and show that OT is able to account for the differences between these languages with respect to the Doubly Filled COMP Filter, something that is far beyond the scope of the Minimalist Program as currently understood. Furthermore, some attention will be paid to the anti-*that*-trace effect in English relative clauses. In the conclusion of this section, we will argue that there are reasons to modify the model of grammar proposed in Section 11.2. This gives us a system which looks more like a 'standard' OT syntax—more specifically, we will suggest that the OT module may choose between derivations, which goes beyond Pesetsky's assumption that the OT module operates on unique LF representations. In Section 11.4, we will argue on the basis of a discussion of the *For-to* Filter in English infinitival relative clauses that this move is indeed desirable. And finally, in Section 11.5, we will go into the interaction of the two components of syntax we have distinguished, and the division of labor between them.

11.2 A Model of Grammar

11.2.1 *The computational system*

Chomsky (1995) assumes that C_{HL} is uniform across languages. He takes C_{HL} to consist of the three operations SELECT, MERGE and ATTRACT/MOVE. The operation SELECT takes elements from the lexicon (or from a Numeration, if indeed such a notion is indispensable, see Section 11.3.8 and further), the operation MERGE creates structures by assembling these elements, and finally ATTRACT/MOVE transforms the structures formed by MERGE, an operation motivated by the need to eliminate uninterpretable features before the derivation reaches the level of LF.

Chomsky (1995, ch.3) argues further that these operations are restricted by global conditions such as Shortest and Fewest Steps. We will assume instead that all conditions in C_{HL} are local in nature, which is in line with Chomsky (1995, ch.4), who interprets the Minimal Link Condition and Last Resort as a defining property of ATTRACT/MOVE. In so far as we need to postulate separate derivational conditions, they should also apply in a strictly local fashion. A good example of such a condition is the one given in (1), which is adapted from Chomsky (1995: 234).

(1)   The derivation is cancelled if α has a strong feature, and is in a category headed by β ($\alpha \neq \beta$).

The general idea is that MERGE may introduce strong features into the structure, which are intolerable and must therefore be eliminated by means of checking before the derivation proceeds. Thus, we ensure that the derivation of LF representations proceeds in a strictly cyclic fashion, with the concomitant result that operations like lowering and yo-yo movement are excluded. Whether we end up with a useful (interpretable) LF representation or not is determined by the bare output conditions imposed by the semantic component on the output of C_{HL}.

At this point, we have a computational system that generates LF structures by making use of the idea that certain features are not interpretable at LF. The basic task of C_{HL} is to eliminate these features through the application of the operation ATTRACT/MOVE, an operation which applies in accordance with the Minimal Link Condition and Last Resort, and is locally constrained by (1).

The question now is: how does C_{HL} feed the PF component? According to Chomsky, C_{HL} sends the PF component (relevant parts of) the structure present at an in principle arbitrary point in the derivation, an operation standardly called *Spell-Out*. The appropriate point of Spell-Out is determined by *Procrastinate*, a principle that demands that Spell-Out apply as early in the derivation as possible (i.e. that movement be postponed as much as possible). Chomsky's strong-weak distinction plays a crucial role here, in that Spell-Out must apply as soon as all strong features are eliminated (elimination of weak features being postponed to a later point in the derivation).

The Minimalist Program meets several problems. First, as a result of the search for explanatory adequacy, the descriptive power of C_{HL} is considerably weaker than that of its predecessors, so that a whole range of language-specific phenomena does not receive an adequate explanation. Secondly, parametrization is difficult to capture in domains that do not involve differences in word order. In order to create a descriptively adequate grammar, we must assume that all that cannot be accounted for by C_{HL} must be explained elsewhere in the grammar, according to Chomsky at PF. Below, we will argue that OT can be taken

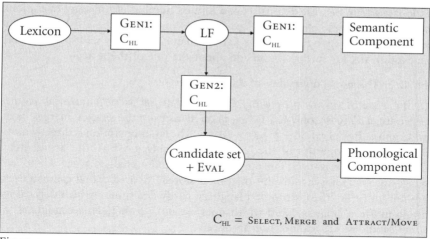

Figure 1.

to be responsible for at least some of these aspects of syntax, in other words, that it mediates between C_{HL} and the phonological component.

If OT is indeed a mediator between C_{HL} and the phonological component, we should wonder whether Chomsky's approach to Spell-Out is the best way to proceed, since there is an obvious alternative, according to which LF structures themselves are spelled out. With respect to A'-movement, this alternative is compatible with Hornstein's (1995) conclusion that A'-movement does not apply covertly, i.e. that all instances of A'-movement must take place before Spell-Out. This means that all movements having a semantic impact will already have applied at the moment of Spell-Out, so that it is indeed justified to consider the structure interpreted by the OT module to be an LF representation, in the sense that all positions relevant for semantic interpretation are filled.

These considerations lead to the model of grammar depicted in Figure 1, which represents the most conservative view on the merger of Chomsky's C_{HL} and OT syntax, since it leaves both systems intact.

11.2.2 Optimality-Theoretic Syntax

11.2.2.1 Generating structure

As we have already mentioned, an important advantage of the model in Figure 1 is the fact that the OT module now has a genuine Generator—i.e. a device that consists of explicit rules. The Generator has received very little explicit attention in the syntactic OT literature (see, however, Samek-Lodovici 1996). In general, it is simply assumed that the Evaluator takes representations as its input, without there being much discussion about the way these structures are created. Although the Generator could have various formats, we prefer Chomsky's computational system, because it consists of a limited number of universal operations, so that in principle all language-specific phenomena can be attributed to the lexicon (feature strength) and the OT Evaluator (Chomsky's PF phenomena); cf. Section 11.5 for further discussion about the role of the lexicon.

11.2.2.2 The non-universality of the candidate set

In the system we are proposing, the candidate set is not universal (contra Legendre *et al.* 1995), only C_{HL} is. C_{HL} takes items from the lexicon, merges them, and applies the operation ATTRACT/MOVE. The latter operation is directly motivated by the properties of the lexical items involved. Thus, the lexical items determine the derivation. Since the lexicon is undoubtedly a place where language-specific, idiosyncratic information is stored, we predict that candidate sets are not universal: the lexicon of a language partly determines which derivations are found in a language, and which ones are not, so that some candidates, or some candidate sets cannot not produced.

If we were to propose that candidate sets are universal, we would for example predict that all languages dispose of the same syntactic categories, which seems to be incorrect. Just because the candidate set is generated by C_{HL} out of lexical items with their own properties, it is language-particular. To put it in the most general of terms, Chomsky's C_{HL} allows us to express that also lexical differences between languages (for example with respect to their inventory of syntactic categories) may have a parametrizing influence on the system.

11.2.2.3 Absolute ungrammaticality

Given the assumption that C_{HL} locally restricts derivations, we predict cases of absolute ungrammaticality, i.e. ungrammatical sentences for which there does not seem to be a grammatical counterpart which blocks it in an OT fashion. For example, it is well known that *Wh*-movement cannot apply from a *Wh*-island. The examples in (2a, b) are both unacceptable, but still cannot be blocked in an obvious way by the construction in (2c), since this construction cannot be interpreted as a matrix question.

(2)   a. *Which book do they remember to whom John gave?
        b. *To whom do they remember which book John gave?
        c. They remember which book John gave to whom.

Chomsky (1995: 294-295) shows that the degraded status of (2a, b) can be accounted for within C_{HL}. The only LF representation with a matrix question interpretation is given in (3). In the embedded cycle, the [+Wh] complementizer attracts the closest *Wh*-element, the DP *which book*. Subsequently, in the matrix cycle, the matrix [+Wh] complementizer must also attract the closest *Wh*-phrase, which is again the DP *which book*, now occupying the specifier of the lower CP. The resulting LF representation in (3) can be argued to be semantically ill-formed, because *which book* must be interpreted both in the main and in the embedded clause, which, by assumption, is not possible (see Chomsky 1995: 291).

(3) $[_{CP_1}$ which book$_j$ do they remember $[_{CP_2}$ t_j John gave t_i to whom]]]

Hence, syntactic representations are illegitimate Output structures if the operations necessary to built them are not available in C_{HL}. The illegitimacy of these output structures can lead to the absence of an entire construction in this language when the (lexical) means to construct alternative structures (e.g. null operators that create the possibility of leaving *Wh*-phrases in situ) with similar semantics are absent. See Ackema and Neeleman, Boersma *et al.*, and Kager (all in this volume) for alternative views on absolute ungrammaticality.

The term *absolute ungrammaticality* as it is used here should not be confused with the phenomenon of gradual acceptability judgements. The former concerns the fact that certain linguistic objects are deviant without there being an alternative, optimal object that blocks it. The latter refers to a situation in which some deviant object is judged to be less deviant than others. At this point, we cannot account for the existence of gradual acceptability judgements, which seems to be a general shortcoming of both the Minimalist Program and OT syntax as they are currently formulated (but see Hayes, this volume).[2]

11.2.3 *Conclusion*

In this section, we have proposed the model of grammar in Figure 1, which we will take as our point of departure in Section 11.3. From the perspective of OT syntax, this model is not entirely satisfactory, since we would like to combine the two Generators. This would give rise to a standard OT system with a Generator that contains both C_{HL} and the operation DELETE. Below, we will see that there are indeed reasons to modify our model in this way.

11.3 The Left Periphery of Finite Relative Clauses

In this section, we examine the surface form of relative clauses. More particularly, we will focus on the realization of the elements in the COMP projection, i.e. the complementizer itself and the relative pronoun in its specifier. As suggested in the previous section, our first step will be to assume that C_{HL} creates the LF structure in (4), which functions as the Input for the OT module responsible for what we could call 'surface syntax', in accordance with Figure 1 (see Kayne 1994 for an alternative proposal). Also in the previous section, we argued that, although C_{HL} is uniform across languages, it may generate LF structures

---

[2] One might speculate that gradual acceptability judgements are the result of the linguist's ability to consciously ignore some principle otherwise operative in the computational system. The relatively acceptable candidate would then be evaluated as the optimal candidate. We leave this suggestion for future research.

that are (weakly) language-specific. We will assume, however, that all externally headed relative clauses have the LF representation in (4), until proof of the contrary is given (see Section 11.3.7 and Section 11.4 for discussion).

(4)   N [$_{CP}$ (P) pronoun$_i$ [$_{C'}$ that [. . . . . . t_i . . . . . .]]]

The Input in (4) is interpreted by GEN2, which gives us a candidate set that consists of the structures given in (5), as a result of the random application of the operation DELETE. This candidate set is evaluated in the standard Optimality-theoretic way, i.e. with respect to a language-particular ranking of (universal) constraints.

(5)   a.   N [$_{CP}$ (P) pronoun$_i$ [$_{C'}$ that [. . . . . . t_i . . . . . .]]]
       b.   N [$_{CP}$ ~~(P) pronoun~~$_i$ [$_{C'}$ that [. . . . . . t_i . . . . . .]]]
       c.   N [$_{CP}$ (P) pronoun$_i$ [$_{C'}$ ~~that~~ [. . . . . . t_i . . . . . .]]]
       d.   N [$_{CP}$ ~~(P) pronoun~~$_i$ [$_{C'}$ ~~that~~ [. . . . . . t_i . . . . . .]]]

11.3.1 *English*

Let us start with a brief discussion of English based on Pesetsky (to appear). In English, relative clauses can take the surface forms in (6). Two generalizations leap to the eye. Firstly, English relative clauses are subject to the Doubly Filled COMP Filter—none of the examples in (6) contains both a phonetically realized relative pronoun and an overt complementizer; at least one of the two must be deleted. Secondly, deletion of the relative pronoun is only allowed if it is not the complement of a preposition.

(6)   a.   the man [$_{CP}$ who$_i$ [$_{C'}$ ~~that~~ [I saw t_i yesterday]]]
       a'.   the man [$_{CP}$ ~~who~~$_i$ [$_{C'}$ that [I saw t_i yesterday]]]
       a''.   the man [$_{CP}$ ~~who~~$_i$ [$_{C'}$ ~~that~~ [I saw t_i yesterday]]]
       b.   the book [$_{CP}$ which$_i$ [$_{C'}$ ~~that~~ [I read t_i yesterday]]]
       b'.   the book [$_{CP}$ ~~which~~$_i$ [$_{C'}$ that [I read t_i yesterday]]]
       b''.   the book [$_{CP}$ ~~which~~$_i$ [$_{C'}$ ~~that~~ [I read t_i yesterday]]]
       c.   the book [$_{CP}$ [$_{PP}$ about which]$_i$ [$_{C'}$ ~~that~~ [he spoke t_i yesterday]]]

Consequently, an analysis of English relative clauses should answer the three questions in (7):

(7)   a.   Why does the Doubly Filled COMP Filter hold?
       b.   Why is deletion of the relative pronoun restricted to those cases that do not involve a PP?
       c.   Why is it possible to delete both the relative pronoun and the complementizer?

Pesetsky argues that these questions can be answered by reducing the pattern in (6) to the interaction of the following tendencies: (i) meaningful elements must be pronounced, unless they are sufficiently close to an antecedent (e.g. a relative pronoun cannot be deleted, unless it is close to the nominal head of the relative construction), (ii) CPs are introduced by a functional head, such as *that*, *for* and *to*, or the verb itself (cf. footnote 12), and (iii) meaningless elements are deleted. Pesetsky provides theoretical correlates for these tendencies by introducing the constraints in (8).[3]

(8)   a. Recoverability (REC): A syntactic unit with semantic content must be pronounced unless it has a sufficiently local antecedent.
      b. Left Edge CP (LE(CP)): CP starts with a lexicalized head from the extended projection of the verb.
      c. Telegraph (TEL): Do not pronounce function words.

The constraints in (8) are used to evaluate the members of the generalized Candidate set given in (5). The particular Candidate sets for the examples in (6a, b) and (6c) are given in (9) and (10), respectively. The structures marked with an asterisk are excluded in English; all others are acceptable:

(9)   a. *N $[_{CP}$ pronoun$_i$ $[_{C'}$ that $[\ldots \ldots t_i \ldots \ldots]]]$
      b. N $[_{CP}$ ~~pronoun~~$_i$ $[_{C'}$ that $[\ldots \ldots t_i \ldots \ldots]]]$
      c. N $[_{CP}$ pronoun$_i$ $[_{C'}$ ~~that~~ $[\ldots \ldots t_i \ldots \ldots]]]$
      d. N $[_{CP}$ ~~pronoun~~$_i$ $[_{C'}$ ~~that~~ $[\ldots \ldots t_i \ldots \ldots]]]$

(10) a. *N $[_{CP}$ P-pronoun$_i$ $[_{C'}$ that $[\ldots \ldots t_i \ldots \ldots]]]$
      b. *N $[_{CP}$ ~~P-pronoun~~$_i$ $[_{C'}$ that $[\ldots \ldots t_i \ldots \ldots]]]$
      c. N $[_{CP}$ P-pronoun$_i$ $[_{C'}$ ~~that~~ $[\ldots \ldots t_i \ldots \ldots]]]$
      d. *N $[_{CP}$ ~~P-pronoun~~$_i$ $[_{C'}$ ~~that~~ $[\ldots \ldots t_i \ldots \ldots]]]$

Let us now turn to the first question in (7), concerning the Doubly Filled COMP Filter. This question consists of the following two subquestions: (i) Why must the specifier of CP be deleted if the complementizer is overtly realized? and (ii) Why must the complementizer be deleted if the specifier of CP is overtly realized? The first subquestion can be answered by taking recourse to LE(CP), according to which the relative clause must be introduced by a lexicalized head. This can only be attained by means of deleting the relative pronoun, as in (9b), as a result of which the complementizer *that* is the first phonetically realized element in the clause. Before we answer the second subquestion, we will first discuss the two other questions raised in (7).

The question in (7b) can be answered by invoking REC. By assumption, deletion of a relative pronoun is possible since it provides semantic information that is also present on the head noun of the construction. Consequently, if LE(CP) can be satisfied by deleting the relative pronoun, as in (9b), REC will not block

---

[3] The definition of LE (CP) given in (8) is taken from Pesetsky (1995). The definitions of the other two constraints are taken from Pesetsky (to appear). We will revise the definitions of REC and TEL in Section 11.3.4.

this. If the relative pronoun is contained in a PP, however, LE(CP) will force deletion of the complete PP. Since the preposition provides non-redundant semantic information, Rᴇᴄ would be violated. Given the unacceptability of (10b), Rᴇᴄ seems to obliterate the requirement that a CP start with a functional element. This leads Pesetsky to the conclusion that Rᴇᴄ outranks LE(CP) in English:

(11)   Rᴇᴄ >> LE(CP)

Let us now turn to the third question in (7): Why is it possible to delete both the relative pronoun and the complementizer in English? This is where the constraint Tᴇʟ enters the picture. Tᴇʟ requires that function words, such as the complementizer *that*, be deleted. This means that two conflicting forces are working on the fate of the complementizer: LE(CP) wants it to be pronounced, whereas Tᴇʟ favors its deletion. Given the fact that (9b) and (9c) are both acceptable, both constraints seem to be equally important: a violation of LE(CP) is as good or as bad as a violation of Tᴇʟ. This can be formalized by taking the two constraints to be in a tie.

(12)   LE (CP) <> Tᴇʟ

There are several ways to define a tie. If two constraints C and D are in a tie, this could mean that they are not ranked—i.e. that C and D are interpreted as one complex constraint. Alternatively, if C and D are in a tie, the language has two equally valued rankings available, viz. C >> D *and* D >> C, as in Pesetsky's definition in (13). We will adopt the definition in (13) here, and motivate this choice in Section 11.3.6, by pointing out a situation where the two definitions make different predictions.

(13)   The output of a set of *tied* constraints is the union of the output of every
       possible ranking of those constraints.

There is independent evidence for the ranking in (12) in English, namely the optionality of the complementizer in complements of epistemic verbs, exemplified in (14a). The Dutch complementizer in (14b), on the other hand, is obligatorily pronounced in this context, which is a first illustration of the fact that constraint ranking is a language-specific matter: in Dutch, the ranking is LE(CP) >> Tᴇʟ.

(14)   a. I think (that) Bill and Bob are incompetent.
       b. Ik vind *(dat) Bill en Bob incompetent zijn.

The ranking in (12) also provides an answer to the second subquestion of (7a), which is still awaiting an answer. If SpecCP is filled, LE(CP) will necessarily be violated. If both the complementizer and the relative pronoun were pronounced (a Doubly Filled COMP configuration), it would only aggravate the situation, in that this would imply a violation of Tᴇʟ on top of the violation of LE(CP).

It goes without saying that it is better to avoid this violation by means of deleting the complementizer.

Above, we have established the ranking of the three constraints in (8) for English, which is repeated in (15).

(15)   English: REC >> LE(CP) <> TEL

This ranking fully accounts for the paradigm in (6). The evaluation procedure for the Candidate Sets in (9) and (10) is given in tableaux (16) and (17).[4] In accordance with the definition in (13), a fatal violation in a tie in only one direction does not suffice to block a candidate.

(16) English		REC	LE (CP)	TEL
	a. the man who that I saw the book which that I saw		*>	<*
☞	b. the man who ~~that~~ I saw the book which ~~that~~ I saw		*>	
☞	c. the man ~~who~~ that I saw the book ~~which~~ that I saw			<*
☞	d. the man ~~who that~~ I saw the man ~~which that~~ I saw		*>	

(17) English		REC	LE (CP)	TEL
	a. the book about which that I spoke		*	*!
☞	b. the book about which ~~that~~ I spoke		*	
	c. the book ~~about which~~ that I spoke	*!		*
	d. the book ~~about which that~~ I spoke	*!	*	

Although this proposal, which is basically the one given in Pesetsky (to appear), accounts for the English data, we are forced to revise it below, because a simple constraint re-ranking will not give us the patterns found in Dutch.

11.3.2 Standard Dutch

In Dutch, nouns can be distinguished on the basis of the article they select: non-neuter singular nouns take the article *de*, while their neuter counterparts take the

---

[4] For ties, we adopt the following tableau conventions:

*>: fatal violation if the tie is read from left to right
<*: fatal violation if the tie is read from right to left
*!:   fatal violation in both directions

Note that only candidates inducing fatal violations on both readings of a tie lose ((*> *and* <*) or *!).

article *het*. In the plural, the gender distinction is neutralized; the article *de* is used in all cases. The two groups also take different demonstratives: *de*-nouns can be combined with the demonstratives *deze* and *die*, while *het*-nouns take the demonstratives *dit* and *dat*. This is demonstrated in (18).

(18)   a.   de man—deze man—die man
                the man   this man   that man

         a′.   de mannen—deze mannen—die   mannen
                the men   these men   those men

         b.   het boek—dit boek—dat boek
                the book   this book   that book

         b′.   de boeken—deze boeken—die   boeken
                the books   these books   those books

At first sight, the relative pronouns seem to be homophonous with the demonstratives *die* and *dat*. The distribution of the two elements (illustrated in (19)) is again determined by gender and number.

(19)   a.   de man die ik gisteren zag
                the man DIE *I yesterday saw*
                'the man I saw yesterday'

         a′.   de mannen die ik gisteren zag
                the men   DIE *I yesterday saw*

         b.   het boek dat ik gisteren las
                the book DAT *I yesterday read*

         b′.   de boeken die ik gisteren las
                the books   DIE *I yesterday read*

Relative d-pronouns are not allowed to be embedded in PPs. Instead, relative w-pronouns are used. Here, the nature of the antecedent plays a crucial role. If the antecedent is human, either the relative pronoun *wie* (as [$_{PP}$ over wie] in (20a)), or the relative R-pronoun *waar*, which precedes the preposition, (as [$_{PP}$ waarover] in (20b)) is used. If the antecedent is not human, only the latter option is available (see also footnote 11).

(20)   a.   de man over wie   ik sprak
                the man about whom I spoke

         b.   de man waarover   ik sprak
                the man what-about I spoke

         c.   het boek waarover/*over   wat ik sprak
                the book what-about/about what I spoke

As will be clear from the examples in (19) and (20), Dutch relative pronouns seem to behave like their prepositional counterparts in English: they never delete. Given the constraints introduced so far, this could only follow from the assumption that the deletion of a relative pronoun violates REC in Dutch. If this is indeed true, we get the evaluations in tableaux (21) and (22) (recall from the discussion of the examples in (14) that LE(CP) outranks TEL in Dutch).

(21) Standard Dutch	REC	LE(CP)	TEL
a. de man die dat ik zag het boek dat dat ik las		*	*!
☞ b. de man die ~~dat~~ ik zag het boek dat ~~dat~~ ik las		*	
c. de man ~~die~~ dat ik zag het boek ~~dat~~ dat ik las	*!		*
d. de man ~~die dat~~ ik zag het boek ~~dat dat~~ ik las	*!	*	

(22) Standard Dutch	REC	LE (CP)	TEL
a. de man waarover/over wie dat ik sprak het boek waarover dat ik sprak		*	*!
☞ b. de man waarover/over wie ~~dat~~ ik sprak het boek waarover ~~dat~~ ik sprak		*	
c. de man ~~waarover/over wie~~ dat ik sprak het boek ~~waarover~~ dat ik sprak	*!		*
d. de man ~~waarover/over wie dat~~ ik sprak het boek ~~waarover dat~~ ik sprak	*!	*	

Of course, the conclusion that deletion of the relative pronoun violates REC in English but not in Dutch is far from desirable. In the next section, we will learn that the situation is even more complex than we have just suggested.

11.3.3 *The Aarschot Dialect*

Both in English and in Standard Dutch, the Doubly Filled COMP Filter seems to be surface-true. This is not the case, however, in the Aarschot dialect, spoken in the Belgian part of Brabant. In this variety of Dutch, a relative clause introduced by a relative pronoun may contain the complementizer *da*. However, this is restricted to those relative clauses that are introduced by the non-neuter relative pronoun *di(e)* or by a prepositional phrase: no examples are attested in which the singular neuter relative pronoun *da* is followed by a complementizer.

This is demonstrated in the examples in (23), taken from Pauwels (1958).[5]

(23)   Aarschot dialect:
    a.   de stoelen di (da) kapot zijn
           the chairs DI *that broken are*

    b.   *'t kind da da   valt
           the child DA *that falls*

    b'.   't kind da valt

    c.   't kind van   wie   (da) 'k spreek
           the child about whom that I talk

The examples in (23) raise two problems. Firstly, the Doubly Filled COMP Filter can be violated in the Aarschot dialect, as shown in (23a,c). It is clear that the three constraints used to explain the English and the Standard Dutch cases cannot be held responsible for any violation of the Doubly Filled COMP Filter. The (a) candidates in tableaux (16), (17), (21), (22) are harmonically bound by the (b) candidates on the three constraints we have adopted, since they incur all constraint violations the (b) candidates do next to their violation of TEL (see Boersma *et al.*, this volume). This means that on all rankings, the complementizer will be deleted if preceded by a relative pronoun, since the effect of the only constraint that disfavors complementizer deletion (LE(CP)) is obliterated if the relative pronoun is phonetically realized.

This can only mean that a fourth constraint is in play. We take this constraint to be Grimshaw's (1997) Obligatory Heads, which is defined as in (24).

(24)   Obligatory Heads (OB-HD): Heads should be filled.

If we assume that, like in Standard Dutch, deletion of the relative pronoun *di(e)* violates REC, the evaluation of the candidate sets related to the examples in (23a,c) takes place as in tableau (25), where OB-HD and TEL are in a tie.[6]

(25) The Aarschot dialect	REC	LE(CP)	OB-HD	TEL
☞ [CP di(e)/van wie da [IP . . .]]		*		<*
☞ [CP di(e)/van wie ~~da~~ [IP . . .]]		*	*>	
[CP ~~di(e)/van wie~~ da [IP . . .]]	*!			*
[CP ~~di(e)/van wie da~~ [IP . . .]]	*!	*	*	

[5] The same seems to hold for Middle Dutch (see Verwijs and Verdam, 1889). The situation in the Aarschot dialect is in fact more complicated than suggested in the main text. The dialect disposes of the three relative d-pronouns given in (i).

(i) a. *di* [di]: [feminine] or [−singular]
    b. *die* [diǝ]: [masculine, +singular]
    c. *da* [da]: [neuter, +singular]

[6] Of course, TEL needs to outrank Obligatory Heads in Standard Dutch and English, where Doubly Filled COMPs are banned.

Secondly, the unacceptability of example in (23b) is a problem for the present analysis. Clearly, the more lowly ranked constraints in tableau 5 are not responsible for this. If we assume, however, that deletion of the relative pronoun *da* does not violate REC, the desired result follows. This is illustrated in tableau (26) (the stars in parentheses will be discussed in the next section).[7]

(26) The Aarschot dialect	REC	LE(CP)	OB-HD	TEL
[$_{CP}$ da da [$_{IP}$ . . .]]		*!		*(*)
[$_{CP}$ da ~~da~~ [$_{IP}$ . . .]]		*!	*	(*)
☞ [$_{CP}$ ~~da~~ da [$_{IP}$ . . .]]				*
[$_{CP}$ ~~da da~~ [$_{IP}$ . . .]]		*!	*	

11.3.4 *Recoverability*

The next step is to account for the fact that the pronouns *di(e)* and *da* seem to behave differently with respect to REC. Apparently, relative pronouns having a local antecedent need not be recoverable after deletion. Let us take another look at the definition of Recoverability, given here in a simplified version in (27).[8]

(27)   Recoverability: Meaningful elements must be pronounced.

The fact that some relative pronouns seem to be recoverable, while others do not, forces us to discuss the notion of what is *meaningful*. In the Dutch determiner system, three semantic features play a role, viz. [±singular] and [±neuter], and [±definite].[9] In Kester (1996: 94ff.), it is argued on the basis of the distibution of the attributive suffix *-e*, among other things, that [+singular], [+neuter], and [−definite] should be considered unmarked in Dutch. In this language, adjectives used attributively appear with this suffix, unless the DP has the aforementioned unmarked features, as illustrated in Table (28).

---

[7] Various people have suggested to us that the impossibility of the sequence *da(t) da(t)* might be the result of a constraint that disallows the occurrence of two adjacent phonetically identical elements. Such an expansion of the constraint inventory is not necessary, since *da(t) da(t)* can be ruled out on independent grounds, as we will see in Section 11.3.5.

[8] We dropped the unless-clause of Pesetsky's definition in (8a), since it is not relevant in the examples we discuss in this chapter. Note that Pesetsky's original formulation of Recoverability in (8a) seems to allow for deletion of a PP if it has a sufficiently local antecedent, so that it is wrongly predicted that (ib) should be acceptable besides (ia). The formulation in (27), on the other hand, correctly excludes (ib), as pointed out to us by João Costa (p.c.).

(i)   a. John cuts the meat with the knife with which he has cut the cheese.

   b.*John cuts the meat with the knife he has cut the cheese.

[9] These features all qualify as interpretable formal features in the sense of Chomsky (1995: ch.4). One might object to the assumption that gender is a semantic feature. Nevertheless, we will assume for the moment that gender is a semantic feature, which is in line with Chomsky (1995: ch.4), who claims that φ-features are interpretable. See footnote 18 for a remark on uninterpretable features and Recoverability.

(28) The inflection of attributively used adjectives

| | singular | | plural | |
	non-neuter	neuter	non-neuter	neuter
definite	de oude man	het oude boek	de oude mannen	de oude boeken
	the old man	the old book	the old men	the old books
indefinite	een oude man	*een oud boek*	oude mannen	oude boeken
	an old man	an old book	old men	old books

If only marked features are syntactically present, as we assume here, we may account for the distribution of the attributive suffix by taking it to be licensed by at least one of the pertinent features. Hence, the assumption that only the marked features are assigned to a lexical element (the unmarked features being inferred by default) allows us to define the notion *meaningful element* as in (29).

(29)   a. A meaningful element is an element that contains semantic features.
        b. Semantic feature: {[–singular], [–neuter], [+definite], . . .}

In the domain of relative pronouns, only the semantic features related to number and gender seem to be relevant. The relative pronoun *dat* does not contain the marked features [–singular] and [–neuter]; as is illustrated in (30), it can only have a singular, neuter noun as its antecedent. The relative pronoun *die*, on the other hand, is specified for these features; in (31a), it takes a non-neuter (singular) noun as its antecedent, and in (31b) a (neuter) plural one.

(30)   a. het boek dat ik las
            the book DAT *I read*

        b. *de jongen dat ik zag
            the boy   DAT *I saw*

        c. *de boeken dat ik las
            the books DAT *I read*

(31)   a. de jongen die ik zag
            the boy   DIE *I saw*

        b. de boeken die ik las
            the books DIE *I read*

Provided that no other features are involved, we may conclude that the relative pronoun *die* is a meaningful element, whereas *dat* is not. This means that only the deletion of *die* violates REC, which is exactly what we want to derive in order to arrive at the evaluations given in tableaux (25) and (26).

Let us now turn to the question of the stars in parentheses in tableau (26). If deletion of *dat* does not violate REC, we should wonder whether its pronunciation violates TEL in (32). If it does, we would end up with a simpler definition of TEL, since we do not have to refer to the (undefined) notion of a *function word*. This would mean that we have to add the stars in question to tableau (26).

(32)   Telegraph (revised): Meaningless elements must be deleted.

In sum, the definition of the notion *meaningful element* given in (27) allows us to give a simpler and more accurate definition of both REC and TEL. Below, we will consider the consequences of the proposed reformulations.

11.3.5 *Relative Clauses in Dutch Revisited*

Let us return now to the examples in tableau (21), and begin with relatives involving *die*. Given the definitions in the previous section, the evaluation is as given in tableau (33). Since OB-HD is irrelevant here, this evaluation is identical to the one in tableau (21).

(33) Standard Dutch	REC	LE(CP)	TEL	OB-HD
a. de man die dat ik zag		*	*!	
☞ b. de man die ~~dat~~ ik zag		*		*
c. de man ~~die~~ dat ik zag	*!		*	
d. de man ~~die dat~~ ik zag	*!	*		*

However, tableau (21) cannot be taken to represent the evaluation of relative clauses introduced by the neuter relative pronoun *dat*, since we have just argued that the deletion of this pronoun does not violate REC. The correct evaluation is therefore as given in tableau (34), from which it follows that the element *dat* should be analysed as a complementizer, and not as a relative pronoun, contrary to what was implied in tableau (21).[10]

(34) Standard Dutch	REC	LE(CP)	TEL	OB-HD
a. het boek dat dat ik las		*!	**	
b. het boek dat ~~dat~~ ik las		*!	*	*
☞ c. het boek ~~dat~~ dat ik las			*	
d. het boek ~~dat dat~~ ik las		*!		*

---

[10] In contrast to what we claim for Dutch, the complementizer *dass* 'that' never surfaces in German relative clauses. This is shown in (i) for a relative construction in which the head of the construction is a neuter noun. Notice that *das* and *dass* are homophones, so we cannot draw any firm conclusions from this example: in the dative, however, the relative pronoun surfaces as *dem*.

(i) das Buch das/*dass er gestern   gelesen hat
     the book DAS/DASS *he yesterday read   has*

This shows that the set of semantic features is not universal: the inventory of semantic features may differ from one language to another, which is illustrated by the fact that English, for example, has no gender distinction at all. Furthermore, the assumption that [+neuter] counts as a semantic feature in German is consistent with the observation that in indefinite, singular, neuter DPs, attributive adjectives are inflected: *ein kleines Buch* 'a small book' (cf. tableau 28). Of course, morphological case marking may also be at work here.

11.3.6 *Relative Clauses in English Revisited*

Our reformulation of the definition of Recoverability has important implications for the analysis of English relative clauses, because the pronouns *who* and *which* clearly contain semantic features. The former refers to human entities only, whereas the latter must combine with a noun that refers to an artifact. In other words, these pronouns are associated with the semantic features [+human] and [−human], respectively (cf. Chomsky and Lasnik 1977, footnote 46).[11] Consequently, deletion of these relative pronouns would violate REC, contrary to what is suggested in tableau (16). Rather, the evaluation proceeds as in tableau (35).

(35) English	REC	LE(CP)	TEL	OB-HD
a. the man who that I saw the book which that I read		*	*!	
☞ b. the man who ~~that~~ I saw the book which ~~that~~ I read		*		*
c. the man ~~who~~ that I saw the book ~~which~~ that I read	*!		*	
d. the man ~~who that~~ I saw the book ~~which that~~ I read	*!	*		*

Tableau (35) differs from tableau (16) in that only candidate (b) is acceptable; the candidates (c) and (d)—optimal in tableau (16)—are now excluded because they violate REC. This leads us to the question how we can account for the fact

---

[11] The Dutch relative R-pronoun *waar* is not recoverable after deletion either: *w*-pronouns which are extracted from a PP cannot be deleted in Dutch (see (ib, c)). The fact that (iic) is acceptable suggests that we are dealing with the deletable relative pronoun *that*. This is probably related to the fact that regular DPs cannot be extracted from PPs in Dutch (unlike R-pronouns), whereas they can in English. The generalization seems to be that *w(h)*-pronouns are never recoverable after deletion in English and Dutch. This might be due to the fact that these pronouns are marked for the feature [±human].

(i) a. Hij kocht het boek waarover ik sprak. (= (20c))
     b. Hij kocht het boek waar ik over sprak.
     c. *Hij kocht het boek dat ik over sprak.

(ii) a. He bought the book about which I talked.
      b. He bought the book which I talked about.
      c. He bought the book (that) I talked about.

That Dutch *w*-pronouns contain the feature [±human] can also be argued on the basis of free relatives, such as (iiia, b). A free relative introduced by *wie* 'who' must refer to human beings, while a free relative introduced by *wat* 'what' is used in the other cases.

(iii) a. Wie dit leest, is gek.   b. Wat Frits gedaan heeft, is onvergeeflijk.
           who this reads is mad   *what Frits done   has   is unforgivable*
           'whoever reads this is mad'   'What Frits has done is unforgivable.'

Furthermore, the assumption that the relative R-pronoun *waar* is marked for the feature [±human] is supported by the fact that some speakers of Dutch object to using the R-pronoun *waar* if the antecedent is [+human]. Those speakers accept only the example in (18a), and reject the example in (18b).

that *the man/book* (*that*) *I saw* is acceptable in English. Since gender and number do not play any role in the English relative pronoun system, we may assume that English has a relative pronoun which is not marked for gender and number, just like the article *the* (note that in accordance with this claim, English does not exhibit attributive inflection: cf. the discussion of Dutch in Section 11.3.4). As a result of its lack of meaning, the pronunciation of this pronoun implies a violation of TEL, while its deletion is free in the light of REC. The evaluation is given in tableau (36), where we take this relative pronoun to be based on the homophonous demonstrative *that*, just like in the case of the Dutch d-pronouns. In the next section, this assumption will be motivated.

(36) English		REC	LE(CP)	TEL	OB-HD
	a. the man/book that that I saw		*>	*<*	
	b. the man/book that ~~that~~ I saw		*>	<*	*
☞	c. the man/book ~~that~~ that I saw			<*	
☞	d. the man/book ~~that that~~ I saw		*>		*

Note in passing that tableau (36) illustrates why we adopted the definition in (13) according to which a tie involves two equally-valued rankings: the ranking REC >> LE (CP) >> TEL >> OB-HD selects option (c) as the optimality candidate, whereas the ranking REC >> TEL >> LE (CP) >> OB-HD picks out candidate (d). If we had assumed that Left Edge (CP) and TEL behave as one complex constraint, in accordance with the alternative definition given in Section 11.3.1, we would have ended up with only one optimal candidate, i.e. option (c), as is shown in tableau (37):

(37) English		REC	LE(CP) and TEL	OB-HD
	a. the man/book that that I saw		**!*	
	b. the man/book that ~~that~~ I saw		**!	*
☞	c. the man/book ~~that~~ that I saw		*	
	d. the man/book ~~that that~~ I saw		*	*!

11.3.7 *The Anti-That-Trace Effect*

In the previous section, we saw that in English the relative pronoun *that* is recoverable after deletion—i.e. that *that* in relative clauses like *the man that I saw yesterday* should be analysed as a complementizer. This conclusion is problematic in clauses in which the subject is relativized. Consider the examples in (38). Given the discussion in the previous section, we would wrongly expect all three options to be acceptable (cf. tableaux (35) and (36)).

(38) a. the man [$_{CP}$ who$_i$ ~~that~~ [$_{IP}$ t_i saw Bill]]
      b. the man [$_{CP}$ ~~that$_i$~~ that [$_{IP}$ t_i saw Bill]]
      b'. *the man [$_{CP}$ ~~that$_i$~~ that [$_{IP}$ t_i saw Bill]]

Of course, other constraints may be involved in the ungrammaticality of example (38b′). One option would be to introduce a soft version of the Empty Category Principle (Chomsky 1981). However, the ECP gives the wrong results here—it rules out the grammatical example in (38b), but accepts the ungrammatical example in (38b′), just as it does with the examples in (39) involving *Wh*-movement.[12]

(39)   a. Who$_i$ do you think [$_{CP}$ t_i ~~that~~ [$_{IP}$ t_i saw Bill]]
        b. *Who$_i$ do you think [$_{CP}$ t_i that [$_{IP}$ t_i saw Bill]]

This observation has been around for a long time; Chomsky and Lasnik (1977) expressed it by means of the *unless*-clause in the *That*-trace Filter in (40).

(40)   *[$_{S'}$ that [$_{NP}$ e] . . .], unless S′ or its trace is in the context: [$_{NP}$ NP ___]

Even if we succeed in giving an independent explanation for the *unless*-clause in (40), that is, for the acceptability of example (38b)—we will still not have accounted for the ungrammaticality of (38b′). We take this to indicate that we attributed incorrect representations to the acceptable structures in (38). What we would like to propose in order to account for the paradigm is that if the subject is relativized, the CP layer is missing.

In Rizzi (to appear), it is proposed that in English main clauses the [+Wh] feature is associated with the inflectional head I. Hence, in the case of *Wh*-subjects, movement to SpecIP should in principle suffice. In this position, the subject is able to check both the case and the [+Wh] feature on I.[13] Movement of the subject into SpecCP and movement of I to C are therefore superfluous, hence blocked. The asymmetry between the examples in (41) follows now: in (41a), the [+Wh] feature on I can be checked by the *Wh*-phrase in SpecIP; in (41b), on the other hand, the [+Wh] feature on I must be moved to C in order to establish a checking relation with the *Wh*-phrase in SpecCP.

(41)   a. [$_{IP}$ who$_i$ I$_{[+Wh]}$ [$_{VP}$ t_i saw Bill]]
        b [$_{CP}$ who$_j$ did [$_{IP}$ you t_{did} see t_j]]

Rizzi assumes that in embedded clauses the [+Wh] feature is associated with the complementizer. If we slightly revise this, and assume that verbs selecting an embedded question must have a projection of a functional head with a [+Wh]

---

[12] In fact, the English constraint ranking makes the same predictions as the ECP (incorrect in the case of subject relatives) if clause-initial *saw* in (38b′) and (39b) satifies LE(CP) (see also Pesetsky 1994). However, the fact that the verb is preceded by a case-marked trace (a variable) in these examples complicates the issue. If variables count as phonetically realized material, LE(CP) is violated in (38b′) and (39b). In the remainder of this chapter we will take case-marked traces to be indeed visible to alignment constraints, an assumption that will be motivated in footnote 16 for English and in Section 11.4.4 for Dutch. See Dekkers (1999).

[13] Rizzi argues for *Wh*-movement of the subject into SpecCP, using additional machinery to avoid *do*-support for English. However, as soon as we allow a position to be both an operator and a case position, the proposal in the main text is fully compatible with Rizzi's assumptions concerning the locus of the [+Wh] feature, and in fact simplifies Rizzi's analysis considerably, which leaves us with an analysis not dissimilar from the one proposed by Grimshaw (1997).

feature in their complement, the categorial status of an embedded question can be either CP or IP, depending on whether the *Wh*-phrase is the subject of the clause or not (see Dekkers 1997, 1999, for arguments in favor of the possibility of evaluating the IP option as the optimal candidate even in cases where the *Wh*-phrase is not the subject of the clause).

If we extend this line of thought to relative clauses, English subject relatives may very well be IPs. Let us assume for the moment that this is correct. When the pronouns *who* or *which* are selected from the lexicon, the IP option gives the same surface form as its CP counterpart. However, when the relative pronoun *that* is used, the *that* that is pronounced can no longer be analysed as a complementizer in the IP scenario. Instead, it should be interpreted as a relative pronoun:

(42)   a.   the man [$_{\text{IP}}$ who$_i$ I [$_{\text{VP}}$ t_i saw Bill]]
       b.   the man [$_{\text{IP}}$ that$_i$ I [$_{\text{VP}}$ t_i saw Bill]]
       b′. *the man [$_{\text{IP}}$ ~~that~~$_i$ I [$_{\text{VP}}$ t_i saw Bill]]

If we are on the right track, the anti-*that*-trace effect boils down to question why the relative pronoun *that* is deleted if it occupies SpecCP, and why it must be overtly realized if it occupies SpecIP. Now, in the first case the pronoun heads an A′-chain, whereas in the latter case it heads an A-chain. We would like to propose that deletion of the head of an A-chain is prohibited, because A-chains carry a θ-role, and should therefore be considered meaningful elements. In accordance with the definition given in (21), deletion would result in a violation of REC.[14] The hypothesis that *that* has pronominal qualities is not new in the generative literature. In a discussion of English subject relatives, Chomsky remarks that *that* has 'quasi-pronominal properties, being preferable with (or for some speakers, limited to) inanimate antecedents' (Chomsky 1981: 245), an observation that seems fully compatible with the analysis proposed here.

Note that we must still account for the fact that the alternative derivation in (38), where the [+rel] feature is associated with the complementizer, is blocked. Following Dekkers (1995, 1999) and Deprez (1994), we will argue that this should be reduced to a matter of economy, since the addition of a CP-layer necessarily involves a larger number of movement steps in the case of subjects. This implies that C_{HL} must be considered an OT-like generator generating structures which are subsequently evaluated in the standard (that is, global) Optimality-theoretic way. This would mean that the structures in (38) violate an additional constraint, namely Grimshaw's (1997) STAY:

(43)   STAY: traces are prohibited.[15]

[14] Cf. Chomsky and Lasnik (1977: Section 11.1.4): 'filters of the core grammar are concerned primarily (or solely) with the complementizer system'. See however footnote 23 for an alternative explanation based on the EPP.

[15] STAY can be considered the OT counterpart of Procrastinate, since both notions disprefer overt movement (see Section 11.5). Chomsky (1995: 228) suggests that Procrastinate is a global condition, despite the fact that he argues for a local interpretation of the other (economy) conditions (see Section 11.2.1). When we substitute STAY for Procrastinate, global economy conditions will have disappeared from the computational system altogether.

This means that the Evaluator must be able to compare distinct syntactic structures (IPs and CPs), which is clearly not in accordance the model of grammar we have been assuming so far (Figure 1, Section 11.2.3). This leads us to derive the model in Figure 2, where distinct structures *can* be compared.

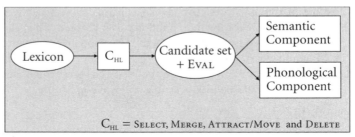

Figure 2.

Figure 2 allows us to assume that the structures in (38) and (42) belong to the same Candidate Set. If we now provisionally assume that sharing the same array of lexical (but not functional elements) is a necessary condition for two structures to be in the same Candidate Set, we get the two evaluations in tableaux (44) and (45).

(44) English	Rec	Stay	LE(CP)	Tel
a. the man [$_{CP}$ who$_i$ that [$_{IP}$ t_i saw Bill]		*!	*	*
b. the man [$_{CP}$ ~~who~~$_i$ that [$_{IP}$ t_i saw Bill]]	*!	*		*
c. the man [$_{CP}$ who$_i$ ~~that~~ [$_{IP}$ t_i saw Bill]]		*!	*	
d. the man [$_{CP}$ ~~who~~$_i$ ~~that~~ [$_{IP}$ t_i saw Bill]]	*!	*	*	
☞ e. the man [$_{IP}$ who saw Bill]			*	
f. the man [$_{IP}$ ~~who~~ saw Bill]	*!			

(45) English	Rec	Stay	LE(CP)	Tel
a. the man [$_{CP}$ that$_i$ that [$_{IP}$ t_i saw Bill]]		*!	*	**
b. the man [$_{CP}$ ~~that~~$_i$ that [$_{IP}$ t_i saw Bill]]		*!		*
c. the man [$_{CP}$ that$_i$ ~~that~~ [$_{IP}$ t_i saw Bill]]		*!	*	*
d. the man [$_{CP}$ ~~that~~$_i$ ~~that~~ [$_{IP}$ t_i saw Bill]]		*!	*	
☞ e. the man [$_{IP}$ that saw Bill]			*	
f. the man [$_{IP}$ ~~that~~ saw Bill]	*!			

For the sake of completeness, we give the evaluation of embedded subject questions in tableau (46), and that of *Wh*-extraction of the subject from the embedded clause in tableau (47). In both cases, the *That*-trace Filter follows.[16] See Dekkers (1995, 1999) for a more detailed discussion.

(46)	English	REC	STAY	LE(CP)	TEL
	a. I wonder [$_{CP}$ who$_i$ that [$_{IP}$ t_i saw Bill]]		*!	*	*
	b. I wonder [$_{CP}$ who$_i$ ~~that~~ [$_{IP}$ t_i saw Bill]]		*!	*	
☞	c. I wonder [$_{IP}$ who saw Bill]			*	

(47)	English	REC	STAY	LE(CP)	TEL
	a. who$_i$ do you think [$_{CP}$ t_i that [$_{IP}$ t_i saw Bill]]		**!		*
	b. who$_i$ do you think [$_{CP}$ t_i ~~that~~ [$_{IP}$ t_i saw Bill]]		**!	*	
☞	c. who$_i$ do you think [$_{IP}$ t_i saw Bill]		*	*	

11.3.8 On Candidate Sets

Our analysis of the anti-*that*-trace effect hinges on the possibility of comparing structures that are built from a distinct set of functional projections. To the extent that functional heads are in the Numeration, we may infer that the Numeration does not play a role in determining the candidate set.

However, we associated the two possible expressions of subject relatives, *the man who saw Bill* and *the man that saw Bill* with two distinct candidate sets, as is shown in tableaux (44) and (45). If indeed the Numeration does not determine candidate sets, we should wonder why the aforementioned expression would not be contained in one and the same candidate set. In fact, if they were,

---

[16] Note that in tableau (44), nothing hinges on the ranking of STAY with respect to LE(CP) and TEL. In tableau (45), however, also candidate (b) is optimal if LE(CP) and TEL outrank STAY, with the result that *the man that saw Bill* corresponds to two distinct syntactic structures. In tableau (46), the actual ranking is again immaterial, while in tableau (47) the ranking LE(CP) <> TEL >> STAY incorrectly gives the candidates (a) and (c) as optimal. This ranking does give the right results in tableau (47) if case-marked traces are invisible to LE(CP), but then we expect candidate (d) to be the only optimal form in tableau (45). Hence we must conclude that case-marked traces are visible to alignment constraints such as LE(CP) (see footnote 12) and that STAY outranks LE(CP) and TEL in English. In Standard Dutch and the Aarschot dialect, on the other hand, LE(CP) outranks STAY, because either C or SpecCP must be filled under all circumstances (see Dekkers 1995, 1999).

Note further that we simplified tableaux (44) and (45) by not taking into account the violations of STAY which are the result of A-movement, assuming that the number of A-movement steps is the same in all cases, and by omitting OB-HD, since this constraint is irrelevant here. Remember also that the additional violations of TEL in the rows (a) and (c) of tableau (45) follow from our earlier assumption that pronunciation of the relative pronoun *that* leads to a violation of TEL, due to the fact that it does not contain semantic features. We did not add an additional violation of TEL in row (e) of tableau (45), because *that* heads an A-chain in this case (it carries a θ-role); this assumption (which becomes crucial in Section 11.3.8, where we argue that Numerations do not determine the Candidate Set) is consistent with our assumption that deletion of *that* violates Recoverability in this case (see row (f) of tableau (45)).

the result would be exactly as it should be, since the optimal candidate violates only LE(CP) in both tableaux.

Similarly, the combined and individual evaluations of the candidate sets in tableaux (35) and (36) give identical results, as is shown in tableau (48). Since LE(CP) and TEL are in a tie, we have to determine the optimal candidates on the rankings REC >> LE(CP) >> TEL >> OB-HD *and* REC >> TEL >> LE (CP) >> OB-HD: on the former ranking, only candidate (48c′) is optimal, while on the latter ranking, (48b) and (48d′) are optimal.

(48)	English	REC	LE(CP)	TEL	OB-HD
	a. the man who that I saw the book which that I read		*>	<*	
	a′. the man/book that that I saw		*>	*<*	
☞	b. the man who ~~that~~ I saw the book which ~~that~~ I saw		*>		*
	b′. the book/man that ~~that~~ I saw		*>	<*	*
	c. the man ~~who~~ that I saw the book ~~which~~ that I read	*!		*	
☞	c′. the man/book ~~that~~ that I saw			<*	
	d. the man ~~who that~~ I saw the book ~~which that~~ I read	*!	*		*
☞	d′. the man/book ~~that that~~ I saw		*>		*

11.4 The Left Periphery of Infinitival Relative Clauses

11.4.1 *Introduction*

We concluded in the previous section that if functional heads are contained in the Numeration, the subject-object asymmetry attested in English relative clauses constitutes evidence in favor of the claim that Numerations do not determine candidate sets, and that this claim is compatible with the analysis presented so far.

In order to avoid structures being blocked by semantically unrelated structures (*Who did you meet?* should not be blocked by the presumably more economical *The Germans lost the war*),we propose to adopt the hypothesis in (49b), instead of the one given in (49a).[17]

---

[17] There are several alternative ways to prevent a structure from being blocked by a semantically unrelated structure, one of which is by the evaluation of output structures with respect to a rich Input (containing a Numeration as well as semantic information concerning predication, quantifier scope, and information structure). Strictly speaking, *the man I saw* would be able to block *the French president*, but only if the latter structure were drastically unfaithful to the Input. In other words, semantically unrelated structures would never be in direct competition if faithfulness plays a dominant role in candidate evaluation.

(49)   a. The members of a Candidate Set are based on identical Numerations.
       b. The members of a Candidate Set are truth-functional equivalents.

In this section, we will argue that infinitival relatives constitute further evidence against the relevance of the Numeration, by showing that candidate sets may have members that contain distinct lexical items (i.c. *who/which* and *that*), which reinforces our choice for (49b). Furthermore, we will see that the fact that we adopted the model of grammar in Figure 2 raises interesting questions with respect to the evaluation of relative clauses involving 'Pied Piping' and Preposition-Stranding.

Before we go on and examine infinitival relatives, we should mention that these clauses pose specific problems which we will not go into here in any detail. One of these problems is that the complementizer *for*, although deletable in clauses that do not contain a lexical subject, must be overtly realized if a lexical subject is present. We will follow Pesetsky (to appear) in assuming that case assignment interferes here. The relevant generalization seems to be the one given in (50).

(50)   The infinitival complementizer *for* is expressed if it assigns case to a lexical DP.

In this chapter, we will not attempt to give a principled account for this generalization. We will merely stipulate that case-assigning *for* is subject to REC, while its non-case-assigning counterpart is not.[18]

11.4.2   *A Book to Read/A Book for John to Read*

In this section, we will discuss infinitival relatives of the type *a book to read*. On the assumption that the relative pronoun in English can be either *who/which* or *that*, and that the complementizer of the relative clause is *for*, we expect the relevant candidates to be the ones in (51) and (52).

Note in passing that it is not evident that the hypothesis in (49a) successfully prevents *Bob wonders who Hank thinks lost the game* from being incorrectly blocked by *Bob thinks Hank wonders who lost the game* (for reasons of economy). We will not go into this problem here, since we reject (49a) on independent grounds.

It must also be noted that abolishing the Numeration has several consequences for the computational system itself, one of which seems to be that we can no longer maintain that MERGE is always preferred to MOVE (Chomsky 1995). This is discussed at length in Broekhuis and Klooster (1997).

[18] This seems to suggest that only case-assigning *for* is a meaningful element, which could very well be related directly to the case feature it is endowed with. This could ultimately lead to a generalization of our formulation of Recoverability in (27) to all elements that contain formal features at Spell-Out—i.e. interpretable features (which C_{HL} does not delete) as well unchecked uninterpretable features.

Note further that this approach to the *For-to*-Filter is compatible with the fact that in some English dialects—e.g. Ozark English as described by Chomsky and Lasnik (1977)—the complementizer *for* can be realized if no overtly realized DP is present: in these dialects OB-HD should outrank TEL, or be in a tie with this constraint.

(51) a. a book [$_{CP}$ which$_i$ for [$_{IP}$ to read t_i]]
     b. a book [$_{CP}$ which$_i$ ~~for~~ [$_{IP}$ to read t_i]]
     c. a book [$_{CP}$ ~~which$_i$~~ for [$_{IP}$ to read t_i]]
     d. a book [$_{CP}$ ~~which$_i$~~~~for~~ [$_{IP}$ to read t_i]]

(52) a. a book [$_{CP}$ that$_i$ for [$_{IP}$ to read t_i]]
     b. a book [$_{CP}$ that$_i$ ~~for~~ [$_{IP}$ to read t_i]]
     c. a book [$_{CP}$ ~~that$_i$~~ for [$_{IP}$ to read t_i]]
     d. a book [$_{CP}$ ~~that$_i$~~~~for~~ [$_{IP}$ to read t_i]]

If we adopt the hypothesis in (49a), the set of options in (51) and the one in (52) correspond to distinct candidate sets, each giving rise to at least one optimal candidate. Since deletion of *which* violates REC, the optimal member of the set in (51) should contain at least the pronoun *which*. Given that the use of this pronoun leads to a violation of LE(CP), the best structure is the one that involves deletion of *for* because this would prevent a violation of TEL. In other words, example (51b) is wrongly predicted to be grammatical, while (52d) is correctly evaluated as the optimal candidate of the set given in (52)).

Hypothesis (49b), on the other hand, does not force us to conclude that at least one example of (51) is acceptable: because the examples in (51) and (52) are now taken to be in the same candidate set, the structures in (51) can be blocked by the members of the set in (52). The evaluation of the examples in (51) and (52) is then as given in tableau (53) (the double line separates the two candidate sets that should be distinguished according to (49a), OB-HD is again irrelevant).[19] Here, candidate (53h) is the only optimal one.

(53) English	REC	LE(CP)	TEL
a. a book [$_{CP}$ which$_i$ for [$_{IP}$ to read t_i]]		*>	<*
b. a book [$_{CP}$ which$_i$ ~~for~~ [$_{IP}$ to read t_i]]		*!	
c. a book [$_{CP}$ ~~which$_i$~~ for [$_{IP}$ to read t_i]]	*!		*
d. a book [$_{CP}$ ~~which$_i$~~~~for~~ [$_{IP}$ to read t_i]]	*!		
e. a book [$_{CP}$ that$_i$ for [$_{IP}$ to read t_i]]		*>	*<*
f. a book [$_{CP}$ that$_i$ ~~for~~ [$_{IP}$ to read t_i]]		*>	<*
g. a book [$_{CP}$ ~~that$_i$~~ for [$_{IP}$ to read t_i]]			*!
☞ h. a book [$_{CP}$ ~~that$_i$~~~~for~~ [$_{IP}$ to read t_i]]			

[19] Like Pesetsky, we assume that LE(CP) is satisfied if *to* is the first expressed element of the clause. We will not consider the structures in which *to* is deleted; according to Pesetsky *to* is responsible for the modal interpretation of infinitival relatives, which entails that its deletion gives rise to a violation of Recoverability. We will not adopt Pesetsky's claim that the expression of *to* gives rise to a violation of TEL; given that deletion of *to* gives rise to a violation of Recoverability, this would not be consistent with our definition of Telegraph in (32). Because all candidates contain *to*, this is innocuous.

In the case of infinitival relatives of the type *a book for John to read* a similar problem arises for the hypothesis in (49a). If we disregard structures in which case-assigning *for* is deleted (see the generalization in (50)), we end up with the candidates in (54) and (55). Since, according to (49a), they are in different candidate sets, at least one of the two structures in (54) should be grammatical. Given that deletion of *which* violates REC, we wrongly predict (54a) to be acceptable.

(54)   a. a book [$_{CP}$ which$_i$ for [$_{IP}$ John to read t_i]]
       b. a book [$_{CP}$ ~~which~~$_i$ for [$_{IP}$ John to read t_i]]

(55)   a. a book [$_{CP}$ that$_i$ for [$_{IP}$ John to read t_i]]
       b. a book [$_{CP}$ ~~that~~$_i$ for [$_{IP}$ John to read t_i]]

If we adopt hypothesis (49b), on the other hand, the examples in (55) may block example (54a). The evaluation of the examples in (54) and (55) is then as given in tableau (56), where only candidate (56d) turns out to be optimal: candidate (56b) is out on both possible rankings because it violates REC; on the ranking LE(CP) >> TEL, the candidates in (56a) and (56c) are blocked as they violate LE(CP), wheras (56d) satisfies this constraint; on the ranking TEL >> LE(CP), candidate (56c) is blocked because it violates TEL twice, whereas (56a) and (56d) violate it only once, and candidate (56a) is blocked because it violates LE(CP) in addition to TEL, whereas (56d) satisfies LE(CP).

(56) English	REC	LE(CP)	TEL
a. a book [$_{CP}$ which$_i$ for [$_{IP}$John to read t_i]]		*!	*
b. a book [$_{CP}$ ~~which~~$_i$ for [$_{IP}$ John to read t_i]]	*!		
c. a book [$_{CP}$ that$_i$ for [$_{IP}$John to read t_i]]		*>	<**
☞ d. a book [$_{CP}$ ~~that~~$_i$ for [$_{IP}$ John to read t_i]]			*

This shows once more that the hypothesis in (49a) cannot be maintained. Our findings are on the other hand in accordance with the hypothesis in (49b), which we will therefore adopt.

11.4.3 *A Topic to Work on/A Topic on Which to Work*

The fact that we adopted the model of grammar in Figure 2 and more particularly that we assumed the hypothesis in (49b) forces us to claim that relative clauses that involve Preposition-Stranding (*a topic to work on*) and ones exhibiting Pied Piping of the preposition (*a topic on which to work*) are contained in one and the same candidate set (see footnote 21 for the prediction based on two alternative sets of assumptions). In this section, we will see that this consequence is not without problems, which may indicate either that our present proposal is untenable, at least in as far as we assume that identity of meaning determines which structures are part of the same candidate set, or that auxiliary assumptions are needed.

But before we go and examine infinitival constructions, we should test if our assumptions give the correct results for finite clauses. Let us therefore consider the examples in (57), which must come out as the optimal candidates.

(57) a. the topic which I am working on
      b. the topic on which I am working
      c. the topic that I am working on
      d. the topic I am working on

The evaluation is given in tableau (58). Since LE(CP) and TEL are in a tie, we have to consider two alternative rankings: on the ranking REC >> TEL >> LE(CP) >> OB-HD, we have four optimal candidates, (58b), (58b′), (58f), (58h′); on the alternative ranking REC >> LE(CP) >> TEL >> OB-HD, there is only one optimal candidate, (58g′). This means that we are forced to include one candidate in the set of optimal candidates that does not belong there, namely (58b′) (the reader may infer that both hypotheses in (49) make the same predictions here).

(58) English	REC	LE(CP)	TEL	OB-HD
a. the topic [CP on which_i that [I am working t_i]]		*>	<*	
a′. the topic [CP on that_i that [I am working t_i]]		*>	<*	
☞ b. the topic [CP on which_i ~~that~~ [I am working t_i]]		*>		*
☞ b′. the topic [CP on that_i ~~that~~ [I am working t_i]]		*>		*
c. the topic [CP ~~on which~~_i that [I am working t_i]]	*!		*	
c′. the topic [CP ~~on that~~_i that [I am working t_i]]	*!		*	
d. the topic [CP ~~on which_i-that~~ [I am working t_i]]	*!	*		*
d′. the topic [CP ~~on that_i-that~~ [I am working t_i]]	*!	*		*
e. the topic [CP which_i that [I am working on t_i]]		*>	<*	
e′. the topic [CP that_i that [I am working on t_i]]		*>	*<*	
☞ f. the topic [CP which_i ~~that~~ [I am working on t_i]]		*>		*
f′. the topic [CP that_i ~~that~~ [I am working on t_i]]		*>	<*	*
g. the topic [CP ~~which~~_i that [I am working on t_i]]	*!		*	
☞ g′. the topic [CP ~~that~~_i that [I am working on t_i]]			<*	
h. the topic [CP ~~which_i-that~~ [I am working on t_i]]	*!	*		*
☞ h′. the topic [CP ~~that_i-that~~ [I am working on t_i]]		*>		*

The problem with candidate (58b′) is independent of the question whether the candidates that involve Pied Piping are in the same candidate set as the candidates that involve Preposition-Stranding; if we had considered the candidates in 18a–d separately, the same result would have arisen. Since we do not have a principled explanation for the ungrammaticality of this candidate, we leave this to future research and postulate the *ad hoc* filter in (59). A similar filter is operative in Dutch (cf. the discussion of (20)).[20]

(59)   a.   English: $*[_{CP} [_{PP}$ P that] C $[_{IP} \ldots]]$
       b.   Dutch: $*[_{CP} [_{PP}$ P die/dat] C $[_{IP} \ldots]]$

Now that we have discussed finite relative clauses, let us consider the results in infinitival clauses. What we would hope to derive is that the examples in (60) are the optimal candidates.

(60)   a.   a book on which to work
       b.   a book to work on

The evaluation of those candidates that do not include the structures that violate the *ad hoc* constraint in (59) is given in tableau (61). We predict only candidate (61h′) to surface, which only violates OB-HD.[21]

Although our proposal predicts there to be only one optimal candidate, we believe that this is not a reason to consider it falsified. In the first place, there are several examples that are in accordance with our predictions. Kester (1994) notes for example that Pied Piping gives rise to a marginal result in sentences like the ones given in (62).

---

[20] Subdeletion of *that* in this construction would involve deletion in an A-chain. Hence, the impossibility of this follows from our present proposal. There may be a link between the filter in (59) and the issue of Preposition-Stranding. In Dutch and English, the filter is active and Preposition-Stranding is allowed, while in Standard German relative d-pronouns may be the complement of a preposition (the filter is not active) and Preposition-Stranding is prohibited. We do not have an explanation for this correlation.

[21] If we had stuck to the grammar in Figure 1 (which entails the hypothesis in (49a)), we would have had the possibility of arguing that Preposition-Stranding and Pied Piping correspond to distinct Input structures, as is argued for by Pesetsky (to appear). Alternatively, if we had adopted the model in Figure 2 in combination with hypothesis (49a), we would have again been able to argue that *a topic to work on* and *a topic on which to work* are in different candidate sets, based on a Numeration containing either *that* (leading to Preposition-Stranding) or *which* (resulting in Pied Piping). As the reader may infer, both alternative sets of assumptions lead to the prediction that the structures b, f, g′ and h′ in tableau (61) are grammatical, which is clearly false.

(61) English	Rec	LE(CP)	Tel	Ob-Hd
a. the topic [$_{CP}$ on which$_i$ for [to work t_i]]		*>	<*	
b. the topic [$_{CP}$ on which$_i$ ~~for~~ [to work t_i]]		*!		*
c. the topic [$_{CP}$ ~~on which$_i$~~ for [to work t_i]]	*!		*	
d. the topic [$_{CP}$ ~~on which$_i$-for~~ [to work t_i]]	*!			*
e. the topic [$_{CP}$ which$_i$ for [to work on t_i]]		*>	<*	
e'. the topic [$_{CP}$ that$_i$ for [to work on t_i]]		*>	*<*	
f. the topic [$_{CP}$ which$_i$ ~~for~~ [to work on t_i]]		*!		*
f'. the topic [$_{CP}$ that$_i$ ~~for~~ [to work on t_i]]		*>	<*	*
g. the topic [$_{CP}$ ~~which$_i$~~ for [to work on t_i]]	*!		*	
g'. the topic [$_{CP}$ ~~that$_i$~~ for [to work on t_i]]			*!	
h. the topic [$_{CP}$ ~~which$_i$-for~~ [to work on t_i]]	*!			*
☞ h'. the topic [$_{CP}$ ~~that$_i$-for~~ [to work on t_i]]				*

(62)   a. ??I am looking for a man to whom to give this book.
      a′. I am looking for a man to give this book to.
      b. ??I am looking for a place to which to travel.
      b′. I am looking for a place to travel to.
      c. ??I am looking for a book to which to refer.
      c′. I am looking for a book to refer to.

Furthermore, Craig Thiersch (p.c.) informs us that in colloquial speech Pied Piping never occurs; the possibility of examples such as (60a) is explicitly taught in school (Thiersch attributes this statement to Howard Lasnik). If so, we may claim that the fact that we are not able to derive (60a) is actually a virtue of our proposal, making it superior to accounts that predict it to be grammatical (such as Chomsky and Lasnik's 1977 Doubly Filled COMP Filter and Pesetsky's, to appear, proposal).

We will conclude by considering infinitival clauses containing an overtly realized subject. In these clauses, there should be only one optimal candidate, namely the one corresponding to the acceptable option given in (63a), its counterpart in (63b) being fully ungrammatical. The evaluation is given in tableau (64). For convenience, we have not included the candidates that go against the generalization in (50) and the filter in (59). The evaluation correctly gives (64d′) as the only optimal candidate.

(63)   a. a topic for John to work on
      b. *a topic on which for John to work

(64)	English	REC	LE(CP)	TEL	OB-HD
	a. the topic [$_{CP}$ on which$_i$ for [John to work t_i]]		*!	*	
	b. the topic [$_{CP}$ ~~on which~~$_i$ for [John to work t_i]]	*!		*	
	c. the topic [$_{CP}$ which$_i$ for [John to work on t_i]]		*!	*	
	c′. the topic [$_{CP}$ that$_i$ for [John to work on t_i]]		*>	<**	
	d. the topic [$_{CP}$ ~~which~~$_i$ for [John to work on t_i]]	*!		*	
☞	d′. the topic [$_{CP}$ ~~that~~$_i$ for [John to work on t_i]]			*	

In conclusion, our proposal comes quite close to being descriptively adequate; especially the fact that we correctly exclude examples such as (63b) is a major improvement over the proposal in Pesetsky (to appear). Nevertheless, the generalization in (50) and especially the filters in (59) still call for a principled explanation.

11.4.4 A Note on Dutch

So far, we have only considered English infinitival relative clauses. If we take into account similar examples from Dutch, our proposal *seems* to make the wrong predictions. Consider the grammatical examples in (65).

(65)   a. een leuke jongen [om   morgen   mee uit te gaan]
         a   nice   boy   COMP *tomorrow with out to go*
         'a nice boy to go out with'

       b. een leuk boek [om   morgen   te lezen]
         a   nice book   COMP *tomorrow to read*
         'a nice book to read tomorrow'

The candidate sets associated with the examples in (65) should be as given in tableaux (66) and (67); in accordance with Pesetsky we will assume that the pronunciation of *om* violates TEL, as does the pronunciation of the relative pronoun *dat*.

(66) Standard Dutch	REC	LE(CP)	TEL
a. een leuke jongen die om morgen mee uit te gaan		*	*!
☞ b. een leuke jongen die ~~om~~ morgen mee uit te gaan		*	
c. een leuke jongen ~~die~~ om morgen mee uit te gaan	*!		*
d. een leuke jongen ~~die om~~ morgen mee uit te gaan	*!	*	

(67) Standard Dutch		Rec	LE(CP)	Tel
	a. een leuk boek dat om morgen te lezen		*!	**
	b. een leuk boek dat ~~om~~ morgen te lezen		*!	*
☞	c. een leuk boek ~~dat~~ om morgen te lezen			*
	d. een leuk boek ~~dat om~~ morgen te lezen		*!	

As we can see in these tableaux, we get the correct result if the relative pronoun is *dat*, but not if it is *die*; since deletion of *die* gives rise to a violation of Rec, we would wrongly expect it to be overtly realized, and the complementizer *om* should be deleted in order to satisfy Tel. Although this result is disappointing, it should be pointed out that we do arrive at the correct result in the case of infinitival interrogatives, where the Specifier of CP is clearly endowed with semantic features. In (68), it is shown that the *Wh*-phrase must always be overtly expressed at the expense of the pronunciation of the complementizer.

(68)   a.   Ik weet niet [$_{CP}$ wie$_i$ ~~om~~ [$_{IP}$ morgen t_i te bezoeken]]
           I   know not   who   tomorrow   to visit
           'I don't know who to visit tomorrow'

       b.   Ik weet niet [$_{CP}$ wat$_i$ ~~om~~ [$_{IP}$ morgen t_i te lezen]]
           I   know not   what   tomorrow   to read
           'I don't know what to read tomorrow'

Because this is precisely what we would expect on the given constraint ranking, there is reason to doubt that the presupposed analysis of the Dutch examples in (65) is correct; the examples in (65) are not relative clauses in the standard sense. Below, we will give some additional reasons for this conclusion.

Firstly, it should be pointed out that in German, relative clauses of the sort under discussion do not occur at all (Kester 1994); examples such as (69) are completely unacceptable.[22] If Dutch resembles German in this respect,

---

[22] In examples such as *ein Buch* [*zum lesen*] and *ein Mädchen* [*zum heiraten*], the bracketed constituent is interpreted as a goal infinitive. Kester (1994) gives two exceptions to the rule that German has no infinitival relative clauses. Firstly, there are examples such as (ia) in which the 'relative pronoun' corresponds to the PRO subject, which are problematic anyway because relative pronouns that correspond to arguments generally originate in case-marked positions. Secondly, there are cases such as (ib) in which the antecedent is necessarily a quantifier-like element. We doubt whether cases like these can be seen as ordinary relative clauses.

(i)   a.   Ich suche   einen Mann$_i$ [um PRO$_i$ für mich einzukaufen].
           I   look-for a   man   um   for me   to-shop
           'I am looking for a man to shop for me.'

      b.   etwas   zu lesen
           something to read
           'something to read'

the examples in (65) must receive a different analysis.

(69) a. *Ich suche ein Buch [um zu lesen]
       'I am looking for a book to read'

      b. *Er fand ein Mädchen [um zu heiraten]
       'He found a girl to marry'

Secondly, examples such as the ones given in (70) are generally analysed as involving *Tough*-movement—i.e. movement of an empty operator into SpecCP (Bennis and Wehrmann 1987).

(70) a. Die jongen is leuk [$_{CP}$ OP$_i$ om [$_{IP}$ PRO t_i mee uit te gaan]]
         that boy   is nice   COMP   *with out to go*

      b. Dat boek is leuk [$_{CP}$ OP$_i$ om [$_{IP}$ PRO t_i te lezen]]
         that book is nice   COMP   *to read*

Being a modifier of the adjective, the infinitival clause can be expected to be placed after the noun when the adjective is used attributively. If so, the examples in (65) can be analysed as cases of *Tough*-movement as well. In other words, SpecCP of the infinitival clause in (65) does not contain a relative pronoun but an empty operator just like in the cases given in (70). This would give rise to the analysis of the examples in (65) in (71).

(71) a. een leuke jongen [$_{CP}$ OP$_i$ om [$_{IP}$ PRO morgen t_i mee uit te gaan]]
      b. een leuk boek [$_{CP}$ OP$_i$ om [$_{IP}$ PRO morgen t_i te lezen]]

Thirdly, infinitival clauses can be used in predicative positions. Some examples are given in (72); being open predicates, the infinitival clauses can again be analysed as involving empty operator movement.

(72) a. Dit kind is [$_{CP}$ OP$_i$ om   [$_{IP}$ PRO t_i te zoenen]]
         this child is   COMP   *to kiss*

      b. Dit boek is [$_{CP}$ OP$_i$ om   [$_{IP}$ PRO in een adem t_i uit te lezen]]
         this book is   COMP   *in one breath   out to read*

As the infinitival clause can be used in predicative position, there is no *a priori* reason not to assume that they may be used as attributive phrases as well. Consequently, examples such as (73) may receive a similar analysis as the examples in (72).

(73) a. een kind [$_{CP}$ OP$_i$ om   [$_{IP}$ PRO t_i te zoenen]]
         a   child   COMP   *to kiss*

      b. een boek [$_{CP}$ OP$_i$ om   [$_{IP}$ PRO in een adem t_i uit te lezen]]
         a   boek   COMP   *in one breath   out to read*

Although examples such as (65) deserve much more discussion, we may conclude that it would be unwise to consider the examples in (65) as decisive counter-examples to our proposal. Hence, we put them aside, while noting that if the clauses in question indeed contain an empty operator in the specifier position, our theory correctly predicts that *om* must be overtly realized. This is shown in tableau (74).

(74) Standard Dutch	R_EC	LE(CP)	T_EL
☞ a. [_CP OP_i om [_IP PRO (XP) t_i te V]]			*
b. [_CP OP_i ~~om~~ [_IP PRO (XP) t_i te V]]		*!	

So far, we have only indicated that there may be reasons to treat the examples in (65) on a par with constructions that are generally analysed as involving empty operator movement. The next step should be to answer the more general question why so-called empty categories are empty, in so far as we want to maintain that these elements are the result of a deletion transformation (see Samek-Lodovici 1996). We leave this for further research.

Finally, in tableau (74) the element *te* is always preceded by the case-marked trace of the empty operator. In order to account for the fact that the complementizer *om* cannot be deleted if XP is empty, we must assume that the presence of this case-marked trace makes it impossible for the inflectional element *te* to satisfy LE(CP) (see footnotes 12 and 16). This is of course reminiscent of the discussion of *wanna*-contraction, which can be blocked by a case-marked *Wh*-trace, but not by an NP-trace or PRO. Apparently, a case-marked trace counts as phonetically realized material.[23]

11.5 Conclusion

In this chapter we have studied a phenomenon that is not likely to be analysed in a satisfactory way in a syntactic system that only disposes of the computational system argued for in Chomsky (1995). In order to meet the requirement of descriptive adequacy, it is necessary to postulate an additional module, which we assumed to have an Optimality-theoretic format. Our point of departure was the model of grammar in Figure 1, in which the computational system and the OT module were strictly separated.

In Section 11.3, however, it became clear that it is possible to combine the two generators into a single one, consisting of the operations S_ELECT, M_ERGE, A_TTRACT/M_OVE and D_ELETE. This resulted in the model in Figure 2, which is

---

[23] If so, the assumption that the head of an A-chain must be pronounced in English (see the discussion of (42a, b) in Section 11.3.7) may be attributed to an E_PP-like constraint, stating that SpecIP must be filled with phonetically visible material. It would follow from this assumption that material which can in principle be deleted under recoverability, such as the relative pronoun *that*, must be pronounced in order to satisfy E_PP if it occupies SpecIP. In other words, the subject relative pronoun *that* can only be deleted if it is A′-moved.

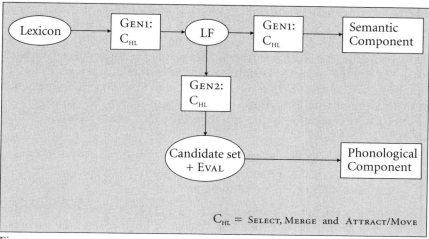

Figure 1.

more or less the model assumed in standard OT approaches to syntax. Finally, in Section 11.4, we showed that the model in Figure 2 is superior to the one in Figure 1.

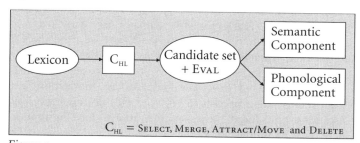

Figure 2.

This leaves us with the question whether the lexicon should still be held co-re-sponsible for parametrization, which (putting the inventory of lexical elements aside and given our earlier assumptions) could be fully reduced to constraint ranking if the OT module can be made to handle the parametrization of A-movement.

We assumed in Section 11.2.1, essentially following Chomsky, that after Spell-Out (or LF, in our terminology), C_{HL} is still operative, in the sense that it con-tinues to manipulate structures until they are ready to be interpreted by the semantic component,—i.e. until they satisfy the bare output conditions imposed by this semantic component. According to Chomsky, word-order parametri-zation reduces to the question whether movement takes place before or after Spell-Out. In English, for example, subjects must be A-moved into SpecIP overtly, whereas overt Object Shift is blocked, which implies that this type of parametrization has taken place before the OT module is reached.

However, it seems fairly simple to develop an OT account that gives exactly the same results (see Broekhuis 1988; Costa 1996; Dekkers 1997, 1999; Grimshaw 1997). For example, we could postulate a violable constraint CASE which forbids arguments in Case-less positions (at the moment of Spell-Out). The interaction of this constraint with STAY could be held responsible for the choice between overt or covert application of the operation MOVE/ATTRACT. The possibilities are given in (75).[24]

(75)   a. CASE >> STAY: obligatory movement
       b. STAY >> CASE: no movement
       c. CASE <> STAY: optional movement

The situation in English with respect to subject and object movement could now be described as in (76), in which EPP stands for a constraint that requires a lexically filled specifier of IP: both the subject and the object may remain in situ as far as CASE is concerned, but the subject must move to SpecIP in order to satisfy EPP.

(76)   EPP >> STAY >> CASE

As far as explanatory adequacy is concerned, the proposal outlined above may even be superior to Chomsky's (1995) proposal. It makes use of ranked constraints, which is independently motivated in the sense that we need the OT module to account for those syntactic phenomena that are not explained within C_{HL}, whereas Chomsky makes use of a distinction between strong and weak features, which does not seem to have any independent motivation (see Chomsky 1996). Importantly, the proposals in (75) and (76) do not imply that we need to introduce constraints for all movement operations, since the application of A′-movement may be motivated by the fact that a given candidate set consists of candidates that are truth-functionally equivalent, so that all semantically relevant operations must have applied before the structure is placed in a certain candidate set.

Besides important issues like this one, various other questions may arise with respect to the mechanisms or constraints employed by the two modules. Let us take two examples to illustrate this point. Firstly, consider Chomsky's assumption that interrogative complementizers contain an interpretable *Wh*-feature. Being interpretable, this feature will survive checking, so that the comple-

---

[24] We can give shape to covert movement in two ways. Possibly, covert movement takes place after Spell-Out, which would mean that in Figure 2, C_{HL} is still operative between EVAL and the Semantic component. Alternatively, covert movement could be seen as movement that strands phonological features, which could apply before EVAL. The first option is argued for by Broekhuis (1998), and the latter by Dekkers (1997, 1999).

mentizer will be adorned with a semantic feature at LF. Given our formulation of REC in (27), this means that deletion of this complementizer will wrongly be blocked:

(77)   John wondered what (*that/if) Bill had said.

We are therefore forced to drop Chomsky's assumption and to conclude that the interpretation of the embedded clause as interrogative follows from the fact that it has a *Wh*-phrase in an operator position (SpecCP). Since cross-linguistically, functional heads such as C, T and Neg need not be realized overtly, these heads never seem to carry an interpretable feature. If A-movement is accounted for in the way suggested above, this conclusion would of course be desirable as it would enable us to eliminate the notion of feature strength from the syntax entirely.

Secondly, consider the assumption that the OT module contains the constraint REC. This constraint has at least one remarkable property: it is always the most highly-ranked and therefore inviolable. If violability is a crucial property of OT constraints, REC seems to be an illicit member of the constraint set. Hence, it is reasonable to assume that recoverability is a condition in the generator. One way to implement this would be to assume that recoverability is a defining part of the operation DELETE requiring that semantic features not be deleted.

The discussion above shows that the model defended in this chapter can be helpful in evaluating the properties assigned to the computational system and the OT part of syntax. This is especially important for defining the proper format of the computational system, discussions about which have so far been fairly remote from empirical considerations and have mainly been led by intuitive, hence vague, ideas about what is or is not conceptually attractive.[25]

11.6 References

Bennis, H. and P. Wehrmann (1987). 'Adverbial arguments.' In F. Beukema and P. Coopmans (eds), *Linguistics in the Netherlands* 1987. Foris, Dordrecht.

Broekhuis, H. (1998). 'Against feature strength: The case of Scandinavian Object Shift'. Ms, University of Amsterdam.

—— and W. Klooster (1997). 'Zinsnegatie: Negatieve woorden en negatief polaire uitdrukkingen'. Ms, University of Amsterdam.

Chomsky, N. (1981). *Lectures on Government and Binding*. Dordrecht, Foris.

—— (1995). *The Minimalist Program*. Cambridge, MA, MIT Press.

—— (1996). 'Some observations on economy in generative grammar'. Ms, Cambridge, MA, MIT.

—— and H. Lasnik (1977). 'Filters and control'. *Linguistic Inquiry* 8.

Costa, J. (1996). 'Word order and constraint interaction'. Ms, Leiden University.

---

[25] We refer the reader to Broekhuis (1998) and Dekkers (1997, 1999) for further discussion and for solutions to some of the empirical issues remaining unsolved in this chapter.

Dekkers, J. (1995). 'Optimal subject extraction'. Ms, University of Amsterdam.

—— (1997). 'French word order: A conspiracy theory.' In J. Coerts and H. de Hoop (eds), *Linguistics in the Netherlands 1997*. Amsterdam and Philadelphia, John Benjamins.

—— (1999). *Derivations and Evaluations: On the Syntax of Subjects and Complementizers*. The Hague, Holland Academic Graphics.

Deprez, V. (1994). 'A Minimal account of the that-t effect.' In G. Cinque *et al.* (eds), *Paths Towards Universal Grammar*. Washington, D.C., Georgetown University Press.

Grimshaw, J. (1997). 'Projection, heads, and optimality', *Linguistic Inquiry* 28, 373–422.

Hornstein, N. (1995). *Logical Form: From GB to Minimalism*. Oxford, Blackwell.

Kayne, R. (1994). *The Antisymmetry of Syntax*. Cambridge, MA, MIT Press.

Kester, E.-P. (1994). *Eurotra Grammar: Adnominal Participles and Infinitives in Germanic and Romance Languages*. Allesandria, Edizioni dell'Orso.

—— (1996). *The Nature of Adjectival Inflection*. OTS dissertations, Utrecht University.

Legendre, G., C. Wilson, P. Smolensky, K. Homer, and W. Raymond (1995). 'Optimality and *Wh*-extraction.' In J. Beckman, L. Walsh Dickey, and S. Urbanczyk (eds), *Papers in Optimality Theory*. University of Massachusetts Occasional Papers 18. Amherst, MA, Graduate Linguistics Students Association.

Pauwels, J. L. (1958). *Het Dialect van Aarschot en Omstreken*. Belgisch Interuniversitair Centrum voor Neerlandistiek.

Pesetsky, D. (1994). 'Optimality Principles of sentence pronunciation'. Cambridge, MA, fall handouts, MIT.

—— (1995). 'Optimality principles of sentence pronunciation'. Papers presented at the University of Amsterdam and the Free University Amsterdam.

—— (1998). 'Some optimality principles of sentence pronunciation.' In P. Barbosa, D. Fox, P. Hagstrom, M. McGinnis, and D. Pesetsky (eds), *Is the best good enough?* Cambridge, MA, MIT Press and MIT Working Papers in Linguistics.

Rizzi, L. (to appear). 'Residual verb second and the WH Criterion'. In A. Belletti and L. Rizzi (eds), *Parameters and Functional Heads*, Oxford/New York, Oxford University Press.

Samek-Lodovici, V. (1996). *Constraints on Subjects: An Optimality Theoretic Analysis*. PhD thesis, Rutgers University.

Verwijs, E. and J. Verdam (1889). *Middelnederlandsch Woordenboek*, vol. 2. The Hague, Martinus Nijhoff (photomechanical reprint 1969), 84–6.

12

Morphological and Prosodic Alignment of Bulgarian Clitics[1]

Géraldine Legendre

12.1 Introduction

Bulgarian clausal clitics include not only familiar object pronouns, but also tense/aspect auxiliaries, modal particles, negative particles, as well as interrogative particles. They display well-known properties associated with clitic elements cross-linguistically. For example, they are typically stressless and they display positional restrictions. In simple sentences, most Bulgarian clitics cluster in second position.

(1)   a.   Az **sŭm mu   go**   dal.
           *I   be-1 him-*DAT *it-*ACC *given*
           'I have given it to him.'

      b.   Dal **sŭm mu go**.
           '(I) have given it to him.'

In the absence of a subject pronoun (pervasive in this null-subject language), the nonfinite verb must appear in clause-initial position, as shown in (1b). More-over, Bulgarian clitics cannot be separated from the verb, except by another clitic. Finally, they typically appear in a sequence or cluster whose internal ordering is fixed.

This brief summary underlines the well-behaved character of Bulgarian clitics from a Balkan as well as universal perspective. What makes them of particular

[1] This paper is a substantially revised version of a talk given at the 1996 Formal Approaches to Slavic Linguistics Meeting in Indiana and of my 1996 JHU Technical Report. I wish to thank the FASL audience, Catherine Rudin, Loren Billings, Andrew Spencer for their comments, as well as Adiamandis Gafos for asking the right question. Special thanks go to my invaluable informants: Marina Todorova, Mariana Lambova, and Boris Nikolov in the United States, Elena Andonova, Gergana Lalova, and Vassil Nikolov in Bulgaria. I am particularly grateful to Paul Smolensky for his suggestions and his feedback on the final outcome. Research for this paper was partially funded by NSF grant IRI–9596120.

interest to a theory of clitics however is the fact that these properties, while typical of Bulgarian, are not obligatory. First, any clitic (other than the question particle *li*) must carry stress in a negative context, if it immediately follows the negative particle *ne* (Hauge 1976). Throughout this chapter, clitics are in bold type while stressed clitics are also in upper case.

(2)   a. **Ne GO**   razbiram.
         NEG *it*-ACC *understand*-1
         '(I) don't understand it.'

      b. **Ne ŠTE sŭm** pročel knigata.
         NEG FUT *be*-1 *read   book-the*
         '(I) will not have read the book.'

Second, some Bulgarian clitics—**šte** (future auxiliary), **da** (modal/complement-izer-like particle) and **ne**—may appear in clause-initial position in violation of the second-position requirement characteristic of other clitics.

(3)   a. **Šte go**   viždaš **li**?
         FUT HIM-ACC *see*-2   Q
         'Will (you) see him?'

      b. **Da ne MI**   ja   dadeš.
         MOD NEG *me*-ACC *it*-ACC *give*-2
         'Don't give it to me!'

      c. **Ne ŠTE li go**   viždaš?
         NEG FUT Q *him*-ACC *see*-2
         'Will (you) not see him?'

      d. Viždal **li go**   e?
         seen   Q *him*-ACC *be*-3
         'Has (he) seen him?'

Third, additional properties displayed in (3) highlight the uniqueness of the interrogative particle **li**, used to mark yes/no questions: (a) it appears in a variety of positions, including second and further down but never first; (b) it does not necessarily cluster with other clitics; (c) in neutral yes/no questions, **li** cannot immediately follow **ne**; as a result it never carries stress.

Finally, even second-position clitics may fail to occur in the overall second position in a clause. This is the case when a clause contains multiple *Wh*-phrases, topicalized phrases, parentheticals, and the like. Examples are from Tomić (1996).

(4)   a. Koj kakvo **mu**   e   dal?
         who what   him-DAT *be*-3 *given*
         'Who gave what to him?'

b. Knigata, Penka **ja**   e   dala na Petko.
   book-the Penka her-ACC *be*-3 *given to Petko*
   'As for the book, Penka gave it to Petko.'

The challenge, therefore, is to provide a unified account of the unmarked as well as the marked properties of all Bulgarian clitics. In this chapter I shall defend the view that clitics are not syntactic atoms generated and moved around in the syntax. Rather, clitics instantiate functional features which are realized morphologically as phrasal affixes, as independently proposed in Anderson (1992, this volume). On a par with lexical affixes, phrasal affixes are subject to alignment constraints (McCarthy and Prince 1993a, b) which favor their realization at the edge of some domain. A competition for realization at the edge of a domain ensues among functional features, which is resolved by ranking the constraints in a language-particular order. Second-position clitics result from the interaction of an alignment constraint whose domain is V′ and one whose domain is the Intonational Phrase.

Additionally, I shall make two other main claims: (a) the question particle **li** is a second-position clitic—the fact that its true nature is often hidden follows from the interaction of morphological and prosodic constraints; (b) despite the complexity of the interaction, the constraint ranking of Bulgarian is modular: I will propose that modularity of constraint ranking be elevated to the status of a meta-constraint of the theory.

The chapter is organized as follows. Section 12.2 is devoted to presenting evidence that Bulgarian clitic auxiliaries and pronouns are syntactically inactive. This leads to the conclusion that they are not in the syntax but rather in the morphology. Section 12.3 focuses on demonstrating that the existing OT theory of morphology (Prince and Smolensky 1993; McCarthy and Prince 1993a, b) can explain all the Bulgarian facts by exploiting the Optimality-theoretic mechanism of ranking applied to simple alignment constraints. The issue of the domain within which clitics are left-aligned is discussed at length. It is concluded, based on Bulgarian, Serbo-Croatian, as well as Tagalog evidence, that the domain of one alignment constraint is prosodic. The other, it is argued, has a phrasal domain. Bulgarian clitics which evade second-position requirements are also shown to fall out of the same formal optimization. Section 12.4 examines the negative particle **ne** and the question particle **li**, with the conclusion that their conditioning is, to some extent, prosodic. Li will be revealed to be a second-position clitic, despite the vagaries of its surface distribution. The interaction of syntactic, prosodic, and morphological constraints in Bulgarian leads to considering the issue of modularity in OT. It is demonstrated that the Bulgarian constraint ranking is in fact modular and leads to the formulation of a meta-constraint, the Constraint Intermixing Ban. Section 12.5 summarizes the main results of the chapter.

12.2 Are Clitics in the Syntax?

One enduring feature of generative grammar is syntactic movement. For example, elements which by virtue of their thematic properties occupy a right periphery position in a clause may instead surface at the left periphery because they have undergone movement to a higher (leftward) position. This is the case for *Wh*-phrases in many languages. This has also been claimed for object clitics in Romance following Kayne (1975). While some scholars have since argued against a movement analysis of object clitics (e.g. Borer 1984; Jaeggli 1986; Suñer 1988), one important assumption behind Kayne's original analysis has gone virtually unchallenged among generative syntacticians. It is the view that clitic elements are generated in the syntax and as such obey syntactic constraints.

This is especially clear in the line of research initiated by Pollock (1989). Word order is taken to result from verb movement around fixed categories such as negation and adverbs, and much tree structure in Balkan languages is built upon functional X° categories which are clitics—i.e. non-standard syntactic elements (Rivero 1994a, b; Rudin 1997; among others). The assumption that clitics are generated in the syntax has gone largely unquestioned despite the fact that its consequences have been theoretically costly. The treatment of Balkan clitics alone has, for example, lead to substantial weakening of various versions of the generative theory of syntax, including Government Binding and the Minimalist Program. Among the adjustements needed, we find the following: lowering of affixes in the syntax (Rivero 1993), adjunction of heads to maximal projections in violation of the Structure Preserving Principle (Halpern 1995), right adjunction of clitics (Rivero 1993; Izvorski *et al.* 1997) generally disallowed in a restrictive theory of phrase structure, such as Kayne (1994), violations of the Head Movement Constraint (Rivero 1994a), proliferation of distinct functional projections such as WP (WackernagelP) and TMP (Tobler-MussafiaP) (Rivero 1994b), as well as movement in the phonology (Halpern 1995).

The present chapter challenges the syntactic status of clitics, arguing instead that they instantiate functional features which are are realized morphologically as phrasal affixes. On a par with lexical affixes—an alternative way in which functional features may be instantiated—phrasal affixes are subject to alignment constraints which favor their realization at the edge of some domain. The argument is made first for clitic auxiliaries, then for pronominal clitics.

12.2.1 *Clitic Auxiliaries*

Many properties of clitic auxiliaries are completely unexpected if they head syntactic projections. Most importantly, clitic auxiliaries systematically differ in syntactic behavior from their non-clitic counterparts, both lexical verbs and auxiliaries. As we will see, the latter are syntactically active while the former are syntactically inert.

Bulgarian auxiliary 'be', for example, is well-known for its differing status depending on tense (Hauge 1976). Present tense 'be' (e.g. first person *sŭm*, third person *e*) is phonologically weak and must procliticize or encliticize to a host; past tense 'be' (e.g. first person *bjax*, third person *beše*) carries stress and has no positional restrictions. In the following discussion past tense forms of 'be' are referred to as lexical auxiliaries. Contrary to lexical verbs and auxiliaries, clitic auxiliaries do not permit subject-auxiliary (SA) inversion in questions. This is shown in (5).

(5) a. Kakvo pročete Ivan?
         what   read-3 Ivan
         'What did Ivan read?'

     b. ?Kakvo beše Ivan pročel?
         what   was-3 Ivan read
         'What had Ivan read?'

     c. *Kakvo e   Ivan pročel?
         what   be-3 Ivan read
         'What has Ivan read?'

     d. Kakvo e pročel Ivan?

In (5a, b) the overt subject follows the lexical verb and auxiliary, respectively *pročete* and *beše*. Other word orders of (5b) are possible and even preferred, having to do with the general preference for sentence-final subjects in neutral contexts. But (5b) is not ungrammatical, it is only stylistically marked. (5c), however, is absolutely rejected by all native speakers, under any discourse conditions. The grammatical counterpart of (5c) is one in which the subject *Ivan* follows the complex clitic auxiliary and past participle: (5d). In other words, the overt subject cannot intervene between a clitic auxiliary and a past participle despite the fact that Bulgarian constituent order is very free (subject only to discourse factors). The ungrammaticality of (5c) does not make sense if *e* heads a functional projection, as is standardly assumed (e.g. Rivero 1994a; Tomić 1996). A similar pattern can be observed in yes/no questions:

(6) a. Pročete **li** Ivan knigata?
         read-3 Q Ivan book-the
         'Did Ivan read the book?'

     b. Beše **li** Ivan pročel knigata?
         was-3 Q Ivan read book-the
         'Had Ivan read the book?'

     c. Pročel **li e**   Ivan knigata?
         read Q be-3 Ivan book-the
         'Has Ivan read the book?'

In particular, the overt subject *Ivan* intervenes between the lexical auxiliary and the past participle in (6b) while it follows the past participle-clitic auxiliary complex in (6c). As we will see shortly, the ungrammaticality of SA inversion with clitic auxiliaries is not an isolated fact but part of a general pattern in Bulgarian. Moreover, this striking feature is shared by other Balkan languages (Legendre 1997; 1998). I propose that clitic auxiliaries do not permit SA inversion because they do not have the status of syntactic head which SA inversion requires. An analysis which does not take the clitic status into consideration must rely on generating various auxiliaries under different functional heads, as proposed in Krapova (1997). This leads to empirical and theoretical problems briefly reviewed below. The impossibility of SA inversion also leads to unsatisfactory analyses of second position clitics which rely on Morphological Merger. For example, Embick and Izvorski (1994) propose that Bulgarian clitics are stranded in clause-initial position in the syntax but appear in second position as a result of obligatory affixation to the adjacent lexical head to their right. They stipulate Short Participle Movement in the syntax to account for the adjacency of the clitic auxiliary and past participle in *Wh*-questions (5c) (though they acknowledge, in a footnote, that it has no independent motivation). But why Short Participle Movement does not feed into Morphological Merger in (5c) is unclear. The formulation of the Morphological Merger rule must consequently stipulate the left clausal boundary and thus merely restates the second-position facts.

An important feature of the theory of head movement which underlies that of functional categories is the Head Movement Constraint (HMC; Travis 1984). Put simply, the HMC prevents a given head from moving across another head dominating it, predicting blocking effects. The existence of Long Head Movement (LHM) in Bulgarian (Rivero 1994a) across a functional head—that is, the absence of blocking effects—is a problem for the HMC. Rivero's solution is to claim that LHM violates the HMC but complies with the ECP under Relativized Minimality. Under Rivero's characterization of the Bulgarian facts, (7a) is grammatical because LHM (a type of A-bar movement) crosses an A-head **sŭm** while (7b, c) are ungrammatical because LHM crosses A-bar heads—i.e. modal and negative operator-like elements.

(7)   a. Pročel **sŭm** knigata.
          read   be-1 book-the
          '(I) have read the book.'

       b. *Pročel **šte**   **sŭm** knigata.
          read   FUT be-1 book-the
          '(I) will have read the book.'

       c. *Pročel **ne**   **sŭm** knigata.
          read   NEG be-1 book-the
          '(I) have not read the book.'

This account faces the empirical problem that (7b) is not ungrammatical but only awkward. As independently reported in Embick and Izvorski (1994) and Todorova (1995), (7b) is possible in certain stylistically marked environments. Thus, šte must be considered an A-head in Rivero's system despite its semantic affinity to ne. The status of A vs. A-bar head becomes a mere stipulation.[2]

In our terms, Bulgarian displays an absence of blocking effects with clitic auxiliaries, not because it violates the HMC but simply because clitic auxiliaries are not present as syntactic heads. Hence they are not subject to the HMC. LHM with ne, despite its clear clitic status, will be argued to result from economy considerations and the fact that ne violates the second position requirement (see Section 12.3.2 for details).[3] Note that the non-syntactic status of clitic auxiliaries brings together the absence of subject-clitic auxiliary inversion and the existence of LHM in Bulgarian and other Balkan languages.

There is yet further evidence for the systemacity of the syntactic contrast between clitic and lexical auxiliaries, as documented in Krapova (1997). Lexical, but not clitic, auxiliaries can be separated from their past participle by VP adverbs and floating quantifiers.

(8)   a. Ivana beše   naburzo pročela knigite.
           Ivana was-3 quickly   read   books-the
           'Ivana had quickly read the books.'

       b. Studentite   bjaxa vsički pročeli knigite.
           students-the were-3 all   read   books-the
           'The students had all read the books.'

(9)   a. *Ivana e   naburzo pročela knigite.
           Ivana be-3 quickly   read   books-the
           'Ivana has quickly read the books.'

       b. *Studentite   sa   vsički pročeli knigite.
           *students-the be-3-*PL *all   read   books-the*
           'The students have all read the books.'

The preferred grammatical counterparts of (9a, b) have the adverb or floating quantifier preceding the clitic auxiliary. The contrast between (8a) and (9a) leads Krapova (1997) to generate clitic auxiliaries under TP and lexical auxiliaries under a separate lower AuxP projection. The difference in adverb placement is for her the result of raising lexical auxiliaries to Agr in the syntax vs. at LF for clitic auxiliaries. From a theoretical perspective, this means that the weak/strong feature distinction is being parametrized within a language, weakening its ex-

---

[2] Another problem in Rivero (1994a) is that *bjax* is phonologically strong hence a lexical auxiliary in her characterization but it allows LHM just like her other functional auxiliaries. See further discussion below.

[3] Optional LHM across a non-clitic auxiliary is analysed in Legendre (1996).

planatory value. From an empirical one, it fails to explain why both types of auxiliaries behave alike with respect to a small class of adverbs like *veče* 'already' and *ošte* 'still'. These adverbs can intervene between any type of auxiliary and the past participle (10a, b) though the preferred word order (or less stylistically marked) for both auxiliaries is (10c):

(10)   a.   Ivana e   veče   pročela knigata.
             Ivana be-3 already read   book-the
             'Ivana has already read the book.'

       b.   Ivana beše veče   pročela knigata.
             Ivana was-3 already read   book-the
             'Ivana had already read the book.'

       c.   Ivana veče e/beše pročela knigata.
             'Ivana has/had already read the book.'

That is, in (10a) the clitic auxiliary **e** appears to have raised across the adverb, despite its weak feature. On the other hand, the adverb appears to be adjoined to TP in (10c) (since **e** heads TP in Krapova's analysis). It is unclear how the adverb order in (10a) can be accomodated within her approach, short of an additional stipulation or giving up the cornerstone of the Pollockian approach to functional categories—i.e. the assumption that adverbs do not move.[4]

From the present perspective which relies on distinguishing clitic from non-clitic elements, **e** is a clitic hence not present in the syntax. The adverb *veče* is also a clitic with the same fate; semantically related adverbial clitics have been documented in another Balkan language, Romanian (Rivero 1994a).

The final contrast among auxiliaries pertains to clitic placement.[5] The position

---

[4] There is in fact no agreement in all previous analyses on what the syntactic positions of various clitics should be. To give a few examples, all clitics but **li** are adjoined to VP in Halpern (1995). In Rivero (1993 1994a) **li** is in C, **sŭm** is in Aux. Pronominal clitics (= XPs) are in WackernagelP in Rivero (1994b). Rudin (1997), however, takes pronominal clitics to be heads of a sequence of Agr-P projections with AgrO-P dominating AgrS-P. For Tomić (1996), all clitics head functional projections, including **li** in C and object clitics in AgrO. Finally, Izvorski (1995) argues that **li** is not in C but heads a separate phrase FocP. The very fact that there is no agreement on clitic positions in the syntax is, in my opinion, further evidence that the assumption that they are in the syntax at all is on shaky ground.

[5] Krapova (1997) further notes that the third person clitic auxiliary *e* may delete under special conditions, e.g. in some renarrated constructions: (i) *Ivana—pročela knigata* '[They say] Ivana read the book.' This is not the case for its lexical counterpart *beše* which can never be deleted. In our terms (i) is not an instance of deletion; rather the feature combination [perfect] [third person] fails to be realized at PF. It is unclear what the explanation for this phenomenon is though it fits into the universal tendency for [third person] to be tied to distinct morphosyntactic properties (e.g. clitic clustering in Romance, split morphological case systems based on person hierarchies, etc.). Note that it cannot simply be related to the fact that *beše* cannot appear in the renarrated construction: (ii) **Az bjax bila pročela knigata* '[They say] I had been reading the book.' Corresponding past participles—*bil*—show all the properties of lexical auxiliaries; contrary to *bjax*, they may appear in the renarrated construction : (ii) *Az sŭm bil pušil tri kutii na den* '[They say] I have smoked three packs a day.'

of clitic pronouns is fixed in the case of clitic auxiliaries but flexible in the case of lexical auxiliaries. Object pronouns follow clitic **sŭm**; but they preferably precede lexical *bjax*, although Hauge (1976) reports (11c) as possible.

(11)   a.   **Az sŭm mu go** dal.
           'I have given it to him.'

       b.   Az **mu go** bjax dal.
           'I had given it to him.'

       c.   Az bjax **mu go** dal.

The question particle **li** shows a related pattern. This time, **li** precedes clitic auxiliaries but follows lexical auxiliaries:

(12)   a.   Pročel **li e** knigata?
           'Has (he) read the book?'

       b.   Beše **li** pročel knigata?
           'Has (he) read the book?'

       c.   Pročete **li** Ivan knigata?
           'Did Ivan read the book?'

As originally discussed in Hauge (1976), **li** must immediately follow the first stressed element in a simple sentence. On the other hand, **e** cannot appear in first position. The past participle *pročel* in first position allows to satisfy both requirements on **e** and **li** simultaneously. How this is formally accomplished will be discussed in Sections 12.3 and 12.4. *Beše*, however, does carry stress; hence *li* may immediately follow it. The same pattern is found with lexical verbs in simple tenses (12c).[6]

To sum up, there is a systematic contrast between two classes of auxiliaries in Bulgarian, exemplified by unstressed **sŭm** and stressed *bjax*. The latter syntactically behaves like a lexical verb; the former, on the other hand, is syntactically inert: in particular, it does not allow SA inversion nor block LHM. This behavior is straightforwardly explained if auxiliary clitics are not heads of functional phrases. This, in turn, suggests that a morphological approach deserves serious consideration.

---

[6] The alternative order *pročel li beše knigata?* is also possible. Marina Todorova (personal communication) reports that such differences in the position of li in the presence of a lexical auxiliary most often relate to differences in the discourse context (though they may be quite subtle). She offers an example of a clear contrast. If someone said the equivalent of 'Yesterday I saw Ivan in the pub', then it would be appropriate for the interlocutor to follow with the question *Beše li se napil?* 'Had he gotten drunk?' If, however, the first comment was something like 'Yesterday I saw Ivan in the pub and he acted strange', then the follow-up question would be formulated as *Napil li se beše?* 'Why? Had he gotten drunk?' In the second case the second speaker is almost offering a guess as to Ivan's state, whereas in the first (s)he is simply asking about it. In the present analysis, these two questions are not discourse-equivalent, hence they correspond to different inputs. They are not part of the same competition.

12.2.2 *Pronominal Clitics*

In colloquial Bulgarian, [+specific] NPs—proper names, emphatic non-clitic object pronouns, and NPs containing the definite article suffix or the specificity-marking indefinite article—appear with a clitic pronoun which agrees with the object NP in number, person, gender, and case (Vakareliyska 1994). While this phenomenon of clitic doubling is obligatory in closely-related Macedonian, it appears to be largely optional in Bulgarian. As Vakareliyska remarks, a topicalized non-clitic object pronoun or a topicalized object NP preceding a subject NP is usually doubled by a clitic. Clitic doubling may then serve to disambiguate the direct object from the subject in the latter case (Bulgarian does not morphologically differentiate nominative from accusative NPs).

(13)   a. Nego/Ivan **go**   viždam.
           him/Ivan   him-ACC *see*-1
           '(I) see him/Ivan.' (= 'as for him/Ivan, (I) see him')

        b. Georgi **go**   gleda   Marija. (Rudin 1986: 17)
           Georgi   him-ACC *watch*-3 *Marija*
           'Marija is watching Georgi.'

        c. Georgi **ja**   gleda   Marija.
           Georgi   her-ACC *watch*-3 *Marija*
           'Georgi is watching Marija.'

Note that doubling generally places emphasis on the object NP; thus in cases where the object and subject NPs are identical in gender and number, clitic doubling favors OVS interpretation (Rudin 1986).

We need not concern ourselves with an exhaustive description of clitic doubling here. It is important, however, to be aware that clitic doubling is alive and well in Bulgarian. The other property of clitic doubling of more immediate relevance to the clitic status issue is case: the object NP appears without a preposition; hence it has case (under standard assumptions) and it violates Kayne's generalization.

Following Suñer (1988), I take clitic doubling to be the mirror image of subject-verb agreement—i.e. a subcase of object-verb agreement. Moreover, keeping in line with OT's economy of structure expressed here and elsewhere (Legendre *et al.* 1995, 1998; Grimshaw 1997a; Legendre 1997, 1998) I wish to adopt the more traditional view of agreement as a relation between an event and its arguments. Concretely, this means two things. One, the input to optimization includes theta roles which get expressed via case (a constraint CASE requires every nominal element to have case). Two, features of arguments (including person, number, case, etc.) get realized twice in the morphology—i.e. on arguments and V/VP as an expression of this relation. In other words, object agreement (including clitic doubling) is the default. Where object agreement/clitic doubling does not occur, a constraint—call it EXPRESS(F)—is violated in order to satisfy a constraint like

DropGiven (which may turn out to be identical to the constraint DropTopic proposed in Samek-Lodovici 1996). It is well-known that pronominal elements like *him, them,* etc. are used for old, given information. Thus, if an input contains the lexical item *John* and the output contains only a double, say a clitic version of *him*, Express(F) is violated but higher-ranked DropGiven is satisfied.

This brief excursion into the technical implementation of clitic doubling serves to highlight the fact that the case properties satisfied by object clitics are not uniquely interpretable as evidence that clitic pronouns are syntactic objects. That conclusion depends on general assumptions concerning case and agreement which, historically, have focused on languages without clitic doubling. In fact, all linguists who have examined languages with clitic doubling have concluded that object clitics could not be handled by movement in the syntax (Borer 1984; Jaeggli 1986; Suñer 1988). The syntactic approach then must rely on alternative treatments for languages with clitic doubling and those without. This does not seem to me to be a theoretically satisfying conclusion.

Returning to Bulgarian clitic doubling, the fact that clitics are indeed agreement markers supports the conclusion reached previously on the basis of clitic auxiliaries: clitics belong to the morphology rather than to the syntax. Moreover, if pronominal clitics were active in the syntax, we would expect blocking effects such as strong crossover effects. No such effects, however, are observed in Macedonian, which has obligatory clitic doubling (Legendre 1998).

(14)   Čovekot$_i$ kogo$_i$ što **go**$_i$ vidov t$_i$.
       man   whom that him saw-1
       'The man whom I saw.'

In Bulgarian, *deto* relative clauses are preferred with a clitic double, according to my main informant.[7]

(15)   Čovekut$_i$ deto **go**$_i$ vidjax t$_i$.
       man-the that him saw-I
       'The man that (I) saw.'

Under the assumption that clitics occupy specifier positions (Rivero 1994b), movement of the antecedent ought to be blocked, for example by Relativized Minimality. But it's not. Alternatively, if clitics are heads of functional projections (Tomić 1996; Rudin 1997), they ought to block movement by virtue of the HMC. But they don't, as numerous examples have shown. One might counterargue that these constraints do not apply to adjoined elements and hence take

---

[7] Rudin (1986: 135) reports that *Wh*-relatives, in contrast to *deto* relatives, normally may not contain what she calls a resumptive pronoun: (i) **Tova e deteto koeto go vidjax včera* 'This is the child who(m) (I) saw yesterday.' My main informant does not reject these as completely ungrammatical though she prefers dropping the clitic double.

pronominal clitics to be adjoined to heads (or to XPs). But if adjunction of clitics is just a strategy to evade syntactic constraints, we have, in fact, an argument against treating clitics as syntactic objects.

To sum up, there is strong evidence that Bulgarian clitic auxiliaries and pronominals are syntactically inert, a conclusion which is inconsistent with the claim that clitics are syntactic atoms. Rather, it supports the view, most prominently put forward in Anderson (1992), that clitics are elements of morphology. In the next section I argue that a particular theory of morphology—the alignment-based theory of Prince and Smolensky (1993) and McCarthy and Prince (1993a, b)—is exactly the theory we need to explain the complex distribution of clitics in Bulgarian.[8]

12.3 Alignment-based Morphology

12.3.1 *Clitics as Instances of Phrasal Morphology*
If we take seriously the fact that the clustering of unrelated categories (auxiliaries, pronouns, etc.) in a single position universally distinguishes clitics from standard syntactic elements and consider the parallels that exist between clitics and word-level affixes, then an alternative view immediately comes to mind. Cross-linguistically, clitics display, within a phrase, the same range of placement options as word-level affixes, including initial, final, second-position, and penultimate position (Klavans 1985; Anderson 1992). Even infixation has a counterpart in clitics which break up the constituency of a phrase. This is possible in Croatian dialects of Serbo-Croation (Anderson 1996, this volume). This is also possible for the Bulgarian question particle **li** (see Section 12.4). Clitics and affixes are both positioned relative to an anchor point (proclitics vs. prefixes, enclitics vs. suffixes). Both are located in the scope of some constituent which constitutes its domain. Finally, the internal order within a clitic sequence is invariant, as is the order of affixes attached to a word.

As Anderson (this volume) also notes, the rigid ordering of clitics does not generally reflect the relative scope of functional categories. For example, first person **sŭm** precedes clitic pronouns but third person **e** follows them in Bulgarian and other South Slavic languages. No syntactic explanation has ever been proposed for this idiosyncracy because there is none: irregularities of this sort are a hallmark of morphology, not syntax. As a result, in all syntactic analyses of South Slavic clitics I am aware of the behavior of **e** requires a distinct mechanism, typically some sort of PF movement.

Finally, syntax is not equipped to deal with the rigidity of clitic order in lan-

---

[8] The validity of the alignment-based OT theory of clitics is independently demonstrated in Balkan (Legendre 1997, 1998), South Slavic (Anderson 1996, this volume), Czech (Richardson 1997), and Romance (Grimshaw 1997b).

guages which are characterized by free-order constituent order (subject to discourse constraints) and fairly free head movement (given the existence of LHM).
Though typically ignored in the literature, the fundamental word-order distinction between clitics and non-clitic elements requires an additional stipulation
under the syntactic approach. This is however naturally captured under a morphological approach because morphology, as opposed to syntax, is characterized
by fixed order of morphemes. This is, I suggest, directly linked to the type of
constraints that operate in both components. Morphological constraints are, to
a large extent, alignment constraints (McCarthy and Prince 1993a, b) while syntactic constraints are typically constraints that force or restrict movement
(Legendre *et al.* 1995, 1998; Grimshaw 1997a).

To give just one example, the question particle **li** exhibits a property which
does not make much sense if **li** is in C, as is commonly assumed (Rivero 1993;
King 1995; Tomić 1996; Rudin *et al.* 1997). A yes/no question may contain the
particle **li**, or alternatively the interrogative complementizer *dali* 'whether', which
is argued to be a true complementizer in Rudin (1986)—hence in C under standard assumptions.[9]

(16) a. Dali   Ivan **e**   otišŭl?
         whether Ivan be-3 left
         'Has Ivan left?'

      b. Otišŭl **li e**   Ivan?
         left   Q be-3 Ivan
         'Has Ivan left?'

Unlike the complementizer *dali*, which can be used only to question a clause,
li can question single constituents in isolation (Rudin 1986: 65).

(17) a. Az **li**?   Kŭštata **li**?   Dnes **li**?   Na masata **li**?
         'Me?'   'The house?'   'Today?'   'On the table?'

      b. *Dali az?   *Dali kŭštata?   *Dali dnes?   *Dali na masata?

It's hard to conceive of a complete clausal structure with **li** in C when all that
is present in (17a) is a single NP or PP constituent, followed by **li**. Consequently,
this distribution leads to recognizing two (accidentally similar) question particles,
li in C for clausal questions and **li** modifying a phrase (possibly adjoined to the
right of the head or the phrase in syntactic analyses). If **li**, however, is a phrasal
affix, then it can attach to any phrasal constituent, whether it be one headed by
V or some other head.

Thus, I proceed with the assumption that clitics are morphological categories

---

[9] Asking a yes/no question with the complementizer *dali* adds a nuance of 'wondering out loud'
(Rudin 1986). Hence the structures with **li** and *dali* do not compete in one single optimization. They
correspond to different inputs and tableaus.

which instantiate properties of phrases, on a par with (word-level) affixes which instantiate properties of words. The functional properties in question are features of the node dominating the relevant phrase.

12.3.2 *Second Position*

Prince and Smolensky (1993: 35ff) define the notions prefix and suffix as morphemes respectively subject to EDGEMOST(LEFT) and EDGEMOST (RIGHT) constraints which align a morpheme edge with a word edge. They demonstrate that Tagalog infixes such as *um* 'Actor trigger' result from the interaction of EDGEMOST(LEFT) with a general constraint against closed syllables (NO-CODA), where NO-CODA outranks EDGEMOST(*um*, LEFT) . They further demonstrate how penultimate stress systems also make use of gradient EDGEMOST. That is, second position from a right edge follows from the interaction of EDGEMOST with a non-gradient NONFINALITY constraint: if NONFINALITY outranks EDGEMOST, a candidate with penultimate stress will violate EDGEMOST once to avoid violating NONFINALITY. A candidate with antepenultimate stress will violate EDGEMOST twice and hence be sub-optimal. EDGEMOST and NONFINALITY are construed as universal constraints. In addition, EDGEMOST is subject to directional parameters (Left, Right), domain parametrization (word, stem, etc.) and parametrization to individual morphemes in the first case. NONFINALITY is also subject to domain parametrization. Thus, EDGEMOST and NONFINALITY represent both universal alignment schemas and families of constraints potentially individualized for particular morphemes.

I propose, along with Anderson (1996, this volume), that phrasal affixes are analysable in terms of Prince and Smolensky's original alignment constraints. For Bulgarian (and, more generally, Balkan languages), the relevance of the left edge of the clause suggests retaining Prince and Smolensky's gradient EDGEMOST(LEFT) as well as making use of a domain-initial counterpart of their NONFINALITY constraint, which I shall refer to as NONINITIAL. In the interest of clarity of presentation, the discussion of the domain of these two constraints is postponed until the basic technical interaction of EDGEMOST and NONINITIAL has been introduced. For the moment, we may assume that the domain is that of the smallest constituent corresponding to the simple null-subject sentences we have exemplified so far: V'. Further refinements will follow.

It is important to keep in mind that no matter how theoretically desirable it is to make use of general alignment constraints in the placement of clitics (Jacobs 1996), one cannot align a sequence of clitics without the use of individualized alignment constraints. This is not a weakening of the theory of alignment; this is just its natural implementation.

That is, clitics not only seek placement at the edge of a domain but they also cluster, a fundamental property typically ignored in syntactic and prosodic discussions of clitics—notwithstanding some important exceptions, including

Perlmutter (1971). Clitics cluster simply because they compete for the same EDGEMOST position. The competition is resolved by ranking individual EDGEMOST constraints (for each feature F) relative to one another. Hence it is not surprising that the ranking of EDGEMOST constraints, to a large extent, reflects the clitic cluster.[10] It is not correct, however, to assume that EDGEMOST constraints may only mirror the surface distribution of clitics. An important demonstration to the contrary is made in Legendre (1998), on the basis of the competition among EDGEMOST constraints in Macedonian.

A strict ranking of EDGEMOST constraints makes an important prediction: the relative order of clitics in the cluster remains the same regardless of where the cluster appears, relative to its anchor point. There is considerable cross-linguistic evidence that this prediction is correct: the change from pro- to encliticization, or vice versa, does not involve rearranging the clitics involved.

Where clitics cluster—e.g. clause-initial vs. second position—results from the relative ranking of EDGEMOST and NONINITIAL. If NONINITIAL outranks EDGEMOST, second-position clitics follow. This is the main Bulgarian pattern, repeated in (18).

(18)   Pročel **săm** knigata.
         '(I) have read the book.'

The competition is made most explicit, by using standard OT tableaus.[11]

(19) NONIN >> E(PERF$_{lc}$)	NONIN	E(PERF$_{LC}$)
a. [$_{V'}$ **săm** pročel knigata] [perf]	*!	
☞ b. [pročel **săm** knigata]		⊛
c. [pročel knigata **săm**]	**!	

The input to optimization is assumed here to include the lexical items *pročel* and *knigata* and their basic propositional structure, plus functional features like [tense], [perfect], [negation], etc. In Macedonian, [tense] competes with other functional features for second position, with the result that the placement of clitics is sensitive to the finiteness of the clause (Legendre 1998). In Bulgarian, however, [tense] does not crucially interact with other functional features, so

---

[10] Any syntactic analysis of clitics must deal with the clustering problem as well and either build it in the structure—either by stipulating the hierarchical order of projections containing the clitics or stipulating the order of adjunction operations—or alternatively, reorder them at PF. In fact, all these solutions have been proposed. But they all involve some additional mechanism besides placing clitics in a certain position in the first place (regardless of whether this is accomplished by base-generation or movement).

[11] Standard OT conventions include the following: ☞ = optimal candidate; * = individual violations of a given constraint; *! = fatal violations; ⊛ = violations incurred by optimal candidates.

I am leaving it out of the discussion for the sake of simplicity. (See Legendre 1998 for an explicit comparison between the two languages.) The first candidate in each tableau is annotated with the relevant features to facilitate interpretation of the forms. The constraint EDGEMOST(PERF) and its subscript 'lc' will be further discussed below.

In tableau (19), candidate (a) loses because it violates higher-ranked NONINITIAL while candidate (c) loses because it incurs two violations of EDGEMOST vs. one for the winner, candidate (b). That is, it is more important in Bulgarian to satisfy NONINITIAL than EDGEMOST(PERF). As discussed further below, EDGEMOST violations are determined by the number of morphemes which separate a target clitic from the left edge of the V' domain.

Note some important properties of this analysis. There is no syntactic movement or LHM of the past participle *pročel*. There is thus no HMC violation, contrary to Rivero (1994a). There is no Prosodic Inversion (Halpern 1995) or Morphological Merger (Embick and Izvorski 1994) either—these are PF movements designed to directly achieve second position.[12] No movement exists because none is needed. By economy, the past participle simply remains in situ. The alignment constraints responsible for the placement of clitics belong to the family of constraints independently needed for affixation.

Consider the first prediction made by Optimality-theoretic constraints: re-ranking. If, contrary to the Bulgarian ranking, EDGEMOST outranks NONINITIAL, clause-initial clitics obtain. This is, in fact, the basic pattern in some other Balkan languages, in particular Romanian and Macedonian(Legendre 1997, 1998).

(20)   R   a. **L-am**   văzut.
               him have seen
               '(I) have seen him.'

      M   b. **Ti go** dade.
               you it gave
               '(He) gave it to you.'

Tableau tableau (21) displays the competition corresponding to the Romanian example. As tableau (21) shows, it is more important in Romanian to satisfy EDGEMOST than NONINITIAL.

---

[12] Prosodic Inversion moves a clitic (generated in the leftmost position in its syntactic domain) immediately to the right of its prosodic host at PF. The host is crucially assumed to be a prosodic word because Serbo-Croatian clitics may appear in second position after the first prosodic word. Morphological Merger is a similar operation but movement is to the right of a lexical head (rather than a prosodic word). As we will see in Section 12.4, Bulgarian effects similar to the Serbo-Croatian ones are naturally handled in the present approach without recourse to movement.

(21) Romanian: E(ACC) >> E(PERF$_{lc}$) >> NonIn	E(ACC)	E(PERF$_{LC}$)	NonIn
☞ a. [$_{V'}$ l-am văzut] [acc] [perf]		⊛	⊛
b. [văzut l-am]	*!	**	
c. [am îl văzut]	*!		*

An important prediction immediately follows from the analysis of a position as resulting from the interaction of two alignment constraints, EDGEMOST and NONINITIAL. A ranking is possible whereby some EDGEMOST constraints outrank NONINITIAL which, in turn, outranks other EDGEMOST constraints. The result is a language where second-position is required of some clitics but not others. This is in fact true of Bulgarian. While the perfect auxiliary and object clitics are strictly second position, the future auxiliary **šte**, the modal particle **da**, and the negative particle **ne** may freely occur in clause-initial position.

(22)   a. **Šte sŭm** pročel knigata.
           FUT *be*-1 *read   book-the*
           '(I) will have read the book.'

       b. **Da ne MI   ja**   dadeš.
           MOD NEG *me*-ACC *it*-ACC *give*-2
           'Don't give it to me!'

       c. **Ne   ŠTE sŭm** pročel knigata.
           NEG FUT *be*-1 *read   book-the*
           '(I) will not have read the book.'

As tableau (23) shows, EDGEMOST(FUT) must outrank NONINITIAL, which in turn must outrank EDGEMOST(PERF) (see tableau (19)). Thus, a subset of Bulgarian clitics behave like Romanian clitics: their preference for being at the clausal edge outweighs their desire to not be in initial position.

(23) E(FUT) >> NonIn >> E(PERF$_{LC}$)	E(FUT)	NonIn	E(PERF$_{LC}$)
☞ a. [$_{V'}$ šte sŭm pročel knigata] [fut] [perf]		⊛	⊛
b. [pročel šte sŭm knigata]	*!		**
c. [sŭm šte pročel knigata]	*!	*	
d. [šte pročel sŭm knigata]		*	**!

The reader might be skeptical of the clitic status of **šte**, **ne** and **da** in view of their conspicuous violation of the basic second-position requirement on Bulgarian clitics. In fact, some scholars have considered them not to be clitics, for that very reason (Dimitrova-Vulchanova 1993; Rivero 1994a). This cannot be correct, however, because **šte** and **da** observe all other basic properties of Bulgarian clitics: (a) they cluster with other clitics, (b) their order is invariant, and (c) they do not carry stress. Note that the latter property alone is evidence against Prosodic Inversion: as (22) shows, a clitic may serve as the host of an enclitic, despite the fact that it itself does not constitute a prosodic word.[13]

Moreover, **šte**, **ne**, and **da** cannot be separated from the verb by a VP adverb.

(24)   a. Ivan burzo **šte** pročete knigata. (Krapova 1997)
         'Ivan will quickly read the book.'

     b. *Ivan **šte** burzo pročete knigata.

     c. Ivan burzo pročete knigata.
        'Ivan quickly read the book.'

     d. Ivana beše naburzo pročela knigite.
        'Ivana had quickly read the books.'

The contrast in (24) remains unexplained under Rivero's claim that **šte** heads a modal phrase. In light of (c) and (d), which respectively involve a tensed verb and a non-clitic auxiliary, one would have to stipulate that manner adverbs must precede **šte** or invoke adverb movement. The adverb pattern extends to **ne** and the particle **da**.[14]

(25)   a. Ivana **ne** burzo beše pročela knigite.
        'Ivana had not quickly read the books.'

     b. *Ivan **ne** burzo **šte** pročete knigata.
        'Ivan will not quickly read the book.'

(26)   a. *Obeštavam **da ne go**   otnovo ostavjam sam.
       promise-1 *to not him*-ACC *again   leave*-1   *alone*
       'I promise to not leave him alone again.'

     b. Obeštavam **da ne go** ostavjam otnovo sam.

It shouldn't come as a surprise that Balkan irrealis particles (which I take to subsume **šte** and **da**) and negation often violate second-position requirements.

---

[13] Tomić (1996) independently claims that **ne** and **šte** are clitics but her analysis does not recognize violable constraints. Hence, she is led to stipulate a PF mechanism of cancellation of prosodic subcategorizations to reconcile the fact that clause-initial **ne** and **šte** are (in her terms) phonologically proclitics while second-position clitics are phonologically enclitics.

[14] Rivero (1994a) assumes that Bulgarian **da** occupies the head of a Modal Phrase, otherwise occupied by the future clitic **šte**. But note the relative order of **ne** and the modal element: **da** precedes **ne** while **šte** follows **ne**. (i) *Ivan da ne xodi tam!* 'Ivan should not go there' (Dimitrova-Vulchanova 1993); (ii) *Ne šte săm mu go dal.* 'I will not give it to him' (Hauge 1976). This shows that **da** and **šte** cannot both be exponents of the same Modal node. Both are clitics and the relevant constraint ranking is: EDGEMOST(MOD) >> EDGEMOST(NEG) >> EDGEMOST(FUT) >> NONINITIAL.

This is presumably linked to the scopal properties of these modal-like elements, though the issue will not be further examined here.

Consider how the present approach naturally handles some other properties of Bulgarian. As noted in Rivero (1994a), LHM is impossible in the presence of **ne**.

(27)   a. **Ne săm** pročel knigata.
          '(I) haven't read the book.'

       b. *Pročel **ne săm** knigata.

There is a very simple explanation for this and it does not require any additional mechanism, such as assuming that NegP is a barrier. The presence of **ne** in clause-initial position sanctioned by the grammar or constraint ranking ensures that auxiliary (and pronominal) clitics automatically satisfy NonInitial. There is absolutely no need to front the past participle. In fact, doing so would result in a crucial violation of Edgemost(neg), now further away from the left edge. Additional violations would include *Structure (economy of structure) and *Trace (economy of movement) though these are omitted in tableau (28). As shown in (28), candidate (b) can never be an optimal candidate in Bulgarian.

(28) E(neg) >> NonIn	E(neg)	NonIn	E(perf$_{LC}$)
☞ a. [$_{V'}$ **ne săm** pročel knigata] [neg] [perf]		⊛	⊛
b. [pročel **ne săm** knigata]	*!		**

The same account extends to imperatives. In prohibitives, **ne** provides the morpheme needed to satisfy Edgemost(acc). See Legendre (1997) for a cross-linguistic analysis of imperatives and prohibitives.

(29)   a. Četi   ja!
          read-IMP *it*-ACC
          'Read it!'

       b. **Ne JA**   četi!
          NEG *it*-ACC *read*-IMP
          'Don't read it!'

Negative gerunds, however, differ from prohibitives. Here, the presence of **ne** does not cause a repositioning of object clitics.

(30)   a. Davaiki **mu**   **go** . . .
          giving him-DAT *it*-ACC
          'Giving it to him . . .'

       b. **Ne** davaiki **mu go** . . .
          'Not giving it to him . . .'

In Legendre (1997, 1998), I argue that Balkan gerunds carry a [gerund] feature, as indicated by the unique morphology of these forms. The pattern in (30) results from the fact that EDGEMOST(GER) outranks EDGEMOST(DAT).

Turning to *Wh*-questions, note that the *Wh*-phrase precedes **ne** in *Wh*-questions, as shown in (31).

(31)   Kakvo **ne**   pročete Ivan?
        what NEG *read*-3 *Ivan*
        'What didn't Ivan read?'

Borrowing two constraints from Grimshaw (1997a), we can easily make sense of (31). One constraint is OPERATOR IN SPECIFIER (OPSPEC) requiring syntactic operators to move to a higher specifier position. The other is OBLIGATORY HEADS (OB-HD) which requires the head of each syntactic projection to be filled. (31) shows that **ne** violates its left edge requirement to allow the *Wh*-phrase to be in a scopal position. Hence OPSPEC outranks EDGEMOST(NEG). The fact that Bulgarian questions take post-verbal subjects, on the other hand, shows that the verb *pročete* has moved to C, to satisfy high-ranked OB-HD. In fact, everything falls into place in this OT analysis of (31) if, as argued above, **ne** is not present in the syntax. If **ne** were to head, say, a NegP necessarily positioned above the projection headed by the verb, then a fatal violation of OB-HD would ensue. This theory-internal argument constitutes independent evidence that **ne** is best analysed as a clitic, subject to a high-ranked EDGEMOST constraint. This analysis of (31) also reveals two important aspects of the overall analysis. One, the position of clitics cannot be identified with a unique syntactic position. Clitics appear wherever V goes, e.g. in VP or in CP. Two, syntactic constraints systematically outrank morphological alignment constraints. We will return to the latter point in Section 12.4.

In frameworks relying on inviolable constraints, the clause-initial position of clitics **šte** and **da** in null-subject sentences is truly idiosyncratic and hard to derive without additional stipulation. In OT, however, this is the kind of behavior that one expects, and it derives from the same mechanism of constraint interaction which results in regular behavior: constraint ranking. There is nothing idiosyncratic about **šte** or **da**. They cluster with other clitics because, like all Bulgarian clitics, they are subject to EDGEMOST constraints strictly ranked with respect to one another. Their overall position in a clause, however, results from the relative ranking of EDGEMOST and NONINITIAL. Bulgarian is an interesting language because NONINITIAL breaks the block of EDGEMOST constraints into two blocks. We will also return to this point in Section 12.4.

As discussed earlier, the distribution of the present perfect auxiliary in Bulgarian and other South Slavic languages depends on its person and number; third person singular 'be' follows object clitics while all other forms of clitic 'be' precede dative and accusative clitics. Under an analysis of 'be' as heading an AuxP projection, it is completely unexpected to have this kind of exception. A special

PF mechanism must be appealed to. From a morphological perspective however, this pattern is not idiosyncratic; rather, it reflects the relative universal flexibility of affix ordering. The single mechanism of constraint ranking readily accounts for this kind of flexibility.

Note that 'be' forms, in fact, instantiate several features, including [perfect], [person], and [number]. For example, **sŭm** is the first person singular form of the perfect auxiliary 'be'. Thus, EDGEMOST(PERF), though a convenient short-cut, is in fact an incomplete characterization of the relevant constraints. The forms are portmanteaux—that is to say, the constraints apply to the same local domain, a morpheme. As argued in Smolensky (1993, 1995), constraints applying to a common local domain can be conjoined. 'Local conjunctions' (Smolensky's term) are, by definition, violated only when the conjuncts are both violated within a common local domain. This is, I propose, what underlies the distribution of 'be' forms in Bulgarian. Specifically, EDGEMOST(PERF) is decomposed into three EDGEMOST constraints, with equally-ranked EDGEMOST(PERF) &EDGEMOST(1,2PERS), EDGEMOST(PERF)&EDGEMOST(PL) outranking EDGE-MOST(PERF). Note the relationship between the higher-ranked, more specific constraints and the lower default one. This reflects Pāṇini's Theorem on Constraint Ranking (Prince and Smolensky 1993).

Consider how the local conjunction applies to first person singular **sŭm**.

(32) Local conjunction of EDGEMOST constraints	NonIn	E(Perf) & E(1,2)	E(Perf) & E(pl)	E(Acc)	E(Perf)
a. [v' **sŭm** go pročel] [perf_{1sg}] [acc]	*!			*	
☞ b. [pročel **sŭm** go]		⊛		⊛⊛	⊛
c. [pročel go **sŭm**]		**!		*	**
☞ d. [pročel go **e**] [perf_{3sg} [acc]]				⊛	⊛⊛
e. [pročel **e** go]				**!	*
f. [**go** e pročel]	*!				*

In, say, second position in V' (candidate (b)), **sŭm** violates the conjunction EDGEMOST(PERF)&(1,2PERS) ranked above EDGEMOST(ACC) as well as the lower-ranked default EDGEMOST(PERF). A first person plural form would violate EDGEMOST(PERF)&EDGEMOST(PL) in addition (the dotted line represents equal ranking). On the other hand, as candidate (d) shows, third person singular **e** violates only the default E(PERF) constraint—the other two being irrelevant. EDGEMOST(PERF) is, of course, ranked below EDGEMOST(ACC). The local conjunction version of EDGEMOST(PERF) is identified throughout the chapter by the subscript 'lc', for simplicity's sake.[15]

To summarize this section, all positional effects result from one mechanism: constraint ranking. The alignment constraints that are ranked (including local conjunctions) are constraints at work elsewhere in morphology and morphophonology. The constraints refer to functional features rather than individual morphemes. That is, they are not specific to Bulgarian, nor even to Balkan or Slavic languages. Clitics universally cluster because they compete for the same position, at the edge of some domain.

12.3.3 *The Domain of Alignment Constraints*

At this point, the question of the precise characterization of the domain of the two alignment constraints needs to be resolved. There are several issues to be adressed. One pertains to EDGEMOST: what is the domain at the left edge of which a given feature is realized?

Bulgarian clitics have long been characterized as syntactic proclitics, meaning they attach to the main verb. This presumably reflects the fact that clitics express properties of the head of the proposition, V. On the other hand, šte, ne, and da satisfy EDGEMOST despite the fact they they do not carry stress. This suggests that the left edge requirement is not prosodic in nature. Rather, it pertains to a phrase structure constituent.

The precise characterization of this syntactic constituent largely depends on one's assumptions about clausal structure. A central concept in much current work in linguistics is that of economy. In OT, this means economy of structure—governed by *STRUCTURE—and economy of movement—governed by *TRACE (Legendre *et al.* 1995, 1998); or STAY (Grimshaw 1997a). In concrete terms, this means that under the VP-internal subject hypothesis, a simple clause need not involve more than a VP, if morphological properties are handled without head movement. In fact, Legendre (1998) argues that EDGEMOST applies to [tense] by documenting crucial competitions between tense and other features in Macedonian. Of course, some clauses do involve verb movement to a higher head position, but only when movement is motivated for other than morphological reasons, e.g. *Wh*-movement.

Another relevant assumption concerns null subjects. If they are instances of pro, then a minimal SVO clause containing a null subject is a VP. If, on the other end, the existence of null subjects is denied (Grimshaw and Samek-Lodovici 1995, 1998), then the same clause is a V'. I shall here adopt Grimshaw and Samek-Lodovici's view that null subjects result from the interaction of constraints pertaining to the syntactic realization of subjects and their discourse

---

[15] Local conjunctions operate in all components of the grammar. See Legendre *et al.* (1998) for an example in syntax and Legendre (1997) for a further example in Romanian morphosyntax.

status and propose that the domain of the EDGEMOST constraint is V′ in Bulgarian and other South Slavic languages.

The crucial evidence comes from simple clauses containing an overt subject. As (33) shows, domain-initial clitics like **šte** follow the subject.

(33)   Az **šte sŭm** pročel knigata.
        'I will have read the book.'

The domain cannot be the maximal projection containing the subject. Hence it cannot be the prosodic constituent corresponding to root clauses either, which presumably is the Intonational Phrase. Otherwise, **šte** would precede neutral subjects. On the other end, the fact that clitics may appear within the C′ projection—under V to C movement in questions—raises the issue of whether the domain should be generalized to X′. But if CPs are only extended projections of V, as proposed in Grimshaw (1991), then V′ is still the relevant domain of clausal clitics.

There is more to EDGEMOST than simply determining its domain. Because being at the edge is a matter of degree, EDGEMOST is a gradient constraint. Hence, degree of violation of EDGEMOST is measured in terms of units which, *a priori*, could be morphological or prosodic. As it turns out, both are relevant to Bulgarian. Two subclasses of clitics can be identified with respect to the units they are sensitive to. Clitic pronouns and auxiliaries count morphemes, as is clear from the fact that they may encliticize to another (stressless) clitic, **šte** or **da**, in initial position: see, for example, (22). In the next section, the question particle **li**, the modal particle **da**, and negative particle **ne** will be shown, however, to count prosodic units generally referred to as prosodic words.

To sum up, the domain of EDGEMOST is V′ for all clitics, the gradiency of EDGEMOST is measured in morphological units for clitic auxiliaries and pronouns but prosodic units for **li**, **da**, and **ne**.

We turn now to the question of the domain of NONINITIAL. At first glance, the generalization appears to be in terms of the notion clause. This is because in phrase structure terms, a second-position clitic like the clitic auxiliary cannot be initial in V′ (in null subject sentences), in VP (in sentences with overt subjects), or in CP (in *Wh*-questions). Relevant examples are repeated here for convenience.

(34)   a. Dal **sŭm mu** go.
            '(I) have given it to him.'

        b. Az **sŭm mu go** dal.
            'I have given it to him.'

        c. Kakvo **e** pročel Ivan?
            'What has Ivan read?'

Now, consider object topicalization in Bulgarian:

(35)   Knigata, Penka **ja**   e   dala na Petko. (Tomić 1997)
       book-the Penka it-ACC *be*-3 *given to Petko*
       'As for the book, Penka gave it to Petko.'

Note that the fronted topicalized object in (35), *knigata*, is separated by an intonational break from the rest of the sentence. Note also that no word order change affects the subject, the verb, and the clitics. For the purpose of counting second-position, it is as if the topicalized NP didn't count. Yet, the whole sentence forms a clause.[16] But in terms of the whole clause, the clitics **ja** and **e** do not cluster in second position.

The same pattern can be observed in *Wh*-structures with object topicalization, and, more generally, in sentences containing sentence-internal pauses.

(36)   a. Knigata, koj **mu**   e   dal? (Tomić 1997)
         book-the who him-DAT *be*-3 *given*
         As for the book, who gave it to him?

      b. Ivan včera   **se**   obadi, vŭrna   **mu**   **gi**,
         Ivan yesterday REFL-ACC *called*-3 *returned*-3 *him*-DAT *them*-ACC
         i   **si**   otide. (Hauge 1976)
         and REFL-DAT *went*-3
         'Ivan called yesterday, returned them to him, and went home.'

Note in particular that clitics occur in second position after each pause marked by a comma in (36b). The presence of intonational breaks marked by commas makes it very clear that the relevant domain is the Intonational Phrase rather than a phrase structure constituent.

Note, however, that the first reflexive clitic, accusative **se**, is in third position in (36b). This is not a counterexample, though. Rather, this follows from the analysis if the present alignment constraints are outranked by constraints which pertain to the placement of adverbs. Given the view of minimal structure outlined above, there is no evidence for a higher functional projection in the absence of verb movement in (36b). Hence the topic subject is presumably in SpecVP and the adverb *včera* is presumably adjoined to V'. A thorough study of adverb positions is clearly needed within the present framework to independently support this assumption. But assuming this can be done, **se**, in fact satisfies both EDGEMOST and NONINITIAL under the present proposal: the former by its position at the left edge of V', the latter by virtue of not being the first element in the Intonational Phrase.

The fact that syntactic constraints outrank morphological ones also explains a similar effect in multiple *Wh*-questions.

---

[16] I am assuming that topicalized phrases are adjoined to the highest maximal projection by virtue of the absence of subject-verb inversion and the effect of the high-ranked constraint *STRUCTURE mentioned previously.

(37)   Koj kakvo **mu**   e   dal?
       who what him-DAT *be*-3 *given*
       'Who gave what to him?'

In Bulgarian, all *Wh*-phrases must move to SpecCP (Rudin 1988). Note that (37) satisfies all relevant constraints if OPSPEC outranks the prosodic and morphological constraints. OPSPEC is satisfied by both *Wh*-phrases. Clitics are at the left edge of V′ and non-initial within the Intonational Phrase. Placing the dative clitic *mu* after the first *Wh*-phrase, on the other hand, would in fact violate EDGEMOST(DAT), because the clitic would not be within V′.

Finally, in embedded clauses with a null subject, Bulgarian clitics immediately follow the complementizer or *Wh*-phrase. The data is from Rudin (1986).

(38)   a. Mislja [$_{CP}$ če **e**   isljazŭl].
          think-1   *that be*-3 *gone out*
          '(I) think that (he) went out.'

       b. Ne znaja [$_{CP}$ dali **e**   isljazŭl].
          NEG *know*-1   *wether be*-3 *gone out*
          '(I) don't know wether (he) went out.'

       c. Tova a knigata [$_{CP}$ deto **ja** kupix].
          this is book-the   that it bought-1
          'This is the book that (I) bought.'

       d. Ne znam [$_{CP}$ kogo **si**   vidjal].
          NEG *know*-1   *who be*-2 *seen*
          '(I) don't know who (you) saw.'

The prosodic structure literature is typically mute about the prosodic structure of syntactic clauses unless they are separated by commas, in which case they are invariably identified as Intonational Phrases. According to Ladd (1996), boundaries of Intonational Phrases need not be defined by a clear pause; other manifestations include a subtle local slowing or pitch change, or a local fundamental frequency fall or rise. Until better understanding of complex prosodic structure is gained, it seems reasonable to assume that syntactic clauses map onto a prosodic constituent bigger than the Phonological Phrase, which might be the Intonational Phrase.[17] My main informant reports that a clear pause is optional before the complementizer/*Wh*-phrase in (38) though one is in fact recommended by the rules of proper enunciation.

With this caveat in mind, I conclude, from the evidence presented in (35)–(38), that the domain within which a clitic must be non-initial is the

---

[17] Beckmann and Pierrehumbert (1986) in fact recognize two types of intonational phrases— roughly, small ones and big ones. Ladd (1986) argues that Intonational Phrases constitute recursive structures.

Intonational Phrase. Clitic placement in simple sentences can obscure this generalization because simple sentences constitute Intonational Phrases.

Evidence that the domain of NonInitial is the Intonational Phrase is not limited to Bulgarian. For example, substantial evidence in Serbo-Croatian is discussed in Radanović-Kocić (1996).

(39)   SC a. Ja, tvoja mama, obećala **sam ti**   igračku.
                I   your mom   promised be-1 *you*-DAT *toy*
                'I, your mom, promised you a toy.'

           b. Ja **sam ti** obećala sam ti igračku.
           c. *Ja **sam ti**, tvoja mama, obećala igračku.
           d. *Ja, tvoja mama, **sam ti** obećala igračku.

Clitics are normally placed after the subject in Serbo-Croatian (39b). But when an appositive is inserted, the placement of the clitic must be delayed: (39a) vs. (39c) vs. (39d). This shows that, just as in Bulgarian, the domain within which a clitic cannot be initial is the Intonational Phrase. Radanović-Kocić (1996) provides substantial additional evidence, including the following contrast between restrictive and unrestrictive relatives.

(40)   SC a. Ona moja sestra koja **je** u Sarajevu **vas se**   sjeća.
                that my   sister who is in Sarajevo you REFL *remembers.*
                'My sister who is in Sarajevo remembers you.'

           b. Moja sestra, koja **je** u Sarajevu, sjeća **vas se**.
                'My sister, who is in Sarajevo, remembers you.'
           c. *Moja sestra, koja **je** u Sarajevu, **vas se** sjeća.

In (40a) the clitics **vas se** cluster in second position after the complex subject *ona moja sestra koja je u Sarajevu* consisting of a restrictive relative clause. In (40b), however, the unrestrictive relative results in intonational breaks, the second of which marks the edge of the domain within which **vas se** cluster in second position. This is confirmed by the ungrammaticality of (40c). Under the assumption that embedded clauses constitute separate Intonational Phrases, the clitic **je** in the relative clause in (40a) obeys the same constraint.

Anderson (this volume) mentions the interesting case of Tagalog clitics, most of which bear their own stress but nonetheless appear in second position.[18] As Anderson comments, there does not seem to be any phonological reason why these could not be initial. Yet the conclusion that Anderson draws from this —that the domain is syntactic rather than prosodic—is incorrect. Kroeger (1993)

---

[18] The fact that Tagalog clitics are prosodically autonomous should not raise eyebrows either. As it turns out, any Bulgarian clitic (though a single one at a time) may also bear stress, provided it is in a very specific context—immediately after **ne** (Hauge 1976). This is one of the issues addressed in the next Section.

provides evidence that the domain of NonInitial in Tagalog is also the Intonational Phrase.

In Tagalog, Adjunct Fronting is distinct from Topicalization: the former does not result in an intonation break after the fronted element while the latter does. As the Intonational Phrase domain hypothesis would predict, clitics must immediately follow the fronted constituent in Adjunct Fronting but clitics follow the verb in Topicalization structures. This is exemplified by the third person singular subject clitic **siya** in (41).

(41)   T   a.   Bukas   **siya** aalis.
            tomorrow he   leave-FUT
            'It.'s tomorrow that he is leaving'

     b.   Bukas,   aalis   **siya**.
            tomorrow leave-FUT *he*
            'Tomorrow, he.'s leaving'

To sum up, the formal characterization of alignment constraints is a complex issue because their domain may, a priori, be prosodic or syntactic; and so may be the units that underlie the gradiency of EDGEMOST. I have argued that Bulgarian, in fact, exploits all the options available. The domain of EDGEMOST is defined in phrase structure terms. Recall the evidence: domain-initial clitics like **šte** follow rather than precede neutral subjects in root sentences. Hence, they are not positioned at the left edge of the Intonational Phrase which coincides with the sentence. Rather, they are realized at the left edge of V'. For most clitics, violations of EDGEMOST are counted on the basis of the number of morphemes which separate the clitic from the left edge of V'. The domain of NonInitial, however, is the Intonational Phrase, hence prosodic. Crucial evidence comes from complex sentences with sentence-internal pauses, in Bulgarian and other languages. Simple sentences, in fact, provide poor evidence for the domain of NonInitial because the Intonational Phrase coincides with the clause.

This double characterization—morphological and prosodic—formally captures the traditional claim that Bulgarian clitics are syntactically proclitics but phonologically enclitics (Tomić 1996). Second-position clitics immediately precede V because they are at the left edge of V' and Bulgarian is a VO language. They cannot be in initial position of an Intonational Phrase. Hence they must be preceded either by a single element within V' or any number of elements outside of V' as long as they belong to the same Intonational Phrase. The present analysis is not merely an implementation of the traditional claim. The morphological theory of clitics these constraints are part of and the Optimality-theoretic character of these constraints have been argued to provide together a more exhaustive and satisfying explanation for the marked and unmarked properties of Bulgarian clitics than previous studies have offered.

The unique Optimality-theoretic character of these alignment constraints raises some further issues relevant to modularity. As the reader may be aware, the candidate representations which undergo optimization are global structures in the sense that these representations combine all traditional levels of representations (syntactic, morphological, and prosodic) into one single level of representation. Furthermore, constraints may refer to any sub-level of representation: some refer to syntax (OB-HD, OPSPEC), others to morphology (EDGEMOST), yet others to prosody (NONINITIAL). These constraints interact, hence the question: is the interaction modular? That is to say, do rankings of constraints freely intermix or do rankings consist of blocks of constraints referring to the same sub-level of representation? In Section 12.4, I will demonstrate that rankings are indeed modular. But first, we turn to the prosodic conditioning of **li** and **ne**.

12.4 Further Prosodic Alignment

The fact that Bulgarian **ne** and **li** obey prosodic constraints has been known since (at least) Hauge (1976). His detailed description of clausal clitics includes the following statements: '**ne** always moves its stress over to the following word, also when this word is a clitic' (p. 18); '**li** is placed immediately to the right of the first stressed element within the verb constituent' (p. 20). While these generalizations are conceived as highly specific rules in Hauge's standard transformational approach, they are, I argue below, best viewed as resulting from the interaction of several constraints. These include already established NONINITIAL and EDGEMOST, as well as prosodic constraints independently needed to handle Bulgarian prosody in general. I proceed by examining the negative particle and then turn to the question particle.

12.4.1 *The Negative Particle* ne

In general, the clitic **ne** directly affects only the prosodic structure of its environment. It is only indirectly that it affects the position of *li*. Consider (42).

(42)   a. **Šte go**   {$_{PrWd}$ VIŽdas}.
        FUT *him*-ACC   *see*-2
        '(You) will see him.'

       b. {$_{PrWd}$ **Ne   ŠTE**} **go**   {$_{PrWd}$ VIŽdas}.
          NEG FUT *him-go*   *see*-2
          '(You) will not see him.'

Curly brackets {} will be used to represent Prosodic Words (PrWd) which, I assume, typically do not include clitic material.[19] Clitics, unlike lexical heads, are in general stressless; this follows if clitics do not head a PrWd. I propose that the

---

[19] Nespor and Vogel (1986) propose that clitics belong to a larger constituent called the Clitic Group. Selkirk (1995), however, argues against the existence of the Clitic Group.

general parsing of clitics outside of a PrWd follows from a constraint which requires them to be parsed in the higher unit of prosodic structure called Prosodic Phrase (PrPh): PARSE(F, PRPH), where [F] stands for any feature (realized as a clitic). In addition, a general alignment constraint on PrWd will be needed: ALIGN(LEXHEAD, L; PRWD, L); it requires the lexical head to be left aligned with the left edge of a PrWd. This constraint is called ALIGN rather than EDGEMOST simply to keep prosodic alignment from morphological alignment apart in our discussion. The reader should keep in mind, however, that they are both instantiations of the same general alignment schema, the only difference here being their domain (prosodic for ALIGN; V′ for EDGEMOST).

Obviously, Bulgarian clitics do get parsed into a PrWd in a negative context, as (42b) above shows. Stress on the future clitic *ŠTE*, I propose, results from the interaction of two constraints. One is PARSE(F, PRPH) which both *ne* and *šte* violate. Given Hauge's generalization, the other constraint pertains to *ne*. It can be stated as another instantiation of the prosodic alignment constraint, ALIGN(NEG, L; PRWD°, L): Align the left edge of *ne* with the left edge of the head of a PrWd°.[20, 21] This constraint is further discussed below.

Putting these proposals together for (42a, b), we can turn to the competition itself, represented in tableau (43). Note that it is a double tableau, with positive context at the top and negative context at the bottom. This format allows us to easily compare the two separate optimizations.

(43) Prosodic structure of *ne*	A(NEG)	A(LEXHD)	P(F, PRPH)
☞ a. [$_{V'}$ šte go {VIŽdas}] [fut] [acc]			
b. [{šte go VIŽdas}]		**!	**
c. [{ŠTE go} {VIŽdas}]			**!
☞ d. [{ne ŠTE} go {VIŽdas}] [neg] [fut] [acc]			⊛⊛
e. [{ne ŠTE go} {VIŽdas}]			***!
f. [{ne ŠTE} {go VIŽdas}]		*!	***
g. [{ne šte go VIŽdas}]	**!	***	***
h. [{NE šte} go {VIŽdas}]	*!		**
i. [{ŠTE ne} go {VIŽdas}]	*!		**

To avoid unnecessary crowding, (43) contains only candidates which are optimal with respect to morphological alignment. For example, an alternative to candi-

---

[20] I am also assuming that lexical heads must be stressed, though this is hardly controversial. The corresponding constraint may be undominated in Bulgarian or in GEN. I leave the matter open for now. That all syllables are parsed into Prosodic Phrases is presumably in GEN.

[21] Thanks to Paul Smolensky for his suggestions in developing this proposal.

date (a) with the order of the two clitics reversed would be sub-optimal because it violates the higher-ranked of the relevant EDGEMOST constraints, EDGEMOST(FUT). The three alternative candidates (a), (b), (c) in (43) represent alternative prosodic parsings of the input. Candidate (a) is optimal because it is perfect: it violates no prosodic requirement. Other candidates violate one or both of ALIGN(LEXHD, L;PRWD, L)and PARSE(F, PRPH).

The bottom competition illustrates how **ne** affects the outcome. The order of clitics results from the ranking of EDGEMOST constraints (not represented), with EDGEMOST(NEG) outranking EDGEMOST(FUT). Note that both pro-sodic alignment constraints, ALIGN(NEG,L;PRWD°,L) and ALIGN(LEXHD,L; PRWD,L), can be simultaneously satisfied if the sequence is parsed into two prosodic words (candidates (d) and (e)) rather than one (candidate (g)). The decision then falls to PARSE(F, PRPH) which favors parsing the clitic *go* outside of either PrWd.

Tableau (43) shows that each of the proposed prosodic constraints is in fact fatal to at least one candidate. For example, ALIGN(NEG,L; PRWD°, L) elimi-nates candidate (i) in which the clitic order within the first PrWd is reversed (candidate (i) also involves an additional EDGEMOST(NEG) violation but the latter is not fatal if prosodic constraints outrank morphological ones, as argued below). Candidate (h) also violates ALIGN(NEG,L; PRWD°,L) though in a dif-ferent way. Ne is at the left edge of the PrWd but it is is stressed.This is where reference to PrWd° rather than PrWd captures the violation incurred by (h). If ALIGN(NEG) referred to PrWd, then it would be satisfied by (h) and (h) would be as optimal as (a), contrary to fact. Because the stresslessness of clausal *ne* is an absolute requirement (Hauge 1976) we could, alternatively, invoke a *NE constraint ('Don't stress **ne**') and keep the domain of ALIGN(NEG) as PrWd. From a theoretical perspective, it is preferable, however, to derive stress proper-ties of various clitics from the interaction of general constraints like ALIGN and PARSE rather than specific constraints like *NE.

12.4.2 *The Question Particle* li

Recall Hauge's generalization according to which **li** must immediately follow the first stressed element. Reference to the 'first element' immediately rings the sec-ond-position bell. In other words, **li**, like most Bulgarian clitics, is a second-position clitic. But here is the twist: while other second-position clitics satisfy EDGEMOST on the basis of the number of morphemes that separate them from the left edge of V′, **li** satisfies EDGEMOST on the basis on the number of PrWds that separate it from the left edge of V′. An explicit formalization of the two EDGEMOST constraints is given in (44).

(44)   a.   EDGEMOST(ACC) = $*[_{V'} ( )_m (ACC)]$ where ( ) represent morpheme boundaries

      b.   EDGEMOST(Q) = $*[_{V'} \{ \}_{PrWd} (Q)]$

Once again, it is important to realize that these constraints simply instantiate the general alignment schema by specifying its two main parameters (the other is directional and it is directly incorporated in (44)). One is the domain at the edge of which the feature favors realization. It is V' for all features, as argued earlier. The other relates to the units in terms of which violations of EDGEMOST are to be measured.

EDGEMOST(Q), in fact, needs further refinement. Rudin *et al.* (1995) report that li may optionally break up a syntactic constituent when, for example, a modifying adjective is the focus of the question.

(45)   a. [$_{NP}$ NOVATA kola] li prodade (ili starata)?
           *new-*FOC *car*   Q *sold-2*   *or old-the*
           'Did you sell your NEW car (or the old one)?'

       b. [$_{NP}$ NOVATA li kola] prodade (ili starata)?

This phrasal analogue to infixation is reminiscent of the one found in mostly Croatian dialects of Serbo-Croatian.[22] Assuming that this patterns violates INTEGRITY(XP) (Anderson, this volume), then the EDGEMOST(Q) constraint in (44) is in need of a slight modification to reflect a wider option of domains: X^n instead of V' (where X^n = V' or XP).[23]

As it turns out, this refinement is needed independently of the pattern in (47). As we have already seen, *li* is used to question any constituent—see (17) above and (50) below.

The competition underlying the surface distribution of li is displayed in the double tableau (46). NONINITIAL is omitted because it does not affect the outcome: it is violated by all candidates.

The competitions of particular interest in (46) are between candidates (a) vs. (b) (top rows) and candidates (g) vs. (h) (bottom rows). They provide evidence for the proper formulation of EDGEMOST. If the units relevant to violations of of EDGEMOST(Q) were the same as those of EDGEMOST(ACC), then candidate (b) would win the top competition—li is closer to the left edge of the domain in terms of morphemes (two morphemes away) than candidate (a) (three morphemes away). Note that the pattern cannot be handled by simply re-ranking the two constraints. If EDGEMOST(ACC) outranked EDGEMOST(Q), then candidate (g) would lose to (h): two violations of EDGEMOST(ACC) for (h) vs. three for (g). It is beyond doubt that EDGEMOST(ACC) violations are measured in terms of morphemes—recall that an unstressed clitic such as šte or da can

---

[22] Rudin *et al.* interpret this pattern as the 'remnant of the second position effects in the placement of li'. The present chapter claims, however, that Bulgarian li is fundamentally a second-position clitic. Its surface distribution to some extent masks this reality, due to the complex interaction of relevant constraints.

[23] Because ne is also used to negate constituents, it is likely that the domain of EDGEMOST(NEG) will also need to be refined along the same lines as that of li. I leave this matter open for now.

provide the support they need to their left. Once the prosodic structure is made explicit, it is also very clear from the minimally different candidates (g) and (h) that PrWds, rather than morphemes, are relevant to **li**.

(46) Prosodic structure of *li*	A(Q)	A(neg)	A(LexHd)	P(F, PrPh)	E(Q)	E(Fut)	E(acc)
☞ a. [$_{V'}$ šte go {VIŽdas} li] [fut] [acc] [Q]					⊛		⊛
b. [šte {VIŽdas} li go]					*		***!
c. [šte li go {VIŽdas}]	***!						**
d. [šte go li {VIŽdas}]	**!						*
e. [{šte go VIŽdas} li]			**!	**	*		*
f. [go šte {VIŽdas} li]					*	*!	
☞ g. [{ne ŠTE} li go{VIŽdas}] [neg] [fut] [Q] [acc]				⊛⊛	⊛	⊛	⊛⊛⊛
h. [{ne ŠTE}go {VIŽdas}li]				**	**!	*	**
i. [{ne ŠTE}{li go VIŽdas}]			**!	****	*	*	***
j. [{ne šte li go VIŽdas}]	***!	***	****	****		*	***
k. [ne šte {VIŽdas} li go]		*!			*	*	****
l. [{ne GO} li šte {VIŽdas}]				**	*	***!	*

Note that the prosodic alignment on **li** differs from that of **ne** in one respect: the directionality of the alignment. The left edge of **ne** must be aligned with the left edge of a PrWd°, hence it is parsed inside the PrWd. The left ledge of **li** must be aligned with the right edge of a PrWd, hence it is parsed outside the PrWd. This follows from the standard assumption that a PrWd minimally consists of a binary foot (see further discussion below tableau (48)). Thus, there remains an irreducible difference between **ne** and **li**, naturally captured in terms of two alignment constraints, ALIGN(Q, L; PRWD, R) and ALIGN(NEG,L; PRWD°, L).

Like EDGEMOST, ALIGN is gradient. In (46), I am assuming that its violations are measured in terms of syllables. (See, for example, sub-optimal candidates (c), (d), (j) and (k)). Alternatively, the units could be construed as morphemes. I leave this matter open for now.

Is the placement of **li** sensitive to the particular clitics involved? That is, does the presence of domain-initial **šte** in (46) affect the competition in any crucial way? The answer is negative, as shown in (47) and corresponding tableau (48).

(47)   a.   Izpratix li **mu**   kniga?
             sent-1   Q *him*-DAT *book*
             'Did (I) send him a book?'

       b.   **Ne MU**   li izpratix kniga?
             not him-DAT Q *sent*-1   *book*
             'Didn.'t (I) send him a book?'

(48) P(F, PRPH) >> E(Q) >> E(DAT)

		A(Q)	A(NEG)	A(LEXHD)	P(F, PRPH)	E(Q)	E(DAT)
☞	a. [ᵥ{izPRAtix} li mu]					⊛	⊛⊛
	b. [li mu {izPRAtix}]	****!					*
	c. [{izPRAtix mu} li]				*!	*	*
	d. [{izPRAtix} mu li]	*!				*	*
☞	e. [{ne MU} li {izPRAtix}]				⊛⊛	⊛	⊛
	f. [{ne MU}{izPRAtix} li]				**	**!	*
	g. [{ne LI} mu {izPRAtix}]	*!			**		**
	h. [{ne izPRAtix} li mu]			*!	*	*	***
	i. [ne {izPRAtix} li mu]		*!			*	***

The closest competitions are between candidates (a) and (c) (top rows) and candidates (e) and (f) (bottom rows). PARSE(F, PRPH), which favors parsing clitics outside of the PrWd is fatal to (c). On the other end, EDGEMOST(Q) is fatal to (f). Note that in both competitions, the fatal constraint is relatively low-ranked in (48).

Candidate (i) deserves further comments. It is sub-optimal because **ne** is outside the PrWd headed by the verb. If it were not for the fact that PrWds minimally consist of a binary foot (McCarthy and Prince 1996), then **ne** could be placed outside the PrWd and right-aligned with the left edge of the PrWd°. This alternative would yield the right result in (46), as the reader may verify. But the alternative does not work in (48): under right-alignment, ALIGN(NEG) is satisfied and candidate (i) becomes optimal, contrary to fact. Thus, **ne** must be left-aligned within the PrWd. This, in turn, constitutes empirical evidence for McCarthy and Prince's claim.

Finally, the placement of **ne** and **li** in the absence of any other clitics falls out of the present analysis.

(49)   {ₚᵣWd **Ne**   ZNAEŠ} li?
             NEG *know*-2   Q
       'Don't (you) know?'

Note that (49), as represented, only violates ALIGN(LexHD,L; PrWD, L). It confirms the ranking ALIGN(NEG, L; PrWD°, L) >> ALIGN(LexHD,L; PrWD, L). Alternative prosodic parsings violate additional constraints, including *STRUCTURE if a second (unnecessary) PrWd is added.

In the analysis of **li** proposed above, prosody plays an important role but prosody alone cannot account for *li*'s distribution. The interaction between EDGEMOST constraints also plays a decisive role (as we just saw in (48)). But movement plays no role at all and no constraint of syntax is violated. This contrasts with an analysis like Rivero (1993) who argues for a type of movement generally banned by the theory she assumes. In her analysis, **li** lowers and left-adjoins to the finite verb in the presence of **šte** or **ne**. It is also proposed as a language-specific rule of Bulgarian. Note that (49) forces her to assume that **li**, upon lowering, may also right-adjoin to the verb. It is unclear how the directionality of adjunction can be predicted, short of an additional stipulation.

Returning to tableaus (46) and (48), note that they provide evidence for the relationship among blocks of constraints. Hence, they can shed light on the modularity of constraint ranking. In Section 12.3, it was argued that syntactic constraints (e.g. OpSpec and OB-HD) outrank morphological alignment constraints (see examples (31) and (37)). The fact that optimal candidates in tableaus (46) and (48) may violate morphological EDGEMOST constraints but not purely prosodic constraints shows that prosodic constraints must outrank morphological constraints. But what about EDGEMOST(Q), which is a mixed constraint? As a clausal clitic, its domain is V' but its violations count PrWds rather than morphemes. (46), in fact, provides crucial evidence that EDGEMOST(Q) outranks all morphological EDGEMOST constraints: under the alternative ranking the competition would yield the wrong optimal candidate.

One other constraint to consider is EDGEMOST(NEG) whose status has been left unspecified so far. As it turns out, formulation as either a purely morphological or a mixed constraint will work. Consider why. Because **ne** is not a second position clitic, it does not violate EDGEMOST(NEG), hence the units relevant to counting violations of EDGEMOST are irrelevant. There is at least one theoretical reason, however, to prefer the mixed formulation. Besides **li**, **ne** is the only Bulgarian clitic subject to strict prosodic alignment constraints. A generalization would fail to be captured if the EDGEMOST constraint on **ne** didn't mirror that on **li**.

Which brings us to the remaining constraint, NONINITIAL. Recall that its domain was argued to be the Intonational Phrase. If our hypothesis about the modularity of the constraint ranking is correct, then the prosodic constraint NONINITIAL must outrank EDGEMOST(Q). Direct evidence for the ranking comes from clauses containing intonation breaks.

(50)   Knigata,   Petko   **li mu**   e   dal? (Tomić 1996)
        *book-the-*TOP *Petko-*FOC Q *him-*DAT *be-3 given*
        'As for the book, is it Petko who gave it to him?'

Li occurs in second position following the focused subject *Petko*; the topicalized object is irrelevant. In (50), the question is no longer a neutral yes/no question. Rather, it takes on a cleft-like interpretation: the question is not about the event but about *Petko* (Rudin *et al.* 1995). In our terms, this means that the NP *Petko* is marked with the features [foc] and [Q] in the input. Economy of structure and absence of evidence for verb movement suggest that *Petko* is in situ (SpecVP). If the hypothesis that clitic placement follows from alignment is correct, then the constraints pertaining to **li** are in fact blind to which element carries Q. The reader may verify that sentence (50) is grammatical because it corresponds to the optimal candidate in (51).

(51) Prosodic constraints >> E(Q)	A(Q)	A(LexHd)	P(F,PrPh)	NonIn	E(Q)	E(Dat)	E(Perf)
☞ a. [$_V${PETko} **li mu** e {DAL}] [foc] [Q]					⊛	⊛⊛	⊛⊛ ⊛
b. {PETko **mu**} **li** e {DAL}			*!		*	*	***
c. {PETko} **mu** e {DAL} **li**					**!	*	**
d. **li** {PETko} **mu** e {DAL}	**!			*		**	***

Consider the fact that in (51), all candidates simply correspond to an Intonational Phrase subconstituent of (50). If we now consider another optimization that takes the whole sentence (50) into consideration, there is a counterpart to (d), say (d') preceded by the topicalized object *knigata*. In that context, ALIGN(Q, L; PRWD, R) is satisfied—the topicalized object provides the necessary host. Candidate (d') still loses to its optimal competitor (a'), but only because it violates NONINITIAL in its Intonational Phrase (as does (d) in (51)). This establishes the partial ranking NONINITIAL >> EDGEMOST(Q) and the claim that prosodic constraints outrank mixed ones. This ranking also yields a surprise result already hinted at at the beginning of the chapter. Recall that this ranking is synonymous with second position. Hence, **li** is indeed a second-position clitic.

The Optimality-theoretic analysis thus achieves two goals. One is to explain the vagaries of **li**'s placement, the other is to reveal the deep regularity of the Bulgarian system. The former has been shown to result from the interaction of prosodic and morphological constraints. The latter results from the basic ranking NONINITIAL >> EDGEMOST which underlies most Bulgarian clitics, including **li**.

Finally, recall that EDGEMOST(NEG) outranks NONINITIAL—since it is not a second-position clitic. The global ranking in Bulgarian can thus be summarized as in (52). The focus is on the interface between the prosodic and morphological constraints, hence other constraints are globally referred to as Syntactic or Prosodic:

(52)   Syntactic constraints >>
            Prosodic constraints >>
                Morpho-prosodic constraints (EDGEMOST(NEG) >>
                NONINITIAL >> EDGEMOST(Q)) >>
                    Morphological constraints (EDGEMOST(FUT) >>
                    EDGEMOST(DAT), etc.)

What (52) shows is that even in a language which displays a complex interaction of an impressive number of constraints, the ranking itself is modular. That is, there is no evidence whatsoever in Bulgarian that constraints may freely intermix. Thus, I interpret the solidity of the Bulgarian case to be indicative of a meta-constraint at work. This constraint on constraint rankings is stated in (53).

(53)   CONSTRAINT INTERMIXING BAN: Constraints belonging to different modules of the grammar may not intermix.

The architecture of standard OT does permit reference to any level of representation. That is, a given alignment constraint may relate structures from one module to another directly, as was demonstrated for the EDGEMOST family. This simply means that some of the alignment constraints argued for in this chapter are interface conditions. As the growing literature on the syntax-phonology interface attests, the need for interface conditions is independent of OT. But it finds a natural implementation in standard OT because, by their very nature, candidate structures are global structures. As we have seen, optimization proceeds in parallel rather than serially.

The alternative approach is one in which the phonology repairs what the syntax produces. This is in fact the prevailing one, under many guises which have been examined throughout this chapter. The repair approach has two major drawbacks: one is empirical, the other is theoretical. As we have seen, clitics do not, in general, share the syntactic properties of their non-clitic counterparts. Reported claims to the contrary have overlooked a great deal of evidence, some of which has been brought to light here. Moreover, from the perspective of the grammar, there is in principle no reason why phonology should undo what the syntax does—and do it, using the same mechanism, i.e. movement. This duplication, alone, raises doubts that the traditional view on the relationship between syntax and phonology is correct.

12.5 Conclusion

To summarize, I have argued in this chapter that the complex distribution of Bulgarian clitics is not the result of syntactic movement. Nor does it result, even partially, from a post-syntactic re-ordering of elements at PF. Instead, I have put forward substantial arguments in favor of analyzing clitics in morphological terms. That is to say, clitics are phrasal affixes whose positional effects mirror those of word-level affixes (see also Anderson, this volume). I have argued in detail that the position of clitics is the product of a complex interaction of alignment constraints. I have shown that an Optimality-theoretic constraint ranking captures their unique properties. This includes their invariant sequences as well as their different anchors, the latter mostly resulting from the fact that constraints are assumed to be violable.

A large inventory of Bulgarian structures have been examined. This has led, among other things, to some novel conclusions. For example, I have argued that second-position clitics result from the interaction of EDGEMOST with NONINITIAL, despite the fact that the alignment domain of the former is defined in terms of phrase structure while that of the latter is defined in terms of prosodic structure. In root sentences, the two domains coincide, but in complex sentences with internal intonation breaks they do not. The interaction of these two constraints explain why Bulgarian clitic auxiliaries and pronouns are in second position in simple sentences but not necessarily in complex ones.

I have also claimed that the Bulgarian question particle li is in fact a second-position clitic though the interplay of constraints thoroughly masks its true nature. Finally, I have argued that despite the complexity of the interaction the constraint ranking of Bulgarian remains modular. I have proposed that modularity of constraint ranking be elevated to the the status of a meta-constraint of the theory.

12.6 References

Anderson, S. R. (1992). *A-Morphous Morphology*. Cambridge, Cambridge University Press.
—— (1996). 'How to put your clitics in their place'. *The Linguistic Review* 13, 165–91.
Barbosa, P., D. Fox, P. Hagstrom, M. McGinnis, and D. Pesetsky (eds) (1998). *Is the Best Good Enough? Proceedings of the Workshop on Optimality in Syntax*. MIT Press and MIT Working Papers in Linguistics.
Beckman, M. E. and J. Pierrehumbert (1986). 'Intonational structure in Japanese and English'. *Phonology Yearbook* 3, 255–309.
Beckman, J., L. Walsh Dickey, and S. Urbanczyk (eds) (1995). *Papers in Optimality Theory*. University of Massachusetts Occasional Papers 18. Amherst, MA, Graduate Linguistics Students Association.
Borer, H. (1984). *Parametric Syntax: Case Studies in Semitic and Romance Languages*. Dordrecht, Foris.
Dimitrova-Vulchanova, M. (1993). 'Clitics in Slavic'. *Working Papers in Linguistics* 18, University of Trondheim.
Embick, D. and R. Izvorski (1994). 'On long head movement in Bulgarian'. In J. Fuller, H. Han, and D. Parkinson (eds), *ESCOL'94*. DMLL Publications, Cornell University, 104–15.
Grimshaw, J. (1991). 'Extended projections'. Ms, Brandeis University.

Grimshaw, J. (1997a). 'Projection, heads, and optimality'. *Linguistic Inquiry* 28, 373–422.

—— (1997b). 'The best clitic and the best place to put it'. Handout to talk presented at the Hopkins Optimality Theory Workshop/University of Maryland Mayfest, Baltimore, MD.

—— and V. Samek-Lodovici (1995). 'Optimal subjects'. In Beckman *et al.* (eds), 589–605.

—— —— (1998). 'Optimal subjects and subject universals'. In Barbosa *et al.* (eds).

Halpern, A. L. (1995). *On the Placement and Morphology of Clitics*. Stanford, CSLI Publications.

Hauge, K. R. (1976). 'The word order of predicate clitics in Bulgarian'. Meddelelser No. 10. University of Oslo.

Izvorski, R. (1995). 'Wh-movement and Focus-movement in Bulgarian'. In R. Eckardt and V. van Geenhoven (eds.), *Console II Proceedings*. The Hague, Holland Academic Graphics, 235–54.

—— T. Holloway King, and C. Rudin. (1997). 'Against *li* lowering in Bulgarian'. *Lingua* 102, 2/3, 187–94.

Jackendoff, R. (1972). *Semantic Interpretation in Generative Grammar*. Cambridge, MA, MIT Press.

Jacobs, H. (1996). 'An Optimality-theoretic analysis of phonological and syntactic aspects of enclisis and proclisis in Old French, Brazilian, and European Portuguese'. ROA-128.

Jaeggli, O. (1986). 'Three issues in the theory of Clitics: Case, double NPs, and extraction. In H. Borer (ed.), *The Syntax of Pronominal Clitics* [*Syntax and Semantics* 19]. New York, Academic Press, 15–42.

Kayne, R. (1994). *The Antisymmetry of Syntax*. Cambridge, MA, MIT Press.

King, T. H. (1995). *Configuring Topic and Focus in Russian*. Stanford, CSLI Publications.

Klavans, J. (1985). 'The independence of syntax and phonology in cliticization'. *Language* 61, 1, 95–120.

Krapova, I. (1997). 'Auxiliaries and complex tenses in Bulgarian'. In W. Browne, E. Dornisch, N. Kondrashova, and D. Zec (eds), *Annual workshop on Formal approaches to Slavic linguistics. The Cornell meeting, 1995*. Ann Arbor, Michigan Slavic Publications, 320–344.

Kroeger, P. (1993). *Phrase Structure and Grammatical Relations in Tagalog*. Stanford, CLSI Publications.

Ladd, D. R. (1986). 'Intonational phrasing: The case for recursive prosodic structure'. *Phonology Yearbook* 3, 311–40.

—— (1996). *Intonational Phonology*. Cambridge, Cambridge University Press.

Lambova, M. D. (1996). *Optional Participle Auxiliary Orders: A Study of the Syntax of Verbal Inflection in Bulgarian*. MA Thesis, Temple University.

Legendre, G. (1996). 'Clitics, verb (non)-movement, and optimality in Bulgarian'. Johns Hopkins University Technical Report JHU-CogSci-96-5.

—— (1997). 'Optimal Romanian clitics: A cross-linguistic perspective'. Johns Hopkins University Technical Report JHU-CogSci-97-9.

—— (1998). 'Second position clitics in a V2 language: Conflict resolution in Macedonian'. Proceedings of ESCOL 1997. CLC Publications, Cornell University, 139–49.

—— C. Wilson, P. Smolensky, K. Homer, and W. Raymond (1995). 'Optimality and Wh-Extraction'. In Beckman *et al.* (eds), 607–36.

—— P. Smolensky, and C. Wilson. (1998). 'When is less more? Faithfulness and minimal links in Wh-chains'. In Barbosa *et al.* (eds).

McCarthy, J. and A. Prince (1993a). *Prosodic Morphology I; Constraint Interaction and Satisfaction*. To appear, MIT Press.

———— (1993b). 'Generalized alignment'. *Yearbook of Morphology*, 79–153.

———— (1996). 'Prosodic morphology 1986'. Technical Report #32, Center for Cognitive Science, Rutgers University.

Nespor, M. and I. Vogel. (1986). *Prosodic Phonology*. Dordrecht, Foris.

Perlmutter, D. M. (1971). *Deep and Surface Structure Constraints in Syntax*. New York, Holt, Rinehart & Winston.

Pollock, J.-Y. (1989). 'Verb movement, Universal Grammar, and the structure of IP'. *Linguistic Inquiry* 20, 365–424.

Prince, A. and P. Smolensky. (1993). *Optimality Theory: Constraint Interaction in Generative Grammar*. To appear MIT Press.

Radanović-Kocić, V. (1996). 'The placement of Serbo-Croatian clitics: A prosodic approach'. In A. L. Halpern and A. M. Zwicky (eds.), *Approaching Second: Second Position Clitics and Related Phenomena*. Stanford, CSLI Publications.

Richardson, M. (1997). 'Czech clitics: 2P or not 2P: that is the question'. In L. Kaiser (ed.), *Yale A-Morphous Linguistics Essays*. Yale Department of Linguistics, 131–50.

Rivero, M. L. (1993). 'Bulgarian and Serbo-Croatian Yes-no questions: V°-Raising to -*li* vs. -*li* hopping'. *Linguistic Inquiry* 24, 567–75.

—— (1994a). 'Clause structure and V-movement in the languages of the Balkans'. *Natural Language and Linguistic Theory* 12, 63–120.

—— (1994b). 'On two locations for complement clitic pronouns: Serbo-Croatian, Bulgarian, and Old Spanish'. To appear in A. van Kemenade and N. Vincent (eds.), *Inflection and Syntax in Language Change*. Cambridge, Cambridge University Press.

Rudin, C. (1986). *Aspects of Bulgarian Syntax: Complementizers and Wh Constructions*. Columbo, OH, Slavica Publishers, Inc.

—— (1988). 'On multiple questions and multiple *Wh*-fronting'. *Natural Language and Linguistic Theory* 6, 445–501.

—— (1997). 'AgrO and Bulgarian pronominal clitics'. In M. Linseth and S. Franks (eds), *Annual workshop on Formal approaches to Slavic linguistics: The Indiana meeting, 1996*. Ann Arbor, Michigan Slavic Publications, 224–252.

—— T. H. King, and R. Izvorski (1995). 'Focus in Bulgarian and Russian yes-no questions'. To appear in proceedings of Amherst Workshop on Focus.

—— C. Kramer, L. Billings, and M. Baerman (1997). 'Macedonian and Bulgarian *li* questions: Beyond syntax'. Ms.

Samek-Lodovici, V. (1996). *Constraints on Subjects: An Optimality Theoretic Analysis*. PhD dissertation, Rutgers University.

Selkirk, E. O. (1995). 'The prosodic struction of function words'. In Beckman *et al.* (eds), 439–69.

Smolensky, P. (1993). 'Harmony, markedness, and phonological activity'. Handout to talk presented at the Rutgers Optimality Workshop 1, New Brunswick, N.J.

—— (1995). 'On the internal structure of the constraint component *Con* of UG'. Handout to talk presented at UCLA.

Suñer, M. (1988). 'The role of agreement in clitic-doubled constructions'. *Natural Language and Linguistic Theory* 6, 391–434.

Todorova, M. (1995). 'Infinitival clauses in Bulgarian and the status of *da*'. Ms, McGill University.

Tomić, O. M. (1996). 'The Balkan Slavic clausal clitics'. *Natural Language and Linguistic Theory* 14, 811–72.

Travis, L. (1984). *Parameters and Effects of Word order Variation*. PhD dissertation, Cambridge, MA, MIT.

Vakareliyska, C. (1994). '*Na*-drop in Bulgarian'. *Journal of Slavic Linguistics* 2(1), 121–50.

Part Four

Acquisition

13

Learning a Grammar in Functional Phonology

Paul Boersma

In this chapter, I will describe how learners can acquire the articulatory and perceptual constraints of segmental phonology and their interactions; specifically, I will show that the substantial content of these constraints does not have to be innate for the learner to be able to acquire an adequate grammar from a realistic amount of overt data.

I will assess the empirical adequacy of the functional learning algorithm with respect to existing algorithms that assume the innateness of constraints, and I will show that it is convergent, realistic, and robust.

13.1 Functional Phonology

The functional hypothesis for phonology (Boersma 1998) maintains that the grammar directly reflects an interaction between the articulatory and perceptual principles of efficient and effective communication. Functional Phonology is a theory that can handle substance-related phonological phenomena without the need for positing innate features and hierarchies; if restricted to the constraints discussed below, its scope equals that of autosegmental phonology and feature geometry.

Functional Phonology thus makes a principled distinction between articulatory and perceptual representations and features, as illustrated in Figure 1, which shows the functional concept of the linguistically relevant systems, processes, and representations of speech production and perception. Figure (1) shows the following representations:

- The *acoustic input* of the speech uttered by another person, as presented to the ear of the listener; written between brackets [ ] because it is a language-independent representation.
- The *perceptual input*: the speech uttered by another person, as perceived by the listener, in terms of perceptual features (periodicity, noise, spectrum) and their combinations; written between slashes / /.

(1)

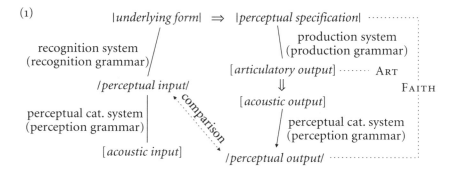

- An *underlying form* in terms of perceptual features, as stored in the language user's lexicon; written between pipes | |. This can be identified with the *perceptual specification* of (a part of) the utterance.
- The *articulatory output* of the speaker, in terms of articulatory gestures (articulator positions, muscle tensions) and their combinations; written between brackets [ ].
- The *acoustic output* of the speaker: an automatic result of her articulatory output; also written between brackets.
- The *perceptual output* of the speaker: her acoustic output, as perceived by herself; written between slashes / /.

Figure (1) shows the following processing systems:

- The speaker's *production system* determines the surface form of the utterance from an underlying perceptual specification. I will assume that it can be described by an Optimality-Theoretic *production grammar*. Its acquisition is the subject of this chapter.
- The listener's *perceptual categorization system* determines how a listener converts the raw acoustic input to a more perceptual representation; she uses the system for the acoustic input from other speakers as well as for her own acoustic output. The system can be described by an Optimality-Theoretic *perception grammar* with PERCEIVE, *CATEG, and *WARP constraints (Boersma 1998: ch.8). The current chapter has no room to dwell much on its acquisition.
- The listener's *recognition system* converts the perceptual input into an underlying form (and helps the categorization system). The current chapter will not address its grammar nor its acquisition.
- The learner can *compare* her own output, as perceived by or self, with her perception of an adult utterance, and take a *learning step* if there is a *mismatch* between these. Note that this comparison is different from the comparison between the perceptual specification and the perceptual output, as evaluated

by the faithfulness constraints: the child should learn to imitate the adult system of faithfulness violations.

13.1.1 Representations in an Adult Production Grammar

A typical production process can be represented with the following tableau:

(2) |spec|	A	B
☞ [art_1] /$perc_1$/		*
[art_2] /$perc_2$/	*!	

This tableau shows the following representations:

- One perceptual specification (underlying form, input) *spec*.
- Many candidate articulatory outputs art_i.
- For each candidate articulatory output, the corresponding perceptual output $perc_i$.

In tableau (2), the two constraints A and B both issue a *protest* against a certain candidate, as shown by the asterisks. Because A is ranked higher than B, the *disharmony* associated with its violation is greater than that of B, and its violation becomes the *crucial violation* for candidate 2, as shown by the exclamation symbol, which is put after the *crucial mark*. Thus, candidate 1 is more *harmonic* than 2, so it becomes the *winner*, as shown by the pointing finger. Some cells are shaded grey because any violations in these cells have not contributed to determining the winner.

13.1.2 Representations in a Learner's Grammar

For the learning situation, two representations have to be added to the tableau:

(3) [*model utterance*] /*model perc*/ |*spec*|	A	B
☞ [art_1] /$perc_1$/		←*
✔ [art_2] /$perc_2$/	*!→	

This tableau shows a *learning pair*: a model (adult) utterance and the corresponding learner's utterance (perhaps from an imitation one way or the other), with the following representations, all of which can be identified in Figure 1:

- The *model utterance*, as it is available to the ear of the learner; not, therefore, the articulatory representation, but the acoustic form that is a direct consequence of that articulation. This is the acoustic input to the learner's perceptual categorization system, and is able to slowly change that system during acquisition.
- The *model perception*: the adult utterance as perceived by the learner. This is the output of the learner's perceptual categorization system.
- The specification is by definition the input to the production grammar. In

early learning, this may be a concatenation of words as stored in the lexicon, equal to the adult overt forms in isolation, as perceived (categorized) by the child (the model perception, in other words). Later on, this may be a more abstract underlying form.

- Many candidate articulations.
- For each candidate articulation: the corresponding output, as perceived by the learner's categorization system.

The learner normally assumes that the perceived model is the *correct form*. She knows that she is in error when her own output, as perceived by herself, is different from that form. If any of the other candidate outputs *is* equal to the correct form, learning may occur. In tableau (3), for instance, the learner's output /perc₁/ may be different from /*model perc*/, but the less harmonic candidate /perc₂/ may be equal to /*model perc*/. If that is the case, the learner will identify the correct form with /perc₂/, as is indicated in (3) with a check mark. The model utterance has now become a *trigger*: the grammar will be changed. The thing that is wrong with the current grammar is that A is ranked too high or B is ranked too low. The learner's strategy could simply be to execute the following learning step:

(4)   Maximal Gradual Learning Algorithm (MGLA)

'Lower the rankings of all the constraints violated in the adult form, and raise the rankings of all the constraints violated in the learner's form (by a little amount).'

In tableau (3), the direction of the ranking change is shown by arrows in the cells with the violation marks.

As we will see, its graduality makes this algorithm robust (resistant against erroneous input or parses), and causes it to exhibit several types of realistic behaviour. Moreover, the algorithm has a property quite desirable for all learning algorithms: it can correctly and quickly learn any target grammar starting from any initial grammar (with the same constraint set). The MGLA also behaves well in situations of variation, as I will show in Section 13.6.1.

13.1.3 *Functional Constraints and Rankings, and the Local-Ranking Principle*

As far as autosegmental phonology is concerned, the grammar consists of constraints that express functional principles of articulation and perception. Some of the constraints can be ranked in a universal way, because of general properties of the human motor and perception systems. The *local-ranking principle* (Boersma 1998: ch.11) maintains that the two members of a constraint pair can have a fixed (near-universal, language-independent) ranking if their arguments or environments differ along only a single parameter, and that all other constraint pairs can, in principle, be ranked freely in a language-specific way.

13.1.3.1 Effort: gestural constraints

The functional principle of *minimization of articulatory effort* is evaluated for each candidate articulation, with a large number of continuous constraint families (Boersma 1998: ch.7), collectively referred to as ART, as shown in (1). The typical representative is

*GESTURE (a: g / d, v, p, t): 'The articulator a does not perform the gesture g along a certain distance d (away from the rest position), and with a certain speed v, reaching a position p for a duration t.'

Basically, articulatory constraints are ranked by *effort*: constraints against gestures that require more effort are universally ranked higher than constraints against easier gestures. The same gesture is more difficult if its distance, speed, duration, or precision is greater, *if everything else is kept equal*; this can lead to a fixed ranking of gestural constraints.

For instance, the ranking of the *GESTURE constraint depends on the distance from the position of the articulator to its neutral position: for two positions p_1 and p_2 on the same side of the neutral position, *GESTURE (a: p_1, t) >> *GESTURE (a: p_2, t) if and only if p_1 is farther from the neutral position than p_2; crucially, the articulator a and the duration t must be equal in both constraints for the fixed ranking to be universal. Likewise, the speaker can be considered aware of the fact that a longer isometric contraction costs more energy than a shorter contraction: *GESTURE (a: p, t_1) >> *GESTURE (a: p, t_2) if and only if $t_1 > t_2$; this ranking, too, is only universal if everything else (articulator, distance, speed, position) is equal in both constraints.

On the other side, it is hard for speakers to compare articulatory effort across articulators (unless the differences are very large): there is no way to universally rank the pair *GESTURE (lips: rounded) and *GESTURE (tongue body: back), and languages are free to vary.

Articulatory constraints can often be written as *implementation constraints*, i.e. constraints against the implementation of a *perceptual* feature. For instance, the ranking of the constraint *[+voiced/obstruent] determines the speaker's idea of how difficult it is to implement voicing under a certain supralaryngeal condition. The height of this constraint is equal to the height of the more fundamental *GESTURE constraint that describes the actual (perhaps language-specific) articulatory gesture that is needed for the implementation of obstruent voicing. Implementation constraints may allow the linguist to work exclusively with perceptual features.

13.1.3.2 Contrast: faithfulness constraints

The functional principle of *minimization of perceptual confusion* is evaluated in terms of the faithfulness of the perceptual output with respect to the perceptual specification, with a large number of constraints (Boersma 1998: ch.9), collectively known as FAITH, as shown in Figure 1. Typical representatives are

TRANSMIT (*f*): 'If any value of the feature *f* is present in the input, the output contains any corresponding (perhaps different) value of this feature.'

*REPLACE (*f*: *x*, *y* / *cond* / *env*): 'The value *x* on the perceptual tier *f* in the input is not replaced with a different value *y* in the output, under a certain condition *cond* and in a certain environment *env*.'

*DELETE (*f*: *x* / *cond* / *env*): 'The value *x* on the perceptual tier *f* in the input is present in the output.' This constraint combines the workings of TRANSMIT (correspondence) and *REPLACE (equality) for features with few categories.

Basically, faithfulness constraints are ranked by perceptual *contrast*: constraints that require the faithfulness of strongly distinctive features are ranked higher than constraints for weakly distinctive features; Boersma (1998: ch.9.5) shows that this is caused by the listener's quest for an optimal recognition strategy. A replacement is more offensive if the contrast between the members of the pair along a certain perceptual dimension is greater, *if everything else is kept equal*; this can lead to a fixed ranking of many pairs of faithfulness constraints.

For instance, it is worse to replace a feature value with a distant value than to replace it with a near value; for instance, a rendering of |ɛ| as [e] constitutes a less offensive violation than a rendering as [i], which is farther from the specification along the perceptual height dimension (first formant). This gives a fixed ranking of *REPLACE (*f*: *x*, y_1) >> *REPLACE (*f*: *x*, y_2) if and only if y_1 is more distant from *x* than y_2 (on the same side of *x*).

On the other side, it is hard for listeners to compare perceptual distinctions across tiers (unless the differences are very large): there is no way to universally rank *REPLACE (place: labial, coronal) with respect to *REPLACE (noise: sibilant, mellow), and languages are free to vary.

As opposed to the local comparisons proposed here, global measures of articulatory effort and perceptual confusion can only predict cross-linguistic *tendencies*, not universals. The typological prediction of the local-ranking principle is that all the constraint pairs that do not receive a fixed ranking, can be ranked in a language-specific way.

As we will see, the local-ranking principle allows the learner to manage the acquisition of continuous constraint families, and speeds up the acquisition process.

13.2 Learning in Functional Phonology

In functional phonology, we have an infinite number of learnable constraints. This state of affairs may pose problems for learnability, because several extant learning algorithms (Gibson and Wexler 1994; Tesar and Smolensky 1993, 1996) need a finite number of innate constraints to work. In the rest of this chapter I will show that neither *finiteness* nor *innateness* is needed for the acquisition of phonology. I'll start with the core algorithm, because that will be used for illustrating every learning stage.

13.2.1 *The Grammar*

I will first present a view of OT grammar and constraints that is fully compatible with nearly all work in OT so far, but allows us to understand more easily several aspects of learning and reranking of constraints. The grammar, in this view, consists of a language-specific finite set of constraints $\{C_1, C_2, \ldots, C_N\}$. Each constraint C has two parts: a pair-evaluation function and a ranking value.

Pair-evaluation function

The evaluation function can compare the harmonies of two output candidates with respect to C. For gestural constraints, the function is ART-EVAL (C, $cand_1$, $cand_2$), where $cand_1$ and $cand_2$ are two articulatory candidates. The function ART-EVAL returns an answer to the question which of the two candidates is the better with respect to C, or whether they are equally harmonic. For faithfulness constraints, the function is FAITH-EVAL (C, $spec$, $output_1$, $output_2$), where $spec$ is the perceptual specification, and $output_1$ and $output_2$ are the perceptual results of two candidates. This function tells us which of the two output candidates, or neither, matches the specification best in a certain respect.

Ranking value

Each constraint is ranked along the *continuous ranking scale*, with a real value between, say, 0 and 100 (though values outside this range must not be excluded). We will see that the continuity of this scale allows us to understand several real-life phenomena.

Comparing a pair of candidates

With the above ingredients, the procedure for evaluating the relative harmony of two candidate outputs runs as follows. Given a perceptual specification and two candidates, all N constraints are asked for their opinions. The constraints that measure no difference of harmony between the two candidates, remain silent. The other constraints issue a *protest*. For instance, if candidate A is less harmonic than candidate B with respect to C_2 and C_5, and B is less harmonic than A with respect to C_3, the constraints C_2 and C_5 issue a protest against A, and C_3 issues a protest against B. The loudness of each protest (the *disharmony*) is determined by the ranking value of the constraint that issues it, and the loudest protest wins. For instance, if C_3 has the highest disharmony of the three protesters, candidate B will be banned, and A emerges as the more harmonic of the two.

Evaluation of all candidates

If GEN (the OT candidate generator) generates 10 candidates, the most harmonic one can be found by starting with a comparison of the first two of these candidates, and going on by comparing the more harmonic of this pair with the third candidate, and so on. After having compared the tenth candidate with the best one of the first nine, we will have identified the winner.

Tableaus

The result of the procedure described above will usually be the same as the result of the usual tableau evaluation. However, as an actual algorithm for finding the winning output, it uses less information (no counting of marks) and memory resources (the evaluations of all the candidates) than the batch algorithm of computing the winner from a tableau. Of course, tableaus were never meant to suggest a psychological reality, and they are particularly useful for explicit communication between linguists. The aim of the current chapter, however, is to show that learning a grammar is as natural as learning anything else, so we need an *explanation* of the learning process in realistic terms.

The view of constraint ranking as exemplified in tableaus is a hybrid representation of grammar: it is meant to represent both the behaviour of the speaker and the properties of the language. A classical OT tableau is totally ranked—i.e. the constraints C_1, C_2, and C_3 written from left to right along the top of the tableau are taken to represent the total ranking $C_1 >> C_2 >> C_3$. There exists a device for indicating in a tableau that two adjacent constraints are not crucially ranked with respect to one another, namely, drawing a dotted vertical line between them instead of a solid line. However, this does not work for all non-crucial rankings. For instance, if we have five constraints with crucial rankings $C_1 >> C_2$, $C_1 >> C_3$, $C_3 >> C_4$, $C_2 >> C_5$, and $C_4 >> C_5$, the freedom of ranking cannot be represented by the usual linear ordering. Instead, the following topology of crucial rankings is more informative:

(5) Linguistically-orientated grammar

For the linguist, it is an interesting quest to find out which constraints are crucially ranked in a language and which are not. However, if the speaker's constraints have ranking values associated with them, she need not know topologies like (5), and there is no point for us in assuming that she does. Rather, her grammar will look like Figure 6.

Note that though the constraints in (6) are written on different heights from those in (5), the two grammars are empirically indistinguishable if used with the fixed-winner systems most phonologists are concerned with. The main reason I think that (6) better represents the cognitive capabilities of the speaker is that

(6) Psychologically-orientated grammar

the learning algorithm that comes with it has the ten desirable properties described in the next section; other evidence for the reality of continuous ranking, though, is found in pragmatic reranking, optionality, and so on, as we will also see.

13.2.2 *The Maximal Gradual Learning Algorithm*

The selection of the winning candidate in Optimality Theory can be seen as an instance of the principle 'minimize the largest problem': the winner is the candidate in which the largest constraint violation is lower than the largest constraint violation of its peers (disregarding shared marks). Likewise, the natural learning algorithm for an Optimality-Theoretic grammar could be equally egalitarian—i.e. demoting the highest uncancelled constraint in the adult form (a Minimal algorithm). However, the following algorithm will be seen to be more realistic under conditions of variation, and show faster recovery from errors:

(7)   Maximal Gradual Learning Algorithm
       'If the learner's current grammar computes a 'winner' that is different from the correct (adult) output form (as perceived by the learner), move the rankings of the constraints violated in the correct adult output form (after mark cancellation) down, and move the rankings of the constraints violated in the incorrect learner's output form up, by a small step along the continuous ranking scale.'

This simple algorithm will prove to have the following desirable properties:

1 The algorithm is *convergent*: it can learn all OT grammars, from any initial state, without ever getting trapped in a local maximum.
2 The learning process is *conservative*: the hypothesis is changed minimally on each step. This ensures the *stability* of the learning process: most of the learned relations are remembered.
3 The algorithm is *local*: only the wrong winner and the correct output form have to be compared. This keeps the necessary computational load within bounds.
4 The algorithm is *oblivious* of previous evaluations of the data: all experience is laid down in the ranking value of every constraint along the scale. This keeps the acclaimed memory resources within bounds.

5 The algorithm is *robust*: if the reranking step is small with respect to the average distance between adjacent constraints on the scale, errors in the input have a small impact as long as they stay a minority; if they do happen to worsen the grammar, correct data received later will remedy this situation.

6 Since the ranking scale is continuous, the algorithm can model the decrease in *plasticity* that comes with the years: for older learners, the reranking steps get smaller.

7 As we will see, a probabilistic interpretation of constraint distances covers several real-life phenomena: closely ranked constraints can sometimes be reversed during evaluation. This causes a *repulsion* of crucially ranked pairs (and thus increases robustness) and an *attraction* of pairs connected by mis-pronunciations or misperceptions.

8 The algorithm can easily be made to allow the input to the grammar to be the overt adult form, until the learner derives underlying forms from the patterns that she discovers in the language.

9 The algorithm can easily be made to actively preserve markedness relations (i.e., honour the local-ranking principle) until the phonology gets really symbolic.

10 The algorithm can easily model *unlearning*: gestural constraints can drift up, faithfulness constraints can drift down.

The distinction between articulatorily-oriented and perceptually-oriented constraints leads to a straightforward account of learning in six stages.

13.2.3 *Three Production Modes*

In all learning stages I will distinguish three modes of sound production:

1 Sound production for the sake of *sound production*. In this 'playing' mode, the child learns the relation between her articulations and their acoustic-perceptual results.

2 Sound production for the sake of *communication*. The child's perception of the adult model utterance is the underlying form, and normal faithfulness constraints apply. The child's speech, like that of the adult, is the result of an interaction between articulatory and faithfulness constraints.

3 Imitation for the sake of *imitation*. In this mode, the child learns to produce articulatory gestures that she does not yet use in speech. Another person's utterance is the underlying form; faithfulness is ranked higher than in normal speech, because the very goal is imitation, not communication (even adults rerank their faithfulness constraints according to the pragmatics of the situation: higher in addressing a crowd, lower in saying an everyday prayer). Also, articulatory constraints may be ranked lower in imitation, because the child need not give any attention to semantics, syntax, or the lexicon (and even adults rerank their gestural constraints—e.g. they raise them when intoxicated).

I will now identify six observable *stages* in the acquisition of (auto-)segmental phonology, and the five developmental *steps* by which the learner goes from one stage to the next. These stages are not to be identified with the stages of the development of vocal production (uninterrupted phonation, interrupted phonation, articulation, prosody, babbling, words) in the baby's first year (MacNeilage 1997; Koopmans-van Beinum and van der Stelt 1998), since I am focusing on the development of linguistic communicative performance. Nor is the ordering presented here meant to be fixed or universal in the sense of Jakobson's (1941) proposal; my main point will be that the acquisition of articulatory coordinations and perceptual categorizations naturally evolves into an adult grammar of learned functional constraints.

13.2.4 *Stage 1: An Empty Grammar*

Acquisition starts with a stage of unlearned perceptual categorization and articulatory coordination. No real constraints exist yet, because no gestures and no categories have been learned. However, we can say that unlearned gestures would pose maximum difficulties for the speaker—i.e. the virtual articulatory constraints ('ART', typically *GESTURE) are undominated. Likewise, we can say that unlearned perceptual categories pose maximum difficulties for the listener—i.e. the virtual faithfulness constraints ('FAITH', typically *DELETE) are at the bottom of the hierarchy. We can illustrate this situation with the following virtual constraint hierarchy:

(8) Stage 1

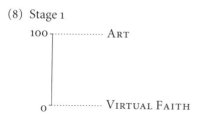

This is the true initial state of the learner: a reservoir of latent articulatory constraints at the top, and a reservoir of latent faithfulness constraints at the bottom: the child will not be able to recognize or produce speech. In such a grammar, no constraints are visible: it is truly a *tabula rasa*; its substance will have to be learned later.

The learner may well be in Stage 1 for a certain phonological feature and in a later stage for another. For instance, a child may have acquired some vowels and coronal stops, but not yet the distinctive sibilancy of /s/ nor, of course, its rather involved articulatory implementation. Using an OT tableau as a descriptive device for this situation, we can represent the child's handling of the adult English form [siː] 'see' as

(9) [siː] /tiː/ = |tiː|	*Delete (coronal)	*Gesture (blade: close and open)
✔ ☞ [tiː] /tiː/		*

The adult produces [siː], which is a language-independent IPA shorthand for 'lung pressure (= release diaphragm and external intercostals), plus fronted and high tongue body (= pull genioglossus and lower longitudinals), plus tongue-tip grooving, adduction, and opening (= upper transverse tongue fibers, etc.), plus glottal adduction (= interarytenoids, etc.)', as well as for its automatic acoustic result. The child perceives /tiː/, which is short for 'coronal (= high-frequency noise), plus high front vowel (= low-F_1 high-F_2 periodic)'. Until further notice, the learner's underlying form, now \|tiː\|, will be equal to this perceived input (as shown by the equals sign). The child generates an articulatory candidate [tiː] and perceives this as /tiː/, fully faithful to her underlying form (no violation mark for *Delete) as well as to the perceived adult form (hence the check mark [tick]: no learning). The child does not generate a candidate [siː] because not even the perceptual input contains a sibilant.

13.2.5 *Step 1 in the Perception Grammar: Acquisition of Perceptual Categorization*

The nativist idea of the universality of phonological feature values is widely held (e.g. Hale and Reiss 1998; Jacobs and Gussenhoven, this volume). It has been found (Eimas, Siqueland, Jusczyk, and Vigorito 1971; Streeter 1976) that very young infants categorize the voice-onset-time (b-p-p[h]) continuum according to criteria that reflect the clustering of plosives that Lisker and Abramson (1964) found in the languages of the world (Cho and Ladefoged 1997 found a much more continuous voice-onset-time [VOT] distribution); this capability is lost in adults, who typically recognize only the contrasts that occur in their language (Abramson and Lisker 1970). However, I will take the less expensive stance that the learner of speech must get by with independently needed strategies of perceptual and cognitive categorization. Firstly, voice-onset-time is not a homogeneous perceptual dimension: it is difficult to regard the [b]-[p] contrast (vocal murmur versus silence) as continuously related to the [p]-[p[h]] contrast (sonorancy versus aspiration noise); in fact, Kuhl and Miller (1978) and Kuhl and Padden (1982) found human-like voicing categories in untrained chinchillas and macaques, suggesting that infant VOT categorization refers to general properties of mammalian audition, not to a linguistic capability specific to the human species. Secondly, for the truly continuous perceptual dimensions of vowel quality (auditory spectrum), we do not find any initial categorization in human infants, and we find clustering only in locations predicted by the hypothesis of contrast maximization (the corners of the vowel triangle, its periphery, and equal height divisions in symmetric systems); a specifically human phenomenon of decreased discriminability of vowel qualities occurred only in the immediate vicinity of language-specific vowel categories (Kuhl 1991). Thirdly, even complicated multidimensional categorization seems not to be restricted to the human species, since Japanese quail have been trained to develop a human-like category /d/, generalizing across different vowel contexts (Kluender, Diehl, and Killeen 1987). For more discussion, see Kuhl (1979), Jusczyk (1986), Werker (1991), Jusczyk (1992), Vihman (1996), MacNeilage (1997), and Behnke (1998).

Thus, the little linguist will listen to her language environment and learn that speakers tend to centre the perceptual feature values of their utterances at certain locations along the continuous perceptual dimensions. This will lead her to construct perceptual categories around these locations, especially when she realizes that the categories are to be associated with differences of meaning and can be used for disambiguation of speech utterances. This part of the learning process can be simulated with any neural-net classification procedure (e.g. Grossberg 1976; Carpenter and Grossberg (eds) 1991; Behnke 1998) that is told to handle acoustic and lexical similarity. The process can also be described within an Optimality-Theoretic model of a perception grammar, namely as the lowering of initially undominated (virtual) *CATEG constraints (Boersma 1998: ch.8); this approach also explains the phenomenon that far outside any language-specific categories, adults perceive the same continuous acoustic feature values as infants (Best, McRoberts, and Sithole 1988).

Perceptual categorization is a prerequisite for both *lexicalization* and the acquisition of production; for instance, the learner should have some values for the perceptual voicing feature before she can replace her unspecified lexical /b̥/ tokens with the correct choice between /b/ and /p/, and before she will start taking the trouble to practise the necessary glottal and supraglottal gestures. In the majority of cases, lexicalization of a contrast precedes its production; for instance, Amahl (Smith 1973: 3) merged all initial |w| and |f| into [w], but when he started to produce a correct [f], he did so 'across the board' in all words that had |f| in the adult language. However, the production of a contrast sometimes precedes its lexicalization: when Amahl (Smith 1973: 54, 77, 97), mastering final [n], acquired the final [nd] cluster ([wɛnd] 'friend', [laund] 'round'), he generalized this to words with final |n| in the adult language ([b̥aund] 'brown'), which suggests that his lexicon did not yet reflect the adult choice between |n| and |nd|. Other examples of lexicalization lagging behind production in Amahl's speech, can be found in Braine (1976), Macken (1980), and Vihman (1982). These facts are important to the hypothesis of functional phonology, because they lend support to the existence of a perception grammar (Fig. 1). As Braine (1976: 495) puts it, 'Auditory encoding laws (. . .) would have adult articulatory features on the left-hand side, indirectly specifying the acoustic input by specifying how adults make it, and the child's auditory features on the right-hand side'. This *perception hypothesis* was evident in the analysis by Waterson (1971), who

wants to explain phonological development in terms of a gradual loosening of constraints on the complexity of internal lexical representations. Permitted complexity constraints are in turn assumed to reflect limitations on what the child is capable of perceiving linguistically, at any given time.   (Queller 1988: 465)

I will take this loosening of constraints literally as OT-style demotion of categorization constraints. The *linguistically* is crucial here: even if the child could hear a certain difference, it is often advantageous (as with Labovian near-merger) to ignore it in the communicative situation.

13.2.5.1   Step 1 in the production grammar: the emergence of faithfulness Constraints

The learner will intend not only to perceive but also to produce the carriers of meaning (or meaning *differences*) in her language environment. Therefore, she will *create* a set of faithfulness constraints (against deletion, insertion, and replacement) for the newly categorizable feature values, or combinations of these. These constraints evaluate the relation between the underlying form (still the adult model, as categorized by the child) and the perceptual output (the sound of the child's utterance, as categorized by herself).

Since the child cannot yet produce the newly developed category, say the sibilant noise of /s/, the learning tableau is especially simple:

		o
(10)	[siː] /siː/ = |siː|	*DELETE (sibilant)
☞	[tiː] /tiː/	←*

Compared to (9), the perceptual input has now been enriched with the feature [sibilant] and is rendered as /siː/, and the underlying form has changed to match this perceptual input. The learner now seems to notice two things: her output /tiː/ is different from her underlying form \|ːsiː\|, giving a *DELETE violation, and her output is also different from the perceptual input \|siː\|, resulting in an *error* that should lead to a learning step. Note that as the perceptual specification is still intimately connected with the adult model, a *DELETE violation and an output mismatch cannot be distinguished; indeed, they are one and the same thing, and so are unfaithfulness and errors.

The error will lead to the learning step of promoting the violated constraint. If the initial ranking is o (zero), as in (10), the new ranking will be above o: the learner will modify the strengths of some neural connections by an amount proportional to the degree of *plasticity* of the neural network. If the current plasticity is 1 on our constraint-ranking scale, the learner's single error-correction step will have the consequence of moving the violated constraint by an amount of 1 up the ranking scale.

Restricted generator

Like (9), but for a different main reason, tableau (10) still does not even *generate* the faithful utterance [siː] as a candidate, because this would require the learner to use a coronal grooving gesture that she has not yet linked to the sound of /s/. This point may require some elaboration. One might think that GEN should be able to generate an output candidate that contains [s], and that the constraint *GESTURE (tongue blade: groove) would be needed to reject that output. According to Section 13.1.1, however, GEN generates articulatory implementations, and there is no point for a speaker in including an unlearned (virtual, latent) gesture in the set of candidates. This is an example of the difference between *universality* and *innateness*, two terms that have often been confounded. In the style of Ellison (this volume):

(11)   Universality versus innateness 1: GEN.
       If GEN is a model for the speaker's generation of output candidates, it will generate no candidates with unmastered articulatory gestures. If, on the other hand, GEN is a device for free hypothesization by linguists, it may generate any articulation that linguists can think of; but this universality will not reflect innateness.

13.2.6 *Stage 2: Violated Faithfulness*

During the acquisition of its categorization, the faithfulness constraints for a language-specific feature value percolate up from the bottom of the grammar. However, the corresponding articulatory constraint is still found at the top of the hierarchy, because the learner's motor control has not yet mastered the relevant gestures. This situation can be pictured as

(12) Stage 2

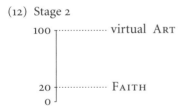

This hypothesis is consistent with the proposal by Gnanadesikan (1995), Smolensky (1996b), and others, that in the initial state markedness (or structural) constraints outrank faithfulness constraints, but inconsistent with Hale and Reiss (1996, 1998), who propose that the reverse holds true (see Section 13.2.7).

    Evidence that articulatory constraints crucially outrank faithfulness constraints at this stage (and of the temporal order of perceptual vs. articulatory acquisition), is found in the phenomenon that children tend not to accept an imitation of their own speech by an adult (the 'fis' phenomenon—Berko and Brown 1960: 321). For instance, if the child produces [tiː] for the English utterance /siː/ 'see', she may still object to her father's pronouncing this word as [tiː], a fact that shows that the child's perceptual target must already be /si:/, and that the output [ti:] is an unfaithful rendering of it (tableau 10).

13.2.7 *Step 2: Sensorimotor Learning*

With high faithfulness constraints, but still higher articulatory constraints, the learner experiences a lot of tension in her system: an average utterance will come out so unfaithful that listeners have trouble understanding her. The acquisition of motor skills will remedy this situation. The articulatory constraints are lowered:

> The child's 'tonguetiedness', that overwhelming reality which Stampe and Jakobson both tried to capture with their respective formal structures, could be handled more felicitously if one represented the heavy articulatory limitations of the child by the formal device of output constraints [. . .]. The child's gradual mastery of articulation then is formalized as a relaxation of those constraints.   (Menn 1980: 35–6)

Again, I will take this relaxation of constraints literally in OT terms.

The learner will be able to learn the relation between articulation and perception with the help of articulatory variation. The learner can interpolate and extrapolate, but because of the many non-linear relationships between articulatory and perceptual parameters, she will also have to *play* a lot.

Once the learner knows that she can produce something that she will perceive as /s/, the constraint *[sibilant] will enter her grammar, perhaps at the height of *GESTURE (blade: groove), if that is the way she chooses to implement this sound. If the learner is a child that has not practised the blade-grooving gesture before, the articulatory constraint will enter at the top of the grammar (with a ranking value of, say, '100'), still resulting in the unfaithful output /ti:/:

(13) [si:] /si:/ = |si:|	100 *[sibilant]	20 *DELETE (sibilant)
☞ [ti:] /ti:/		←*
✓ [si:] /si:/	*!→	

In this tableau, the finger points to the learner's output (her production, as perceived by herself), and the check mark identifies the form that the learner assumes to be correct: the adult output form, as perceived by the learner. Thus, tableau (13) results from a pair of utterances: one by the adult, one by the learner. Given the learner's capabilities of perceptual categorization, we can assume that she notices the discrepancy.

The learner will tackle the problem by moving *[sibilant] down the ranking scale, perhaps by practising the grooving gesture, and by moving *DELETE (sibilant) up:

(14) [si:] /si:/=|si:|	99 *[sibilant]	21 *DELETE (sibilant)
☞ [ti:] /ti:/		←*
✔ [si:] /si:/	*!→	

Now, fundamental questions arise. Do these tableaus show an output mismatch or a *DELETE violation? Is the remedy to practise a gesture or to demote *GESTURE? In other words, does the learner acquire a production system or a grammar? From the Universal Grammar standpoint, these have been clearly distinguished; Hale and Reiss (1996, 1998) would argue that in (14), faithfulness actually has to dominate the structural constraint because the learner perceives /si:/, and knows that the output should be /si:/; so /si:/ would be the output of the *grammar*, and /ti:/ the output of the *body*. The idea is that the recognition process mirrors the production process, so that they should share (a part of) the grammar, and the up and down arrows in (1) should be intimately connected (for the top part). This may be true for the more 'lexical' parts of phonology, but if we see the grammar as a description of human behaviour, we should include the more superficial parts that allow functional explanation, all the way up to the actual articulation. Moreover, the procedure of *robust interpretive parsing* (Smolensky 1996a; Tesar and Smolensky 1996; Tesar, this volume) allows initially high-ranked structural constraints in a grammar that can be used for production as well as for comprehension.

13.2.8 *Stage 3: Faithful Imitation*

After some practice (e.g., 30 unit steps as in (13)), the articulatory constraints become so low, and faithfulness constraints so high, that a special situation of FAITH-raising and ART-lowering would result in a faithful rendering of the perceptual target, though during normal speech production the articulatory constraint still dominates:

(15) Stage 3: normal speech   Stage 3: imitation

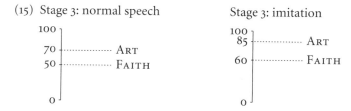

This mode-dependent constraint reranking counters a certain criticism against ascribing the large input-output disparity to performance difficulties:

claiming that children don't produce, say, a particular segment because their motor control hasn't yet mastered it, can run afoul of the fact that children who systematically avoid a given structure in their linguistic productions can often easily imitate it.   (Smolensky 1996a: 720)

If we accept the possibility of pragmatics-based reranking, the argument vanishes. What's more, we have a second explanation (after play) for an otherwise awkward bootstrapping problem: how could we know that we should practise a certain gesture to drag down a constraint, if we do not know that its demotion will result in a more faithful grammar? Answer: we perform an experiment by temporarily ranking a faithfulness constraint above it, and this experiment results in a correct output (which, still equivalently, satisfies *DELETE):

(16) imitation of [si:] /si:/=|si:|	85 *DELETE (sibilant)	60 *[sibilant]
[ti:] /ti:/	*!	
✔ ☞ [si:] /si:/		*

Thus, free variation of faithfulness adds to the learner's confidence in the choice of articulatory gestures to practise.

13.2.9 *Step 3: The Learning Curve*

Some practice of producing the new gesture (perhaps aided by a few faithful imitations) will dramatically facilitate its implementation, and some practice of perceiving the new category will raise its importance in communication. These events draw the anti-gesture constraint and the relevant faithfulness constraint into each other's vicinity:

(17) [si:] /si:/=|si:|	61 *[sibilant]	59 *DELETE (sibilant)
☞ [ti:] /ti:/		←*
✔ [si:] /si:/	*!→	

The result is still unfaithful (= incorrect). The next learning step will bring the two constraints up to an equal height. Two synaptic strengths are never exactly equal, so we should assume that this situation gives rise to two possible evaluations, a faithful one and an unfaithful one, both with a probability of 1/2. The faithful (= correct) evaluation gives

(18) [si:] /si:/=|si:|	60 *DELETE (sibilant)	60 *[sibilant]
[ti:] /ti:/	*!	
✔ ☞ [si:] /si:/		*

and the unfaithful (and incorrect) evaluation gives

(19) [siː] /siː/=|siː|	60 *[sibilant]	60 *DELETE (sibilant)
☞ [tiː] /tiː/		←*
✔ [siː] /siː/	*!→	

Because the learner will still interpret half of her utterances as incorrect, another learning step will soon follow, giving a stable grammar:

(20) [siː] /siː/=|siː|	61 *DELETE (sibilant)	59 *[sibilant]
[tiː] /tiː/	*!	
✔ ☞ [siː] /siː/		*

Learning has succeeded; no errors are to be expected; the grammar will not change any further. Note that learnability along this discrete ranking scale prohibits the existence of *ties*, in the sense of constraints with equal harmonies that pass the buck to lower-ranked constraints:

(21)   No ties
   The marks incurred by a constraint can never be cancelled by the marks incurred by a different constraint with the same ranking.

13.2.9.1 Stochastic evaluation

The process described above shows some unrealistic behaviour: the learner has a 0% correct score for some time, then a 50% correct score for a very short time, and then a 100% correct score for the rest of the time. Real learning shows a much smoother behaviour. We therefore interpret constraint ranking in a probabilistic manner. With a neural-net analogy, the loudness of the protest of a constraint is the value of an inhibitory postsynaptic potential: it depends on the synaptic strength (the ranking as specified in the grammar) as well as on some things like the accidental amount of locally available neurotransmitter. At evaluation time, therefore, the disharmony (the 'effective' ranking) of the i-th constraint C_i is something like

$$\text{disharmony}(C_i) = \text{ranking}(C_i) + \text{rankingSpreading} \times z$$

where z is a Gaussian random deviate with mean zero and standard deviation 1. Now the problem of ties automatically vanishes: the probability that the disharmonies of two different constraints are equal is zero. The learning algorithm is very resilient against the actual value of *rankingSpreading*, but in the examples of this chapter I will take it to be 2.0.

We will also have fuzzy reranking steps. In the above examples, the plasticity was held constant at 1 per learning step. A more realistic view holds that it contains a noise component, and that it decreases with the age of the learner (children learn and unlearn some things faster than adults):

(23) $plasticity = plasticity_0 \times (1 + relativePlasticitySpreading \times z) \times \left(\frac{1}{2}\right)^{age/plasticityHalfTime}$

In this formula, *plasticity₀* is the *day-one plasticity*: the value on the first day. As far as learnability is concerned, *relativePlasticitySpreading* may be anything, including zero, but I'll keep it fixed at 0.1. Finally, *plasticityHalfTime* is the time needed for the plasticity to decrease by a factor of two: if day-one plasticity is 1, and the plasticity half-time is 1500 days, the plasticity will have decreased to 1/2 at an age of 1500 days, and to 1/4 at an age of 3000 days; the advantage of this decrease is that young learners learn fast, and older learners learn more accurately. For this chapter, I will ignore this exponential decrease in plasticity, setting *plasticityHalfTime* to an infinite value.

Now, with a ranking spreading of 2.0, the grammar of tableau (20) is not yet stable. When it comes to an actual evaluation, *DELETE (sibilant) may be ranked at, say, 61 − 1.34, and *[sibilant] may be ranked at 59 + 0.78 or so, which is higher. This will result in an incorrect (= unfaithful) output again:

(24) [siː] /siː/=|siː|	59 + 0.78 *[sibilant]	61 − 1.34 *DELETE (sibilant)
☞ [tiː] /tiː/		←*
✔ [siː] /siː/	*!→	

So the gestural constraint is demoted again, and the faithfulness constraint is raised. As the distance between the two constraints increases, the probability of a reversal decreases, and the reranking will nearly come to a halt when *[sibilant] has fallen below 55, and *DELETE (sibilant) has risen above 65:

(25)   Constraint repulsion
        A crucially ranked pair of constraints repel one another and end up maintaining a safety margin.

Simulation (26) shows how the ranking of *[sibilant] becomes lower as a function of time (= the number of received /s/ data), and how the percentage of correct productions rises smoothly from 0% to 100% (with a plasticity of 0.2)[1]

We see that the 50%-correct point is reached only a short time after the first correct utterance, but that it takes a relatively long time after that before speech

---

[1] The algorithm for the rankings G and D of the two constraints *GESTURE and *DELETE is:

$G[0] := 100; D[0] := 20; p := 0.2;$
for t from 1 to 500
    if $G[t-1] + 2 \cdot z > D[t-1] + 2 \cdot z$
    then $G[t] := G[t-1] - (1 + 0.1 \cdot z) p; D[t] := D[t-1] + (1 + 0.1 \cdot z) p$
    else $G[t] := G[t-1]; D[t] := D[t-1]$

Realizing that the spreading of the difference of two Gaussian distributions with spreadings of 2 is $2\sqrt{2}$, we can compute the percentage correct at time t as $\frac{1}{2} \times (1 - erf(\sqrt{2}/2 \times (G[t] - D[t])/(2\sqrt{2})))$.

(26) OT learning curve

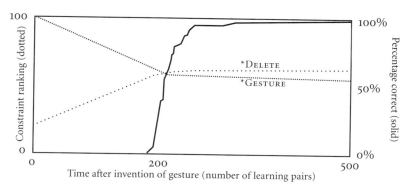

becomes flawless (even with constant plasticity), because the probability that a datum triggers a grammar change decreases.

Figure (26) shows the learning curve as seen from the learner. From the point of view of the adult there are two complications. Firstly, the gesture-invention day cannot be seen. Secondly, whether the learning curve rises as steeply as in the figure depends on whether the learner has had enough time since her categorization day to lexicalize all occurrences of /s/.

13.2.9.2 Continuous constraint families

Even with fuzzy ranking and demotion, the /siː/ example has a knack of discreteness. After all, it is not so important *whether* we can produce sibilant noise but *how similar* our output is to sibilant noise. For instance, the candidate [θiː] would be more faithful than the candidate [tiː] because it has a greater chance of being categorized as /siː/. With discrete *DELETE constraints, we would say

(27) [siː] /siː/ = |siː|	*GESTURE (blade: groove)	*DELETE (noise)	*GESTURE (blade: protrude)	*DELETE (sibilant)
[tiː] /tiː/		*!	*	*
☞ [θiː] 40% /siː/			←*	
✔ [siː] /siː/	*!→			

but a more realistic account would involve a continuous noisiness scale. If course, there is a universal local ranking *DELETE (noise) >> *DELETE (sibilant), or, more explicitly locally ranked: *DELETE (noise: ≥ mellow) >> *DELETE (noise: ≥ sibilant) 'It is more important to have at least mellow noise than to have at least sibilant noise'. If you cannot get it all, settle for a little less.

This is an example of *acoustic faithfulness*: the speaker minimizes the confusion probability by seeking maximum distances between sounds along a continuous acoustic dimension. Generally, the more effort we spend, the less confusing (unfaithful) we are. The optimum is found where the problem of articulatory effort *equals* the problem of confusability (Boersma 1998: ch.10).

We also understand now why /s/ is the universal unmarked fricative: *not* because it would be easier to make than /θ/, but because it sounds better: the alveolar fricative is 10 dB louder than the dental fricative.

13.2.9.3 Probabilistic categorization

As another example, consider the acquisition of the voicing contrast in plosives. When a Dutch learner already has correct categories /d/ and /t/, but has not yet mastered the voicing and devoicing gestures, both inputs will be pronounced with neither gesture, typically as a lenis voiceless plosive [d̥] (like English initial 'd'), which may be perceived (by the adult, and also already by the learner) as the fortis voiceless plosive /t/ in, say, 70% of all cases, and as the lenis voiced plosive /d/ in the other 30% of the cases. Because the majority of utterances will give /ta/, the learner will probably evaluate her candidates as if [d̥] would result in /t/.

Consider the input /ta/. Before production, the learner will evaluate the main candidates as

(28) [ta] /ta/ = |ta|	*[−voiced/plosive]	*Delete (−voice)
✔ ☞ [d̥a] /ta/		
✔ [ta] /ta/	*!	

In 70% of the cases, the winner's perceptual output /ta/ equals the prediction of this tableau and also equals the correct adult form, so these cases will cause no change in the grammar (= would not force learning of a devoicing gesture). In the remaining 30% of the cases, however, the learner will perceive the actually produced output as /d/. This will call for a reanalysis, now with a violation of *Delete (−voice):

(29) [ta] /ta/ = |ta| reanalysis	*[−voiced/plosive]	*Delete (−voice)
☞ [d̥a] /da/		←*
✔ [ta] /ta/	*!→	

The winning articulatory candidate [d̥] has not changed. However, it is no longer equal to the correct adult form, so it will induce reranking. The net result of a large number of /ta/ input data is the demotion of the gestural constraint past *Delete (−voice), caused by the simultaneous acquisition of a devoicing gesture and strengthening of the perceptual voicing feature. Thus, error-driven learning manifests itself as minimization of confusion probabilities.

In general, error-driven learning is used by humans to increase the reproducibility of the external results of their motor actions. In phonology, it acts as a local strategy for implementing the globally defined functional principle of minimization of confusion by way of perceptual invariance.

Now consider the input /da/. The learner will initially evaluate the candidates as

(30) [da] /da/=|da|	*[+voiced/ /plosive]	*DELETE (plosive)	*DELETE (+voice)	*[+voiced/ /–obstruent]
☞ [d̥a] /ta/			←*	
✔ [da] /da/	*!→			
[na] /na/		*!		*

For the purposes of illustration, this tableau shows the candidate [na], which represents a way of faithfully parsing the [+voice] specification. If *DELETE (plosive) (or *INSERT (nasal)) dominates *DELETE (+voice), this candidate cannot win. Note that the constraint *[+voiced/–obstruent] is still ranked very low; in fact, it is universally ranked below *[+voiced/plosive] because of the monotonically decreasing relation between the ease of phonation and the degree of supralaryngeal constriction.

The result of (30) will give rise to a promotion of all the constraints violated in the learner's form, i.e. *DELETE (+voice), and a demotion of all constraints violated in the adult form, i.e. *[+voiced/plosive]. In 30% of the cases, however, the produced result will be analysed as /da/, contrary to the predicted output /ta/ (in the row with the pointing finger), and the reanalysis will give

(31) [da] /da/=|da| reanalysis	*[+voiced/ /plosive]	*DELETE (plosive)	*DELETE (+voice)	*[+voiced/ /–obstruent]
✔ ☞ [d̥a] /da/				
✔ [da] /da/	*!			
[na] /na/		*!		*

This reanalysis will cause the output to be equal to the correct form /da/, and no reranking will occur.

13.2.10 *Stage 4: Faithfulness Outranks Gestural Constraints*

With faithfulness still in the same position as in Stage 2, the output is now equal to the specification, which still equals the perceived adult model:

(32) Stage 4

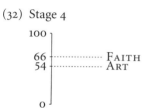

All relevant faithfulness constraints outrank all relevant articulatory constraints. Learning seems to have succeeded. There are no *DELETE violations, because the learner's perceptual output equals her underlying form. And there are no output mismatches (learning triggers) because the learner's perceptual output equals her perceptual input (the overt adult model utterance, as perceived by the learner). As the underlying form is still identified with the perceptual input, these two statements refer to the same phenomenon. Until now, we have used the powerful device of an OT tableau with five representations just for massaging a grammar into a state of pronounceability. We will need its full resources when grammar (32) will have to change by the only way it can ever change—breaking the identity between the perceptual input and the underlying form.

13.2.10.1 Timing

The learning stages may have different timing for different features. If place contrasts are mastered but voicing contrasts are not, we have the following ranking:

(33) Place but no voice

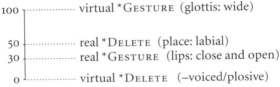

13.2.10.2 Phonation

Some innate sound-producing articulations can be used for communicative purposes exceptionally fast: crying requires glottal adduction, so the articulatory constraint *GESTURE (glottis: adduct) must be low at the time of the first steps into language. As soon as the perceptual features [voiced] and [sonorant] have been acquired, the implementational constraints *[+voiced/–obstruent] and *[sonorant/–obstruent] must be low, because *GESTURE (glottis: adduct) is low[2] Note that the voicing of non-obstruents is not automatic; it is just *easy* because the necessary gesture (controlled interarytenoid activity to move away from the neutral breathing position of the vocal folds) is mastered early. For phonation, therefore, step 1 will immediately lead to Stage 4.

13.2.11 *Step 4: Sentence-Level Phonology*

The form of a word in isolation is usually acquired earlier than the form of a

---

[2] I would like to reserve the term *sonorant* for the perceptual feature that refers to full periodicity (voicing) with clearly defined spectral components (formants). I use *obstruent* as a cover term for all the articulations that do not allow air to flow freely between the upper larynx and the outer air.

word in the sentence. Since the learning strategy has involved a fairly high ranking of faithfulness (in order to overcome the articulatory problems), we can expect the child to remain pretty faithful in Stage 4. For instance, Dutch four- or five-year-olds tend not to implement adult sentence-level phenomena like degemination and nasal place assimilation (judging from my own observation of the speech that prevails in my children's school classes; Hernández-Chávez, Vogel and Clumeck 1975 showed that Spanish-speaking children, too, proceed from unassimilated to assimilated clusters across word bounderies). In these adult processes, certain position-dependent faithfulness constraints fall below gestural constraints as a result of the low perceptual contrast between [np] and [mp] or between [pp] and [p], which admits the replacement of the faithful form by an articulatorily easier candidate. For the learner, this means that she will eventually lower some faithfulness constraints.

As an example, consider the acquisition of the place assimilation of Dutch /n/ to following labial or dorsal consonants (plosives do not assimilate; labials and dorsals do not assimilate). In Stage 4, the grammar is

(34) Nasal place assimilation, Stage 4

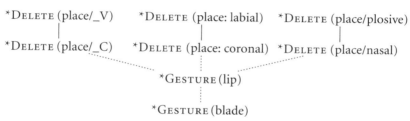

This grammar already shows four local rankings that the learner can be assumed to know, based on the dependence of the confusion probability on the availability of acoustic cues (for position-dependent *DELETE and manner-dependent *DELETE; see Jun 1995), on an adaptation by the listener to asymmetries in frequency of occurrence (for place-dependent *DELETE; see Boersma 1998: ch.8.5), and on an alleged effort difference between two articulators (reflecting a markedness relation identified by Prince and Smolensky 1993: ch.9).

In this grammar, the learner will produce an underlying |an#pa| as [anpa], and she will categorize this as /anpa/. Previously, the learner may only have taken isolated word forms as evidence for learning phonology. From the moment that the learner takes into account sandhi phenomena, an error will be generated when she hears that an adult speaker uses something that the learner perceives as /ampa/ (we know that the child can hear the difference, because some languages do assimilate and some do not). Instead of questioning her underlying form (which in isolation would be a correct word form), the learner will signal an offending faithfulness constraint in her analysis:

(35) [ampa] /ampa/ \an#pa\	*Delete (place/nas)	*Delete (place: cor)	*Delete (place/_C)	*[lab]	*[cor]
☞ [anpa] /anpa/				*	←*
✔ [ampa] /ampa/	*!→	*→	*→	*	

With *Delete violable, the connection between perceptual input and underlying form has been severed, as has the link between faithfulness and correctness.

Three *Delete constraints incur uncancelled marks in the correct form, and they are demoted; one constraint has an uncancelled violation mark in the learner's winner, and it is promoted.[3] The three *Delete constraints will trickle down the hierarchy, and *[cor] will trickle up, until the three have fallen to some safe distance below *[cor]. If *[cor] rises above *[lab] and this is inappropriate, other learning steps will raise *[lab] above *[cor] again; Section 13.6.1 will show that the whole procedure converges to the correct ranking. The resulting grammar will be:

(36) Nasal place assimilation, Stage 5

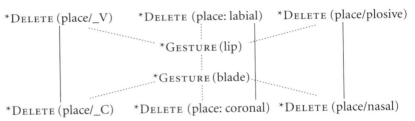

In this grammar, all the local rankings have been preserved.[4]

13.2.12 *Stage 5: Alternating Levels of Constraints*

We now have virtual Art >> real Faith >> real Art >> real Faith >> virtual Faith. Ignoring the latent faithfulness constraints, such a grammar exhibits a chain of three crucial dominations (from a universal viewpoint): it has a *depth* of three. Phonology has now gone from the word to the sentence, and postlexical phenomena have been learned.

---

[3] The error-driven constraint demotion (EDCD) algorithm of Tesar and Smolensky (1996) would immediately drop all three *Delete violators in tableau (35) below the constraint that incurs the highest mark in the winner that is not cancelled by a corresponding mark in the output; therefore, below *[coronal]. The EDCD step, therefore, changes the grammar in such a way that the correct adult form becomes more harmonic than the learner's original winner. The properties of the two algorithms are compared in Section 13.4.

[4] The local rankings actually allow a language with assimilation of /m/ and not of /n/. The non-existence of such a language must lead us to question the status of the alleged local ranking of the gestural constraints.

13.2.12.1 Optionality

The optionality of a thing like place assimilation of nasals can be explained by a pragmatically-determined reranking of constraints. In a communicative situation that requires extra understandability, all *DELETE constraints may go up by a distance of, say, 20 along the continuous ranking scale, and several *GESTURE constraints will fall prey to this rising faithfulness. However, markedness relations are preserved here, too: high-ranked *GESTURE constraints and low-ranked *DELETE constraints will experience a relatively low degree of optionality.

13.2.13 *Step 5: Emergence of Underlying Forms*

The learner grows to see patterns in the words of the language, based on morphological alternations, and may construct more or less abstract underlying forms. The input to the learner's grammar shifts from the adult word form to this new underlying representation. The output is no longer equal to the input; as in step 4, the learner may learn that faithfulness constraints can be violated in an adult grammar, but this step will also introduce morphologically-conditioned ranking, output-output constraints, perhaps suspension of local ranking, and language-dependent symbolic relations that are hard to describe with functional constraints.

For word-internal phenomena that allow descriptions in terms of functional constraints, like vowel harmony, step 5 will introduce the necessary negative evidence against certain word-internal combinations of gestures (for an example, see Section 13.3.5).

13.2.14 *Stage 6: The Adult Phase*

The adult phase has heavily interacting gestural and faithfulness constraints for postlexical phonology and some autosegmental lexical phenomena, and a language-specific symbolic constraint set based on alternations in the lexicon and some sentence-level phenomena. Some typical levels of constraints are, from top to bottom:

- Depth 0: unlearned gestures (virtual and other).
- Depth 1: obligatory perceptual features.
- Depth 2: difficult gestures.
- Depth 3: unimportant perceptual features.
- Depth 4: easy gestures.
- Below all: unlearned categories (virtual).

At the top, we see the latent articulatory gestures: most of them play no role for speakers until they want to learn a new language; likewise, the latent faithfulness constraints at the bottom can be considered to be outside the grammar. These two types of virtual constraints are maximally high or low not because they have been ranked as such but because the speakers have no experience whatsoever with them (unless they have ghost segments in underlying forms). Therefore, these constraints have no claim on *psychological reality*. For all practical purposes we can assume that the speaker only uses the 'real' constraints in the middle, and these have obviously emerged during the processes of perceptual categorization and motor learning:

(38)   Finiteness
        'Gestural as well as faithfulness constraints are learned, not innate. Each
        language uses a finite set of these constraints, learned in the processes
        of perceptual categorization and motor learning.'

Because crucial rankings deeper than four or five levels seem to be quite rare, the question arises whether a grammar consisting of crucial rankings (instead of rankings along a continuous scale) could be psychologically real and learnable. Such a grammar would be expressible with unviolated declarative constraints; the 'unimportant perceptual features' of depth 3, for instance, could be reworded in terms like 'pronounce except if'. In this chapter, however, I will stay with OT.

13.2.15 *Second-Language Acquisition*

After the learning of the first language, a part of the initial state is still there: unused gestures will still be invisible to the grammar—i.e. they will be represented by undominated constraints; and unlearned categories will still be invisible—i.e. their faithfulness constraints will be ranked at the bottom; their workings in the initial stage of second-language acquisition are fully automatic.

The average Germanic-speaking adult is still in the initial stage with respect to e.g. the acquisition of ejectives. Upon hearing [k'a], she will first analyse this as /ka/ and imitate it as [ka] (Stage 1); after some more exposure, she will recognize the ejective burst and categorize it as /k'a/ (Stage 2), though her pronunciation will still be [ka]; after some practice, she will be able to pronounce [k'a], first in imitation (Stage 3), later on in communicative situations (Stage 4). At some time during Stages 2, 3, or 4, she will have lexicalized the ejective, so that after learning the patterns of the language, she may know that some underlying /k'/ tokens have positionally-neutralized [k] variants (Stage 5, 6).

13.2.16 *Acoustic Versus Linguistic Faithfulness*

A criticism uttered by Smolensky (1996a) against the performance hypothesis (the hypothesis that performance problems account for the relative poverty of production with respect to perception), is the fact that children's replacements of certain gestures do not seem to have anything to do with articulatory problems. For instance, Smith (1973: 150) mentions a child who renders the adult /θɪk/ 'thick' as [fɪk], but not as a result of problems with the production of a dental fricative, since the same child renders the adult /sɪk/ 'sick' as [θɪk].

The solution of this problem lies in a perceptual asymmetry. Initially, the child will try to imitate the adult model as faithfully as possible, but this faithfulness will be evaluated in acoustic terms, since adaptation to different speakers must also be learned. Consider an example from a different domain: the adult utterance [ɛ] may have a first formant of 600 Hz, defining the vowel as lower-mid. If it is true that the child's initial classification system yields psychophysical rather than phonetic categories (Section 13.7.5), the child will reproduce this formant and produce a vowel which adults may perceive as [e] because they have learned to correct spectral structure for the length of the vocal tract of the speaker, probably with the help of the fundamental frequency; and indeed, the child has articulated a higher-mid vowel. Thus, the adult utterance [i e ɛ a] is perceived by an adult as [high higher-mid lower-mid low] on her perceptual relative [vowel height] tier, and it is perceived by a young child as [250Hz 400Hz 600Hz 850Hz] on her perceptual absolute F_1 tier. In their reproductions of this utterance, both the adult and the child may be absolutely faithful in their own terms. The adult/child difference seems to reflect the usual order of the acquisition of entities versus relations in cognitive development.

The same reasoning may apply to the imitation of adult [θɪk]: the child may perceive her candidate [fɪk] as closer to the original than her candidate [θɪk] because of its somewhat lower spectral content. We thus expect chains like [ɔ] → [o] → [u] and [s] → [θ] → [f], and the child's productions must be considered as more or less equal to her underlying forms (= perceptual targets).

13.2.17 *Puzzles*

Another apparent chain shift is Amahl's (Smith 1973: 55, 149) rendering of 'puzzle' as [pʌdl] and 'puddle' as [pʌgl]. Smith's derivational phonology has to take recourse to the *counterfeeding* ordering of the rules d → g / _l and z → d / _l. Likewise, a naive OT account would have that if [dl] is the optimal candidate for /zl/, it would also be the optimal candidate for /dl/. However, there is a partly universal ranking of functional constraints that produces the attested facts:

(39) Puzzles and puddles

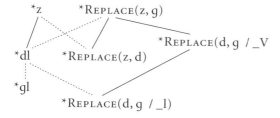

We can consider the ranking of *z above *dl as near-universal, because [z] requires a precise (controlled) movement of the articulator, which is not needed in the ballistic thrust of [d] (Hardcastle 1976). Of course, this is the reason

Amahl (and most children) pronounced *all* |z| as [d]. The ranking of *REPLACE (z, g) above the other faithfulness constraints is also universal, because the perceptual distance between /z/ and /g/ (different place and manner) is larger than that between /z/ and /d/ (same place) or between /d/ and /g/ (same manner); this corresponds to a property of Gnanadesikan's (1997) *ternary scales* (which are a first cautious step in the ultimately inevitable generalization from binary hybrid features to multi-valued perceptual features). As noted by McCarthy (1998), this type of chain shift is one of the few examples of opaque rule ordering that a monostratal OT grammar can handle. The constraint *REPLACE (d, g/_l) is very low, because the perceptual distance between /dl/ and /gl/ is very small (Kawasaki 1982). Most rankings in (39) are, therefore, expected to occur during the acquisition of any language. The ranking of *dl above *gl could be due to the asymmetric motor learning of the gestures associated with the abundant initial |gl| and the absent initial |dl| in English. The remaining crucial property of (39) is the high ranking of *REPLACE (z, g), even before [l]. The functional correlate of this high ranking is the strength of the coronal place cue in [zl]: the continuancy and sibilance of /z/ ensure a good acoustic reflex of coronality, quite differently from that of /d/, which almost vanishes before [l].

Chain shifts are often associated with the idea of contrast preservation. As far as Amahl is concerned, Kiparsky and Menn (1977: 69) hold that he 'displaced the contrast'. However, when Amahl started to pronounce |z| as [d], his 'puzzle' surfaced with an adult-like fricative, but he kept on merging |dl| with |gl|. Also, he always seemed more interested in faithful production than in contrast preservation: at first, he pronounced |s| as /t/ (faithful place), and later as /l/ (faithful place and continuancy). More likely, Amahl's [dl] for |zl| is an instance of his general [d] for [z], and his [gl] for |dl| is a result of his perception of the adult [dl] as a laterally-released stop. Smith's (1973: 150) assertion that 'this clearly is false' since the child distinguished adult [dl] and [gl], is only valid for those who believe in universal underlying feature values. English |dl| sequences are very limited in distribution, and it is no surprise that a child should perceive them primarily as 'laterally released stops' [dˠ‿l], with a secondary place cue (the transition from the previous vowel) that distinguishes them from [gˠ‿l], giving the ranking *DELETE (lateral release) >> *REPLACE (place: coronal, dorsal/ unreleased). Thus, the relevant part of (39) will look like this:

(40) Puddles

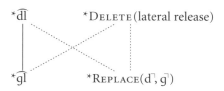

13.3 Example: The Acquisition of Tongue-Root Harmony

The example of the previous section involved the learning of the implementation of a single feature value (e.g. sibilant noise) by a possibly complex combination of gestures (e.g. a grooved tongue-tip held at a critical position near the dental alveoli, combined with sufficient lung pressure, a closed velum, and an open glottis). In this section, I will show how the local-ranking principle helps in learning the ranking of continuous constraint families.

The example of this chapter will be the acquisition of a tongue-root-harmony system. The largest vowel space for tongue-root-harmony languages that we will consider (Archangeli and Pulleyblank 1994; Pulleyblank 1993; Pulleyblank 1996; Pulleyblank, Ping, Leitch, and Ọla 1995), is a product of the dimensions of vowel height (low, mid, high), place (front, back), and tongue-root position (advanced = ATR, retracted = RTR):

(41)

	front		central		back	
	ATR	RTR			RTR	ATR
high	i					u
		ɪ		ʊ		
mid	e					o
		ɛ		ɔ		
low			ə ATR			
			a RTR			

In order to find out what articulatory constraints are involved in the production of these sounds, we will have a look at the gestural and acoustic correlates of the height and tongue-root features.

Phonetically, a specified vowel height (F_1) can be implemented with the help of an oral tongue-body constriction and a mid-pharyngeal width adjustment. Abstracting away from the effects of lip-spreading, tongue-body position, and damping, a specified F_1 must be implemented by adjusting the *quotient* of the cross-sectional area of the oral tongue-body constriction and the area at the mid pharynx: increasing these two areas by the same factor will roughly leave the F_1 unchanged, because the relative deviations of the resonance frequencies of a tract from those of a straight tube with the same length depend, in first approximation, only on the relative areas of the various regions, not on their absolute areas (Fant 1960: 23–67; Flanagan 1972: 69–72). Table (42), therefore, shows an idealized account of the gestures that implement four F_1 values.

From this table, we see that the ternary 'height' feature in (41) corresponds to the degree of oral constriction, and that the 'TR' feature corresponds to the width of the pharynx. For instance, [e] has the same F_1-based height as [ɪ] (400 Hz), but it has the same constriction-based height as [ɛ] (2 cm²).

Many tongue-root harmony languages lack the advanced low vowel /ə/, or the retracted high vowels /ɪ/ and /ʊ/, or both of these sets. Archangeli and Pulley-

(42)

1-dim height	F_1	A_{phar}/A_{oral}	retracted implementation			advanced implementation		
			A_{phar}	A_{oral}	sound	A_{phar}	A_{oral}	sound
high	250 Hz	20				10	0.5	[i]
higher-mid	400 Hz	4	2	0.5	[ɪ]	8	2	[e]
lower-mid	600 Hz	0.6	1.2	2	[ɛ]	4.8	8	[ə]
low	850 Hz	0.1	0.8	8	[a]			

(A_{phar} and A_{oral} measured in cm²)

blank (1994) ascribe these asymmetries to the following phonetically motivated *grounding conditions* on possible *paths* (simultaneous pairs of feature values):

1   Lo/Rtr: 'If a vowel is low, it has a retracted tongue root'
2   Hi/Atr: 'If a vowel is high, it has an advanced tongue root'

In later work, Pulleyblank (1993, 1996) translates these grounding conditions directly into OT-able constraints with the same names. From the viewpoint of functional phonology, however, these constraints must be regarded as surface constraints: they adequately describe a tendency that occurs in the data, but their functional explanation may involve articulatory as well as perceptual arguments. The difference between such constraints and constraints directly derivable from functional principles may be subtle, but will be seen to have empirical consequences under a strict-ranking regime (Section 13.3.3).

13.3.1 *Universal Ranking of Articulatory Constraints*

From the functional point of view, the grounding constraints (43) could be articulatory constraints against the performance of tongue-root gestures, say *Gesture (pharynx: width / body: position)*. These constraints have some universal rankings: it is easier to achieve a specified large pharynx width if the

(44) Local ATR effort

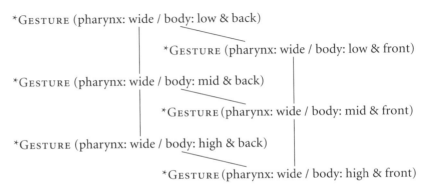

tongue body is pulled up or to the front than if the tongue body is pulled down or backwards. These fixed rankings are shown with solid lines in Figure (44).

The universality of the rankings in this figure is subject to the local-ranking principle, which maintains that only pairs of minimally different (i.e. adjacent) constraints can ever be ranked in a universal manner, and that all other pairs (like the high-back versus mid-front pair) can be ranked freely in a language-specific way. Analogously to (44), the constraints against a narrowing of the pharynx are ranked as

(45)   Local ATR effort

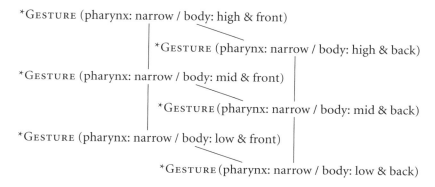

If we assume, as a rather crude idealization, that the perceptual effects of tongue-root movement are a function of the realized pharynx width only (disregarding the interaction with the perceptual results of higher articulations), and that the perceptual feature values [front], [back], [high], [mid], and [low] correspond with horizontal and vertical tongue-body positions, we can write the articulatory constraint families (44) and (45) as implementation constraints for certain perceptual feature values. Respecting the local-ranking principle, we get Figure (46).

(46)   Local tongue-root implementation effort

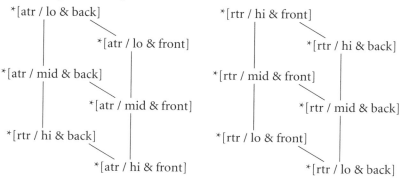

Note that all features in this picture are *perceptual* features, as opposed to those in (44) and (45), which are articulatory gestures. The equivalence between the two representations is a coincidence (and an idealization).

The local-ranking principle tells us that the [atr] hierarchy in (46) is not connected to the [rtr] hierarchy because [atr] and [rtr] must be implemented by different muscle groups, if we assume that [atr] represents a tongue position forward from the neutral position and that [rtr] represents a backward tongue movement.

13.3.2 *Universal Ranking of Faithfulness Constraints*

The partial universal grammar (46) contains an idealization of *perceptual invariance*: it shows how difficult it is to implement articulatorily the given perceptual feature values [atr] and [rtr]. Real languages will also show effects of *articulatory invariance*: for the implementation of a given perceptual feature, the amount of effort considered worth spending will tend not to diverge much for the various possible environments. Thus, the feature value [atr], if implemented with the same genioglossus activity, will surface perceptually much more clearly for high front vowels than for low back vowels. For [rtr], the situation is the reverse: tongue-root retraction will be most clearly audible for high vowels.

If the relationship between the distance from the neutral position and the required articulatory effort is superlinear (e.g., $0.5^2 + 1.5^2$ for high and low vowels versus $1^2 + 1^2$ for mid vowels), this means that with invariance of articulatory effort, the perceptual contrast between the two tongue-root values will be largest for mid vowels, and smaller for high and low vowels. This can be translated into the following somewhat tentative fixed ranking of faithfulness constraints:

(47)   Local tongue-root contrast

Real languages will trade some, but not all, perceptual invariance for articulatory invariance, so that they will combine (47) with a shrunk version of (46).

13.3.3 *Typology of Tongue-Root Systems*

A combinatorial typology of possible tongue-root systems results from combining (46) and (47), subject to the local-ranking principle, which fixes the rankings that are represented with solid lines in these figures. Ignoring the back vowels, I will show two of the possible grammars. The system of Wolof (Pulleyblank 1996; Archangeli and Pulleyblank 1994: 225–39), which disallows the high RTR vowels /ɪ/ and /ʊ/ while the high ATR vowels are transparent to tongue-root harmony, and which does allow the low ATR vowel /ə/, will look like this (not yet distinguishing ATR and RTR faithfulness):

(48)   Wolof inventory

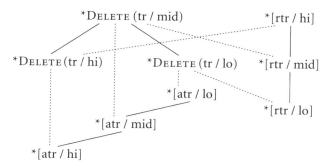

The fixed rankings are drawn with solid lines, and the crucial Wolof-specific rankings with dotted lines. Most tongue-root-sensitive systems are defined by the ranking of *DELETE (tr / mid) above *[atr / mid] and *[rtr / mid]—i.e. by the occurrence of an [e]–[ε] contrast.

A topology equivalent to (48) allows the generalization of some constraints, with a homogeneous *DELETE (tr):

(49)   Wolof inventory (equal contrast)

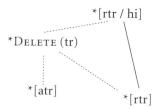

This grammar minimizes the number of constraints. Figure (49) also shows the technical possibility of an 'elsewhere' formulation of *[rtr], licensed by its ranking below a more specific constraint.

Now we see the difference between positing phonetically motivated grounding constraints and the functional approach: though the constraint *[rtr / hi] (or HI / ATR) comes out on top, the constraint *[rtr / mid], which is universal in the sense that every language with a retracted mid vowel has to deal with it, 'causes' other languages to have no tongue-root contrasts for mid vowels. The only restriction that the fixed ranking of these two constraints places upon possible grammars, is the fact that if a language licenses RTR in high vowels it also licenses RTR in mid vowels.

An empirically slightly different formulation of (48), with a reversal of the

*DELETE (tr / hi) and *[atr / hi] constraints, would generalize all articulatory constraints:

(50)   Wolof inventory (equal effort)

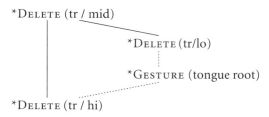

This expresses the idea that if there is no tongue-root contrast for high vowels, the speaker will not bother to make either the advancing or the retracting gesture. In other words, if *DELETE (tr / hi) is ranked below *[rtr / hi], there is no tongue-root contrast for high vowels, and the contrast-dependency of the ranking of faithfulness will cause *DELETE (tr / hi) to fall even further, right to the bottom of the constraint-ranking continuum; specifically, below *GESTURE (tongue root: advance / high).

Other tongue-root systems vary as far as the freely rankable pairs are concerned, but keep the locally rankable pairs fixed. For instance, a pre-lexical stratum of Akan (Archangeli and Pulleyblank 1994: 212–25), which has no lexical tongue-root contrast for low vowels, can be analysed as

(51)   Akan inventory

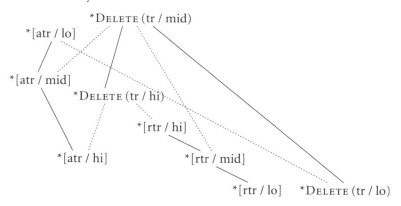

though constraint generalizations will result in something analogous to (49). The ranking of *[rtr / lo] versus *DELETE (tr / lo) is depicted as ambiguous in order to allow both possible interpretations of Akan-like systems: if *[rtr / lo] is the higher of the two, the *GESTURE constraints can be regarded as homogeneous, and /a/ must be considered as having no articulatory specification for tongue-root movement; if *DELETE (tr / lo) is higher, the *DELETE constraints can be regarded as homogeneous, and /a/ contains [rtr]. An empirical difference between these two systems could be found in the spreading of the retracted-tongue-root gesture from /a/, which should be possible only in the latter case, under the assumption that only articulatory gestures can spread but perceptual feature values cannot.

From a combinatorial typology of tongue-root systems, we can derive two implicational universals, which are assumed by Pulleyblank and Turkel (1995, 1996):

1 If a tongue-root language with three vowel heights has [ɪ], it also has [ɛ] and [a].
2 If a tongue-root language with three vowel heights has [ə], it also has [e] and [i].

According to the local-ranking principle, these universals are independent from each other—i.e. the probability of a language having [ɪ] does not depend on whether it has [ə].

13.3.4 *The Learning Process for Continuous Families*

As I argued above, all learners start from the same empty grammar. As speakers, they start out with undominated *GESTURE constraints because no articulatory speech gestures and coordinations have yet been learned. As listeners, they start out with undominated *CATEG constraints because no perceptual categorizations have yet been established. As far as categorization is concerned, we can assume that every learner of a tongue-root language that includes /i/, /e/, /ɛ/, and /a/, learns to categorize the perceptual correlate of the constriction-based vowel-height dimension (perhaps with the help of the presence of harmony) into three classes (low, mid, and high) because these occur in the acoustic input; and that she learns to categorize the perceptual tongue-root dimension in two classes (ATR and RTR), because both of these values occur in the listener's input.

Initially, therefore, the learner is not capable of making either the tongue-root-advancing or the tongue-root-retracting gesture: they will still have to be learned.

For the learning process, therefore, we must consider a binary perceptual feature, with values [atr] and [rtr], and a ternary production feature: the advancing gesture, the retraction gesture, or no tongue-root gesture at all. If a vowel is pronounced without a tongue-root gesture (which I will denote with a diaeresis diacritic), it must still be perceived as either [atr] or [rtr], with probabilities like those in the following table:

(53)

↓ produced perceived →	atr	rtr
[ä]	0.1	0.9
[ë]	0.4	0.6
[ï]	0.8	0.2

The fact that none of these probabilities is zero will guarantee that the learner will at some time perceive some utterances without tongue-root gestures as unfaithful (cf. Section 13.2.9).

Initially, none of the constraints in (44) and (45) is dominated by a faithfulness constraint. This gives one of the typologically possible systems: one without any tongue-root contrasts.

The local-ranking principle asserts that *[atr / lo] is always ranked above *[atr / mid], so that if motor learning causes the demotion of *[atr / lo], the universally lower constraint *[atr / mid] (and the infinite number of constraints in between along the height dimension) will be pushed along down the hierarchy:

(54)

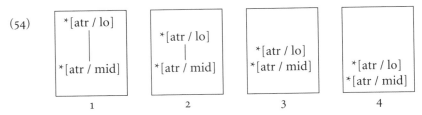

13.3.5 *The Learning of Simplified Wolof*

As an example, we will look at a language that is unlearnable with the greedy and conservative error-driven learning algorithm by Gibson and Wexler (1994). This is a simplified version of Wolof, as used by Pulleyblank and Turkel (1995, 1996) in a three-parameter account of the typology of tongue-root harmony. Boersma, Dekkers, and van de Weijer (this volume) show that parameter-setting learners of this language ('B') can end up in an absorbant cycle of two hypotheses, both of which cannot account for the perfect Wolof sequence /ɛti/. By contrast, constraint-sorting algorithms, including the gradual algorithm advocated in this chapter, always end up in a hypothesis that accounts for /ɛti/.

We will thus follow the stages in the acquisition of a minimal Wolof-like language, all utterances in which are V_1tV_2 sequences, where V_1 and V_2 are chosen from the set of six non-round vowels {a, ə, ɛ, e, ɪ, i}. Wolof honours the Hɪ/Aᴛʀ grounding condition, so that /ɪ/ does not occur on the surface, but it does not honour Lo/Rᴛʀ, so that /ə/ *is* a licit segment. Thus, possible VtV surface forms include the 13 harmonic utterances /iti/, /eti/, /ite/, /ita/, /əti/, /ete/, /ɛtɛ/, /etə/, /əte/, /ɛta/, /atɛ/, /ətə/, and /ata/, and do not include any of the 11 thinkable utterances with at least one /ɪ/.

For the remaining 12 VtV words, we have to examine the fact that Wolof shows tongue-root *harmony*, i.e. there is a structural constraint, say *[TR contour], which disallows an ATR and an RTR vowel to occur together in a word, and this constraint must outrank at least one faithfulness constraint. I will follow Pulleyblank and Turkel (1995, 1996) in their choice of faithfulness constraints (though with a perceptual interpretation), suppressing the dependence of *Dᴇ-ʟᴇᴛᴇ on vowel height but letting it depend on the value of the tongue-root feature; thus, the constraints are *DELETE (atr) (which for binary categorization is the same as *REPLACE (tongue root: advanced, retracted)), and *DELETE (rtr). If the dominated constraint is *DELETE (rtr), then the harmony constraint will force an underlying |ete| to become [ete]. However, Pulleyblank and Turkel state that Wolof is RTR-dominant, which means that *DELETE (rtr) >> *DELETE(atr), so that *DELETE(atr) must be the dominated constraint and |ete| will surface as [ɛtɛ]. In either case, the eight disharmonic surface forms /ate/, /eta/, /əte/, /ɛta/, /ete/, /etɛ/, /ata/, and /əta/ will never occur.

However, Archangeli and Pulleyblank (1994) report no underlying disharmonic forms for actual Wolof, so RTR dominance must be assessed in a different way. Wolof allows the surface forms /ɛti/ and /ati/, which can be explained by the ranking *[rtr / hi] >> *DELETE(rtr) >> *[TR contour] >> *DELETE(atr): for underlying |ɛti|, the candidate [ɛtɪ] would violate *[rtr / hi], and /eti/ would violate *DELETE(rtr). Thus, because RTR faithfulness dominates harmony, our simplified Wolof allows /ɛti/, /ite/, /ati/, and /ita/ (for real Wolof, see Section 13.3.9). This concludes our description of the adult forms.

13.3.5.1 Stage 1

The initial state is the same for all languages, see figure (8). I assume that in the initial state of the acquisition of tongue-root contrasts, three abstract (constriction-based) vowel heights have already been learned. If the perceptual distances *within* the tongue-root pairs {e, ɛ} and {ə, a} are smaller than the distances *between* the pairs, this may simply result from similarity-based categorization. In Stage 1 of the acquisition of a tongue-root inventory, the three possible non-back vowels are pronounced as [ä ë ï] (using the umlaut diacritic to denote tongue-root neutrality), and even the adult vowels are perceived as the equally undifferentiated set /ä ë ï/.

13.3.5.2 Step 1

In a language environment that makes extensive use of the tongue-root contrast, the learner will acquire a perceptual dimension not exploited in other languages: the perceptual [tr] feature. The chances that a separation of the two spectrum-based perceptual tiers for [height] and [tr] will occur increases as the number of vowel qualities grows. The minimal categorization along the [tr] dimension is binary, and that is probably also the maximal one, lest confusion probabilities should get out of hand.

13.3.5.3 Stage 2

We may conjecture that the binary tongue-root contrast is perceptually less salient than a ternary height contrast or a binary place (front unrounded/back rounded) contrast (on the average; the local-ranking principle allows variation here). The categorization step may well therefore have led to a ranking like (55) This ranking will be similar for many tongue-root languages. The learner now perceives the adult set /a ə ε e i/, but still produces only the no-tongue-root vowels [ä ë ï].

(55)   Tongue-root language, Stage 2

*REPLACE (height)   *REPLACE (place)

*REPLACE (tongue root)

13.3.5.4 Step 2

Sensorimotor learning will push the necessary gestural constraints into the grammar from above. They will include the familiar *[atr] and *[rtr] constraints, plus, crucially for a tongue-root harmony language, constraints against tongue-root gestures within an utterance or within a word: things like *GESTURE (tongue root: from advanced to retracted). I will collapse the various harmony constraints simply under the name of *[TR contour].

Also, the first Wolof-specific phenomenon will emerge: the language does not allow [ɪ], so that the learner will not practise the tongue-root retraction gesture for high vowels, and the constraint *[rtr / hi] will be undominated and can be left out of the grammar. One might think that when the 'rich base' comes with an input that contains /ɪ/, we need *[rtr / hi] to keep it from surfacing.

(56)   Universality versus innateness 2: richness of the base
        Richness of the base is a concept useful for typological study, and can predict the behaviour of humans when they borrow words from another language, but cannot be proved to be psychologically real.

This is somewhat harsh on the constraint *[rtr / hi] because that is just a member of the *[rtr] family. To show the difference with linguistically relevant but invisible constraints and those irrelevant constraints that are left out of the pictures by reason of space (like *[front] or *DELETE(front)), I shall include constraints like *[rtr / hi] in my figures, but they will be clinging to the ceiling or to the floor, as in (57).

13.3.5.5 Stage 3

Disregarding the height and place features, the constraints will be

(57)   Wolof, Stage 3

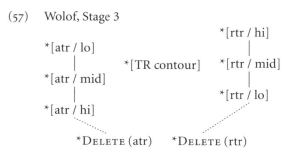

This figure shows the local rankings as solid lines and the crucial rankings as dotted lines; the constraint *[rtr / hi] hangs (ehh . . . hung) from the ceiling, since it is not a real part of the learner's inventory of constraints.

The output of grammar (57) will always be an utterance without any tongue-root gestures, surfacing only with the vowels [ä], [ë], and [ï] (which will be perceived according to Table 53). The harmony constraint *[TR contour] is, therefore, automatically satisfied, so it is not yet crucially ranked with respect to any of the other constraints. As far as production is concerned, the articulatory tongue-root feature must at least be ternary; adult speakers, however, will never use the null gesture because that would cause a large probability of confusion, according to table (53).

In *imitation*, the *DELETE constraints are raised, and a lot of performances are possible, depending on the accidental relative heights of the gestural constraints. We can get an example by putting the *DELETE constraints on a horizontal line in (57) just above *[atr / mid]. The result is

(58)   Wolof, Stage-3 imitation

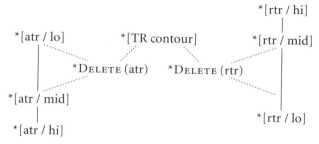

In this example, a model [e] will be pronounced faithfully, because *DELETE (atr) dominates *[atr / mid]. At the same time, a model [ɛ] will be imitated as [ë] because *[rtr / mid] still outranks *DELETE (rtr), resulting in a faithful /ɛ/ perception only 60% of the time, according to table (53), and in an unfaithful /e/ 40% of the time; of course, this is still better than producing an [e] outright:

(59) [ɛ]	/ɛ/=|ɛ|	*[rtr / mid]	*DELETE (tr)	*[atr / mid]
	[ɛ] /ɛ/	*!		
☞ [ë]	60% /ɛ/			
	40% /e/		40% *	
	[e] /e/		*	*!

Because of the high anti-contour constraint, the Wolof utterance /ita/ would be rendered with vowel harmony:

(60) [ita] /ita/ = |ita|	*[rtr / hi]	*[TR contour]	*Delete (tr)
[ita] /ita/		*!	
☞ [itə] /itə/			*
[ɪta] /ɪta/	*!		*

13.3.5.6 Step 3

On hearing /ə/, the Wolof learner will have to demote *[atr / lo] and raise *Delete (atr); because of local ranking, the constraint *[atr / mid] will be pushed
along, causing the advanced pronunciation of the sound [e] suddenly to become
licensed in the learner's grammar, without her needing any [e] data. For the
demotion of the two *[rtr] constraints, the learner will need some [ɛ] data, and
if these are presented to the learner, she will acquire the correct tongue-root
gesture for [a] automatically. Finally, because Wolof allows the harmony violations /ɛti/ and /ati/, the anti-contour constraint has to be demoted below the
*Delete constraints. During the course of all these rerankings, the learner may
go through a lot of different grammars, of which a grammar topologically equivalent to (58) is just one example.

Of all the possible articulatory tongue-root contrasts with neutral gestures,
only [e ë] and [ɛ ë] come close to implementing a perceptual contrast (according
to (53)). Because of local ranking, *[atr / mid] will always pass the *Delete
constraints before *[atr / lo] does, so that if the learner produces a faithful
tongue-root contrast for low vowels, she will always be able to make some sort
of contrast for mid vowels as well. Thus, the implicational universals (52) are
satisfied at any moment during acquisition, and adult markedness relations reflect acquisition order.

13.3.5.7 Stage 4

The acquisition of the gestures comes to an end when all relevant constraints
have fallen below the *Delete constraints, which have risen:

(61)   Wolof, Stage 4

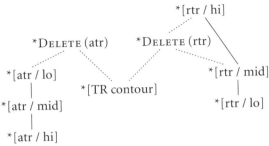

The segment inventory has been learned correctly in this grammar of depth-2

(i.e. with at most two cascaded non-universal crucial rankings, denoted by the dotted lines). The two possible tongue-root contours, however, have been generalized, so that the learner would now allow in her grammar (= be able to pronounce) [ɛte], [ate], [atə], and [ɛtə]. To get rid of these, she needs evidence for the violability of a *DELETE constraint.

13.3.5.8 Step 5

Once the learner reconstructs by morphological analysis that a certain form is underlyingly |at+e| (this is no longer real Wolof), she will pronounce this faithfully as [ate], according to (61). However, when hearing that an adult actually pronounces this as /atɛ/, the learner is confronted with an output mismatch. She now has the negative evidence needed to rule out [ate]:

(62) [atɛ] /atɛ/ |at+e|	*DELETE(rtr)	*DELETE(atr)	*[TR contour]
☞ [ate] /ate/			←*
[ətе] /ətе/	*!		
✔ [atɛ] /atɛ/		*!→	

The learner discovers that it is not at all very important to pronounce an underlying |e| faithfully, or that the harmony is more important than she had in mind. She will therefore demote *DELETE(atr), and promote *[TR contour]. The constraint *DELETE(rtr) will stay where it is: apparently, this is an RTR-dominant language (the [rtr] specification of |a| dominates the [atr] specification of |e|). Note that the learner does not need to know that this has anything to do with RTR dominance, nor with the interaction with a harmony constraint: it occurs automatically, and no innate parameters are needed. After some of these data, *DELETE (atr) will fall down past *[TR contour]; if *[TR contour] happens to rise above *DELETE (rtr) as a result of this procedure, disharmonic data like /ati/ will push *[TR contour] down and raise *DELETE (rtr). Eventually, a stable ranking *DELETE (rtr) >> *[TR contour] >> *DELETE (atr) will emerge.

While *DELETE (atr) is falling, it may come near *[atr / low]. In this case, the learner will probably experience some mismatches when comparing her output with adult /ə/ data, and she will demote the *[atr] family, with the idea of keeping [ə] pronounceable. When *DELETE (atr) finally drops below the anti-contour constraint, the situation is likely to be as in (63).

This is the correct grammar of our simplified 'Wolof'. It is four crucial rankings deep: along the dotted path we see the grounding condition for high vowels (the top constraint), tongue-root harmony (the contour constraint dominating at least one faithfulness constraint), RTR dominance (the contour constraint sandwiched between two *DELETE constraints), and the availability of schwa (the domination of *[atr / lo]).

It is possible that the demotion of *DELETE (atr) below the harmony constraint actually precedes the demotion of *[atr / low]. In that case, [ə] would temporarily become unpronounced (not unpronounceable) in some cases (see Section 13.3.7), but the output mismatches that result from it will eventually draw the *[atr] family to the bottom of the relevant hierarchy. In all thinkable cases, grammar (63) will result.

(63)   Simplified Wolof, Stage 6

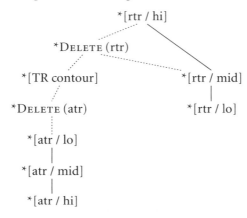

13.3.6 *An Alternative Wolof: Articulatory Versus Perceptual Candidates*

Most OT work is performed within the generative tradition of hybrid phonological features. So let us try to restrict GEN to a binary tongue-root constraint, analogous to our perceptual feature, instead of to a ternary (in reality: continu-

(64)   Simplified Wolof, binary GEN

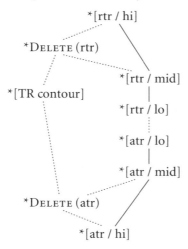

ous) gestural constraint. Wolof can then be described with an alternative grammar (see Figure 64). But this is the wrong grammar: [ə] surfaces not because *DELETE(atr) outranks *[atr / lo], but because *[rtr / lo] outranks *[atr / lo]. From the functional standpoint, this is outrageous: while not *perceiving* a feature as [atr] may mean that you perceive it as [rtr] (because of the binary categorization), not *producing* a gesture never means that you have to make the opposite gesture: a prohibition on a gesture can never force another gesture; only *DELETE constraints can do that (from the generative standpoint with its hybrid features, there would be no problem, because there would be no *[rtr / lo] constraint). Instead of a forced choice between two gestures, there should always be the possibility of no gestures at all; if articulatory constraints are unviolated, the result should be *no gesture*, not the default gesture.

13.3.7 *Wolof with Schwa Licensing*

One of the possible grammars that are one step removed of converging onto simplified Wolof, has a depth of five:

(65)   Simplified Wolof with schwa licensing

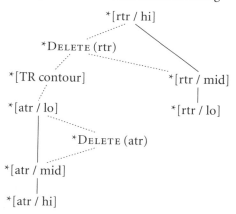

This is a peculiar language indeed: it disallows an isolated *[ə], and it disallows *[ətə]. An underlying |ətə| will surface as [ata] because the grounding condition *[atr / lo] dominates *DELETE (atr). However, the other schwa words [əte] and [əti] are allowed, because *[TR contour] dominates *[atr / lo]. In other words, the ATR gesture of [e] and [i] licenses ATR in a low vowel. Note that this [ə] is not just a positional variant of |a|: underlying |ati| still surfaces faithfully because *DELETE (rtr) dominates the harmony constraint (and *[atɪ] is out because of *[rtr / hi]). Thus, |ə| is fully contrastive, though it requires an adjacent non-low ATR vowel to survive.

This example involves five crucial rankings in cascade. The free ranking allowed by the local-ranking principle (as well as the standard account with grounding constraints) would predict that this is a possible language.

13.3.8 *Learning Unnatural Local Rankings*

The learning of certain combinations of gestures often involves the demotion of the relevant gestural constraints below 'universally' easier gestures.

For instance, speakers of Dutch are used to implementing the /b/–/p/ contrast in such a way that both plosives require active gestures to make them voiced or voiceless; these same speakers have trouble pronouncing the English or German lenis voiceless plosive [b̥], though that sound would be easier than either Dutch plosive because it requires no active voicing or devoicing gesture. Likewise, speakers of tongue-root languages may learn to have trouble *not* performing any tongue-root gestures in vowels.

As a more dramatic example, consider the cross-linguistically abundant /i/–/u/ contrast. Most speakers of a language with exactly these two high vowels will have trouble pronouncing the unrounded high back vowel [ɯ], though that sound should be universally easier than [u] because it does not involve a lip gesture. The reason that /i/ is a spread front vowel and /u/ is a rounded back vowel, is that the perceptual contrast of 'front' (high F_2) versus 'back' (low F_2) is best implemented by varying the lip shape as well as the tongue-body position. It is highly unlikely that articulatory ease is involved in rounding back vowels: first, rounding the lips costs energy; second, there is no innate anatomical or functional relationship between rounding and backing; third, the prevalence of unrounded velar obstruents proves that even in speech the relation is not automatic.

Requirements of faithful voicing or F_2 contrasts thus lead to learning complex coordinative gestures, and the single gestures are unlearned. This is a normal procedure in human motor behaviour; one of its advantages is the reduction of cognitive load—i.e. the number of high-level neural commands. Still, we may suspect that in the early stages of acquisition the single gestures are still easier for the child than the complex gestures. Thus, the first plosive that the Dutch (or any other) child will learn, before trying to implement or even recognize the voicing contrast, is one without any active voicing or devoicing gestures: typically, a lax voiceless stop. Likewise, we would expect Turkish children, if they recognize a four-way contrast in the high vowels, to have less trouble with the pronunciation of [ɯ] than with [u].

There are also things that seem to go against the local-ranking principle. Adult speakers of Proto-Indo-European may have had trouble pronouncing [b] even though they had [d] and [g] (and [p]), and [b] is allegedly easier to voice. However, all Indo-European languages hurried to fill up the original gap at /b/, suggesting that learners may have considered it to be an accidental gap in their lexicon, not in their grammar. This suggests that the local-ranking principle may be valid into adulthood.

13.3.9 *Real Wolof*

The simplified Wolof described above was chosen for its known problems with parameter-setting learning algorithms. It differs from real Wolof (Archangeli and Pulleyblank 1994: 225–39) in a number of respects. I will now show that the differences do not require us to pull into question our functionalist approach.

First, Wolof has long and short vowels, and /ə/ is allowed only as a short vowel. The constraint *[atr / lo] must therefore split, so that *[atr / long low] is unviolated. Whether the acquisition process involves constraint splitting (of *[atr / lo]) or constraint generalization (of e.g. *[atr / long mid] and *[atr / short mid]), or both, is a question that has no bearing on the nativist/environmentalist issue, since any OT account of Wolof will have to introduce a diacritic here; for instance, Pulleyblank (1996) summarizes the /ə/ facts with the ranking Lo/Atr$_{\mu\mu}$ >> Lo/Atr, where μ denotes a timing unit (the mora).

Secondly, Wolof tongue-root harmony is directional: it works only from left to right. Consider the form /doːraːtɛ/ 'to hit usually'. The vowel in the medial syllable can never be /ɔː/, because of the high ranking of *[atr / long low]. Because the harmony constraint outranks *Delete (atr), the form would have to be */dɔːraːtɛ/, i.e. every word containing an underlying RTR specification or a long vowel, and no high vowels, would have to be entirely RTR. As it is, the initial ATR /doː/ is allowed, and only the final syllable /tɛ/ must share its retraction with the preceding /aː/. Pulleyblank (1996) accounts for this phenomenon with a constraint of which the simplest form could be written as Align (RTR, right; Word, right); e.g. the form */doːraːte/ would violate this constraint by one syllable, since the right edge of the RTR span /raː/ is one syllable away from the right edge of the word. Since alignment constraints are highly language-specific (they are often morphologically conditioned), their specific forms cannot be innate anyway, so they must be learned; perhaps they are created automatically for every pair of learned features and/or morphological constituents (as suggested by Mark Ellison).

Opacity effects, like the opacity of /aː/ for rightward spreading of ATR, are expected for articulatory harmony constraints: opacity reduces the number of contours. The third distinguishing property of real Wolof, however, is that it also shows a transparency effect: Wolof allows forms like /tɛkːilɛːn/ 'untie!', but not */tɛkːileːn/. Apparently, RTR spreads to the right through the high vowel, which is not allowed to become RTR itself because of the high ranking of *[rtr / hi]. Instead of reducing contours, this kind of harmony maximizes the number of vowels that carry RTR. Functionally, the RTR specification tries to express itself maximally, in order that it be heard optimally. We could call this constraint Maximum(RTR); Wolof thus seems to have articulatory harmony (opacity) as well as perceptual harmony (transparency). Pulleyblank (1996), however, uses the same alignment constraint as above, but alignment is not only to the Word, but also to the nearest RTR value. Thus, /tɛkːilɛːn/ violates it only once, because /tɛ/ is only one syllable away from the RTR sequence /lɛːn/, while */tɛk:ile:n/ violates it twice, because /tɛ/ is two syllables away from the right edge of the word. Note that the two approaches are empirically different: with MAXIMUM (RTR) you would not expect a non-underlying RTR value (i.e. one that is forced by a long low vowel) to spread through a high vowel (/do:ra:tɛbɔ:bule/); with Pulleyblank's ALIGN (RTR, rightWord, right), you would: /do:ra:tɛbɔ:bulɛ/. Of course, Pulleyblank's prediction for this hypothetical sequence will be correct.

The fourth difference is that the word-initial forms /itɛ/ and /ita/ (with short /a/) are not allowed in real Wolof. Apparently, an underlying RTR must always be realized on the first syllable; if this is impossible because of high-vowel grounding, RTR must be deleted. Pulleyblank (1996) accounts for this with a ranking like $\text{HI}/\text{ATR} \gg \text{ALIGN}(\text{RTR}_{\text{root}}, \text{left}; \text{Root}, \text{left}) \gg {}^*\text{DELETE}(\text{RTR})$—i.e. with an alignment constraint that refers to the underlyingness of its material.

Since constraint splitting, constraint merger, and alignment constraints are devices that must be learned regardless of whether structural and faithfulness constraints are learned or innate, the differences between real Wolof and our simplified Wolof do not constitute any threat to the hypothesis that all constraints can be learned. The least expensive starting-point, then, is that there are no innate phonological constraints.

13.4 Comparison with Other Learning Algorithms

The Maximal Gradual Learning Algorithm (MGLA) differs from other learning algorithms in a number of respects, nearly all of which seem to favour the choice of the MGLA as a realistic model of the language learner.

13.4.1 *Convergence*

The gradual learning algorithm described above is *error-driven* (response only to output mismatches), *incremental* (small changes at a time) and *greedy* (only changes that directly aim at improving the grammar). It shares these properties with the Triggering Learning Algorithm (TLA) of Gibson and Wexler (1994). The TLA, however, works within a Principles-and-Parameters (P&P) framework and is known not to converge in all cases; in the introduction to this book (Boersma, Dekkers and van de Weijer, this volume) we show that the TLA, when applied to a three-parameter problem of tongue-root harmony, has problems with *local maxima* due to *superset grammars* and other *sinks*, including *absorbing cycles*. By contrast, the MGLA leads to the learnability of any three-parameter tongue-root-harmony system.

13.4.2 *The Initial State*

In the initial state, all the gestural constraints should be on top. However, in a theory with hybrid binary features they are inherently conflicting: if it should honour the two grounding constraints, the underlying form /ita/ should surface as [ita]; but this form violates the harmony constraint, so the three universal constraints are in conflict. By contrast, the three gestural correlates *[atr], *[rtr], and *[TR contour] can be satisfied all at once: just make no active tongue-root gestures at all. Underlying /ita/ will surface as [ïtä], and be perceived according to (53). With the MGLA, all tongue-root-harmony languages with these constraints are learnable. In Stage 4, their grammars will look much like (61): zero, one, or two grounding constraints at the top, two *DELETE constraints at the first level, and the harmony constraint and the remaining gestural constraints at the second level.

13.4.3 Genetic Algorithms

Genetic algorithms (Clark and Roberts 1993; Turkel 1994; Pulleyblank and Turkel, this volume) improve on the convergence on P&P learning algorithms. Still, they do not guarantee convergence onto the global maximum, and they require the learner to maintain several grammar hypotheses at the same time. By contrast, the Maximal Gradual Learning Algorithm is guaranteed to converge, even with a single hypothesis.

13.4.4 Robustness

While the most obvious difference between the Triggering Learning Algorithm and our Gradual Learning Algorithm is convergence, another possible source of concern is the lack of robustness of the TLA: one erroneous input will change the setting of a parameter, and if we arrive in a superset language, we will not be able to get out.

13.4.5 Reliance on Underlying Forms

A fundamental problem with our MGLA seems the following. To arrive at the correct grammar, the learner will need to know underlying forms, at least in Step 6. This seems like a dirty trick. The MGLA has this in common with the OT learning algorithms of Tesar and Smolensky (1993, 1996) and Tesar (1995), which have been criticized for this reason by Turkel (1994) and Pulleyblank and Turkel (this volume). In learning Wolof, for instance, a learner can only reintroduce the workings of the harmony constraint if she encounters underlying forms like |at+e| that should surface as /atɛ/.

We could reverse the argument. The question is how a P&P learning process of Wolof would handle this. If a P&P learner is in a superset language, as Stage-4 Wolof (61) is as compared with adult simplified Wolof (63), how could she ever learn that the surface form [ate] is forbidden? The answer is that she cannot. In the MGLA, on the other hand, all learners of 'Wolof' arrive in this superset language, and if there are alternations of the form described, they *will* adopt the more restrictive hypothesis: any low ranking of faithfulness can only be learned if faithfulness is violated—i.e. if there are differences between underlying and surface forms.

13.4.6 *Optimality-Theoretic Learning*

The constraint-sorting algorithm by Tesar and Smolensky (1993, 1996) solves the convergence problem of P&P and genetic algorithms. Apparently, grammars are organized not around parameters, but around constraints.

In Tesar and Smolensky's original algorithms, the necessary losing candidate was randomly supplied by GEN. In later work, Tesar (1995) and Tesar and Smolensky (1996) propose that this loser is to be identified with the correct adult output form: Error-Driven Constraint Demotion (EDCD). An example of the workings of this algorithm is given in our footnote below tableau (35). EDCD is as simple as our algorithm, and it shows convergence, conservatism, and oblivion.

Some differences remain, though: EDCD is not very *robust* against errors: a single error may destroy the grammar in such a way that it can cost on the order of N^2 learning steps (N is the number of constraints) to climb out of the wrong grammar (though in practice, a typical number is N). In the Maximal GLA, the number is exactly 1: after taking an incorrect adult uterance at face value, the constraints are shifted by a little amount, so that the probability of an error increases somewhat; once such an error occurs, the same constraints are shifted back to their original positions. Finally, EDCD does not show the flexibility or realism of an algorithm based on a continuous scale (Section 13.2.9).

13.4.7 *The Initial State in an Optimality-Theoretic Grammar*

In Tesar and Smolensky's (1993) initial state, all constraints are born equal. But this raises some problems.

Consider Tesar and Smolensky's example of a language that only allows CV syllables. If an underlying form /CVCVC/ surfaces as [CVCV], this is a sign that NO-CODA is honoured. But presumably, some of those languages have no underlying codas in the lexicon. Still, according to the principle of 'richness of the base' (Prince and Smolensky 1993; Smolensky 1996), NO-CODA must be high-ranked in these languages, and some evidence for this is found in the adaptation of loanwords, which will either lose their codas or be supplied by an epenthetic vowel. But how should anyone be able to learn this ranking? The only evidence that the learner is confronted with is /CVCV/ → [CVCV]. In Tesar and Smolensky's algorithm, NO-CODA will still vacuously come out on top because it is not violated in any winner, and thus never demoted: the default position for a constraint in the hierarchy is at the top. Thus, invisible means undominated, just as with the gestural constraints described earlier.

But e.g. *DELETE (click) will come out on top, too, and still we would imagine that an underlying [!a] would surface as [ka] (i.e., a heard [!a] would be pronounced as [ka], even if the click were categorized as a click). Therefore, the default ranking for faithfulness constraints should *not* be at the top. To remedy this situation, Smolensky (1996) and Tesar and Smolensky (1996) propose that the initial state should have all structural constraints dominating all faithfulness constraints.

This, as we saw, is the generic solution to the subset problem, and is reminiscent of the *subset principle* (Berwick 1985; Wexler and Manzini 1987). But this solution had to be *posited*. By contrast, a functional division between constraints can derive it, as we have seen: the difficulty of an articulatory gesture decreases as it is practised, and the importance of a perceptual feature increases as it is practised. The real solution, therefore, is that constraints are learned, not innate.

13.4.8 *Innateness*

In Tesar and Smolensky's algorithm, it is crucial that No-Coda is a universally available constraint: even though (or because) the learner has never had to learn its ranking, she must know that it is at the top of the hierarchy, or it could not do its work in determining the surface shape of consonant-final loanwords. Therefore, No-Coda must be *innate*.

A functional theory of phonology can hardly accept the innateness, or even the existence, of a constraint like No-Coda: it must be an epiphenomenon of an interaction between gestural and faithfulness constraints. Besause the articulatory effort of an initial consonant cannot be very different from the effort of a final consonant, the asymmetry must lie in perceptual confusion. Some place cues, for instance, depend on transient effects like release bursts, so that the average contrast between initial consonants is greater than the average contrast between final consonants. Together with the fact that the place cues of intervocalic consonants are better than those of consonants adjacent to other consonants, this leads to a preference of CV over VC syllables. The relevant constraint ranking is therefore something like:

(66)   CV language

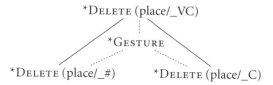

The empirical consequences of this ranking are different from those of the single No-Coda constraint. It predicts, for instance, that coda-avoiding languages tend to have simple onsets—i.e., that languages with an apparent high-ranked No-Coda also appear to have a high-ranked *ComplexOnset.

The grammar of (66) can be learned by the usual demotion of *Gesture from the top, given a local ranking of *Delete (place/_V) >> *Delete (place/_C). If this local ranking is valid, grammar (66) will have been arrived at in Stage 4, without the need for underlying forms with codas. Only if a learner accidentally manages to get *Gesture below all the *Delete constraints, will she need the evidence of Step 5 to learn that underlying codas do not appear in the output.

13.5 Algorithm

I will now show in pseudocode how you could simulate the handling of a single learning pair for the Maximal Gradual Learning Algorithm if you already have a classical tableau-oriented evaluation algorithm. For simplified tongue-root-harmony languages, for instance, you would only use the two grounding constraints, the two *DELETE constraints, and the harmony constraint.

We start with a hypothesized grammar *H*, consisting of an unordered constraint set $\{C_i\}$, $i = 1 \ldots N$. Every constraint is assumed to have a ranking value.

(a) Generate an adult utterance. You could draw it randomly from a vocabulary list, or compute it from a random input evaluated in the target grammar like:

adultInput := get_random_input   // from richness of the base, for instance
adultOutput := get_winner (*targetGrammar*, *adultInput*) // classical GEN, H-EVAL, etc.

(b) Compute the learner's underlying form for this utterance.

if *age* ≥ UNDERLYING_FORM_START_AGE
    learnerInput := *adultInput*
else
    learnerInput := *adultOutput*

Instead of just copying the adult output, the young learner could try robust interpretive parsing (Smolensky 1996a; Tesar and Smolensky 1996), or possibly an iterative version of it (Tesar 1995, 1996, this volume), modified, of course, to include stochastic evaluation.

(c) Compute the disharmonies for all constraints C_i:

for *i* from 1 to *N*   // *N* is the number of constraints
    C_i.disharmony := C_i.ranking +
    + RANKING_SPREADING * z
                            // z is a Gaussian random deviate, with $\mu = 0$ and $\sigma = 1$

(d) Sort the constraints by disharmony from high to low.

(e) Compute the learner's output with your favourite OT implementation:

learnerOutput := get_winner (*H*, *learnerInput*)

(f) Adjust the rankings of all non-cancelling constraints:

if *learnerOutput* ≠ *adultOutput* // error-driven
    for *i* from 1 to *N*
        adultMarks := number_of_marks (*H*, *adultOutput*, C_i)
        learnerMarks := number_of_marks (*H*, *learnerOutput*, C_i)
        if adultMarks > learnerMarks
            demote_constraint (C_i)
        else if learnerMarks > adultMarks
            promote_constraint (C_i)

The demotion procedure is recursive:

procedure demote_constraint (*C*)
    demotionStep := DAY_ONE_PLASTICITY
        * (1 + RELATIVE_PLASTICITY_SPREADING * z)   // z is Gaussian (0, 1)
        * (0.5 ** (*age*/PLASTICITY_HALF_TIME))
    C.ranking := *C*.ranking − *demotionStep*
    if *age* < LOCAL_RANKING_SUSPENSION_AGE
        for all C_i that are locally ranked below *C*
            while C_i.ranking $\geq$ *C*.ranking
                demote_constraint (C_i)

The promotion procedure is analogous to this, with '−', 'below', and '$\geq$' replaced by '+', 'above', and '$\leq$'.

(g) Sort the constraints by ranking value from high to low.

13.6 Proof of Correctness

I will now show that the Maximal Gradual Learning Algorithm can learn the class of stochastic OT grammars, which is a superclass of the class of stratified grammars, which again is a superclass of the totally crucially ranked grammars.

13.6.1 *Stochastic Grammars*

We will call two grammars *equivalent* if they give equal probabilities for all the thinkable outputs for any thinkable phonological input, and we will call acquisition *successful* as soon as the child's grammar is equivalent to that of the adult. I will show that the Maximal Gradual Learning Algorithm is guaranteed to make acquisition succeed.

Suppose that there are K candidates, each of which has a probability P_k^L ($k = 1 \ldots K$) of being chosen by the learner, and a probability of P_k^A of being chosen by the adult. Suppose that the grammar contains N constraints with rankings r_n ($n = 1 \ldots N$). As a result of the demotion of all the adult's violated constraints and the promotion of all the learner's violated constraints, the ranking of constraint n will increase upon the next learning pair by an amount Δr_n, whose expectation value is

$$(67) \quad \mathrm{E}[\Delta r_n] = p \times \sum_{k=1}^{K} (P_k^L - P_k^A) m_{kn}$$

where p is the plasticity constant, and m_{kn} is 1 if candidate k violates constraint n and 0 otherwise (for now, we consider only constraints that can be violated only once).

We can see that if a candidate occurs with greater probability in the speaker than in the adult, its violated constraints will rise on average, so that the probability of this candidate in the speaker will decrease. The expected ranking change thus seems to decrease the gap between the two grammars. We can see immediately that if the learner's grammar equals the adult's grammar—i.e. if P_k^L equals P_k^A for all k—the expected ranking change of every constraint n is zero—i.e. the expected change in the learner's grammar is zero. To prove learnability, however, we have to show the reverse—namely, the convergence of the learner's grammar upon the adult's grammar. An important part of the proof involves showing that the learner cannot end up in a grammar incompatible with the adult's. Suppose the learner does end up in such a *local maximum*, i.e. $E[\Delta r_n]$ is zero for every constraint n. We can write this situation in vector-matrix notation:

$$(68) \quad \mathbf{m}^T\,(\mathbf{P}^L - \mathbf{P}^A) = 0$$

Given a violation matrix $\mathbf{m}$, the learner can end up in any grammar that satisfies (68). As we know from linear algebra, however, the vector must be zero if the matrix $\mathbf{m}$ behaves well. In Boersma (1998: Section 15.A) I consider the three simplest cases of ill-behaved violation matrices and show that all of them still lead to probability matching (i.e. $\mathbf{P}^L - \mathbf{P}^A$), if the adult grammar is a stochastically evaluating OT grammar.

13.6.2 *Stratified Grammars*

A large difference between Tesar and Smolensky's algorithms and MGLA seems to be that the former learn a *totally ranked* grammar while the hypothesized grammars are *stratified* (have different constraints whose marks can cancel each other), so that during the acquisition process the learner does not yet possess a grammar of a possible language. The gradual algorithm, on the other hand, learns the larger group of *crucially-ranked* grammars, and the hypotheses do not contain crucial ties, so that every grammar hypothesized during the learning process represents a possible language.

13.6.3 *Subset Problems*

The criterion in Section 13.6.1 for assessing the success of the acquisition procedure allows the learner to arrive in a *superset* grammar—i.e. a grammar that allows not only all attested data but also some more. The child will, however, not produce these data during normal language behaviour, since she will take her own form, if deviant from the adult's, as negative evidence along the lines of the MGLA, thus drifting to a grammar that does not produce unattested data given the language's set of input forms. However, L2 acquisition behaviour points to the high ranking of those structural constraints that are never violated in L1 data. For instance, because native Japanese does not have heterorganic consonant clusters, foreign loanwords in Japanese will not have these clusters either, although a grammar that did allow them would be compatible with Japanese if the lexicon did not contain any such clusters.

For the case of learned perceptual categories and articulatory gestures, the solution to this problem is that unused categories and gestures will be *unlearned*: all faithfulness constraints will slowly drift down the grammar, and the gestural constraints will drift up. In order for the child to learn to match the performance of an adult, she will have to compensate this unlearning by reinforcement learning in the case of the categories and gestures that she uses a lot.

13.7 Acquisition Time

Suppose that all N constraints start out with the same ranking, and the target grammar is totally ranked. To reach its target ranking, the average constraint will have to travel up or down by a distance of $\frac{1}{4}N$ multiplied by the safety margin (the minimal stable distance between two adjacent crucially-ranked constraints), divided by the plasticity. For instance, if the plasticity is about 5 per cent of the ranking spreading, it will be about 1 per cent of the resulting safety margin. With N constraints, the minimum number of constraint rerankings is $\frac{1}{4}N \times N \times 100$.

During acquisition, however, the number of non-triggers increases. When all rerankings but one have been performed, only one constraint pair out of the total of $\frac{1}{2}N(N–1)$ pairs is out of rank, and the probability of finding it on the next learning pair may well be as small as 1 part in $\frac{1}{2}N(N–1)$ (from the schwa-licensing example of Section 13.3.7, we see that the last step of learning simplified Wolof may involve a probability of 1/17 of encountering the disambiguating /ətə/). The acquisition time, therefore, scales as the fourth power of N. For 100 constraints, the minimum number of required constraint evaluations is on the order of $10N^4 = 1,000,000,000$. Since constraints are often reranked in the wrong direction, the real number of constraint evaluations will be higher than the minimum by a factor that our simulations show to be consistently around 3. However, the average learning step will rerank three constraints, so the expected number of data needed to convergence upon a 100-constraint totally-ranked target grammar is about 10^9.

For a grammar of crucial rankings, the situation greatly improves. The acquisition time scales as the fourth power of the *depth*. If a grammar with 100 constraints has a depth of 5, the *width* of the grammar is approximately $N/(depth + 1) = 100/6$, and the expected number of required data before convergence is on the order of $width \times 10 \times (depth+1)^4 = 216,000$, a marked improvement over the total-ranking case.

If the demotion procedure honours the local-ranking principle, the effective depth of the grammar decreases. If it becomes 4 instead of 5, the number of required data is on the order of $216,000 \times (5/6)^4 \approx 104,000$ (the width is not changed). Thus, local ranking may reduce the acquisition time with a factor of 2 or so.

At 36 pieces of data a day, the required 104,000 data are provided in eight years; after one half of that time, the grammar will on average have been acquired up to a depth of 4, and the learner has the remaining four years to acquire the deepest level.

Apparently, large segmental grammars can be learned even with a modest plasticity and a low degree of exposure to language data.

13.8 Conclusion

Making a principled distinction between articulatory and perceptual constraints within functional phonology leads to a straightforward learning process in which all articulatory constraints enter at the top of the hierarchy, and all faithfulness constraints enter at the bottom. The procedure moves on by promoting faithfulness constraints in the process of the acquisition of perceptual categorization, and demoting gestural constraints in a process of motor learning, aided by the bootstrapping power of play and temporary variation of constraint ranking. Continuous constraint families are handled with the help of the local-ranking principle, which ensures that moving constraints must push along their locally easier or less contrastive neighbours. In this way, universal markedness relations in adult phonology come to reflect the child's acquisition order. Under an error-driven learning scheme, all segmental phonological grammars are learnable. The Gradual Learning Algorithm is thus the first of the constraint-sorting or parameter-setting algorithms that can be connected to the actual acquisition process (Boersma and Levelt, to appear).

This chapter has shown that any segmental constraint set can be learned, without assuming any set of innate constraints, and that any segmental phonology can be learned unambiguously. Universal Grammar appears to contain no substance; the main innate things in phonology seem to be the desire and the ability to learn articulatory and perceptual features, the propensity to organize functional principles into an Optimality-Theoretic grammar, and the large plasticity in the acquisition of this grammar.

13.9 References

Abramson, A. S. and L. Lisker (1970). 'Discriminability across the voicing continuum: cross-language tests.' In B. Hala, M. Romportl, and P. Janota (eds), *Proceedings of the 6th International Congress of Phonetic Sciences*. Prague, Academia, 569–73.

Archangeli, D. and D. Pulleyblank (1994). *Grounded Phonology*. Cambridge, MA, MIT Press.

Behnke, K. (1998). *The Acquisition of Phonetic Categories in Young Infants: A Self-Organising Artificial Neural Network Approach*. Doctoral thesis, University of Twente. MPI Series in Psycholinguistics, 5.

Berko, J. and R. Brown (1960). 'Psycholinguistic research methods'. In P. Mussen (ed.), *Handbook of Research Methods in Child Development*. New York, Wiley, 517–57.

Berwick, R. C. (1985). *The Acquisition of Syntactic Knowledge*. Cambridge, MA, MIT Press.

—— and P. Niyogi (1996). 'Learning from triggers.' *Linguistic Inquiry* 27, 605–22.

Best, C. T., G. W. McRoberts, and N. M. Sithole (1988). 'Examination of perceptual reorganization for nonnative speech contrasts: Zulu click discrimination by English speaking adults and infants.' *Journal of Experimental Psychology: Human Perception and Performance* 14, 345–60.

Boersma, P. (1997). 'How we learn variation, optionality, and probability.' *Proceedings of the Institute of Phonetic Sciences of the University of Amsterdam* 21, 43–58. ROA-221.

—— (1998). *Functional Phonology: Formalizing the Interactions Between Articulatory and Perceptual Drives*. PhD dissertation, University of Amsterdam. The Hague, Holland Academic Graphics.

—— and C. C. Levelt (to appear). 'Gradual constraint-ranking Learning Algorithm predicts acquisition order'. In E. Clark (ed.), *Proceedings of the 30th Child Language Research Forum*. Stanford, April 1999.

Braine, M. D. S. (1976). 'Review of N. V. Smith, The Acquisition of Phonology'. *Language* 52, 489–98.

Carpenter, G. A. and S. Grossberg (eds) (1991). *Pattern Recognition by Self-Organizing Neural Networks*. Cambridge, MA, MIT Press.

Cho, T. and P. Ladefoged (1997). 'Variations and universals in VOT: evidence from 17 endangered languages'. *UCLA Working Papers in Phonetics* 95, 18–40.

Clark, R. and I. Roberts (1993). 'A computational model of language learnability and language change'. *Linguistic Inquiry* 24, 299–345.

Eimas, P. D., E. R. Siqueland, P. W. Jusczyk, and J. Vigorito (1971). 'Speech perception in infants'. *Science* 171, 303–6.

Fant, G. (1960). *Acoustic Theory of Speech Production*. The Hague, Mouton.

Ferguson, C. A. and C. B. Farwell (1975). 'Words and sounds in early language acquisition'. *Language* 51, 419–39.

Flanagan, J. L. (1972). *Speech Analysis, Synthesis and Perception* (2nd expanded edn.) Berlin, Springer.

Gibson, E. and K. Wexler (1994). 'Triggers'. *Linguistic Inquiry* 25, 407–54.

Gnanadesikan, A. (1995). 'Markedness and faithfulness constraints in child phonology'. Ms, U.Mass. ROA-67.

—— (1997). *Phonology with Ternary Scales*. PhD dissertation, U.Mass.

Grossberg, S. (1976). 'Adaptive pattern classification and universal recoding: A parallel development and coding of neural feature detectors'. *Biological Cybernetics* 23, 121–34.

Hale, M. and C. Reiss (1996). 'The initial ranking of faithfulness constraints in UG'. Ms, Concordia University. ROA-104.

—— and C. Reiss (1998). 'Formal and empirical arguments concerning phonological acquisition'. *Linguistic Inquiry*.

Hardcastle, W. J. (1976). *Physiology of Speech Production. An Introduction for Speech Scientists*. London, Academic Press.

Hernández-Chávez, E., I. Vogel, and H. Clumeck (1975). 'Rules, constraints and the simplicity criterion: An analysis based on the acquisition of nasals in Chicano Spanish'. In C. A. Ferguson, L. M. Hyman, and J. J. Ohala (eds), *Nasálfest*. Stanford, Stanford University Press, 231–48.

Jakobson, R. (1941). *Kindersprache, Aphasie und allgemeine Lautgesetze*. Uppsala.

Jun, J. (1995). 'Place assimilation as the result of conflicting perceptual and articulatory constraints'. *West Coast Conference on Formal Linguistics* 14.

Jusczyk, P. W. (1986). 'Toward a model of the development of speech perception'. In J. S. Perkell and D. H. Klatt (eds), *Invariance and Variability in Speech Processes*. Hillsdale, NJ, Lawrence Erlbaum, 1–35.

—— (1992). 'Developing phonological categories from the speech signal'. In G. A. Ferguson, L. Menn and C. Stoel-Gammon (eds), *Phonological Development: Models, Research, Implications*. Timonium, York Press.

Kawasaki, H. (1982). *An Acoustical Basis for Universal Constraints on Sound Sequences*. Doctoral thesis, University of California, Berkeley.

Kiparsky, P. and L. Menn (1977). 'On the acquisition of phonology'. In J. Macnamara, (ed.), *Language Learning and Thought*. New York, Academic Press, 47–78.

Kluender, K. R., R. L. Diehl, and P. R. Killeen (1987). 'Japanese quail can learn phonetic categories'. *Science* 237, 1195–7.

Koopmans-van Beinum, F. J. and J. M. van der Stelt (1998). 'Early speech development in children acquiring Dutch'. In S. Gillis and A. de Houwer (eds), *The Acquisition of Dutch*. Amsterdam and Philadelphia, John Benjamins.

Kuhl, P. K. (1979). 'The perception of speech in early infancy'. In N. J. Lass (ed.), *Speech and Language: Advances in Basic Research and Practice*, vol 1. New York, Academic Press, 1–47.

—— (1991). 'Human adults and human infants show a "perceptual magnetic effect" for the prototypes of speech categories, monkeys do not'. *Perception and Psychophysics* 50, 93–107.

—— and J. D. Miller (1978). 'Speech perception by the chinchilla: Identification functions for synthetic VOT stimuli'. *Journal of the Acoustical Society of America* 63, 905–17.

—— and D. M. Padden (1982). 'Enhanced discriminability at the phonetic boundaries for the voicing feature in macaques'. *Perception and Psychophysics* 32, 542–50.

Lisker, L. and A. S. Abramson (1964). 'A cross-language study of voicing in initial stops'. *Word* 20, 384–422.

McCarthy, J. J. (1998). 'Sympathy and phonological opacity'. Ms, U.Mass.

MacNeilage, P. F. (1997). 'Acquisition of speech'. In W. J. Hardcastle and J. J. Laver (eds), *The Handbook of Phonetic Sciences*. Cambridge, MA and Oxford, Blackwell, 303–32.

Macken, M. A. (1980). 'The child's lexical representation: The 'puzzle-puddle-pickle' evidence'. *Journal of Linguistics* 16, 1–17.

Menn, L. (1980). 'Phonological theory and child phonology'. In G. H. Yeni-Komshian, J. F. Kavanagh, and C. A. Ferguson (eds), *Child Phonology, vol. 1: Production*. New York, Academic Press, 23–41.

Prince, A. and P. Smolensky (1993). 'Optimality Theory: Constraint interaction in generative grammar'. Ms, Rutgers University and University of Colorado.

Pulleyblank, D. (1993). 'Vowel harmony and Optimality Theory'. In *Actas do workshop sobre fonologia*. University of Coimbra, 1–18.

—— (1996). 'Neutral vowels in Optimality Theory: A comparison of Yoruba and Wolof'. *Canadian Journal of Linguistics* 41, 295–347.

—— J.-K. Ping, M. Leitch, and Q. Ọla (1995). 'Typological variation through constraint rankings: Low vowels in tongue root harmony'. In *Proceedings of the Arizona Phonology Conference: Workshop on Features in Optimality Theory*. University of Arizona.

—— and W. J. Turkel (1995). 'Asymmetries in feature interaction. Learnability and constraint ranking'. Ms, University of British Columbia.

—— —— (1996). 'Optimality Theory and learning algorithms: The representation of recurrent featural asymmetries'. In J. Durand and B. Laks (eds), *Current Trends in Phonology: Models and Methods*. Salford, Manchester, University of Salford Press.

Queller, K. (1988). 'Review of N. Waterson, *Prosodic Phonology*'. *Journal of Child Language* 15, 463–7.

Smith, N. V. (1973). *The Acquisition of Phonology: A Case Study*. Cambridge, Cambridge University Press.

Smolensky, P. (1996a). 'On the comprehension/production dilemma in child language'. *Linguistic Inquiry* 27, 720-31.

—— (1996b). 'The initial state and 'richness of the base' in Optimality Theory'. Technical report, 96–4, Department of Cognitive Science, Johns Hopkins University, Baltimore. [Rutgers Optimality Archive, 154, http://ruccs.rutgers.edu/roa.html]

Streeter, L. A. (1976). 'Language perception of 2-month-old infants shows effects of both innate mechanisms and experience'. *Nature* 259, 39–41.

Tesar, B. (1995). *Computational Optimality Theory*. Doctoral thesis, University of Colorado, Boulder.

—— (1996). 'An iterative strategy for learning metrical stress in Optimality Theory'. To appear in *Proceedings of the 21st Annual Boston University Conference on Language Development*.

—— (1997). 'An iterative strategy for language learning'. *Lingua* 104, 131–45.

—— and P. Smolensky (1993). 'The learnability of Optimality Theory: An algorithm and some basic complexity results'. Ms, Department of Computer Science and Institute of Cognitive Science, University of Colorado, Boulder. ROA-2.

—— —— (1996). *Learnability in Optimality Theory (long version)*. Technical report, 96–3, Department of Cognitive Science, Johns Hopkins University, Baltimore. ROA-156.

Turkel, W. J. (1994). 'The acquisition of Optimality Theoretic systems'. Ms, University of British Columbia. ROA-11.

Vihman, M. M. (1982). 'A note on children's lexical representations'. *Journal of Child Language* 9, 249–53.

—— (1996). *Phonological Development. The Origins of Language in the Child*. Cambridge, MA and Oxford, Blackwell.

Waterson, N. (1971). 'Child phonology: A prosodic view'. *Journal of Linguistics* 7, 179–211.

Werker, J. (1991). 'The ontogeny of speech perception'. In I. G. Mattingly and M. Studdert-Kennedy (eds), *Modularity and the Motor Theory of Speech Production*. Hillsdale, NJ, Lawrence Erlbaum, 91-109.

Wexler, K. and M. R. Manzini (1987). 'Parameters and learnability in binding theory'. In T. Roeper and E. Williams (eds), *Parameter Setting*. Dordrecht, Reidel, 41–76.

14

The Universal Constraint Set: Convention, not Fact[1]

T. Mark Ellison

All languages make the same phonological generalizations. This is the remarkable claim of Optimality Theory (OT).

In early generative phonology (Chomsky and Halle 1968), phonological generalizations were expressed by ordered rewrite rules. Each language, however, required its own set of rules as well as its own ordering. Later, underspecification phonology (Archangeli and Pulleyblank 1989, 1994) emphasized default rules. Universal tendencies in the rules were apparent, but characterizing all languages with a single set of rules remained an unreachable dream.

In OT, phonological generalizations are expressed as ranked defeasible constraints. Ranking provides so many distinct but plausible grammars that it seems feasible that a universal set of phonological generalizations could account for the diversity of phonological systems.

The question we face is no longer whether the assumption of such a universal set is theoretically tenable, but whether it is justifiable.

There are two senses in which such an assumption could be justified: either as a fact or as a convention. If a fact, it claims that all language users objectively instantiate the same set of generalizations. If a convention, it encourages phonologists to describe languages using an agreed but arbitrary system of generalizations. In this interpretation, the universal constraint set is as arbitrary, but as useful, as the international phonetic alphabet (IPA).

This chapter examines seven kinds of argument for one or other status of the universality of phonological constraints. These are the arguments from empirical evidence (Section 14.2), restrictiveness (Section 14.3), simplicity (Section 14.4), universal markedness, acquisition (both Section 14.5), learnability (Section 14.6), and convention (Section 14.7). Close examination finds all but the last of these arguments to be wanting.

[1] I would like to thank the following people for their comments on an earlier version of this chapter: Ash Asudeh, Paul Boersma, Patricia Cabredo Hofherr, Frank Keller, Alice Turk, Markus Walther, and one anonymous reviewer. I would also like to thank the editors for their patience and interest.

The conclusion that remains is that universality, like the IPA, makes a better convention than fact. It should be used rather than believed.

14.1 Optimality Theory and Universals

Optimality Theory (Prince and Smolensky 1993; for an introduction see Archangeli and Langendoen 1997) is first and most frequently applied to phonology.[2] In this domain, the theory defines a metalanguage for stating generalizations about phonological sequences and representations, and at the same time it determines how these generalizations interact when combined to form complex analyses. Although the individual concepts of OT are presaged in earlier literature, its combination of sweeping generalizations with a simple mechanism of combination has proved very popular in the phonological community.

Since the scientific study of phonology began, its practitioners have intuited many powerful generalizations, but exceptions have plagued attempts to give these generalizations a precise expression. Optimality theory offers a mechanism for protecting generalizations from the pernicious effects of exceptions: all exceptions to any constraint are either lexically required or achieved by a conspiracy of more highly-valued constraints. While the lexical exception was a part of earlier phonological theories, they lacked principled mechanisms for capturing patterned exceptions.

Other chapters in this book have introduced and exemplified the basic concepts of Optimality Theory, so there is no need to present a detailed account of OT here. Rather, I propose to highlight those aspects of OT which play a role in the material found later in the chapter.

14.1.1 *Three Optimality Theories*

The basic components of OT are: a lexicon which can provide input candidate sets, a ranked set of violable constraints, and an evaluation function which eliminates non-optimal candidates. These components, on their own, define a pure theory of constraint interaction, which we may refer to as *Pure Optimality Theory* ($OT_{\emptyset}$). $OT_{\emptyset}$ does not include any assumptions about what can be in the lexicon, how the candidate sets are generated, or what the constraints are. It only stipulates the generation mechanism.

Supplementing this theory with two further assumptions defines what I will call *Standard* OT ($OT_{P\&S}$), the theory proposed by Prince and Smolensky (1993). These additional assumptions are: GEN and UNIV. The first of these assumptions (1) concerns the relation between the lexicon and candidate sets.

---

[2] The formalism has also been applied to morphology (e.g. Benua 1995, Golston and Wiese 1995, Orgun 1994, Russell 1995) and syntax (Dickey 1995, Grimshaw and Samek-Lodovici 1995, Legendre *et al.* 1993, Sells *et al.* 1994, Speas 1995, Woolford 1995).

(1) The candidate sets for each utterance are generated from lexical representations by a universal function GEN.

The second assumption, UNIV, is discussed in Section 14.1.2.

The initial statement of OT was very like Declarative Phonology (Bird 1990, 1995; Bird and Ellison 1994; Scobbie 1991, 1997; Scobbie *et al.* 1995) in its monostratal formulation: constraints acted only on surface forms, combining to eliminate all but the correct forms from those offered by GEN.

More recent work (McCarthy and Prince 1995; McCarthy 1996) has seen a shift towards incorporating a second level of *phonological* representation, usually identified with the lexical input to GEN. Phonological derivation therefore includes input and output levels of representation,[3] and constraints control the relationship between these.

Note that this two-level approach is reminiscent of the finite-state transducer models of morphology and phonology (Koskenniemi 1983; Antworth 1990), an observation made by Orgun (1995).

In this two-level theory of OT (OT_{2-L}), constraints on the phonological output, the so-called *structure* constraints, supplement constraints matching lexical forms to surface forms, the *faithfulness* constraints.[4] The ranking of phonological structure and faithfulness constraints determines the compromise made between the demands of the lexical input and the pressure for unmarked surface forms.

14.1.2 *The Universal Constraint Set*

The Optimality Theory of Prince and Smolensky (1993) assumes two universal components beyond the basic mechanism of constraint ranking. The first of these, GEN, creates candidate surface forms from lexical entries. The second defines the set of constraints, common to all languages. Variation between languages is accomplished not by having different constraints but by modifying the priority rankings between them. In Prince and Smolensky's words (1993: 5): 'Constraints are essentially universal and of very general formulation.' For ease of reference, UNIV will denote this assumption of universality. UNIV lends itself to two distinct interpretations. According to the the stronger of these, it states a fact about the mental reality of language users (2). This strong assumption will be denoted UNIV-FACT.

(2) UNIV-FACT: There is (at least) one hierarchy of constraints objectively present in the mind of each language-user. Furthermore, the same constraint set is used in each hierarchy of each and every user.

This strong form of UNIV is implicit in a good deal of OT work, including the

---

[3] Prince and Smolensky (1993: 192) do presage the two-level approach.
[4] McCarthy and Prince 1995 also introduce the notion of constraints controlling correspondence between surface forms.

original technical report. As a typical example, Prince and Smolensky (1993: 5) refer to the constraint hierarchy as a cause: 'interlinguistic differences arise from the permutations of constraint-ranking'—they do not arise from differences in the constraint set.

In a similar vein, Smolensky equates language acquisition with the manipulation of constraint rankings. 'In Optimality Theory, learning a target adult language requires a child to determine the relative rankings of universal constraints' (1996: 17). Here, the child is assumed to have a mentally-objective constraint hierarchy replete with universal constraints.

Archangeli (1997) also makes this assumption of universality a cornerstone of her account of Optimality Theory (p. 15).

Con, as a universal set of constraints, is posited to be part of our innate knowledge of language. What this means is that every language makes use of the same set of constraints. . . . This is the formal means by which *universals* are encoded

In this chapter, I offer an alternative interpretation of Univ, which takes the uniformity of constraint description to be a methodological desideratum rather than a statement of fact (3).

(3) Univ-Conv: Languages should be analysed (as much as possible) using a constraint set common to the community of phonologists.

Some of the arguments presented in this chapter contrast Univ, as either Univ-Fact or Univ-Conv, with the lack of this assumption. For ease of reference, this lack will be given the name No-Univ.

(4) No-Univ: Languages may or may not use the same constraints.

Like the original statement of Univ, No-Univ is ambiguous, referring to a lack of uniformity among either mentally real constraints, or the purely descriptive constraints of linguistic analyses. The context will serve to distinguish the senses, when the distinction is relevant.

Now that we have a precise notion of constraint universality to work with, we can proceed to the question of whether linguistic evidence could ever empirically show that objective constraints are universal—i.e. that Univ-Fact is true.

14.2 Empirical Evidence

The argument for a universal constraint set from empirical evidence is one I have never seen put forward, but it is certainly imaginable, and so, for the sake of completeness, takes its place here.

Many kinds of empirical evidence are imaginable, but few are found. We could, in a flight of fancy, imagine autopsies revealing neurons carefully inscribed with the names of their corresponding phonological or syntactic constraints. In reality, however, all empirical evidence for linguistic generalizations in the mind is indirect. We have access to: surface forms, variation in surface forms, meanings, and the results of elicitation. A generous interpretation of this evidence would claim that it suffices to identify both lexical candidate sets and the corresponding optimal forms. Supposing this evidence were available, an empirical argument for a universal set of constraints might develop as follows.

(A) The argument from empirical evidence

    A1 Empirical evidence about the selection of optimal candidates from lexical candidate sets is collected for many languages.

    A2 In each language language L, the empirical evidence forces us to conclude that users employ a particular constraint hierarchy H_L.

    A3 All of these hierarchies H_L use the same constraints.

    ∴ All languages use the same constraints.

The weak assumption in this argument, without which it cannot succeed, is (A2). We show below that for any constraint hierarchy there is another that uses a different set of constraints but always selects the same candidates as optimal. Thus no amount of data can force us to conclude that a particular language uses a given constraint set: there is always an equally well-supported alternative.

14.2.1 *Constraint Addition*

The basis for the counterargument is an operation for combining two constraints, an operation we can call *addition*. The addition C+D of two constraints C and D designates a distinct third constraint which assigns to each candidate the sum of the number of violations assigned by constraints C and D.

To illustrate addition, Table 1 shows the evaluations assigned to various phoneme sequences, Portuguese words in this case, by the two well-known constraints ONS, requiring onsets, and NO-CODA, prohibiting codas, and by their sum ONS+NO-CODA. There is, of course, nothing special in the choice of the two constraints for this example. Any other two constraints would have sufficed equally.

Table 1. The evaluation of candidates under summed constarints. The full stop is used to mark the absence of violations.

			ONS	NO-CODA	ONS + NO-CODA
Portuguese					
para	*for*	/pɐ.rɐ/	.	.	.
amores	*loves* (noun-PL)	/ɐ.mo.riʃ/	*	*	**
torneadas	*round*	/tur.ni.a.dɐʃ/	*	**	***
alcohol	*alcohol*	/al.ku.ɔl/	**	**	****

The word /alkuɔl/, orthographically ⟨alcool⟩, 'alcohol', has two onsetless syllables and two codas, and so engenders two violations each to Ons and No-Coda. Consequently, it incurs four violations of the sum constraint Ons + No-Coda.

I should emphasize here that summed constraints, such as Ons + No-Coda, are independent, singleton constraints. They bear no relation to their component constraints, except the mathematical relationship in the number of exceptions.

14.2.2 *Two Equivalent Hierarchies*

Now consider the action of the two two-constraint hierarchies Ons >> No-Coda >> and Ons >> Ons+No-Coda. Table 2 shows these two hierarchies selecting among some candidate syllabifications of /subʃtitue/, 'substitute (3s subj)'.

Table 2. Equivalence of hierarchy with summed constraints

	Ons	No-Coda	Ons	Ons+ No-Coda
Portuguese				
substitua *replaces* ☞ /su.bʃ.ti.tu.e/	*	*	*	**
/sub.ʃ.ti.tu.e/	**	**	**	****
/sub.ʃ.tit.u.e/	***	***	***	******
/su.bʃ.tit.u.e/	**	**	**	****

The optimal candidate from the two hierarchies is the same, /su.bʃ.ti.ti.tu.e/. This is not a coincidence. Two hierarchies C >> D and C >> C + D will select the same optimal candidate whenever applied to the same candidate set. In both cases, the higher-ranked constraint elects candidates optimal to it, and the lower-ranked constraint need only choose between these.

In the first hierarchy, this means that of the optimal candidates according to C, the candidate(s) with the fewest violations to D will be regarded as optimal. In the second hierarchy, once again C dominates, and so of the candidates optimal according to C the candidates showing the least violations of C+D will be optimal to the hierarchy. But all candidates optimal in C will have the same evaluation for C, and thus the only differences in C+D's evaluation of these candidates is provided by differences in D. Consequently, of the candidates optimal in C, those optimal in D will also be optimal in C+D. Thus precisely the same candidates incur minimal violations according to these two constraints. These two small hierarchies therefore select the same optimal candidates.

14.2.3 *Constructing Distinct but Equivalent Hierarchies*

Given any hierarchy with more than one constraint, we can construct a distinct, but functionally equivalent, second hierarchy by the simple expedient of replacing its second-ranked constraint by the sum of the second-ranked constraint and the first-ranked. For example, if the two highest-ranked constraints in the first hierarchy were Ons and No-Coda in that order, then replace No-Coda with Ons+No-Coda, keeping all other constraints the same, to make a new hierarchy.

This new hierarchy has a different constraint set from the first; No-Coda is missing from the second constraint set. But as we have seen, the combined selective action of the first two constraints in both hierarchies is the same. Because all subsequent constraints are identical, the action of the two hierarchies as a whole is identical. The two hierarchies can be regarded as notational variants for the same function. Because the constraints in the two hierarchies are different, they cannot both accord with a putative universal candidate set.

Empirical evidence cannot ever distinguish between two functionally-equivalent hierarchies. Consequently, empirical evidence alone can never identify a unique constraint set for a given language. The evidence which supports the putative universal constraint set in a language also always supports alternatives using different constraints.

It might be argued that C >> D and C >> C+D are uninteresting notational variants, lacking distinctive linguistic value. This is not the case, for precisely the reason that is important to this discussion. Reversing the rankings of these two hierarchies results in hierarchies that make different decisions on certain candidate sets.

For example, suppose C is Ons and D is No-Coda. The hierarchies Ons >> No-Coda and Ons >> Ons+No-Coda always select the same optimum from a candidate set. If the rankings are reversed, however, this is not the case. The candidate /kal/ violates No-Coda once, while /a.ka.la/ violates it not at all. However, /a.ka.la/ violates Ons once. Both candidates violate Ons+No-Coda the same number of times. So in the reversed ranking Ons+No-Coda >> Ons, it is the candidate best satisfying Ons which is optimal. The corresponding ranking No-Coda >> Ons prefers /akala/ because it offers no violations to the higher-ranked constraint No-Coda. These comparisons are tabled in Table 3.

Table 3. Parallel tableaus showing the different selective power of No-Coda >> Ons and Ons+No-Coda >> Ons

	No-Coda	Ons		Ons + No-Coda
Portuguese				
cal *chalk-powder* /kal	*!	.	☞	*
scala /a.ka.la/ ☞	.	*		*

So while the two hierarchies offer the same weak generative capacity when ordered in these hierarchies, reversing the ordering results in different predictions. And although the two hierarchies are notational variants, the differences in notation are linguistically important.

14.2.4 *Notational Variants*

These notational variants pose a serious problem for an objective interpretation of Univ. They mean that the hypothesis is not proven empirically. Furthermore, it fails to meet a primary criterion for psychological reality. Harman (1980: 21) speaks of a true theory—namely, one that is in accordance with the empirical evidence, in which aspects 'not shared by its notational variants are not taken to have psychological reality'. Coherence with a putative universal constraint set is not a property shared by all notational variants of any OT analysis of an individual language. The constraint set cannot, therefore, be ascribed psychological reality.

The conclusion, therefore, is that if we can analyse linguistic data using one constraint hierarchy, we can always use another hierarchy with a different constraint set to do the same job. The assumption (A2) of the argument from empirical evidence always fails. Consequently, argument A can provide no support for Univ-Fact. Univ-Fact cannot be proved empirically.

Furthermore, by not being independent of notational variance—i.e. non-empirical variance—in language analyses, the universal constraint set fails a major criterion for psychological reality.

It might be argued, however, that the impetus for Univ-Fact is not simply empirical but indirect. The next four sections consider indirect arguments for Univ.

14.3 Restrictiveness

The second argument for a universal constraint set relies on the frequently cited desideratum of restrictive linguistic hypotheses. Smolensky (1996: 3) includes restrictiveness among the advantages of encapsulating systematic cross-linguistic variation within constraint-ranking.

In much linguistic literature, including the article just cited, it is unclear whether restrictiveness refers to limitations on structure underspecified by the linguistic evidence, or whether it refers to predictive limitations of what might be observed. However, some works do emphasize the importance of predictive or empirical restrictiveness in allowing hypotheses to be tested. Chomsky (1978: 9) identifies this, and the consequent property of refutability, as vital for both particular grammars and grammatical theories.

It is worth noting that the desideratum of predictive restrictiveness is closely allied to Popper's (1959) theory of scientific development. Popper claims that unless there is empirical evidence to distinguish among them, the better of two competing hypotheses is the one which is compatible with the smallest number of distinct predictions. In other words, the more restrictive hypothesis is the better one.[5]

---

[5] As an example, imagine that you have tossed a coin of unknown reliability 1,000 times, and each time gained heads. One can imagine three hypotheses about the coin's behaviour: it always returns tails; it always returns heads, it returns anything. The first contradicts the data and is so eliminated. Of the remaining two, the second is more restrictive and so is preferred.

An argument for UNIV-FACT on the grounds of empirical restrictiveness might be formulated as follows.

(B) The argument from restrictiveness
  B1 UNIV-FACT cannot be proved empirically.
  B2 UNIV-FACT is not falsified by current evidence.
  B3 UNIV-FACT is more restrictive than NO-UNIV.
  B4 More restrictive unfalsified hypotheses are to be preferred.
  ∴ It is better to assume UNIV-FACT than NO-UNIV.

There is no problem accepting assumption (B1); it is, after all, what we saw proved in the previous section. We shall for the purposes of this argument presume that (B2) is also true. And because (B4) suffers some serious problems, we shall not tackle these here, but rather focus on assumption (B3)

The counter-argument to (B3) is not direct. It relies on assuming the validity in general of arguments from restrictiveness. An alternative hypothesis is shown to be more restrictive than UNIV-FACT, and so preferable to it. Furthermore, so long as this alternative is held, UNIV-FACT lacks all restrictive power, and so the argument from restrictiveness can offer it no support.

14.3.1 UNIV-FACT *is Restrictive*

We begin by showing that UNIV-FACT is restrictive. This is important, not so much for the result itself but for what the argument shows about *how* UNIV-FACT is restrictive. The reader should recall that we are only considering standard OT in which constraints are assumed to be subject to a total ranking: constraints cannot enter disjunctive relationships.

Suppose that some language uses two forms x and y for the same lexical input[6] in free variation.[7] As languages use single, fixed hierarchies, then this free variation must result from the equal harmony of these two candidates: they form a *tie*.

Now suppose that for some lexical input in a second language GEN produces a candidate set which contains both x and y. In this language, however, only candidate x surfaces as optimal. There is only one possible conclusion in this circumstance. The two languages must be employing different constraint sets.

Because x and y are both optimal in the first language, they must incur precisely the same number of violations for each constraint in force in this language. If one of them is optimal in the second language, while the other is not, they must incur a different number of violations for at least one constraint. It follows, therefore, that the two languages cannot be using the same constraint set.

It is worth noting what knowledge we have assumed to be accessible in order

---

[6] For example, in my idiolect, /plant/ and /plænt/ occur in free variation as realizations of ⟨plant⟩.

[7] Markus Walther (p.c.) suggests that this presupposition could not hold if the lexical entry were derived by lexical optimisation. If this is the case then the SINGLE given below always holds, and UNIV-FACT is not restrictive.

to create this falsification of UNIV-FACT; these are the same assumptions we made in section 14.2. We have assumed that we could identify two distinct surface forms which differ phonologically. This presupposes that phonological differences could be isolated from differences in phonetic implementation.

Secondly, we have presumed that it is possible to tell whether a second language uses these same candidates in a lexical competition. This is particularly difficult if, as in OT$_{2\text{-L}}$, candidates carry considerable non-surface structure with them. It may be that the second language has candidates with the same phonetic structure as the two optimal forms in the first language but which carry different hidden structure, allowing the common constraint set to evaluate them differently.

These difficulties notwithstanding, there are circumstances in which the evidence we have assumed to be potentially available could falsify UNIV-FACT. Thus it is, albeit in theory, an empirically restrictive hypothesis.

14.3.2 UNIV-FACT *is Restrictive Only With Free Variation*

It so happens that UNIV-FACT can only be falsified if there is a language showing free variation between two forms. We can show this by assuming the condition fails, and then proving that if any OT analysis of a set of languages is possible, one respecting UNIV-FACT is also.

Suppose we are examining a set of languages, and we analyse each of them using a different set of constraints. In each language, however, there is no free variation: from each candidate set only a single optimal candidate is returned. For ease of reference, we will give this restriction a name, SINGLE.

(5) SINGLE: For every possible candidate set which GEN can output, the constraint hierarchy in each language selects only a single optimal candidate.

It should be noted that speakers of languages conforming to SINGLE may realize the same word in a number of different ways, so long as the differences are ascribed to either phonetic implementation or separate lexical choice. SINGLE, as used here, deals only with phonological constraint systems.

If SINGLE holds throughout our analyses of each language, then we can construct another hierarchy for each language obeying both SINGLE and UNIV. This is done by appending to each constraint hierarchy all of the other constraints used in the analyses of the other languages. Because these are lower-ranked than the original constraints, the latter have priority in making their unique selection from the lexical candidate sets. The 'foreign' constraints are able to select only from within a singleton set of candidates. Thus for every input to GEN, the new, augmented hierarchies select the same optimal candidates as the original hierarchy. The action of the constraint hierarchies are precisely the same in the old and new analyses.

But notice that all of the new hierarchies use the same constraints. Consequently, they adhere to UNIV-FACT.

So any OT analyses of any languages can be modified to conform to
Univ-Fact without changing their empirical behaviour, so long as none of the
original analyses allowed multiple winning candidates. In other words, any falsification of Univ-Fact must also falsify Single.

14.3.3 *A More Restrictive Alternative*

The problem for Univ is not that it lacks restrictive power but that other
hypotheses have more. In fact, Single is more restrictive, and by the argument
from restrictiveness should be preferred.

We have already seen that if linguistic data from a number of languages
allows Single then it also allows Univ-Fact. Single is therefore at least
as restrictive as Univ-Fact. It is easy to imagine sets of languages analysable
with the same set of constraints in different rankings, but which permit more
than one optimal phonological form per lexical input. These would contradict
Single. So while every contradiction to Univ is a contradiction to Single, the
reverse is not the case. Thus Single is more restrictive than Univ.

In the argument from restrictiveness, assumption (B4) bids us prefer unfalsified restrictive hypotheses. Until Single is disproved, it should be preferred to
Univ.

14.3.4 *Both Hypotheses Together*

Single and Univ are not incompatible. If they are both restrictive, is there not
a case that both be accepted? The answer is that although they can be enter-
tained simultaneously, the argument from restrictiveness provides no reason that
they should be.

We saw above that Single is disproved by all counter-examples to Univ-
Fact, and more. Counter-examples to the conjunction of the two constraints
will be the union of two counter-example sets. This will be identical to the
counter-example set for Single. So Single and Univ-Fact combined are no
more restrictive than Single on its own.

In summary, then, if empirical restrictiveness is to be a desideratum, then it
is not one which Univ-Fact maximises. In fact, a more restrictive hypothesis,
Single, robs Univ-Fact of any restrictive power. Until Single can be
convincingly falsified, the argument from restrictiveness offers no support to
Univ-Fact.

The next section examines whether simplicity can offer any support to Univ-
Fact.

14.4 Simplicity

The third argument for Univ departs from empirical considerations and resorts
to that most powerful of non-empirical arguments: simplicity.

(C) The argument from simplicity

    C1 UNIV is simpler than NO-UNIV.

    C2 Simpler hypotheses should be preferred.

    ∴ UNIV should be preferred to NO-UNIV.

This argument both succeeds and fails. It succeeds when UNIV is interpreted as a convention—i.e. when UNIV is UNIV-CONV. But when UNIV denotes a fact about psychological reality, assumption C1 fails, and the argument consequently lends no support for UNIV-FACT.

The one successful simplicity criterion requires models to be evaluated in their complete description. The simplicity of a hypothesis cannot be evaluated independently of how it affects the representation of the data it accounts for, the probability of phenomena it is to explain, or the *ad-hoc*ness of the theoretical infrastructure it entails. The feature-counting measures of simplicity of phonological analyses were examples of this kind of simplicity measure precisely when they balanced the complexity of rules systems against the elimination of redundancy from the lexicon.

In fact, this complete view of simplicity defines the machine-learning method known as minimum message-length (Wallace and Boulton 1968; Wallace and Freeman 1987) or minimum description length (Rissanen 1978, 1982, 1987) which has close links to Bayesian probability and algorithmic complexity (Li and Vitanyi 1989, 1993). The same method has been used to computationally select between different phonological analyses (Ellison 1992). It behoves us then to evaluate the simplicity of UNIV together with the theoretical edifice it entails.

14.4.1 *The Simplicity of* UNIV-CONV

Let us first consider the simplicity argument for UNIV-CONV. In this case, we need only consider the analysis as a description. Descriptions have neither a causal effect, nor do they need to be explained as the result of particular causes. Rather, they are formally self-contained. Thus it is only the components of the analysis itself which need to be measured in a simplicity argument.

An OT description of one language needs five components: lexical inputs, GEN, a list of constraints, a ranking of the constraints and EVAL.[8] Being willing to assume the universality of GEN and EVAL, for the purposes of this argument, we do not need to express each of these components anew for every different language. A description of the, say, 6,000 languages of the world consequently needs fewer than 30,000 components. Grossly measured, for 6,000 languages, we need 18,002 components: GEN, EVAL, 6,000 sets of lexical inputs, 6,000 constraint sets and 6,000 constraint rankings. This is the component count if NO-UNIV is adopted and languages vary in their constraint sets. Does UNIV-CONV make things simpler?

---

[8] We assume that the expression of the constraint set, e.g. as a bitmap, does not imply any rank ordering.

If the same constraint set is used in each description, then we need only 12,003 components: GEN, EVAL, the universal constraint set, 6,000 sets of lexical inputs and 6,000 constraint rankings. So the comparison is between 18,002 components, or 12,003. This is not a definitive proof that UNIV is better. It may be a comparison of 18,002 simple, transparent components with 12,003 components of fiendish complexity. *Ceteribus paribus*, however, it is reasonable to assume that analyses with fewer components are simpler.

So UNIV-CONV is well supported by the argument from simplicity. Its realist counterpart UNIV-FACT, however, falls foul of the need for explanatory causes.

14.4.2 *The Simplicity of* UNIV-FACT

The objective components needed for any OT model of the cognitive language processes include those needed for language description: lexical inputs, GEN, constraints, constraint rankings and EVAL.

A principle emphasized by Isaac Newton (1953) and more recently by Reichenbach (1956), Salmon (1975, 1978, 1984) and Sober (1988) requires that to the same natural effects common causes should be assigned. In its more modern formulation, correlations should be explained by means of a common cause. Salmon offers the example of word-for-word identical assignments being submitted by two students. It is possible they were created independently; it is more plausible that at least one of the students is guilty of plagiarism.

This principle applies to universal tendencies in language structure: they need to be explained by a common cause, which can justify the assumption of a universal GEN, a universal EVAL and a universal constraint set. One possible such cause will be discussed in more detail in Section 14.5. For the current argument, the important implication of this principle is that if we assume that each language speaker's mind embodies the same GEN, EVAL and constraint set, then we must present common causes for these to account for their uniformity.

Because we are interested here only in the contrast between UNIV and NO-UNIV, we will presume that explanations are found for universal GEN and EVAL. So we need only seek a common cause for the uniformity of the constraint set across humanity.

This need for a common cause arises with the constraint ranking as well. Speakers of the same dialect use the same ranking. Such a correlation needs to be explained. The explanation given in OT is that the linguistic environment provides evidence, and a learning procedure re-ranks constraints until the adult, correct ranking is achieved. So the OT model of the language-user involves linguistic input and a re-ranking procedure.

UNIV-FACT applies not only to adults but to children as well. It follows that children at all ages must in fact share the same constraint set as adults. Consequently, the common constraint set cannot be acquired. It must be innately, presumably genetically, specified.

Many other domains, apart from language, can be modelled by an OT-like system of ranked constraints. For example, driving a car may be reduced to a number of constraints, some of which take priority over others. These constraints interact to select optimal actions for the driver. Highly-ranked will be 'Don't hit anyone', more lowly-ranked will be 'Go as fast as you can'.

While some of these constraints might be universal, and be shared with many other skills, such as 'Don't hit anyone', others, like 'Depress the clutch before changing gear', will not. Since we learn to drive vehicles nonetheless, the human mind requires a mechanism for learning such constraints.

Now let us return to language.

If the phonological constraint set is innate, then it cannot be the result of learning, and so a cause beyond that used to acquire constraints for other skills —e.g. driving—must form part of our model of cognitive development and function, adding to its complexity.

We can evaluate UNIV-FACT in terms of the complexity of the model it requires for the language user. UNIV-FACT requires that the speaker begin with the following objects: (i) GEN, (ii) EVAL, (iii) linguistic input for learning the lexical inputs and the constraint ranking, (iv) a mechanism for ranking constraints, (v) a mechanism for learning constraints in other domains, and (vi) a genetic stipulation of the common constraint set.

Without UNIV-FACT, we can have a simpler model because all constraints can be created by the same mechanism, a learning device. The components needed by the model are: (i) GEN, (ii) EVAL, (iii) linguistic input for learning the lexical inputs and the constraint ranking, (iv) a mechanism for ranking constraints, and (v) a mechanism for learning constraints in all domains. This model is simpler than that needed for UNIV-FACT.

Of course, even without adopting UNIV-FACT, we could propose that constraints were determined genetically. Different gene combinations would be needed to account for different constraint sets. At first glance, this might appear as complex as having a genetic specification for a universal constraint set. The principle of similar effects' having similar causes means, however, that the uniformity of constraints under UNIV-FACT must be the result of uniform genetic specifications. But why should the genetically-specified constraint set not vary genetically, as does body-shape, eye-colour or fingerprints? A further causal mechanism is needed to explain the uniformity of the genetic specification for the constraint set.

So the genetic specification of the universal constraint set does no more than move the uniformity under contention from the speakers' minds to their genes. The need for a common cause explanation to account for UNIV-FACT remains.

When placed in its complete setting, UNIV-FACT makes for a more complex model of language than does No-UNIV. Uniformity in the real world is a simplifying assumption only so long as it can be attributed naturally to an otherwise-motivated common cause. If the uniformity comes at the expense of added ontological assumptions, such as a relatively uniform genetic specification of the constraint set, then it makes for a more complex, not a simpler, assumption.

In summary then, we have two very different evaluations of UNIV. The factual version UNIV-FACT is not well supported by a simplicity argument: in fact, simplicity favours NO-UNIV. But in its application to phonological descriptions, UNIV-CONV seems a natural step towards constructing simpler and more concise simultaneous analyses of many languages without the burden of ontological claims.

14.5 Markedness and Acquisition

The next two arguments for the universality of constraints are treated together for two reasons. Firstly, they have much in common. Both rely on UNIV-FACT as necessary for the explanation of certain phenomena. Secondly, a single response counters both arguments.

The first of these two arguments for UNIV-FACT is the argument from cross-linguistic markedness. It is based on the observation that certain phonological structures seem to be preferred in all languages.

(D) The argument from cross-linguistic markedness
    D1 Languages regard the same structures as unmarked.
    D2 UNIV-FACT offers an explanation of this.
    D3 There is no other explanation of this.
   ∴   UNIV-FACT.

One example of markedness, in the sense of (D1), concerns voiceless stops. Languages generally have either both voiced and voiceless stops, or only voiceless stops. No language uses only voiceless stops. Voiceless stops are therefore said to be unmarked.

Similarly, all languages seem to use /CV/ syllables even though they may have more elaborate syllable types as well. Although there are languages which allow only this kind of syllable and no other, there are no clear cases of languages which prohibit it.

The second of the two arguments for UNIV-FACT has the same form as (D) but addresses the order in which particular linguistic constructions are acquired. UNIV-FACT is needed to account for the correlation between the order of acquisition of phonological structures and increasing cross-linguistic markedness.

(E) The argument from acquisition-ordering
    (E1) Children learn to produce more marked phonological structures later.
    (E2) UNIV-FACT offers an explanation of this.
    (E3) There is no other explanation of this.
   ∴   UNIV-FACT.

The basis of this second argument—namely assumption (E1)—can be termed the Jakobsonian Generalization after the linguist who first stated it (Jakobson

1968). It has been pursued in linguistic theory by Stampe (1979) and recently Smolensky (1996).

14.5.1 *Explanations With* UNIVFACT

Optimality theory with UNIV-FACT offers an account for both (D1) and (E1). The account of (D1) is quite simple: markedness is equated with constraint violation.

All languages share the same constraints. The least marked forms in any language will be the ones which incur no violation to any constraint. Forms which violate no constraints will also be optimal in all other rankings of the same constraints, and thus, under UNIV-FACT, be universally unmarked.

Smolensky (1996) offers an OT_{2-L} account of (E1). His account relies on the demotion algorithm for learning constraint rankings developed with Tesar (1995; Tesar and Smolensky 1993, 1996). Boersma (this volume) offers an alternative algorithm for the same task. These algorithms require the learner to know *a priori*, or deduce, the lexical input as well as the complete surface representations of words it hears. With the lexical input, GEN can be used to construct the lexical constraint set.

If the correct candidate—that is, the form actually appearing in the language—is ruled non-optimal in the current ranking, all constraints which prefer other candidates to it are demoted below the highest-ranked constraint which will eliminate these competitors. This algorithm can be proved to arrive at a ranking which selects as optimal the right surface forms, provided such a ranking exists. Smolensky proposes that children learn language by demoting constraints in this way.

In order to explain (E1) with constraint demotion, two problems must be solved. First, how does the child determine the lexical input for new words it hears? Second, what relates phonological markedness to acquisition order?

In answer to the first question, Smolensky stipulates that the learner treats the perceived form as the lexical input. GEN acts on this form, pairing it with all possible surface forms. If the only constraints which were to apply were faithfulness constraints, then the child would reproduce the input exactly.

The second question is also answered by stipulation. The learner begins with a constraint hierarchy which ranks all phonological structure constraints above all faithfulness constraints. As the child receives input which conflicts with phonological markedness preferences, the structure constraints are demoted, and the undemoted faithfulness constraints effectively percolate higher in the constraint ranking. If, however, the child never receives input which contradicts a particular well-formedness constraint, in the way for example that a child raised in a Hawaiian-speaking environment will not hear codas, then the constraint is never demoted and so remains to outrank faithfulness constraints. In maturity, the hierarchy will result in borrowed lexical items being realized in conformance with the undemoted phonological structure constraints.

That UNIV-FACT contributes to an explanation of these two phenomena offers little support for UNIV-FACT if there are simpler alternatives. The next section provides one such alternative.

14.5.2 *Acquisition Without* UNIV

The starting-point for a universal-less account of markedness and acquisition order is the common human development in physiology and coordination. Very young infants face two problems in the production of the words they hear:[9] the shape of the mouth makes some segments impossible to produce, and their lack of general coordinative skills also preclude the reliable production of some segments and/or sequences (Kent 1992a, b; Kent and Miolo 1995: 307–9).

During the process of development children outgrow their physiological limitations and, more selectively, the limitations on their ability to coordinate sounds. With the addition of two further assumptions, this provides the basis for the universal-less explanation. The first assumption we make is that children learn constraints which internalize the structures of those words they say repeatedly. This assumption is shared by the psycholinguistic model of Menn (Kiparsky and Menn 1977; Menn 1983), and later Matthei (1989), in which developing children store their own utterances as well as those perceived in their linguistic input.

The second assumption is that children tend to use words which they know they can articulate successfully. While they continually try new ones, they do not continue to repeat words by means of which they have failed to communicate. Three different kinds of evidence can be adduced for this assumption. Firstly, in their earliest meaningful utterances children tend to reuse syllables used in babbling (Vihman 1992). Secondly, at a later age, children are found to actively avoid words and phonemes which they cannot produce accurately (Ferguson and Farwell 1975; Schwartz and Leonard 1982). Further, children spontaneously self-correct and repair following a failure to communicate (Clark 1978).

From these two assumptions we conclude that a child at any stage of development will be revising the phonological constraint system to account for the intersection of the language it is exposed to, and the capabilities it has within the physiological and coordinative limitations of its developmental stage. While these limitations may be quite similar between children, there is no evidence or necessity to suppose that the constraints which the child uses to internalize these limitations do *not* vary significantly from child to child. It is the function of the constraint system as whole, not of its components, which matters.

It is this internalization of the child's own articulatory limitations which accounts for the broad similarities in cross-linguistic markedness judgements. But to complete this account we need the assistance of one final assumption: that children retain permanently the linguistic knowledge gleaned at previous stages

---

[9] I leave aside the question of perceptual development here, although it must certainly form a component of any complete theory.

of development. Later development only adds to this knowledge, supplementing the constraints which modelled the limitations on structure and articulation present at earlier stages.

On the basis of this assumption, the child always retains the constraints which modelled its articulatory skill at earlier stages of development. These constraints may be outranked by later-developed constraints, constraints which are perhaps similar to the faithfulness constraints in OT$_{2-L}$. In any case, the most optimal word forms will be those which conform to all of the constraints, including those learned during the period of limited articulatory prowess. Thus the least-marked utterances will be those that were possible at the earliest stages of physiological and coordinative development.

Where constraints describing outgrown limitations are outranked by new constraints developed in response to linguistic input, the child learns to articulate more marked structures. Where they are not, the limitations of child physiology and coordination are reflected in the corresponding aspects of the adult pronunciation. The adult may remain incapable of articulatory feats not because his or her tongue lacks agility, but because the model of lingual articulation he or she has internalized has not been revised since a less agile stage of development.

For example, consider a child's attempting to produce the word /snɔʊ/, 'snow'. When it first attempts speech, the child will find itself unable to reproduce the initial consonant cluster of the word, producing perhaps [nɔ] or [soʊ] instead. It will internalize this limitation in its cognitive model of phonology. At some point in development, the child will attain both the physical and coordinative ability to say the cluster /sn/. But more is required, namely continued pronunciation of such clusters by the child. The impetus for the pronunciation of certain clusters is present in the language: if the child pronounces a word with an onset cluster, and succeeds in better mimicking adult pronunciation, then this behaviour is reinforced, and the child is likely to use that pronunciation again. With continued use, the child reviews its cognitive model of the articulation system to account in a comprehensive way for the forms it now finds itself saying.

In OT terms, this review of the articulation model need be no more than the addition of new constraints. There is no need for re-ranking of the constraints describing earlier stages. The child learning to pronounce complex onsets may dominate its previous hierarchy with a constraint which forces the realization of the perceived sequence /sn/ as a complex onset. Even if all earlier models of the articulation system had precluded consonant clusters, the dominance of this constraint will allow clusters to surface where lexical forms contain them.

So we now have an account of both phenomena, (D1) and (E1), which does not depend on UNIV-FACT. This account also does not need the mechanism of constraint demotion. Rather, all change is effected by the construction of new constraints which may override the constraints reflecting earlier, developmental limitations. In this account we have used as causes only linguistic input, a learning device, and the child's own physiological and coordinative development.

In any OT account of language development using UNIV-FACT, these facts remain, but must be supplemented by an added mechanism to force constraint uniformity. As pointed out in the discussion of simplicity in Section 14.4, this kind of additional requirement renders the explanation from UNIV-FACT more complex.

Taking the universal-less view to its limit, we might assume that once an initial set of well-formedness constraints are learned, further constraints specify morpheme classes, or in the extreme case, individual morphemes in the lexicon. The adult constraint system, after such a learning process, would look like that proposed by Russell (1995). Russell contended that rather than being the inputs to GEN, lexical specifications are constraints which limit a single universal candidate set. These morphemic constraints can be ranked among the phonological constraints, and it is the interaction of the two that produces morphophonological complexity.

In this model, complex, later-learned articulation patterns such as morpheme-specific phonological effects are reified in constraints of higher rank. This is appropriate because these phenomena are supplementary cases of the 'except when' behaviour which motivated much of Prince and Smolensky's (1993) argument for OT.[10]

In summary, then, this section has presented an alternative account of both cross-linguistic markedness effects and the correlation of markedness with acquisition order. This account, while making use of the totally ordered constraint hierarchy of OT, does not assume a universal constraint hierarchy. Instead, constraints are learned to reflect the growing articulatory capabilities of the child and the demands of the language being learned. These constraints are not given but made.

In that this alternative account requires only the staged development of the child from a common, very limited, state, and does not require wholesale stipulation of linguistic, non-physiological universals, it is simpler than explanations built from UNIV-FACT, and so forms a preferable explanation. Consequently, the arguments for UNIV-FACT from markedness and from acquisition have little weight.

14.6 Learnability

The penultimate argument for UNIV is the argument from learnability. This argument is one shared, at least in part, with other theories of linguistics which rely on the notion of Universal Grammar.

(F) The argument from nativism
    (F1) Adults speakers use constraint hierarchies to define their language.
    (F2) These hierarchies must have come from somewhere.

---

[10] Thanks to Markus Walther (p.c.) for pointing this out.

(F3) Learning constraints and hierarchies from positive data alone is in general too difficult for children to accomplish.

(F4) Children have access only to positive data.

∴.   The constraints are not acquired.

(F5) What is not acquired is innate.

∴.   The constraints must be innate.

(F6) Humans are all equally capable of learning all languages.

(F7) If humans had different innate constraints, they could not learn all languages equally well.

∴.   All speakers have the same innate constraints.

(F8) All languages use all constraints.

∴.   UNIV-FACT All languages use the same constraint set.

The view that Universal Grammar is the result of genetically-specified mental structures specific to language is widely held in the linguistic community (for a recent popular exposition, see Pinker 1994). This view has, however, recently come under attack from connectionism (Elman *et al.* 1996; Quartz and Sejnowski 1996) and statistical learning (e.g. Finch and Chater 1992).

The argument above is an example of how the universality of the constraint set might be linked with the innateness. If we need the genetic specification of universal grammar to make languages learnable, then it is reasonable to assume that the genes specify the constraint set. If this is so, then all languages will use the same constraint set in the same way that (almost) all people are born with four fingers and a thumb on each hand.

There are, however, three points where this argument can be challenged: assumptions(F4), (F7), and (F8). The remainder of this section discusses problems with each of these assumptions in turn.

14.6.1 *Poverty of the Stimulus (F4)*

The first of these three assumptions states that children have access only to positive information—that is, information about what is *possible* in the language they hear. In contrast, they receive no information which indicates that a certain form or construction is *impossible*—they receive no negative evidence.

This premiss is based on the evidence that children do not seem to receive care-taker instruction that ungrammatical utterances they make are improper. On the occasions that they do receive this kind of input, they seem to ignore it (Brown and Hanlon 1970; Pinker 1989). This view of child input has not, however, gone unchallenged (Sokolov and Snow 1994).

One form of functional negative evidence that is available to the language acquirer is failure to communicate. If a child asks for an icecream, and is met with blank stares, this offers significant evidence that the construction has failed. Reasons for the failure may be pragmatic, lexical or grammatical. If there is other evidence to show that the pragmatics and lexicon are satisfactory, then grammatical infelicity is the likely cause of the failure to communicate. Negative evidence has been gleaned about the grammar.

It would intuitively seem to be the case that the lack of a particular construction in the ambient linguistic input could also act as negative evidence. However, it is argued in the literature that this is not the case (Valian 1990). The reason for this is not so much the nature of language as the nature of current linguistic models.

Most current models of language do not regard information about the frequencies of items or structures as part of the systematic specification of the language. Consequently, the incorporation of a particular construction in a language gives no indication, and in fact, *can* give no indication, of how frequent that construction is. Consequently, its lack in available data may merely result from the construction's having low frequency, not from its systematic prohibition.

Note that this ignorance of distributional evidence is a vital assumption in Gold's (1967) proof of the necessity of negative evidence for learning one of a suitably large class of languages.

In contrast, a language model of language which regards frequency information as part of the specification of a language can be subject to negative evidence, albeit not *absolutely* conclusive evidence, if a form which should occur in the language with relative frequency f does not occur. As the number n of constructions in which the form could occur but does not increases, the probability $(1-f)^n$ of not seeing an example of the form tends to zero. Bayes' theorem then implies that the likelihood of a grammar which predicts this frequency f for the form must also tend towards zero.

In other words, the absence of expected constructions can act as negative evidence to the right sort of language model. Conversely, the lack of negative instruction only implies a lack of negative evidence if the language model is too impoverished to make substantive claims about frequency. There seems little evidence that a child model is so impoverished.

An alternative form of negative evidence occurs if the relations between language structures are topographic (see Ellison (1997) for a discussion of learning with topographic mapping, and its potential application to language). If a language has a topographic mapping from meaning to phonological form, then similar meanings, at e.g. the sentence level, relate to similar phonological forms. This offers implicit negative evidence in the following way. If meaning A is similar to meaning B, and the output form of A is **A**, then the output form of B is (probably) not dissimilar from **A**.

In Optimality-theoretic terms, this amounts to the restriction that similar lexical inputs should result in similar optimal candidates. For example, if the Old Irish lexical input /berami/ results in an optimal output form /bermai/, then we would expect the input /gerami/ not to result in /graim/ in preference to /germai/. This is because /germai/ is more similar to /bermai/ than is /graim/.

If learners distinguish successful interactions from unsuccessful, if grammars specify distribution, or if grammars make use of topographic mappings, then negative evidence is available to language learners even without negative instruction. If the learner is using language to achieve a goal, then failure to achieve this goal may indicate an improper construction. If the learner has distributional expectations, or expectations based on similarity, failure of these may also indicate a need for grammatical revision.

Of course, the best response to this assumption of poverty of the stimulus would be to build a system that was capable of learning language structure without negative evidence, perhaps using distribution or topographicality assumptions to achieve this end. Unfortunately, approaching this problem is beyond the scope of this chapter, and a final solution is still lacking.

In summary, then, the claim that children receive no negative evidence is definitely controversial, relying on isolating the task of learning about grammar from considerations of motivation, distribution and topographicality.

14.6.2 *Innate Constraints Must Be Uniform (F7)*

Another assumption that can be challenged states that languages could only be learned with equal facility if all learners had the same innate constraint set. Let us leave for Section 14.6.3 the possibility that learners need not use all of their innate constraints. Even without this option it may be the case that the space of human languages is accessible using a number of different constraint sets.

It may be the case, for example, that variation is restricted to constraints which are applicable only in a very restricted range of situations. Variation in these constraints would offer no more handicaps to speakers than the variation which occurs in the inclusion of low-frequency words in our individual vocabularies.

For example, constraints controlling the fine prosodic interaction of words cross-clausally may be present in some people and absent in others. This will allow the former group a finer poetic ear than the latter. If other parts of linguistic behaviour have a genetic basis, there is no particular reason to think that this kind of individual difference cannot have a basis in genetic variation in the same way that eye-colour, skin-tone or height have.

Of course, these low-frequency constraints may be so outranked that any effect they might have on the language of the individual is overshadowed by other influences. The individual differences offered by these constraints might then be curtailed by an appropriate conspiracy of shared constraints.

The important point to take from this section is that while uniformity of constraints may be important for the most frequently-active constraints, it is by no means certain for the less frequently-applied constraints. For these cases a lack of uniformity in the innate constraint set results in little communicative cost.

14.6.3 *All Languages Must Use All Innate Constraints (F8)*

Another assumption open to challenge is (F8). This assumption claims that all the innate constraints must be used in all languages. Without it, even a shared human gene-complex specifying a uniform constraint set will allow different individuals and/or different languages to make use of distinct subsets of the common constraint set, and consequently, the constraint sets used in language hierarchies will not be universal. UNIV-FACT will fail.

Specifying a set of constraints a priori is a great help to learning, but once present, constraints can be readily eliminated.

The argument for innateness presumes an inborn candidate set in order to make the task of language learning tractable. Language learning is the task of identifying the correct grammar in a large space of possible grammars. The argument for innateness claims we need a language-specific genetic endowment to reduce the space of possible grammars to a size at which it can be feasibly searched.

In OT, the space of grammars is the space of constraint hierarchies. The innate specification of CON reduces complexity by limiting possible hierarchies to those using a single common constraint set. This, it is argued, makes learning tractable, because it involves only the task of constraint re-ranking.

But the innate specification of a common constraint set need not force all languages to use the same constraints. Different languages might make use of different subsets of the constraint set. This could be achieved in two ways: so that language development consists of removing constraints from an all-encompassing initial state, or of adding constraints to a constraint-poor initial state.

In the former case, a child is born with a hierarchy that includes all of the innately possible constraints. As the child gathers linguistic evidence, certain constraints are eliminated when they are seen not to participate in the hierarchy.

The most direct evidence for constraint deletion is free variation. Suppose that for a particular lexical input, two different surface forms are equally acceptable in the target language, and what is more, these two candidates differ only in the evaluation of one constraint. Because no hierarchy, stratified hierarchy, or even hierarchy with disjunction, can account for this kind of free variation, it follows that the constraint which distinguishes the two forms cannot be part of the hierarchy defining this language.

As a concrete example, let us imagine that syllable structure is defined by the constraints ONS, NOCOMPLEX, NO-CODA, PARSE and FILL. Suppose free variation occurs in which an high vowel followed by a low vowel can be parsed as the head of its own syllable, or as an onset to the following vowel. These two cases might be /i.a/ and /ia/. In the first case, ONS is violated twice, but no other constraint is violated: there are no complex onsets or codas, and there is no deletion or epenthesis. The same is true of the second syllabification except that ONS incurs no violations; the only syllable has an onset.

If these two syllabifications occur in free variation, then ONS cannot form part of the hierarchy, or the variation would not be free. No reordering, or even disjunction, of these constraints can account for this variation. Thus ONS cannot form part of the constraint hierarchy for this language.

It does not matter that in a different hierarchy this free variation might be analysed by constraint disjunction. Nor is it important that this kind of free variation might not actually occur. The point is that a single example of free variation is enough to eliminate an unwanted constraint from a hierarchy without any great computational expense. Subset hierarchies are, therefore, learnable.

We might also choose to remove constraints which never serve to eliminate non-optimal candidates. For example, Ons might be removed in a language with a highly ranked Parse dominating NoComplex which in turn dominates No-Coda, simply because these three constraints combine to force any intervocalic consonant to be parsed as an onset. If the language does not permit syllabic consonants, then the only alternatives to parsing a consonant as an onset are deletion or parsing it as a coda. These two alternatives are precluded by the highly-ranked Parse and No-Coda constraints. Thus eliminating the Ons constraint would have no effect on the syllabification of lexical material. The constraint could then be deleted.

That Ons *can* be dispensed with does not mean that it necessarily *is* removed from the hierarchy. What it does mean, however, is that if the learning algorithm does dispense with the constraint, it will not affect the language of the learner. Univ-Fact is not required to make language learning feasible.

In an alternative model, constraints are inserted into a hierarchy rather than removed from it. Suppose we begin with a hierarchy that contains only structural constraints and no faithfulness constraints. Whenever the constraints in the hierarchy are violated and re-ranking will not alleviate the problem, a faithfulness constraint could be introduced from the innate constraint set which requires just enough faithfulness in the input-output mapping to make the correct candidate optimal.

The new constraint could subsequently be ranked within the hierarchy using an algorithm like that of Boersma (this volume) or of Tesar and Smolensky (1996).

There is an interesting implication of this model which distinguishes it from accounts, like Smolensky's (1996), in which faithfulness constraints are present but ranked low in the initial stage of acquisition. In both models, early articulations will be largely the effect of structural constraints. The difference between the models is that having faithfulness constraints within the infant's grammar from the beginning means that up to the limits of their linguistic prowess, children will always attempt to produce real, well-formed words.

In contrast, if children begin with no faithfulness constraints in the initial stages, then we might expect an initial stage of unmarked and also meaningless articulation: babbling. This is what does occur in babies. Babbling is devoid of word content. This supports the proposal that faithfulness constraints are absent, rather than dominated.

In summary, then, babbling offers some evidence that constraints are inserted into the constraint set as the child language learner develops.

At issue in this section is not so much the contingent fact of whether or not all of the putative innate constraints are used in all languages, but the necessity that this is the case. Given that procedures to insert or delete constraints are not computationally taxing, learnability offers no basis for assuming this consistency.

14.6.4 *Summary*

We have looked at three assumptions used in the argument for universality from learnability via innateness. The poverty of the stimulus premiss (F4) can be countered by incorporating motivational, distributional or topographic information into the language model.

The assumption that all innate constraint sets must be the same (F7) can also be challenged: even if the difficulty of learning forces us to presume that constraints are innate, there is no necessity that we all have the same innate set. All that is required for the relative homogeneity of our linguistic capabilities is that variation predominately occurs in constraints with a low frequency of application, much as variation in native-speaker vocabularies occurs primarily in the low-frequency items.

Nor is the third assumption, that all users must incorporate all innate constraints into their hierarchies (F8), a self-evident truth. Identifying situations in which constraints can or must be deleted from hierarchies is computationally tractable, as is identifying when they should be inserted. Furthermore, an insertion model makes the correct prediction that the initial stage of language should be arbitrary babbling, not merely the reduction of meaningful forms to unmarked articulations.

The conclusion, then, is that the argument for innate language knowledge from the poverty of the stimulus premiss, does not of itself offer significant support to the claim that the constraint hierarchies of the world's languages use the same constraint set.

14.7 Convention

The final argument for Univ is the most powerful.

(G) The argument from ease of communication
  (G1) Using a uniform constraint set makes it easier for phonologists to communicate analyses of languages to each other than if they used different constraints for each language.
  (G2) The easier it is for phonologists to communicate language descriptions, the better.
  ∴   Phonologists should use a standard constraint set in analysing languages.

It is very difficult to contest either assumption in this argument. If language descriptions are sought using a common constraint set, and individual descriptions differ only in the rankings of the constraints, then linguists can quickly grasp the distinctive content of new language descriptions. This is particularly so if they are already familiar with a number of different rankings of the same constraints.

On the other hand, if the burden of understanding the grammar of another language includes mastering the implications of a new set of constraints *as well as* grasping the implications of the constraint ranking, then the task will be much more difficult.[11]

This argument, then, seems sound. A standard set of constraints makes a useful tool for furthering communication between linguists.

14.8 Conclusion

In the introduction to this chapter I set out to show that UNIV made a better tool than fact. Sections 14.2 to 14.6 discussed arguments which sought to establish UNIV as a fact, through empirical means, restrictiveness, simplicity or as a necessary explanation for features of markedness, acquisition order, or learnability. Each time, UNIV-FACT as fact proved to be an escapable conclusion. In contrast to these arguments, the case for UNIV as a conventional usage to make the sharing of linguistic descriptions straightforward is robust. The conclusion is that UNIV is not a fact but a promising convention.

The international phonetic alphabet (IPA) makes an excellent parallel. More than any theory or linguistic fact, this convention has allowed each conforming linguistic description and analysis access to a wider audience. A conventional set of constraints for language description, independent of any theory-particular claim of Universal Grammar, cross-linguistic markedness or mental reality, would serve similarly to make language descriptions more accessible, more understandable, and more readily matched against theoretical speculations.

If UNIV is taken as a convention, then our attitude towards it can be more flexible. For example, requiring that all constraints are present in all languages is as useful as requiring that every language employ all the sounds tabulated in the IPA. Rather, the common constraint set becomes a resource for language description from which the linguist can draw according to his or her needs.

Secondly, if the phonologist needs a constraint not found in the universal constraint set, there is no need to create another grand concept to be found in all languages. Instead, a diacritical rider on an existing constraint, like diacritics on phonetic symbols, will make easier the communication of the phenomenon. This is particularly so if the standard constraint set comes replete with standard riders. These might include 'except at the beginning of a word', or 'in open syllables'.[12]

---

[11] Markus Walther has noted (p.c.) that if declarative constraints are used, the problem is also simplified: no rank ordering needs to be considered, and the independent action of declarative constraints makes it possible to understand each in isolation.

[12] This does not have the same effect as ranking another constraint higher or lower. Applying such riders to a constraint would have the effect of making the whole hierarchy more permissive, rather than less.

OT offers a remarkable opportunity. For the first time, the linguistic community can define a common language for phonological generalizations akin to the phonetic alphabet. For the first time, the means of combining phonological generalizations is sufficiently flexible to allow the same ones to analyse many different languages. But we should shy away from making a category error, confusing description with content, alphabet with inventory. UNIV makes a rich device, but a poor fact.

14.9 References

Antworth, E. (1990). *PC-KIMMO: A Two-Level Processor for Morphological Analysis*. Dallas TX, Summer Institute of Linguistics.

Archangeli, D. (1997). 'Optimality Theory: An introduction to linguistics in the 1990s'. In Archangeli and Langendoen (eds), 1–32.

—— and D. T. Langendoen (eds). (1997). *Optimality Theory: An Overview*. Malden, MA, Blackwell.

—— and D. Pulleyblank (1989). 'Yoruba vowel harmony'. *Linguistic Inquiry* 20, 173–217.

—— —— (1994). *Grounded Phonology*. Number 25 in Current Studies in Linguistics Series. Cambridge, MA, MIT Press.

Beckman, J., L. Walsh Dickey, and S. Urbanczyk (eds), (1995). *Papers in Optimality Theory*, number 18 in University of Massachusetts Occasional Papers in Linguistics. Amherst, MA, Graduate Linguistic Student Association

Benua, L. (1995). 'Identity effects in morphological truncation.' In Beckman *et al.* (eds), 77–136. ROA-74.

Bird, S. (1990). *Constraint-Based Phonology*. PhD thesis, University of Edinburgh. Revised as Bird 1995.

—— (1995). *Computational Phonology: A Constraint-Based Approach*. Studies in Natural Language Processing. Cambridge, Cambridge University Press.

—— and T. M. Ellison (1994). 'One level phonology: autosegmental representations and rules as finite automata'. *Computational Linguistics* 20, 55–90.

Brown, R. and C. Hanlon (1970). 'Derivational complexity and order of acquisition in child speech'. In J. R. Hayes (ed.), *Cognition and the Development of Language*. New York, Wiley, 11–53.

Chomsky, N. (1978). 'A theory of Core Grammar'. *Glot* 1, 7–26.

—— and M. Halle (1968). *The Sound Pattern of English*. New York, Harper and Row.

Clark, E. V. (1978). 'Awareness of language: Some evidence from what children say and do'. In A. Sinclair, R. Jarvella, and W. Levelt (eds), *The Child's Conception of Language*. New York, Springer, 17–43.

Dickey, M. (1995). 'Inversion in child English and acquisition in Optimality Theory'. In Beckman *et al.* (eds), 575–588.

Ellison, T. M. (1992). *The Machine Learning of Phonological Structure*. PhD thesis, University of Western Australia, Perth.

—— (1997). 'Induction and inherent similarity'. In M. Ramscar and U. Hahn (eds), *Proceedings of Simcat '97*, 83–90.

Elman, J. L., E. A. Bates, M. H. Johnson, A. Karmiloff-Smith, D. Parisi, and K. Plunkett (1996). *Rethinking Innateness*. Cambridge, MA, MIT Press.

Ferguson, C. A. and C. B. Farwell (1975). 'Words and sounds in early language acquisition'. *Language* 51, 419–39.

——— L. Menn, and C. Stoel-Gammon (eds) (1992). *Phonological Development: Models, Research, Implications*. Timonium, MD, York Press.

Finch, S. P. and N. Chater (1992). 'Bootstrapping syntactic categories using statistical methods'. In W. Daelemans and D. Powers (eds), *Background and Experiments in Machine Learning of Natural Language*. Tilburg, ITK, 229–36.

Gold, E. M. (1967). 'Language identification in the limit'. *Information and Control* 16, 447–74.

Golston, C. and R. Wiese (1996). 'Zero morphology and constraint interaction: Subtraction and epenthesis in German dialects'. *Yearbook of Morphology*, 1996, 115–42.

Grimshaw, J. and V. Samek-Lodovici (1995). 'Optimal subjects'. In Beckman *et al.* (eds), 589–606.

Harman, G. (1980). 'Two quibbles about analyticity and psychological reality'. *The Behavioral and Brain Sciences* 3, 21–2.

Jakobson, R. (1968). *Child Language: Aphasia and Phonological Universals*. Janua linguarum. The Hague, Mouton.

Kent, R. D. (1992a). 'The biology of phonological development'. In Ferguson *et al.* (eds), 65–90.

——— (1992b). 'Phonological development as biology and behavior'. In R. S. Chapman (ed.), *Process in Language Acquisition and Disorders*. St Louis, MS, Mosby-Year Book, Inc., 67–85.

——— and G. Miolo (1995). 'Phonetic abilities in the first year of life'. In P. Fletcher and B. MacWhinney (eds), *The Handbook of Child Language*. Oxford, Blackwell.

Kiparsky, P. and L. Menn (1977). 'On the acquisition of phonology'. In J. Macnamara (ed.), *Language Learning and Thought*. New York, Academic Press.

Koskenniemi, K. (1983). 'Two-level model for morphological analysis'. In *Proceedings of the Eighth International Joint Conference on Artificial Intelligence*, 683–5.

Legendre, G. , W. Raymond, and P. Smolensky (1993). 'Optimality-Theoretic typology of case and grammatical voice systems'. In *Proceedings of the 19th Meeting of the Berkeley Linguistics Society*. ROA-3.

Li, M. and P. M. B. Vitanyi (1989). 'Inductive reasoning and Kolmogorov complexity'. In *Proceedings of the Fourth Annual Conference on Structure in Complex ity Theory*, 165–85.

——— (1993). *An Introduction to Kolmogorov Complexity and its Applications*. Texts and Monographs in Computer Science. Springer Verlag.

McCarthy, J. (1996). 'Extensions of faithfulness: Rotuman revisited'. ROA-110.

——— and A. Prince (1995). 'Faithfulness and reduplicative identity'. In Beckman *et al.* (eds), 249–384. ROA-60.

Matthei, E. (1989). 'Crossing boundaries: More evidence for phonological constraints on early multi-word utterances'. *Journal of Child Language* 16, 41–54.

Menn, L. (1983). 'Development of articulatory, phonetic and phonological capabilities'. In *Language Production*, vol. 2. London, Academic Press, 3–50.

Newton, I. (1953). *Newton's Philosophy of Nature: Selections from His Writings*. New York, Haffner.

Orgun, C. O. (1994). 'Monotonic cyclicity and Optimality Theory'. In M. Gonzalez (ed.), *Proceedings of the 24th Annual Meeting of the North-East Linguistic Society*,

Amherst, MA. Graduate Linguistic Student Association, 461–474. ROA-123.

—— (1995). 'Correspondence and identity constraints in two-level OT'. ROA-62.

Pinker, S. (1989). *Learnability and Cognition: The Acquisition of Argument Structure*. Cambridge, MA, MIT/Bradford.

—— (1994). *The Language Instinct*. Harmondsworth, Penguin Books.

Popper, K. (1959). *The Logic of Scientific Discovery*. London, Hutchinson.

Prince, A. and P. Smolensky (1993). 'Optimality theory: Constraint interaction in generative grammar'. Technical Report TR-2, Rutgers University, Center for Cognitive Science. Same as Prince and Smolensky (to appear).

—— (to appear). *Optimality Theory: Constraint Interaction in Generative Grammar*. Cambridge, MA, MIT Press. Same as Prince and Smolensky (1993).

Quartz, S. R. and T. J. Sejnowski (1996). 'The Neural Basis of Cognitive Development: A Constructivist Manifesto'. *The Behavioral and Brain Sciences*, 20, 537–96.

Reichenbach, H. (1956). *The Direction of Time*. Berkeley, University of California Press.

Rissanen, J. (1978). 'Modelling by shortest data description'. *Automatica* 14, 445–71.

—— (1982). 'Estimation of structure by minimum description length'. *Circuit systems signal Processing* 1, 395–6.

—— (1987). 'Statistical complexity'. *Journal of the Royal Statistical Society*, B49, 223–39, 252–65.

Russell, K. (1995). 'Morphemes and candidates in Optimality Theory'. ROA-44.

Salmon, W. (1975). 'Theoretical explanation'. In S. Korner (ed.), *Explanation*. Oxford, Blackwell, 118–45.

—— (1978). 'Why ask "why"?' *Proceedings and Addresses of the Americal Philosophical Association* 51, 683–705.

—— (1984). *Scientific Explanation and the Causal Structure of the World*. Princeton, NJ, Princeton University Press.

Schwartz, R. and L. Leonard (1982). 'Do children pick and choose: An examination of phonological selection and avoidance in early lexical acquisition'. *Journal of Child Language* 9, 319–36.

Scobbie, J. M. (1991). *Attribute Value Phonology*. PhD thesis, University of Edinburgh.

—— (1997). *Autosegmental Representation in a Declarative Constraint-Based Framework*. New York, Garland.

—— J. Coleman, and S. Bird (1996). 'Key aspects of declarative phonology'. In J. Durand and B. Laks (eds), *Current Trends in Phonology: Models and Methods*, vol. 2. European Studies Research Institute, University of Salford Publications, 685–710.

Sells, P., J. Rickford and T. Wasow (1994). 'An Optimality-Theoretic approach to variation in negative inversion in AAVE'. Stanford University. ROA-53.

Smolensky, P. (1996). 'The Initial State and "Richness of the Base" in Optimality Theory'. Technical Report JHU-CogSci-96-4, Department of Cognitive Science, Johns Hopkins University. ROA-154.

Sober, E. (1988). *Reconstructing the Past*. Cambridge, MA, MIT Press.

Sokolov, J. and C. Snow (1994). 'The changing role of negative evidence in theories of language acquisition'. *Input and Interaction in Language Acquisition*. London, Cambridge University Press, 38–55.

Speas, M. (1995). 'Generalized control and null objects in Optimality Theory'. In Beckman *et al.* (eds), 637–54.

Stampe, D. (1979). *A Dissertation on Natural Phonology*. New York, Garland.

Tesar, B. B. (1995). *Computational Optimality Theory*. PhD thesis, University of Colorado.

—— and P. Smolensky (1993). 'The learnability of Optimality Theory: An algorithm and some basic complexity results'. Technical report, Department of Computer Science, University of Colorado, Boulder. ROA-2.

—— —— (1996). 'Learnability in Optimality Theory' (long version). Technical report, Department of Cognitive Science, Johns Hopkins University and Center for Cognitive Science, Rutgers University. ROA-156.

Valian, V. (1990). 'Logical and psychological constraints on the acquisition of syntax'. In L. Frazier and J. de Villiers (eds), *Language Processing and Language Acquisition* Dordrecht, Kluwer, 119–45.

Vihman, M. M. (1992). 'Early syllables and the construction of phonology'. In Ferguson *et al.* (eds), 393–422.

Wallace, C. and P. Freeman (1992). 'Single-factor analysis by minimum message length estimation'. *Journal of the Royal Statistical Society*, B54, 195–209.

Wallace, C. S. and D. M. Boulton (1968). 'An information measure for classification'. *Computer Journal* 11, 185–195.

Woolford, E. (1995). 'Object agreement in Palauan: Specificity, humanness, economy and optimality'. In Beckman *et al.* (eds), 655–702. ROA-55.

15

Learning Phonology: Genetic Algorithms and Yoruba Tongue-Root Harmony[1]

Douglas Pulleyblank and William J. Turkel

15.1 Introduction

This chapter presents an implementation of a genetic algorithm which acquires the constraint rankings of an Optimality-theoretic grammar. The chapter begins by sketching the structure of a grammar within Optimality Theory, goes on to outline the nature of an acquisition model employing genetic algorithms, and finally, applies genetic algorithms to Optimality Theory, using as a case study the acquisition of tongue-root harmony systems. The basic structure of a phonological grammar in Optimality Theory is established by the appropriate ranking of a universally determined set of violable constraints. This structure is well suited for an acquisition model based on genetic algorithms, a form of evolution that occurs on a computer. In a genetic algorithm, a problem of some sort is encoded in the form of strings of symbols. In the case of an Optimality-theoretic grammar, each such string of symbols directly corresponds to a ranked set of constraints. A population of these strings (ranked constraint sets) is randomly generated, each corresponding to a possible grammar. The goodness (or 'fitness') of each of the strings is then assessed for how well it describes the sort of data encountered. The fitness of most of the randomly generated strings will be very poor—especially if the search space is large—but some strings are better than others. This relative fitness gives direction to the search for a stable phonological grammar. Those strings with the highest fitness are preferentially selected to reproduce, and the whole process is iterated. Over time, the average fitness of

[1] We would like to thank Paul Boersma, Robin Clark and Mark Hewitt for comments on this work, as well as audiences at the University of Calgary, Rutgers University, University of Pennsylvania, SISSA (Trieste), University of Arizona, Holland Institute of Generative Linguistics, and the 1996 Girona International Summer School in Linguistics. This work was supported by a standard research grant from the Social Sciences and Humanities Research Council of Canada.

the population climbs. The case study here is the tongue-root harmony system of Yoruba. Using positive evidence only, we demonstrate that the algorithm succeeds in converging on the pattern of Standard Yoruba as well as on a related pattern referred to as Absolute Alignment. In concluding, we discuss implications of the approach for both phonological theory and for language acquisition.

Even for a linguistic system defined by a fairly small number of parameters, the problem of acquisition can be a formidable one. The patterns defined by natural language acquisition are therefore somewhat perplexing. While it can be argued that the richness of attested language patterns requires a reasonably large number of dimensions of variation, we nevertheless observe that children are able to learn languages even under quite adverse circumstances, and in a fairly short period of time.

This chapter presents a model of acquisition for Optimality-theoretic grammars based on genetic algorithms. To begin, the structure of a grammar within Optimality Theory will be sketched, focusing on the formal nature of the properties that must be learned during the course of acquisition. We then lay out the structure of an acquisition model employing genetic algorithms, and demonstrate how genetic algorithms can in principle be applied to the acquisition of Optimality-theoretic grammars. Finally, we present a case study of the tongue-root harmony system of Standard Yoruba, a Niger-Congo language of Nigeria. We demonstrate that a genetic algorithm can successfully converge on the attested grammar of Standard Yoruba, and discuss implications of the observed patterns for both acquisition and phonological theory. The basic proposal is that the combination of genetic algorithms and Optimality Theory allows for an account both of complex phonological patterns, and for rapid acquisition of such patterns.

15.2 The Structure of an Optimality-Theoretic Grammar and the Nature of the Acquisition Problem

As we will demonstrate at some length below, the intrinsic structure of an Optimality-theoretic grammar makes it eminently suitable for acquisition via genetic algorithms. The basic tenet of Optimality Theory is that phonological effects result from the interaction of a set of ranked, violable constraints, drawn from a universal pool.[2] Consider these properties individually, focusing on their relation to acquisition.

As a crucial starting-point, it is assumed that a grammar consists of a set of constraints, and it is assumed that all constraints are determined by Universal Grammar. Language-specific phonological patterns are attributed to particular

---

[2] For an introduction to Optimality Theory, including a discussion of the sorts of featural effects discussed here, see Archangeli and Langendoen (eds) (1997).

rankings of universally-determined constraints, not to the introduction of special language-specific constraints. This proposal has an immediate consequence for acquisition: language learners do not need to deduce some set of phonological constraints, they have only to correctly establish the ranking of the predetermined set of universal constraints.

Given the universal nature of the constraint pool, not all constraints will be surface true for all languages—that is, constraints are violable. Consider a set of representations involving two constraints. In configurations where both constraints can be satisfied, the *optimal* representation, and therefore the representation predicted by the grammar to be attested, must satisfy both constraints. But consider some representation where one constraint can only be satisfied at the expense of the other—that is, where the two constraints are in conflict with each other. Optimality Theory proposes that such cases of conflict are resolved by rankings: each individual grammar imposes a ranking on the set of constraints; violation of a constraint is tolerated only when necessary to allow the satisfaction of a higher-ranked constraint.

A grammar is thus determined by establishing a ranking for the set of constraints provided by Universal Grammar.

To illustrate this sketch of Optimality Theory, we present a pair of constraints that play a crucial role in the particular case study discussed later in this chapter, the case of vowel harmony. The basic pattern of vowel harmony is one where some vocalic feature takes an entire constituent as its domain. For example, the feature for a retracted tongue root (RTR) in Yoruba is realized throughout the domain of the phonological word.[3] Consider the case of mid vowels, for example. In order to be fully harmonic, such vowels must agree in their retraction value; no combinations of retraction and advancement are allowed within a single word composed entirely of mid vowels. We assume for the implementation presented here that retraction (RTR) is phonologically specified, while advancement is the phonetic realization of a vowel unspecified for RTR. This is for simplicity only. Assuming that both retraction (RTR) and advancement (ATR) are present is equally possible, as we have demonstrated in Pulleyblank and Turkel (1996). Assuming that only retraction is present phonologically, a word with completely advanced vowels has the phonological structure of (1a), while a word with completely retracted vowels has the structure of (1b). (Illustrations are taken from forms involving consistently front unrounded vowels for the sake of expositional clarity only.)

---

[3] For treatments of Yoruba vowel harmony within rule-based theories, see Archangeli and Pulleyblank (1989, 1994) and the references therein. For two different approaches to Yoruba within Optimality Theory, see Archangeli and Pulleyblank (1993) and Pulleyblank (1996). For a discussion of the role of domains in Yoruba harmony, see Akinlabi, Archangeli, Ọla and Pulleyblank (in preparation).

(1) Fully harmonic forms

a. $\begin{bmatrix} & \\ e & e \end{bmatrix}$ b. $\begin{bmatrix} R_{TR} \\ \widehat{\varepsilon\ \varepsilon} \end{bmatrix}$

ebè	'heap for yams'	ɛsè	'foot'
ègè	'dirge'	ègɛ́	'cassava'
èké	'lie'	ɛké	'forked stick'

Forms which mix mid advanced vowels with mid retracted vowels are ruled out, as schematised in (2).

(2) Impossible forms

a. $^*\begin{bmatrix} R_{TR} \\ | \\ e\ \ \varepsilon \end{bmatrix}$ b. $^*\begin{bmatrix} R_{TR} \\ | \\ \varepsilon\ \ e \end{bmatrix}$

To achieve the desired distinction, we assume that Universal Grammar includes constraints forcing the alignment of vocalic features such as RTR with the edges of the phonological word (Kirchner 1993; Smolensky 1993; Pulleyblank 1993, 1996; Akinlabi 1995, 1996). For the Yoruba case, one constraint forces the alignment of RTR to the right edge of the word (ALIGNRIGHT) while a second constraint forces the alignment of RTR to the left edge of the word (ALIGNLEFT).

The basic alignment constraints interact with substantive constraints governing the legitimacy or illegitimacy of particular combinations of feature values. In Yoruba, for example, there are three vowel heights, high [i, u], mid [e, ɛ, o, ɔ], and low [a]: RTR may co-occur with mid and low vowels, but may not co-occur with high vowels. That is, high vowels must be advanced in Yoruba [i, u]; they cannot be retracted *[ɪ, ʊ]. This constraint, which will be referred to as the RTR/HI constraint (Archangeli and Pulleyblank 1994), interacts with alignment in interesting ways.

Consider a configuration involving a *mid-vowel high-vowel* sequence, in conjunction with a lexical specification of RTR. If the RTR specification is associated with both vowels, then the form is fully harmonic (specifically, ALIGNRIGHT is satisfied); RTR/HI is violated, however, because the final vowel is high and retracted (3a). If the substantive prohibition against high retracted vowels is respected, then the form is not fully harmonic (3b).

(3) Conflicting Constraints

a. $\begin{bmatrix} R_{TR} \\ \widehat{\varepsilon\ \ ɪ} \end{bmatrix}$ ALIGNRIGHT satisfied
   RTR/HI violated

b. $\begin{bmatrix} R_{TR} \\ | \\ \varepsilon\ \ i \end{bmatrix}$ ALIGNRIGHT violated
   RTR/HI satisfied

Since it is impossible for both constraints to be satisfied, a grammar must make a choice to rank one as more important than the other. Standard Yoruba, which absolutely prohibits high retracted vowels, ranks RTR/HI above ALIGNRIGHT; other languages allow the derivation of high retracted vowels in such configurations by assuming the opposite ranking, resulting in a larger inventory of vowels (for example, Akan and Maasai (Archangeli and Pulleyblank 1994)).

These two possible rankings are illustrated in (4). In this and subsequent tableaux, left-to-right presentation of constraints corresponds by convention to top-down ranking. An asterisk (*) indicates a constraint violation, while the inclusion of an exclamation mark (!) graphically locates a violation that serves to eliminate a form as a nonoptimal candidate. The pointing finger (☞) graphically identifies the optimal representation.

(4)   Illustration of ranking possibilities

GRAMMAR 1 ALIGNR >> RTR/HI	ALIGNR	RTR/HI
☞ a. $\begin{bmatrix} \text{RTR} \\ \overset{\wedge}{\varepsilon\ \ \text{I}} \end{bmatrix}$		*
b. $\begin{bmatrix} \text{RTR} \\ \overset{\mid}{\varepsilon\ \text{i}} \end{bmatrix}$	!*	

GRAMMAR 2 RTR/HI >> ALIGNR	RTR/HI	ALIGNR
a. $\begin{bmatrix} \text{RTR} \\ \overset{\wedge}{\varepsilon\ \ \text{I}} \end{bmatrix}$	*!	
☞ b. $\begin{bmatrix} \text{RTR} \\ \overset{\mid}{\varepsilon\ \text{i}} \end{bmatrix}$		*

By ranking ALIGNRIGHT above RTR/HI, Grammar 1 selects the fully harmonic form as optimal (Grammar 1, form *a*: [ɛ C ɪ]). By ranking RTR/HI above ALIGNRIGHT, Grammar 2 selects the form respecting substantive constraints as optimal (Grammar 2, form *b*: [ɛ C i]).

For such a theory of phonology, a large part of the acquisition problem is the correct determination of the relative rankings of the various constraints supplied by Universal Grammar. In this simple example, the problem is quite trivial. Observation of a form with the vowel sequence [ɛ . . . ɪ] is only compatible with Grammar 1, while observation of a form like [ɛ . . . i] is only compatible with Grammar 2.

(5)   The acquisition problem: how to determine whether ALIGNR ranks above RTR/HI or vice versa
    Primary Linguistic Data: { . . . [ɛ . . . ɪ] . . . } ⇒ Grammar 1.
    Primary Linguistic Data: { . . . [ɛ . . . i] . . . } ⇒ Grammar 2.

The problem immediately ceases to be trivial, however, once a larger set of constraints is considered. Consider the addition of even a single constraint. Mathematically, the number of possible constraint rankings for a set of N con-

straints is *N!*.[4] For two constraints, there are two possible rankings (as seen in
(4)); for three constraints, the number increases to six.

(6)   Possible grammars with three constraints

      Language 1: AlignR >> Rtr/Hi >> MaxRtr
      Language 2: AlignR >> MaxRtr >> Rtr/Hi
      Language 3: Rtr/Hi >> AlignR >> MaxRtr
      Language 4: Rtr/Hi >> MaxRtr >> AlignR
      Language 5: MaxRtr >> AlignR >> Rtr/Hi
      Language 6: MaxRtr >> Rtr/Hi >> AlignR

For the illustration in (6), the third constraint is MaxRtr, a correspondence
constraint that requires that any Rtr value found in a lexical input be retained
in the output.

The acquisition problem is immediately rendered more severe by the introduction of even this fairly minimal level of complexity (see Pulleyblank and
Turkel 1997, 1998). Pulleyblank and Turkel 1998, for example, notes four relevant
problems. First, there are ambiguities in the mapping from a phonetic signal to
a surface phonological representation. Second, there are comparable ambiguities
in the relation between surface phonological representations and corresponding
underlying representations. Third, the establishment of an underlying/surface
relation underdetermines grammatical constraint rankings. Fourth, even if a
ranking has been established, there is indeterminacy in the establishment of
underlying representations.

15.3 Acquisition as Combinatorial Optimization

If language variation is characterized by configurations or permutations of innate, universal principles, then the acquisition process can be seen as a search
through a space of possible languages. Comparing acquisition in Optimality
Theory with parameter setting models is instructive.

A system of N binary parameters can specify at most 2^N different possible
languages. Put another way, changing the number of parameters from N to $N+1$
causes the space of possible grammars to become twice as large. The impact that
this change will have on the acquisition process depends on the degree to which
the parameters are *independent*.

If each parameter is completely independent of the others, then that parameter may be set without making reference to the settings of any of the other parameters. A system of 20 parameters can be set via a process of 20 questions: 'Is
parameter one plus or minus?', 'Is parameter two plus or minus?', and so on.
Under such an account, the addition of another parameter will double the num-

---

[4] The notation *N!*, read '*N* factorial', denotes $N \times (N-1) \times (N-2) \times \ldots \times 2 \times 1$. So $3! = 3 \times 2 \times 1 = 6$.

ber of possible languages distinguished by the system, but will only add a single question to the acquisition process.

The idealization of parameter independence is not tenable. Parameters show some degree of *interdependence*, and thus a parameter can only be set in the context of the settings of some of the other parameters. In the limit, each of the N parameter settings would be dependent on the settings of the other $N-1$ parameters—a case which Edwin Williams described as 'paralysing interconnectedness'.

The 20 questions model of parameter setting cannot work when the parameters are interdependent. One method which would work (but which we must reject because it is psychologically implausible and computationally infeasible) is *brute force enumeration*. Each possible vector of parameter settings is tried, one at a time. On average, half of the total number of vectors will be enumerated before the target settings are discovered (although in any given case, the number could be much larger). Under this account, the addition of a new parameter will double the number of possible languages, but it will also double the number of hypotheses the learner must entertain during acquisition.

Consideration of the problem of parameter interdependence led Clark (1992) to suggest that parameters should be set as a group, rather than one at a time. Formulated like this, the problem of parameter setting becomes a problem of *combinatorial optimization*. In a combinatorial optimization problem, the interdependence of variables forces you to search for an optimal collection of settings. Such problems tend to be very hard computationally. Clark proposed a parameter setting model based on *genetic algorithms*. A genetic algorithm is a form of evolution which occurs on a computer, and which is capable of solving combinatorial optimization problems.

In Clark's model, a number of vectors of parameter settings are randomly generated. Each vector is assigned a value (known as the *fitness*) which indicates the degree to which that vector of parameter settings generates the target language. The vectors with higher fitness values are preferentially *recombined* to give rise to new vectors. These vectors are tested for fitness, and the whole process is iterated until the vector which generates the target language is discovered.

Now consider a system of N constraints. As previously mentioned, there will be $N!$ possible constraint rankings. The learner's task is to find a constraint ranking which matches the rankings of the speakers of the target language. The factorial function grows much more rapidly with increasing N than 2^N does. Changing the number of constraints from N to $N+1$ causes the space of possible grammars to become $N+1$ times as large. Although we do not intend our estimates of acquisition time in (7) as serious estimates of the length of time required to learn rankings of particular lengths, it is instructive to keep in mind that even at an extremely rapid rate of acquisition, a stroll through the constraint ranking space cannot be a possible account of acquisition even for a finite, and indeed small, number of constraints.

(7)   The N! Problem

Number of constraint rankings per number of constraints	Back-of-the-envelope acquisition time (1 ranking per second, examining half the rankings)
$2! = 2$	1 second
$3! = 6$	3 seconds
$4! = 24$	12 seconds
$5! = 120$	1 minute
.	.
.	.
.	.
$11! = 39,916,800$	231 days
.	.
.	.
.	
$20! = 2,432,902,008,177,000,000$	38,573,408,298 years ($\pm$)

The idealization of constraint independence cannot be adopted as an acquisition strategy because constraint functionality is crucially dependent on interaction. While it is unlikely that a given constraint is crucially-ranked with respect to each of the other *N-1* constraints, it is possible. There is no upper bound to constraint interaction, and the degree of interdependence is likely higher than that of parameters.

In addition, Optimality-theoretic systems are subject to a *compounding problem*: increasing the number of constraints increases the class of possible inputs. As a result, the interdependence between the success of a particular constraint ranking and the set of postulated underlying representations is accentuated (Pulleyblank and Turkel 1998).

The rapid growth of *N!*, crucial interdependence of constraints, and the compounding problem suggest that acquiring a target constraint ranking can also be viewed as a problem in combinatorial optimization. In fact, finding a constraint ranking is analogous to solving the Travelling Salesperson Problem (TSP), the prototypical combinatorial optimization problem.

In the TSP, the object is to find a tour through *N* cities which minimises some cost function. Depending on the cost function, the problem can be either *symmetric* or *asymmetric*. Say that we find that the shortest route through cities A, B, C, and D is ABCD. This is a symmetric problem, because the salesperson would travel the same distance on the route DCBA. If, however, we want to minimise some combination of cost and distance, then the tour ABCD is not necessarily as good as DCBA, even though they are the same distance. The salesperson may be able to take advantage of airline seat sales by travelling via the latter route. In this case the problem is asymmetric. Finding a ranking for *N* constraints is an asymmetric problem, because A >> B >> C is not the same as C >> B >> A.

The genetic algorithm has been used successfully in finding solutions for the

TSP,[5] and thus forms a natural hypothesis for the core of a global optimization model for Optimality Theory. Of particular interest, the genetic algorithm exhibits striking formal similarities to the evaluation mechanism of Optimality Theory (Turkel 1994). Hence in exploring the applicability of genetic algorithms to OT, very little theoretical apparatus needs to be added to OT's intrinsic ability to determine optimal candidates.[6]

15.4 Finding OT Constraint Rankings with a Genetic Algorithm

In this section we describe the structure and operation of the genetic algorithm, a program which optimizes by simulating the process of natural selection. We modify the algorithm so that it can optimize in a space of constraint rankings. We then describe an implementation of an Optimality-theoretic acquisition model constructed around the modified genetic algorithm.

15.4.1 *The Standard Genetic Algorithm*

Two processes characterize evolution by natural selection. The first of these is *heritability with variation*. A population of offspring inherit the genetic makeup of their parents, but the transmission is disrupted by random fluctuations (*mutations*) and by more systematic alteration (*recombination*). The second process is *selection*. Individuals must compete for scarce resources; those individuals which are more *fit* are more likely to reproduce. Taken in conjunction, the two processes lead to species which are increasingly *adapted* to their environments.[7]

The standard genetic algorithm (Goldberg 1989; Forrest 1993) operates in a fashion directly analogous to natural selection. A problem of interest forms the environment in which a population of artificial creatures 'lives'. Those creatures which are better suited to the problem environment are preferentially selected to reproduce. Over time, the population adapts to the environment, and in so doing, solves the problem posed by that environment. The suitability of a given creature to the environment is measured by the *fitness function* (or, in the terminology of optimization, the *objective function*).

The operation of the standard genetic algorithm is shown in (8). A collection of solutions to the problem of interest are generated. These solutions (known as *chromosomes*) are encoded in some way, usually as fixed-length binary strings.

---

[5] It may not be the case that the genetic algorithm finds some provably optimal solution for the problem (Wetzel 1983; Goldberg and Lingle 1985; Goldberg 1989; and many others)—in fact, the TSP does not yet have a provably optimal solution. This may not be important for its application to language, however, since imperfect learning can characterize language variation and guide language change (Clark and Roberts 1993; Niyogi and Berwick 1995; Pulleyblank and Turkel 1996).

[6] This does not mean, of course, that genetic algorithms are the only algorithms that could solve either the TSP or OT problems; consider, for example, simulated annealing and taboo search.

[7] This sketch is not intended to do justice to evolutionary biology but rather to convey the metaphor upon which genetic algorithms are based.

It is customary in working with genetic algorithms to make the simplifying assumption that the artificial creature can be equated with its chromosome. The leftmost box in (8) shows an initial population of chromosomes. Each completely specifies a possible solution to the problem. The key point is that some of these solutions are better than others, and the chromosomes encoding the better solutions have a correspondingly better chance of survival and reproduction in the problem environment.

The *fitness* of each chromosome is assessed, and the more fit chromosomes are preferentially selected to form the *mating pool*, the centre box in (8). The population sizes in the genetic algorithm are usually kept constant, so the mating pool will have the same number of chromosomes as the initial population, although the composition will be somewhat different. In particular, there is often more than one copy of a high fitness chromosome in the mating pool, allowing that chromosome to have a number of offspring.

Members of the mating pool give rise to the population at time *t+1* (shown in the rightmost box of (8)) in one of four ways. The simplest thing that can happen to a chromosome is that it can be *cloned*: copied without alteration into the population of the next generation. A single chromosome may also be *mutated*: copied into the next generation with some minimal disruption. Typically, mutation is implemented as the toggling of a randomly-chosen bit. Two chromosomes from the mating pool may also be *recombined*. The recombination algorithm illustrated in (8) is *one-point crossover*. Two chromosomes are lined

(8)   Operation of the genetic algorithm

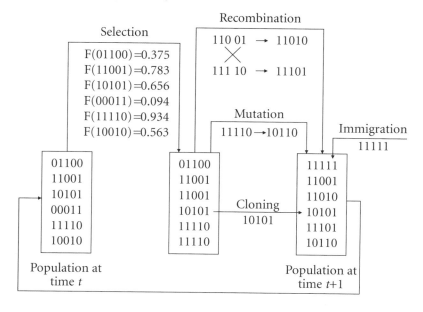

up and cut at the same randomly-chosen location. The head of each is then joined to the tail of the other. The two resulting chromosomes are placed in the population of the next generation. Finally, a chromosome from the mating pool may be replaced in the next generation by a randomly-generated chromosome.

The whole process is iterated, so that the population of time $t+1$ undergoes selection, disruption, and so forth, giving rise in turn to the population at time $t+2$.

Two aspects of the genetic algorithm are particularly problem-dependent; the encoding of potential solutions to the problem as chromosomes, and the evaluation of fitness. In order to apply the genetic algorithm to the problem of optimization within a space of constraint rankings, we must address each of these issues.

The modifications required for encoding hypothesised constraint rankings are shown in (9). We chose to use permutations of constraints as chromosomes, where each such permutation ABCDE represents a strict dominance hierarchy A >> B >> C >> D >> E. There is exactly one occurrence of each constraint per chromosome, and in a system of N constraints, $N!$ possible chromosomes.

Mutation can be implemented as the swap of a randomly-chosen pair of adjacent constraints. *Recombination* can be achieved by 'mark cancellation crossover' (Turkel 1994; cf. Prince and Smolensky 1993). A pair of chromosomes are cut at a randomly-chosen point. The constraints which appear in the head of each are eliminated from a copy of the other chromosome. The resulting copies are then appended to the heads. This process is illustrated schematically in (9). *Cloning* and *immigration* required no modification.

(9)   Genetic algorithm modified for constraint ranking

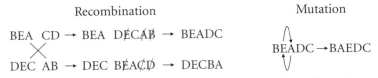

Although we experimented with various combinations of the disruption operators, the results reported on here involve mutation, cloning and immigration only.

The evaluation of fitness for hypothesised constraint rankings is somewhat more complicated, and will be developed piece by piece. We begin with an overview of the whole process.

The learner receives a datum drawn from the set of primary linguistic data (PLD). Such a datum is assumed to be minimally structured—consistent with what Ken Wexler has termed the 'fundamental assumption about the input' (Wexler 1995; see Pulleyblank and Turkel 1998 for discussion within the context of Optimality Theory). In the case we implement, we assume that the learner is able to delineate words, recognize vowel features, and determine whether a surface representation violates constraints. We do not assume any knowledge at the stage we examine of morphology (for example, paradigms) nor do we assume any knowledge of correct lexical forms (structured underlying representations). We return to this issue in more detail in Section 15.7.2, where we lay out details of the actual implementation.

A set of possible pairings of underlying representation (UR) and surface representation (SR) are generated. These pairings correspond to the datum the learner has received. There are a number of such pairings for any surface form, as discussed earlier. For each hypothesised ranking and for each UR/SR pairing, the following steps are performed. The learner determines which constraints are relevant for fitness (more about this later). Those constraints are entered into a tableau, and UR/SR pairings are assessed for constraint violations. A tally of the violations of relevant constraints is represented as a binary number, which is converted into a fitness measure. The maximum fitness value is chosen to represent the fitness for the hypothesised constraint ranking with respect to the input datum being considered. The fitness values are scaled and used for selection of the mating pool.

The evaluation of a constraint ranking hypothesis is schematically illustrated in (10). Each of the rankings in the population is taken out to be tested for fitness. A datum is sampled from the PLD, and a set of UR/SR pairings are generated which are compatible with the datum. These pairings form the rows

(10)   Schematic illustration: evaluating a constraint-ranking hypothesis

Underlying	Surface	RTR/HI	MAXRTR	ALIGNR	DEPRTR	DEPPATH	Binary	Fitness
$\begin{bmatrix} \text{E I} \end{bmatrix}$	$\begin{bmatrix} \text{RTR} \\ \varepsilon\ \text{i} \end{bmatrix}$	0	0	1*	1*	1*	00111	0.78125
$\begin{bmatrix} \text{RTR} \\ \text{E i} \end{bmatrix}$	$\begin{bmatrix} \text{RTR} \\ \varepsilon\ \text{i} \end{bmatrix}$	0	0	1*	0	1*	00101	0.84375
$\begin{bmatrix} \text{RTR} \\ \varepsilon\ \text{I} \end{bmatrix}$	$\begin{bmatrix} \text{RTR} \\ \varepsilon\ \text{i} \end{bmatrix}$	0	0	1*	0	0	00100	0.87500

of a tableau. If a particular constraint is violated by a UR/SR pairing, then a 1 is entered into the corresponding cell in the tableau. Otherwise, a 0 is entered into the cell.[8]

Reading across each row, the binary number obtained reflects the fitness for the ranking and a given UR/SR pairing. We note that by encoding the fitness of a particular ranking as a binary number, we automatically encode the claim made in Prince and Smolensky (1993), as well as most subsequent work, that any high-ranking violation counts as worse than the sum of any set of more lowly-ranking violations. That is, 1000 is a worse violation than 0111.

To facilitate comparison of rankings with different numbers of constraints, the binary number is converted to a decimal fitness value between zero and one. The maximum such fitness value is returned as the fitness for the ranking—it reflects the fitness that the ranking receives under the best possible interpretation of lexical organization.

The tableau method for evaluating constraint rankings has to be adjusted so that vacuous satisfaction of constraints cannot boost the fitness of a ranking. The genetic algorithm is sensitive to statistical regularities; unless controlled for, statistical generalizations may conflict with linguistic generalizations. The learner checks for *fitness relevance*: it scores only those constraints for which the universally quantified argument is present in the UR/SR pair.

To illustrate the importance of fitness relevance, consider a case where the population on iteration t happens to include the two (partial) rankings given in (11).

(11)   a. RTR/HI >> LINKRTR >> ALIGNL
        b. ALIGNL >> RTR/HI >> LINKRTR

For a language such as Standard Yoruba (see below), the actual ranking is that given in (11a). If appropriate existing Yoruba forms including RTR specifications and high vowels are used to evaluate such pairs, (11a) will indeed be assigned a

(12)   Comparison of rankings with relevant data

Underlying	Surface	RTR/HI	LINKRTR	ALIGNL	Binary	Fitness
$\begin{bmatrix} \text{RTR} \\ \text{I E} \end{bmatrix} \Leftrightarrow \begin{bmatrix} \text{RTR} \\ \text{i } \varepsilon \end{bmatrix}$		0	0	1 (*)	001	0.875

Underlying	Surface	ALIGNL	RTR/HI	LINKRTR	Binary	Fitness
$\begin{bmatrix} \text{RTR} \\ \text{I E} \end{bmatrix} \Leftrightarrow \begin{bmatrix} \text{RTR} \\ \text{i } \varepsilon \end{bmatrix}$		1 (*)	0	0	100	0.500

---

[8] Note that gradient violation information is lost in this algorithm. We could modify the algorithm to keep an arbitrary amount of information about gradient violation, but it has not been necessary so far. See Prince and Smolensky (1993: section 10.2.2).

fitness that is higher than that assigned to (11b). Using a single input/output pairing to illustrate, consider the case in (12).

Because the ranking of RTR/HI >> LINKRTR >> ALIGNL is assigned a higher fitness value than the alternative, its properties are more likely to be inherited by members of the $t+1$ population.

Consider, however, the fitness scores that would occur if the same two rankings were evaluated, but where a PLD with no RTR value present is used to evaluate them.

(13)   Comparison of rankings with irrelevant data

Underlying	Surface	HI/RTR	LINKRTR	ALIGNL	Binary	Fitness
$\begin{bmatrix} I\ E \end{bmatrix}$	$\Leftrightarrow$ $\begin{bmatrix} i\ e \end{bmatrix}$	0	0	0	000	1.000

Underlying	Surface	ALIGNL	HI/RTR	LINKRTR	Binary	Fitness
$\begin{bmatrix} I\ E \end{bmatrix}$	$\Leftrightarrow$ $\begin{bmatrix} i\ e \end{bmatrix}$	0	0	0	000	1.000

In such a case, both rankings attain perfect scores since no violations of the three constraints are incurred.

Imagine now that both rankings are members of a population of rankings being evaluated during a particular generation. Imagine further that the ranking in (11a) receives a datum exactly as in (12), while the ranking in (11b) receives a datum as in (13). This means that the desired ranking would receive a lower fitness than the less desired ranking, but on the basis of an irrelevant datum.

One could imagine correcting this problem by presenting the same datum to all constraint rankings in any generation. As such, if one ranking gets a relevant datum, then all rankings get the same relevant datum; and if one gets an irrelevant datum, then so do the others. Such a modification would alter somewhat the problem being considered, but it would not eliminate it. Consider the distribution of low vowels in a typical five-vowel system of the type [i, e, a, o, u]. Assuming that all five vowels occur with equal frequency, this means that there is 0.2 (i.e. 1/5) chance of having a low vowel in a word of one syllable, and a 0.36 (1/5 + (4/5 × 1/5)) chance of having at least one low vowel in a two-syllable word. Assume in addition that the language exhibits a distinction between advanced and retracted tongue roots, with a 1/2 chance of a word having vowels from the advanced set , and 1/2 of having vowels from the retracted set. Putting these two factors together, the probability at any given time of encountering a one-syllable word with a low vowel and advancement would be 1/2 × 0.2, i.e. 0.1, and the probability of encountering a two-syllable word with at least one low vowel and advancement would be 1/2 × 0.36, i.e. 0.18. So if there was a constraint on the co-occurrence of lowness with advancement, less than 18% of forms would be expected to be relevant. Consider what this would mean. If a poor ranking achieved a perfect score on the relevant constraint because the constraint passes vacuously, then the fitness would be relatively high, but for an invalid reason. The odds of encountering crucial data is relatively low. So even though the right ranking will do better occasionally, between 10% and 18% of the time, a bad ranking can do well between 82% and 90% of the time! The algorithm can end up preferring a ranking whose high fitness was a function of irrelevant data.

To prevent such undesirable skewing of results, we implemented fitness relevance, scoring only those constraints whose universally quantified variable is observed in the datum. For example, LINKRTR universally quantifies over tokens of 'RTR': *all* tokens of RTR must be linked. RTR/LO (If RTR then LO) universally quantifies over the variable 'RTR': for *all* tokens of RTR, the implication must hold (note that no such quantification holds of low values in such a case). Hence constraints like LINKRTR and RTR/LO are *relevant* for any representation containing an RTR specification.

15.5 The Application of Genetic Algorithms to Optimality Theory

We report here on a test of the performance of a genetic algorithm in a case study of tongue-root harmony. The formal hypothesis that we assume is that vowel harmony results from the interaction of three families of constraints: *faithfulness* (Prince and Smolensky 1993; McCarthy and Prince 1993a; Itô, Mester and Padgett 1995), *alignment* (Prince and Smolensky 1993; McCarthy and Prince 1993a, b; Kirchner 1993; Smolensky 1993) and *grounded conditions* (Archangeli and Pulleyblank 1994).

With regard to faithfulness, we assume a model of correspondence (McCarthy and Prince 1995). The basic effect of faithfulness is to require that input forms and corresponding output forms be identical. Specifically, any feature present in the input must also be present in the output (MAXF), any feature in the output must be present in the input (DEPF), and any association to a feature that is present in the output must be present in the input (DEPPATH).[9] Informally, the effect of MAXF is to prohibit featural deletion, the effect of DEPF is to prohibit feature insertion, and the effect of DEPPATH is to prohibit the spreading of a feature. To simplify the case somewhat, we did not entertain candidates where a feature is delinked; that is, we did not consider cases where MAXPATH might be relevant.

In conflict with faithfulness, we assumed that alignment constraints are directly responsible for harmony. Specifically, harmony results from aligning a feature with the left and right edges of some harmonic domain. Here, we distin-

---

[9] Following Lombardi (1995), Myers (1997), etc., we assume that evaluations of correspondence are on a feature-by-feature basis, hence we posit MAXF and DEPF, F a featural element, and we do not posit any class of IDENT constraints.

guish between two domains: Root, a morphologically-defined domain, and (Phonological) Word, a phonologically-defined domain.

Finally, we assume that feature co-occurrence conditions of both sympathetic and antagonistic types govern the distribution of harmonic features. Sympathetic constraints require the presence of one feature in the presence of some other feature (If F then G); antagonistic constraints prohibit the co-occurrence of two features (If F then not G). Sometimes such conditions work in tandem with alignment to produce harmony; sometimes they work against harmony.

In concrete terms, we assumed representations specified for values of the Retracted Tongue Root (RTR) feature, and instantiated these three constraint families with constraints appropriate for RTR (for treatments of tongue-root harmony in Optimality Theory, see, for example, Akinlabi 1997; Pulleyblank 1996; Pulleyblank *et al.* 1995; Li 1996; Shahin 1997).

With regard to faithfulness, three constraints result:

(14)   Instantiation of faithfulness constraints with respect to RTR

MAXRTR: An RTR element in the input must be in the output.
DEPRTR: An RTR element in the output must be in the input.
DEPPATHRTR: A path between RTR and a vowel that is in the output must be in the input.

Note that although we implement faithfulness constraints, we do not assume that the learner has determined correct underlying representations for morphemes at the stage of learning that we examine. That is, we assume what Wexler (1995) has referred to as the Fundamental Assumption on the Input (see Pulleyblank and Turkel 1998). We will discuss this in detail when we describe the implementation in Section 15.7.2.

For alignment, an RTR specification may be aligned to the left or right of the root, or it may be aligned to the left or right of a phonological word.

(15)   Instantiation of alignment constraints with respect to RTR

$[\text{ALIGNR}]_{RT}$: The right edge of any root RTR specification is aligned with the right edge of the root.
$[\text{ALIGNL}]_{RT}$: The left edge of any root RTR specification is aligned with the left edge of the root.
ALIGNR: The right edge of any RTR specification is aligned with the right edge of the word.
ALIGNL: The left edge of any RTR specification is aligned with the left edge of the word.

Following Pulleyblank (1996), we assume that any specification subject to a root domain alignment constraint must be a part of the root, while any specification subject to a word alignment constraint must be part of the word.

Finally, for our simulation we assume four grounded conditions with regard to RTR, derived as follows. Three surface vowel heights are identified, *high, mid, low*, specified by two monovalent features: HI defining high vowels, LO defining low vowels, and mid vowels defined by the absence of specification. Retracted vowels are defined by the monovalent feature RTR, while advanced vowels are unspecified. Following Archangeli and Pulleyblank (1994), low vowels are preferentially retracted while high vowels are not, and retraction preferentially results in a low vowel, not a high vowel – that is, the full set of phonetically-motivated implications involving RTR and the two height features LO and HI are posited, with conditions involving positive antecedents only allowed:

(16)   Instantiation of grounded constraints with respect to RTR and height
        features
        Lo/RTR: If LO then RTR.
        Hi/RTR: If HI then not RTR.
        RTR/Lo: If RTR then LO.
        RTR/Hi: If RTR then not HI.

In concluding this brief introduction to the constraints used in this implementation, we note two additional points. First, although we assume a monovalent RTR specification in this chapter, nothing depends on such an interpretation. Interpreting 'RTR' as '[–ATR]' would lead to equivalent results for the specific purposes of this chapter. Second, we assume for the purposes of simplification that only RTR is present in the representations, but not ATR. That is, the feature of tongue-root retraction (RTR) is found to the exclusion of the feature for tongue-root advancement (ATR). In a fuller account, both could be present, with the domination of one over the other resulting from the way the relevant constraints are ranked. See Pulleyblank and Turkel (1996).

15.6 The Grammars of Standard Yoruba and Absolute Alignment

In order to test the ability of a genetic algorithm to acquire an appropriate grammar for some set of data, it is necessary to have both a data set and an analysis of it. To this end, we targeted first the pattern of vowel harmony in Standard Yoruba, and then a closely related variant of it, one we refer to as Absolute Alignment. We assume the approach to harmony developed in Archangeli and Pulleyblank (1989, 1993, 1994), and specifically assume the optimality analysis of Pulleyblank (1996). We summarize the relevant data and analysis here; for details and motivation, the reader is referred to the cited works. We begin with a brief account of Standard Yoruba.

15.6.1 *Standard Yoruba*

Standard Yoruba has seven oral vowels which co-occur in monomorphemic disyllabic forms as shown in the chart in (17).

(17)   Standard Yoruba Vowel Co-occurrence Patterns

	i	e	ε	a	ɔ	o	u
i	+	+	+	+	+	+	+
e	+	+				+	+
ε	+		+	+	+		+
a	+	+	+	+	+	+	+
ɔ	+		+	+	+		+
o	+	+				+	+
u							

Examples of these vowel patterns are given in (18).

(18)   Examples of permissible Yoruba disyllabic forms

	Form	Gloss			Form	Gloss
a.	igi	'wood'		q.	akī	'manly fellow'[10]
b.	ilé	'house'		r.	ate	'hat'
c.	ilὲ	'land'		s.	àɟὲ	'paddle'
d.	ilá	'okro'		t.	ara	'body'
e.	itɔ́	'saliva'		u.	aʃɔ	'cloth'
f.	ìgò	'bottle'		v.	àwo	'plate'
g.	iʃu	'yam'		w.	ahū	'miser'; 'tortoise'
h.	ebi	'hunger'		x.	ɔtí	'spirits'
i.	ebὲ	'heap for yams'		y.	ɔ̀bε	'knife'
j.	ekpo	'oil'		z.	ɔɟà	'market'
k.	eku	'bush rat'		aa.	ɔkɔ́	'vehicle'
l.	ὲbi	'guilt'		bb.	ɔdū̃	'year'
m.	εsὲ	'foot'		cc.	orí	'head'
n.	ὲkpà	'groundnut'		dd.	olὲ	'thief'
o.	ὲkɔ	'pap'		ee.	owó	'money'
p.	ὲwu	'clothing'		ff.	oɟú	'eye'

Note that there are no forms in Standard Yoruba which begin with the high vowel [u]. The grammar of harmony that we assume does not account for this presumably unrelated fact, although the exclusion of such forms from the corpus does affect the frequency of high-vowel-initial forms.

With regard to the pattern of tongue-root harmony discernible in these data, several points are crucial. First, sequences of mid vowels must agree in their harmonic value. Second, mid vowels preceding a low vowel must be retracted,

---

[10]   Except for a handful of exceptions, the four sequences a . . . i, a . . . u, ɔ . . . i, ɔ . . . u do not occur unless the second vowel is nasalised; see Clements and Ṣonaiya (1990). We abstract away from this prohibition in the implementation here, assuming that such sequences do occur even with oral vowels.

but no such restriction holds of mid vowels following a low vowel. Third, high vowels co-occur with mid vowels of both the advanced and retracted sets. These patterns are derived by the ranking of constraints given in (19).

(19)   Standard Yoruba constraint ranking

Lo/RTR, HI/RTR, RTR/HI >> MaxRTR >> [AlignR]rt, DepRTR >> [AlignL]rt, AlignL >> DepPathRTR, RTR/Lo >> AlignR

Although we do not give detailed motivation of this portion of the grammar of Yoruba, we do provide a summary of the basic motivation for the various crucial rankings. In addition, although we only give a full set of two syllable examples here, we included all possible two-syllable and three-syllable forms in the implementation.

The three constraints Lo/RTR, HI/RTR and RTR/HI are undominated in this set. All low vowels must be retracted (Lo/RTR), no high vowels may ever be retracted (HI/RTR), and no retracted vowels may ever be high (RTR/HI). Thus the three vowels *[æ], *[ɪ], *[ʊ] are all ruled out of the Standard Yoruba vowel inventory (where the symbol [æ] is used for an advanced low vowel). For Lo/RTR, the crucial ranking in this regard is its domination of DepRTR: it is better to insert an RTR value on a low vowel than to violate Lo/RTR. For the two conditions involving high (HI/RTR, RTR/HI), it is crucial that at least one of these constraints dominate MaxRTR: as such, it would be better to delete an RTR value if the only alternative were to have a high retracted vowel. Similarly, at least one of HI/RTR or RTR/HI must dominate all of the alignment constraints, since misalignment is preferred to the retracting of a high vowel (*èbi* 'guilt', *ilè* 'land', etc.).

With regard to the ranking of MaxRTR with respect to [AlignR]rt, it is more important to preserve an RTR feature than to respect right-edge alignment. That is, MaxRTR dominates [AlignR]rt. This can be seen in examples like *èbi* 'guilt', *ɔtí* 'spirits', and *ɛtiri* 'difficult'.

Proceeding down the ranked set of constraints, DepRTR must dominate both AlignL and AlignR since misalignment with the left or right edge cannot be improved by the insertion of an RTR value not present underlyingly. The importance of this particular ranking can be seen only in words of more than two syllables, specifically words with medial high vowels, such as *èlùbɔ́* 'yam flour' (*ɛ̀lùbɔ́*). Note that the impossibility of *ɛ̀lùbɔ́* also depends on ruling out inputs with two RTR specifications (see Pulleyblank 1996 for discussion). For the purposes of our simulation, we assumed an unviolated OCP.

Similarly, MaxRTR must dominate DepPathRTR. The linking or spreading of an RTR feature, which causes a DepPathRTR violation, cannot be resolved by deleting the RTR value.

Perhaps the most central rankings of the harmonic system involve the dominance of Lo/Rtr, [AlignR]rt and AlignL over DepPathRtr. Crucially, the prohibition against new relations between Rtr and anchors (DepPathRtr) must be overridden by the need to retract low vowels (Lo/Rtr), to spread root values of Rtr to the right ([AlignR]rt), and to spread all values of Rtr to the left (AlignL). The need to retract low vowels can be seen in the complete absence of advanced low vowels; the need to align root values to the right can be seen in the fact that root Rtr values always appear as far to the right as possible, and the need for left-edge alignment can be seen by the fact that Rtr values extend as far to the left as possible. Note that if all vowels are non-low, then any Rtr value must be a root value (ɛsɛ̀ 'foot', ɛ̀kɔ 'pap'); if there is a low vowel, then the Rtr value may be a root value (afɔ 'cloth') or it may be a non-root value whose presence is forced by Lo/Rtr. In the latter case, such a value must be left-aligned (ɛ̀kpà 'groundnut', *e/oCa), but need not be right-aligned (afɔ 'cloth', ate 'hat'). Cases where an Rtr specification are left-aligned but not right-aligned (ate 'hat') also demonstrate that the prohibition on adding associations (DepPathRtr) must dominate AlignR.

Longer morphemes that involve medial high vowels demonstrate that right-edge alignment of a lexical Rtr specification is satisfied to the detriment of left-edge alignment: ɛ̀lùbɔ́ 'yam flour', *ɛ̀lùbó. This motivates the ranking: [AlignR]rt >> AlignL, [AlignL]rt.

Finally, note that Rtr/Lo prohibits the assignment of Rtr to a non-low vowel. Since harmony regularly produces retracted mid vowels (àɟɛ́ 'witch', ɛ̀kpà 'groundnut', ɔkɔ 'vehicle', etc.), this means that the constraints producing harmony must overrule this co-occurrence condition: [AlignR]rt, AlignL >> Rtr/Lo. Similarly, MaxRtr must dominate Rtr/Lo. By ranking faithfulness above the co-occurrence condition, it is ensured that satisfaction of the co-occurrence condition is not achieved by simply deleting the potentially offending Rtr value.

15.6.2 *Absolute Alignment*

In addition to the case of Standard Yoruba, we implemented a case that is minimally different, a case that we refer to as Absolute Alignment. This case is virtually identical to Standard Yoruba, except that a harmonic value cannot be misaligned with respect to the right edge. As such, if the rightmost vowel is advanced, then any vowel to the left is similarly advanced; only if the rightmost vowel is retracted can other vowels also retract. For example, Standard Yoruba words such as ɛ̀wu 'clothing' and ɛ̀bi 'guilt' (seen in (18)) have Rtr values that are not right-aligned; longer examples are also attested, such as ɛtiri 'difficult' and ɛ̀bùrú 'shortcut'. In an Absolute Alignment grammar, such misaligned forms are impossible: a sequence of Rtr vowels must appear at the extreme right edge of a word, or else not appear at all. All else remaining equal, Standard Yoruba ɛtiri 'difficult' would be realized as etiri in an Absolute Alignment dialect. Such patterns are attested in various dialects of Yoruba (Akinlabi *et al. in preparation*), in mirror-image form in Wolof (Ka 1988; Archangeli and Pulleyblank 1994;

Pulleyblank 1996), and are found in other languages and types of harmony as well (Akinlabi 1995, 1996).

The distinction between relative and absolute alignment results from the ranking of alignment with respect to faithfulness. Where MAXF is ranked above ALIGNF ('F' = some feature), alignment is relative; where ALIGNF is ranked above MAXF, alignment is absolute (Akinlabi 1996; Pulleyblank 1996).

(20)   Relative Alignment: MAXF >> ALIGNF
        Absolute Alignment: ALIGNF >> MAXF

To compare the results of the learner for two closely-related grammars, in our simulation we targeted a grammar that is minimally different from that of Standard Yoruba. This grammar does not correspond exactly to any dialect of Yoruba because the dialects exhibiting absolute alignment exhibit certain additional differences. We therefore refer to this language as 'Absolute Alignment' and it should be kept in mind that is not an occurring dialect of Yoruba.

The vowel co-occurrence patterns assumed for two-vowel sequences in Absolute Alignment are shown in (21). To facilitate comparability with Standard Yoruba, we assumed that u-initial words are impossible. Patterns for three vowel sequences are similarly comparable to Standard Yoruba with the exception of the relative vs. absolute alignment cases.

(21)   Absolute Alignment vowel co-occurrence patterns

	i	e	ɛ	a	ɔ	o	u
i	+	+	+	+	+	+	+
e	+	+				+	+
ɛ			+	+	+		
a	+	+	+	+	+	+	+
ɔ			+	+	+		
o	+	+				+	+
u							

The four types of data in which this language differs from Standard Yoruba are shaded in (21): *ɛCi, *ɛCu, *ɔCi, and *ɔCu.

As noted above, to distinguish Standard Yoruba from Absolute Alignment, exactly one ranking is crucially different, shown in bold in (22).

(22)   Absolute alignment dialect constraint rankings

Lo/RTR Hi/RTR RTR/HI	>>	[ALIGNR]RT	>>	MAXRTR DEPRTR	>>	[ALIGNL]RT ALIGNL	>>	DEPPATHRTR RTR/LO	>>	ALIGNR

The goal of the implementation, to which we now turn, was to see how effectively a genetic algorithm could acquire the grammars of Standard Yoruba and

Absolute Alignment when presented with positive data consisting of possible two-vowel and three-vowel sequences.

15.7 Implementation

In this section, we discuss first the architecture of the implementation, and then the method employed in simulating the acquisition of Yoruba tongue-root harmony.

15.7.1 *Architecture*

The genetic-algorithm-based acquisition model was implemented in ANSI C on a Sun workstation. The architecture of the implementation is shown schematically in (23). The implementation consists of a learner, an environment, and a

(23) Architecture of the implementation

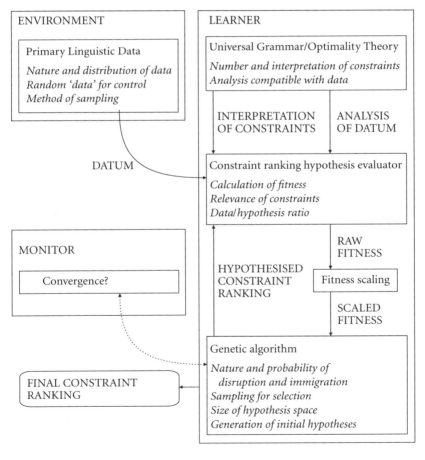

monitor who observes the learner but does not aid the learner in any way.

The learner is based on a genetic algorithm which operates over a population of hypothesised constraint rankings. The genetic algorithm passes a hypothesis into a module which evaluates the hypothesis in the context of data received from the environment and the learner's own inductive bias (provided by the UG/OT module). The evaluator returns a fitness for the hypothesis to the genetic algorithm, which optimizes the fitness values of the learner's hypotheses.

The monitor observes the progress of the learner, and stops it when it has converged on the constraint ranking of the target language. The monitor does not teach or train the learner, or provide any form of negative evidence to it.

Since the system considers a constraint ranking in the context of a limited amount of data, the fitness measure is not particularly accurate, and fitness values tend to fluctuate. For example, many ranking hypotheses return no stars for a given datum, and thus receive a perfect raw fitness. For this reason, the learner performs much better if fitness values are scaled (Baker 1985; Winston 1992). Scaling the fitness has the effect of eliminating the magnitudes of differences in fitness, while retaining relative value. We use a linear scaling algorithm from Baker (1985), as shown in (24). We also use the scaling to make the search more aggressive—the worst candidate of each population is eliminated during scaling.

(24) Scaled fitness values for the purposes of selection

Scaled Raw Fitness	Raw Fitness	Ranked Fitness	Scaled Ranked Fitness
0.044629	1.000000	31	0.062500
.	.	.	.
.	.	.	.
0.044629	1.000000	25	0.050403
0.044629	1.000000	24	0.048387
.	.	.	.
.	.	.	.
0.032949	0.738281	17	0.034274
0.031206	0.699219	16	0.032258
.	.	.	.
.	.	.	.
0.022271	0.499023	9	0.018145
0.020811	0.466309	8	0.016129
.	.	.	.
.	.	.	.
0.009675	0.216790	1	0.002016
0.005535	0.124023	0	0.000000
1.0	22.4067	496	1.0

Members of population $n+1$ are selected from population n according to the *scaled ranked fitness* values. That is, the probability of a particular member of the population being selected is equal to its scaled ranked fitness value.

There are two possibilities for determining when the learner has acquired the target grammar. The first, which we call *system-external convergence*, involves a monitoring program which stops the learner when the monitor decides that the learner's current hypothesis is close enough to the ranking independently established by the linguist. The second possibility, *system-internal convergence*, has the learner monitor its own progress and determine when it is close enough to the target. We use system-external convergence here. Work by Gold (1967) on finite identifiability and Osherson, Stob and Weinstein (1986) on self-monitoring learners suggests that attempting system-internal convergence makes learning more difficult. In fact, system-internal convergence may not be possible at all.[11] The monitor needs to compare the constraint rankings generated by the learner with those provided by the linguist. It is necessary to be able to determine at what point the acquired grammar is sufficiently close to the target grammar for the learner to stop changing its grammar. In order to compare two constraint rankings, we define a distance measure which is illustrated in (25). The dominance relations of each constraint ranking are encoded in the upper triangular portion of a matrix, and then the matrices are compared on a cell-by-cell basis. If A >> B in one ranking and B >> A in the other, then the distance is incremented. (In figure (25), 'F' means 'follows' and 'P' means 'precedes'.)

(25) Comparing rankings: the distance between matrices reflecting constraint rankings
   a. Target ranking: B >> A >> D >> {C E}

	A	B	C	D	E
A		F	P	P	P
B			P	P	P
C				F	
D					P
E					

   b. Source ranking: C >> E >> A >> B >> D

	A	B	C	D	E
A		P	F	P	F
B			F	P	F
C				P	P
D					F
E					

[11] Thanks to Robin Clark for pointing out to us the work on self-monitoring learners.

In (25), the distance between B >> A >> D >> {C E} and C >> E >> A >> B >> D is 7, out of a maximum of 10 for this illustration with 5 constraints.

15.7.2 *Method*

Experiments
The learner was run to (external) convergence or 20,000 iterations, whichever came first, in two conditions. In the experimental conditions, the learner was presented with data uniformly sampled with replacement from the PLD of Standard Yoruba or Absolute Alignment (to be described below). In the control conditions, the learner was presented with randomly generated 'data'.

Primary Linguistic Data
All input data consisted of two- or three-vowel sequences that were admissible by the target language. The learner received no negative evidence. There were 196 Standard Yoruba data: 32 two-vowel sequences and 164 three-vowel sequences. There were 168 Absolute Alignment data: 28 two-vowel sequences and 140 three-vowel sequences. In the control conditions, the learner received two- and three-vowel sequences created by randomly sampling from the ten-vowel inventory with replacement. There were 100 possible two-vowel sequences and 1000 possible three-vowel sequences. The proportion of two-vowel to three-vowel data in the control conditions was the same as the corresponding experimental conditions (Standard Yoruba and Control 16.33% two-vowel vs. 83.67% three-vowel; Absolute Alignment and Control 16.67% two-vowel vs. 83.33% three-vowel). All runs used one datum paired with one constraint ranking.

We stress here that the learning problem that we examined did not involve the postulation of prior knowledge of correct input forms.[12] Data were supplied to the learner in output form only. In this respect, the problem under examination differed from work such as Tesar and Smolensky (to appear), where the problem of deriving the correct ranking for a language is considered given the assumption that structured representations are available—that is, outputs for which the correct input is known.[13] In addition, we assumed no knowledge of morphology other than the possibility of categorising a form as either root or word; we assumed knowledge of the distinction, but did not assume that the learner had access to information on whether a particular form encountered was correctly assigned to the root class or the word class. The learning stage that we consider is therefore a very early one, a stage prior to the stage where detailed morphological analysis takes place and where lexical growth is rapid (Goad 1993). Our learner postulated input/output pairings as data were encountered, but had no information on the correctness of the postulated pairings, and did

---

[12] See also Boersma (this volume) for a learning algorithm making this assumption.

[13] In more recent work, Tesar and Smolensky embed their constraint demotion algorithm in a system which hypothesises structured representations rather than being provided with them.

not retain any pairings once an assessment of the fitness of a particular ranking was reached. The learner is therefore consistent with the requirement discussed by Wexler (1995) that early learning be based solely on information present in a surface string.

Genetic Algorithm

The genetic algorithm operated over a population of 32 constraint ranking hypotheses at one time. Disruption operators were applied with a probability of 0.5. Only mutation was implemented. Cloning was applied with a probability of approximately 0.49985 and immigration with a probability of approximately 0.00015.

UR/SR Pairings

All possible pairings of underlying representation and surface representation were generated for a given datum, subject to an assumption that we refer to as the Containment Assumption (Ingram 1992; Prince and Smolensky 1993).

(26)   Containment Assumption
        Upon encountering an output datum, the learner will posit inputs that contain a subset of the phonological content of the encountered output.

The effect of this assumption is that inputs may contain fewer specifications than found in a corresponding output, but inputs may not contain features *not* encountered in the relevant output. Hence specifications of RTR will not be posited in an input form where the output contains no such value. The effect of the Containment Assumption will be obscured at later stages of learning where morphological relations are considered. For example, if one allomorph were posited without an RTR value, and a second allomorph were posited including an RTR value, then the unification of the two could produce an input that includes an RTR value. Such cases are not considered here, however, since a stage prior to such morphological analysis is the stage under consideration. Given our assumptions concerning featural specifications, a datum such as (27a) could therefore have the possible input/output pairings in (27b); input/output pairings such as in (27c) would be impossible since they contain either specifications or associations that are not motivated in the surface form encountered.

(27)   The class of possible input/output pairings
        a. [ε i]
        b. $\begin{bmatrix} \\ \text{E I} \end{bmatrix} \longleftrightarrow \begin{bmatrix} \text{RTR} \\ | \\ \text{ε i} \end{bmatrix}$

           $\begin{bmatrix} \text{RTR} \\ \text{E I} \end{bmatrix} \longleftrightarrow \begin{bmatrix} \text{RTR} \\ | \\ \text{ε i} \end{bmatrix}$

           $\begin{bmatrix} \text{RTR} \\ | \\ \text{ε I} \end{bmatrix} \longleftrightarrow \begin{bmatrix} \text{RTR} \\ | \\ \text{ε i} \end{bmatrix}$

c. $\begin{bmatrix} \text{Rtr Rtr} \\ \text{E} \quad \text{I} \end{bmatrix} \longleftrightarrow \begin{bmatrix} \text{Rtr} \\ | \\ \epsilon \text{ i} \end{bmatrix}$

$\begin{bmatrix} \text{Rtr} \\ \diagdown \\ \epsilon \text{ i} \end{bmatrix} \longleftrightarrow \begin{bmatrix} \text{Rtr} \\ | \\ \epsilon \text{ i} \end{bmatrix}$

The number of available pairings depended on the datum under consideration, and ranged from two to nine.

Fitness
The raw fitness for each ranking and UR/SR pairing was calculated with the following formula

$$\frac{2^N - \text{Dec}}{2^N}$$

where N is the number of relevant constraints and Dec is the decimal value of the binary fitness from the tableau. The maximum such ranking was returned as the fitness for a constraint ranking. When fitness scaling was used, chromosomes in the population were ranked from best to worst according to raw fitness, and assigned fitness values of 31/496, 30/496, . . . , 0/496 respectively.

Convergence
The learner was considered to have converged when eight separate rankings in the population of a single iteration were within a distance of two or less from the target, based on crucial rankings only.

15.8 Results for Standard Yoruba and Absolute Alignment

We discuss here the results of the simulations, first for Standard Yoruba, then for Absolute Alignment.

15.8.1 *Performance of the Learning Algorithm for Standard Yoruba*

The learner successfully converged on the target constraint rankings for Standard Yoruba and Absolute Alignment when presented with data drawn from the PLD of the languages. When presented with randomly-generated data, (the control condition) the learner converged on the target constraint rankings only by chance.

Figure (28) shows the distance (mean of population distances) of the learner's current hypothesis from the target for the first trial of Standard Yoruba (solid line) versus the first trial of the control (dotted line). Convergence in the experimental condition occurred in less than 2,500 iterations. Convergence in the control condition took more than 18,000 iterations. In the simulations in (28), the disruption rate was 0.5 and fitness values were scaled.

As previously mentioned, raw fitness values were not accurate or stable enough to allow the learner to operate efficiently. Nevertheless, with a low

(28)   Convergence of a single run: Standard Yoruba vs. Control

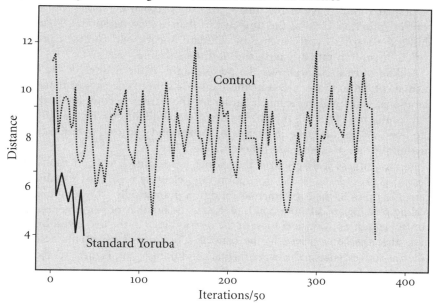

(29)   Iteration to convergence: Standard Yoruba vs. Control, raw fitness and low disruption

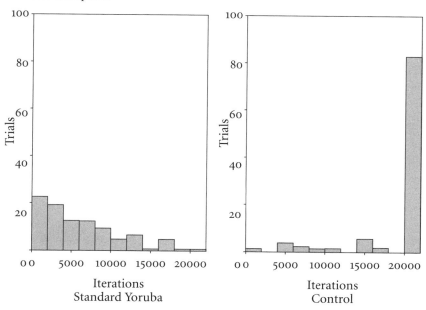

enough disruption rate the learner was able to converge reliably in the experimental condition (99% of the time in less than 20,000 iterations) but not the control condition (17% of the time in less than 20,000 iterations). Figure (29) shows the learner's performance in Standard Yoruba and control conditions, with a disruption rate of 0.0625 and no fitness scaling.

Adding fitness scaling leaves the performance of the learner in the experimental condition more or less unaffected (98% convergence in less than 20,000 iterations) while making it much harder for the learner to converge in the control condition (4% of the time in less than 20,000 iterations). Figure (30) shows the learner's performance in Standard Yoruba and control conditions, with a disruption rate of 0.0625 and fitness scaling.

Because fitness scaling makes the learner less sensitive to fluctuations in fitness, it is possible to set the disruption rate relatively high, thus speeding convergence times in the experimental condition dramatically. The combination of scaling plus higher disruption also increases the number of convergences in the control condition. Consideration of the distributions in the two conditions suggests that the convergence in the control conditions is essentially accidental, whereas convergence in the experimental conditions is not. Figure (31) shows the learner's performance in Standard Yoruba and control conditions, with a disruption rate of 0.5 and fitness scaling. Convergence in the experimental condition occurred 100% of the time in less than 4,300 iterations. Convergence in the

(30)   Iteration to convergence: Standard Yoruba vs. Control, scaled ranked fitness and low disruption

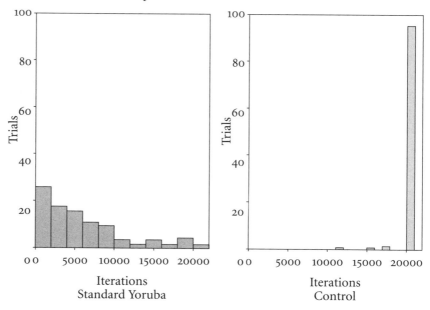

(31)   Iteration to convergence: Standard Yoruba vs. Control, scaled rank fitness
and high disruption

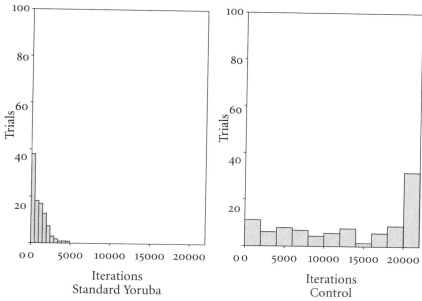

Iterations
Standard Yoruba

Iterations
Control

control condition occurred 18% of the time in less than 4,300 iterations and 68% of the time in less than 20,000 iterations.

15.8.2 *Linguistic Results for Standard Yoruba*

To assess the results obtained by the learner from a linguistic perspective, we considered the rates of success for acquiring pairs of crucial rankings. The full set of pairwise comparisons are given in (32). The values there are for rankings that are both crucial and noncrucial.

In many cases, the rankings are exactly as desired. For example, according to the linguistically-established grammar it is crucial that H$_I$/R$_{TR}$ outrank A$_{LIGN}$L; this ranking is found in 100% of the grammars produced by the learning algorithm. In contrast, H$_I$/R$_{TR}$ is not crucially-ranked with respect to R$_{TR}$/H$_I$ according to the target grammar; the results of the learner are that in 51.1% of the observed grammars H$_I$/R$_{TR}$ is ranked above R$_{TR}$/H$_I$, while in 48.9% the opposite ranking is attested. That is, operation of the learner results in randomly-ranked constraints where the ranking is not crucial. In many instances, therefore, the learner acquired the desired rankings.

To assess these results more critically, the pairs of crucially-ranked constraints are summarized in (33).

A consideration of these rankings reveals only one serious problem (shaded in (33)). The learner assigned rankings to D$_{EP}$R$_{TR}$ and A$_{LIGN}$L essentially at

(32) Standard Yoruba: Percentages for all constraint ranking pairs, organized by constraint ranking

	Lo/Rtr	Hi/Rtr	Rtr/Hi	MaxRtr	[AlignR]rt	DepRtr	[AlignL]rt	AlignL	DepPathRtr	Rtr/Lo	AlignR
Lo/Rtr	0.0	17.5	10.0	22.9	87.9	99.9	88.4	90.0	100.0	99.6	99.9
Hi/Rtr	82.5	0.0	48.9	90.8	99.4	100.0	100.0	100.0	100.0	100.0	100.0
Rtr/Hi	90.0	51.1	0.0	89.9	99.8	100.0	100.0	100.0	100.0	100.0	100.0
MaxRtr	77.1	9.2	10.1	0.0	98.5	100.0	96.8	99.8	100.0	100.0	100.0
[AlignR]rt	12.1	0.6	0.2	1.5	0.0	93.5	75.5	83.9	100.0	100.0	98.6
DepRtr	0.1	0.0	0.0	0.0	6.5	0.0	26.1	42.8	83.9	82.1	94.0
[AlignL]rt	11.6	0.0	0.0	3.2	24.5	73.9	0.0	50.6	92.9	86.4	83.2
AlignL	10.0	0.0	0.0	0.2	16.1	57.2	49.4	0.0	99.8	98.6	85.0
DepPathRtr	0.0	0.0	0.0	0.0	0.0	16.1	7.1	0.2	0.0	50.7	65.9
Rtr/Lo	0.4	0.0	0.0	0.0	0.0	17.9	13.6	1.4	49.2	0.0	45.9
AlignR	0.1	0.0	0.0	0.0	1.4	6.0	16.8	15.0	34.1	54.1	0.0

random—indeed favouring the incorrect ranking of these two constraints. This incorrect ranking would affect sequences of /Mid HIGH MID/ vowels in morphemes with an RTR specification. That is, occurring forms like [èlùbɔ́] 'yam flour' would be expected to be suboptimal, with the ungrammatical *[èlùbɔ́] predicted to be optimal. The ranking in question would affect a total of 12 forms out of the total number of 196 forms observed in Standard Yoruba. There are three types of changes that might correct such a result: (i) a modification of the learning algorithm, (ii) adjustment in the frequency of occurrence of individual

(33) Standard Yoruba: Success in converging on a crucial ranking, expressed as a percentage

Lo/Rtr >> DepRtr	99.9	[AlignR]rt >> DepPathRtr	100.0
Hi/Rtr >> MaxRtr	90.8	AlignL >> DepPathRtr	99.8
Rtr/Hi >> MaxRtr	89.9	DepPathRtr >> AlignR	65.9
MaxRtr >> [AlignR]rt	98.5	[AlignR]rt >> AlignL	83.9
DepRtr >> AlignL	42.8	[AlignR]rt >> [AlignL]rt	75.5
DepRtr >> AlignR	94.0	[AlignR]rt >> Rtr/Lo	100.0
Lo/Rtr >> DepPathRtr	100.0	AlignL >> Rtr/Lo	98.6
MaxRtr >> Rtr/Lo	100.0	Rtr/Hi >> AlignL	100.0
MaxRtr >> DepPathRtr	100.0	Hi/Rtr >> [AlignL]rt	100.0
Hi/Rtr >> AlignL	100.0	Rtr/Hi >> [AlignL]rt	100.0

data types (currently, all data are assumed to occur with equal frequency), (iii) a modification of the set of constraints employed by the grammar and learner. We leave this matter for further investigation.

In closing this brief discussion of the linguistic implications of the results, we note an interesting class of cases where the learning algorithm results in grammars that favour a particular ranking, but where the ranking in question does not appear to be crucial. For example, it does not appear to be the case that Lo/RTR and HI/RTR are crucially-ranked. Nevertheless, the results of the simulation were that HI/RTR outranked Lo/RTR in 82.5% of the trials. It is unclear whether such results are desirable or undesirable. It may be that certain properties of the data or learner skew results in a direction that would prove problematic in a language where it is important to rank Lo/RTR above HI/RTR. On the other hand, it might be the case that the observed skewing accounts for a pattern of linguistic change discernible from consideration of a range of related languages. Since we have no evidence either in favour of such skewing or against it, and since noncrucially-ranked constraints derive correct surface forms under either ranking, we do not currently consider such rankings problematic.

15.8.3 *Performance of the Learning Algorithm for Absolute Alignment*

We ran the learner in Absolute Alignment and control conditions with a disruption rate of 0.5 and fitness scaling. The results are similar to those for Standard Yoruba, and are shown in (34). The learner converged 100% of the time in less than 5,500 iterations in the experimental condition. In the control condition, the learner converged 8% of the time in less than 5,500 iterations, and 20% of the time in less than 20,000 iterations.

(34)   Absolute Alignment: number of iterations required for convergence

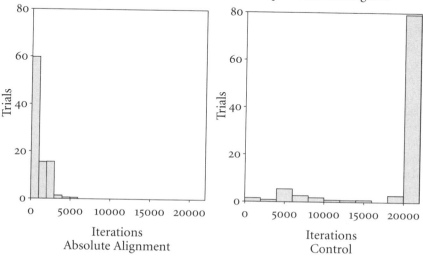

15.8.4 *Linguistic Results for Absolute Alignment*

Pairwise results showing the rankings acquired by the learner for Absolute Alignment are given in the table in (35).

(35) Absolute Alignment: Percentages for all constraint ranking pairs, organized by constraint ranking

	Lo/Rtr	Hi/Rtr	Rtr/Hi	[AlignR]rt	DepRtr	MaxRtr	[AlignL]rt	AlignL	DepPathRtr	Rtr/Lo	AlignR
Lo/Rtr	0.0	39.9	40.9	86.6	100.0	81.6	96.6	97.8	100.0	100.0	98.0
Hi/Rtr	60.1	0.0	51.9	93.1	100.0	98.9	100.0	99.9	100.0	100.0	98.5
Rtr/Hi	59.1	48.1	0.0	90.8	100.0	99.0	100.0	100.0	100.0	100.0	99.2
[AlignR]rt	13.4	6.9	9.2	0.0	98.9	61.0	96.5	98.6	100.0	100.0	95.4
DepRtr	0.0	0.0	0.0	1.1	0.0	5.5	27.0	51.1	83.4	82.6	68.2
MaxRtr	18.4	1.1	1.0	39.0	94.5	0.0	85.8	90.0	99.2	98.9	87.6
[AlignL]rt	3.4	0.0	0.0	3.5	73.0	14.2	0.0	60.2	92.0	91.9	70.6
AlignL	2.2	0.1	0.0	1.4	48.9	10.0	39.8	0.0	98.0	98.9	62.0
DepPathRtr	0.0	0.0	0.0	0.0	16.6	0.8	8.0	2.0	0.0	47.5	45.8
Rtr/Lo	0.0	0.0	0.0	0.0	17.4	1.1	8.1	1.1	52.5	0.0	35.4
AlignR	2.0	1.5	0.8	4.6	31.8	12.4	29.4	38.0	54.2	64.6	0.0

The degree of success shown by the learner on crucial rankings for Absolute Alignment is shown in (36).

(36) Absolute Alignment: Success in converging on a crucial ranking, expressed as a percentage

Lo/Rtr >> DepRtr	100.0		[AlignR]rt >> DepPathRtr	100.0
Hi/Rtr >> MaxRtr	98.9		AlignL >> DepPathRtr	98.0
Rtr/Hi >> MaxRtr	99.0		DepPathRtr >> AlignR	45.8
[AlignR]rt >> MaxRtr	61.0		[AlignR]rt >> AlignL	98.6
DepRtr >> AlignL	51.1		[AlignR]rt >> [AlignL]rt	96.5
DepRtr >> AlignR	68.2		[AlignR]rt >> Rtr/Lo	100.0
Lo/Rtr >> DepPathRtr	100.0		AlignL >> Rtr/Lo	98.9
MaxRtr >> Rtr/Lo	98.9		Rtr/Hi >> AlignL	100.0
MaxRtr >> DepPathRtr	99.2		Hi/Rtr >> [AlignL]rt	100.0
Hi/Rtr >> AlignL	99.9		Rtr/Hi >> [AlignL]rt	100.0

Two significant problems can be seen in these results: the ranking of DepRtr with respect to AlignL, and the ranking of DepPathRtr with respect to AlignR are assigned more or less randomly (both are shaded in (36)). This means that in roughly half the grammars there will be problems with certain forms. When ALIGNL is ranked above DEPRTR, forms like [èlùbɔ́] 'yam flour' would be expected to be surface as the ungrammatical *[èlùbɔ́]—this is the same problem already noted for the simulation of Standard Yoruba. When ALIGNR is ranked above DEPPATHRTR, forms like [ate] 'hat' and [àwo] 'plate' should surface as [atɛ] and [awɔ]. Note in this case that forms with a low vowel followed by a retracted mid vowel are perfectly grammatical in all dialects of Yoruba—they are indeed the maximally harmonic form for a low-mid sequence. The problem is how to allow for the disharmonic sequence of a low vowel followed by an advanced mid vowel. We leave both these problems for future investigation.

With regard to the ranking that distinguishes Standard Yoruba from Absolute Alignment, the simulation is a qualified success. The correct ranking of [ALIGNR]RT over MAXRTR is achieved in 61% of the trials. While imperfect, this result appears significant for two reasons. First, it should be compared with the 98.5% success rate for acquiring the ranking of MAXRTR over [ALIGNR]RT when the learner is presented with data from Standard Yoruba. It is clear that the learner is responding in a strikingly different fashion in the two cases. Second, it is important to consider the nature of the Absolute Alignment pattern.

In a two-vowel sequence, there are four possible combinations of mid and high vowels:

(37) Possible combinations of mid and high vowels in a two-vowel sequence

		Advanced	Retracted
a.	Mid Mid	e/o . . . e/o	ɛ/ɔ . . . ɛ/ɔ
b.	High Mid	i/u . . . e/o	i/u . . . ɛ/ɔ
c.	Mid High	e/o . . . i/u	ɛ/ɔ . . . i/u
d.	High High	i/u . . . i/u	—

Two points should be kept in mind as background: (i) all combinations in the 'advanced' column are grammatical for all relevant grammars since they are fully harmonic, (ii) all high vowels are systematically advanced given the high ranking of HI/RTR. Since the issue under consideration is alignment with respect to the right edge, the only pattern that is relevant for comparing right-edge alignment vs. faithfulness is therefore the retracted Mid High sequence (37c): in the *relative alignment* grammar of Standard Yoruba, the retention of a lexical RTR value on the mid vowel forces a violation of right-edge alignment; in the *absolute alignment* grammar, the loss of any lexical RTR value results in a violation of faithfulness (MAXRTR). Hence a putative input form of the type /E . . . I, RTR/ would be realized as [ɛ . . . i] under relative alignment and [e . . . i] under absolute alignment.

There is an important point to note, however. While it is impossible for the absolute alignment grammar to produce a surface form [ɛ . . . i], a surface form [e . . . i] can be produced in both grammars by simply positing an underlying sequence devoid of RTR values: /E . . . I/. That is, all occurring surface forms of an Absolute Alignment language can be produced even if MAXRTR is (incorrectly) ranked above [ALIGNR]RT. Ungrammatical surface forms would only result from the combination of a particular ranking with a particular underlying form. Moreover, the actual language data encountered by an Absolute Alignment learner would not motivate the postulation of underlying forms that would be problematic. That is, data devoid of RTR values on the surface would not motivate the postulation of RTR values underlyingly—particularly given the Containment Assumption (26).

This is an instance of the *subset problem* (see, for example, Manzini and Wexler 1987). The relative alignment grammar of Standard Yoruba evaluates as grammatical all eight of the following: [eCi], [eCu], [oCi], [oCu], [εCi], [εCu], [ɔCi], [ɔCu]. In contrast, the Absolute Alignment grammar evaluates only a subset of these forms as grammatical, namely: [eCi], [eCu], [oCi], [oCu]. The problem is the asymmetric nature of the learning problem. If the learner happens to postulate an *absolute alignment* grammar, and then encounters a form from the set [εCi], [εCu], [ɔCi], [ɔCu], then the learner will perform poorly, unable to assign a grammatical analysis to such a form. Such failure will drive the learner to seek a more adequate grammar, which in this case would the the relative alignment grammar. In contrast, if the learner happens to postulate a *relative alignment* grammar, and then encounters only data from the class [eCi], [eCu], [oCi], [oCu], the learner is not under any particular pressure to shift to the grammar characterising the subset language since the superset grammar successfully analyses all data encountered. There is little pressure, therefore, to switch to the *absolute alignment* grammar from the *relative alignment* grammar. It is of interest, therefore, that the learner correctly achieves the subset grammar, Absolute Alignment, in the majority of trials: 61%.

15.9 Results and General Conclusion

This chapter reports on a simulation that used a genetic algorithm to learn two divergent grammars of tongue-root harmony. In broad terms, the simulation was successful in that the learner acquired both of the target grammars for which it was presented data, responding in a qualitatively and quantitatively different fashion to actual language data as compared to control data.

In conducting such a simulation, a number of issues arise, and we conclude by raising some of these issues briefly. This discussion serves in some instances as a conclusion for the work already conducted, and in other instances as the formulation of a hypothesis defining the direction for future research.

With regard to the problem of acquisition, the learner presented here is stochastic without constituting a random search. It is guided by errors, and yet it is not an error-driven learner (Gibson and Wexler 1994; Niyogi and Berwick

1993, 1995)—that is, it can change state even when its current grammar is able to successfully analyse data that are encountered. Similarly, it is optimizing, without being 'greedy'—it can modify its grammar even if the modification is not demonstrably an improvement. Because of such properties, we hypothesise, the genetic algorithm is able to avoid problems of local maxima and subset relations.

We note that the learner makes use of only positive evidence to converge, and that it seems to be psychologically plausible in terms of time and space requirements. Moreover, the central properties of the learner are not specific to the type of phonological problem examined. As such, by increasing the grammatical coverage (increasing the number of constraints in the OT/UG module) and by changing the nature and distribution of the PLD, the genetic algorithm learner should be able to converge on other OT analyses. We note that the learner considered here could easily complement other components of learning that could also be modeled using genetic algorithms. For example, it would be possible to select for fitness of lexical entries. Indeed, one might suppose that as candidate hypotheses for grammatical analyses begin to converge, there would be a lexical explosion as the learner began also to converge on lexical entries. As pointed out to us by Mark Hewitt, the learner also makes predictions as to patterns of overgeneralization during the learning process.

A learner such as the one examined here makes numerous predictions for phonological theory. By being stochastic rather than deterministic, it predicts that speakers' idiolects may differ in subtle ways even if gross grammatical properties are shared. As such, it constitutes a step towards a model for idiolectal variation, as well as constituting a move towards a model for diachronic change. The genetic algorithm makes no distinction between constraints that are crucial in a grammar and constraints that are not—it seeks to optimize both classes. Hence a learner such as the genetic algorithm causes even noncrucial constraints to be organized in particular ways, resulting in 'sub-grammars' that may emerge synchronically or diachronically given appropriate circumstances. In general terms, we suggest that learners such as the genetic algorithm may be used to test hypotheses on underspecification, the status of particular substantive features with relation to others, as well as hypotheses concerning markedness and lexicon optimization.

15.10 References

Akinlabi, A. (1995). 'Featural affixation.' In Akinbiyi Akinlabi (ed.), *Theoretical Approaches to African Linguistics*. Lawrenceville, Africa World Press, 217–37.
—— (1996). 'Featural affixation'. *Journal of Linguistics* 32, 239–89.
—— (1997). 'Kalabari vowel harmony'. *The Linguistic Review* 14, 97–138.
—— D. Archangeli, Q. Qla, and D. Pulleyblank (in preparation). 'An optimal account of ATR harmony in Yoruba dialects'. Ms, Rutgers University, University of Arizona, Tulane University, University of British Columbia.

Archangeli, D. and D. T. Langendoen (1997). *Optimality Theory: An Overview*. Malden, MA, Blackwell Publishers.

—— and D. Pulleyblank (1989). 'Yoruba Vowel Harmony'. *Linguistic Inquiry* 20, 173–17.

—— —— (1993). 'Two rules or one . . . or none? [ATR] in Yoruba,' *Proceedings of BLS* 19, 13–26.

—— —— (1994). *Grounded Phonology*. Cambridge, MA, MIT Press.

Baker, J. E. (1985). 'Adaptive selection methods for genetic algorithms.' In J. J. Grefenstette (ed.), *Proceedings of the First International Conference on Genetic Algorithms*. Hillsdale, NJ, Lawrence Erlbaum, 101–11.

Clark, R. (1992). 'The selection of syntactic knowledge'. *Language Acquisition* 2, 85–149.

—— and I. Roberts (1993). 'A computational model of language learnability and language change'. *Linguistic Inquiry* 24, 299–345.

Clements, G. N. and R. Ṣọnaiya (1990). 'Underlying feature specification in Yoruba'. *Studies in the Linguistic Sciences* 20, 89–103.

Forrest, S. (1993). 'Genetic algorithms: Principles of natural selection applied to computation'. *Science* 261, 872–8.

Gibson, E. and K. Wexler (1994). 'Triggers'. *Linguistic Inquiry* 25, 407–54.

Goad, H. (1993). *On the Configuration of Height Features*. PhD dissertation, USC.

Gold, E. M. (1967). 'Language identification in the limit'. *Information and Control* 10, 447–74.

Goldberg, D. E. (1989). *Genetic Algorithms in Search, Optimization and Machine Learning*. Reading, MA, Addison-Wesley.

—— and R. Lingle (1985). 'Alleles, loci, and the travelling salesman problem'. *Proceedings of an International Conference on Genetic Algorithms and their Applications*, 154–59. Cited in Goldberg (1989).

Ingram, D. (1992). 'Early phonological acquisition: A cross-linguistic perspective.' In C. A. Ferguson, L. Menn, and C. Stoel-Gammon (eds), *Phonological Development: Models, Research, Implications*. Timonium, MD, York Press, 423–35.

Itô, J., A. Mester, and J. Padgett (1995). 'Licensing and Underspecification in Optimality Theory'. *Linguistic Inquiry* 26, 571–13.

Ka, O. (1988). *Wolof Phonology and Morphology: A Non-Linear Approach*. PhD dissertation, University of Illinois at Urbana-Champaign.

Kirchner, R. (1993). 'Turkish vowel disharmony in Optimality Theory'. Paper presented at ROW–1, Rutgers University.

Li, B. (1996). *Tungusic Vowel Harmony: Description and Analysis*. The Hague: Holland Academic Graphics.

Lombardi, L. (1995). 'Why place and voice are different: Constraint interactions and feature faithfulness in Optimality Theory.' Ms, University of Maryland, College Park. [ROA-105.]

McCarthy, J. and A. Prince (1993a). Prosodic morphology I: Constraint interaction and satisfaction, Ms, U.Mass, Amherst and Rutgers University.

—— —— (1993b). 'Generalized alignment.' In G. Booij and J. van Marle (eds), *Yearbook of Morphology 1993*. Dordrecht, Kluwer, 79–153.

—— —— (1995). 'Faithfulness and reduplicative identity.' In J. Beckman, L. Walsh Dickey, and S. Urbanczyk (eds), *Papers in Optimality Theory*, University of Massachusetts Occasional Papers in Linguistics 18. Graduate Linguistics Student Association, Amherst, MA, 249–384.

Manzini, M. R. and K. Wexler (1987). 'Parameters, binding theory, and learnability'. *Linguistic Inquiry* 18, 413–44.

Myers, S. (1997). 'OCP effects in Optimality Theory'. *Natural Language and Linguistic Theory* 15, 847–92.

Niyogi, P. and R. C. Berwick (1993). 'Formalizing triggers: A learning model for finite spaces'. AI Memo 1449, CBCL Paper 86, MIT.

—— —— (1995). 'The logical problem of language change'. AI Memo 1516, CBCL Paper 115, MIT.

Osherson, D. N., M. Stob, and S. Weinstein (1986). *Systems that Learn*. Cambridge, MA, MIT Press.

Prince, A. and P. Smolensky (1993). 'Optimality Theory: Constraint interaction in Generative Grammar'. Technical Report #2 of the Rutgers Center for Cognitive Science, Rutgers University.

Pulleyblank, D. (1993). 'Vowel harmony and optimality theory'. *Proceedings of the Workshop on Phonology*. University of Coimbra, Portugal, 1–18.

—— (1996). 'Neutral vowels in Optimality Theory: A comparison of Yoruba and Wolof'. *Canadian Journal of Linguistics* 41, 295–347.

—— P. Jiang-King, M. Leitch, and Ọ. Ọla (1995). 'Typological variation through constraint rankings: Low vowels in tongue root harmony.' In K. Suzuki and D. Elzinga (eds), *Proceedings of South Western Optimality Theory Workshop 1995*, Arizona Phonology Conference vol. 5, 184–208.

—— and W. J. Turkel (1996). 'Optimality Theory and learning algorithms: The representation of recurrent featural asymmetries'. In J. Durand and B. Laks (eds), *Current Trends in Phonology: Models and Methods*, vol. 2. Salford, Manchester: University of Salford Press, 653–84.

—— —— (1997). 'Gradient Retreat.' In I. Roca (ed.), *Derivations and Constraints in Phonology*. Oxford, Oxford University Press, 153–93.

—— —— (1998) 'The logical problem of language acquisition in optimality theory.' In P. Barbosa, D. Fox, P. Hagstrom, M. McGinnis, and D. Pesetsky (eds), *Is the best good enough? Optimality and competition in syntax*. Cambridge, MA, MIT Press.

Shahin, K. (1997). *Postvelar Harmony: An Examination of its Bases and Crosslinguistic Variation*. PhD dissertation, University of British Columbia.

Smolensky, P. (1993). 'Harmony, markedness, and phonological activity'. Paper presented at ROW-1, Rutgers University.

Tesar, B. and P. Smolensky (to appear). 'The learnability of optimality theory: An algorithm and some basic complexity results'. *Linguistic Inquiry*.

Turkel, W. J. (1994). 'The acquisition of Optimality-theoretic systems'. ROA–11.

Wetzel, A. (1983). 'Evaluation of the effectiveness of genetic algorithms in combinatorial optimization'. Unpublished manuscript, University of Pittsburgh, Pittsburgh. Cited in Goldberg (1989).

Wexler, K. (1995). 'On the learnability problem for constraint orderings in Optimality Theory'. Workshop on Optimality in Syntax–'Is the Best Good Enough?' MIT.

Winston, P. H. (1992). *Artificial Intelligence*. Reading, MA, Addison-Wesley.

16

On the Roles of Optimality and Strict Domination in Language Learning[1]

Bruce Tesar

This chapter examines the possible contributions to language learnability of two defining properties of Optimality Theory (Prince and Smolensky 1993): optimization and strict domination. The fact that Optimality Theory is based upon the optimization of harmony makes it possible to adapt some optimization-based ideas from statistical learning theory to the questions of language learning. The important properties of optimization-based learning procedures are discussed in Section 16.2.

Strict domination among the violable constraints makes it possible for a learner to efficiently identify a ranking making a particular candidate optimal. This is because strict domination restricts the possible ways for constraints to interact (as compared to, say, distinguishing the relative importance of constraints by assigning numeric values). As a result, if a hypothesis ranking does not make the correct description optimal, it is possible to quickly determine a way of changing the ranking to one which is closer to the correct ranking. By indicating the direction in which to move in the hypothesis space, strict domination guides learning so that it may reach the correct ranking quickly. Section 16.3 discusses how strict domination may be exploited, and presents an algorithm for learning constraint rankings from grammatical structural descriptions.

The optimization-based nature of Optimality Theory permits an approach to the problem of the underdetermination of structural descriptions by the observed overt forms available to the learner. A learner can assign a 'best possible interpretation' to an observed form by finding the most harmonic description matching that form, using a hypothesis ranking. This can be done even if the overt form is not grammatical according to the hypothesis ranking. Thus a

---

[1] The author would like to thank Alan Prince and Paul Smolensky for many valuable discussions. Exceptionally useful comments were also provided by two anonymous reviewers. The author's full address is: Department of Linguistics, Rutgers University, New Brunswick, NJ, 08903, USA.

learner may use a hypothesis ranking to interpret observed overt forms, and then use those interpretations to modify his or her hypothesis ranking. This 'iterative' approach is presented in Section 16.4, and some empirical simulation results from the application of this algorithm to learning metrical stress rankings are briefly presented.

16.1 The Challenges of Learning

16.1.1 *What Can Make Learning Difficult?*

Learning is difficult when the relationships between the hypotheses and the observed data are not directly apparent. It is possible that the empirical consequences of any particular hypothesis may not be immediately obvious. If the hypothesis/data relationship is sufficiently complicated, it may be a non-trivial task just to identify hypotheses that are consistent with a particular datum. Typically, the hypothesis space is not just a random collection of possibilities but is structured by dimensions of variation, and hypotheses can be identified by where they fall along these dimensions. For example, a hypothesis space might be structured by a set of parameters, each admitting several values. Each hypothesis would be identified with a set of values assigned to the parameters[2]. A common learning strategy is to try to identify relationships between specific dimensions (e.g. parameters) and specific elements of the data. The challenge of determining which dimensions of variation are responsible for a given pattern of data is sometimes called 'the credit assignment problem' (Minsky 1961; Dresher 1996).

In language learning, the data are the overt forms of utterances, and the hypotheses are grammars. The language learner attempts to infer the correct grammar from the overt forms presented. Complex data/hypothesis relations can arise because of a gap between the overt form (the actual acoustic realization of an utterance) and the full structural description (of which the overt form is only a part). The gap consists of the *hidden structure*—that is, the part of the description that is not overtly realized. The problem is that the same overt form may be shared by several distinct full structural descriptions. This underdetermination of the full structural description by an overt form makes language learning challenging because the linguistic principles shaping the grammatical hypotheses make crucial reference to the non-overt portions of the description (that is why the non-overt portions are hypothesized to exist in the first place). This problem can be compounded when, for a given overt form, different full structural de-

---

[2] It should be emphasized that this characterization does not assume that the values of the different dimensions of variation are necessarily independent; the hypothesis space may well place limitations on what values may co-occur—e.g., some combinations of values for different parameters might be prohibited by Universal Grammar.

scriptions are consistent with different grammars. If each observable overt form is consistent with several hypotheses, distinguishing one hypothesis as correct will require a number of other pieces of data.

Even relationships between hypotheses and full structural descriptions can be non-trivial. In Optimality Theory, the grammaticality of a full structural description is not a relationship between the description and the ranked constraints in isolation; it is dependent on the other candidate structural descriptions. Determining that a full structural description is consistent with a hypothesis requires showing that the description is more harmonic (better satisfies the ranked constraints), under that hypothesis, than the other candidates (of which there may be infinitely many).

The challenges just described hardly exhaust the challenges of language learning. Another factor that can make learning difficult is data with errors. In language learning, this would amount to overt forms that have no grammatical description in the target language. An already competent speaker of the target language can identify such ill-formed utterances, but it is commonly assumed that the language learner receives no consistent external indication that immediately identifies ungrammatical forms (Pinker 1989). Other challenges include the acquisition of the lexicon of a language, including underlying phonological forms and syntactic features. This chapter focuses on the learning of the core grammar of a language, and specifically on the challenges created by the relationship between grammatical overt forms and grammar hypotheses.

16.1.2 *Formal Learnability in Linguistics*

Early work on formal language learnability focused on the learnability of general classes of formal languages, typically characterized in terms of the computational capacity needed to process the classes. Gold (1967) demonstrated that there exist computationally simple classes of languages, like the regular languages, that are unlearnable with only positive data. Angluin (1980) illustrated the intricacies of classes of languages containing subset relations. Important issues in this work were contending with infinite classes of languages, and learning using only positive data.

The focus of much linguistic learnability work changed with the advent of the principles and parameters framework (Chomsky 1981). That framework hypothesizes that core grammars may vary only in a finite, prespecified number of ways, expressed as parameters. A particular grammar is determined by assigning each parameter one of its permissible values. Given that there are only a finite number of parameters, and each takes only a finite number of possible values, the number of possible grammars is finite. If the class of possible grammars is finite, then the 'in principle' learnability of that class is guaranteed. This provided at best minor comfort, for a few reasons. For one, not all of linguistics succeeded in adopting the principles and parameters framework; the only part of phonology so far admitting serious principles and parameters analyses is Metrical Stress Theory. Further, the in principle proofs of learnability for the finite classes typically rely on listing the entire set of possible grammars, and testing them one by one. While this approach makes many classes learnable in a finite amount of time, that finite amount is nevertheless unrealistically long, as the size of the class of grammars grows exponentially with the number of parameters.

Thus, the achievement of in-principle learnability leads to the question of how 'difficult' it is to learn a given class of grammars. The difficulty of learning can be measured in at least two ways. One is the amount of data required to determine the correct hypothesis. Another is the amount of computational effort required, often measured in terms of time. The two are not unrelated; if a large amount of data is required to successfully learn, then the amount of computational effort will be at least as much as required just to examine all of the required data.

Recent work on linguistic language learnability has focused on approaches that do not list out the entire class of grammars. One approach, the Triggering Learning Algorithm (Gibson and Wexler 1994), performs a kind of 'greedy' random search. When presented with an overt form, it attempts to parse it using its current grammar. If parsing is successful, then the overt form is consistent, so the grammar is not changed. If the overt form cannot be parsed, a parameter is selected at random and its value changed. If the change produces a grammar that can parse the overt form, the changed value is kept. Otherwise, the original value is kept. In any event, the algorithm quits processing the overt form after one guess. A variation on the triggering learning algorithm, due to Niyogi and Berwick (1993), keeps the changed parameter value whether it renders the overt form parsable or not.

A significant property of the triggering algorithm is the limited use it makes of overt forms. The algorithm only uses the overt form to determine if it is consistent with the current grammar hypothesis. If the overt form is not consistent, a random guess is made for an alternative hypothesis. The overt form is used only to test grammars in a binary fashion; no use is made of the content of the overt form to suggest which alternative hypothesis to consider.

A rather different approach, also within the principles and parameters framework, is Cue Learning (Dresher and Kaye 1990; Dresher 1996). A cue learner does not attempt to parse overt forms into full structural descriptions; in fact, cue learning makes no use of full structural descriptions at all. A cue learner searches for specific patterns in the overt forms, called cues. The learner associates a cue with each value of each parameter, and watches for each cue, usually in a prespecified order. If a cue occurs in an overt form at a time when the learner is looking for that cue, then the learner sets the associated parameter to the appropriate value.

In contrast to the triggering learning algorithm, which can be applied to nearly any parametrically-specified space of hypotheses, the cue-learning approach only produces a working algorithm after a full-scale analysis of a particular system has been conducted. This is because the selection of a particular cue for a given parameter value must be made in light of all possible interactions with the possible values of the other parameters. Any changes made to the parametric system can necessitate a complete reanalysis of the system and result in a completely different set of cues.

While the triggering learning algorithm and cue learning are at opposite extremes in some respects, they also have some properties in common. First, both depend upon the principles and parameters framework. Second, both treat the relationship between overt forms and grammar settings in monolithic terms, without employing the full structural descriptions which mediate the relationship within linguistic theory itself. Tesar and Smolensky have proposed a decomposition of the learning problem that explicitly employs full structural descriptions (Tesar and Smolensky 1996; Tesar and Smolensky 1998). This proposal decomposes learning into the subproblems of

• reconstructing the full structural descriptions for overt forms
• determining the grammar from the full structural descriptions.

This decomposition is motivated by proposals for solving each of the two subproblems. The primary objective of this chapter is to show how specific, defining principles of Optimality Theory make it possible to apply these learning proposals that take advantage of the mediating role of full structural descriptions.

16.1.3 *Learning and the Structure of Optimality Theory*

Language learning within Optimality Theory encounters the credit problem in full force. The relationships between the constraint rankings and the structural descriptions involve complex interactions between violable constraints, and comparisons within a (potentially infinite) space of competitors. While determining the constraint violations assessed a particular structural description is usually assumed to be straightforward, determining whether a description is optimal is not a trivial matter, let alone determining what specific constraint ranking relationships are properly held accountable. The auditory signals received by the learner are taken to underdetermine the full structural descriptions in Optimality Theory as in other linguistic theories.

The learning proposals presented in Sections 16.3 and 16.4, the Error-Driven Constraint Demotion algorithm and the Iterative Learning algorithm, take advantage of strict domination and the optimization-based nature of Optimality Theory. The iterative learning algorithm, like the triggering learning algorithm but unlike cue learning, maintains a working grammatical hypothesis at any given time, and evaluates overt forms for consistency with the working hypothesis. However, unlike the triggering learning algorithm, the iterative learning algorithm uses the specific information in the overt form to determine what alternative hypotheses ought to be tried when the current one fails.

16.2 Optimization in Learning and Processing

16.2.1 *Optimization-Based Learning*

16.2.1.1 Error Minimization

A very common mathematical formulation of learning is in terms of error minimization. An error is a discrepancy between the prediction made by a hypothesis and the actual observed data. For a given set of data and a given set of hypotheses, the goal of learning is to find the hypothesis that has the least error with respect to the data. If there is a hypothesis with no error relative to the data, then that hypothesis is guaranteed to be optimal. This is a standard formulation in computational learning theory. One motivation for this formulation is that it permits the application of computational optimization techniques. A related formulation common in statistical learning is to select the hypothesis that maximizes the probability of occurrence of the observed data. Another optimization-based statistical method is the Minimum Description Length (MDL) method (Wallace and Boulton 1968; Rissanen 1989). This method examines possible patterns in a corpus of data, and tries to find the shortest description of the data that can be constructed via the patterns. The patterns considered are the possible hypotheses; the best hypothesis is the one that permits the shortest description of the corpus (its patterns best and most broadly characterize the data). These types of formulations can in general be characterized as maximizing some goodness function relating the data and the hypotheses. In the case of error, the goodness function is the negative of the error, so that maximizing goodness is the same as minimizing error.

Another motivation for characterizing learning in terms of optimization is the possibility of data that contains errors. Defining learning as finding the hypothesis that is consistent with all of the data is of little use if there is no hypothesis consistent with all of the data. Optimization provides a kind of approximation: a hypothesis with zero error is clearly optimal, but short of that the hypothesis with the minimum error is the goal. Notice that the criterion is now comparative; the goal hypothesis is defined not in terms of the hypothesis in isolation, but in terms of a relationship between it and all other hypotheses. The same thing commonly happens with statistical learning: unless all but one of the hypotheses have probability 0 (given the observed data), no hypothesis will have probability 1 (given the observed data). The desired hypothesis is identified not by its probability in isolation but by its probability relative to the probabilities of the other hypotheses.

16.2.1.2 Gradient Ascent

The mere possibility of characterizing a particular learning problem in terms of optimization doesn't necessarily mean very much by itself. Any learning problem can be characterized as optimization by using a goodness function which assigns 1 to the correct hypothesis and 0 to all others. The interesting computational effect comes when non-optimal hypotheses have differentiated comparison. One computational strategy permitted by such differentiation, called the *greedy strategy*, exchanges one hypothesis for another only if the new one is better than the old one (according to the goodness function). The greedy strategy is often combined with a topology in the form of a distance metric on the hypothesis space, treating the hypotheses as points in the space. The distance metric is simply a way of saying that some pairs of points are 'nearer' to each other than others. Commonly, the distance metric defines for each point a *neighbourhood* consisting of the points nearest to it.

Combining a differentiating goodness function with a topology permits a computational strategy called *hill-climbing*. An algorithm of this type starts with a particular hypothesis, and looks for a better one near by, in that hypothesis' neighbourhood. If it finds a better one, it switches to that (better) hypothesis. This continues until a hypothesis is reached which is better than all of the other ones in its neighbourhood. Such a hypothesis is a *local optimum*. If a hypothesis is not only a local optimum but in fact the best hypothesis of all, then it is the *global optimum*. The hill-climbing strategy is motivated by the intuition that the optimal hypothesis will be surrounded by good ones, and lesser hypotheses will be further away. A common variant of hill-climbing is *gradient ascent*, which picks as its next hypothesis the best of the hypotheses neighbouring the current one, provided that it is better than the current hypothesis (gradient ascent is distinguished from, for example, selecting a neighbour at random, and adopting it if it is better).

One issue that must be distinguished from the use of gradient ascent itself is the choice of data presentation between batch and on-line algorithms. A *batch* algorithm collects all of the available data ahead of time, and then operates on all of it. A batch hill-climbing algorithm can evaluate a hypothesis with respect to all of the data, and decide whether to adopt a new hypothesis on the basis of its performance with respect to all of the data. An *on-line* algorithm receives data one instance at a time, processing one piece of data fully before moving to the next. On-line gradient ascent algorithms frequently (but not necessarily) proceed by making a small change that increases the goodness measure with respect to the current piece of data. Then, when that piece of data is discarded and the next received, another small change is made with respect to the new piece of data. Batch algorithms have the advantage of considering all of the data at each step, at the cost of requiring large amounts of memory and the imposition of a (possibly arbitrary) finite bound on the amount of data to be used. For these reasons, algorithms for natural language learning are frequently on-line algorithms.

In some domains it is possible for hill-climbing algorithms to use information available at the current hypothesis to determine what hypothesis to try next. One such method, gradient ascent, has already been mentioned. This technique is especially common when the hypothesis space is continuous; in that case, it is often possible to compute the gradient of the goodness function at that point, which tells the direction in which the goodness function is increasing the fastest, without requiring the algorithm to explicitly evaluate a hypothesis for every possible direction. Backpropagation (Rumelhart *et al.* 1986) is an example of a continuous gradient-directed learning algorithm. Other search strategies, for example genetic algorithms (Holland 1975) and simulated annealing (Kirkpatrick *et al.* 1983), use a graded goodness function, but replace hill-climbing with probabilistic acceptance mechanisms (which are not greedy procedures). Such algorithms are capable of escaping from local optima, but at the cost of losing the rapid directedness of hill-climbing.

16.2.1.3 Optimization in Language Learning

The triggering learning algorithm is a greedy on-line algorithm, and can be characterized as optimizing in the minimal, all-or-nothing sense. The topology is determined by the parameters: two hypotheses are neighbours if they differ in the value of only one parameter. The goodness measure is the parsability of the currently observed overt form. If the current hypothesis cannot parse the overt form, but the randomly-selected neighbouring hypothesis can, then the neighbouring hypothesis is adopted. Two points should be emphasized. The first is that the goodness measure is really an all-or-nothing criterion: either the overt form can be parsed or it cannot. The second is that the neighbouring hypothesis checked when an error occurs is selected at random; the algorithm does not attempt to determine which neighbour is 'more likely' to be successful.

While the triggering learning algorithm was proposed for grammar spaces within the principles and parameters framework, its strategy is largely independent of specifically linguistic principles. In fact, a version of the triggering learning algorithm has been proposed for Optimality Theory (Pulleyblank and Turkel 1995, this volume). What is required is a topology for the space of possible grammars and a procedure for evaluating a piece of data with respect to a given grammar.

Optimization-based learning algorithms are not a panacea. Many complex hypothesis spaces contain local optima, at least with respect to the most apparent topologies. But these algorithms have given good results on a variety of learning problems where the hypothesis space is simply too vast to be searched exhaustively. This good performance is usually achieved when the function defining the goodness of the hypotheses is more complex and graded, so that it can direct the search. Section 16.3 will explain how strict domination facilitates a kind of hill-climbing strategy that is very effective for learning in Optimality Theory.

16.2.2 *Optimization Approaches to Hidden Structure*

Hidden structure, as discussed in Section 16.1.1, is also an issue of interest in learning theory generally. In statistical learning theory, the problem is often framed as having missing values for variables in the data. In the case of underdetermination of linguistic structural descriptions, the variables with missing values represent the hidden structure. The grammar hypotheses evaluate structural descriptions in terms of the values of all their variables.

There is a class of algorithms for dealing with the problem of missing values that has received a lot of attention in recent years. This is the class of Expectation-Maximization, or EM, algorithms (Dempster *et al.* 1977). Such an algorithm has two phases, and it alternates between the two. The algorithm assumes that you have a starting hypothesis that is a reasonable first guess. The correct hypothesis is, of course, what the procedure is trying to learn, so in general the first guess will be an incorrect hypothesis. Nevertheless, the first phase (the expectation step) uses this hypothesis to compute the expected values of the missing variables. Having calculated values for the hidden variables in that way, the second phase (the maximization step) then uses those values, along with the attendant overt variable values, to find the best hypothesis for those observations. The goal of the second phase is to determine, using the full sets of values for all the variables, the hypothesis that makes those observations most probable. This gives a new (and hopefully improved) hypothesis. The first phase can then be repeated, using the new hypothesis to get new expected values for the hidden variables. The two phases can be repeated in alternating fashion.

For several classes of problems, this algorithm can be proved to always increase the goodness of the hypothesis until it converges, meaning that the hypothesis and the expected values of the hidden variables stop changing. Thus, a local optimum is guaranteed to be reached, despite the back-and-forth nature. An example of this kind of algorithm is the Baum-Welch algorithm (sometimes called the Forward-Backward algorithm) for training hidden Markov models (Baum 1972; Rabiner 1989 for an overview).

One adaptation of this strategy to the domain of language learning is as follows. Start with a grammar hypothesis. Use it to arrive at the 'expected' full structural description for each observed overt form. That would be the language counterpart to the 'expectation' step. Then use those full structural descriptions to select a new grammar hypothesis. That would be the language counterpart to the 'maximization' step. Section 16.4 will explain how the optimizing structure of Optimality Theory makes it possible to apply this kind of strategy to learning constraint rankings with overt forms that underdetermine the full structural descriptions.

16.2.3 *Parsing as Optimization*

In Optimality Theory, grammatical descriptions are the descriptions which are optimal with respect to their corresponding underlying forms. The function being optimized is called *Harmony*, and is defined by the ranked universal constraints. The constraint ranking assigns a harmony value to each candidate structural description. The structural description which, of the many candidates for a given underlying form, has the highest harmony is the optimal candidate. The mapping from an input to its optimal description can be taken as a (highly idealized) characterization of the language production task: language production is an optimization process[3] (Tesar 1996; Ellison 1994). The process of computing the optimal structural description for an underlying form, given a constraint ranking, will be called *production-directed parsing*.

Filling in the hidden structure of a structural description for an observed overt form is the task of the language comprehender. A competent speaker of a language is able to assign the correct description to an utterance, and is thereby able to understand it. While it is not logically necessary, it seems intuitively plausible that a child would use the same basic language faculty to attempt to interpret utterances while learning, the same faculty that becomes the comprehension faculty of a competent speaker. That intuition underlies the comprehension proposal presented here.

(1) The relationship between production-directed and interpretive parsing

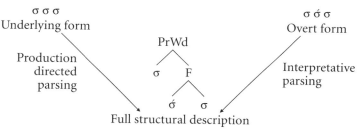

Full structural description

The proposal is that language comprehension, like production, is an optimization process. The hearer is presented with an overt form, and selects the description of that overt form that is optimal with respect to his or her current constraint ranking. The difference is that here the candidate structural descriptions competing for optimality are candidates whose overt portions match the observed overt form. The interpretation assigned to an observed overt form is that structural description which, out of all descriptions whose overt portion matches the observed form, best satisfies the ranked universal constraints. The process of

---

[3] Algorithms which compute this optimization for various classes of Optimality-theoretic grammars have been developed (Tesar 1995, 1996; Ellison 1994). The iterative learning algorithm described in Section 16.4.3 uses a dynamic programming procedure to compute the optimal descriptions assigned to underlying forms by hypothesis constraint rankings (Tesar to appear). The learning algorithm also uses another dynamic programming procedure to compute the optimal descriptions assigned to overt forms, as required for interpretive parsing. The dynamic programming procedures operate by building up a small set of partial descriptions as they work through the input, so that only a few entire descriptions need be compared by the time all of the input has been processed. Space does not permit a lengthier description of these algorithms.

computing the optimal structural description for an overt form, given a constraint ranking, will be called *interpretive parsing*.

One critical property of this approach to comprehension is that it is 'robust' in the following sense: the process can assign a description to an overt form even if there is no description matching that overt form which is grammatical according to the current ranking. A description will still be assigned to the form, even if there is another description with the same underlying form (but different overt form) which is more harmonic. The comprehender can be aware that the observed form is not grammatical according to his or her current ranking but can nevertheless do the best he or she can to interpret the form. This reflects the observation that competent speakers can often offer consistent interpretations of overt forms they simultaneously judge to be ungrammatical.

What is proposed, then, is optimization-based processes for both language production and language comprehension. When competent speakers, possessing the correct constraint ranking, interpret an overt form, they arrive at the same structural description as when they apply production processing to the corresponding underlying form. Both processes are defined in terms of optimization with respect to the same constraint ranking. This optimization-based framework plays a central role in the learning proposal.

One important addition must be made to the optimization defined by Optimality Theory. In the course of learning, hypotheses will be considered in which the domination relation is not defined for some pairs of constraints. The ranking hypotheses used by the learning algorithm are of a particular form, called a stratified hierarchy. A *stratified hierarchy* consists of ranked strata, in which each stratum contains one or more of the constraints. A stratified hierarchy with only one constraint in each stratum is called a *total ranking*; total rankings are what Optimality Theory formally takes as defining actual grammars. This freedom to have hypotheses that aren't totally ranked is important to the success of the learning algorithm. The typological predictions of total-ranking OT are not altered: the learning algorithm will always converge to a stratified hierarchy consistent with at least one total ranking; this is discussed further in Section 16.3. However, the definition of optimality must be extended to stratified hierarchies in general. This is done by 'pooling the marks' of all of the constraints in a stratum. Two competing candidates are compared on an entire stratum, such that the candidate with fewer total constraint violations of all the constraints in the stratum is the more harmonic candidate. If the two candidates have the same number of violations for the top stratum, the decision passes to the second stratum of constraints, and so forth.

16.3 Using Strict Domination to Guide the Search

The first subproblem of the decomposition of the learning problem presented in section 16.1.2 is the problem of reconstructing full structural descriptions for overt forms. This section will assume that correct full structural descriptions can be determined for the overt forms, and focus on the second subproblem. The procedure presented here—constraint demotion—determines a correct ranking for the constraints from full structural descriptions. Section 16.4 will then complete the story with an approach to determining the full structural descriptions for the overt forms.

16.3.1 *Constraint Demotion*

The challenge specific to the learning of constraint rankings is illustrated in tableau (2). The problem is posed in terms of two competing structural descriptions of the same input. One of the descriptions, called the *winner*, is the grammatical structural description, the one assigned by the target grammar. The other description, the *loser*, is a competitor that is (necessarily) suboptimal under the target ranking. The rows of tableau (2) give the constraint violations of the structural descriptions. The goal is to find a constraint ranking that makes the winner more harmonic than all of its competitors, one of which is the competitor here labeled loser. By definition, for the winner to be more harmonic than the loser, at least one of the constraints violated more times by the loser must dominate all of the constraints violated more times by the winner.

(2)   The Disjunction Problem; $\langle * \rangle$ indicates a canceled mark

	DEM	SUP	MID	ORG	BET
winner	$*$	$\langle * \rangle$			$*$
loser		$\langle * \rangle$		$*$	

To simplify the discussion slightly, the violations of a constraint by a candidate will be referred to as *marks*: a constraint assigns a candidate one mark for each violation of that constraint. When two competitors are being compared, and they both violate the same constraint, corresponding marks will be canceled, so that the only remaining marks, the uncanceled marks, are those indicating greater violation of a constraint by one candidate, as compared to its competitor. In tableau (2), both candidates violate SUP, but the loser violates it one more time than the winner. The violation mark in common is canceled, leaving the mark indicating that the loser has greater violation of the constraint. If two competitors violate a constraint the same number of times, all marks for that constraint are canceled, properly indicating that the constraint has no say in determining the relative harmony of the two competitors. Because marks are identified with constraints, it is convenient to talk about the relative ranking of uncanceled marks, where one mark is more highly-ranked than another precisely when the constraint assigning the one mark is more highly-ranked than the constraint assigning the other. The less harmonic of a pair of candidates, on a given constraint hierarchy, is thus the one receiving the highest-ranked uncanceled mark.

The precise information contained in the loser/winner pair of tableau (2) is given in Equation (3).

(3)   (Sup or Org) >> (Dem and Bet)

The tricky part is the disjunction (the logical 'or') of the constraints violated by the loser: we know one of them must dominate the constraints violated by the winner, but we don't know which one (if not both). In systems with a larger number of constraints it may be possible for a single loser/winner pair to have quite a few constraints in the disjunction, and attempting to maintain and reconcile all such information across many examples could be difficult.

A solution to this problem is *constraint demotion* (Tesar and Smolensky 1995, 1998). Constraint demotion identifies the highest-ranked uncanceled mark of the loser. Every constraint which (a) assigns an uncanceled mark to the winner, and (b) is not currently dominated by the highest-ranked constraint assigning an uncanceled loser mark, is *demoted* to immediately below the highest-ranked constraint assigning an uncanceled loser mark. This ensures that the resulting ranking will hold the winner more harmonic than the loser. The central idea is referred to as the principle of constraint demotion.

(4)   **The Principle of Constraint Demotion**
For any constraint C assessing an uncanceled winner mark, if C is not dominated by a constraint assessing an uncanceled loser mark, demote C to immediately below the highest-ranked constraint assessing an uncanceled loser mark.

Constraint demotion is illustrated in tableau (6) for the loser/winner pair of tableau (2). The highest-ranked uncanceled loser mark is Sup. One constraint assigning an uncanceled winner mark, Bet, is already dominated by Sup, and so is left alone. The other constraint assigning an uncanceled winner mark, Dem, is not so dominated. Thus, constraint demotion demotes Dem to the stratum immediately below Sup (effectively creating a tie between Dem and Mid). The resulting constraint hierarchy is given in Equation (5).

(5)   Sup >> {Dem,Mid} >> Org >> Bet

With respect to this hierarchy, the winner is more harmonic than the loser.

(6)   Constraint Demotion (only uncanceled marks are shown)

	(Dem)	Sup	Dem	Mid	Org	Bet
winner	(*)		*			*
loser		*			*	

As previously discussed, the ranking hypotheses used by the algorithm are stratified hierarchies. The hierarchy in Equation (5) is an example of a constraint hierarchy that is not a total ranking: DEM and MID are not ranked with respect to each other (but each is ranked with respect to all of the other constraints).

The demotion illustrated in tableau (6) ensures that the winner is more harmonic than the loser. It does not guarantee that the winner is optimal; for the winner to be optimal it must be more harmonic than all competitors. What is important is that while the learner may not have yet reached a correct ranking, the learner has made demonstrable progress. Further progress can be made if a different loser is now selected, one that is currently more harmonic than the winner. A competitor that is more harmonic than the grammatical candidate for a given hypothesis constraint hierarchy is called *informative*; a winner combined with an informative loser is called an *informative pair*. Constraint demotion applied to this new loser along with the winner will produce a hierarchy by which the winner is more harmonic. This process can be repeated until a ranking is arrived at which holds the winner as the optimal candidate. The procedure can also be performed with other grammatical structural descriptions used as winners.

Each application of constraint demotion moves the learner to a hypothesis closer to a hierarchy generating the language. To see why, recall that the grammatical descriptions are all generated by some total ranking R of the constraints. Some constraint C_1 is the highest-ranked constraint in R. Any grammatical structural description violates C_1 as many or fewer times than all of its competitors; otherwise, it would not be the grammatical description. It follows that C_1 will never be demoted because only constraints violated by a winner more times than the loser are eligible for demotion on a given loser/winner pair. Eventually, every constraint that is required by the language to be below C_1 will be demoted below (if it was not already below C_1). The only informative losers will then be competitors that match their grammatical counterpart in the number of violations of C_1. The same reasoning used for C_1 now recursively applies to the second-highest constraint in R, C_2. No informative competitor violates C_2 fewer times than the winner, by virtue of the fact that the winner is optimal with respect to R. So from that point forward C_2 will not be demoted. Overall, C_2 will only ever be demoted if it is above C_1.

The challenge posed by the disjunctions in the mark-data pairs is met as a consequence of the use of demotion, and not promotion, of constraints. Attempting to satisfy a mark-data pair through promotion would mean choosing a constraint violated more by the loser and promoting it to above all constraints violated more by the winner. This forces a direct confrontation with the disjunction: *which* constraint violated more by the loser should be promoted? Demotion, on the other hand, focuses on the conjunction: *all* constraints violated more by the winner must be demoted if they are not already dominated appropriately. No uninformed choice need be made.

16.3.2 *Selecting Competitors*

An informative competitor for a grammatical description is one that is more harmonic on the current hypothesis hierarchy than the grammatical description. There are an infinite number of competitors, however, so an informative competitor, if one exists, cannot be identified simply by checking every competitor. A solution to this problem is to use production-directed parsing to identify an informative competitor, if one exists (Tesar 1995, to appear). When presented with a grammatical description, compute the description for the same input[4] (underlying form) that is optimal with respect to the current hypothesis hierarchy. If it does not match the grammatical description, then the grammatical description is made the winner and the description currently optimal is made the loser. If the currently optimal description matches the given grammatical one, then there is no informative competitor, so no learning takes place.

A mismatch between the grammatical description and the description optimal for the current hypothesis hierarchy can be termed an *error*; such a mismatch indicates that the current hierarchy is not a correct one, because the wrong description is optimal. Learning is triggered by such errors, and for that reason the algorithm is called *Error-Driven Constraint Demotion*, shown in (7).

(7)   The error-driven constraint demotion algorithm

    Given: an initial hierarchy *start-H* and a grammatical
    structural description *winner*
    set *H* to be *start-H*
    set *U* to be the underlying form of *winner*
    repeat
        apply production-directed parsing, with *H*, to *U*, getting description *loser*
        if *loser* ≠ *winner*
            cancel the violation marks in common to *loser* and *winner*
            apply constraint demotion to the uncanceled marks and *H*, getting *new-H*
            set *H* to be *new-H*
        end-if
    until *loser* = *winner*
    return *H*

The measure (over constraint ranking hypotheses) being optimized by error-driven constraint demotion is the relative harmony of the grammatical structural description (the winner) with respect to the description that is optimal according to the hypothesis (the loser). As the algorithm works to make the winner optimal, the uncanceled violations by the winner appear in lower and lower strata in the successive hypothesis rankings. The measure compares hypotheses on the basis of the relative 'height' of the constraints violated more by the winner.

This measure differs from those used in many of the optimization approaches to learning mentioned in Section 16.2.1 in that it applies strictly on a form-by-

---

[4] Full structural descriptions contain their input, so the input for the grammatical description may be extracted. Learning inputs is beyond the scope of this chapter, but the issue is discussed in Section 16.5.1.

form basis. The goodness measure of the ranking hypotheses is defined with respect to some given winner; as of yet there has been no definition of how to compare the performance of different hypotheses upon different winners. For the current task, such a comparison is unnecessary; given grammatical full structural descriptions, error-driven constraint demotion can reach a correct hierarchy by processing one winner at a time, using the goodness measure defined by each winner as it is processed. The winner relativity of the goodness measure is reflected in the conservatism of constraint demotion: constraints violated more by the winner are demoted only as far as necessary, and no further.

The error-driven structure of the algorithm makes it convenient to measure data complexity in terms of the number of errors (mismatches that result in constraint demotions) that can occur prior to convergence on a hierarchy generating the correct language. There is a mathematically provable bound on the worst-case number of errors that can occur prior to convergence: $N(N–1)$ errors, where N is the number of constraints. In practice, this worst case is a large overestimate, and the algorithm reaches the correct ranking far more quickly. This demonstrates that the amount of data required to learn a ranking does not scale anything like the number of total rankings; values of both for a few choices of numbers of constraints are shown in tableau (8). Both the convergence of error-driven constraint demotion and the data complexity are theorems. The full formal analysis, including the proofs of the theorems, can be found in Tesar and Smolensky (1998).

(8)   Data complexity of constraint demotion

Constraints	Total Rankings	Max. # Errors (before convergence)
5	$5! = 120$	$5(5–1) = 20$
10	$10! = 3,628,800$	$10(10–1) = 90$
11	$11! = 39,916,800$	$11(11–1) = 110$
110	$20! = 2,432,902,008,176,640,000$	$20(20–1) = 380$

16.3.3 *The Advantages of Strict Domination*

Error-driven constraint demotion is successful because it can assume that strict domination holds among the constraints. For any loser/winner pair, the correct ranking must assign the loser the highest-ranked uncanceled mark. Therefore, the learner is always justified in demoting constraints assigning uncanceled winner marks down at least as far as the constraint assigning the highest-ranked uncanceled loser mark. The resulting hierarchy may still not be correct, but that can only be because some constraints need to be demoted even further down.

To see how advantageous strict domination is, it may be helpful to compare it to a hypothetical alternative. Consider a theory by which the relative importance of the constraints is determined not by a ranking but by assigning a negative integer number to each constraint, expressing the strength of the constraint. The possible strengths would be the first N integers, where N is the number of constraints. The more important constraints in a particular grammar will have larger (in magnitude) harmony numbers assigned to them. The harmony of a structural description would be determined by adding together the harmony numbers for the violated constraints (the strength of a constraint is added to the total once per violation of the constraint). Different structural descriptions would then be compared on the basis of their numeric harmony. For any pair of descriptions, the description with the higher harmony (the harmony value that is closer to 0) is the more harmonic. A description which does not violate any constraints will have a harmony value of 0. The linguistic viability of such a theory is not of interest here; what is of interest is the computational difficulty of learning within such a system.

In this scheme, the language learner's task is to assign harmony strengths to the constraints in the form of numeric values. Consider tableau (9) in which the violation marks have been replaced by numbers expressing the strengths of the constraints:

(9)   Harmony with negative integral values

	DEM	SUP	MID	ORG	BET
winner	−5	−1			-2
loser		−1 −1		-3	

The harmony of the winner is now (DEM + SUP + BET) = −8, while the harmony of the loser is (SUP + SUP + ORG) = −5. What does this information tell us? One possibility is that DEM should exchange its strength with ORG or SUP or MID (which is assumed to have strength -4). For instance, changing the strength of DEM to −3 while changing the strength of ORG to −5 would result in the winner, with a harmony of −6, being more harmonic than the loser, with a harmony of −7. That situation appears much like those with strict domination: the strongest of the differentiating constraints is violated more by the loser.

However, it is also possible that each of the constraints violated by the loser is weaker than one of the constraints violated by the winner, but much stronger than the other one. For example, suppose the strengths are changed to those shown in tableau (10).

(10) The winner is more harmonic, but also violates the strongest constraint.

	DEM	SUP	MID	ORG	BET
winner	−5	−4			−1
loser		−4 −4		−3	

This arrangement also makes the winner more harmonic than the loser, despite the fact that the winner has greater violation of the strongest constraint, DEM. Such a possibility has the intriguing property of making the winner fare better against the loser by *decreasing* the absolute harmony of the winner from −8 to −10. All of these options are possible. There is no single constraint that must have its strength changed, given only this single loser/winner pair.

The difficulty with the integer strengths case is that there is no single clear direction to take in changing the strengths of the constraints. That is not the case with strict domination because of the restrictive structure placed on constraint interactions. Lower-ranked constraints cannot 'gang up' on a higher-ranked constraint. The information contained in the pair shown in tableau (2) really is that given in equation (3): (SUP **or** ORG) >> (DEM **and** BET). If constraint demotion demotes both DEM and BET to below ORG, and later data reveals that ORG must be demoted to below SUP, then DEM and BET will need to be further demoted to below SUP. But that does not indicate that the earlier demotion of DEM and BET was in the wrong direction; on the contrary, it means that the demotion did not move far enough in that direction to get DEM and BET all the way down (in one step) to where they ultimately need to be.

The crucial point is that a single instance of constraint demotion is guaranteed to be progress. The new constraint hierarchy is better than the previous one, better in that it is closer to a correct hierarchy. A mismatch between the known grammatical candidate and the currently optimal candidate does more than just tell the learner that his or her current hierarchy is wrong; it provides real information about what the right hierarchy must be like. By obeying the constraint demotion principle, the learner can take an informed step without having to reach all the way to a hypothesis consistent with the current form. It is this capacity that makes constraint demotion efficient: you can reach your destination much more quickly when you know which way to go.

To be clear, the claim is not that any strength scheme other than strict domination will have a more difficult associated learning problem. It is certainly possible to design schemes with special structure that permit efficient learning. But it is easy to design general strength schemes that don't permit efficient learning. The claim made here is that strict domination provides a special structure that does permit efficient learning, and strict domination is part of an empirically successful linguistic theory, Optimality Theory.

16.4 Using Optimality to Compensate for Incomplete Data

The previous section showed how the correct constraint ranking can be determined, given the correct full structural descriptions for the overt forms. This section presents a strategy for dealing with the gap between the actually observed overt forms and the desired full structural descriptions. The strategy depends crucially on the fact that OT grammars are defined in terms of optimization.

16.4.1 *An Iterative Strategy*

At any given time, there is a hypothesis ranking held by the learner. Given an overt form, the interpretive parsing algorithm, as described in Section 16.2.3, is used to determine the most harmonic structural description for that overt form, relative to the hypothesis ranking. That full structural description includes an underlying form (the underlying form of the interpretation). Production-directed parsing, also described in Section 16.2.3, is then applied to the underlying form of the interpretation to obtain the optimal structural description for that under-lying form, relative to the hypothesis ranking. If the optimal interpretation of the overt form matches the optimal description of the underlying form, the ranking is not changed. So far as can be determined from this overt form, the hypothesis ranking is the correct one: the current grammar's expression of the underlying form matches the observed overt form.

If, on the other hand, the interpretation of the overt form given by interpre-tive parsing does not match the structural description generated by production-directed parsing, an error has occurred. Such a mismatch is the indication that learning needs to take place. What could be the source of the error? One possi-bility is that the interpretation of the overt form, given by interpretive parsing, is incorrect, due to the incorrectness of the learner's current hypothesized con-straint ranking. Another possibility is that interpretive parsing gave the correct interpretation but that the structural description given by production-directed parsing is incorrect; again, this would be due to the incorrect ranking (the two possibilities are not mutually exclusive). In either case the constraint ranking needs to be changed.

The ultimate goal of the learner is to find a ranking such that the interpreta-tion of each overt form matches the optimal description for the corresponding underlying form. Changing the hypothesis ranking may change what the optimal description is for the underlying form of the prior interpretation. But it may also change the interpretation assigned to the overt form by interpretive parsing. Consequently, the learner must, after changing the ranking, re-apply interpretive parsing to the overt form, using the new ranking. The resulting interpretation under the new ranking (which may or may not be the same description as as-signed under the previous ranking) then provides the underlying form to which production-directed parsing is applied. If under the new ranking the interpreta-tion matches the optimal description, then the learner stops working on that overt form; for that form, learning would appear to be successful. If another mismatch occurs, then the learner must change the constraint ranking again.

When an error occurs, indicating that the hypothesis ranking needs to be changed, the key question is: *how* should the ranking be changed? The strategy advocated here is to assume that the interpretation (obtained using the current ranking) is correct, and therefore that the structural description generated by production-directed parsing is in error. The immediate goal is then to change the constraint ranking so that the interpretation is more harmonic than the description optimal by the current ranking. But that is precisely what constraint demotion accomplishes. The learner thus applies constraint demotion to find a new constraint ranking, using the interpretation as the winner, and the description produced by production-directed parsing as the loser.

What results is an iterative procedure that alternates parsing and grammar-changing. The hypothesis ranking is used to determine a 'best guess' at the interpretive structural description, including the hidden structure, for an overt form. This 'best guess' is then used to determine a new hypothesis ranking. The new hypothesis ranking is then used to determine a new 'best guess' at the hidden structure, and so forth. Learning is successful if the iterations converge upon a stable ranking: the interpretation matches the optimal description. The iterative learning algorithm is shown in (11). It may help to compare the iterative learning algorithm with the error-driven constraint demotion algorithm of (7).

(11)   The Iterative Learning Algorithm

Given: a constraint hierarchy *start-H* and a grammatical overt form *F*
set *H* to be *start-H*
repeat
    apply interpretive parsing, with *H*, to *F*, getting interpretation *winner*
    set *U* to be the underlying form of *winner*
    apply production-directed parsing, with *H*, to *U*, getting description *loser*
    if *loser* ≠ *winner*
        cancel the violation marks in common to *loser* and *winner*
        apply constraint demotion to the uncanceled marks and *H*, getting new
        hierarchy *new-H*
        set *H* to be *new-H*
    end-if
until *loser* = *winner*
return *H*

The intuition behind this strategy is that even when the current hypothesis ranking is wrong, the best interpretation of the overt structure is likely to be informative because it is constrained to match the observed overt structure. Even when the best interpretation is itself incorrect, treating it as correct (at least temporarily) can allow the learner to make progress.

The strategy just described is inspired by the EM algorithms discussed in Section 16.2.2. The analogy is not an exact one, due to differences between OT grammars and probability models. Probability models assign greater or lesser likelihood to a set of possible outcomes. By contrast, Optimality Theory has a 'winner-take-all' spirit: the most harmonic structural description is fully grammatical, while all suboptimal structural descriptions are completely ungrammatical. This spirit is carried over to the expectation step analogue in the iterative learning algorithm. The hidden structure is not filled with an 'average' of the values across different candidate interpretations, as is done in EM algorithms. The most harmonic interpretation, and it alone, gets to fill the hidden structure values, in keeping with both the nature of OT optimization and the view of robust interpretive parsing as a competence model of language comprehension. In this way, the iterative learning algorithm is even more optimization-based than the EM algorithms are.

16.4.2 Examples: Success and Failure

16.4.2.1 Success: Learning with an incorrect interpretation

The starting ranking for this example is given in Equation (12)

(12)   A-F-L >> A-F-R >> IAMB >> MAIN-R >> TROCH >> {the rest}

Only five of the 11 constraints are shown in the tableaus. The first overt form presented to the learner is [o o o 1 o]. This is a five-syllable word; the numbers indicate the stress level for each syllable, 1 indicating primary stress, 2 secondary stress, and o unstressed (the form in this example does not have any syllables with secondary stress). The correct, grammatical description of this overt form is [o o o (1 o)], a right-aligned trochaic foot.

The learner applies interpretive parsing to this overt form, using the constraint ranking in (12). The result of interpretive parsing is the full structural description, [o o (o 1) o], shown in the Winner row of tableau (13). The learner then applies production-directed parsing to the underlying form, which consists of five syllables without stress levels, and obtains the description [(o 1) o o o], shown in the Loser row of tableau (13).

(13) The production-directed parse (loser) of 5 syllables better satisfies the ranked constraints than the optimal interpretation (winner) of overt form [o o o 1 o].

	A-F-L	A-F-R	IAMB	MAIN-R	TROCH
Loser [(o 1) o o o]		***		***	*
Winner [o o (o 1) o]	**	*		*	*

Constraint demotion is then applied, which demotes ALL-FEET-LEFT to below ALL-FEET-RIGHT, into the stratum already occupied by IAMBIC. Tableau (14) shows the same loser/winner pair after this demotion.

(14) After the first demotion, the winner is more harmonic.

	A-F-R	IAMB	A-F-L	MAIN-R	TROCH
Loser [(o 1) o o o]	***			***	*
Winner [o o (o 1) o]	*		**	*	*

Now, the learner reapplies both interpretive parsing and production-directed parsing, using the new constraint ranking. The resulting loser and winner are shown in tableau (15) along with their constraint violations.

(15)   Loser/Winner pair before the second demotion.

	A-F-R	Iamb	A-F-L	Main-R	Troch
Loser [o o o (o 1)]			✶✶✶		✶
Winner [o o o (1 o)]		✶	✶✶✶		

The learner then applies constraint demotion again, this time demoting Iambic to below Trochaic. The result is shown in tableau (16).

(16)   Loser/Winner pair after the second demotion

	A-F-R	A-F-L	Main-R	Troch	Iamb
Loser [o o o (o 1)]		✶✶✶		✶	
Winner [o o o (1 o)]		✶✶✶	✶		✶

The learner now has a stable ranking. When interpretive parsing is applied to the overt form, the resulting structural description is [o o o (1 o)], the same as the winner on the previous step. Applying production-directed parsing to the underlying form results in the identical description: the winner now matches the loser. Further, it is the correct structural description. Notice that, at the beginning, the interpretation used by the learner, [o o (o 1) o], was not correct, due to the incorrect hypothesis ranking. Nevertheless, the learner made progress when he or she used that description as a winner for constraint demotion. Despite being incorrect, that initial interpretation contained enough correct information to allow the learner to make progress, and ultimately converge on a correct constraint hierarchy.

16.4.2.2 Failure to converge

While convergence is possible despite early misinterpretations, it is not guaranteed for all cases. An interesting case of failure to converge is one where the learner assigns to an overt form an interpretation which is not only incorrect but impossible: the interpretation is not optimal under any constraint ranking.
    Consider the example given in tableau (17).

(17)   The winner causes the demotion of Iambic.

	Parse	A-F-L	Main-R	Iamb	Troch
Loser [(o 2) (o 1) o]	✶	✶✶	✶		✶✶
Winner [(2 o) (o 1) o]	✶	✶✶	✶	✶	✶
Correct [(2 o) o (1 o)]	✶	✶✶✶		✶✶	

The overt form is [2 o o 1 o]. The correct interpretation is [(2 o) o (1 o)]. However, the ranking of All-Feet-Left over Main-Right and the foot-form constraints makes [(2 o) (o 1) o] the currently optimal interpretation, hence the winner. Notice that this interpretation has inconsistent footing, with one trochaic foot and one iambic foot. The OT system being used here, however, does not have inconsistent footing in optimal descriptions under any total rank-ing (descriptions with inconsistent footing are possible candidates generated by GEN but they always lose to some other candidate for any total ranking). Any persistent effort to find a ranking making this description optimal is guaranteed to fail.

The iterative learning algorithm, however, has not been granted any special knowledge of such cases, and proceeds as usual. The loser/winner pair of tableau (17) results in the demotion of IAMBIC to below TROCHAIC. This makes the winner more harmonic than that loser. The re-application of parsing using the new constraint ranking produces the same winner but a new loser; these are shown in tableau (18).

(18)   The winner causes the demotion of TROCHAIC.

	PARSE	A-F-L	MAIN-R	TROCH	IAMB
Loser [(2 0) (1 0) 0]	*	**	*		**
Winner [(2 0) (0 1) 0]	*	**	*	*	*
Correct [(2 0) 0 (1 0)]	*	***			**

The loser has changed; the reversal of the ranking of the footform constraints results in a reversal of footform for *both* feet in the optimal description (loser). The winner remains the same because it still satisfies PARSE and ALL-FEET-LEFT better than any other interpretation of [2 0 0 1 0]. The learner, in his or her effort to make the winner optimal, now demotes TROCHAIC to below IAMBIC. But this puts the learner right back to where he or she started, as in tableau (17). The situation reveals a cyclic pathology: the learner repeatedly demotes the foot-form constraints, one below the other and then vice versa.

16.4.3 *Some Experimental Results*

To empirically test this approach to grammar learning, some simulations were run. Due to space restrictions, the results are discussed only briefly here; the work is reported in full in (Tesar, to appear). The linguistic domain was metrical stress theory. The overt forms consisted of words of between two and seven syllables, with stress levels (main stress, secondary stress, and unstressed) as-signed to the syllables. What was not included in the overt forms was the foot structure within the prosodic word. The Optimality-theoretic system included 11 freely rankable constraints, sufficient to capture a variety of metrical phenom-ena, including trochaic vs. iambic footing, main-only vs. main and secondary stresses, leftward vs. rightward iterativity of footing, and extrametricality effects. Quantity sensitivity was not included (but see Tesar 1997 for simulation results on an OT system that includes quantity-sensitive phenomena). In this experi-ment, a language is a stress pattern on six words (length two through seven). There were a total of 104 distinct possible languages in the system (recall that a possible language is one generated by at least one total ranking of the constraints).

The first set of simulations ran the algorithm on all 104 languages, using an initial ranking hypothesis with all of the constraints tied in a single stratum (the *monostratal* hierarchy). The program converged upon a correct constraint hierarchy for 87 of the 104 possible languages. For the other 17, the algorithm failed to converge. All of the failures exhibited the pathology illustrated in Section 16.4.2.2.

The second set of simulations ran the algorithm on all 104 languages, this time with an initial ranking hypothesis placing the two footform constraints IAMBIC and TROCHAIC in the top stratum, and the rest of the constraints in the second stratum. This time the program converged for all 104 languages. Placing the footform constraints at the top has the effect of enforcing consistent footform: the dominant footform constraint, determined early on, has priority over the constraints determining placement of the feet. Enforcing consistent footform avoids the cyclic pathology.

A significant aspect of these simulations is the speed at which the iterative learning algorithm converges. On the correctly-learned cases the program always converged after at most 10 instances of demotion. Because the system had 11 rankable constraints, the number of distinct total rankings of the constraints is $11! = 39,916,800$. The actual working hypothesis space is the space of all possible stratified hierarchies, including ones that are not total rankings; for 11 constraints, the number of possible stratified hierarchies is 1,622,632,573, which is two orders of magnitude greater. The learning algorithm is powerful enough to converge quickly despite the large size of the hypothesis space.

16.4.4 *The Advantages of Optimality*

Optimality can be used to compensate for the incompleteness of overt forms by providing a basis for filling in the values of hidden structure: the values that result in the most harmonic overall structural description are selected. Further, the procedure, interpretive parsing, is not an extra processing mechanism solely for the purpose of learning; it is an entirely plausible proposal for language comprehension, both during and after learning.

There is no in principle reason why non-optimizing procedures could not be found which would successfully fill in hidden structure during learning. But there are obvious questions. What would those procedures be? What principles would govern their operation? Would they fit into a general plan for language comprehension? The most common parsing procedures used with the principles and parameters framework respond with a simple 'No' to an overt form that is inconsistent with the grammar in use; no further attempt is made to interpret such an overt form. The nonviolable constraints employed in the principles and parameters framework can reject structural descriptions as ungrammatical but do not otherwise assess the rejected forms relative to one another. This may underlie the lack of utilization of full structural descriptions in the principles-and-parameters learning literature, despite the central role of full descriptions in the linguistic theory itself.

The iterative approach for solving 'chicken and egg' hidden structure problems is an option for Optimality Theory because Optimality Theory is based upon optimization. Interpretive parsing can do more than just tell whether or not an overt form is consistent with the current grammar: it can return the most harmonic interpretation, including the hidden structure, of that overt form, whether or not the overt form is grammatical. That is the Optimality-theoretic equivalent of finding the expected values for hidden variables according to a particular statistical model. The best interpretation can then serve as a target for the learner, providing an informed estimate of the direction to move along. Because the linguistic theory is based on optimization, an overt form causing an error provides much more useful information than a mere indication that the current grammar hypothesis is incorrect.

16.5 Further Issues

16.5.1 *Underlying Forms and Output Correspondence*

According to the principle of 'richness of the base' (Prince and Smolensky 1993), the set of linguistic inputs is universal. Following the assumption that knowledge of universals need not be learned, in a sense there is no learning problem for *possible* underlying forms; the possible underlying forms are the permissible inputs. There does remain, however, the matter of learning the lexicon—that is, of learning which of the universally available inputs are paired with which morphemes. This issue is particularly apparent in phonology, where the same morpheme can appear differently in different contexts, according to the phonology of a specific language.

As it happens, this problem was addressed by Prince and Smolensky (Prince and Smolensky 1993), who proposed an optimization-based approach in the form of the principle of *lexicon optimization*. This principle states that if several different underlying forms surface with overt forms that match the overt forms of a given morpheme, then the underlying form of which the surface forms in various contexts are collectively the most harmonic is selected as the underlying form for that morpheme. Because all the candidate underlying forms have identical surface realizations in each context, the most significant differences between them will usually be differences of faithfulness. The optimal underlying form selected by lexicon optimization for a morpheme will likely be the one with minimal disparities between it and the surface realizations of that morpheme.

Lexicon optimization could be adopted as part of the optimizing approach to language learning. Interpretive parsing will have to select underlying forms, because underlying forms are part of full structural descriptions. Thus, the use of a hypothesized lexicon, along with a hypothesized constraint hierarchy, to estimate full structural descriptions for overt forms is already part of the approach. Lexicon optimization could then be added to the learning of the grammar from the estimated full structural descriptions, so that both a new hypothesized constraint hierarchy and a new hypothesized lexicon are produced. Again, this approach is made possible by optimality; the faithfulness of the correspondence between underlying forms and surface forms is determined by optimization over violable constraints. See (Tesar and Smolensky 1996) for further discussion of this kind of approach.

The addition of lexicon optimization to the learning approach makes the role of cross-form interactions in learning even more apparent. It requires that the learner examine the optimal descriptions of several inputs, where each input includes a particular morpheme as an element, in order to determine an underlying lexical entry for that morpheme. Such a requirement shouldn't come as any great surprise—the entire issue of learning underlying forms arises because the same morpheme is observed to surface differently in different contexts. The significance of cross-form interactions is perhaps made even greater by recent work on output-output correspondence in Optimality Theory (Benua 1994; Burzio, this volume), which suggest that cross-form comparisons are part of the determination of the optimal description of a single input. Whether the underlying forms stored in the lexicon are taken to be separate representations for individual morphemes or full representations of multi-morphemic words subject to cross-form restrictions, it is clear that cross-form interactions must be accounted for in an overall learning theory. Lexicon optimization suggests a way for integrating the learning of lexical entries into the overall optimization-based iterative strategy for learning Optimality-theoretic grammars.

16.5.2 *Dealing With Errors in the Data*

As mentioned in Section 16.2.1, the issue of data errors is often approached via optimization-based learning, commonly by minimizing some measure of error between the predictions of hypotheses and the observed data. If a learning strategy is already based upon minimizing discrepancy between hypothesis and observation, the same strategy can carry over as an approach to learning with observations which may contain errors. If the observed data are guaranteed to be error-free, then learning is expected to produce a hypothesis with no discrepancy; if the observed data contain errors, then only a hypothesis with minimal discrepancy can be expected.

The approach to learning given in Section 16.4 might be characterized in terms of overall optimization. This would involve optimizing the discrepancy between the winner and the loser assigned to a set of overt forms. If the overt forms contain no errors, then the correct ranking will give a perfect match between the winner and the loser for each overt form, a discrepancy of zero under any reasonable measure. If the overt forms do contain errors, then any constraint hierarchy will have a mismatch between winner and loser for at least some of the overt forms. A measure of harmony similar to that used to determine grammaticality might be used to measure the discrepancy by applying it to the constraint violations that differ between the winners and losers of the overt forms. There is a non-trivial challenge here. As discussed in Section 16.3.2, the standard OT definition of harmony applies when comparing candidates in a single competition for a form. It does not include any way of combining harmony measures across different forms, such as would be required to assign a single harmony value to a set of forms. Whereas it is not hard to imagine ways in which this might be done, justifying a particular method, and getting it to work effectively, will be more difficult.

16.6 Summary

The principles of Optimality Theory were originally arrived at because they provided powerful linguistic explanations. The strict domination approach to the relative strength of violable constraints was adopted because it made the right empirical predictions, both in analyses of phenomena in specific languages and in cross-linguistic typological observations. However, these principles make possible powerful strategies for language learning. Strict domination provides the basis for efficient determination of the direction in hypothesis space that will lead to a hypothesis with increased goodness as a consequence of reduced discrepancy between the winner and the loser. The performance value of this directional information is indicated by the speed of convergence of the procedure exploiting the information, error-driven constraint demotion.

Optimality provides the basis for an optimizing approach to learning hidden structure. The hidden structure values that do best with respect to ranking are selected as the interpretation of an overt utterance. This approach has the advantage of using procedures that any language user will perform anyway. Language comprehension always involves assigning a structural description to an utterance; the semantic interpretation is dependent on the structural analysis, at all linguistic levels. This is also a quite plausible account of what language learners are doing: they interpret the utterances they hear as best they can, and adjust their grammars to better conform to their interpretations. In such ways, Optimality-theoretic principles provide the basis for significant progress in language learnability.

16.7 References

Angluin, D. (1980). 'Inductive inference of formal languages from positive data'. *Information and Control* 45, 117–35.

Baum, L. E. (1972). 'An inequality and associated maximization technique in statistical estimation for probabilistic functions of Markov processes'. *Inequalities* 3, 1–8.

Benua, L. E. (1994). 'Identity effects in morphological truncation'. In J. Beckman, L. Walsh Dickey, and S. Urbanczyk (eds), *Papers in Optimality Theory*. U.Mass, Amherst, MA. University of Massachusetts Occasional Papers in Linguistics 18, 77–136.

Chomsky, N. (1981). *Lectures on Government and Binding*. Dordrecht, Foris.

Dempster, A. P., N. M. Laird, and D. B. Rubin (1977). 'Maximum likelihood from incomplete data via the *EM* algorithm'. *Journal of the Royal Statistical Society B* 39, 1–38.

Dresher, B. E. (1996). 'Charting the learning path: Cues to parameter setting'. Ms, University of Toronto, revised version to appear in *Linguistic Inquiry*.

—— and J. Kaye (1990). 'A computational learning model for metrical phonology'. *Cognition* 34, 137–95.

Ellison, T. M. (1994). 'Phonological derivation in optimality theory'. In *Proceedings of the Fifteenth International Conference on Computational Linguistics*, 1007–13.

Gibson, E. and K. Wexler (1994). 'Triggers'. *Linguistic Inquiry* 25, 407–54.

Gold, E. M. (1967). 'Language identification in the limit'. *Information and Control* 10, 447–74.

Holland, J. (1975). *Adaptation in Natural and Artificial Systems*. Ann Arbor, MI, The University of Michigan Press.

Kirkpatrick, S., C. Gelatt Jr., and M. Vecchi (1983). 'Optimization by simulated annealing'. *Science* 220, 671–80.

Minsky, M. L. (1961). 'Steps toward artificial intelligence'. *Proceedings of the Institute of Radio Engineers* 49(1), 8–30.

Niyogi, P. and R. Berwick (1993). 'Formalizing triggers: A learning model for finite spaces'. A. I. Memo No. 1449. Artificial Intelligence Laboratory, MIT.

Pinker, S. (1989). *Learnability and Cognition*. Cambridge, MA, MIT Press.

Prince, A. and P. Smolensky (1993). 'Optimality Theory: Constraint interaction in generative grammar'. Technical report, TR-2, Rutgers University Cognitive Science Center, and CU–CS–696–93, Department of Computer Science, University of Colorado at Boulder. To appear in the *Linguistic Inquiry* Monograph Series, MIT Press.

Pulleyblank, D. and W. J. Turkel (1995). 'Traps in constraint ranking space'. Handout of talk given at the 1995 MIT Conference on Optimality in Syntax.

Rabiner, L. R. (1989). 'A tutorial on hidden Markov models and selected applications in speech recognition'. *Proceedings of the IEEE* 77(2), 257–86.

Rissanen, J. (1989). *Stochastic Complexity in Statistical Inquiry*. Singapore, World Scientific Publishing,

Rumelhart, D., G. Hinton, and R. Williams (1986). 'Learning internal representations by error propagation'. In D. Rumelhart and J. McClelland (eds), *Parallel Distributed Processing*. Cambridge, MA, MIT Press, 318–62.

Tesar, B. (1995). *Computational Optimality Theory*. PhD thesis, University of Colorado, Boulder. ROA-90.

—— (1996). 'Computing optimal descriptions for Optimality Theory grammars with context-free position structures'. In *Proceedings of the 34th Annual Meeting of the Association for Computational Linguistics*, 101–7.

—— (1997). 'An iterative strategy for learning metrical stress in Optimality Theory'. In E. Hughes, M. Hughes, and A. Greenhill (eds), *The Proceedings of the 21st Annual Boston University Conference on Language Development*, Somerville, MA, Cascadilla Press, 615–626.

Tesar, B. (to appear). 'Error-driven learning in Optimality Theory via the efficient computation of optimal forms. In P. Barbosa, D. Fox, P. Hagstrom, M. J. McGinnis, and D. Pesetsky (eds), *Is the Best Good Enough? Papers from the Workshop on Optimality in Syntax*. Cambridge, MA, MIT Press and MITWPL.

—— (to appear). 'An iterative strategy for language learning'. *Lingua*.

—— and P. Smolensky (1995). 'The learnability of Optimality Theory'. In *Proceedings of the Thirteenth West Coast Conference on Formal Linguistics*, 122–37.

—— —— (1996). 'Learnability in Optimality Theory' (long version). Technical Report JHU–CogSci–96–4, Department of Cognitive Science, The Johns Hopkins University. ROA-156.

—— —— (1998). 'Learnability in Optimality Theory'. *Linguistic Inquiry*.

Wallace, G. and D. M. Boulton (1968). 'An information measure for classification'. *Computer Journal* 11, 185–95.

Subject Index

Index of Languages

Index of Names